Writers on Writing

Epictetus	If you wish to be a good writer, write.
George Meredith	The art of the pen is to rouse the inward vision.
Elizabeth Janeway	Great writers leave us not just their words, but a way of looking at things.
Joanne Greenburg	Your writing is trying to tell you something. Just lend an ear.
W. H. Auden	Language is the mother, not the handmaiden, of thought: words will tell you things you never thought or felt before.
Annie Dillard	The writer […] is careful of what he reads, for that is what he will write.
Mark Twain	A powerful agent is the right word.
Ralph Waldo Emerson	Good writing is a kind of skating which carries off the performer where he would not go.
Gabriel Fielding	Writing to me is a voyage, an odyssey, a discovery, because I'm never certain of precisely what I will find.
Henry Miller	Writing, like life itself, is a voyage of discovery.
John Updike	Writing and rewriting are a constant search for what one is saying.
Robert Hayden	As you continue writing and rewriting, you begin to see possibilities you hadn't seen before.
William Stafford	I don't see writing as a communication of something already discovered, as "truths" already known. Rather, I see writing as a job of experiment. It's like any discovery job; you don't know what's going to happen until you try it.
Leslie Marmon Silko	The reason I write is to find out what I mean.

The Longwood Guide to Writing

Brief Edition

Ronald F. Lunsford

University of North Carolina
at Charlotte

Bill Bridges

Sam Houston State University

Allyn and Bacon

| Boston | London | Toronto |
| Sydney | Tokyo | Singapore |

Vice President: Eben W. Ludlow
Editorial Assistant: Grace Trudo
Executive Marketing Manager: Lisa Kimball
Editorial-Production Administrator: Susan Brown
Editorial-Production Service: Lifland et al., Bookmakers
Text Designer: Melinda Grosser for *silk*
Composition Buyer: Linda Cox
Manufacturing Buyer: Suzanne Lareau
Cover Administrator: Linda Knowles

Copyright © 2000 by Allyn & Bacon
A Pearson Education Company
160 Gould Street
Needham Heights, MA 02494
Internet: www.abacon.com

Library-of-Congress Cataloging-in-Publication Data

Lunsford, Ronald F.
    The Longwood guide to writing / Ronald F. Lunsford, Charles W. Bridges.
    —Brief ed.
      p.   cm.
    Includes index.
    ISBN 0-205-27207-X
      1. English language—Rhetoric.   2. English language—Grammar.
  3. College readers.   4. Report writing.   I. Bridges, Charles W.   II. Title.

PE1408.L883   2000
808'.042—dc21

                                               99-052643

Printed in the United States of America
10 9 8 7 6 5 4 3 2 1   03 02 01 00 99

Acknowledgments appear on pages 595–602, which constitute a continuation of the copyright page.

Brief Contents

Contents

Part Two Writing Occasions 125

5 Personal Essays 131

6 Informative Essays 165

7   Evaluation Essays 211

Part Three Research 447

12 Researching and Writing 449

Part Four Special Writing Tasks 497

Part Five Style 535

15 Working with Words 547

What Is a Word? 547

The Symbolic Nature of Words 548

A Rhetorical Perspective 549
Strategies for Writing That Spotlights the Subject 549 / Strategies for Writing That Spotlights the Writer 556 / Strategies for Writing That Spotlights the Reader 564

16 Shaping Sentences 571

Sentence Structure 572
Time Out 573

A Rhetorical Perspective 573
Strategies for Writing That Spotlights the Subject 573 / *Time Out* 575 / *Time Out* 577 / *Time Out* 580 / Strategies for Writing That Spotlights the Writer 582 / *Time Out* 584 / *Time Out* 585 / Strategies for Writing That Spotlights the Reader 590

Acknowledgments 595

Index 603

Preface

In one sense, this book began twenty-five years ago, when the two of us met at Florida State University in a graduate rhetorical theory course taught by our mentor, James M. McCrimmon. Thanks to the many conferences we have attended together since that time and to advances in technology that have allowed us all but immediate communication, we have collaborated more and more, eventually coauthoring several articles and three books. We even confer with each other in our teaching; these days, we seldom if ever take a writing exercise to class that the other has not read, critiqued, and, ultimately, made better. Over the years we have worked together, we have written and talked our way to the writing theory that provides this book's framework. We can best describe this theory as one that views writing as rhetorical, personal, and communal.

WRITING AS RHETORICAL   Professor McCrimmon introduced us to the work of Kenneth Burke, and through Burke to Aristotle. The result is a heavy commitment to writing as rhetorical—that is, to the view that the quality of a piece of writing is judged by its effectiveness in achieving its writer's purpose for the intended reader. That commitment is made evident in our use of the rhetorical triangle as a means of structuring the chapters in Part Two that treat various writing occasions. It should also be clear in our treatment of argument and persuasion in Chapters 9 and 10 and in the rhetorical perspective we bring to our treatment of style in Chapters 15 and 16.

WRITING AS PERSONAL   Good writing is personal. That is, it conveys the significance the writer sees in her subject. *The Longwood Guide to Writing* reveals our commitment to the personal nature of writing in our emphasis on significance in all types of writing. Whether a personal essay or a fully developed, researched argument, good writing conveys the significance or meaning the writer sees in her topic.

WRITING AS COMMUNAL   Writing, as we have come to know it, is not a solitary act. Our work on this book—and on numerous projects before it—has taught us that good writing does not happen in a vacuum, or even in a writer's garret—unless it has an e-mail hook-up. At times, it is hard for us to know who is responsible for what. For example, one of us drafts a chapter, and the other responds, rewrites, and then ships it back. From there, the chapter's initial writer revises. This back-and-forth process continues until, in the end, the product is a joint one. Through e-mail, we have even worked with each other's students by serving as readers and editors at a distance. Our work together has helped us develop more and more collaborative exercises for our writing classes. We have included many of these exercises in this text.

DISTINCTIVE FEATURES OF *THE LONGWOOD GUIDE TO WRITING*

WRITING AS A PROCESS   We have attempted to make writing process an integral part of this book, without falling into the trap of acting as if there were only one writing process that all writers either do or should employ for all types of writing. What makes our approach distinctive is the availability of process throughout the text. We begin by devoting an entire section to writing process: Part One, with chapters on invention, shaping, revising, and reading. Further, in the first three of these chapters, we follow a student writer's process as she begins thinking and freewriting about her topic, then writes an initial discovery draft, and then revises that rough draft three more times until she completes the assignment. The attention to process is continued with an Assignment and Guidelines for Writing section in each of the writing occasion chapters in Part Two. Finally, our discussion of diction and sentences in Part Five emphasizes that good writing develops over time by means of a process.

THE RHETORICAL TRIANGLE   What is good writing? As a way of answering this question, think for a moment about the various situations in which writing takes place. We write notes to family members and friends. We write grocery lists and to-do lists. We write terse letters to credit card corporations, asking to be taken off their mailing or telephone lists. Some of us write books. Many of us write e-mail messages to our teachers, students, and friends. What do all of these writing situations have in common? Each involves a subject, a writer, and a reader. These elements are often referred to as the *rhetorical triangle:*

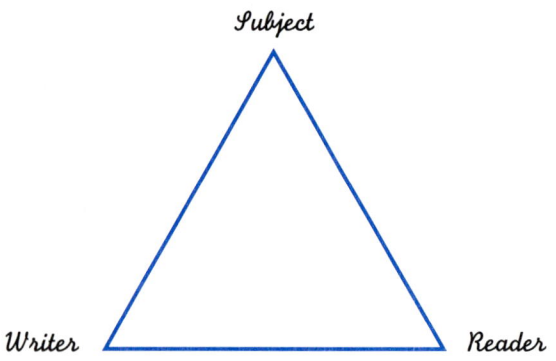

This triangle suggests that good writing results from a process in which a writer shares meaning with a reader. It also suggests that writing requires some sort of balance among writer, subject, and reader. The writer must fit the subject to the reader. The writer must identify with the audience in such a way as to predict what readers want to learn from the writing and what information they need as background before they can understand the essential information in the text. This is difficult enough when writing for one reader—for instance, when writing a note to a family member about how to program the VCR. It becomes increasingly difficult as the readers become more numerous and more varied in their interests and knowledge. In writing an instruction booklet that includes a section on programming a VCR, a writer must arrive at some concept of a typical reader in order to decide what information to include.

In Part Two, we use the rhetorical triangle extensively. Each chapter in this part has three sections corresponding to the corners of the rhetorical triangle: spotlighting the subject, spotlighting the writer, and spotlighting the reader.

EMPHASIS ON INVENTION   We devote the first chapter of *The Longwood Guide to Writing* to invention and return to invention activities in the Guidelines section of each chapter in Part Two. These activities range from the informal (e.g., freewriting and brainstorming) to the formal (e.g., using a comprehensive set of questions for analyzing a topic, discovering insights or information to use in an essay, and shaping those materials into an essay). This set of questions is consistent with our commitment to a Burkean approach to rhetoric, for it derives from Burke's logological analysis.

MODES AS INVENTION AND ORGANIZATIONAL STRUCTURES   We see modes as powerful tools in the writing process. However, it seems wrong to us to equate types of writing with modes. In *The Longwood Guide to Writing,* we are careful to illustrate how each mode may be, and often is, employed in writing with any aim. For example, even though the overall structure of an informative essay will likely be provided by one of the expository modes, there is no one-to-one correlation between expository modes and informational or explanatory writing. In fact, informational writing may well make use of an argumentative thesis and employ narrative or descriptive modes or both. The same could be said for writing with any other aim; that is, the writer may well use any mode to help achieve any aim. In the Guidelines sections of several of the writing occasion chapters, we present modes as tools for generating and shaping material rather than as constraints or containers that limit writing.

CONNECTIONS BETWEEN WRITING AND READING   Writing and reading are very closely connected, and *The Longwood Guide to Writing* contains a chapter devoted to this connection. In Chapter 4, we focus on ways in which students' reading can inform their writing and on ways in which writing can help students understand what they are reading. This chapter includes a comprehensive range of reading and writing strategies that students may use before they read, while they are reading, and after they have read to enhance their reading of a given text and then to use that text in fulfilling a writing assignment.

WRITING ABOUT AND FROM LITERATURE   In Chapter 8, we offer two ways of responding to literature: writing about literature and writing from literature. Writing about literature requires the writer to analyze a piece of literature and write an interpretation of it, whereas writing from literature involves using a piece of literature as a springboard to an essay. These essays tend to be personal, but they can be argumentative or even informational. Both types of literature essays—writing *about* and writing *from*—begin with reading closely to derive an understanding of the literature at hand. Chapter 8 discusses how to develop this understanding.

ARGUMENT AND PERSUASION   We have chosen to deal with argument and persuasion in two chapters rather than one. In Chapter 9, we attempt to help students strengthen their abilities to think through an argument, both from their own perspectives and from the perspectives of those who would disagree with them. The writer's goal in this type of writing is not to persuade a person holding an opposite point of view to agree with him, but rather to gain the respect and understanding of those who disagree. To do so, the writer must show respect and understanding for those who hold an opposing point of view.

In Chapter 10, we follow two important tenets of Kenneth Burke. The first is that persuasion occurs only when writer and reader can identify with each other. This identification cannot occur when writer and reader begin with opposing positions on arguments that, in part, determine their identity. The second Burkean principle follows from the first, namely, that in persuasive writing the writer must carve out an audience that suits the topic of persuasion. Thus, if a writer wants to persuade readers to take some action to promote the goals of those who hold a particular view on a controversial topic, such as abortion, she must choose an audience that can be persuaded on this topic. To do otherwise is to do pretend, rather than real, writing.

USING THE INTERNET   We introduce students to the Internet as a tool for research. We discuss how to assess the reliability of Internet sources, and we provide samples of electronic documentation formats following the guidelines established by the fifth edition of the *MLA Handbook for Writers of Research Papers* (1999) and the fourth edition of the *Publication Manual of the American Psychological Association* (1994).

STUDENT WRITING   We make ample use of student writing, featuring essays written by our students as examples in a number of chapters. In addition, each chapter in Parts Two and Three presents a piece of student writing in its entirety from prewriting to final draft. The collaborative nature of writing is emphasized by the inclusion of actual peer reviews and teacher comments students received during the writing process, whether in prewriting and planning or between drafts.

REALISTIC PROFESSIONAL MODELS   We have chosen professional writing that can serve as models for student writing. Most of these essays are comparable in length to those written by our students. Thus, students should be able to see structural parallels between these essays and those they will be writing. The Questions for Review after each essay encourage students to reflect on the ways in which each one illustrates the concepts being treated in the chapter in which it is presented.

STRUCTURE OF *THE LONGWOOD GUIDE TO WRITING*

Part One, Strategies for the Writing Process, introduces students to various parts of the writing process, moving from generating ideas (Chapter 1), to organization (Chapter 2), to rewriting (Chapter 3). The final chapter in this part (Chapter 4) helps students hone their reading skills as a means of both generating ideas for writing and becoming more critical readers of their own writing.

Part Two, Writing Occasions, consists of seven chapters that guide students through writing assignments for papers with various discourse aims. Each of these chapters contains several professional essays and at least two student samples. One of those student essays is traced from the beginning of the writing process through to the final draft. Each of these chapters also contains a discussion of the key elements in writing designed to achieve the aim in question, with attention given to each element in the rhetorical triangle: subject, writer, and reader. Finally, each of these chapters contains numerous exercises designed to help students explore the concepts being introduced and apply them to their own writing. The seven chapters in this section are further categorized as follows:

Writing That Spotlights the Writer	Chapter 5, Personal Essays
Writing That Spotlights the Subject	Chapter 6, Informative Essays
	Chapter 7, Evaluation Essays
	Chapter 8, Essays About and From Literature
Writing That Spotlights the Reader	Chapter 9, Position Essays
	Chapter 10, Persuasion Essays
	Chapter 11, Problem/Solution Essays

Part Three, Research, consists of one chapter, Chapter 12. In it, we discuss various types of research students are likely to do in college and after they graduate, and we guide them through the writing of a research project, giving special attention to the use and documentation of information from the World Wide Web.

Part Four, Special Writing Tasks, consists of two chapters. In Chapter 13, we analyze essay-examination questions from various disciplines and categorize them into four types based on the response called for: summary, synthesis, evaluation, or interpretation. We also offer strategies for writing these types of essays and analyze sample essay examinations. In Chapter 14, we model two different approaches to writing portfolios and include parts of two sample portfolios.

Part Five, Style, comprises two chapters, both related to the rhetorical triangle presented in Part Two. Chapter 15 examines word choice in terms of writing that spotlights the subject, writing that spotlights the writer, and writing that spotlights the reader. Chapter 16 examines sentence structures in the same manner. The intent of these chapters is not to suggest that various strategies are limited to specific types of writing, but to look at general principles of diction and syntax. We approach style as something of a paradox, both inseparable from content and yet one of the ultimate marks of the polished writing that careful revision leads to.

HOW TO USE *THE LONGWOOD GUIDE TO WRITING*

We have written this book as a tool to be used in writing classes; we do not envision ourselves as the teachers of those classes. Another way of putting this is to say that we have not written this book as a tutorial, which students can work their way through from start to finish without other guidance—though we certainly believe they could gain insights into writing in general and into their own writing process by doing so. Our intent was to write a book teachers can use to suit their purposes, rather than one that would constrain and limit teachers. We do not imagine that many teachers will be able to assign all of the chapters in this text, and we have not designed it in such a way as to make this necessary. Some teachers will be working in courses that place relatively little emphasis on persuasion and thus may well omit most, if not all, of the chapters spotlighting the reader in Part Two. Other teachers, working in courses focusing on argument, may devote most of their attention to those chapters. We believe this book can be successful in both of these situations.

As we have indicated, we do not envision this book as a linear text in which one begins with Chapter 1 and finishes it before moving on to Chapter 2, and so forth. But there is a basic design within which teachers can work. That design suggests that the teacher begin by deciding which of the chapters in Parts Two, Three, and Four the course will include. The choice of chapters will be determined by such considerations as the nature of the course (e.g., whether it is the first or second in a two-course sequence) and the types of writing assignments the teacher intends to make. Once this decision is made, the teacher can then use the selected chapters as the course's major units. Within these units, the teacher can include readings from the chapters in Parts One and Five.

We imagine that teachers will assign various parts of the first three chapters as students work through the first chapter assigned from Part Two, so that students apply the invention, shaping, and revision strategies presented in Part One while they are writing their first formal essay. Further, Chapter 4 may be assigned at any point during the course. Some will no doubt want to assign it first, so that students can apply the reading strategies it presents not only in their writing course but in other courses as well.

Depending on what type of writing is being done, the teacher may well move ahead to sections from Part Five. For example, if the first chapter assigned from Part Two is Chapter 5, Personal Essays, a teacher may want to assign the section from Chapter 15 on Strategies for Writing That Spotlights the Writer and the section from Chapter 16 on Sentence Strategies for Writing That Spotlights the Writer.

SUPPLEMENTS FOR *THE LONGWOOD GUIDE TO WRITING*

The Longwood Guide to Writing is supported by a variety of helpful supplements for instructors and students.

SUPPLEMENTS FOR INSTRUCTORS

- The *Instructor's Resource Manual* we wrote contains an introductory section that provides sample syllabi for various courses in which *The Longwood Guide* might be used; a section in which we discuss each chapter individually, providing background information about what we hope students will achieve as they work through the material, as well as responses to many of the exercises in the text; and a theoretical section, in which we discuss, in three separate articles, the essential ingredients of a process approach to writing, various ways of giving students feedback about their writing, and the theories of Kenneth Burke that are the foundation of our text. Finally, a separate section, written by Nancy Pfingstag, a member of the English Language Training Institute faculty at UNC–Charlotte, covers teaching writing to students for whom English is a second language.
- *The Longwood Guide to Writing Website* enables instructors to access online writing activities as well as links keyed to specific chapters, to post and make changes to their syllabi, to hold chat sessions with individual students or groups of students, and to receive e-mail and essay assignments directly from students. *http://www.abacon.com/lunsford*
- *An Introduction to Teaching Composition in an Electronic Environment,* developed by Eric Hoffman and Carol Scheidenhelm, both at Northern Illinois University, offers a wealth of computer-related classroom activities. It also provides detailed guidance for both experienced and inexperienced instructors who wish to make creative use of technology in teaching composition.
- *The Allyn and Bacon Sourcebook for College Writing Teachers,* Second Edition, compiled by James C. McDonald of the University of Louisiana at Lafayette, provides instructors with a varied selection of readings written by composition and rhetoric scholars on both theoretical and practical subjects.
- *Teaching College Writing,* an invaluable instructor's resource guide developed by Maggy Smith of the University of Texas at El Paso, is available to adopters who wish to explore additional teaching tips and resources.
- *CompSite Website* is an easily navigable and informative forum for instructors and students of composition. Instructors can share teaching strategies with colleagues. New resources include material on writing across the curriculum, teaching tips for newer instructors, and advice on using technology in the composition classroom. *http://www.abacon.com/compsite*

SUPPLEMENTS FOR STUDENTS

- *The Longwood Guide to Writing Website* presents chapter summaries, writing activities, the course syllabus, links keyed to specific text sections, and chat and e-mail functions for communicating with classmates and the instructor. *http://www.abacon.com/lunsford*
- *CompSite Website* offers resources and instructional materials for students, including helpful information on using computers for writing, techniques for using the Internet for research, and a forum for exchanging papers and writing ideas. *http://www.abacon.com/compsite*

ACKNOWLEDGMENTS

A project like this leaves us indebted to many more people than we can properly thank. We would like to begin with the many students we have taught and who have taught us through the years. We especially thank those whose essays are included in this text.

We thank those colleagues who have given us the benefit of their expertise in reading drafts of this text and suggesting ways we might improve it: Joseph A. Alvarez, Central Piedmont Community College; Paul Heilker, Virginia Polytechnic Institute and State University; Elizabeth Kiszely, Fullerton College; Sue V. Lape, Columbus State Community College; Joe Law, Wright State University; Sarah Liggett, Louisiana State University; James C. McDonald, the University of Louisiana at Lafayette; and Charlton Ryan, University of Memphis.

We thank Allyn and Bacon for giving us the opportunity to write this text. We especially thank Eben Ludlow for believing in the project from the start. We also wish to thank Donna de la Perrière, our developmental editor, and Susan Brown, our production editor, for taking the project into their capable hands and making it happen.

In this, as in every professional endeavor we have undertaken since coming under his powerful and generous influence, we are indebted to our inspiring mentor, James M. McCrimmon.

Ron wishes to thank Reba, his mother, for her undying love; Mell, for her continual friendship and support; Tamara and Christopher, for their love and patience; and Nancy, for the light in her eyes.

Bill wishes to thank Mary Beth, Mark, David, and Matt, for their love, support, patience, and good humor at having just about everything but this text put on hold, but especially Mary Beth, who makes it all possible.

Bill also has a special acknowledgment: Shortly after completing the manuscript of this text, I became chair of the Department of English and Foreign Languages at Sam Houston State University and so left New Mexico State University, after having been a faculty member there for 23 years. This acknowledgments section would be incomplete without my thanking several of my colleagues at NMSU for their friendship and support in this project and beyond: Christopher Burnham, with whom I've had innumerable talks about life and about writing, literature, and the teaching of both; Reed Dasenbrock, who offered a sympathetic ear on more than one occasion; Stuart Brown, who always entertained yet one more question; Stacey Somppi, who, as co-director with me of the New Mexico State Writing Project, taught me about teaching by dint of example; and Meghan Flisakowski, whose work as our graduate assistant researcher proved invaluable. Finally, to Bruce and Tom—not a bad sojourn, no?

Strategies for the Writing Process

WHY WRITE?

In the current computer-rich business climate, it seems that paper is on its way out, that the paperless office is increasingly taking over. Computers are replacing pen and paper as the medium of choice for writing. The implication is that writing will soon be unnecessary, for all we really need to do to communicate is pick up the phone and call or get on-line and send an e-mail message. But the concept of the paperless office should not lead us to expect an end to, or even a lessening in the importance of, writing. Even though there may be less and less paper, there is, in fact, more and more writing. All of that work we do at keyboards is writing; any time we use words to compose our thoughts, using a medium that lets us review the words we have written and revise if we choose to, we are writing. So, despite the pervasiveness of telecommunications, writing will remain an important part of our attempts to communicate.

Writing will be crucial to your success after college, and you'll no doubt find many opportunities to hone your writing skills in college. You'll write in response to tests and assignments such as essays, research papers, and laboratory reports. You'll keep notes on reading assignments, class lectures, and lab experiments. You'll probably write for personal reasons as well—letters, journal or diary entries, to-do lists, to name but a few. Writing clearly has a number of purposes, and it can help us do at least these things:

REMEMBER   "Write it down—paper remembers." This old saying is true. If we write a grocery or to-do list, we use writing to help us remember what we need to do. But writing can also help us remember important people, places, and events as we record them in journals or diaries. When we ask our students who keep journals why they do so, the overwhelming response is this: "To remember what happened."

RECORD   We use writing to record what happened in a given situation. Sometimes this written record may take the form of minutes of a meeting or a step-by-step description of what occurred during a biology lab. Creating such records is important because we often need to document an event; we need to create a history.

UNDERSTAND AND THINK CRITICALLY   As we write, we often pause to reflect and consider what we think about a particular person, event, or concept. Why did your boyfriend or girlfriend break up with you? Why did you pick the major you did? Why do you think you want to change your major? What were the principal causes of a historical event? Your writing can help you find answers to these and many other questions. Writing can be especially powerful when you analyze and interpret the ideas of others, that is, when you couple writing and reading. As you write about the ideas of other writers, you strengthen your own critical reading skills; you strengthen your abilities to summarize, analyze, and interpret.

LEARN   One of the most powerful uses of writing is to learn. As a physical act, writing seems to be connected directly with the mind; there's just something about consciously creating words and ideas on the page (whether we're using a ballpoint pen, a typewriter, or a word processor) that causes us to retain those words and ideas longer. We create knowledge by writing things down; at the same time, we transfer that knowledge from the page to the mind, from the page to the brain's idea warehouse.

Writing to learn begins when you take notes from your readings and from lectures and labs, and it continues as you write essays in response to formal writing assignments. As you review your notes (and even take notes on those notes), you'll work at learning their important parts. As you write to prepare for essay exams, you'll learn the subject matter better than you would otherwise and so improve your chances for a good grade. And, as you work through an extended essay assignment, you'll discover things you didn't know about the topic. In making such discoveries, you'll come to know the subject in more comprehensive ways.

CREATE ORDER   We use language to bring order out of chaos. Think, for example, about a camper who hears the banging of garbage cans as something tries to knock off their lids and get at whatever scraps of food they contain. What's the effect of his saying, "Oh, that's just raccoons after bacon"? The mere naming of the noisemaker makes familiar the unfamiliar; it shrinks the two-headed beastie with twelve-inch claws and razor-sharp fangs to something much smaller and more manageable—raccoons after bacon. Although this example is simple, it illustrates how you can use language to create order in, and so obtain more control over, your world.

The Longwood Guide is designed to help you explore the ways in which you can use writing to achieve these purposes.

HOW DOES WRITING HAPPEN?

Let's begin with this scenario: Late at night, the professional writer sits down to compose another masterpiece. She thinks for a bit, mulling over her day as she enjoys a glass of wine; then, out of nowhere, inspiration strikes! She grasps an idea, perhaps jots a note or two or a quick outline to make sure the idea doesn't escape, and then dashes off a poem, essay, short story, play, or novel effortlessly, without stopping, without making a mistake. She smiles contentedly as she prints a copy of the work. Then she either ships the text electronically to her agent or places it in an envelope for the next day's mail, confident of immediate publication and critical acclaim, if not a sale of movie rights.

Here's a second scenario: Having put off beginning his writing assignment until the absolute last minute, the writer drags himself over to his writing desk and sits down. He dreads the laborious task he's about to undertake, but he knows he has to get it done. So he begins. He thinks up a topic. He thinks about this topic. He writes a thesis sentence. He writes an outline. He writes the essay. He reads the essay only once, correcting errors in spelling, grammar, and mechanics as he goes. He staples the pages together and stuffs the draft into his backpack. He smiles ruefully, knowing that he hasn't written a very good paper, but he does have something to hand in the next day.

These scenarios are very much overdrawn and unrealistic. Yet the first scenario reflects the ideal that many students aspire to, whereas the second scenario is much more like their actual writing practices. In our experience, however, writing is something much less magical than the first scenario implies and much less predictable than the second one does. Writing is a recursive process in which the writer engages in considerable trial and error, looping backward while moving forward. She may begin by freewriting or asking questions about her topic, then compose a rough outline for her essay, move to a draft, move forward to experimentation with words, trying to find the right word for a specific thought, then hit a snag in a certain passage and move back to freewriting about what seems to be bothering her in the passage, get some insight into an entirely new section that needs to be added, return to the rough outline and revise it to allow for this new section, and then write a second draft of her essay. Just like the preceding sentence, the writing process is fluid and ongoing.

STAGES IN THE WRITING PROCESS

How can you manage something as seemingly chaotic as writing? One way is to break your writing task into several parts, or stages, each with specific activities you may complete along the way, rather than trying to deal with the assignment as a whole. Now, we really can't divide the writing process neatly into separate units, but it is useful and convenient to talk about three stages—prewriting, drafting, and revising—as if they were discrete units. This separation allows us to deal with smaller parts than the whole of the writing process. Learning to work from one stage to the next can help you manage a writing project from start to finish.

Prewriting, which occurs before the writer produces the first rough draft, is a planning and preparation stage. In prewriting, the writer selects a subject and begins to discover what he wants to say about it and how best to present his thoughts to his intended audience. This stage provides the foundation for discovery; it is the germination, or gestation, period, the stage in which ideas begin to take shape. Our first chapter, "Invention: Finding Something to Say," offers strategies for getting started on an essay and for finding things to say in your writing.

Drafting is the stage in which the writer produces a rough draft of the paper. Here the writer should concentrate on actually writing his ideas; he should not be concerned with such matters as finding exactly the right word, restructuring sentences or paragraphs, or correcting errors in spelling or punctuation. Too much attention to these matters may constrict or stop the flow of ideas, and the free flow of ideas is essential during this stage. "Shaping an Essay," our second chapter, offers advice on how to structure your writing so that you can produce a rough draft from the information you generated during your prewriting.

Revising is that part of the process in which the writer takes stock of his draft and decides what he needs to do to strengthen and improve it. Revision is an important part of writing that is at times neglected by many writers. This stage requires the writer to make decisions that determine the final shape and effectiveness of his writing; thus, revising is fundamental.

We like to think of revision as a stage in which the paper is examined by a quality checker who has an idea of what the final paper should look like—or, more correctly, who will know it when she sees it. She may look at a draft and see that it needs only minor changes, a word here and there, or that it needs some tightening of sentence structure and some attention to editing conventions. In other cases, this quality checker will find big gaps in the paper, places that can be filled in only by the writer's returning first to prewriting to generate more information and then to drafting.

If a writer is to produce a piece of good writing, he must revise—deleting what doesn't fit in the final draft, making what remains stronger, creating new information that will clarify parts of the draft, leaving alone what is satisfactory, or discarding everything and starting again. Whatever the changes at this stage, they must come in light of decisions already made in the other stages of the process. The writer is not bound, however, by these previous decisions. Changes made at this stage reflect the writer's ability to see the previous stages of the writing process from a new vantage point. To revise is to see again and to change the paper as this "seeing again" dictates. Thus, revising is creating anew. Our third chapter, "Revising," offers a number of strategies to help you revise and edit your writing.

As we stated earlier, it is not easy to make neat distinctions among the three stages of the writing process. Sometimes they come together. Think about your own writing. When you have been writing a rough draft or answering an essay examination, how many times have you combined writing and rewriting by scratching out a word, sentence, or paragraph and substituting a more appropriate choice? You've probably done so many times. In all likelihood, you've written sentences or paragraphs (drafting) in your exploration of a subject (prewriting) and revised them on the spot (revising) before incorporating them into a paper. The fact that these stages frequently occur simultaneously reinforces our statement that writing is a recursive process that involves considerable trial and error as the piece of writing unfolds and takes shape.

WRITING AND READING

Writing and reading are very closely connected, and good writers often make extensive use of readings before and while they write. They read to get ideas, to consider the ways other writers have written, and to enjoy someone else's insights and language. "Responding to Readings," our fourth chapter, offers a number of comprehensive reading strategies and then suggests ways in which you may use reading as an important element of your writing process.

COMPUTERS AND WRITING

Computers and word processing have had a profound impact on writing in many ways. Probably the most dramatic impact has been on the ease of revision. Before computer use became so widespread, writers relied on pencils, pens, and typewriters to produce their drafts. Changing more than a word or two of a handwritten or typed draft often meant redoing the entire thing, so many writers were reluctant to revise. Today, computers make it easy to revise. It takes very little effort to insert a word here, move a paragraph from one place in the draft to another, or import text from other files into a piece you're working on.

Computers hold other benefits for writers as well. They make storage of drafts and other materials, such as your prewriting, easy. And when you're ready to print and submit a final draft of a paper, you may print only that draft, so that all of your other materials reside on a single floppy disk. With access to the

Internet, computers provide a powerful means of communicating with others through e-mail and of researching a topic. It's possible for you to sit at a keyboard in your room and retrieve information from a library located hundreds or thousands of miles from your school. And computers can help you produce a professional-looking paper, through the range of typefaces, fonts, and graphics typically available in most word-processing software packages.

How much you'll use a computer in your writing will depend on availability and on your level of comfort in using one. Throughout the first four chapters, and where appropriate in the rest of *The Longwood Guide*, we'll offer advice on using the computer while you write. Writing with a word processor and becoming computer-literate will be important for you, not only during your college career but once you graduate and enter the work force. Because of this importance, we advise you to take classes or at least tutorials in basic word processing and desktop publishing.

Exercise

COMPUTER FACILITIES   Does your campus have computer centers or clusters or labs, where machines are available to all students? If so, visit one, and find out the following:

Hours—when is it open?
Computers—how many are available? What kind (DOS machines, Apples, both)?
Printers—how many are available? What kind (laser, dot matrix, inkjet)?
Staff—how many staff members are available to help you?
Services—what instructional support is offered? Formal, credit-bearing classes? Tutorials? One-on-one help in response to specific questions?
Costs—is the cost of your using the facility already supported by the fees you paid to register, or are there additional costs? If the latter, what are these?

WRITING CENTER   Does your campus have a writing center designed to help students with their writing? If so, visit it, and find out the following:

Hours—when is it open?
Staff—how many staff members are available to help you? Will they work with you one-on-one or in small groups?
Services—what writing support is offered? Tutorials? Individual or small-group conferences with a tutor? Handouts?
Costs—is the cost of your using the center already supported by fees you paid during registration, or are there additional costs? If the latter, what are these?
Computers—are computers available for writing in the center itself? If so, how many, and how readily available are they?

You sit in class, and your teacher assigns your first essay. What do you do now? Where, how to begin? Getting started on a writing assignment is not difficult, if you plan your route through the assignment carefully. When is the due date? What kind of essay does the assignment call for? What steps has your professor recommended or required you to follow? Learning to manage an assignment is an important part of learning to write well.

Whether you have been given an assignment or you have an idea to explore on your own, you may ask yourself three questions as you begin:

1. What do I know about my subject?
2. What else do I want or need to know?
3. What is important, interesting, or significant enough about this subject that I want to tell someone else about it?

This last question is of particular importance, because the best writing matters both to the writer and to the reader. That is, good writing is marked by a sense of significance, by a sense that the writer has something she wants to say and has taken particular care in presenting that something to a reader. Your job as a writer is to discover this significance, this something that you want to say, and then to discover the best ways to present that to a reader. In this chapter, we'll offer you some strategies that can help you find this significance. We suggest that

Invention: Finding Something to Say

C H A P T E R 1

you work through each strategy at least twice, so that you get a feel for how each can help you generate information to use in a paper.

FINDING TOPICS

Choosing a topic for your writing is important, and you need to take care to pick one that interests you and that you can make interesting for your reader. You'll live with an essay's topic from the time you begin until you submit your final draft, and you'll invest a good bit of time and energy in writing your essay. Writing requires you to make choices all along the way, from start to finish, and the better the choices you make, the better your writing is likely to be. To begin, then, select your topic; don't simply settle for one. To help you discover potential topics for your writing, we offer this assignment.

WRITING ASSIGNMENT

Answer as fully as you can each question under at least five of the following six topic headings. This assignment is designed to help you select topics for your writing that are meaningful to you—there are no right or wrong answers, only *your* responses.

Interest Inventory

1. Community
   a. Where do you live?
   b. What type of community is your hometown or neighborhood?
   c. What especially interests or disturbs you about your community? Why?
   d. What particular places or events in your community do you enjoy? Why?
   e. What things about your community would you like to see changed? Why?
2. Family, Friends, and Acquaintances
   a. What about your family is unique?
   b. Which of your relatives are especially interesting or important to you? Why?
   c. What special customs does your family have? (For example, is there anything special about how you celebrate such events as birthdays, religious holidays, or Thanksgiving?)
   d. Which of your friends are especially interesting or important to you? Why?
   e. Do you know any unusual people? If so, what makes them unusual?
   f. Which of your neighbors are especially interesting or important to you? Why?
3. Education
   a. What type of educational background do you have? (Consider kindergarten, elementary school, and so on. Think about such things as class and school size, what you learned, and teachers who impressed you.)

    b. What types of courses have you taken or are you taking? Which are your favorites? Why? Which do you dislike? Why?

    c. If you could change anything about any of the schools you have attended, what would you change? How would you change it? Why?

    d. What informal (not strictly related to school) educational experiences have you had? How were they educational?

4. Jobs

    a. What types of jobs have you had? What about them interested or disturbed you? Why?

    b. What career do you hope to have? Why have you chosen this particular field?

5. Leisure

    a. What hobbies do you enjoy? What makes each enjoyable?

    b. What kinds of movies, music, and reading material do you like? Why?

    c. What types of vacations or travel do you enjoy? If you could travel anywhere, where would you go? Why?

    d. What types of extracurricular activities do you engage in? Why?

6. Attitudes and Issues

    a. Have you experienced a change in your attitude toward such things as politics, religion, school, family, or friends? If so, what was that change, and what caused it?

    b. What events in the past year or so have interested you or disturbed you most? Why?

    c. What types of issues (for example, political or environmental) interest you? Why? Identify one or two specific events that represent these interests.

    d. Have the technological advances or changes you've seen been for the best? Why? What technological developments would you like to see take place? Why?

    e. Have the societal changes you've seen been for the best? Why? What changes in society would you like to see take place? Why?

    f. What particular social customs interest or disturb you? Why?

Your responses to these questions will, in all likelihood, reveal broader rather than more narrow interests. As you look to this inventory for topic ideas, keep in mind that you'll have to work with any topic you select, narrowing it and probing or exploring it until you discover a subject that's manageable in the context of your writing assignment.

Computer Tip

Create a file named INTINV. Type in the first question of the Interest Inventory and answer it, then the next question, then the next, and so on until you've completed your Interest Inventory. Be sure to save your work frequently. When you finish answering the inventory's questions, print a copy and keep it available for handy reference, either in your Writer's Notebook or pinned to a bulletin board near your study desk.

WRITING ABOUT AN ASSIGNED TOPIC

In many writing situations, your topic will be assigned. At times, the topic will be well-defined; at other times, less so. Your writing begins as you read the assignment to see what your instructor wants you to do. Consider this assignment, which we have taken from Chapter 5:

> Describe an event from which you learned something. Your job is to use your language to recreate the event so that your readers will feel that they have been at least observers of this important event with you, if not participants in it.

What does this assignment call for? One way to decide is to examine its key terms: "describe," "important event," "use your language to recreate." Your first step is to pick an event that you count as important. Once you have selected this event, you can begin to work with your language to recreate it for the reader. For all assigned topics, identify the key terms of the assignment and use those key terms as an initial guide in completing the assignment.

EXPLORING TOPICS

Once you have either selected or been assigned a topic, how can you explore it? How can you generate information or ideas about it? Five approaches that many writers find helpful are brainstorming, freewriting, clustering, visualizing, and asking questions.

BRAINSTORMING

To brainstorm, list quickly any and all ideas that come to mind. As you brainstorm, do not censor any ideas; just list. Below is an example of brainstorming that Bill wrote in response to this prompt: Spend 15 minutes listing every event you've participated in that comes to mind, no matter how serious or inconsequential.

> band at Tarleton
> trumpet in Joey's closet
> Jake & Dot's café
> Homer's thick milkshakes
> TSC dorms
> beating the drum—homecoming
> Lake Proctor
> Thanksgiving float trip
> Gus, Larry, Lynn, Harvey

kicked PAT
move from Tallahassee
Ol' Mullet
kids' cradle
fishing—Sam Rayburn Res. (7 lb. bass)
hiking and backpacking
Three Rivers Camp (fell in river, wasps)
Eagle projects
Willow Creek—building step-down dams
conservation work at Aguirre Springs
setting up double-wide trailers
FSU track—jogging
Pittsburgh—early a.m. runs (park, llamas)
Mark—worm
Pirates/Expos game
bus rides
Dad's old red pickup
van—hauling kids
soccer—Roswell tourney
road trips—soccer, football, choir, Scouts
conference in Nashville (OpryLand, Grand Ole Opry)
DFW airport

Note the informality of this list. Bill was not concerned with writing complete sentences, only with getting down whatever came to mind. He simply jotted down events he remembered until he had listed thirty-one possible topics for an essay. How many of these could serve as the basis for an essay? Each one could, depending on what Bill found important, which topic or topics he thought might be worth exploring.

Computer Tip

Create a file named BRAIN or BRNSTRM. Use this file for at least one brainstorming session, as outlined in the following exercise. After you finish brainstorming, consider how using a computer affected the process.
How does your computer-generated list compare to any you completed by hand?

Exercise 1.1

Brainstorm about potential topics for an assignment. If your instructor has already made an assignment, then use this exercise to begin work on it. If you do not have an assignment yet, then brainstorm about significant events or about problems you have encountered since enrolling at your university. List every idea that comes to mind, whether you think it a good one or not. Do not censor any idea. Write for 10 minutes or until you fill at least a page from top to bottom.

FREEWRITING

Freewriting is just what its name suggests—to freewrite, you simply write. Once you start, do not stop. Do not lift your pen or pencil off the page; do not lift your fingers off the keyboard—write! If you get stuck, if the thoughts will not come, then write a single word—"stuck, stuck, stuck"—or write a nonsense phrase—"wet ducks, wet ducks, wet ducks"—or write a sentence about your frustrations—"this is dumb, this is dumb, this is dumb." It doesn't really matter what you write, so long as you continue to write. Eventually, writing that word, nonsense phrase, or sentence should get you past your stuck point and back to what interests you. As you write, do not stop to correct grammar and spelling errors. Freewriting is designed solely to uncover ideas, so grammar and mechanics do not count, and worrying about them at this point in the writing process can cause you to lose focus on your subject and the ideas you will discover. The key thing to remember is this: Do not censor, do not correct, just write.

The following examples of freewriting were written by Arlene Yusnukis, a composition student at New Mexico State University (NMSU). Arlene began with a particular assignment: to write a personal essay about a place or event that affected her deeply. In the first freewrite, Arlene's job was to write about places and events that stood out in her mind.

> I remember being sprayed in the face with a chemical fire extinguisher at 2:30 in the morning, backpacking in the pecos wilderness the rams eating crackers, waterskiing for the very first time, cliff jumping, the green station house with the card rack when mom and I got off the train, riding my tricycle in circles around a big red ant, my grandmother dying of cancer & being there for a month going to school in Spokane, the hot lunch cart getting bronchitis and letters from dad c/o my aunt my cousins picking on my brother my grandfather and his horses. Flicka a horse bit my brothers hand. Meeting Kelli and Paul my boyfriend and the initiation into the band, going to Denver and freezing the huge Bronco football players, stepping on head phone, sleeping by the bathroom. Sneaking out to play frisbee in the middle of the night and getting caught cuz the frisbee was loud cuz we never caught it. trying to make poptarts quietly in the dark. My dog dying. Our toilet getting stuck flushing. Being in two accidents in less than a year seeing the front grill of the truck before it hit us. Physical therapy migraines, pills for schizophrenics. The old age home and smell—

Is this a finished piece of writing? Obviously not. But it is a very good example of what an initial freewrite is supposed to do because it uncovered a number of topics that Arlene could have written about. How many topics are in this freewrite? At least a dozen. And note the range of things Arlene wrote about. Some of the topics she remembers from her childhood (riding the tricycle in circles around the ant), others from events that happened as recently as the preceding semester (the band trip to Denver). Some of the topics are very serious (her grandmother's death, being in two accidents), others far less so (making Poptarts). What is most important to note is that Arlene just wrote; she did not censor herself, did not judge any particular topic as better or worse than any other, did not stop to mull any topic over, did not scratch anything out, did not try to correct errors in grammar, spelling, or punctuation. She started writing and kept writing until the time allotted for freewriting was over.

**Exercise
1.2**

Pick an entry from your Interest Inventory or one of the topics you listed while brainstorming and freewrite about it for 10 minutes. Once you get started, don't stop until this time is up. Don't worry about grammar or spelling. Don't lift your pen or pencil off the page; don't stop writing—just write. When you finish, let the freewrite sit for a few minutes, then read through it. How many potential topics can you identify? Did any of what you wrote surprise you? If so, why? Did you uncover something you didn't think you would? If so, what?

Next, Arlene selected one of the potential topics she had uncovered—"backpacking in the pecos wilderness the rams eating crackers"—and did a second freewrite to see whether she would be interested in writing an entire paper about it. At first, it may seem that such a small detail would hardly let Arlene develop a paper about a place or event that affected her deeply, but then, that was her task as a writer—to show that the event or place was important to her. Here is her second freewrite:

> Driving up there the road dirt for so long and our caddy not liking the drive but tolerating it. Trying to get everyones packs into the trucks and trunks. The storm clouds over the pecos mountains as we drove up. The quaint little town inside the canyon, Jack's creek. The beautiful campground at the top where we started from. Climbing up and up at a steep angle and looking down to my left at a vertical nearly drop. Switchbacks, losing my sleeping bag having to bring up the rear with Brad and Chip, fellow workers, up front slowpokers in back. Hard to get transportation. Chip not wanting to charge for gas. Rain in the late afternoon. The big highcountry meadow with posts to mark trail in snow. The smell, clear sky, critters heaviness of pack & Brad taking lighter stuff as trip goes on. Cold in rain. Finally stop near Pecos baldy lake. Small lake. Pecos baldy bald! Just flat rocks—shale? Wet, brad no warm clothes water cold to wash face in. Brad sick. Starting Svea stove quick! Finally getting all kids in tents in bed. Teresa & I talking for a long time. Boys growl whole camp awake. Sunny next morning. Better tempers cute people in morning messy hair, buffalo breath.
> One ram one ewe big horn sheep come down embankment near camp. Ewe no hair on neck, radio collar rubbed off. Eat out of Ross hand knock over packs a camp away & eat crackers. Climbing saddle to leave PB area. Switchbacks a tight-zipper. Relief on other side. Walk forever that day. Walking just behind storm. See hail everywhere but not on us. Worry that won't get out in time. Boys tell steve to eat skunk cabbage cabonions. Pest bad news hard to get in the swing of walking after them. Knives of pain on top of shoulder. hip strap much too big for me. Ross gets stuck between rock & log. Steve fell over one. Don't stop where we were supposed to. Have to go on Pretty golden meadow. Clumps of trees on mntn on either side. Narrow with stream in middle Horse Thief meadows. Finally stop to camp on top of flat hill base of mtn sparse trees

no camp in meadow Steve sick. Cabbage poison could die. Gets dry heave scares us. We eat rest, massage shoulders me no hiking boots only tennies, no blisters yet. We eat wash up in red stream below. Notice old forbidden trails. Steve ok we sleep. Me with a stick in my middle. Go on. Next day.

See Stewart and Spirit lakes. Rain no fun my poncho—day-glo orange—rips. We know where we want to camp—by Santa Fe baldy. Some want to climb. I do. send rest to camp spot. Climb steep hill above timber line. Takes longtime. Big rocks. On top see into eternity rest on rocks. Marmits whistle at us. We see SFB lake—glacier lake Finally leave. Run down jumble insides, cow almost charges us. Join group and play. Sleep Rain.

Chip & Brad too anxious to leave. They go ahead. I take poky ones like me later. We catch up go to rondevous and wait for 1½ hrs. I told them no rush. rain. Mr Tatro watermelon yum. Ski basin pretty home. limp blisters cut open by bad surgeon. Relief bath. sleep.

Danielle Corder, a first-year writing student at NMSU, used freewriting in a different way. First, she generated a short list of potential topics for a persuasive essay. Then, she completed a freewrite about each of those topics to see what kind of interest she had in them.

Things I feel strongly about:

- Parents have a responsibility to bring their children up in a good way.
- Bringing a weapon to school is unjustifiable.
- Children should be encouraged to participate in extracurricular activities.
- A legal adult—can do anything but purchase and consume alcoholic beverages. Either the age of consumption should be lowered or the legal adult age should be raised. Maybe. Hmmm . . .
- I'm running out of ideas!
- Gender roles aren't a bad thing. Yes, men and women are different, but they should still have equal rights & privileges & etc.
- I can't think!

1. Parents and their responsibility to their children.
   First off, let me start by saying anyone mature enough to make the child should be prepared to raise and be there for that child throughout their life. I believe parents have the major and primary responsibility to be in that child's life. They have a responsibility to provide for the child emotionally and physically. Parents need to be role models for the next generation, avoiding drugs, excessive drinking, and mental and physical abuse. They need to be a large part of their children's lives.
2. Weapons at school.
   I understand that at times a person feels as if they need to defend themselves, so they bring a gun to school. It's still wrong. A gun is used for one thing—to kill. Not to wound, to kill. There are many other options. In the movie "Friday," a father says something to his son that should really hit home to the youth who find it necessary to bring weapons to school: You don't need a gun, when you have your fists and they're all you need. If you can't use those your a wimp. Yes, you lose some. Yes, you win some. The one thing is you're still alive and *that's* the most important thing.

3. Children in extracurricular activities.
  It's not too much of an outrageous statement to tell someone that children involved are children who stay out of trouble. I would even bet statistics say the same. Growing up is a difficult process. It's hard to find oneself and to find what you enjoy. Often times boredom and limited acquaintances lead children to other "not-so-nice" extracurricular activities. Encourage children to try new things. Thousands of things are available. Schools alone offer tons of activities: club, organizations, sports. There's such a variety, it'd be hard to not find something for your child. The city and community also offer activities along with churches and other organizations. So don't let your child think there's nothing to do.
4. Legal adults not being able to drink.
  Okay, so my point is this: Why can an 18 year old do anything but drink. They take on all other responsibilities—why are they incapable of just this one. Yes, it is a big one and I know a lot of 18 year olds I wouldn't want drinking. I'm not very decided on this one.
5. Yuck! I don't even want to write about gender roles or gender discrimination.

For her essay, Danielle selected the third entry—children and extracurricular activities. Through freewriting, she found that she had enough interest in this topic to work with it as the basis for an entire essay.

Computer Tip

Create a file named FREEWRIT. Use this file to complete the following exercise; then compare your computer writing to any freewriting you did by hand.

Exercise 1.3

From your initial freewrite, identify a particular topic or idea that interests you. Then do a second freewrite about it, this time taking 20–30 minutes to write.

In comparing the two examples of freewriting given here, we find that Danielle used her freewriting to decide whether she had enough interest in a particular topic to base an essay on it, whereas Arlene used her freewriting to discover a topic and then to generate a fair amount of detail about it. Danielle wrote in complete sentences; Arlene did not. Each writer used freewriting well, with each discovering a topic for her essay.

We want particularly to note the detail that Arlene began to generate about her camping experience in the Pecos Wilderness. She even implied what may have been significant about the experience when she wrote, "On top see into eternity." Note also how little attention Arlene paid to correctness. For example, how many sentence fragments did she write in the first paragraph alone? How many words are misspelled? Arlene generated a substantial amount of information, not all of which found its way into her final draft. Arlene's final draft is presented in Chapter 5 (see pp. 138–139).

Exercise 1.4

Compare your two freewrites from Exercise 1.3. How detailed is the second? How does it relate to the first? Did any of what you wrote surprise you? If so, why? Did you uncover something you did not remember? If so, what? Did you discover any gaps in your knowledge, anything you either need or want to know more about? If so, what will you need to do to fill those gaps? Does any of this second freewrite point toward the significance of the topic? If so, identify it.

CLUSTERING

Clustering can help you generate ideas and show potential relationships among them. You start by capturing your topic idea in a single word or short phrase and placing it in a box or circle in the center of a sheet of paper. Then, write down things about the topic that come to mind, circling each item and connecting it with a line to the main topic or to other circles, whichever connection seems more appropriate. You'll build individual clusters of ideas that relate to each other and to the main topic idea.

Clustering works on the principle of association. The more ideas you generate, the more ideas are likely to occur to you, and so you compile a group of ideas and show how they relate to one another. Seeing how things relate can help you discover the significance that is characteristic of good writing. And in showing specifically how different ideas relate, clustering can give you a visual representation of the relative importance of particular ideas—the more circles in a given cluster, the more important that cluster is likely to be. [For an extended discussion of clustering, see Gabriele L. Rico's *Writing the Natural Way* (Los Angeles: Tarcher, 1983).]

Figure 1.1 is an example of clustering Bill did with his children's literature class in connection with Frances Hodgson Burnett's *The Secret Garden*. You'll find the topic of the cluster, "gardens," in the middle of the page, with those things Bill associated with gardens connected to that term. But you'll also see that this exercise took him over a range of territory and subjects, some directly related to gardens, some only brought to memory by one of the other terms. Note the power of association this cluster shows—from the main topic, "gardens," to "backyard" (a reference to flowers in Bill's backyard), to "gladiolas (dead)," to "Altha, FL." Bill made the tie from gladiolas to Altha because Mary Beth, his wife, taught in Altha's elementary school. Gladiolas are grown around Altha, and Mary Beth's students often brought her armfuls of fresh-cut gladiolas.

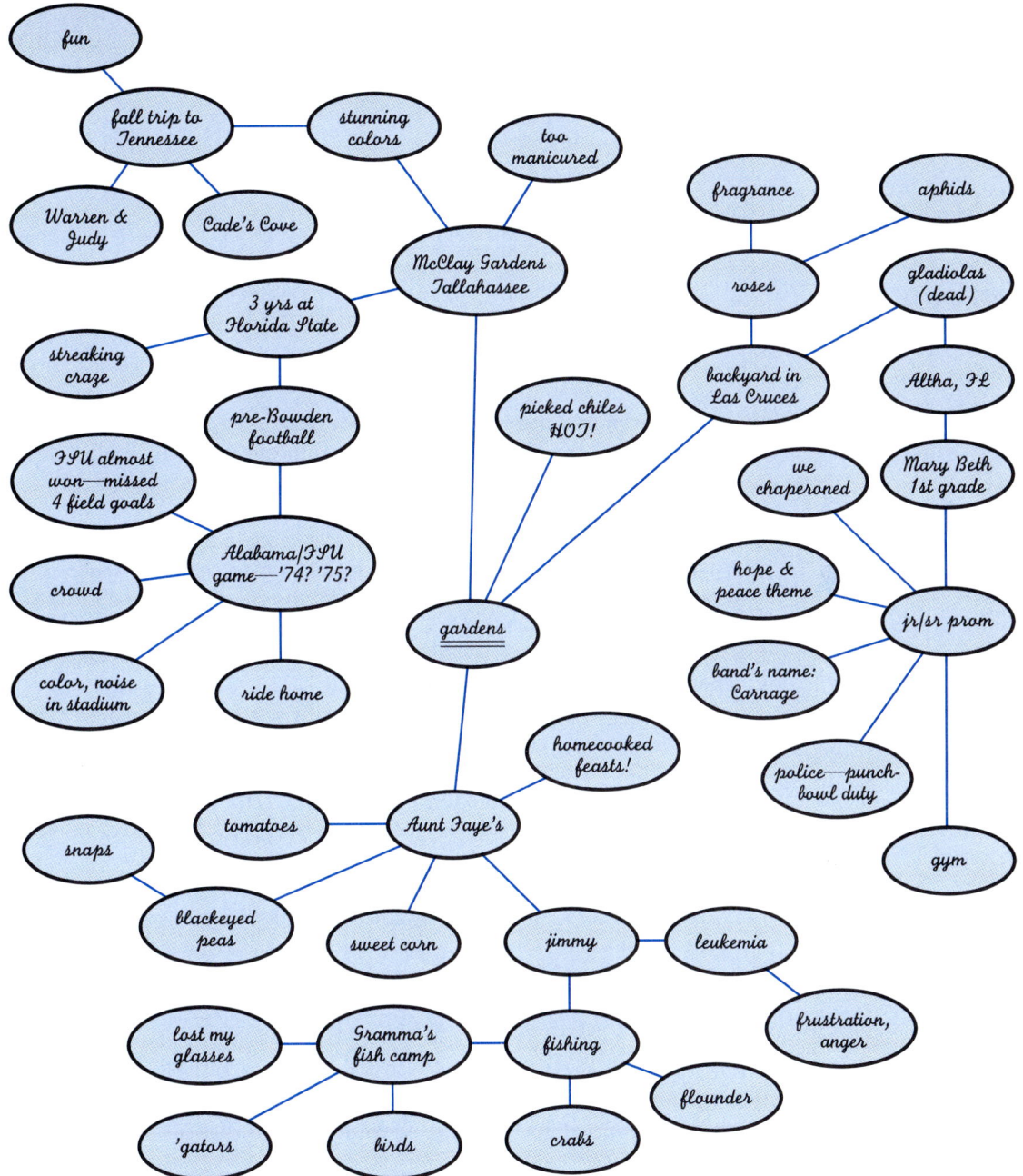

FIGURE 1.1 Prewriting Strategy: Clustering

How many papers could come from this single clustering? If we focus only on those clusters of three or more terms, then Bill could be interested enough in these topics:

chaperoning a junior/senior prom
the Alabama/Florida State football game (either 1974 or 1975)
remembering Jimmy (his cousin who died from leukemia at the age of 52)
spending time at his grandmother's fish camp
Florida panhandle home cooking

Exercise 1.5

1. Pick an event that was important in your life. If you cannot think of a specific event immediately, look again at your Interest Inventory or at the events you listed in brainstorming. Then cluster that event, following the directions given for clustering. What major clusters or idea groups emerge? How do these point toward the significance of the event for you? Does your clustering point toward any gaps in your knowledge of the topic? If so, what do you need to do to fill them?

2. Cluster at least three of these topic ideas: fear, happiness, fifth grade, winner, pain, family, college, backyard, the future, today, the past, flying, running, racing. What major clusters or idea groups emerge? How do these point toward the significance these terms have for you? Does your clustering point toward any gaps in your knowledge of the topic? If so, what do you need to do to fill them?

3. Use your major as the key term for a cluster. If you haven't declared a major, then pick some topic you're interested in and use it as the key term for a cluster. What major clusters or idea groups emerge? How do these point toward the significance of the term you selected? Does your clustering point toward any gaps in your knowledge of the topic? If so, what do you need to do to fill them?

4. Select a topic that has at least some controversy surrounding it, such as a campus issue or a community or political issue, and use it as the key term for a cluster. What do you learn about the topic and your interest in it from completing this cluster?

VISUALIZING

Another effective technique for developing detail is visualizing. This technique helps you "see" your topic—create it in your mind so that it comes to life as much as possible.

Exercise 1.6

We invite you to travel in your mind to your favorite place. First, find a quiet spot, one in which you can relax as completely as possible. Throughout this exercise, be as still and as attentive as possible to the detail you will generate. Below is a set of directions for you to follow. Do not respond out loud to any of them—visualize first, then respond in writing. The first few times you try this, you may need to have a friend read the directions aloud so that you can work through the exercise completely. Eventually, with enough practice, you'll be able to do this exercise on your own.

1. Close your eyes and take several deep breaths. Sit very still in as comfortable a position as possible.
2. Identify the place, naming it in your mind.
3. Bring this place to life by recreating it in your mind's eye.
4. Stand in the center of the scene you have created. Turn very slowly in a complete circle, letting your eyes pan up and down like a camera taking in scenery. What do you see? What particular features dominate the scene? What colors stand out? When you have completed one turn, stop. Stand absolutely still.
5. Let your senses other than sight come into play.
   a. Is there a dominant odor in this place? Is it pleasant, sweet, acrid, faint, strong, pungent, foul? Identify its source.
   b. Is there a dominant sound? Is it loud, soft, pleasant, harsh, unpleasant, bright, muted? Identify its source.
   c. Is there anything you can touch? Does it feel cold, hot, wet, dry? What is its texture? Smooth? Rough?
   d. Does this place have a dominant taste, perhaps something in the air? Is this taste pleasant or unpleasant? Identify its source.
6. Is anyone with you in this place? If so, who? Name the person(s) there. What are you (both or all) doing? What kind of conversation is taking place—small talk, argument, important discussion? Try to capture as much of the conversation and action as possible.
7. What is the dominant mood of this place? Why is this place important to you? Why is it your favorite place?
8. Slowly, take one last look around, stopping to examine dominant or important aspects of this place in as much detail as you think necessary.
   When you are ready, leave this place and come back to where you are now.

Write a paragraph in which you detail this place. Your task is to write so that a reader can see that this place is meaningful to you without your having to say that. Do not use such words as "favorite" and "meaningful"; instead, let the detail you give the reader carry this message.

As you read over the paragraph you wrote, did you find any surprises? Did you remember anything about the place that you didn't think you would? Did anything startle or please you? Identify that element. Why does it stand out? Are there any noticeable gaps in your memory of the place? If so, what do you need to do to fill them?

Once you have completed this exercise, try it again; visualize your favorite place a second time. When you have written the second descriptive paragraph, compare it with your first, looking for similarities but also for differences, such as increased detail.

The following five paragraphs, each very different in its topic from the others, were written as part of an in-class visualization exercise. You'll note that these examples are in some ways similar to Arlene's and Danielle's freewrites in that they are not polished pieces of writing. They were written in class under timed conditions, and you'll find some grammatical and mechanical mistakes. For now, ignore any errors you spot, and respond to these questions: How easy is it for you to understand that the place described is a favorite or significant one for each writer? Which details or images show you the significance? What makes these effective?

No worry. No stress. No cares. No school. No homework. Just life. I wonder so often what I am missing in the real world when I am at school. Everything is a book, or so it seems. My head aches from each test. Am I happy? I think to those summer days of plenty. I do so wish I was there right now. On that bicycle, riding endlessly just because. "Time is on my side" now. I don't fight the clock for every second. I enjoy each one instead. I smile, I laugh, I play. I see a goal. I am on this bicycle, and I know where it is going. Everything is so clear, and then school comes around again. Am I cut out for this? I wonder if college is the be all end all. Can I be all I want to be without it? Maybe. I don't have the answer. I wish I did. What do I want? Is this it? Maybe it is just one of those days, but I have those too often. I wish I could find my place. I wish I had directions to this life. What am I good at? What makes me tick? The bicycle just keeps on spinning regardless. I can't stop it now. Where would I be then?

Kara Edewaard

The overall mood of this place is extremely excited and intense. This place is the Bulldog Bowl and it's five minutes before kickoff. The Artesia Bulldogs will try to win their 20th state football championship today. I can feel the electricity in the air. The crowd screams along with the cheerleaders. Everyone is pumped up. I look to the left where the flag is blowing in the breeze. it is barely cool enough for the fans to have to wear jeans and long-sleeved shirts. However, I am so exhilerated that I won't have any trouble staying warm. As I sit down on the 50 yard line to stretch my back, I glance up into the stands and try to find my parents. However, everyone looks alike in the bright waves of orange. I also see a steady stream of orange overflowing onto the grass beside the seats. I hear fragments of sentences and phrases coming from the crowd. All I can understand are things like "c'mon dogs" or "win." The crowd begins to boo so I turn around. The Silver City Colts take the field in their deep blue uniforms. The other side of the stadium looks like a deep ocean.

Greg Tutak

As I sit upon these rocks I feel the wind delicately caress my hair, my face, my eyes. The moon casts its soft beams down upon the landscape, illuminating everything in its reach. towering over me is the immense mountainside. The size and shape of the mountain cause it to emanate a sense of security and power. The blacks, greys, and dark blues ooze over the landscape like a thick oil. In the distance I hear the gentle hum of a car passing. The smell of the air is crystal clean, like a rain storm on a cool afternoon. All is quiet. The only sound is the presence of life around me. The trees, the grass, the earth, the moon, and the stars. I touch the rock beneath me letting my hands explore every crevice.

Daniel Martinez

I walk into Sonic at the beginning of the closing shift and instantly my heart rate starts to climb and I feel the need to put my whole self on fast forward. Everything is chaotic. The switchboard is beeping a high-pitched beep, customers are ordering, the cooks are yelling for beef patties and fries, and the manager is persuading the carhops to hustle just a little bit faster. My stomach tightens slightly from the odors drifting from the kitchen. Chicken and bacon are frying. Tator tots and onion rings are in the friers. The rush is on and every employee is running about mad at the insistence of the manager, or even me sometimes. We bump into each other, apologize, and carry on. It is so hectic. The clock only says 6:15. 6:15. Can that be? Surely it's at least 7:00. The ice machine is empty now, and the cups need to be restocked. "We're out of slush," someone yells. More customers come still. There is food on the tray table still waiting to go out. 8 feet of table filled with orders all waiting to go out. the monitors overhead show that there are still drinks and banana splits and shakes to be made. It seems to go on forever sometimes.

Ayn Leslie-Cook

I step out of the warm car into the snow. No one else has stepped in it yet. The cold stings my nose, to make me realize how clean and fresh the air is. I put on my brown velvet gloves and follow Thomas out into the snow meadow. The only sounds present are feet crunching through the top layer of snow and the occasional scream of glee from a nearby child. All at once my view of the pine-covered mountain is changed to the absolute blue sky. My Thomas, a little boy at heart, has just tackled me and I'm lying out flat in the snow. I never realized snow smells, but it does, like the cleanest water with a touch of earth, the smell of pines accenting the snow makes me want to eat it. I take a bite and just like the appearance it is pure in its taste. Even at the age of a hundred I think I will act like a child in the snow, lost in its innocence.

Andrea Gonzalez

Exercise 1.7

Repeat the steps listed in Exercise 1.6 for visualizing two or three of the following topics, and then write a paragraph detailing your visualization: your school's orientation or registration sessions, friendship (or a friend), patriotism (or a patriot), racism (or a racist), sexism (or a sexist).

You'll note that these topics lend themselves to writing that could be more argumentative than personal in nature. If, for example, you were to decide to write an essay examining problems you had with your school's registration system and proposing solutions to those problems, you could use visualization to relive your experiences and thus sharpen the focus of your writing. Visualization is one way to explore a topic, whether intensely personal or very public.

ASKING QUESTIONS

One of the best ways to explore a topic is to ask questions about it, so we've developed a set of questions designed to help you generate a lot of information. It won't always be necessary to ask every question every time you use this technique, but until you get used to asking these questions about a topic, you should ask and try to answer all of them. Begin by identifying or defining your topic, either in a word or two (e.g., "college football") or in a phrase ("reintroducing wolves in New Mexico wilderness"). Then substitute your word or phrase for *"your topic"* in each question.

The questions are given in the present tense, but if your topic is an event that has already taken place, then consider varying the tense you use. For example, if you are writing about a football game you played a year ago, you can rephrase the question "What are the implications of the game?" to "What were the implications of the game?" But you can also use the present-tense form if you want to consider how your present-day view of the topic contrasts with that from the past. Similarly, if your topic is set in the future, you may want to ask several of the questions in the future tense.

Finally, a particular question may not seem to apply to your topic. If this occurs, then skip that question for a moment, but return to it later and try to see how it might fit.

Questions of association enable you to

define, state what something is
classify, sort or group like things with like
compare, state how something is like something else
describe the physical attributes of something
create a context, place something in its environment

Each of these activities involves you in generating ideas you associate with your topic, things that go or fit with your topic. Here are questions based on association:

How do you define *your topic?* What is it?
What do you associate with *your topic?*
What are the physical elements or characteristics of *your topic?*
Where does *your topic* take place? In what context does it occur?
What has been written or said in favor of *your topic?*
How does *your topic* compare with other things like it?

Questions of opposition enable you to

look at opposites and opposition
contrast, see how something is unlike something similar
examine tensions, see how something does not fit with its surroundings
look for what does not quite add up, for what may be out of line with
    other things

Each of these activities requires you to consider those aspects of your topic that set it apart from other things. Here are questions based on opposition:

Who or what opposes *your topic*? Why? What is the nature of this opposition?

What has been written or said against *your topic*?

How is *your topic* unlike other similar things? What sets it apart from those things?

How does *your topic* stand out against its context?

What about *your topic* seems odd, incongruous, or unusual?

Questions of sequence enable you to

consider how something evolved
examine cause and effect
look at the order of something
consider the order of steps or stages from start to finish

Each of these activities asks you to examine the origin, order, or development of your topic. Here are questions based on sequence:

What is the specific sequence in *your topic*? What comes or happens first, then second, then third, and so on?

How did *your topic* come to be?

What are the causes of *your topic*?

What steps, if any, are involved in *your topic*?

Questions of consequence enable you to

consider knowledge gained from exploring a topic
examine problems and solutions
ask, "What if?" and "Why?"
make a value judgment

Each of these activities requires you to consider the worth or implications of your topic. Ultimately, these activities require you to assess your topic and so to discover your understanding of its significance. Here are questions based on consequence:

What did you learn from *your topic*?

What did you learn from your investigation of *your topic*?

What problems are inherent in *your topic*? What are their solutions?

What results from *your topic*?

What opportunities does *your topic* offer?

What are the implications of *your topic*?

What about *your topic* is good? Bad? Desirable? Undesirable? Necessary?

Should *your topic* be? Not be? Why or why not?

When should you use these questions? At any point as you work to generate ideas. You may use them as the starting point in working up a topic; you may select a topic from your Interest Inventory and begin asking the questions. You may also use them to continue exploration of a topic that was the basis for any brainstorming, freewriting, clustering, or visualizing you may have done. And you may use them as you revise an essay. Whenever it is necessary for you to generate detail and ideas, the questions are available to you.

Writing Strategy

QUESTIONS FOR ANALYSIS

To explore a possible writing topic, ask yourself these questions:

Association

How do you define *your topic*? What is it?
What do you associate with *your topic*?
What are the physical elements or characteristics of *your topic*?
Where does *your topic* take place? In what context does it occur?
What has been written or said in favor of *your topic*?
How does *your topic* compare with other things like it?

Opposition

Who or what opposes *your topic*? Why? What is the nature of this opposition?
What has been written or said against *your topic*?
How is *your topic* unlike other similar things? What sets it apart from those things?
How does *your topic* stand out against its context?
What about *your topic* seems odd, incongruous, or unusual?

Sequence

What is the specific sequence in *your topic*? What comes or happens first, then second, then third, and so on?
How did *your topic* come to be?
What are the causes of *your topic*?
What steps, if any, are involved in *your topic*?

Consequence

What did you learn from *your topic*?
What did you learn from your investigation of *your topic*?
What problems are inherent in *your topic*? What are their solutions?
What results from *your topic*?
What opportunities does *your topic* offer?

What are the implications of *your topic*?

What about *your topic* is good? Bad? Desirable? Undesirable? Necessary?

Should *your topic* be? Not be? Why or why not?

APPLICATION: THE FUZZWORT REFINING COMPANY

The following application focuses on a fictitious refining or smelting company, the Fuzzwort Refining Company (FRC). If you have ever seen a plant like a smelter in operation, its smokestacks probably stand out in your memory. Such stacks are large and, because of the smoke they emit, highly visible. Try to visualize the plant or plants you have seen as we proceed with our application of the Questions for Analysis to FRC. In the application, *"your topic"* in each question is replaced by the subject, "FRC." And the investigator of the topic, the student writer, is represented by "I."

QUESTIONS OF ASSOCIATION

What is FRC?

It's a refining corporation that refines such metals as copper from raw ores. It's a heavy industry, with smelters capable of polluting its surrounding environment.

What do you associate with FRC?

Last year there was a big flap about the plant's smoke emissions. At the request of a concerned group of citizens, a team from the Environmental Protection Agency (EPA) inspected the plant and found that it was emitting at least twice the pollution allowed by EPA standards. Nearly every local newspaper covered the story, all of them praising the EPA's attempts to restrict this pollution. But nothing was done, thanks to court action brought by FRC attorneys. FRC seems to have little, if any, concern for the public's or the environment's well-being. Other things— the plant has a big payroll (I don't know how much) and pays a lot of local and state taxes. It employs a lot of people in all (I don't know how many).

What are the physical elements or characteristics of FRC?

The actual physical plant covers a number of acres, mostly devoid of plant life. It's a bleak place, grimy, with a large parking lot, usually full of the cars of commuting workers. It has several smokestacks, all in use twenty-four hours a day, the smaller ones up to 750 feet high, the largest one a 1,200-foot-high giant. At times these stacks belch a thick, black, sooty smoke that hangs over the countryside like a pall. Things to find out: What's the particulate composition of that smoke? What kinds of chemicals are those stacks putting into the air?

Where does FRC take place? In what context does it occur?

The context is a broad one. First is the immediate context, the countryside surrounding this plant. It's set in a rural area with cultivated fields on three sides. Within four or five miles of the plant are several small towns, each having a population under 5,000. Within thirty miles is a large city with a population of close to 1,000,000. Nearly all the workers at this plant commute from the city; only a small part of the workforce comes from the smaller nearby towns. A larger context involves the economical setting; that is, FRC is set in a context of industrialism and big business.

What has been said or written in favor of FRC?

Company officials ran a big ad campaign not too long ago—newspapers, radio, billboards. The general message was that FRC is the county's friend because it employs a lot of people, pays a lot of taxes, and produces materials vital to national security. All this put the company in a very positive light, presenting only the company's point of view. I need to find these and look at them again.

How does FRC compare to other things like it?

It's like other businesses that emit smoke and pollutants. In this sense, it's like chemical plants that release toxic wastes into rivers as well as into the air. It's also like power plants fueled by oil and coal. It's also like other businesses that employ large numbers of people; it contributes to the county's economy.

QUESTIONS OF OPPOSITION

Who or what opposes FRC? Why? What is the nature of this opposition?

Two years ago, a group of concerned citizens formed a special-interest group and became a watchdog of this plant. They called in the EPA inspection team, and since that team's visit this group has filed suit in the federal courts to force strict compliance by FRC with EPA guidelines. In addition, three local newspapers have begun writing about the plant's continued pollution and so have begun exposing FRC to public scrutiny. The group's and the papers' goal is to see the plant stop its pollution entirely or shut down. Lately, there has been much concern over the acid rains afflicting much of the northern United States, and great debate between environmentalists and businesspeople has ensued. Environmentalists offer much opposition, though not just to this plant.

What has been said or written in opposition to FRC?

All the local newspapers ran negative stories about the pollution. These stories discussed plants dying, greater incidence of respiratory illnesses the closer you got to the plant, and so on. Several investigative reporters really took company officials apart. I need to find copies of these articles. Then there are the articles on acid rain published by *National Geographic* and other environmentally oriented magazines. Because FRC has been accused of contributing to this problem, these articles might set the company's problems in a broader context. I need to locate these articles also.

How is FRC unlike other similar things?

Where can I find a refining plant that doesn't pollute the environment.

How does FRC stand out against its context?

The plant provides a stark contrast with the countryside immediately surrounding it. That countryside is lush and green and is characterized by cultivated fields seemingly carved out of forest. As far as standing out against the larger context of industrialism or big business, this particular plant does not; rather, it blends right in and is actually indistinguishable from other plants and similar businesses.

What about FRC seems odd, incongruous, or unusual?

There's a real incongruity at work, given the company's ad campaign (everything's just fine and dandy) in light of the reality of the plant itself. It looks like a plant in Eastern Europe.

QUESTIONS OF SEQUENCE

What is the specific sequence in FRC? What comes or happens first, second, third, and so on?

There's been something of a sequence at work as company officials responded to increasing criticism. At first, they simply ignored their critics. But as the media attention created increased concern, the officials' response escalated as well. I need to go back and look at the sequence of events here.

How did FRC come to be?

It began as a turn-of-the-century company, responding to the need to deal with raw ore being taken from the surrounding mountains. It grew up in an era when there was little concern for pollution standards, because the U.S. public seemed simply to want more and more material goods. The plant continued to expand until it reached its current size about thirty years ago. It has quadrupled in size since it was first built. It's a very profitable plant for its owners, hence the dynamic growth. Just how profitable is it? I don't know.

What are the causes of FRC?

A response here is implicit in the preceding question, where I talked about the need for a smelter and then the expansion in response to demand by the U.S. public.

What steps are involved in FRC?

I guess I could talk about the actual process of refining ore, tracing it step-by-step as it moves through the various stages of refining until an ingot of metal is produced.

QUESTIONS OF CONSEQUENCE

What did you learn from FRC?

How to put an advertising campaign together. Theirs was really a slick production designed to shift public concern away from the negative aspects of the plant so that the public would consider only the benefits (jobs, taxes, payroll).

What did you learn from your investigation of FRC?

The language of the ad campaign was incredibly manipulative. Its goal was to hide the pollution the plant produced, not to deal with the problem of the pollution itself. So I learned to be wary of big business and advertising—actually, I was already wary, so I guess my wariness got reinforced.

What problems are inherent in FRC? What are their solutions?

Obviously, the problem this plant poses is pollution of the countryside. Given the way tall stacks disperse pollutants into the atmosphere, FRC may pose an environmental problem to areas many miles away as well. The solutions are complex. The plant should either clean up its emissions or shut down. To clean up the emissions would require expensive scrubbers for the smokestacks; to shut down would result in the loss of jobs at the plant as well as the loss of business to those businesses that support the plant—a railroad, chemical suppliers, equipment suppliers, and companies subcontracted to perform maintenance at the plant.

What results from FRC?

Two primary products: the refined copper, which is beneficial, and the pollution, which is not. And, of course, accompanying the copper is the plant as an economic entity, with its jobs and so on.

What opportunities does FRC offer?

Another expansion is planned; so there will be more jobs, ranging from jobs for construction workers during the building of the expansion to jobs for more FRC workers to staff and run the expansion.

What are the implications of FRC?

Continued emissions at the present level will do the environment no good whatsoever. Continued operation of the plant will do the local and, by extension, the national economy much good.

What about FRC is good? Bad? Desirable? Undesirable? Necessary?

Okay, so I need to make a value judgment. That judgment is: The FRC plant is necessary, but at present not at all desirable. I could propose that the plant be required to install the scrubbers necessary to clean up its emissions and that antipollution devices and procedures be required in the new expansion, so that the expansion will not aggravate the problem. I don't want the plant to shut down because of its importance to the local economy, but I don't want it to continue polluting the environment.

Should FRC be? Not be? Why or why not?

Well, we have to have metals, and the only way to get them is to refine ore. So it's difficult to say that the company should shut down, especially since many people will be directly hurt economically by a shutdown. I guess the bottom line is what I said in the preceding question: The smelter has to clean up its emissions, or it has to shut down.

In examining FRC as the subject for a paper, we uncovered a great deal of material a writer could use in an essay. We also discovered aspects of this topic that called for more investigation. Were we to investigate them, we would generate still more information. Obviously, a writer could not use all this information, nor would he wish to. Instead, he would have to take a stance on the subject and then use only the information relevant to an argumentative essay. If, for example, the writer agreed with our value judgment, he could mention the benefits of the FRC plant, but he would focus on the problem of the plant's pollution and then on solutions to that problem.

Computer Tip

Create a file named QUESTION. Use it to complete the following exercise:

1. Type in the name of the first topic you select.
2. Type in each question and your response to it in turn.

3. When you complete the questions for your first topic, enter a page break or 4–5 line spaces, then type in the name of your second topic.
4. Type in each question and your response to it in turn.
5. Let your responses sit for a day; then reopen the file. Read your responses, and respond to the exercise's questions asking you to consider the kinds of detail you generated.

Exercise 1.8

Identify two topics, one concrete (e.g., an event, a person, a place), the other more abstract (e.g., morality, ethics, government, religion). Write two or three sentences in answer to each of the Questions for Analysis. If a particular question doesn't seem to work, don't give up on it entirely; instead, skip it, leaving space in your responses to come back to it later. When you have finished, consider the kinds and amount of information you generated. How much detail did you generate? Did you find anything that surprised you? If so, what, and why was it a surprise? Did you remember anything that you didn't think you would? If so, what? What gaps in your knowledge did your use of the questions reveal? What will you need to do to fill them? And what kinds of statements did you make in response to the questions about consequence?

SAMPLE STUDENT PROCESS—PREWRITING

To illustrate how you may move from prewriting through writing to revising, we'll follow a first-year composition student's process from start to finish. Marisol Vargas was assigned to write a personal essay in response to this prompt, which is one of three we present in Chapter 5:

> Describe an event from which you learned something. Your job is to use your language to recreate the event so that your readers will feel that they have been at least observers of this event with you, if not participants in it.

Bill, Marisol's instructor, specified that the paper be 1,000–1,500 words long, about 4–6 pages.

Bill suggested that his students freewrite for 15 minutes about important moments or events they remembered. But Marisol didn't do that; instead, she remembered immediately what she counted as a major turning point in her life and spent the entire 15-minute period on it.

FREEWRITE I

> I remember the changing point in my life. It was when I really began to realize that I did need other people, and that was when I became happy again. My friend Erika had been gone for an entire month in the summer and I missed her. That summer when she got back we did things. One of these days she called me to help her pack and visit a friend. I remember we went to visit Ed. I gave him a plant because it was his birthday. Erika and I had planned to go out to eat that

day and to talk. After we made up an excuse to leave Ed's we got in the car to drive to the restaurant. I did not feel like myself that day. I felt somehow apart from everything and everyone. I was also extremely tired. I usually get that way before a huge storm, so I told her how I felt and she felt the same. We went out to eat and we talked forever about the past. About our broken hearts, lost loves. Both of us were trying to get some guys out of our heads. They had made an incredible impact in our lifes. These guys were so similar. I got out of the restaurant feeling refreshed. Then it came. The rain storm. We were so excited. We wanted to go the park to play. As I was driving it poured. The windows were open wide and we took it all in. We went to her house to change. Then to the park. It poured the afternoon for almost an hour. That is unusual for NM. We danced outside played on the swings, sang, and did belly slides. When it stopped raining I noticed a little D on my arm. I still don't know how I got it. It was crazy. I remember that day I felt like everything I thought was important didn't matter anymore. Broken heart was for nothing. It all was washed away by the rain. Erika was the only person who I know of who would go out in the rain with me like that. The next day I woke up feeling so clean. Like I had taken a hot bath in roses for hours. My thoughts were so clear. It was that day that I forgot about the past. I realized I had all I needed. I have never had a friend as wonderful as Erika and never will. She helped me realize that things aren't as important as the ones that stay. We moved. She is the one that I miss. I realize now that I need her friendship. It is because of her that I got out of my depression and I will never forget her or that day for that.

This freewrite clearly is not a polished piece of writing. But that's the nature of a freewrite. It's designed to help the writer get as much on the page about her thoughts as possible, and that's what Marisol did here. However, after considering whether she wanted to base her first essay on this freewrite, she decided to find another topic. So she produced a second freewrite, again without worrying about grammar or spelling.

FREEWRITE 2

I remember when I went with my mom to feed the homeless. When I first got there I was a little scared. I didn't really know what to expect. We got out of the car with pans of food. They all just looked at us. I tryed not to make eye connect. I remember when we got into the building we went into the kitchen, a small separated area. It was hidden from the dining area. I just wanted to stay in there, but the other volunteers sent me out with a fruit bowl. I had to ask people if they wanted fruit. I am a shy person so this was a hard job for me. But I did it. How they crowded me wanting the fruit. They asked for bananas especially for potassium they said. By the second bowl I felt better. I lifted my eyes from the bowl to make sure I got everyone and survey the area. There were family's in there. The children looked so sad. There were people with animals who were outside. They were really nice and thanked me so much for the fruit. I remember this one man who wanted some fruit. He reminded me of Santa Claus with a sweet rosy smile. He had coffee in his hand and plate. "Sir would you like some fruit," I asked. He looked at me as if to say where can I put it. With a shaky hand he took it with the hand of his coffee. Some of the coffee split. I think it burnt him. He just thanks me so sweetly and walked off clumsily. I'll never forget the way he looked. It was at that moment that I realized how stupid and selfish I was. I had tryed to hard not to make eye connect. What for it it is not as though they were going to kill me with their eye. Homeless are just like everyone else and there is no reason that they should be viewed differently. We look business men in the eye. A homeless person could have once been a business man. Sometimes we treat the homeless worst than animals. At that moment I realized one day I could be in that position or maybe a friend or family member. I would be greatful of the person who took the time to look me in the eye and smile. There was an indian man who wanted a banana, but there were not more. When I got my new batch I found him to give him the banana. We are so lucky with what we have. Getting almost anything we want, the least we can give is a banana. I learned humility that day.

Marisol decided that this topic—volunteering at a homeless shelter—was one she wanted to work with, so she was then ready to work this freewrite into a longer, more detailed piece of writing. We'll continue working with Marisol's drafting process in Chapter 2.

FROM INVENTING TO DRAFTING

Once you have worked through one or more of these invention devices, you'll proceed to drafting. Your task will be to shape many of the details you generated into an initial draft of an essay. Keep in mind that you probably won't use all of the information you generated, but the writer's task is to choose the details that best represent her topic to her reader, which oftentimes means not using everything she generates. Just as a reminder here, look again at the details Arlene generated in her two freewrites about the backpacking trip. She discovered a lot of detail, but she wasn't able to use all of it in her final draft, simply because it didn't fit.

The next chapter, on shaping an essay, is designed to help you move from your inventing to writing a first rough draft of an essay.

Once you've generated some ideas and information in your prewriting, your next job is to shape those ideas into a rough draft, one ready for peer review. In this chapter, we'll offer some practical strategies for drafting that should help you do this.

INITIAL SHAPING STRATEGIES

WRITING FOR A READER

As you begin writing your first draft, your discovery draft, consider who your audience may be. Who might want or need to read your paper? Identify this person or persons, and then respond to these questions:

1. What do my readers already know about this topic?
2. What do I want them to know, understand, or learn from reading my writing?
3. Why do I want them to know this?

Writing answers to these questions can help you focus your drafting by identifying things you want to cover and why you want to cover them. Your job at this point is not to write a final draft for this initial audience; instead, it's to find out as much as you can about your topic and what you think and feel about it. When

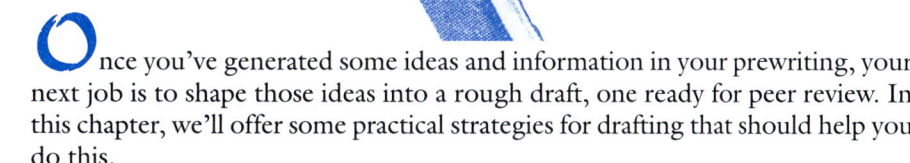

Shaping an Essay

CHAPTER 2

we move to discussion of revising, you'll work with your audience more extensively. For now, it's enough for you to speculate about who your audience might be and what information you'll need to present to those readers.

FOCUS STATEMENTS

To develop an initial focus for your paper, consider what you might want readers to learn from your paper and why you want them to learn it. As you speculate about what and why, you should be able to develop a tentative focus statement for your paper. This statement, which should be at least three sentences long, is an initial speculation about purpose, about what you think you want your essay to accomplish or do. Here is an example of a focus statement for an essay on a meaningful event:

> The event I want to write about is the time I failed to pass a swimming merit badge class at Scout camp. I want to talk about the experience of failing the class. I learned that it's ok to fail. I didn't learn it at that time; instead, I came to realize it only a couple of years after the fact. And I learned that it's ok to fail, as long as you try, and I want my readers to see that failure isn't always a bad thing.

A writer using this statement would have several tasks to accomplish: (1) to describe the class, what he did, how he came to fail, which parts of the class worked for him and which did not; (2) to describe what it felt like to fail; and (3) to talk about what he eventually realized from having experienced that failure.

Writing a focus statement can suggest an initial structure or direction for a paper. In this example, the writer could divide the paper into three major sections, one for each of the tasks listed: first, a description or narration of the events of the class; second, a description of that key moment when he learned that he had failed and how that felt; third, a discussion of what he eventually learned. Although hardly a detailed blueprint of the essay's structure, this three-part division could serve as an initial look at that structure.

Another way to use a focus statement is to project what a potential reader would need to know about your topic. Below are two statements, the first by Katherine Ozment, the second by Adam Castoreno, both first-year composition students at New Mexico State University (NMSU). These statements were developed as essay proposals that identified a topic and then stated an initial position on it at the drafting stage in a researched essay assignment. During class, these students circulated their statements to members of their peer groups, who asked questions raised by the statements.

KATHERINE'S FOCUS STATEMENT AND HER READERS' QUESTIONS

> I would like to write my paper on a recent proposal to the education system—inclusion. Inclusion refers to classrooms that have a wide variety of students or, more specifically, completely integrating special ed students into regular ed classrooms. I would like to oppose this idea.

In this brief statement, Katherine identifies her topic (first sentence), defines it (second sentence), and then takes a stance or position on it (third sentence). The members of Katherine's group posed these questions in response:

1. Why do you oppose inclusion?
2. What are the implications for approving or disapproving inclusion?
3. What's a detailed definition of inclusion?
4. What is wrong with the current system?
5. What is wrong with inclusion?
6. What would happen if the two systems were integrated?

ADAM'S FOCUS STATEMENT AND HIS READERS' QUESTIONS

Adam's focus statement is more fully developed, more detailed, than Katherine's. But at this point, Adam doesn't know whether he thinks gene therapy (the topic of his paper) is a good idea or not. There is a tentative nature to his third paragraph, especially in the last sentence, that suggests he will use the assignment to explore the topic so that he can determine what he feels or thinks about gene therapy. He would like to be positive about it, but he needs to work through this paper to help him decide whether he can be. Here's his focus statement:

Imagine one day possessing the knowledge, the ability to alter the human DNA and correct serious genetic defects in a developing fetus. By performing "Gene Therapy," a particular gene can be taken out, altered or cloned, and placed back into the DNA, where it can perform as "programmed." According to many critics, this type of brilliant technology is not without flaws. Do we have the right to manipulate the human DNA? How far is genetic research going to take us? Can we one day develop the technology to make human beings "superhuman," possessing only superior genes or those deemed acceptable?

These kinds of philosophical questions carry some validity. However, the knowledge and information we can gain from carrying on with genetic research is enormous. Disease and genetic disorders could become dilemmas of the past. We must remember that the driving force behind gene manipulation is not to create further problems for society, but to help solve some.

Gene therapy is a serious issue facing our society which needs to be considered more deeply. As it stands currently, the knowledge base in the field of genetics is doubling every five years and will continue to increase at an even faster rate. Researching an argument in favor of my possible career choice is essential if I ever want to work in the field with any strong convictions.

The members of Adam's group posed these questions:

1. What has been done with this so far?
2. What positive things can come from this research?
3. What negative things can come from this research?
4. Are you in favor of this process? If not, how can this research be stopped or prevented? If so, how do we make sure people don't try to form "superhumans"?
5. What are the ethical problems/questions?

6. What is the procedure?
7. Could this result in more bad than good? Could someone abuse this technology?

Both Katherine and Adam created expectations in their potential readers, as reflected in the questions their group members asked. These questions helped Katherine and Adam generate still more ideas as they thought about the kinds of information potential readers would need and want. These questions also helped them consider various arguments they might have to respond to or questions they might have to answer in their papers.

Once you've developed a focus statement, either ask someone else to read and respond to it by asking several questions, as in the examples here, or prepare your own questions, listing what you would want to know if you were the intended reader of the essay. These questions can point the way to specific elements you should include in your writing and thus can help you organize your paper.

SAMPLE STUDENT PROCESS— DISCOVERY DRAFT

Your writing task now is to produce a *discovery draft*—a tentative first draft, one that probably will not be nearly as complete or as fully developed as the final draft you write. A discovery draft continues the exploration of the topic you began in your prewriting, connecting the bits and pieces of insights and information you created or uncovered while prewriting into a larger piece of writing, an essay. To begin, use your initial consideration of audience and your focus statement as reminders of what you want to cover and for whom. You may also want to develop a quick outline or list of the points you want to make. As you write, don't be concerned with grammar and mechanics, with finding the exact word, or with creating a perfectly structured final essay. Instead, concentrate on getting as much information on the page as possible. Your goal is to produce a draft that you may then revise into a rough draft for review.

Below we continue working through the drafting of Marisol Vargas's essay on her experience helping at a homeless shelter. After completing the two freewrites you read in Chapter 1, Marisol felt that she wanted to base her essay on her experience at the homeless shelter. As she moved from her second freewrite toward a discovery draft, she wrote an initial audience analysis and a focus statement to provide guidance for her writing.

INITIAL AUDIENCE ANALYSIS

My audience is the members of this English class, so it's a group of 21 NMSU students, most freshmen, different majors and hometowns. Probably a good cross-section of NMSU's student body.

1. What do my readers already know about this topic?

Like me, they probably don't have too many good feelings about the homeless, because of what we've all seen—beggars, street persons pushing shopping carts, dirty, raggedy. Television also shows this stereotype as well.

2. What do I want them to know, understand, or learn from reading my writing?

That the homeless can be just about anybody and that meeting and dealing with them isn't bad.

3. Why do I want them to know this?

Because homelessness is a problem in this country. The more we stay away from the homeless, the more they'll stay faceless. And that just keeps the problem from being solved.

FOCUS STATEMENT

I want my readers to understand how I felt at the beginning and the end of the day I spent at the homeless shelter. I want them to see what I thought and felt. In order to do this I must be very descriptive. I have to describe the area, the way people looked, the families. I have to show the emotion I felt while I was serving the fruit. I have to show the other people's reactions. I have to show my change in thought.

DISCOVERY DRAFT

It is the experience that stands out in my mind the most.

The stop light turned red and as the car slowed to a halt, I opened my eyes to my surroundings. I had been asleep for most of the journey and now the change in the car's momentum awakened me. As I looked around I noticed groups of people walking.

The steady momentum, rhythm of my life changed when I went with my mother to feed the homeless. Through this experience I learned to view people in a different light. Feeding the homeless made me realize that others people's suffering may be greater than my own. Therefore, I have learned to be more considerate.

The light turned green and we turned heading for in the same direction as the crowd.

"We're here," my mom said. I remember thinking that it wasn't as large as I expected. In front of us was a small grey building surrounded by an old chain like fence. It reminded me of a warehouse.

This was the first time I had come with my mother to feed the homeless. She had asked me many times before, but because the comfort of my bed in the early morning, I had always declined. This time, however, I worked up the energy to go.

We got out of the car with casseroles and bags of fruits. As we walked toward the shelter, I felt as though everyone was watching us and I tried not to make eye connect. "Just look straight," were the only thoughts in my head.

We entered the building through narrow doors and went toward the kitchen, a small area hidden from the rest of the cafeteria. I helped some of the other volunteers warm the food that everyone had brought. I decided that if I stayed in the seclusion of the kitchen I would be "safe."

Then we were called out to the dining area for a short breakfast prayer. I went out nervously. When it was over I hurried to the kitchen and started to serve the food, but the volunteers had a different job for me. They wanted me to go out with a bowl full of fruit and offer it to everyone. I am a shy person so the thought of having to approach unfamiliar faces scared me.

As I filled up my dish, I prepared myself for the worst. I got up, clenched my fruit bowl and slowly walked out to the dinning area. As I looked around all of my foolish thoughts and fears diminished.

Many people crowded around me waiting to get their fruit. They were very polite, thanking me with smiles and kind words. When the bowl was empty I raced back into the kitchen to refill it and I hurryed back out.

The room was filled with people of different gender and race. There were families, and single men and women, and outside there were people with animals.

Watching the families made me sad. There were little girls who's dresses were loose from hunger and the stresses of living of the street. Their eyes resembled that of an older person with lines of stressful days and sleepless nights.

As I walked outside one man caught my eye. He reminded me of Santa Claus because of his sweet eyes and big rosy cheeks. "Sir would you like some fruit," I asked. He looked at me and smiled bashfully. He looked down at his hands. He was holding coffee and an empty plate. He looked back at the fruit, he was wondering if he had room in his hands to carry it. He carefully took it into the hand that held his coffee. It split from his shaky, nervous movements. Then he thanked me sweetly and slowly walked away.

At that moment I realized how foolish I had been. Fear had kept me away so long. As I walked around I couldn't quiet figure out what it was that I feared. The people I was looking at could have easily been me or a family-member. I was lucky to have my comfortable warm bed to sleep in at night and wake up to in the morning. I couldn't imagine how it would be to have a sidewalk for a bed.

As we walked out of the shelter that day, I made it a point to look people in the eye and smile, a genuine smile. As we drove away that morning I remember my mom saying, "I think we fed over a hundred people today." All I could do was think of the faces I had seen, and I realized how much they looked like me.

How tightly structured is this essay? Not very. For example, the first six paragraphs jump back and forth between the narrative (the story Marisol wants to tell) and Marisol's commentary on it. Further, this draft lacks a good bit of detail; what she saw and felt just doesn't come alive on the page. But it serves its purpose—in drafting it, Marisol got her thoughts about that day at the homeless shelter on the page. Keep in mind that this is not her final draft; in fact, Marisol wrote another rough draft and then revised it into an essay to submit. Finally, she revised her essay one last time, following the recommendations of Bill, her instructor. We'll present these three drafts in Chapter 3.

DEVELOPING AN ESSAY'S STRUCTURE

All of the elements of an essay come together as you work to develop a discovery draft, that tentative first draft we mentioned at the start of this chapter. Once you establish at least an initial focus, either in a focus statement or a thesis sentence, you'll need to develop a structure—a shape or form—to guide you in writing your discovery draft. What follows are some practical suggestions for developing a structure. Again, keep in mind that your goal is not to produce a finished paper at this stage but to use your writing to explore your topic further. Developing an initial structure can help you in that exploration.

SHAPING STRATEGIES

Gilbert Highet offers this insight on the need for a piece of writing to have a shape, a form:

> The next thing is to devise a form for your essay. This, which ought to be obvious, is not. I learned it for the first time from an experienced newspaperman. When I was at college I earned extra pocket- and book-money by writing several weekly columns for a newspaper. They were usually topical, they were always carefully varied, they tried hard to be witty, and (an essential) they never missed a deadline. But once, when I brought in the product, a copy editor stopped me. He said, "Our readers seem to like your stuff all right, but we think it's a bit amateurish." With due humility I replied, "Well, I am an amateur. What should I do with it?" He said, "Your pieces are not coherent; they are only sentences and epigrams strung together; they look like a heap of clothespins in a basket. Every article ought to have a shape. Like this" (and he drew a big letter S on his pad) "or this" (he drew a descending line which turned abruptly upward again) "or this" (and he sketched a solid central core with five or six lines pushing outward from it) "or even this" (and he outlined two big arrows coming into collision).
>
> I never saw the man again, but I have never ceased to be grateful to him for his wisdom and for his kindness. Every essay must have a shape. You can ask a question in the first paragraph, discussing several different answers to it till you reach one you think is convincing. You can give a curious fact and offer an explanation of it. You can take a topic that interests you and do a descriptive analysis of it: a man's character [. . .], a building, a book, a striking adventure, a peculiar custom. There are many other shapes which essays can take; but the principle laid down by the copy editor was right.
>
> Gilbert Highet, *Explorations*

That principle is a simple one: Every essay you write should be shaped or structured for a purpose. You can use the following strategies to marshal support for your focus statement, to shape your essay's content.

LISTING

Read your focus statement and look back over the information you generated while inventing. Then develop a list of the important ideas, topics, or points you want to include in your paper. Your list can be as elaborate or as sparse as necessary. Its sole function is to guide you through your writing by reminding you of what you wanted to cover. Try these steps:

1. Write down all of the points about your topic that seem important to you. Derive these from your prewriting, from whatever freewriting, clustering,

visualizing, or questioning you may have done to get started. It's important not to censor yourself while making this list. Don't argue with yourself; don't worry about the order in which you list the points—simply list.

2. Number the points in the sequence in which you think they will appear in your paper. You may, for example, rank your entries in order of importance, from most to least important or from least to most important. Or you may place your entries in chronological order, taking a first-to-last approach.

3. Look again at your list, considering its completeness in light of your focus statement. If something needs to be added or deleted, then do so. If you think it would be helpful at this point to recopy the list, putting each entry in order, then do so. Otherwise, start writing.

4. As you write, refer every now and then to your focus statement and list, to see whether you're covering what you thought you needed to. If you aren't, don't be too concerned, because you may well discover a new focus as you write this discovery draft.

If you find while writing that you need to add a point not on your list, then add it. And if you decide while writing that something on the list doesn't fit after all, then delete it.

TOPIC OUTLINES

A topic outline is a listing of the topics, or subjects, and the order in which you think they will appear in a paper. It is most helpful when you let it serve as a tentative itinerary for your trip through the paper. That is, you will need to be flexible enough to depart from your outline if your writing calls for you to do so. To develop your topic outline, identify the main idea in your focus statement and then order the support for that idea in an outline format.

Below is a topic outline for a paper on assisted suicide for people with terminal illnesses.

Thesis sentence: A terminally ill patient should have the legal right to ask for death or help in dying without legal repercussions.

   I. Introduction (include thesis)
  II. History of euthanasia
     A. Greeks: acceptance of suicide and death
     B. Modern: accepting death
 III. Issues, views
     A. Right-to-die
     B. Right-to-life
     C. Physicians' dilemma
 IV. Legal aspects
     A. Past laws
     B. Current laws
     C. Future laws
  V. Conclusion

The entries marked by Roman numerals represent major sections of the paper, and the entries under these represent paragraphs and topics to support and develop the thesis. (See pp. 46–47 for discussion of thesis sentences.) This is not a detailed outline; instead, it presents an overview of the paper's structure. It identifies the main points of an essay and support for them, and it provides a guide for drafting and then, later, a checklist for completeness.

Kent Sallee, a first-year writing student at NMSU, wrote a humorous essay about how to be a pest. One of his writing strategies was this informal outline, which includes possible examples to support the points he thinks he may make in his essay. As in freewriting, Kent paid little attention to formal concerns. That is, the entries aren't strictly parallel, and you'll find a few misspelled words. But because this wasn't a final draft, Kent didn't worry about such concerns.

How to irritate people

A recipe in irritation

In a world where ignoring someone is expected, the best way of getting attention is irritation.

irritation is the term used in making people displeased at your presence.

- never push them too far—releases the tension
- should seem to be unintentional
  example: when your roommate is studying
  talk about pointless things
  make as much noise as possible
  ask questions they know you know the answer to
  if they ask you to be quiet or go away, act hurt at their rudeness
  if you have any sort of musical instrument, play a popular tune, messing up often and starting the phrase over again
- a group of irritating people is much more powerful than one
  example: eating at a restaurant
  more volume = more irritating
  gaudy subjects are good
  have very strong opinions on the wrong side of a subject
  say the exact same thing as the person said before you
- pretend to be considerate
  example: going on a date
  ask many pointless questions, refusing to accept the answer they give you
  ask the same questions with different phrasing: "your sure?" "your absolutely positive?" "your absolutely positively sure?"
- irritate someone by helping them
  example: "helping" someone with a math problem. first thing: take as long as possible to find the problem their talking about. "what number is it?"
  immediately say "this is easy"
  start doing the wrong problem
  write very large on their paper, preferably in a different colored ink
  do the problem once, exactly the way they did it, and then give up, saying "I give up."
  for best results, as you walk away, in a sarcastic "whisper," mutter "your welcome"
- become an expert in something you know nothing about
- the art of movie watching
  comment as often as possible

nitpick on every detail in the movie, giving examples of why the scene was "physically impossible" using physics terms as gravity, force, initial momentum, and the popular "compound refraction of light"

yell at the characters in the movie as if they could actually hear you—"don't do that" & "you idiot!"

ALWAYS complain constantly about the quality of the film as you watch it, especially about the last scene

Kent used this outline as a guide, expanding his notes in the examples listings into sentences and paragraphs. Not everything in the outline appeared in the paper. For example, Kent didn't use the section headed "pretend to be considerate" for two reasons: First, the example he listed there didn't illustrate a lack of consideration; second, the other entries provided more than enough material for him to use in his paper.

BLOCKING

Blocking enables you to create "bins" to hold the content of the various sections of your essay. Each block represents a major section of the paper and will probably contain several paragraphs. To begin, identify the main idea from your focus statement and then draw several blocks. Into each block, jot notes of support for the main idea you generated in prewriting. If you wish, you can subdivide larger blocks to create a block for each paragraph.

Were you to write about the problem of inadequate lighting on your campus, you could block your essay as shown in Figure 2.1.

Blocking can give you an overview of the essay's structure, representing that structure as a whole (the biggest block) divided into its parts (the smaller blocks). Such a representation can help you see how the various parts of the essay fit together. Blocking is useful at two points in your writing. Early on, it can help you shape a discovery draft by providing you with places to put the information you generated while exploring your topic. Think of a block as a bin into which you place information related to the subject of that block. In the case of the problem/solution essay presented in Figure 2.1, all information generated about the problem during prewriting would go into the problem block, or bin, and all information about the solution would go into the solution block. Later, as you revise, blocking can help you examine your draft's structure for consistency. To use blocking for this second function, summarize each paragraph's content in a phrase and place these summaries in the appropriate blocks. You may well find that a paragraph is out of place and that you need to move it or delete it altogether.

FIGURE 2.1   Organizing Strategy: Blocking

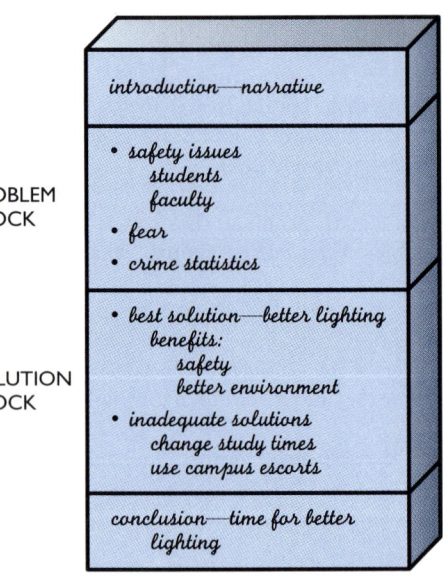

PROBLEM BLOCK

SOLUTION BLOCK

introduction—narrative

- safety issues
  students
  faculty
- fear
- crime statistics

- best solution—better lighting
  benefits:
    safety
    better environment
- inadequate solutions
  change study times
  use campus escorts

conclusion—time for better lighting

MAPPING

Mapping is similar to clustering (see Chapter 1), in that the writer uses clusters of ideas to direct, or map, the essay. Daniel Martinez, a first-year composition student at NMSU, developed the map in Figure 2.2 to guide his writing of an essay on deadbeat parents. As the map suggests, Daniel's essay involved interviews of two people, a young man who hadn't paid child support and a young mother who wasn't receiving child support. Daniel made notes in each of the blocks, creating a list of what to include. This map will probably seem chaotic to you, but it's a personal guide that Daniel used effectively. As long as the writer can read his own map, that's what counts.

FIGURE 2.2 Organizing Strategy: Mapping

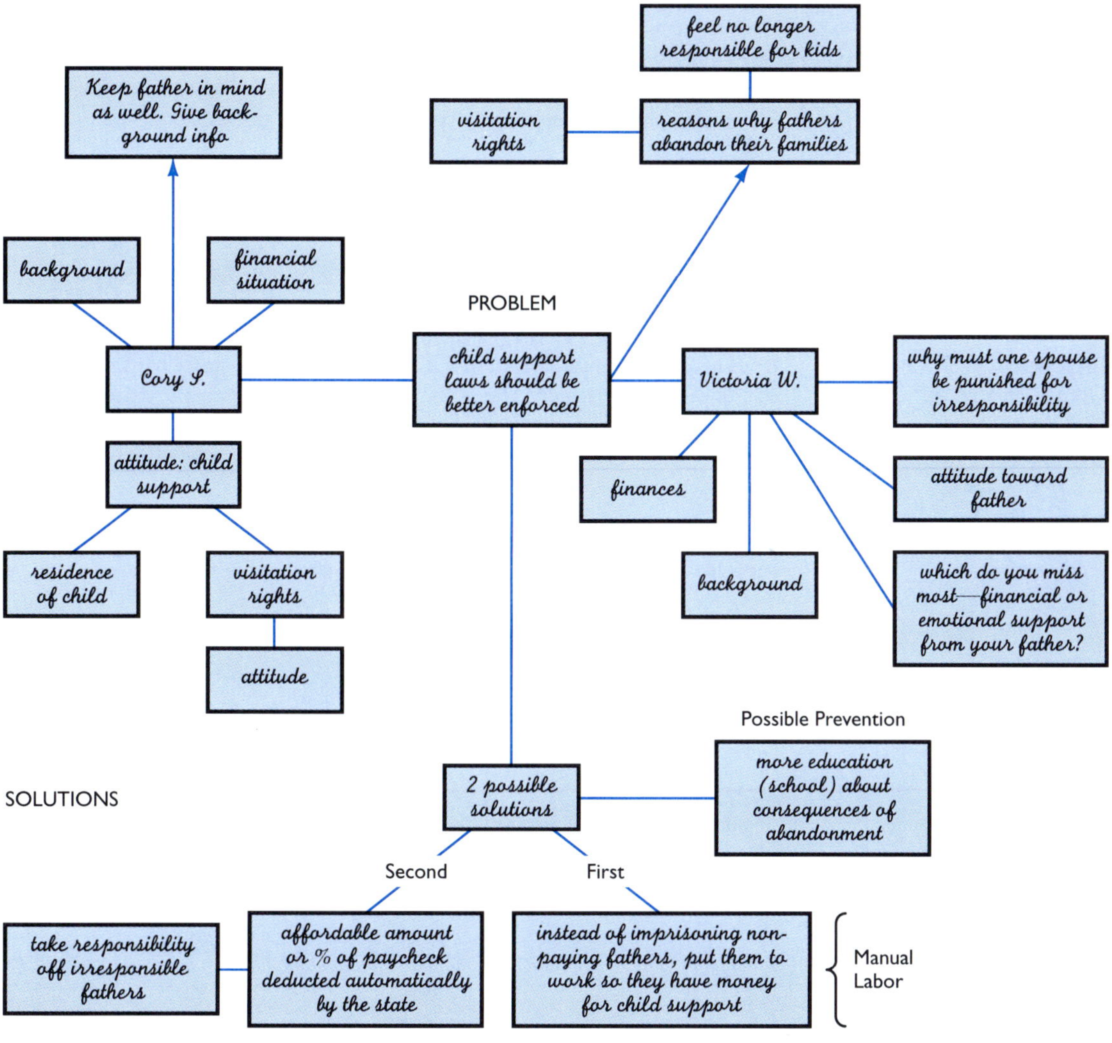

DRAWING

Another way to structure a paper is to draw a shape for it. Mike Tietsworth, a writing tutor at NMSU, has his students use a fish skeleton (see Figure 2.3) to help them remember structure. In this skeleton, the head represents the introduction and the tail the conclusion, with the ribs ready to hold the supporting details, so that the writer puts meat on the bones of the essay.

Another visual aid that has been helpful for some students is a bookshelf. In Figure 2.4, the bookends represent the introduction and conclusion, and the books represent either individual paragraphs or major sections of a paper.

Or you could think of your essay as a pearl necklace: Each pearl is a paragraph or major section of your essay that is tied tightly to the next. When the clasp is closed, the necklace forms a circle, so that the end connects to the beginning and completes the circle, as shown in Figure 2.5.

Skeletons, bookshelves, and pearl necklaces provide ready-made representations of structure, and you may use them for just about any paper you need to write. But you may also draw your own figure for a given paper. Here's an account of one such drawing that Bill created to help him solve a structural problem with a formal essay he was preparing to submit for publication:

> Committing to a shape is a technique I use for arranging the material generated in my prewriting, and I've found that drawing my paper is a very good way of finding a shape. Recently, I was stuck on discerning a workable shape for a paper describing the rationale and then the structure of a course I teach designed to prepare teachers of writing. The course has several strands, which derive from a central theme—that by employing the best we know of theory and research on writing, we create a student-centered class—and I was having trouble organizing discussion of the strands. I tried drawing a hamburger, but that suggested there was a central meaty issue, with the other elements being simple garnishes for that issue. The breakthrough came when, in one of those heavy rains rare to New Mexico, I saw the paper's

FIGURE 2.3
Organizing Strategy:
Fish Skeleton

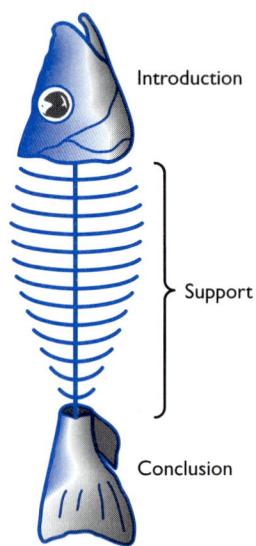

Introduction

Support

Conclusion

FIGURE 2.4   Organizing Strategy: Bookshelf

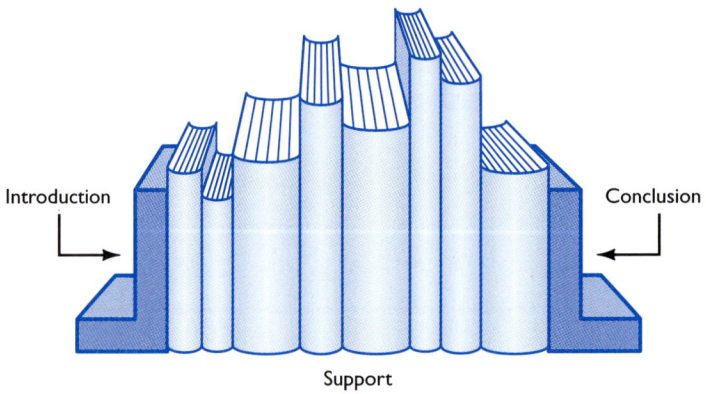

Introduction

Conclusion

Support

FIGURE 2.5 Organizing Strategy: Pearl Necklace

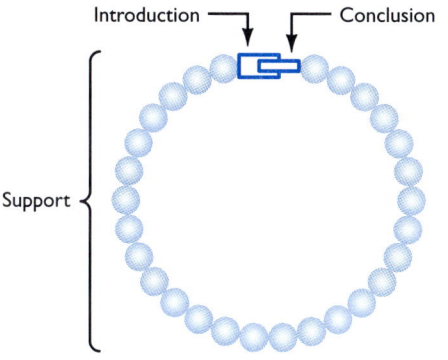

FIGURE 2.6 Organizing Strategy: Umbrella

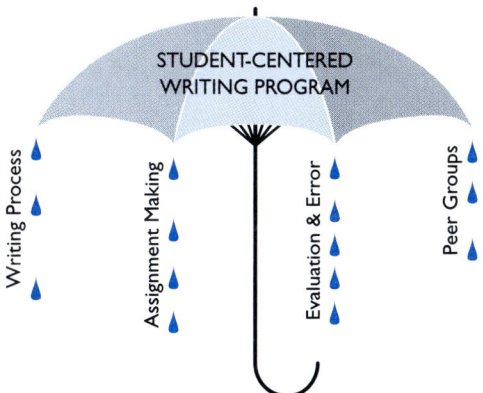

shape as an umbrella, with the umbrella providing the overall rubric and each strand represented by raindrops streaming from the umbrella. This drawing worked by letting me see the parts of my course as equally important and necessary, with each deriving from the central theme.

Figure 2.6 shows the drawing Bill made.

ELEMENTS OF AN ESSAY

For our purposes, we define an *essay* as a sequence of paragraphs that support and develop the essay's main idea. Similarly, each paragraph is a sequence of sentences that develop the paragraph's main idea. We can view the elements of an essay as pieces of a puzzle, with sentences working together to build paragraphs—sections of the puzzle—and paragraphs working together to build the essay—the complete picture. We will discuss several of the specific puzzle pieces that are elements of an essay: thesis sentences, introductions, paragraphs, and conclusions.

WRITING A THESIS SENTENCE

The thesis sentence provides a center of gravity for the paper, capturing its significance in a single sentence. This sentence can do a number of things, including

1. make an assertion: "Clearly, the current pandering of politicians to lobbyists and political action committees for contributions shows that campaign laws must be reformed."
2. issue a call to action: "Somewhere in New Mexico a sanctuary for the Mexican gray wolf must exist, and I urge you to actively support its reintroduction to the Gila Wilderness."

3. direct a reminiscence: "That summer I spent in Ireland continues to be vivid in my memory nearly twenty years later."
4. offer an evaluation: "*Grumpier Old Men* is one of those rare sequels that works; it is funnier than *Grumpy Old Men*."

By capturing the writer's thinking on the essay topic in a single sentence, the thesis provides direction for the reader. And it makes promises to the reader that the writer must keep. It differs from the focus statement in both length and wording. Whereas a focus statement should be a minimum of three sentences long, a thesis sentence is a single sentence. Although a focus statement may suggest the writer's stance or position on the subject, a thesis sentence clearly reveals the writer's stance. In showing that position, the thesis sentence promises the reader the specific direction the writer intends to take.

Look again at Katherine Ozment's and Adam Castoreno's focus statements (pp. 34, 35). Katherine states a position on her topic of inclusion: "I would like to oppose this idea." Compare this statement with her paper's thesis sentence: "Regardless of the degree of severity [of a student's handicap], inclusion is an educational policy that does more harm than good and should be stopped." Katherine's focus statement is a fairly simple statement of opposition, whereas her thesis sentence makes specific assertions that Katherine has to support in the rest of her essay. What promises does Katherine's thesis imply? What expectations does it create about the kinds of support that Katherine will develop?

Although Adam hints at his position on gene therapy in the last sentence of his focus statement—"Researching an argument in favor of my possible career choice is essential if I ever want to work in the field with any strong convictions"—he doesn't state a specific position. A reader could infer from the focus statement that although Adam might think he approves of gene therapy, he is still undecided and will use this essay to explore this topic. The thesis sentence from Adam's essay—"Gene therapy is a vital technology which should be researched further, enabling numerous doors to be opened with regard to a plethora of ailments which plague our society"—shows that he is in favor of research into gene therapy. In this thesis sentence, Adam takes a specific stance; he asserts that gene therapy has great potential and should be the subject of further research. What expectations about essay direction and supporting details does this thesis create for you as a potential reader of Adam's essay?

Where does a thesis sentence appear in an essay? It can appear anywhere, but most often it appears near the beginning, as part of the introduction. Certain kinds of essays may have a different thesis placement. For example, an essay presenting the writer's solution to a problem could fairly neatly divide into two parts: a section for discussion of the problem and a section for discussion of the solution. The statement of the solution would be the essay's thesis, and it would probably come at the beginning of the second part. So in this case, the thesis would appear near the middle of the essay.

Should every paper have a thesis? Most will, because in the thesis the writer makes commitments to the reader. Although three of the four examples at the beginning of this section would appear in persuasive essays, a thesis statement is also useful in essays that explain, as this thesis illustrates: "As health care becomes more and more expensive and as our health care delivery system becomes more and more complicated, many individuals in our society find that the quality of their health care becomes worse and worse." As we discuss in Chapter 6, such an argumentative thesis may well be used in informative writing, because it allows the writer to make her promises to the reader clear. Personal essays, however, often do not have a specific sentence that can be identified as a thesis. Instead, the writer uses his language to present an event or a person to the reader and lets the reader infer the importance of that event or person for the writer. But a personal essay needs direction just as much as any other essay, and a clearly written focus statement can provide this direction.

It's important to remember that you may change your thesis to fit the paper as it develops. If the thesis does not fit the paper as you proceed with your writing, then either the paper or the thesis has to change. Having a clearly stated thesis can provide you with a helpful revision tool as you make sure during revising that your essay fully develops your thesis.

Writing Strategy

WHEN SHOULD YOU WRITE A THESIS SENTENCE?

Some writers develop a thesis sentence early in their drafting and use it as a guide throughout their writing. Others will write a tentative statement that doesn't qualify as a thesis sentence as we've defined it. Only when these writers have written their way to discovering exactly what they want to say will they write a thesis sentence, one that truly reflects the essay's purpose. So the answer to the question about when you should write a thesis sentence is this: It depends. You may write one at the start of your process; then again, your thesis may not come to you until you're in the middle of or perhaps nearly finished with your drafting. If you can't develop a strong thesis sentence right at the start of your drafting, don't worry. Just write a statement to point the way you think you want to go, and then follow it until you have a firmer understanding of what you want your writing to say.

INTRODUCTIONS

An introduction forms the reader's entrance into the paper. This introduction, which may consist of a single paragraph or several paragraphs (depending on the essay's length and the writer's purpose), plays an important role in the essay. It prepares the reader for the essay that follows. It orients the reader to the paper, laying out the paper's general topic and suggesting, if not stating clearly, the writer's position on or attitude toward that topic. It catches the reader's attention. It may present a thesis sentence; then again, it may not, for as we have noted, a thesis sentence may appear anywhere in an essay. Below we present five introductions taken from essays reproduced in later chapters in this text. After reading each, respond to these questions:

1. What is the essay's general subject? What is the writer's position on or attitude toward this subject?
2. How effectively does each introduction catch your attention as a potential reader of the essay? What information or details does the writer present to catch your attention?
3. What expectations does the introduction create in you? What promises does it make that its writer must keep?
4. If a thesis sentence is presented, how effective is it? What does it reveal of the writer's purpose? If a thesis sentence is not presented, does its omission hamper the introduction? Why or why not?

The first introduction, by Datus Proper, opens his personal essay "Dark Hollow." In this introduction, Proper raises the question of ownership of a trout stream and points toward potential conflict.

> Fish a place long enough and it becomes a homestead, a personal stretch of boulders and water and trout. I've been proving my claim on Dark Hollow Run for twenty years now, so I wondered about the other car parked on Skyline Drive, right where I always start my hike down to the stream. Maybe the visitor was just the usual refugee from the city, out for a stroll on the Appalachian Trail, but then again I might find a fisherman ahead of me. I hurried down the mountainside with my rod and rucksack.
>
> The visitor was easy to catch. "Hill's getting hard to pull," she said. Her hair was more gray than red where it fell over the lace collar of her dress. Her name was Betty Cave and her only burden was a bunch of flowers, but it established a claim 200 years older than mine. I read the names of her family when we got to what used to be the Dark Hollow settlement.
>
> There were more headstones in the clearing than Betty had flowers to decorate—rough fieldstones, big ones and little ones, lots of little ones. One of the unmarked stones was for the Cave who brought the family's red hair from Ireland to the Blue Ridge long ago. The oldest legible marker was for John G. Cave of the Virginia Light Artillery, C.S.A. Near it were stones for Betty's parents and her sister Lula Belle.
>
> Not far away was a fireplace, stones chinked with mud, standing lonely in the woods. Betty Cave had stories to go with that old hearth. It had been part of her family's cabin once, and she remembered the days when her mother tended the fire and her father came home with food.

The second example, by Camille Paglia, opens "Rape and Modern Sex War," a piece of persuasive writing, with a strong, startling statement:

> Rape is an outrage that cannot be tolerated in civilized society. Yet feminism, which has waged a crusade for rape to be taken more seriously, has put young women in danger by hiding the truth about sex from them.

Gloria Naylor begins "Mommy, What Does 'Nigger' Mean?" by identifying the subject of her essay as language, but not specifically the language of racism.

> Language is the subject. It is the written form with which I've managed to keep the wolf away from the door and, in diaries, to keep my sanity. In spite of this, I consider the written word inferior to the spoken, and much of the frustration experienced by novelists is the awareness that whatever we manage to capture in even the most transcendent passages falls far short of the richness of life. Dialogue achieves its power in the dynamics of a fleeting moment of sight, sound, smell and touch.
>
> I'm not going to enter the debate here about whether it is language that shapes reality or vice versa. That battle is doomed to be waged whenever we seek intermittent reprieve from the chicken and egg dispute. I will simply take the position that the spoken word, like the written word, amounts to a nonsensical arrangement of sounds or letters without a consensus that assigns "meaning." And building from the meanings of what we hear, we order reality. Words themselves are innocuous; it is the consensus that gives them true power.

Stacy Birch, a first-year composition student at NMSU, opens her essay considering the potential effectiveness of a new legal program by summarizing it, providing the reader with information about the program.

> On October fifteenth of this year [1997] a new project, called Project Amnesty, was adopted throughout the state of New Mexico. Project Amnesty has been specifically designed to decrease the number of parents, especially fathers, who do not pay child support or provide medical insurance for their children. These parents who are not currently financially supporting their sons and daughters have now been given a forty-five day amnesty period to make child support payments, or at least provide health care insurance. If no action is taken during this amnesty period, penalties, including heavy fines and even arrest, could and will be levied. Project Amnesty will be an overall benefit to the children of New Mexico because it will force deadbeat parents to provide money and insurance that rightfully belongs to their children.

Each of these introductions does its job differently.

Proper: Proper structures his introduction as a narrative that establishes the place (Dark Hollow Run in the Appalachians), but it also establishes potential conflict with the introduction of Betty Cave, who has a much longer "claim" to the land Proper fishes.

Paglia: Paglia opens with a very strong statement, first with a definition of rape ("an outrage that cannot be tolerated"), and then with an intriguing assertion: "feminism [. . .] has put young women in danger by hiding the truth about sex from them." This assertion is hardly what we expect to hear because of the feminist movement's strong advocacy of women's rights.

Naylor: By offering a statement of her topic—"Language is the subject"—Naylor provides something of a scholarly counterpoint to her essay's title. Naylor forecasts the thrust of her essay in the last sentence of her introduction, focusing on what gives words their "true power."

Stacy: Stacy gives a quick synopsis or summary of Project Amnesty's main provisions—that deadbeat parents have to make arrangements to pay up or be prepared for legal sanctions—and then her evaluation of this project.

Three of these introductions contain a thesis sentence, an assertion that the essay will support or attempt to prove.

Paglia: Yet feminism, which has waged a crusade for rape to be taken more seriously, has put young women in danger by hiding the truth about sex from them.

Naylor: Words themselves are innocuous; it is the consensus that gives them true power.

Stacy: Project Amnesty will be an overall benefit to the children of New Mexico because it will force deadbeat parents to provide money and insurance that rightfully belongs to their children.

Having made an assertion, each writer then had to offer arguments, examples, anecdotes, and other kinds of support for that statement.

Only Proper's introduction doesn't contain a thesis sentence. But he does provide a sentence that helps structure the remainder of his essay: "Betty Cave had stories to go with that old hearth." Proper builds his essay around several of Betty Cave's stories about her family, alternating her stories with his own story of his day fishing Dark Hollow Run. Near the end of the essay, Proper makes an assertion that reveals a significant dilemma when he comments on the meaning he's gleaned from his fishing and from listening to Betty Cave: "Something beautiful had been saved for me—and taken from the Caves."

Although these sample introductions are varied, each achieves its primary purpose—to identify the topic and the writer's stance on it and to bring the reader into the paper.

Writing Strategy

WHEN SHOULD YOU WRITE AN INTRODUCTION?

Although some writers may begin writing by composing the introduction, we suspect that most do not. In order to start at the beginning and proceed straight through the essay to its end, a writer would have to have thought through her writing completely and so know fully everything she wanted to say in the essay before actually composing it. Some writers find this possible, but most do not. Thus, in many cases, the introduction will be one of the last sections the writer composes.

Exercise 2.1

Select an essay in another chapter in this text and look at its introduction. How effective is that introduction? What does the introduction do for the reader? How well does it establish a context for the essay it introduces?

PARAGRAPHS—TOPIC SENTENCES

A well-written paragraph displays a certain logic; it has a tight structure that leads the reader through the development of its content. One element of this logic is the topic sentence, which makes a statement that the paragraph then develops, explains, or supports. The topic sentence is a signal to the reader that identifies what the paragraph is about and so directs or guides the reader through the paragraph's content.

Most often, the topic sentence appears at the beginning of the paragraph, but it can occur anywhere in the paragraph. We've underlined the topic sentence of each of the following paragraphs. After you read each paragraph, respond to the questions that follow.

This paragraph appears in Susan Jacoby's essay "Common Decency," which offers a counterpoint to Camille Paglia's "Rape and Modern Sex War":

> The immorality and absurdity of using mixed signals as an excuse for rape is cast in high relief when the assault involves one woman and a group of men. In cases of gang rape in a social setting (usually during or after a party), the defendants and their lawyers frequently claim that group sex took place but no force was involved. These upright young men, so the defense invariably contends, were confused because the girl had voluntarily gone to a party with them. Why, she may have even displayed sexual interest in *one* of them. How could they have been expected to understand that she didn't wish to have sex with the whole group?

1. What focus does the topic sentence provide? What promises does it make? How well does the paragraph develop this focus and so keep its promises?
2. How well does the topic sentence guide you through the paragraph?

In this paragraph, Jacoby derides one of the more prevalent defenses offered in cases of gang rape. The language she chooses—"the immorality and absurdity" of the mixed-signals defense—focuses the reader immediately on her attitude toward this defense. The paragraph then develops the attitude implicit in the topic sentence through irony, if not outright sarcasm. Jacoby labels the accused rapists "upright young men" with whom the rape victim had gone "voluntarily" to a party. Continuing her attack, Jacoby uses conversational language that has a sneering quality to it: "Why, she may have even displayed sexual interest in *one* of them. How could they have been expected to understand that she didn't wish to have sex with the whole group?" Jacoby, then, presents a well-structured paragraph that develops its topic sentence well, showing clearly the "immorality and absurdity" of a mixed-signals defense for gang rapists.

In this paragraph from "Clean Up or Pay Up," Louis Barbash places a topic sentence near the middle:

> The athlete's first priority is to play pro ball. Forty-four percent of all black scholarship athletes, and 22 percent of white athletes, entertain hopes of playing in the pros. That's why they will play four years for nothing. But in fact, the lure of sports that keeps kids in school is a false hope and a cruel hoax. "The dream in the head of so many youngsters that they will achieve fame and riches in professional sports is touching, but it is also overwhelmingly unrealistic," says Robert Atwell, president of the American Council on Education. The would-be pro faces odds as high as 400–1: of the 20,000 "students" who play college basketball, for example, only 50 will make it to the NBA. The other 19,950 won't. Many of them will wind up like Tom Scates, in minimum wage jobs, or like Reggie Ford, who lost his football scholarship to Northwest Oklahoma State after he injured his knee and now collects unemployment compensation in South Carolina.

1. Do you agree or disagree with our designation of this paragraph's topic sentence? Why?
2. What focus does the topic sentence provide? What promises does it make? How well does the paragraph develop this focus and so keep its promises?
3. How well does the topic sentence guide you through the paragraph?
4. What is the function of the sentences preceding the topic sentence?

Barbash wishes to decry the common belief among college athletes that they'll make it to the NFL or NBA. To do that, he has to show that this is indeed a prevalent belief—hence the statistics he cites in the first sentence. The topic sentence focuses on the "false hope and [. . .] cruel hoax" of playing in the pros, which Barbash implies is the primary reason many student-athletes stay in college. Having made this statement, Barbash must support it, and he does so through statistics and by quoting an authority in the field. To make his assertion even more convincing, Barbash closes the paragraph by referring by name to two athletes whose experience in collegiate sports didn't send them into professional sports. Barbash has written an effective, convincing paragraph that develops its topic sentence well.

Our third sample paragraph is from Julie Titone's "Balance of Power: Can Endangered Salmon and Hydroelectric Plants Share the Same Rivers?" Titone places her topic sentence at the paragraph's end.

In the early 1900s, as many as 16 million wild salmon traveled up the Columbia River and its tributaries each year. Today there are only 2 million, all but 300,000 of which are from hatcheries. As salmon sport-fishing declined in recent decades, many Idaho riverside communities lost an important source of income. Now the misery is flowing downstream, as fishing communities on the Lower Columbia and along the Pacific coast face up to rough new harvest restrictions. <u>The fish just aren't there.</u>

1. Do you agree or disagree with our designation of this paragraph's topic sentence? Why?
2. What focus does the topic sentence provide? What promises does it make? How well does the paragraph develop this focus and so keep its promises?
3. How well does the paragraph lead to the topic sentence?
4. Titone could well have opened her paragraph with the last sentence. What would she have lost or gained by doing so?

By placing the topic sentence at the end of the paragraph, Titone uses her writing to accomplish two goals. First, she creates some suspense by layering detail upon detail, showing the impact of the severe decline in the number of salmon initially on upstream "riverside communities" and now on "fishing communities" downstream. As readers, we want to know the writer's interpretation of all the details. Titone makes us wait, withholding her interpretation until the end, so that it has a greater impact than it would have at the beginning of the paragraph. Second, by leading us from one detail to the next, Titone forces us to make sense of those details with her, enabling us to recognize more clearly the validity of her interpretation. The placement of this topic sentence is effective.

Although a paragraph may sometimes not contain a topic sentence, each paragraph should develop what we call a topic idea. A paragraph without a topic sentence must nonetheless contribute to the essay's development, and it may do so by developing an extended example or by developing an idea from a preceding paragraph in more detail. The following excerpt from "Politics and the English Language" illustrates this point. In this essay, George Orwell talks about defending the English language from those who misuse it. He closes one paragraph dealing with various minor misuses and ways to remedy them with this statement: "The defence of the English language implies more than this, and perhaps it is best to start by saying what it does *not* imply." Orwell then goes on to this paragraph:

To begin with, it has nothing to do with archaism [. . .] or with the setting up of a Standard English which must never be departed from. On the contrary, it is especially concerned with the scrapping of every word or idiom which has outgrown its usefulness. It has nothing to do with correct grammar and syntax [. . .] or with the avoidance of Americanisms, or with having what is called a "good prose style." On the other hand it is not concerned with fake simplicity and the attempt to make written English colloquial. Nor does it even imply in every case preferring the Saxon word to the Latin one, though it does imply using the fewest and shortest words that will cover one's meaning. What is above all needed is to let the meaning choose the word, and not the other way about.

George Orwell, "Politics and the English Language, *"Shooting an Elephant" and Other Essays*

This paragraph has no topic sentence. Instead, it is guided by the last sentence in the preceding paragraph, and it develops that sentence. Note Orwell's use of pronouns to connect the two paragraphs. If you write a paragraph that does not carry a topic sentence, you must make very clear connections between that paragraph and the idea that guides it.

Exercise 2.2

Select an essay in another chapter of this text and examine each paragraph of the body for its topic sentence. What idea does the topic sentence imply the paragraph will develop? How well does the paragraph develop this idea? Where does the topic sentence appear? Is it where it should be? If a paragraph does not have a topic sentence, does it develop a topic idea expressed in a preceding paragraph? If not, should it have its own topic sentence? Why or why not?

PARAGRAPHS—COHESION

A well-written paragraph hangs together; it consists of related sentences that further the point the writer wants to make. We can talk of this hanging together as cohesion. A well-written paragraph is cohesive; its sentences fit together, one sentence working with the next and the next and then the next until the paragraph is structured. Three important cohesive devices, illustrated below, are repetition of key terms, repetition of sentence structure, and transition.

REPETITION OF KEY TERMS

A key term is an important word or phrase that adds meaning to a paragraph and essay. In the following paragraph, Loren Eiseley repeats key terms, which we've underlined, to create cohesion. How effective are they?

> Some years ago the old elevated railway in Philadelphia was torn down and replaced by a subway system. This ancient El with its barnlike stations containing nut-vending machines and scattered food scraps had, for generations, been the favorite feeding ground of flocks of pigeons, generally one flock to a station along the route of the El. Hundreds of pigeons were dependent on the system. They flapped in and out of its stanchions and steel work or gathered in watchful little audiences about the feet of anyone who rattled the peanut-vending machines. They even watched the feet of crowds who gathered between trains. Probably very few among the waiting people who tossed a crumb to an eager pigeon realized that this El was like a food-bearing river, and that the life which

haunted its banks was dependent upon the running of the trains with their <u>human freight</u>.

Loren Eiseley, "The Brown Wasps," *The Night Country*

REPETITION OF SENTENCE STRUCTURE

Repeating a particular sentence structure works to create cohesion, as the two sample paragraphs below will illustrate. In the first paragraph, from "Clean Up or Pay Up," Louis Barbash repeats a sentence pattern we may label subject-verb-complement (SVC). That is, Barbash begins a sentence with a subject and follows that immediately with the sentence's verb and then the complement, the rest of the predicate. The subject in the second, third, and fourth sentences is the pronoun "it"; the verb is "is"; the complement is cast as a relative clause beginning with the relative pronoun "that." How well do you think this paragraph hangs together?

> One scarcely knows where to start in on a statement like that. It's appalling that an accredited state university would admit a functional illiterate, even re-cruit him, and leave him illiterate after four years as a student. It's shocking that it would do all this in order to make money from his unpaid performance as an athlete. And it is little short of grotesque that an educator, entrusted with the education of 20,000 young men and women, would argue that the cynical arrangement between an institution of higher learning and an uneducated high school boy was, after all, a fair bargain.
>
> Louis Barbash, "Clean Up or Pay Up"

In the next paragraph, a bread maker and aspiring cookbook writer repeats a sentence structure that uses an introductory clause (the "if" clause at the start of the sentence) and an explanatory clause (the "because" clause at the end of the sentence) to emphasize the relationship among the paragraph's sentences. How effectively does this repetition work to create cohesion?

> As you make bread, experiment with adding various ingredients to enhance the flavor and nutritional value of each loaf. If you add honey instead of sugar as a sweetener, your bread will taste better, because honey adds its own distinc-tive flavor as well as sweetness. If you add wheat bran, your bread will be more healthful, because the bran fiber adds the bulk necessary for proper digestion. And if you add wheat germ, your bread will be more nutritious, because wheat germ adds vitamins. What you choose to add to your bread dough determines whether what you bake will be merely bread or B*R*E*A*D.

USE OF TRANSITIONAL WORDS AND PHRASES

Transitional words and phrases are the connectors we all use in speaking and writing. Here is a partial list of transitions and the relationship each signals:

> *addition*—and, also, in addition to, further, furthermore, similarly, not only/ but also, both/and, moreover, either/or, another, like
>
> *contrast*—but, contrary to, yet, still, in opposition to, however, notwith-standing, although, whereas, while, neither/nor, on the other hand

example—for example, that is

time—when, as, already, then, after, afterwards

sequence—next, then, soon, after, afterwards, following, since, first, second, finally

result—thus, therefore, since, so, because, for

Writers use transitional words and phrases to connect parts of sentences, to connect sentences within a paragraph, and to connect paragraphs within an essay. In the following passage, the various transitions are underlined. How effectively do they create cohesion within the paragraph?

One recourse we do have is to teach our daughters how to talk back to and make fun of the mass media. This is especially satisfying since, thanks to Nickelodeon, we sometimes see them watching the same stuff we grew up with. In an episode of *Lassie* my daughter and I watched one morning, a ranger comes to the house to warn the mom that there are some mountain lions in the area. As he tries to show her, on a map, where they'd been spotted, she demurs, confessing that she can't read maps and they just confuse her. Then, on her way to meet Dad and Timmy at a Grange dinner, she gets a flat—which, of course, she hasn't a clue how to change—and then gets caught in one of the traps set for the mountain lions. Lassie—a dog—has more brains than she does and has to save her. Such scenes provide the feminist mom with an opportunity to impart a few words of wisdom about how silly and unrealistic TV can be when it comes to women.

But this was an exception. I don't want to monitor my daughter's TV viewing on Saturday morning, I want to go back to bed. How many mothers have the time or the energy for such interventions? Why should such interventions be so constantly necessary? And even the most conscientious and unhurried mom can't compensate for the absences, the erasures, of what their daughters don't see, may never see, about women and bravery, intelligence, and courage. And this is just what little white girls don't see. What of my little girl's best friend, who is Asian? She will confront even more erasures, and more glib stereotypes. Of one thing I am certain. Like us, our daughters will make their own meanings out of much that they see, reading between the lines, absorbing exhortations to be feisty side by side with exhortations to be passive. Like us, they will have to work hard to fend off what cripples them and amplify what empowers them. But why, after all these years, should they still have to work so hard and to resist so much?

Susan Douglas, *Growing Up Female with the Mass Media*

Exercise 2.3

Select an essay in another chapter of this text and examine its paragraphs for unity and coherence. Does each paragraph follow the direction established by its topic sentence? If a particular paragraph does not contain a topic sentence, does it develop a topic idea, perhaps an idea stated in a preceding paragraph? If so, how well does it develop that idea? Mark any transitional words and phrases used. Are these appropriate? Why or why not? Mark any repetition of key terms. Are these appropriate? Why or why not?

Writing Strategy

PRINCIPLES OF PARAGRAPH DEVELOPMENT

To check the development of your paragraphs, keep these principles in mind:

1. A paragraph is a sequence of content-related sentences that develops an idea in some detail.
2. A paragraph usually contains a topic sentence. This sentence serves to guide both writer and reader through the paragraph's content. The topic sentence can occur anywhere in the paragraph, though it usually comes at the beginning.
3. In some cases, a paragraph may not have a topic sentence, developing instead a topic idea stated in a preceding paragraph. (If you find that you have written a paragraph without a topic sentence, check to be sure that the paragraph does develop some aspect of your paper's purpose, some topic idea. Be sure to identify where that topic idea is stated.)
4. Paragraphs should be unified; each should develop one particular aspect of an essay's main thesis.
5. Paragraphs should be coherent; the sentences in each should be logically connected by transitional words and phrases, by repetition of key terms, and/or by repetition of sentence structure.

Writing Strategy

ONE PAGE, ONE PARAGRAPH

Some of our students have found it helpful to give each paragraph a separate page for drafting. Here is how this works:

1. At the top of a sheet of paper, place a topic idea or topic sentence, something that represents support for the essay topic you want to write about. This idea may come from your focus statement, or it may be an

entry on an outline or a list. (For discussion of topic sentences, see pp. 51–54.)

2. Write a paragraph that explores this topic idea or sentence. As you write, do not stop to worry about the appropriateness of what you are writing or whether what you are writing will find its way into the final essay—just write.

3. When you have completed a first draft of each paragraph, you will have several individual sheets of paper. Arrange these in what appears to be their logical or most effective order. (As you revise these paragraphs to form a whole paper, you will have to be sure to provide an introduction, a conclusion, and appropriate transitions between the paragraphs to tie them together.)

Students who have used this technique report that having to concentrate on developing only one paragraph at a time helps them manage writing the whole essay better, because focusing on only one part seems less worrisome than trying to focus on that one part and the rest of the essay at the same time.

CONCLUSIONS

There is quite a difference between ending an essay and merely stopping it. The ending, or conclusion, of an essay is the final section; it completes the background against which the material in the body is to be placed and thus helps shape the overall meaning of the essay. It is more than a simple summary, though it may include a summary in certain situations, especially when the essay is long and involved.

Below are the conclusions to the essays from which we took the introductions given earlier (see pp. 48–49). As you read these conclusions, keep these questions in mind:

1. How effectively does the writer provide insight into his or her purpose for writing the essay? Is there a statement or implication of the paper's significance for the writer?

2. What is the nature of the conclusion—a summary, a call to action, a reiteration of the thesis?

3. How effective does the conclusion seem? (Although we have not presented the entire essay, speculate about this effectiveness.)

Datus Proper structures his essay as something of a dialogue with Betty Cave, alternating one of her stories with a narrative of part of his day's fishing. He repeats this structure throughout the essay and ends the essay by describing the significance Dark Hollow holds for him, following his talk with Betty Cave. Here is the conclusion of his essay, with Proper's commentary in regular type and Cave's final story in italics:

> Change would have come to the settlement in time, even if the old families had been allowed to stay in their homes. Somebody would have driven a car to the cabins and the world would have followed, one vehicle at a time. People

who had been part of nature would have erected television antennas in the heart of Dark Hollow.

With humans gone, the original vegetation returned, and if the young hardwoods drank some of the stream's water, they also protected the watershed from erosion. The trout were not big, but they were doing better here than in most parts of their ancestral range. I expected to find the native wildlife waiting for me as long as I could manage the hard pull.

Something beautiful had been saved for me—and taken from the Caves.

When they first built Skyline Drive, I would hike up there and sell little paper flowers. Mama made 'em for me. I'd charge a dime, but some of the guests would stop their cars and give me a dollar. I was five years old.

After awhile, the government pushed us off our land and made it part of Shenandoah National Park. That was before the war started—1939 or the edge of '40, I think. Daddy got a dollar an acre. Friends gave us use of a house outside the Park—they knew we couldn't pay rent. We wanted to go back to Dark Hollow, but the government burnt down all eight cabins. Burnt the church, too.

Daddy didn't have any work. All he knew was farming and hunting and fishing. I remember him sitting outside every evening, cryin' and cryin'.

By following his statement of the significance Dark Hollow holds for him with Betty Cave's story about the impact of having to leave the Hollow on her family and particularly on her father, Proper creates a powerful ending for his essay. By continuing the pattern of alternating stories, he maintains the essay's cohesion. And through his use of "hard pull," he echoes Betty Cave's words in the introduction, providing a thread that helps tie the introduction and conclusion together.

Camille Paglia closes "Rape and Modern Sex War" by repeating her theme of the truth about sex.

As a fan of football and rock music, I see in the simple, swaggering masculinity of the jock and in the noisy posturing of the heavy-metal guitarist certain fundamental, unchanging truths about sex. Masculinity is aggressive, unstable, combustible. It is also the most creative cultural force in history. Women must reorient themselves toward the elemental powers of sex, which can strengthen or destroy.

The only solution to date rape is female self-awareness and self-control. A woman's number one line of defense is herself. When a real rape occurs, she should report it to the police. Complaining to college committees because the courts "take too long" is ridiculous. College administrations are not a branch of the judiciary. They are not equipped or trained for legal inquiry. Colleges must alert incoming students to the problems and dangers of adulthood. Then colleges must stand back and get out of the sex game.

Paglia's conclusion maintains the stark, terse tone established by her essay's introduction. Given that her purpose was to upbraid feminism for failing young women while maintaining a pro-women stance, Paglia's conclusion works. Whether readers will agree with her stance or not, Paglia offers a provocative essay, framed by a strongly worded introduction and conclusion.

Following discussion of the various contexts in which she heard the term "nigger" used, Gloria Naylor explains how blacks she knew—her family and her family's friends—defused the term, refusing to see it as inherently racist.

> I don't agree with the argument that use of the word "nigger" at this social stratum of the black community was an internalization of racism. The dynamics were the exact opposite: the people in my grandmother's living room took a word that whites used to signify worthlessness or degradation and rendered it impotent. Gathering there together, they transformed "nigger" to signify the varied and complex human beings they knew themselves to be. If the word was to disappear totally from the mouths of even the most liberal of white society, no one in that room was naive enough to believe it would disappear from white minds. Meeting the word head-on, they proved it had absolutely nothing to do with the way they were determined to live their lives.
>
> So there must have been dozens of times that the word "nigger" was spoken in front of me before I reached the third grade. But I didn't "hear" it until it was said by a small pair of lips that had already learned it could be a way to humiliate me. That was the word I went home and asked my mother about. And since she knew that I had to grow up in America, she took me in her lap and explained.

Throughout her essay, Naylor has explained the various contexts in which she has heard the term "nigger" applied. In exploring these contexts, Naylor supports the assertion of her thesis sentence: "It is the consensus that gives [words] true power." Her conclusion maintains this position. But by presenting the ultimate context in which "nigger" was discussed—her grandmother's living room—Naylor brings to life the abstract concept of the consensus generating true power, claiming, "the people in my grandmother's living room took a word that whites used to signify worthlessness or degradation and rendered it impotent." So in her conclusion Naylor returns to her introduction, proving a final example in support of her thesis's asssertion.

In her conclusion, Stacy Birch acknowledges the speculative nature of her evaluation of Project Amnesty.

> Since Project Amnesty has only begun, we cannot gauge its final outcome. It is Project Amnesty's goal to at least double the amount of child support payments currently being paid in New Mexico. I believe that the amount of child support payments will increase, maybe even meet that goal, because of this program. If payments do increase, if children do benefit from this program, then the effort to push the program forward will have been worth it, even if some deadbeat parents are fined or jailed for not supporting their children.

At the time Stacy wrote the paper, Project Amnesty had been in effect only a short time, so she really couldn't say with any certainty that it would work. However, her conclusion derives quite logically from her essay; the evidence and support Stacy presented throughout the essay led her to believe that Project Amnesty would be effective and that, ultimately, children in New Mexico would benefit from the program. Her conclusion, then, forms an effective ending for her paper.

Read the essays by Datus Proper and Steven Barboza in Chapter 5 and draw a structure for each. What did you draw? How effectively does your drawing represent the structure for each? What do your drawings suggest to you about potential structures for your own writing?

We close this chapter with an exercise that brings together the principles of essay and paragraph development we've discussed. Read the questions in the exercise first, followed by the essay; then respond to the questions.

1. What is Rebecca Thomas Kirkendall's point in this essay? How effectively does she present and support it?
2. Does this essay have a thesis? If so, identify it and comment on its effectiveness. If not, do you think it needs one? Why or why not?
3. How cohesive are the essay's various paragraphs? Select any two paragraphs and comment specifically on how Kirkendall works to achieve cohesion. Pay particular attention to topic sentences.
4. Block the essay; identify the paragraphs that constitute the introduction, body (its supporting paragraphs), and conclusion. Further, divide the body into miniblocks; that is, identify the major sections of the essay's body. Justify your divisions.
5. How effective is the introduction? What does the introduction reveal of Kirkendall's attitude toward the topic? How does Kirkendall show this to her readers?
6. How effective is the conclusion? How does it work to bring the essay to an end?
7. Beginning with the first paragraph, identify this essay's key terms. How do they work to create a cohesive essay?

REBECCA THOMAS KIRKENDALL

WHO'S A HILLBILLY?

1 I once dated a boy who called me a hillbilly because my family has lived in the Ozarks in southern Missouri for several generations. I took offense, not realizing that as a foreigner to the United States he was unaware of the insult. He had meant it as a term of endearment. Nonetheless, it rankled. I started thinking about the implications of the term to me, my family and my community.

2 While growing up I was often surprised at the way television belittled "country" people. We weren't offended by the self-effacing humor of "The Andy Griffith Show" and "The Beverly Hillbillies" because, after all, Andy and Jed were the heroes of these shows, and through them we could comfortably laugh at ourselves. But as I learned

about tolerance and discrimination in school, I wondered why stereotypes of our lifestyle went unexamined. Actors playing "country" people on TV were usually comic foils or objects of ridicule. Every sitcom seemed to have an episode where country cousins, wearing high-water britches and carrying patched suitcases, visited their city friends. And movies like "Deliverance" portrayed country people as backward and violent.

3   As a child I laughed at the exaggerated accents and dress, never imagining that viewers believed such nonsense. Li'l Abner and the folks on "Hee Haw" were amusing, but we on the farm knew that our work did not lend itself to bare feet, gingham bras and revealing cutoff jeans.

4   Although our nation professes a growing commitment to cultural egalitarianism, we consistently oversimplify and misunderstand our rural culture. Since the 1960s, minority groups in America have fought for acknowledgment, appreciation and, above all, respect. But in our increasingly urban society, rural Americans have been unable to escape from the hillbilly stigma, which is frequently accompanied by labels like "white trash," "redneck" and "hayseed." These negative stereotypes are as unmerciful as they are unfounded.

5   When I graduated from college, I traveled to a nearby city to find work. There I heard wisecracks about the uneducated rural folk who lived a few hours away. I also took some ribbing about the way I pronounced certain words, such as "tin" instead of "ten" and "agin" for "again." And my expressed desire to return to the country someday was usually met with scorn, bewilderment or genuine concern. Co-workers often asked, "But what is there to *do*?" Thoreau may have gone to Walden Pond, they argued, but he had no intention of staying there.

6   With the revival of country music in the early 1980s, hillbillyness was again marketable. Country is now big business. Traditional country symbols—Minnie Pearl's hat tag and Daisy Mae—have been eclipsed by the commercially successful Nashville Network, Country Music Television and music theaters in Branson, Mo. Many "country" Americans turned the negative stereotype to their advantage and packaged the hillbilly legacy.

7   Yet with successful commercialization, the authentic elements of America's rural culture have been juxtaposed with the stylized. Country and Western bars are now chic. While I worked in the city, I watched with amazement as my Yuppie friends hurried from their corporate desks to catch the 6:30 line-dancing class at the edge of town. Donning Ralph Lauren jeans and ankle boots, they drove to the trendiest country bars, sat and danced together and poked fun at the local "hicks," who arrived in pickup trucks wearing Wrangler jeans and roper boots.

8   Every summer weekend in Missouri the freeways leading out of our cities are clogged with vacationers. Minivans and RVs edge toward a clear river with a campground and canoe rental, a quiet lake resort or craft show in a remote Ozark town. Along these popular vacation routes, the rural hosts of convenience stores, gift shops and corner cafés accept condescension along with personal checks and credit cards. On a canoeing trip not long ago, I recall sitting on the transport bus and listening, heartbroken, as a group of tourists ridiculed our bus driver. They yelled, "Hey, plowboy, ain't ya got no terbacker fer us?" They pointed at the young man's sweat-stained overalls as he, seemingly unaffected by their insults, singlehandedly carried their heavy canoes to the water's edge. That "plowboy" was one of my high-school classmates. He greeted the tourists with a smile and tolerated their derision because he knew tourism brings in dollars and jobs.

9   America is ambivalent when it comes to claiming its rural heritage. We may fantasize about Thomas Jefferson's agrarian vision, but there is no mistaking that ours is an

increasingly urban culture. Despite their disdain for farm life—with its manure-caked boots, long hours and inherent financial difficulties—urbanites rush to imitate a sanitized version of this lifestyle. And the individuals who sell this rendition understand that the customer wants to experience hillbillyness without the embarrassment of being mistaken for one.

10   Through it all, we Ozarkians remind ourselves how fortunate we are to live in a region admired for its blue springs, rolling hills and geological wonders. In spite of the stereotypes, most of us are not uneducated. Nor are we stupid. We are not white supremacists, and we rarely marry our cousins. Our reasons for living in the hills are as complex and diverse as our population. We have a unique sense of community, strong family ties, a beautiful environment and a quiet place for retirement.

11   We have criminals and radicals, but they are the exception. Our public-education system produces successful farmers, doctors, business professionals and educators. Country music is our favorite, but we also like rock and roll, jazz, blues and classical. We read Louis L'Amour, Maya Angelou and the *Wall Street Journal.* And in exchange for living here, many of us put up with a lower standard of living and the occasional gibe from those who persist in calling us "hillbillies."

Writing Strategy

BEATING THE DREADED WRITER'S BLOCK

Sometimes you'll get stuck while writing, and no matter how long you stare at the page or computer monitor before you, the words just won't come. How to get unstuck? Try any of these:

1. Go back to the beginning of your essay and read through to your stuck point.
2. Look back at your focus statement to see how much of it you've developed and what's next.
3. Use invention techniques—brainstorm, freewrite, cluster, visualize, ask questions.
4. Freewrite about why you're stuck—what you want the essay to do, where you want it to go, why you can't seem to get there.
5. Map your essay—where you began, where you think you are, where you think you want to go. Then write about how you can get to your destination.
6. Talk it out with your roommate, a classmate, or your instructor. E-mail a friend or your instructor and ask for a response.
7. Read something related to your topic.

8. Take a break—walk the dog, throw a load of clothes in the washer, mow the lawn, make a grocery list, fix a glass of iced tea, watch a couple of innings of a baseball game. Sometimes a short break can help you refocus when you return to your writing.

9. Let it sit for a day. If all else fails, then leave your writing alone for at least 24 hours. This is especially helpful if you're tired.

The myth: The writer sits down, turns on the faucet, and writing pours out—clean, graceful, correct, ready for the printer.
The reality: The writer gets something—anything—down on paper, reads it, tries it again, rereads, rewrites, again and again.
Donald M. Murray, *The Craft of Revision*

What does it mean to revise a piece of writing? It means rethinking, reviewing, reseeing, and reconsidering what you have placed on the page. It means looking at each aspect of the paper, from its purpose to individual words, sentences, and paragraphs. It means reworking the paper you have written, whether you change only a word or two or start your writing process all over again with an entirely new topic. Ultimately, your goal in revising is to make sure that you have said to your reader what you intended to say.

Don Murray is absolutely right—the reality of writing is that the writer must revise. Revising is one of the most important parts of the writing process, so important that many composition instructors will tell you that writing is revising, that in order to write successfully the writer must rewrite. When you revise, you must be ruthless, ready to cut out and throw away what must be cut and thrown. It may be hard for you to eliminate words you struggled to find and whole paragraphs you labored to write, but if those words and paragraphs don't fit, they have to go—you have to give them up.

Revising

CHAPTER 3

Computer Tip

ADDING, DELETING, AND MOVING TEXT AROUND

One of the advantages of computers is that they make revising easy. To add text, you simply place the cursor at the appropriate location, make sure the Insert function is on (if necessary), and then type in the additional text. You can also add text by typing entire paragraphs or sections in a different file and then using the Insert function to combine the two files. You can move existing paragraphs or sections from one place to another by using the Copy function. And you can delete words, sentences, and paragraphs by high-lighting them and then pressing the Delete key.

Even the best writers must learn to delete lengthy passages that aren't work-ing to achieve their purposes. For example, in one part of a manuscript he was working on, Aldous Huxley (author of *Brave New World*) scratched out an en-tire passage three paragraphs long and began a revision of it in the margin, but scratched that out, too.

James Jones (author of *From Here to Eternity*) had a different revision prob-lem. An original passage from one of Jones's novels read:

> Solid and dense, sweeping away to the foothills in the distance, it might have been an ancient avalanche of green lava which had rolled down from some vol-cano to form this flat-topped plateau a hundred feet high.

The revised version reads this way:

> Solid and dense, sweeping away to the foothills in the distance, it might have been an ancient green lava flow laid down by some volcano centuries ago to form this flat-topped plateau a hundred feet high.

Jones made few revisions in this sentence, but those he made strengthened the sentence and thereby the entire passage in which it appears. Consider the change in the verb "rolled." Jones listed four choices in the margin before he decided to change "rolled" to "laid." By choosing "laid," he attributed an active role to the volcano—the lava didn't merely flow from it; instead, the volcano assumed a life of its own and laid the lava down to form the plateau. It's important to note that Jones didn't stop while writing to find the right term but returned to the draft to work on it only after he had gotten his thoughts down on the page.

These two examples illustrate two approaches to revision. Huxley engaged in what we may call global revision—that is, revision of fairly extensive propor-tions. Global revision may involve such activities as reorganizing an entire piece of writing, considering the development of ideas as a whole, or, as Huxley did, discarding a lengthy passage and starting over again. Jones engaged in local revision, that is, revision that focuses on smaller details. Local revision may involve working with individual sentences, working with diction (individual word choice), as Jones did in the second example, or editing. Your focus in revision, whether global or local, will be on strengthening your writing, on deciding whether to rework longer passages, perhaps even the entire essay, or to reconsider individual word choice to ensure that you present your reader with the right word rather than one that is almost right.

Global and local revision may take place at any point in the writing process, but global revisions tend to be made relatively early on. A typical writing process may resemble the following scenario: Following some prewriting, the writer composes a first draft—a discovery draft—and puts it aside for a short while to get some distance from it. She returns to the draft and reads it, probably making a few local revisions, tinkering with a sentence here, a word there, perhaps correcting a misspelled word or two. She then sets the draft aside for a longer period, perhaps as much as 24 hours. Next, she considers global revisions—matters of overall meaning and structure, for example—to produce a second draft. She repeats this process with the second draft, getting a little distance before considering local revisions and then more distance before attempting global revisions. She continues this process until she completes the draft.

We need to say again that, in practice, you cannot separate global and local revision. We have separated them in our discussion to encourage you to be sure to incorporate global revision in your process. All too often, the only kind of revision that takes place is local. Unless you are an exceptional writer, failure to consider global revision will undermine the quality of your writing.

To help you work through both kinds of revision, in the rest of this chapter we present several strategies that focus on these specific aspects of revision: distance, meaning, audience, structure, sentences, words, and peer review.

REVISING STRATEGIES
GETTING DISTANCE

To begin revising, get some distance from your writing. When a writer rewrites immediately after completing a draft, he more often than not reads what he intended to write rather than what he actually wrote. So our first piece of advice for revising is this:

1. Finish the paper at least two days before its due date. Meeting this deadline will require you to have the discipline to begin your writing well ahead of time to avoid the "night before the due date" rush to write the entire paper.
2. Once you have completed it, set the paper aside for at least 24 hours before you turn to revising it.
3. After that 24-hour period passes, read the paper at least twice. The first time through, read without marking anything in your draft. Take the time to review your writing as a whole before considering reworking its

parts. The second time through, mark places in the paper that you think are particularly strong as well as those that you think may need work.

4. Read the paper aloud. Reading aloud will cause you to slow your reading down so that you will have a better chance to find places that need work.

5. Focus first on broader concerns—whether the meaning you intended is clear and well supported, whether you have written for your audience, whether the overall structure of the paper and the structure of each paragraph provide an effective framework for your ideas.

6. Focus next on matters of style and diction—whether each sentence effectively represents your thinking, whether each word carries the precise meaning it should.

REVISING FOR MEANING (GLOBAL)

You already have good starting points for considering whether your paper says what you intend it to say in your focus statement and your thesis sentence, both of which make promises to the reader (see Chapter 2). Your job at this point is to decide what promises you made and how well you kept them. As you think about your paper's content, write a short response to each of these questions:

1. What is the purpose of your paper?
2. What parts of the paper develop that purpose? How do they do so?
3. Are there any parts of the paper that do not specifically develop your purpose? If so, what will you need to do to remedy this (e.g., add more detail to those parts or simply delete them)?
4. What details have you provided to support your purpose?
5. Identify your thesis sentence. What promises does it make? Point to places in the paper that have kept those promises. How effectively have you kept your promises to the reader?
6. What are the major points you wanted to make to support your thesis sentence? Which of these have you made? Which have you not made? If there are points you haven't made, do you need to make them?
7. What is the significance you want your writing to carry? How clearly does this significance come through? What parts of the paper keep it obscured or hidden? What do you need to do to clarify the significance you intended?

Steve Duran wrote this assessment of his essay "The Intricacies of an Idiot," an evaluation of Homer Simpson as a funny cartoon character. Although he didn't write in strict response to the questions above, Steve nonetheless addressed most of them.

> The purpose of my essay is to evaluate why I think Homer Simpson is the most entertaining cartoon character on TV. I believe my paper gives good examples of the intricacies of this particular idiot, although to truly understand

why Homer is so funny, one must watch the show. That is another goal of this paper; to get an Anti-Simpsonite to watch the show and laugh at one man's stupidity. It's great fun. I think the introduction is a good description of Homer and different views of him. The conclusion shows that although Homer is insanely incompetent, it is funny because somehow he comes out on top. He gets through life on dumb luck, and sometimes we can all use luck instead of skill (i.e., pulling a Homer). I believe the part of the audience that still doesn't like Homer might not understand my concluding sentence, my semi-idolization of Mr. Simpson.

I couldn't come up with any blanket criteria about what makes all cartoon characters funny, so my criteria was basically any reason why I think Homer is funny. I used many quotes from different shows, although there are so many different episodes that I couldn't include (or remember) all that I would like to have included in this paper. Many of the situations that I think are just hilarious would not have been good to include in this paper because they are either all in the animation, or are too complicated to write in less than forty pages. I hope I used quotes and situations that accurately show Homer's stupidity and comedic value. But, alas, I am a biased writer, so pretty much everything involving Homer is funny as hell to me.

The language I used was hopefully humorous and descriptive. The language will be good for those who watch the Simpsons, but I am not sure about how well the language fits the non–Simpsons watching audience. I tried to relate it to them, but I'm not sure how well I did that. (I have a friend in Texas who doesn't like Homer or the rest of the Simpsons, and I tried to aim this paper at her, to convince her that the Simpsons are worth watching.) I think my language is good for my purpose, if it is descriptive and funny enough.

I already gave my paper a title after the discovery draft. I like using a big word like "intricacy" with a smaller word that also starts with an "I," "idiot." It shows exactly what Homer is like. He is an idiot, yet he tries to be smart. Although, it was very hard trying to find all kinds of different words for "stupidity." (As I am writing this, just remembered a perfect example of one of Homer's funniest moments. So, I am going to add something, and print out yet another draft of this paper.)

Steve discovered something very important from writing this statement—he remembered another example that would support his analysis of Homer Simpson, so he stopped his assessment and returned to his essay to add the example. His finding that he wanted to add one more example reinforced the fact that revision can occur at any point during the writing process, even when the writer thinks he's finished.

REVISING FOR AUDIENCE (GLOBAL)

Earlier, we advised you to pick an initial or tentative audience for your paper and use that audience to help provide direction for your discovery draft. As you revise that draft and continue writing, you need to give greater attention to audience. "To whom should I direct this paper?" is a question you will need to answer in some detail, because defining your audience will help you determine the final form and details of your paper. Begin by writing about your audience in response to such questions as these:

> Who are your intended readers? Who would benefit from reading your paper?
> What are these readers' tendencies in matters of politics and social beliefs?
> What social class(es) do your readers come from?
> Where do your readers live—in one particular region or type of community (e.g., rural, urban, or something else)?
> What kinds of work might your readers do?
> What types of reading do your readers do? What magazines, books, or newspapers might they be familiar with?
> What kinds of issues might particularly concern your readers?

Although this list is not exhaustive, these questions can help you begin to define your audience. And with this initial understanding of your readers, you can begin to develop the kinds of information you need to use in your writing. The better you understand your readers, the better your chance at presenting them with an effective piece of writing.

For an essay entitled "Vim," which details her positive experiences with yoga, Marisol Vargas wrote this initial definition of audience:

> My audience will be a group of people who wonder how I can get up so early to go to yoga. They already will know a little about this exercise from others, but have never experienced it, or heard a detailed description. They are open-minded about yoga and are likely to respond to its effectiveness. How it combines mind, body, and soul.

Because she assumes a receptive audience, Marisol shaped her draft as more of an informative than an argumentative essay, relying on specific examples to develop an assertion that yoga is an effective exercise because it's holistic, focusing on "mind, body, and soul."

Once you have defined your audience, respond to these questions about your paper and your readers:

1. What do you want your readers to understand or gain from reading your paper?
2. What attitudes are your readers likely to have toward your topic? What aspects of those attitudes have you addressed in your paper?
3. What do your readers already know about your topic? What do they need to know?
4. What questions will your readers have about your topic? How effectively have you answered them?
5. What particular action do you want your readers to take, if any? Is your writing compelling enough to make them want to take this action? Why or why not?

6. Is there any part of your paper that may make your readers reject your thinking? If so, how effectively have you prepared them for this material?
7. Is there any aspect of your paper that is likely to surprise your readers? If so, does this surprise serve your purpose? If not, how may you more effectively prepare your readers for this material?

After completing a draft, Marisol wrote this response to the questions:

1. I want my reader to gain a better understanding of yoga and how its combinations are effective.
2. My reader has a positive attitude and is open-minded about this exercise.
3. My reader only knows what he has heard secondhand. He knows a little about the yoga postures, but needs clarification on how they work and their benefits.
4. My reader will wonder how it has affected me as well as how it can help with ailments.
5. I would like my reader to go to a yoga class; my thoughts are too jumbled to be clear.
6. Since my reader is open-minded, he won't reject the information given to him.
7. The meditation contemplation may be a surprise. I think explaining it fully will help him to better understand this concept.

Three points derive from this second analysis:

1. Marisol's realization that she needed to clarify yoga's postures for the reader (3) led her to add detail to her discussion of those postures as she moved from her rough draft to her final draft.
2. Her statement "my thoughts are too jumbled to be clear" (5) was important; Marisol identified a problem in her paper and revised accordingly.
3. Marisol's understanding that the reader could be surprised by the "meditation contemplation" aspect of yoga (7) led her to make sure to provide enough detail so that the reader would understand it.

If you can, get someone to assume the role of an intended reader and to read from that perspective. Ask this person to point to places in your draft that work as well as to those that do not. Having an outside reader—someone other than yourself or your teacher—can help you identify which parts of your writing you can keep and which you need to rework.

REVISING FOR STRUCTURE (GLOBAL)

In Chapter 2, we talked about paragraph cohesion. The structure of your writing sends important messages to your readers. As you look at the overall structure and how the various parts of your essay fit, consider such questions as these:

1. What shape did you intend for your paper? Did you draw it? If so, how effectively does the paper follow that shape? If you didn't draw it, do so

now. Does this shape seem appropriate for your purpose and audience? Why or why not?

2. What transitional words and phrases have you used to move the reader smoothly through the paper? How effectively have you used them?

3. How unified and coherent is the paper overall? How well does it develop one primary point? How effectively does each paragraph develop that point? Are there any paragraphs that do not develop the point? If you need to keep such paragraphs, what do you need to do to ensure that they develop part of the paper's purpose?

4. In what order have you presented your support? Have you presented your strongest or most important first? Last? How effective is this order likely to be? Why?

Computer Tip

Your computer has functions that help with global revisions, such as

Cut and Paste: move blocks of text around in your essay
Insert: add text from another file
Delete: highlight and delete portions of text that must be cut out

Be sure to provide a transition that ties any moved or inserted text tightly to the rest of the essay.

REVISING FOR SENTENCES (LOCAL)

Once you have looked at larger concerns, such as the overall structure of the essay and the structure of individual paragraphs, turn your attention to how the sentences fit together to form the essay's paragraphs. (Refer to Chapter 16 for a detailed discussion of how sentences function and how they may be structured for emphasis and variety.)

In looking at sentences, consider such questions as these:

1. How long are your sentences? In a given paragraph, what is the longest sentence? The shortest? If all of your sentences are approximately the same length, how might you combine sentences to vary the length?

2. How much sentence variety is at work? Do you rely too heavily on sentences that consist of only one simple clause with a subject and verb? Do you make use of introductory phrases and clauses and a variety of sentence types? (See Chapter 16 for a full discussion of strategies for varying sentence structure.)

3. Identify any sentence fragments in your paper. Did you intend to write each one for emphasis? How effective is each intended fragment?

4. What kinds of transitions do you use between sentences?

For a sample of a revision that focuses on sentences, see the example that accompanies the next strategy.

REVISING FOR WORDS (LOCAL)

As you read your essay, you need to make sure that each word carries the meaning you intended, that each is vivid or accurate enough to help the reader understand your point. (Refer to Chapter 15 for an extended discussion on such matters as diction and word choice.)

In looking at the words you have chosen to represent your thinking, consider such questions as these:

1. How vivid is the detail you have presented to your readers? Are there any bland or overused words (e.g., good, bad, nice, pleasant, mellow, lovely, nasty) that don't convey your thinking accurately?
2. How accurate is the language you have used? How accurately have you interpreted events or data?

The following revision of a paragraph by Chris Miller deals primarily with sentences and words. In the essay from which this paragraph is taken, Chris talks about the problem of cyclists riding on sidewalks at New Mexico State University (NMSU). This particular paragraph offers discussion of a similar problem and an attempted solution to it. First, we present the paragraph as it appeared in Chris's paper; next, we'll see how it was revised during a whole-class discussion of revision; and finally, we'll offer the revised paragraph.

> This has also been a problem in places other than college campuses. The city of Albuquerque, for example, recently had a problem with bicycles and pedestrians having accidents on sidewalks. Their solution to the problem was to ban all bicycles on its sidewalks. This ended up causing more problems and accidents than it solved. The people who still ride their bikes are left with two choices: ride on the sidewalk and break the law, or ride in the street with the cars. The ones who ride on the sidewalk are stopped by the police and even ticketed. The ones who ride in the street are put in a much greater danger than accidents with pedestrians ever cause. Many of Albuquerque's streets have no bike lanes so the cyclists are forced to ride in the right hand lane. This has caused many accidents. Cars speed down the road going 45 or 50 m.p.h., not expecting to see a bike. If they turn a corner and suddenly there is one going 10 m.p.h. they can't do anything except swerve into the next lane and pray there isn't a car there. Unfortunately, many times there is a car there and they hit each other. It has happened time and time again. Cars have even hit the bikes. Since the onset of this law, the number of accidents has decreased, but the seriousness has increased. This is another example of a failed way to solve this problem.

Bill, Chris's teacher, photocopied the paragraph on an overhead transparency and, with Chris's permission, based a revision workshop on it. The sentences in the version on page 74 are numbered, to make discussion easier. To begin, we'll note that half of the paragraphs's sixteen sentences consist of one simple clause with only one subject and verb (sentences 1, 2, 3, 4, 8, 9, 13, and 14).

Following an initial reading, the students in the class made these comments on the paragraph:

1. It's wordy. What's said here can be said more concisely. Try to tighten things up.
2. It plods along; it has too much of the same kind of sentence structure. Try some sentence combining to make it read more smoothly.
3. The language seems a little bland in a couple of places. Think about verbs like "wreck" for "hit each other" in sentence 12. Try to cut such expressions as "there are" and "this is" if you can.
4. The paragraph has a few grammatical errors in it that need fixing, including a problem with parallelism (sentence 5), a couple of run-on sentences (8 and 12), and a dangling modifier (sentence 10).

With these comments as a guide, the class revised the paragraph. The handwritten annotations in the following version are the revisions recommended by the class.

(1) This has also been a problem in places other than college campuses. (2) The city of Albuquerque, for example, recently had a problem with ~~bicycles~~ *cyclists running into* and pedestrians ~~having accidents~~ on sidewalks. (3) ~~Their~~ *Albuquerque's* solution to the problem ~~was~~ to ban all bicycles on ~~its~~ sidewalks. (4) ~~This ended up~~ caus*ed* more problems and accidents than it solved. (5) ~~The people who still ride their bikes are left with~~ *In effect, cyclists have* two choices: ride on the sidewalk and break the law, or ride in the street ~~with the cars.~~ *and take their chances* [||ism] (6) ~~The ones~~ *Those* who ride on the sidewalk are stopped by the police and even ticketed. ~~(7) The ones~~ *but those* who ride in the street are ~~put in a~~ *in* much greater danger ~~than accidents with pedestrians ever cause.~~ (8) Many of Albuquerque's streets have no bike lanes*,* so the cyclists are forced to ride in the right hand lane*, which* ~~(9) This~~ has caused many accidents. (10) Cars ~~speed down the road going~~ *travel at a normal rate of speed, their drivers* 45 or 50 m.p.h., not [dm] expecting to see a bike. (11) If they turn a corner and suddenly ~~there is~~ *come up behind* one going 10 m.p.h.,*'* they can't do anything except swerve ~~into the next lane~~ and pray ~~there isn't a car there.~~ *for a clear lane* (12) Unfortunately, many times ~~there is a~~ *they meet another* car ~~there~~ and they ~~hit each other.~~ *crash* ~~(13) It has happened time and time again.~~ [ro] (14) Cars have even hit the bikes. (15) Since the onset of this law, the number of accidents has decreased, but their seriousness has increased,*'* ~~(16) This is~~ another example of ~~a failed way to solve the problem.~~ *this solution's failure*

||*ism* = parallelism problem
ro = run-on sentence
dm = dangling modifier
⌗ = delete indicated material

Here's a summary of the specific revisions the class suggested:

1. Reword sentence 2 to focus on cyclists hitting pedestrians—"cyclists and pedestrians having accidents" isn't as forceful or quite as accurate as "cyclists running into pedestrians."
2. Combine 3 and 4 to decrease wordiness; create emphasis by setting off the definition of the solution with dashes.
3. Open 5 with transition ("in effect"); use fewer words; clear up parallelism problem at the end of the sentence.
4. Combine 6 and 7; repeat "those" for emphasis; delete unnecessary words.
5. In 8, add comma after "lanes" to work with the coordinating conjunction "so" to clear up the run-on sentence; combine 8 and 9 (9 becomes a relative clause subordinate to 8).
6. Add a subject ("drivers") to the participial phrase in 10 to clear up the dangling modifier ("dm")—cars can't expect to see a bike, but drivers can.
7. Reword 11 to delete repetition of "there"; set off introductory clause with a comma.
8. In 12, add a comma after "car" to work with the coordinating conjunction "and" to clear up the run-on sentence; reword to delete repetition of "there."
9. Delete 13 because it really doesn't add much to the paragraph.
10. Combine 15 and 16; delete unnecessary words.

Here's a clean copy of the revised paragraph. This version has eleven sentences and a total of 198 words, compared to 240 words in the original version. Only three of the revised sentences are simple one-clause ones; the rest have been made more complex structurally. How effective do you think these revisions are? Why?

> This has also been a problem in places other than college campuses. The city of Albuquerque, for example, recently had a problem with cyclists running into pedestrians on sidewalks. Albuquerque's solution—to ban all bicycles on sidewalks—caused more problems and accidents than it solved. In effect, cyclists have two choices: ride on the sidewalk and break the law, or ride in the street and take their chances. Those who ride on the sidewalk are stopped by police and even ticketed, but those who ride in the street are in much greater danger. Many of Albuquerque's streets have no bike lanes, so cyclists are forced to ride in the right hand lane, which has caused many accidents. Cars travel at a normal rate of speed, their drivers not expecting to see a bike. If they turn a corner and suddenly come up behind one going 10 m.p.h., they can't do anything except swerve and pray for a clear lane. Unfortunately, many times they meet another car, and they crash. Cars have even hit the bikes. Since the onset of this law, the number of accidents has decreased, but their seriousness has increased, another example of this solution's failure.

PEER REVIEW (GLOBAL AND LOCAL)

In peer review, someone else reads your writing and comments constructively on it. At times, you'll be able to call on another writer or group of writers in the class for which you're writing. When this is the case, that person or group will be aware of your paper's context and so should be able to give you an idea of how well you have fulfilled the assignment. At other times, you may ask someone unfamiliar with the paper's context to review it for you. In either case, you have a responsibility to provide your reviewer with more than the paper itself. You should give your reviewer a quick assessment of how well you think the paper works and where you think there are trouble spots. To prepare this assessment, write a note to the reviewer in which you

1. state your intended purpose and audience,
2. identify those parts of the paper that you think work well, and
3. ask for help.

If you think there is a trouble spot in the paper but don't know quite how to fix it, then point to it and ask the reviewer to pay particular attention to that spot.

One principle to keep in mind concerning any form of peer review is that ultimately, you, the writer, are responsible for deciding which pieces of your reviewers' advice to heed and which to ignore. Your readers are expressing their opinions about your paper and offering support for them, but the final decision about how to revise your writing is yours.

WORKING ONE-ON-ONE

Working with another person one-on-one, you may each read the other's paper silently, paying attention to the writer's assessment (see above) and responding in writing to the parts that worked as well as to those that didn't. Next, you should talk through your reactions to the piece of writing, one at a time, focusing on both strengths and weaknesses. After such a peer-review session, your job is to consider your reviewer's comments and decide which ones you want to use to guide your revising.

Another one-on-one strategy requires each of you to read the other's paper aloud, so that the writer hears her words in someone else's voice. The writer listens but may not comment. As you read your partner's essay aloud, mark in the margins where you think the writing works and where it doesn't work, so that you and the writer may discuss these sections later. Once you've finished reading the paper, talk with the writer about the parts you've marked. The writer's role is to listen, to take notes, and to ask questions, but not to argue with your reading of the essay.

WORKING WITH A GROUP

Working with a group of students in your writing class is a good way to get outside opinions about your writing. To make this strategy work, groups need guidelines to follow. If your instructor doesn't provide these for you, your group should establish its own ground rules, and then each member should agree to abide by them. Begin by discussing these aspects of working successfully in a group:

1. *Attending group meetings.* Attendance is obviously crucial, since group meetings are not possible if the members don't attend.
2. *Being prepared.* If you don't have your rough draft ready for your group workshop, then you can't get the help you need.

3. *Being helpful, not hypercritical.* If your group is to work, you have to be willing to critique your peers' papers honestly. But all group members need to remember what we've told our students is the Golden Rule of Peer Criticism: Nobody says or does anything willfully mean.

4. *Being receptive to group critiques.* Receiving criticism is the other side of the coin, and you have to accept your group members' assessments of your work in the same spirit in which you critique their work. The ability to receive criticism is one you'll have to cultivate.

Your group may wish to incorporate these four principles, along with others you may devise, into a contract that each member helps to write and then signs. Should your group not function as well as you would like, consult with your instructor about how to make it work better.

Once you have the principles in place, you're ready for group sessions, which usually will take two class periods or at least two hours outside of class. It's important to structure these sessions carefully so that all writers receive the maximum benefit from them. To conduct a review session, follow these steps:

1. Before reading any of the essays of the group members, read through the directions your instructor provides. If your instructor doesn't provide a critique sheet—a list of specific questions and directions to use in a review session—you'll have to develop your own. To do so, you may use several of the strategies for revision presented above and focus on the following aspects of a paper:

   a. *Purpose.* What is the essay's purpose? How effectively has the writer achieved it?

   b. *Strengths.* What do think is particularly effective about the paper? Identify at least two aspects of the essay that work well and tell the writer why you think they're effective.

   c. *Weaknesses.* What seems ineffective? Identify at least two aspects of the essay that need work and make specific suggestions for revision.

   d. *Essay structure.* Identify the paper's beginning, middle, and end, describing what the writer has done in each section. How effective is each section? What makes it so? Make specific suggestions for revision.

   e. *Paragraph structure.* How effectively is each paragraph structured? Does each have a topic sentence? How effectively is that topic sentence supported? Make specific suggestions for revision.

   f. *Sentence structure.* How varied are the sentences (length, word order)? How effectively does each sentence fulfill the writer's purpose? How effectively has the writer used such devices as transition and repetition of key terms to create connections between and among sentences? Make specific suggestions for revision.

   g. *Details and word choice.* How effective are the details the writer has chosen? Are there specific words or phrases that don't support the writer's purpose? Make specific suggestions for revision.

h. *Overall assessment.* When you've finished responding to the various parts of the paper, write a statement giving your final impressions of the paper, summarizing its strengths and offering the writer suggestions for improvement.

2. Read a given paper once without marking anything on it. Read it as a whole, paying attention to its impact on you. Then read it again, this time marking your responses to the critique sheet on the paper itself.

3. After this second reading, respond in writing to the various parts of the critique sheet.

4. When all the papers presented have been read and critiqued, talk with the writer. The writer's drafts are returned, along with all written criticism from the group, and then each group member tells the writer his or her impressions of the essay. The writer isn't to quibble or argue about these points, but to consider them as attempts to be helpful.

Note that different instructors may suggest different group procedures. For example, Ron often has a writer distribute a copy of an essay to each group member and then read the paper aloud twice before the group begins work on it. During the first reading, group members simply listen. During the second reading, they make notes on the draft where there is something they want to discuss with the writer.

Each of these strategies is designed to provide a means for peers to offer you insights that might help make your paper better. But once you have their thoughts, what do you do with them? How much of the group's criticism do you use? Whatever you think is helpful. If a majority of your group members mark a place in the paper as needing work, then you should consider making revisions at that point. If only one member marks a place as needing work, you should consider that criticism as well, though it may not carry as much weight in your mind as it would if the majority had commented on that place. Remember that, ultimately, you are responsible for your writing, and decisions about what to revise and what to let stand are yours to make.

EDITING STRATEGIES

Although *editing* and *revising* are often used interchangeably, we make an important distinction between the two terms. *Revising* is a much broader term than is *editing*. In revision, you consider substantive changes to every aspect of your paper. Editing involves carefully proofreading and then making those final changes in grammar and mechanics (e.g., spelling and punctuation) that make for a finished product. Some successful proofreading strategies include reading backwards, spotlighting problems, and using a word processor.

READING BACKWARDS   Often, writers read their best intentions instead of what they actually put on the page. To counteract this tendency, read each word from the last to the first, so that you read each out of its context.

SPOTLIGHTING PROBLEMS   If you know that you have a particular grammatical or mechanical problem, then spotlight that problem during proofreading. If, for example, your instructor has told you that you tend to use comma splices, then you should look at every comma you use in your essay; if a comma separates two independent clauses without being accompanied by a coordinating conjunction, then you've committed a comma splice and need to decide how best to fix it. Or, if you tend to write sentence fragments that are relative clauses, then you need to look at every relative pronoun; if that pronoun opens a clause, then you need to make sure that the clause is attached to a sentence rather than standing alone.

USING A WORD PROCESSOR   One very effective tool for proofreading and editing is a word processor. You should always use the Spellcheck function before you submit a draft for peer review or to your instructor. A word of caution, though—spelling checkers aren't totally reliable because they don't check to make sure you've written the right word and they don't distinguish between homophones (words that sound alike but are spelled differently). Here's a paragraph that a spelling checker considered correct:

> Its vary clear that the computer can bee a useful tool, butt you half two read draughts carefully too ensure their correct. Other ways, you mite assume you're draughts are all together finished and sew ready too bee handed inn for grating. How ever, you're teacher cud get the idea that you should of proof red a printed copy, to.

The Search function (sometimes known as Seek or Replace) can prove valuable for editing. If you have trouble with homophones, you may find each instance of these in your paper to make sure you have the right word. Common homophones include "to," "too," "two" and "there," "their," "they're." You can also use the Search command to help you correct grammatical problems. For instance, if you have a tendency to write dangling modifiers, you can type "ing" in the Search For box, because most dangling modifiers have an *ing* verbal as part of their structure. Here's an example:

> While pitching wide to the trailing halfback, the ball popped loose and was recovered by the defense.

The dangler in this sentence is the introductory phrase "While pitching wide to the trailing halfback." In its position in the sentence, the introductory phrase must modify the sentence's subject, in this case, "ball." But the ball cannot pitch itself; someone (probably the quarterback) has to do the pitching. So the modifier (the introductory phrase) is said to dangle because it does not refer clearly to the subject. Here is one possible revision to correct this problem:

> While pitching wide to the trailing back, the quarterback was hit by a linebacker, and the ball popped loose, only to be recovered by the defense.

In this revised sentence, it is clear who was doing the pitching, so the introductory phrase no longer dangles. If you can identify each instance of an *ing* verbal in your paper, then you have the chance to correct the ones that are dangling.

You can use the Search function to identify instances of other aspects of your writing that may need attention as well. If you tend to use such listless constructions as "There is" and "There are" in your writing, finding and replacing them will make your writing stronger. If you tend to overuse such verbs as "have" and "be" (including "to be," "been," "was," "is," "are," and "were"), find them and consider whether you can substitute a more lively verb. The Search function will facilitate your editing by enabling you to find quickly and easily every occurrence of a word or phrase that you know gives you trouble.

Exercise 3.1

After you've written your final draft of an assigned paper, let it sit a day or two, and then answer the following questions. Then write a self-assessment paragraph in which you identify your essay's strengths and weaknesses. What will you do differently the next time you write?

1. What is the purpose of this essay? To what extent does your draft fulfill that purpose? What revisions do you think will be necessary?
2. How well does the introduction work? What, specifically, did you intend the introduction to do? Is it appropriate for your audience? If not, what will you need to do to make it appropriate for your audience?
3. How well does the conclusion work? What, specifically, did you intend the conclusion to do? Is it appropriate for your audience? If not, what will you need to do to make it appropriate for your audience?
4. How appropriate is the language you have used in the paper? Have you provided enough detail? Is the tone appropriate for your audience? For your purpose? Why or why not?
5. What sentence strategies have you used? Are your sentences primarily all of one type (e.g., short or long, loose or periodic)? Is there enough variety in your sentences to keep your writing from being choppy?
6. Are your paragraphs unified and coherent? Does each paragraph develop some aspect of your thesis sentence?
7. What grammatical or mechanical problems do you see?
8. What title will you give your paper? What word, phrase, or sentence do you think will best represent your paper to your reader?

Computer Tip

Your word-processing program offers you a wide range of features that will help you prepare a professional-looking manuscript.

HEADERS AND/OR FOOTERS   Use the Header/Footer command to create headers and/or footers. You may include an identifying label for your paper in a header or footer and continuous page numbers as well. A header for Marisol Vargas's essay might be one of these:

Vargas—p. 2
Vargas, "Mirror Image," 2
"Mirror Image"—p. 2.

MARGINS   Word processors usually have a default margin of one inch all the way around. But you can change the margins if you need to. For instance, you'll want to change the left-hand margin if you need to inset a quotation that is more than four lines long.

FONTS   Word processors offer a number of fonts and type sizes. For your writing, you should select one of the common text fonts. Typical fonts for essays include Times New Roman, Courier, and Arial. You shouldn't use a fancier font, such as an Old English, or a script font, such as ShellyVolante, for your papers, though such fonts work well when you're creating a certificate or when you're trying to create a special effect in your paper. Also, select a point size (size of type) of either 10 or 12, as these are standard sizes. Use larger or smaller sizes only when you're trying to create a special effect.

Be sure your papers conform to the specifications your teacher requires for manuscript preparation. If you have any questions about format, consult your instructor.

SAMPLE STUDENT PROCESS—REVISION

We'll continue working with Marisol's personal essay here, focusing on the revisions she made, particularly in light of advice she received from her writing group and from Bill, her teacher. Marisol began revising by reading back over her discovery draft, identifying parts she thought needed work, and then revising, producing the rough draft that follows. As you read this draft, identify three or four changes that Marisol made. How effective do you think they are? How greatly did she change the essay? Did she strengthen or weaken it? Why?

ROUGH DRAFT

1   The steady rhythm of my life changed when I went with my mother to feed the homeless.

2   Through this experience I learned not to take things for granted. For what may seem common to me, may be a luxury for another. It is this occurrence that stands out in my mind the most.

3   The stop light turned red and as the car slowed to a halt, I opened my eyes to my surroundings. I had been asleep for most of the journey and now the

change in the car's momentum awakened me. As I looked around I noticed groups of people walking. The light turned green and we turned, heading in the same direction as the crowd.

4   "We're here," my mom said. I remember thinking that it wasn't as large as I expected. In front of us was a small grey building surrounded by an old chain-link fence. It reminded me of a warehouse.

5   This was the first time I had come with my mother to feed the homeless. She had asked me many times before but, because of the comfort of my bed in the early morning, I always declined. This time, however, I worked up the energy to go.

6   We got out of the car with casseroles and bags of fruits. As we walked toward the shelter, I felt as though everyone was watching us and I tried not to make eye contact. "Just look straight," was the only thought in my head.

7   We entered the building through narrow doors and went directly toward the kitchen, a small area hidden from the rest of the cafeteria. I helped some of the other volunteers warm the food that everyone had brought. I decided that if I stayed in the seclusion of the kitchen, I would be "safe."

8   Then we were called out to the dining area for a short breakfast prayer. I went out nervously. When it was over, I hurried to the kitchen and started to serve the food, but the volunteers had another job for me. They wanted me to go into the dining area and offer fruit to everyone. I am a shy person, so the thought of having to approach unfamiliar faces scared me.

9   As I filled up my dish, I prepared myself for the worst. I got up, clenched my fruit bowl and slowly walked out to the dining area. As I looked around, all of my foolish thoughts and fears diminished. Many people crowded around me waiting to get their fruit. They were very polite, thanking me with smiles and kind words. When the bowl was empty, I raced back into the kitchen to refill it and I hurried back out.

10   The room was filled with people of different gender and race. There were families, and single men and women. Outside there were people with animals. Watching the families was heart breaking. There were little girls whose dresses were loose from starvation and the stresses of living on the street. Their eyes resembled that of an older person, with lines of stressful days and sleepless nights.

11   As I walked outside one man caught my eye. He reminded me of Santa Claus, because of his sweet eyes and big rosy cheeks. "Sir, would you like some fruit," I asked. He looked at me and smiled bashfully. He looked down at his hands. He was holding coffee and an empty plate. He looked back at the fruit, wondering if he had room in his hands to carry it. He carefully took it into the hand that held his coffee. It spilt from his nervous, shaky movements. Then he thanked me and slowly walked away.

12   At that moment I realized how foolish I had been. Fear had kept me away so long. As I walked around I couldn't quite figure out what it was that I feared. The people I was looking at could have easily been a family member or me. I was lucky to have a comfortable bed to sleep in at night and wake up to in the morning. I couldn't imagine having to use a concrete sidewalk as my bed.

13   As we drove away that morning, I remember my mom saying, "I think we fed over a hundred people today." All I could do was think of the faces I had seen, and I realized how much they looked like me.

Marisol provided each member of her review group with a copy of this rough draft. Over two class meetings, group members read, marked, and responded to the questions on the following review sheet:

Follow these instructions in reviewing the essays from your group members: (1) Before you read any essays, read the questions below. (2) Read each essay through once without marking anything. (3) Read the essay again, this time marking places in the paper that you think are strong and that you think need work. (4) Using the markings from 3 as a guide, respond in writing to the questions below. (5) Talk about your reading of the essay with its author.

Above all else, remember the Golden Rule of Peer Review: Nobody says or does anything willfully mean.

1. What event is the essay about?
2. What did the writer learn from having experienced the event; that is, what is the significance the writer sees in the event? How clearly does this significance come through? Make specific suggestions for revision.
3. Identify two places you think are particularly strong. What makes them strong?
4. Identify two places you think need work. What, specifically, should the writer do to strengthen these?
5. How effective is the detail the writer has written? On what do you base your assessment? If you see the need for revision, make specific suggestions to help the writer.
6. What is your overall assessment of the essay's effectiveness? Remember that your job is to help the writer make the essay better.

One group member commented:

1. The essay is about the time she went with her mother to feed the homeless.
2. She extinguishes any fear of the homeless she once had through this experience. Not quite sure what fear was (shyness, fear of them, etc.)? Might be helpful to expand on feelings of fear. Staying in kitchen—¶6—keeps her "safe" from what?
3. One great part is ¶10—the description of the "Santa Claus." She uses great imagery. Great description. Helped me see the man in my head. Another great part is the last sentence. If you do decide to expand closing, from my point of view the last sentence is a great closing thought.
4. A couple areas I would like to see more description is your time spent in kitchen away from homeless. More of your thoughts/images/actions. Why fearful. Maybe the conclusion and opening ¶s could be expanded. I would like it if opening, you worked way towards shelter. Maybe not come right out and state essay about feeding homeless. I love your usage of "steady rhythm of life" in the first sentence.
5. I loved the details you recalled about "Santa Claus." It would be great if you could talk about other people with that detail. Overall the detail used to describe things was good. I could get the picture in my head of this place.
6. The essay is very effective. It is a very positive reflection to read. Good essay to read even if don't want to make any changes.

A second member commented:

1. About the time the author went to feed the homeless.
2. The writer learns not to take for granted the luxuries she has. I don't think it comes through very clear, though, because it seems to me that she learned more about humanizing the homeless, than really appreciating material objects. She learns not to fear them and that are just like you & me. very little writing is given to appreciating what she has.
3. I really like the last sentence of the 6th paragraph. It conveys the author's insecurities very well, and by putting "safe" in quotations it also shows how she feels those insecurities were silly, now. I also liked the first sentence, or rather the part I underlined. It starts off the essay with a bang. It says "this is an extremely important event in my life" and it makes you want to read on.
4. I think if the author really wants to convey the lesson of not taking things for granted, she should expand on this paragraph, but like I said it seems to me the greater lesson was humanizing the homeless.
5. Her detail is wonderful, I think. for example, the 10th paragraph about Santa Clause is detailed very well and I particularly liked the description of the little girls at the end of paragraph 9.
6. I believe it is an effective essay and she writes well and I've already harped on my one concern enough in questions 2 & 4.

These comments are typical of first reading sessions. You'll note that the readers are a bit reluctant to say very much that's openly critical, and they tend to overpraise the essay's effectiveness. This is not to say that Marisol's writing at this point isn't effective. Instead, we're saying that the essay, however much promise it may show, still has a way to go before it will stand as a finished piece of writing. And both group members point to places that need revising.

DRAFT FOR INSTRUCTOR EVALUATION

Taking into consideration her group's advice, Marisol revised her rough draft, creating the essay that follows.

1   One Sunday morning my mother invited me to volunteer with her at a homeless shelter. Volunteering at a shelter taught me that no one can be excluded from poverty. It is not prejudice towards race, gender, or age. This realization changed the steady rhythm of my life.

2   The stop light turned red and as the car slowed to a halt, I opened my eyes to my surroundings. I had been asleep for most of the journey and now the change in the car's momentum awakened me. As I looked around I noticed groups of people walking. The light turned green and we turned, heading in the same direction as the crowd. "We're here," my mom said. I remember thinking that it wasn't as large as I expected. In front of us was a small, warehouse-like building surrounded by an old chain-link fence.

3   My mom and I unloaded casseroles and bags of fruits from the car. We entered the building through narrow doors and went directly toward the kitchen, a small area, secluded from the rest of the cafeteria. Our food was combined with that of the other volunteers, making a diverse potluck. My first job was to help warm the food. Then we were called out to the dining room for a short breakfast prayer. I went out nervously, not knowing what to expect. When the prayer was over, I hurried to the kitchen and started to serve the food, but the volunteers had another job for me. They wanted me to go into the dining area and offer fruit to everyone.

4   As I filled up my dish, I prepared myself for my task. I got up, clenched my fruit bowl and slowly walked out to the dining area. Many people crowded around me waiting to get their fruit. They were very polite, thanking me with smiles and kind words.

5   The room was filled with people of different gender and race. There were families, and single men and women. Outside there were people with animals. There were little girls whose dresses were loose from starvation and the stresses of living on the street. Their eyes resembled that of an older person, with lines of stressful days and sleepless nights.

6   As I walked outside one man caught my eye. He reminded me of Santa Claus, because of his sweet eyes and big rosy cheeks. "Sir, would you like some fruit," I asked. He looked at me and smiled bashfully. He looked down at his hands. He was holding coffee and an empty plate. He looked back at the fruit, wondering if he had room in his hands to carry it. He carefully took it into the hand that held his coffee. He spilt from his nervous, shaky movements. Then he thanked me and slowly walked away.

7   Outside animals greeted me. There were beautiful dogs who seemed to be unaware of their misfortune. Some of the people took care of their animals' hunger before their own. One man had a litter of puppies that needed homes. He tried to convince me to take one with me. His puppies were playful and healthy. They seemed very content.

8   After breakfast was over, I helped the crew clean everything. It was then that I realized my fortune. I had a comfortable bed to sleep in at night and wake up to in the morning. I never had to be tortured by the rumbling growls of hunger in my stomach. I could not imagine having to use a concrete sidewalk as my bed or a cardboard box as my home.

9   As we drove away that morning, I remember my mom saying, "I think we fed over a hundred people today." All I could do was think of the faces I had seen, and I realized how much they were like mine.

Marisol submitted this draft to Bill for his evaluation. After he read it, Bill wrote this comment:

> Marisol—thanks for this essay. It's a quiet affirmation of you, and I appreciate your letting me see it. You need more; it needs to be longer so that the details become sharp and clear. Let's have a conference before you revise it.

The draft wasn't long enough to meet the minimum length requirement specified in the assignment (4–6 pages, 1,000–1,500 words), and it had some grammatical errors. The more important consideration was that Marisol hadn't provided enough detail for a reader to truly understand her feelings and her experience. In conference, Bill suggested that she consider working with the introduction, to detail her reluctance to go with her mother, and that throughout the essay she pay attention to these three words: detail, detail, detail. Marisol subsequently submitted this revised final draft of her essay.

REVISED FINAL DRAFT

MIRROR IMAGE

MARISOL VARGAS

1   "Please come with me tomorrow," my mother begged as we wrapped up the chicken casserole preparing it for its journey to the homeless shelter. It wasn't the first time my mother asked me to accompany her, and my argument always was the same: I can't get up. I don't want to go. I just can't peel myself out of bed that early in the morning. As if anticipating these words, my mom quickly said, "You can sleep in the car on the way."

2   Defeated, I shrugged my shoulders, and reluctantly answered, "Okay."

3   The next morning when my alarm rang, I quickly turned it off and tried to resume slumber, hoping my mother would forget about the agreement we made the night before. I could hear her rummaging through the kitchen. Soon the sound of her movements headed toward my room. The door creaked open. "Wake up, Marisol, I made you breakfast," she said. A human alarm clock whose words forced me to arise. I reluctantly dragged myself out of bed, and stumbled into the kitchen, where my breakfast was neatly placed. Although grateful of her generous gestures, I still wanted to return to my warm, comfortable bed. Instead I ate in silence. As I put my empty plate on the kitchen sink, I saw my mom frantically preparing for our trip. I wanted to beg off, to tell her I'd go with her next week, even though I knew I wouldn't want to. But she looked so energetic and happy that I could not bear to disappoint her, so I sluggishly picked up a bag of fruit, headed for the car, and plopped myself onto the front seat. My mom swiftly placed the casserole on my lap, and we were off. My eyes slowly began to close, and I nodded off.

4   A red stop light caused the car to slow to a halt, and I opened my eyes to my surroundings. I had been asleep for most of the journey, and now the change in the car's momentum awakened me. As I looked around, I noticed a variety of people walking. People of different genders, races, and ages. The light turned green and we turned, heading in the same direction as the crowd. "We're here." my mom said. I remember thinking that it wasn't as large as I expected. In front of us was a run-down, grey, warehouse-like building surrounded by asphalt and an old chain-link fence. For some reason, I thought it would look more like a restaurant. Instead, it reminded me of an elementary school cafeteria.

5   My mom and I unloaded the casserole and bags of fruit. We entered the building through narrow doors and went directly to the kitchen, a small area, secluded from the rest of the cafeteria. Combining our food with that of the other volunteers, we concocted a diverse potluck filled with a variety of casseroles, enchiladas, beans, and tortillas, as well as desserts and fruit. The volunteers split up the work of preparation, and my job was to warm the food.

6   Then we were called out to the dining room for a short prayer. I went out nervously, not knowing what to expect. I imagined the homeless as they are portrayed on TV—crazy people with rotten teeth who talk to themselves on street corners. I realized my ignorance and slowly walked out. Scanning the room, I noticed people of all different shapes and sizes, yet none looked crazy nor foamed at the mouth. I stood by my mom and waited for the opening prayer, a universal blessing that was written as not to favor any one religion. When it was over, I hurried to the kitchen and began serving the food, but the volunteers had another job for me. They wanted me to go into the dining area and distribute fruit.

7   As I filled the large plastic bowl with apples, oranges, bananas, and the odd peach or two, I prepared myself for the task. How would I approach or address them? "Mom," I whispered. "What do I say to them? Can't somebody else do this?" She shook her head. "Just treat them like people, Marisol, just treat them like you'd treat anybody else." I got up, clenched my fruit bowl tightly, and left the kitchen. Many people crowded around me waiting to receive their fruit. They were very polite, thanking me with smiles and kind words, "Thank you, ma'am," or "God bless you" immediately dissolved all of my tension. It was almost a shock to hear so many grateful words. I felt uplifted with the loss of my fears.

8   Again I looked around the room, but this time I saw more than just "people." Families, single men, and women filled the room. Little girls whose dresses were loose from starvation and the stresses of living on the street, their eyes resembling those of an older person, with lines of stressful days and sleepless nights. Women and men whose appearances could easily hide their poverty, and others who looked tired and weak. Smiling faces headed outdoors to get a whiff of the morning air and converse with others.

9   I began to walk outside with my fruit bowl, when one man caught my eye. He reminded me of Santa Claus, because of his sweet eyes and big rosy cheeks. "Sir, would you like some fruit?" I asked. He looked at me and smiled bashfully. He looked down at his hands. He was holding coffee and an empty plate. He looked back at the fruit, wondering if he had room in his hands to carry it. Carefully, he took a banana into the hand that held the coffee, and spilled it with his nervous movements. He thanked me and slowly walked away.

10   Sorrow stricken, I continued to walk outside and was greeted by jumping dogs, beautiful dogs that seemed to be unaware of their misfortune. The owners satisfied their dogs' appetites before their own. One man had a litter of puppies that needed homes. He tried to convince me to take one, but they seemed very content there, with him.

11   After breakfast was over, I helped the crew clean. As we washed the empty casserole bowls and pots, my mind began to wander. It was then that I realized my fortune. I had a comfortable bed to sleep in at night and wake up to in the morning. I never had to be tortured by the rumbling growls of hunger. I could not imagine having to use a concrete sidewalk as my bed or a cardboard box as my home. Volunteering that day taught me that poverty can come for any of us—it is not prejudiced towards race, gender, or age. This realization changed the steady rhythm of my life.

12   As we drove away that morning, I remember my mom saying, "I think we fed over a hundred people today." All I could do was think of the faces I had seen, and I realized how much they looked like mine.

Exercise 3.2

Revisit each draft of Marisol's essay. How effectively does the revised final draft fulfill the promises Marisol makes in her discovery draft (pp. 37–38)? In her freewriting (p. 30)? Point to at least two places in the revised final draft that you think are particularly strong. Why do you think these are effective? Point to at least two places in this draft that you think need revising. Why do you think these are less effective? What advice would you offer Marisol, were she to revise this paper for her portfolio?

Writing Strategy

REVISION TIPS

Get some distance. Give yourself enough time to let the paper sit at least 24 hours before you begin revising.

Revise for meaning. Decide whether you've kept the promises your focus statement and thesis sentence made.

Revise for audience. Try to read from your reader's perspective, or ask someone else to read your essay from that perspective.

Revise for structure. Look at the overall structure or shape of the essay first, then at the structure of each paragraph.

Revise for sentences. Consider the variety of your sentences, including sentence type and length.

Revise for words. Make sure your words are accurate and appropriate.

Use peer review. Participate in review sessions with your classmates.

Edit. After you've worked through all these revision strategies, proofread your paper to correct problems in spelling, grammar, and mechanics.

any students approach reading as though it were a spectator sport. You can see this by watching them move from their written homework to the reading they have been assigned. While they write, they generally sit at a desk or table. But when it comes time to read, they move to a soft chair or even a bed and get comfortable—they take off their shoes and kick back, reclining into what looks like a very passive state in which the only thing that moves is their eyes. It's no wonder that reading has often been prescribed as a cure for insomnia. But your reading process, just like your writing process, should be far more active than this.

In "How to Mark a Book," Mortimer J. Adler advocates reading actively and explains how the active reader can come to "own" the books she reads.

> There are two ways in which one can own a book. The first is the property right you establish by paying for it, just as you pay for clothes and furniture. But this act of purchase is only the prelude to possession. Full ownership comes only when you have made it a part of yourself, and the best way to make yourself a part of it is by writing in it. An illustration may make the point clear. You buy a beefsteak and transfer it from the butcher's icebox to your own. But you do not own the beefsteak in the most important sense until you consume it and get it into your bloodstream. I am arguing that books, too, must be absorbed in your bloodstream to do you any good.

To get what you're reading "into your bloodstream," you have to become an active reader. And as Adler suggests, one of the best ways to own a book, or any other

Responding to Readings

C H A P T E R 4

kind of reading, is through writing in it and about it. (A disclaimer here: While you were in high school, you were probably told repeatedly not to mark in your books, so actually writing in a text may not be an easy thing for you to do. A little later in this chapter, we'll suggest some alternatives to writing in the text itself. See p. 99.)

Reading and writing are so tightly connected that we can say they're intertwined. That is, your ability to write is strengthened by your ability to read, and vice versa. And although we may argue that writing is the most powerful learning tool we have, we could also argue for the powerful ways we learn by reading. Reading gives us information that we would not have access to otherwise. However—and here the inseparability of reading and writing becomes clear—we often learn more by writing about what we read. Many of your teachers in college will require you to write about the readings they assign because they believe that you will retain more of the readings by writing about them. Obviously, you should complete these assignments as thoroughly as possible. But even when you aren't given such a writing assignment, you'll find it helpful to write about assigned readings. For one thing, you'll engage a given text more actively by writing about it than by simply reading it and closing the book until your next class meeting. For another thing, you may find that you can expand your ideas for writing on a topic by reading and responding to what others have said about that topic.

Reading thoroughly and well will be extremely important for you during your college career. Remember, take the time necessary to read and respond to class readings, whether written response is assigned or not. You'll strengthen your reading and study skills, and that should lead, in turn, to improved grades. In this chapter, we'll discuss specific reading and writing strategies that should help you strengthen your abilities to use writing while reading and then reading while writing.

SAMPLE READINGS

Read each of the following texts and consider the questions that accompany them. The first selection, "No Hunting Here, Please," is a persuasive essay by Denise D. Knight that appeared in *Newsweek*.

DENISE D. KNIGHT

NO HUNTING HERE, PLEASE

1   Three years ago my husband and I built our dream house in the country. It was exhilarating. We blazed trails through the woods, dug ponds and placed birdhouses and feeders throughout our 143 acres. Our efforts were richly rewarded. We have watched blue herons wading in our ponds, turtles sunning on the shore and mallards swimming with their young. We have been visited by turkeys, opossums, coyotes, deer, skunks, raccoons, rabbits, foxes and groundhogs. More than 50 varieties of birds have dined at

our feeders, from the tiny ruby-throated hummingbird to the exotic ring-necked pheasant. Friends who spent a week with us last summer christened our place "Shangri-La."

2 During our first autumn in the country, we placed NO HUNTING signs around our property to discourage trespassers, then hoped for the best. Deer-hunting season in mid-November brought a measurable increase in traffic on our seldom-traveled road. Cars and trucks filled with orange- and camouflage-attired hunters crept slowly by. Those who stopped to ask us permission to hunt were turned away disappointed. Before long, things took a turn for the worse. Our closest neighbors were relaxing in their living room one quiet Sunday when a bullet shattered their window and dropped to the floor. Police investigators traced the slug to the rifle of a hunter on an adjacent property. While he was more than 500 feet away from the residence—the minimum distance required by New York state law—his ammunition was powerful enough to travel more than 1,000 feet.

3 Hunters in New York who apply for a license need not demonstrate any proficiency at hitting a target, moving or fixed. Rather, they pay a licensing fee and take a safety course on how to render first aid should they shoot a fellow hunter (which some of them inevitably do each year). Then they take to the woods, often with willful disregard for posted signs on private land. Although the state has thousands of acres of land open to hunters, many of them seek out the less crowded conditions found on private property.

4 Despite the conspicuously posted signs on our land, we've had numerous trespassers. The second Monday of last fall's hunting season started out magically, as many of our days do. As the sun crept up over a distant hill, my husband spotted the silhouettes of three deer that had bedded down on the hill behind a pond, seeking rest and solitude after a long night of foraging for food. I was working at home that morning and welcomed the opportunity to observe these creatures in their habitat. A few minutes after 8 A.M. a shot rang out at such close range that the walls of my study shook, and a flock of turkeys that had been feeding in the backyard scattered. When I ran to a front window, I saw a trio of hunters—two in their car and the one who had fired the shot standing next to it. He had shot right over the top of a NO HUNTING sign and onto our property. Had he hit and killed the deer, I have no doubt that he would have brazenly marched onto our land to claim his prize. When the hunter finally saw me, he returned to his car and made a hasty retreat. Within minutes, an environmental-conservation officer located the trio, who denied any wrongdoing. When they were confronted with the retrieved shell and the threat that their weapons might be confiscated, the driver of the car came clean. He was charged with two misdemeanors: firing from the road and discharging a weapon at an unsafe distance from a residence. Although he had broken the law, shattered my sense of safety and deprived the deer of the sanctuary that our property was intended to provide, he was immediately released to resume his hunting. Eventually, he paid a $200 fine.

5 While my husband and I are non-hunters, we are not altogether anti-hunting. We are, however, vehemently opposed to encountering armed intruders on our own land. We have the right to enjoy our property 12 months of the year without the threat of being harassed or harmed by strangers bearing lethal weapons.

6 Last hunting season brought even more problems. While my husband was out walking one afternoon, he came upon an 18-year-old hunter wandering the property with a rifle slung over his shoulder. When my husband questioned him, he denied having seen our signs. During the subsequent investigation, the teen's father revealed that his son had trouble controlling his temper. When I asked him if he thought it was prudent for someone with a violent temper to be handling a rifle, he told me that his son was of age and there was nothing he could do to stop him. So, back to the woods he went. Then in February, two rabbit hunters, a man and his neighbor's 14-year-old

son, walked right past our posted signs as if they were invisible. When questioned by the authorities, the man said he'd hunted those grounds for years. He'd just never been caught before.

7 These experiences have taught us that signs are no more effective against trespassers than restraining orders are against the stalkers or batterers who are intent on harming their victims. They are merely pieces of paper for which the violaters feel outright contempt. While trespassing is not as serious as the crimes that often plague more populated areas, it is a manifestation of the same social illness that causes some people to believe that they are above the law. With children also bearing arms and taking to the woods (the legal age for hunting small game in New York is 12), the adults who ignore NO HUNTING signs are setting the example that it's OK to trespass.

8 Living in the country rejuvenates the spirit, but it also has its price. We have to guard against such hazards as Lyme disease and rabid raccoons. But more worrisome than any natural danger is the weapon-toting human whose reckless disregard for the law is far more insidious.

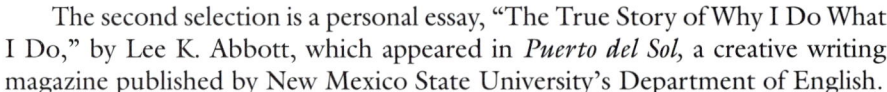 *Questions for Review*

1. What is the purpose of Knight's essay?
2. Identify two or three instances of vivid language that you noticed as you read. What makes these passages noteworthy or interesting?
3. How effectively does Knight use specific examples in her essay?
4. To what extent do you agree or disagree with Knight? Why?

The second selection is a personal essay, "The True Story of Why I Do What I Do," by Lee K. Abbott, which appeared in *Puerto del Sol,* a creative writing magazine published by New Mexico State University's Department of English.

LEE K. ABBOTT

THE TRUE STORY OF WHY I DO WHAT I DO

1 All stories are true stories, especially the artful lies we invent to satisfy the wishful thinker in us, for they present to us, in disguise often and at great distance, the way we are or would want to be. Told to us in a lingo as unique as a fingerprint, they address our up-and-down, our here-and-now. They come, I think, from a desire, as irresistible as love itself, to fix on the page a moment, suffered or made up, when something—one puny thing or idea or person—revealed itself and so turned off the Boom-Boom-Boom which usually deafens us to ourselves. Happily-ended or not, stories are the truth we leave behind, like crumbs, to say how we've come and what was there to see.

2   To be inspirational, as high-minded and upward-looking as the foolish half of me mostly aims to be, I have to tell you about my father—as crazed, driven and cross-hearted a hero as I have ever known. His analogues have appeared in dozens of my stories: he's the gentleman, in golf togs or business suit, throwing the epic tantrum, careening hither and thither in a men's locker or banker's office; he's the one, in the fiction I invent, with the outraged moral intelligence, the one who hectors and harangues, the one telling another (usually me, you can guess) how to behave and when to beware and what is likely to be the dry end of things we love.

3   In fiction, he is imperious, forbidding as a Puritan God, sharp-minded as an out-of-town lawyer, stiff as pig bristle, wiry and unforgiving; in fiction, the made-up landscape I am a sometime citizen in, he suffers and is redeemed (or he is not), does the wrong thing and is shamed (or is not), comes to insight and is crushed (or is not). In fiction, given its unities and shape and its epiphanies, I comprehend my father. I know exactly what he meant when he told me that you could tell a gentleman by his hand shake and his shoe shine. I know, and can articulate, what significance there is in the properly mowed lawn, what wisdom there is in the order of dried dishes. In fiction, I know—maybe as Flannery O'Connor did—why the heathen rage.

4   In life, however—which, messy and improbable and ephemeral, is not good fiction—I had no idea what made his world spin round and round. The facts were clear to me, not the flesh. He went to Dartmouth, I knew. He pole-vaulted cross-handed. One brother died on the Bataan Death March; his sister in a boating accident on Lake Sasebo in Maine. His father went blind in the last years of his life; his mother squandered an inheritance of at least one million dollars. He was a roué, I heard, a slick-haired rake who hung out on the pier at Old Orchard Beach and went down to Miami in the winter. He married my mother, the over-pampered daughter of a Canadian insurance executive, in Harlingen, Texas, while he was at gunnery school in VMI. They lived in Panama, where I was born. He ran the National Guard in Illinois, where my brother was born. He played one year of professional golf. He became a career military man, went to England, Korea, Germany, resigned his commission twice because somebody, or something, infuriated him.

5   If it is true, as Willa Cather says, that the "basic material a writer works with is acquired before the age of fifteen," then by the time I was a sophomore in high school in Las Cruces, New Mexico, already telling my teachers and myself that I was going to be a writer, the material I had acquired I'd got from him: a duke's mixture of soirees, of country clubs and officers' clubs, of colorful compadres named Red and Goonch and Uncle Inches—the whole of it tragic and tearful to the aggressively poetic kid I was then. My mother was a drunk, institutionalized when I was twelve; my father was a drinker.

6   He had psoriasis on his knobby knees and knobby elbows, he smoked like the dickens, he threw a wedge at the TV, he dressed in pink polkadots for the Club Championship, he banished me to my room forever, he expected my brother and me to know the truth and speak it invariably—this was my material, a hodgepodge of goo and muck and human blah-blah-blah the responsibility for which I was absolutely unaware of until the inspirational summer afternoon I am partly here to yap about.

7   Once upon a time (Isn't this the rhetoric, in truth, that opens every fairytale we survive and want to write about?), my father and I found ourselves alone at home. I want to say it was a Sunday, for in my memory the day, if not the events themselves, have a liturgical, quasi-holy "feel." In my memory, that attic atop the shoulders where everything truly felt is found, there is that Sunday light, crooked and mote-filled and lazy, and that Sunday time, heavy and ever in danger of wobbling to a halt. My father, in his bermuda shorts and golf shirt, is in the TV room, drinking the rum thing he preferred;

he had the habit, annoying I think now, of dumping his half-used ice cubes back in the freezer, a habit the girl who became my wife told me was disgusting every time I made her a Coke and it tasted like hooch. I am in the living room, I think, listening to records; more likely, I am reading—*Sports Illustrated,* the *National Geographic, Life* magazine.

8   My taste in those days ran to the quick, the immediate—prose of the slash-and-burn kind. *Mila 18* by Leon Uris, *The Naked and the Dead* (still an excellent book, by the way), Alistair MacClean's high seas adventures. I saw myself writing a book like those one day—a book, conceived out of testosterone and *Nugget*-style macho, a book as pithy and direct as a dust jacket blurb: "Mr. Abbott," the endorsement would run, "writes like an assassin. He's the 'Aaarrgghh' the yellow yammer when they spy the vast What-Not opening to greet them." I had, I thought then, no experience (this was long before I realized that Henry James was correct when he said that "experience was an atmosphere of the mind"). I was just a kid, after all. Skinny, with a flat-top and fifteen pimples, half my mind tilted toward girls, the other half tilted toward glory (which would, in the reasoning I was the victim of, get me girls).

9   The hours passed that Sunday afternoon as they always do when I cast myself back into the dangerous tides that are my past: the clock above the antique writing desk chiming on the quarter-hour, the father wandering between the refrigerator and liquor cabinet, Pee Wee Reese or Dizzy Dean saying in the TV room what the Dodgers were doing; the son in another room cobbling together in his fertile but screwy imagination a tale of swashbuckling and hair-raising, a narrative of guns and grateful bimbos and nick-of-time derring-do. We were in our elements, him and me: one, the older, tuned to the stupid clatter of the exterior world; the other, the younger flesh of him, tuned to the twilight interior world of fetch-and-keep, of fantasy. Then he burst into the living room, eyed me as if wondering for the last time whether I was up to the burden he was about to pitch my way, and said, a little drunkenly, "Come with me."

10   He had been thinking about himself, it is clear now. An inventory, check mark after check mark after check mark, had been taken: three heart attacks, a fist-sized hunk of his lung removed at William Beaumont General Hospital in Ft. Bliss, the yips on the putting green, Homeric-like anger, frustration at a life twisted which-away, hopes high as heaven he believed in, bitterness at being less than the hero he'd promised himself he'd be. I didn't know this at the time I followed him outdoors and into the utility rooms at the end of the car port. I knew only that he was semi-sloshed. I knew only that he was fifty-six years old, gray-headed and tough. I knew he hated going to work at the post office, his job in those days, where he supervised and inspected and, unhappiest of all for him, had to tattle on those who stole money or stamps or swiped somebody's *Playboy* magazine.

11   "See this, Kit?" he said. He was standing in the center of the utility room, lawn mower here, gas can there, the walls hung with tools I never got the sense of. Golf clubs were in there, a bucket of practice balls, cans of oil, greasy rags, a hoe, a rake, a cheap hardware store of goodies that smelled old and used and too sweet. "You want to be a writer, huh," he said, sweeping his arms, then pulling me after him. He snarled the word; it was sound which scorned ignorance and innocence. Against the wall, high as the ceiling, were stacked his footlockers and steamer trunks, from the Army of the United States and from the regiments that were the families of his own father, innkeeper Layman Kittredge Abbott of Portland, Maine. I like to think now that I knew we were coming to something, my father and me, that he was going to say words to me and I, perhaps for the first time, was going to understand him precisely. I like to think now that I was smart enough to know that I was in the presence of a truth grander than the two of us, a truth the price of which we go on paying forever, a truth

more dire than the knowing that we die and do not rise. This is the moment, I like to think of myself thinking then, when you discover how hard the world is, when what you've cleaved to is cleaved from you with an broadaxe.

12   Then he assaulted those lockers and trunks. In a fury, huffing and puffing, he snatched them down, one by one, hollering "Timber!" when the uppermost went tumbling. They crashed and banged, and I tried backing up a little, as he flung one behind him and scrambled over another to reach a third. He was hollering, you have to know, all the New England notes of his voice echoing in that now cramped room, and maybe I was some scared. This was the temper I'd witnessed elsewhere—on the golf course, behind the wheel of his Ford, in the living room when someone in the big world made a ding-a-ling out of himself. But there was more than anger here: there was pain, the particular kind of which was personal and buried deep in his bones, pain for which there is no Latin name or medicine or machine, other than fiction, to account for.

13   "Write it all down!" he was shouting. "Write it all goddam down!"

14   And it was here, from a certain X-spot in the world, 1855 Cruse, that my father, teetering from booze and the awful weight of his own life, was taking seriously, in a manner I couldn't yet, what purpose writing ought to have. Here it is, he was in effect saying. Crated and stored, catalogued and preserved, year by used-up year, place by rotten place. Here it is: the come and go of it, the building and collapse of it, the joy and weep of it. Here it is, he was saying. All the tissues and nerves and human jingle-jangle, that want and excess of it, the rigamarole and whirling, damaged creatures we are. And all you have to do, son and boy, is write it down. Write it all goddam down.

15   This, I submit, is the inspirational part. If we write for any larger purpose than a simple good time—and, believe me, there is nothing at all wrong with a good time—it is, I think, because we all feel, less and more, the obligation we have to our fathers, to our mothers, to all the folks, linked by biology or not, who have raised us; an obligation, as essential to our moral natures as our hearts are to long life, to the places we were raised in and to the knowledge we learned there. We want, I hope, because there is no other way to do it, to write it down, to transform it, to set it straight. At our best, we do not write for the money alone, though money is nice; nor do we write for fame, though fame is likewise nice. We write, beginner and professional alike, because, though half-frightened, we want to know what is in the trunks and lockers we lug forward through time, what vital secrets they can be sprung to reveal.

Questions for Review

1. How effectively does Abbott's essay develop the promise of its title?
2. Identify two or three instances of vivid language that you noticed as you read. What makes these passages noteworthy or interesting?
3. How effectively does Abbott use specific examples in his essay?
4. Were any parts of the essay confusing? If so, which ones? What did you do to understand them?

"Freeway 280," the third selection, is a poem by Lorna Dee Cervantes that appeared in *Emplumada*, a collection of her poetry.

LORNA DEE CERVANTES

FREEWAY 280

1　　　Las casitas near the gray cannery,
　　　nestled amid wild abrazos of climbing roses
　　　and man-high red geraniums
　　　are gone now. The freeway conceals it
5　　　all beneath a raised scar.

　　　But under the fake windsounds of the open lanes,
　　　in the abandoned lots below, new grasses sprout,
　　　wild mustard remembers, old gardens
　　　come back stronger than they were,
10　　trees have been left standing in their yards.
　　　Albariciqueros, cerezos, nogales . . .
　　　Viejitas come here with paper bags to gather greens.
　　　Espinaca, verdolagas, yerbabuena . . .
　　　I scramble over the wire fence
15　　that would have kept me out.
　　　Once, I wanted out, wanted the rigid lanes
　　　to take me to a place without sun,
　　　without the smell of tomatoes burning
　　　on swing shift in the greasy summer air.

20　　Maybe it's here
　　　en los campos extraños de esta ciudad
　　　where I'll find it, that part of me
　　　mown under
　　　like a corpse
25　　or a loose seed.

Translations of Spanish words and phrases:

Las casitas—the little houses
abrazos—bear hugs
Albariciqueros, cerezos, nogales—apricot trees, cherry trees, walnut trees
Viejitas—old women (*-itas,* the diminutive, connotes affection)
Espinaca, verdolagas, yerbabuena—spinach, purslane, mint
en los campos extraños de esta ciudad—in the strange fields of this city

Questions for Review

1. In this poem, Cervantes includes Spanish words and phrases. How effectively does she do so?

2. How do the translations of Spanish words and phrases at the poem's end help you to understand the poem?
3. Why do you think Cervantes mixed Spanish and English in this poem? What would have been lost had she used only Spanish? Only English?

Exercise 4.1

How did you read each of these texts? Think back for a moment to your reading, and write a brief description of your reading process. Where did you read them? What did you do while you read? Did you make any notes? Write a brief response to each piece in which you comment on whether you liked it or agreed or disagreed with it and why.

READING STRATEGIES

In this section, we list a number of reading strategies. We don't want to prescribe exactly how you should read, and we recognize that you probably won't use all of the strategies we suggest every time you read an assigned text. However, we do suggest that you try them all as you work through the section. Once you've done this, then you may choose those you think work best for you.

Reread Abbott's personal essay and Cervantes's poem, and apply each strategy in turn. Then consider how your application of these strategies enhances your reading of each piece.

BEFORE YOU READ

1. *Give yourself enough time to read.* Far too many students leave reading assignments to the last minute, thinking that saving them until the eleventh hour will mean that the material will be fresher in their minds. This is a shaky rationalization at best. You may be able to remember enough details to get through a test, but waiting until the last minute is like cramming—you may retain information in the short run but not over the long term. And long-term retention of facts and ideas is what we're after here. So the first piece of advice is to give yourself enough time to complete the reading assignment. That means you'll have to plan your reading time carefully, perhaps dividing a longer assignment into manageable chunks.

2. *Try to read assignments more than once.* This seems absolutely untenable to many students. They have reading assignments in all their classes, and for each class major assignments and tests seem to be due within a week of one another. And it may not be possible to read longer assignments (e.g., a novel) twice. But when you can, plan your time so that you read assignments at least twice. You really can't expect to uncover all (or even most) of a text's meaning on the first reading. Complex texts, those rich in ideas or data, take time to absorb and digest, and a single reading just won't provide enough exposure to a given text to "get it into your bloodstream," to use Adler's analogy.

3. *Jot down some of the expectations you bring to the kind of reading you have been assigned.* What kind of reading have you been assigned—a piece of fiction, an autobiography or biography of a historical figure, a poem, a chapter in a chemistry textbook, an essay from your composition textbook? What expectations do you have for the reading? For example, if you have been assigned to read a novel, consider what you know about fiction (about characters, plot, and conflict, to name three elements of fiction) that will inform your reading. If you have been assigned to read a biography of a major historical figure, what do you expect to learn from reading that text? What do you already know about that figure? What do you want to learn from reading about the person? If you have been assigned a chapter from your chemistry text, what do you expect to learn from this reading? How will the reading fit with your work in the chemistry classroom or laboratory? What do you know about the author? Is the author known or unknown to you?

4. *Preview the assigned reading, jotting brief responses to the following questions.* Before you begin reading, take a look at the text's title, subtitle, headings, and any graphics (i.e., visual aids) and their captions. What orientation to the text do these elements offer? What does the title tell you about the text to come? How does the subtitle expand or clarify the title? How do the headers break up the text itself? What do they suggest about how the text is structured? What graphics—tables, charts, maps, diagrams, drawings, photographs—are present? How do they support the text? What is their purpose?

When you have finished this initial survey, read the first section of the text and then the last. What is the content of each section? What does the writer say in each? What material does the writer present in each? What does the first section suggest about the rest of the text? What is the writer's purpose? What is the writer's attitude toward the subject and toward the reader? What does the last section tell you about the writer's purpose? How does the writer end the text?

From this preview, write a statement of purpose or a summary of what you think the text's main idea is. Also write two or three questions you want the text to answer or write about two or three aspects of the text you find interesting or curious.

Writing Strategy

THE TIME IT TAKES

The second strategy above may raise the question of just how much time you should devote to studying. We tell our students that, as a general rule of thumb, they should allot 2 hours' time outside class for each hour in class, so that your 16-hour load would require 32 hours of study time in addition to the time spent in class and labs. Although this may seem like an inordinate amount of time, you need to treat your schoolwork as you would a job—you have to put in the time to get out of it what you need.

WHILE YOU READ

5. *Consider the sequence—the text's beginning, middle, and end.* One way to think about the flow of a text is to see it as proceeding from a beginning, through a middle, and to an end. As you read, identify these three parts of the text. How does the writer begin the text? What information or material does the writer provide in the introduction? Where does the beginning move into the middle, and what does the writer present in that middle? Where does the middle move into the ending, and what does the writer do to end the text? What transitions does the writer use to make moving from beginning to middle to end smooth and clear? How does each part support the others?

6. *Pause at natural breaks to write about what you have read.* As the writer moves from one major section of the text to the next, stop reading and write a one- or two-sentence summary of what you have just read or write one or two questions you have about your reading. Are there aspects of what you've read that have made you curious or that you don't understand? If so, write a note or a question about these.

7. *Mark and annotate the text as you go, preferably on your second reading.* Highlight or underline (or mark in some other way) important passages while you're reading. If you simply cannot stand to mark a book, make your notes on index cards or on pieces of paper that are slightly smaller than the pages of your book and insert them between pages themselves, so that you have everything together. Jot a quick note in the margins of the text to create a topic index or to indicate an important section. If you're just not a text marker, then use small, stick-on note strips to create this index, and write on each strip why the section is important.

A word of caution—don't mark everything. Some parts of a text are more important or carry more freight than others. How do you decide what to mark? Look for words and ideas that are repeated. Look also for parts you found interesting, you agreed with, or you disagreed with. Mark these, and return to them later; these sections may provide a starting point for your written response.

The following is a sample annotation of Denise Knight's "No Hunting Here, Please." What would you mark and comment on that we didn't? Why?

DENISE D. KNIGHT

NO HUNTING HERE, PLEASE

1   Three years ago my husband and I built our <u>dream house </u>in the country. It was <u>exhilarating</u>. We blazed trails through the woods, dug ponds and placed birdhouses and feeders throughout our 143 acres. Our efforts were <u>richly rewarded.</u> We have watched blue herons wading in our ponds, turtles sunning on the shore and mallards swimming with their young. We have been visited by turkeys, opossums, coyotes, deer, skunks, raccoons, rabbits, foxes and groundhogs. More than 50 varieties of birds have dined at our feeders, from the tiny ruby-throated hummingbird to the exotic ring-necked pheasant. Friends who spent a week with us last summer christened our place <u>"Shangri-La."</u>

an ideal place, an Eden in NY

hunting season in fall—a threat

2   During our first autumn in the country, we placed <u>NO HUNTING signs</u> around our property to <u>discourage trespassers,</u> then hoped for the best. Deer-hunting season in mid-November brought a <u>measurable increase</u> in traffic on our seldom-traveled road. Cars and trucks <u>filled</u> with <u>orange- and camouflage-attired hunters</u> crept slowly by. Those who stopped to ask us permission to hunt were turned away disappointed. Before long, things took a turn for <u>the worse.</u> Our closest neighbors were relaxing in their living room <u>one quiet Sunday</u> when a <u>bullet shattered</u> their window and dropped to the floor. Police investigators traced the slug to the rifle of a hunter on an adjacent property. While he was more than 500 feet away from the residence—the minimum distance required by New York state law—his ammunition was powerful enough to travel more than 1,000 feet.

2nd time for "No Hunting"

problem—stray bullet & neighbors

3   Hunters in New York who apply for a license need not demonstrate any proficiency at hitting a target, moving or fixed. Rather, they pay a licensing fee and take a safety course on how to render first aid should they shoot a fellow hunter (which some of them inevitably do each year). Then they take to the woods, often <u>with willful disregard</u> for posted signs on private land. Although the state has thousands of acres of land open to hunters, many of them seek out the less crowded conditions found on private property.

a bit sarcastic— reduces Hunter Safety course to the lowest common denominator

sound like criminals

4   Despite the conspicuously posted signs on our land, we've had numerous <u>trespassers.</u> The second Monday of last fall's hunting season started out magically, as many of our days do. As the sun crept up over a distant hill, my husband spotted the silhouettes of three deer that had bedded down on the hill behind a pond, seeking rest and solitude after a long night of foraging for food. I was working at home that morning and welcomed the opportunity to observe these creatures in their natural habitat. A few minutes af-

problem—hunters who trespass

ter 8 a.m. <u>a shot rang out at such close range that the walls of my study shook</u> and a flock of turkeys that had been feeding in the backyard scattered. When I ran to a front window, I saw a trio of hunters—two in their car and the one who had fired the shot standing next to it. <u>He had shot right over the top of a NO HUNTING sign and onto our property.</u> Had he hit and killed the deer, I have no doubt that he would have brazenly marched onto our land to claim his prize. When the hunter finally saw me, he returned to his car and made a hasty retreat. Within minutes, <u>an environmental-conservation officer</u> located the trio, who denied any wrongdoing. When they were confronted with the retrieved shell and the threat that their weapons might be confiscated, the driver of the car came clean. He was charged with <u>two misdemeanors:</u> firing from the road and discharging a weapon at an unsafe distance from a residence. Although he had broken the law, shattered my sense of safety and deprived the deer of the sanctuary that our property was intended to provide, he was immediately released to resume his hunting. Eventually, he paid a $200 fine.

5   While my husband and I are non-hunters, we are not altogether anti-hunting. We are, however, <u>vehemently opposed</u> to encountering <u>armed intruders</u> on our own land. We have the right to enjoy our property 12 months of the year without the threat of being harassed or harmed by strangers bearing lethal weapons.

6   Last hunting season brought even more problems. While my husband was out walking one afternoon, he came upon an 18-year-old hunter wandering the property with a rifle slung over his shoulder. When my husband questioned him, he denied having seen our signs. During the subsequent investigation, the teen's father revealed that his son had trouble controlling his temper. When I asked him if he thought it was prudent for someone with <u>a violent temper</u> to be handling a rifle, he told me that his son was of age and there was <u>nothing he could do</u> to stop him. So, back to the woods he went. Then in February, two rabbit hunters, a man and his neighbor's 14-year-old son, walked right past our posted signs as if they were invisible. When questioned by the authorities, the man said he'd hunted those grounds for years. He'd just never been caught before.

7   These experiences have taught us that signs are no more effective against trespassers than restraining orders are against the stalkers or batterers who are intent on harming their victims. They are merely pieces of paper for which the violators feel <u>outright contempt</u>. While trespassing is not as serious as the crimes that often plague more populated areas, it is a manifestation of the same <u>social illness that causes some people to believe that they are above the law.</u> With children also bearing arms and taking to the woods (the legal age for hunting small game in New

ideal shattered

total disregard by hunters for property owners

3rd time—"No Hunting"

language—not a game warden but "an environmental-conservation officer"

no real teeth to these laws

crux of the conflict—property rights v. hunters' wishes

another example, this time a troubled teen

some arrogance on the hunters' part

good analogy—ineffectiveness of notices

heavy duty significance here—hunters as a sign of society's increasing disregard for the law

4th time—
"No Hunting"

York is 12), the adults who ignore NO HUNTING signs are setting the example that it's OK to trespass.

8   Living in the country rejuvenates the spirit, but it also has its price. We have to guard against such hazards as Lyme disease and rabid raccoons. But more worrisome than any natural danger is the weapon-toting human whose reckless disregard for the law is far more insidious.

hits lawlessness
theme again

8. *Index and analyze the text's key terms.* The index of a book is a listing of that book's main, or key, terms and where to find them. You may create your own index by identifying a text's key terms and then, after you finish your reading, writing about the meaning of each and how it supports the writer's purpose. In a novel, for example, you may identify particular symbols or characters that are important. What are these, and why are they important? In a chapter in a physics text, you may identify concepts (e.g., heat transfer or masses in motion) that are important. Define these concepts, and speculate about why they are important to the chapter.

How do you identify a key term? Look for terms that appear frequently in the text. Look for terms used in the title, subtitle, and headers that recur in the body of the text. Such repetition often signals that terms are key terms. Also look for terms that appear in an essay's thesis, topic sentences, introduction, and conclusion and reappear throughout the essay.

9. *Identify words and terms whose meaning you don't know.* As you read, you're likely to encounter unfamiliar terms. When you do, mark them in some way so that you may return to them later and work to fully understand them. Then, try to guess their meaning. What is their context? What word or term would make sense as a substitute? Sound the unfamiliar word or term out. Do prefixes or suffixes hint at its meaning? If you're working through a first reading, don't stop to look up the definition of a term unless you think the term is so important that the entire reading won't make sense without a definition. But before you begin your second reading, take time to write a definition of those terms you have marked.

10. *Consider the context of words and terms.* Often, you'll find that the meaning of a word or term will shift, so that the word or term takes on a meaning you may not ordinarily associate with it. In his essay, Lee K. Abbott uses the word "inspirational" three times, in paragraphs 2, 6, and 15. Because it's repeated, "inspirational" looks like a key term, and it is. But each time, the meaning of this term shifts. In paragraph 2, "inspirational" suggests that Abbott's been asked to write a piece that offers insight into writing and the life of the writer and so is "inspirational" for the reader. In paragraph 6, Abbott shifts the meaning of this term away from the reader and uses it to describe the summer afternoon and its events that inspired him to write, so "inspirational" becomes more personalized. And in paragraph 15, Abbott shifts the meaning slightly once again, so that "inspirational" remains personalized but also takes on a larger meaning, one that suggests the true nature of the writer's inspiration to write: "the obligation we have to our fathers, to our mothers, to all the folks,

linked by biology or not, who have raised us; an obligation, as essential to our moral natures as our hearts are to long life, to the places we were raised in and in the knowledge we learned there." Although the shifts in meaning are subtle, they are nonetheless important. The larger meaning of the last use of "inspirational" is particularly important for the aspiring writer. "Inspirational" is customarily used to describe something that is positive, something that helps motivate us to think better thoughts or to do good works—"this morning's talk was not only informative but inspirational." But in this last use, Abbott suggests that the writer is driven to write by his past—not simply motivated to write but driven by obligation. So in this last use, "inspirational" takes on less positive connotations. And in taking on those less positive connotations, the term expands in meaning, so that it becomes more comprehensive in its meaning than it was when we first encountered it in the second paragraph.

For another example, how does Lorna Dee Cervantes's use of Spanish terms and sentences in "Freeway 280" fit with the rest of the poem, which is in English? Cervantes is fluent in both Spanish and English, so why did she choose to present important elements of this poem in Spanish? And for another example, look at Sherman Alexie's poem "That Place Where Ghosts of Salmon Jump" (p. 271). What does the term "senseless magic" (line 6) mean? How does the context of this poem make us read "senseless" as a term that's more complicated than it would be in the phrase "a senseless act of violence"?

11. *Take note of places where your knowledge of history, language, culture, or some other specialized subject (e.g., music or mathematics) helps you create meaning with the author.* Writers depend on our knowing a great deal. They must do so, because they simply don't have enough time and space to tell us everything we might need to know in support of their writing. But even if they could do so, they wouldn't, because part of the pleasure of reading is working to figure out what the writer means. For example, in "The True Story of Why I Do What I Do," Lee K. Abbott says this:

> The hours passed that Sunday afternoon as they always do when I cast myself back into the dangerous tides that are my past: the clock above the antique writing desk chiming on the quarter-hour, the father wandering between the refrigerator and liquor cabinet, Pee Wee Reese or Dizzy Dean saying in the TV room what the Dodgers were doing; the son in another room cobbling together in his fertile but screwy imagination a tale of swashbuckling and hair-raising, a narrative of guns and grateful bimbos and nick-of-time derring-do. We were in our elements, him and me: one, the older, tuned to the stupid clatter of the exterior world; the other, the younger flesh of him, tuned to the twilight interior world of fetch-and-keep, of fantasy.

This passage offers two allusions that help contrast Abbott and his father. By naming Pee Wee Reese and Dizzy Dean and the Dodgers, Abbott identifies his father's interest in baseball and identifies the particular time of the passage. (Reese and Dean were television announcers for the Dodgers baseball organization from the mid 1950s to the early 1960s.) By alluding to the adventures at work "in his fertile but screwy imagination," Abbott reveals his own romantic nature as a hero wannabe, one who overcomes overwhelming odds to rescue "grateful bimbos," always at the risk of great personal danger, always threatened by gunfights and the like. Abbott assumes that the reader has some knowledge of baseball in the first instance and of escapist fiction in the second; he thereby invites the reader to share particular scenes from his previous experience to help heighten the contrast between father and son that he is drawing.

At times, you may not understand something in a reading because you may not have the knowledge or background you need to interpret it. For example, Cervantes writes part of "Freeway 280" in Spanish. Although you may be able to infer at least part of the meaning of the Spanish terms from their context, you won't understand important elements of this poem unless you read Spanish. Cervantes provided definitions of these terms for you, but if she had not, you would have had to find someone to interpret them for you to get the full import of the poem.

12. *Take note of particularly creative uses of language. Paraphrase these; that is, put them into your own words.* We expect poets to use such devices as metaphor, simile, and personification to convey meaning to their readers. However, prose (whether fiction or nonfiction) can be just as rich as poetry in these devices. For example, Datus Proper uses personification (attributing human qualities to an inanimate object) in "Dark Hollow": "The fly rights itself, shimmies its peacock body at the trout, and flashes you a V-for-victory sign with white wings." Using the verbs "rights," "shimmies," and "flashes," Proper attributes purposeful action to a fishing fly, making the fly come to life and seem to be a conspirator with Proper against the trout. Another example from Proper's essay involves a description of the size of a sycamore tree: "The trunk was as thick as four Dark Hollow girls standing back to back, pale toes wriggling down into the pool." Just how big is this tree? A rough paraphrase might be "The sycamore tree's trunk was about three feet in diameter, and its roots were down into the water." What is lost in such a paraphrase? As you consider that question, you'll be developing insight into one of the most significant characteristics of good writing.

Exercise 4.2

Writing a paraphrase means rewriting a passage in other words. A paraphrase is a complete rendition of the original passage and generally approaches the original's length. Although paraphrases are most often used in connection with research, the following exercise is designed to help you focus on the power of creative uses of language.

What images are evoked by the following examples of figurative language? After you read each example, paraphrase it. What differences do you notice between the original and your paraphrase?

> And on this afternoon, the sense of illness lay so heavy you could have gathered it in your hands like snow and rounded it into balls to throw.
> Henry Louis Gates, Jr., "Change of Life," *Colored People*

> She moved quickly, darting through the field like a rabbit startled by a hunter.

The cat moved sideways as it approached the mouse, looking for all the world as if a stiff wind were blowing it into the helpless prey.

By "language using" here I am referring to the employment of any system of symbols in order to make sense of the world—the primary means by which all of us run order through chaos, thereby giving ourselves the identities we have.

William E. Coles, Jr., *Seeing Through Writing*

Writing Strategy

ON PARAPHRASING

To paraphrase is to restate a piece of writing (e.g., a sentence or a paragraph) in your own words, so that you accurately rephrase its content. A paraphrase should be approximately the same length as the original passage on which it's based.

As a reading strategy, paraphrasing can help you understand a difficult passage more clearly, because it forces you to read the passage carefully. As a writing strategy, paraphrasing can help you make things easier for your reader to understand. In essence, when you paraphrase, you translate the language of the original passage into terms your reader may more readily grasp.

When you paraphrase, whether only a sentence or a longer passage, you must document your source; that is, you must cite the source in the text of your writing and then document it as part of a "Works Cited" page. For more information on documenting sources, see Chapter 12.

AFTER YOU HAVE READ

13. *Write answers to the questions you raised; write responses to the "curiosities" you identified; or write a response to the writer about points of interest, agreement, and/or disagreement (see 4, 6, and 7 above).* How did your reading answer your questions? How did those curiosities you identified figure in the text? At what points did the writer truly pique your interest? On what points did you agree or disagree? Why?

14. *Define the terms you didn't know (see 9 above).* Write the term and then a definition of it in the margins of the text and on an index card. Keep these cards to create a text-specific or course-specific key-term dictionary. Be sure to identify the text and page number on each card.

15. *Write a summary of the text.* When you finish reading the text, review it, taking note of what you've marked as important, and write a brief summary

of the text's major points. If you didn't understand something, jot down a couple of questions to ask when your class discusses the reading or in a conference with your teacher.

Writing a summary begins in your identifying the important parts of the text and then capsulizing, or creating an overview of, the text. Think about a time recently when you told a friend about a movie you had seen. What was the movie? What did you tell your friend? In all likelihood, your discussion followed one of these two structures:

1. You talked about the movie's plot by giving its highlights, from start to finish, so that you followed the plot line (the events of the movie) fairly closely.
2. You retold the movie's highlights—things you remembered as important or dramatic or humorous; things that stood out in your memory.

In either case, you retold parts of the movie in your own words, giving your friend enough of an overview of the movie, enough of its flavor, to tempt her to see it, perhaps even with you. Summaries of written texts can function the same way.

As you prepare to write a summary, consider what you identified while reading as the text's highlights, points you marked as important or arguable, and so on. Then make a list of those points, so that you have at least a checklist of things to include in your summary. Your goal in summarizing a text is to report the text's main idea (or ideas) as accurately as you can, so that someone who hasn't read the text can gain an overview of it just from reading your summary. How long should a summary be? Generally, the length is determined by the length of the piece being summarized. A 500-word passage should be summarized in only a few sentences, but an entire book probably can't be summarized well even in 500 words.

Writing Strategy

CHECKLIST FOR WRITING A SUMMARY

1. Have you given the author's name, the text's title, and complete publication information?
2. What is the text's main idea? How accurately have you reported it?
3. Have you directly quoted key words or terms, perhaps even entire sentences? If so, have you identified direct quotations by placing them in quotation marks?
4. If you have included specific details (e.g., data or examples), is the information absolutely essential for the summary to make sense?

5. How long is it? If you've summarized a shorter piece, does your summary run more than 150–200 words? If you've worked with a longer piece, is your summary long enough to capture the spirit and content of that piece?

6. If you then use information from the summary as part of your own writing, remember that you must document it; that is, you must provide both a citation in the body of your essay and a reference to the source as part of a "Works Cited" page. For more information about documenting sources, see Chapter 12.

Compare this short passage by Otto Friedrich with the summaries that follow it. How accurately do the two summaries report the passage's contents?

> In medicine, the computer, which started by keeping records and sending bills, now suggests diagnoses. CADUCEUS knows some 4,000 symptoms of more than 500 diseases; MYCIN specializes in infectious diseases; PUFF measures lung functions. All can be plugged into a master network called SUMEX-AIM, with headquarters at Stanford in the West and Rutgers in the East. This may sound like another step toward the disappearance of the friendly neighborhood G. P., but while it is possible that a family doctor would recognize 4,000 symptoms, CADUCEUS is more likely to see patterns in what patients report and can then suggest a diagnosis. The process may sound dehumanized, but in one hospital where the computer specializes in peptic ulcers, a survey of patients showed that they found the machine "more friendly, polite, relaxing, and comprehensible" than the average physician.
>
> Otto Friedrich, "The Computer Moves In," *Time*

The following summary of this passage focuses on the computer's role in making diagnoses and, in particular, on the amusing idea that a computer may be more personable than a human:

> In "The Computer Moves In" (*Time,* January 3, 1983, pp. 14–24), Otto Friedrich notes that computers are applied widely in medicine to enhance a doctor's diagnosis of a patient's symptoms. And while computers do not yet replace doctors, in at least one hospital, patients seemed to prefer the bedside manner of a computer able to deal with peptic ulcers to that of a typical physician.

This summary emphasizes the specific functions computer diagnosis makes available to doctors:

> In "The Computer Moves In" (*Time,* 1/3/83, pp. 14–24), Otto Friedrich tells readers that while the computer was originally used by doctors to keep records of patients, it has now become a crucial tool for diagnosing illnesses. Friedrich mentions such programs as CADUCEUS, which knows 4,000 symptoms of 500 diseases; MYCIN, which specializes in infectious diseases; and PUFF, which measures lung functions.

The content of any summary you write will be determined by your interpretation of the passage's significant or key points.

1. Select two or three stories from a weekly magazine such as *Newsweek, Time,* or *Sports Illustrated* and write a summary of each. Bring the articles with you to class and exchange one article and summary with a classmate. Read your classmate's article and summary and discuss with him his summary's accuracy.

2. Read and summarize an essay selected by your instructor from one of the chapters in this textbook. Exchange your summary with those of two of your classmates. How are their summaries similar to yours? Different? How do you account for any differences you find? How accurate do you think their summaries are, even though they may be different from yours?

SAMPLE READING RESPONSE

To illustrate the kinds of information you can generate using these various strategies, Bill wrote the following response to Lee K. Abbott's essay, "The True Story of Why I Do What I Do." As we noted earlier, you probably won't use each strategy for every reading you're assigned. However, Bill has used each in turn to indicate the kinds of information each strategy may help you generate as you complete a reading assignment. The number for each response corresponds to the number of the particular strategy.

1. and 2. no written response necessary, except to say that I read the essay twice, marking the text only on the second run through. I did, however, take some notes on first reading.

3. Expectations
personal essay, so I expect some kind of statement Lee will make about learning something or coming to realize something important from personal experience.
author—Lee K. Abbott. I know a little bit about him, having met him on several occasions. He's a graduate of Las Cruces H. S. and NMSU. got an MFA in creative writing. published several collections of short stories (e.g., *The Heart Never Fits Its Wanting*—good stories). currently a faculty member in the English department at Ohio State. Lee gives very good readings of his stories.

4. Preview
15 ¶s, so it's not very long. no headers or graphics, just the title: "The True Story of Why I Do What I Do." "true story" might seem oxymoronic, perhaps ironic, since stories are sometimes made up, a fiction. reminds me of a line from a country and western song: "That's my story, and I'm stickin' to it."
first section—read first ¶. Lee talks about "true stories" as being "artful lies." They reveal things to us. They're the "truth we leave behind." So stories—"artful lies"—are important.
How can "true stories" be "artful lies"? terms a bit incongruous, at odds.
last section—¶15. Lee says, "This . . . is the inspirational part." What's the "this" that's "inspirational"? He says we have an "oblig-

ation" to those (parents & others) who "raised us," to the "places we were raised in" & the "knowledge we learned there." He closes by saying we write to understand, to know what our past & experiences mean.

main idea? I expect Lee to talk about why he's a writer or a teacher of writing and why he has to write.

5. Beginning, middle, end

Beginning—¶s 1–6. Once I got into the essay, I had to change my mind about the first section. It actually consists of the first six paragraphs, not just the first paragraph as I'd originally thought. Lee talks about writing, stories, artful lies. talks about his father (a complex man), understandable in fiction but not life. writer's material comes from early experience (Cather).

Middle—¶s 7–14. tells story of an afternoon when he was about 16 and his father showed him what it meant to be a writer, what the writer's job is—to "write it all down."

End—¶15. Lee draws conclusions about why he writes and why other writers write. He's compelled, they're compelled to write; writers are obligated to see what "vital secrets" their writing may reveal.

6. Natural breaks

first major break comes between ¶s 6 & 7 as Lee moves into the narrative of the afternoon. "inspirational" appears again (second time)—but it's shifted slightly in meaning. question: Is "inspirational" a key term? Why the shift in meaning?

second major break comes between ¶s 14 & 15 as Lee ends the story about the afternoon with his dad and begins the conclusion. And there's "inspirational" again. And it's shifted in meaning again, seems broader in scope here than before. question: How do the three instances of "inspirational" work together? What do the shifts in meaning signal?

7. Markings

there was pain, the particular kind of which was personal and buried deep in his bones, pain for which there is no Latin name or medicine or machine, other than fiction, to account for.

13 "Write it all down!" he was shouting. "Write it all goddam down!" — *climactic (key) moment*

14 And it was here, from a certain X-spot in the world, 1855 Cruse, that my father, teetering from booze and the awful weight of his own life, was taking seriously, in a manner I couldn't yet, what purpose writing ought to have. Here it is, he was in effect saying. Crated and stored, catalogued and preserved, year by used-up year, place by rotten place. Here it is: the come and go of it, the building and collapse of it, the joy and weep of it. Here it is, he was saying. All the tissues and nerves and human jingle-jangle, that want and excess of it, the rigamarole and whirling, damaged creatures we are. And all you have to do, son and boy, is write it down. Write it all goddam down. *stuff of writing*

to ¶ 6, 2

15   This, I submit, is the inspirational part. If we write for any larger purpose than a simple good time—and, believe me, there is nothing at all wrong with a good time—it is, I think, because we all feel, less and more, the obligation we have to our fathers, to our mothers, to all the folks, linked by biology or not, who have raised us; an obligation, as essential to our moral natures as our hearts are to long life, to the places we were raised in and to the knowledge we learned there. We want, I hope, because there is no other way to do it, to write it down, to transform it, to set it straight. At our best, we do not write for the money alone, though money is nice; nor do we write for fame, though fame is likewise nice. We write, beginner and professional alike, because, though half-frightened, we want to know what is in the trunks and lockers we lug forward through time, what vital secrets they can be sprung to reveal.

¶ 11 & 12

8. Key terms
Lee Abbott—"I" first person narrator throughout. reports himself as a skinny, pimply, testosterone-driven, 15–16-year old aspiring writer
father—mercurial, drinker, anger, pain, unpredictable
footlockers & steamer trunks—literal lockers and trunks in ¶s 11 & 12; figurative or metaphorical meaning in ¶15. literal meaning—holders or containers of stuff, of physical reminders of life, of past, of keepsakes. metaphorical meaning—holders or carriers of significance, things remind us of significant events and people
writing, purpose of writing (specific references in ¶s 1, 5, & 8)
inspirational (¶s 2, 6, & 15)—more to say on this later
write it all down (¶s 13 & 14)—advice from Lee's father that eventually proved true and inspirational

9. Terms to define
Flannery O'Connor (¶3)—short-story writer who lived in Georgia. wrote also about the writer's craft
Willa Cather (¶5)—American novelist who wrote about the Midwest, also wrote *Death Comes for the Archbishop* (a novel set in NM)
wedge (¶6)—golf club used for hitting high, arcing shots from within 75 yards or so of a green
Nugget (¶8)—a men's magazine, lots of nudity, cheesecake
Henry James (¶8)—American novelist and short-story writer. sometimes called the father of psychological realism, so he got into his characters' heads as much as possible.
Pee Wee Reese & Dizzy Dean (¶9)—professional baseball players in the '40s and '50s who also were a popular team as sports announcers in the '50s. broadcast the Falstaff Game of the Week every Saturday.

10. Terms that shift meaning in context
inspirational—appears in three ¶s (2, 6, & 15). It's significant that it appears at the juncture of the beginning and middle and then of the middle and end. (For a complete discussion of the significance of this term, see Reading Strategy 10, pp. 102–103.)

11. Specialized knowledge
    Lee refers to three prominent American writers of this century: O'Connor, Cather, and James. As an English teacher, I understand their importance and know that each wrote about the writer's craft. I particularly remember one of James's statements: "If you would be a writer, be one on whom nothing is lost." seems to me that that's what Lee's father was telling him.

12. Creative uses of language
    Lots of such uses, and here's a sampling of things I marked— *Boom-Boom-Boom* (¶1)—the noise of daily life that can deafen us to what we need to hear
    The description of the father particularly stands out (¶3)—lots of adjectives (imperious, forbidding), similes (stiff as pig bristle). And the structure of the first sentence is pretty much vintage Abbott.
    moment of discovery (¶13)—"when you discover how hard the world is, when what you've cleaved to is cleaved from you with a broad-axe." play on "cleaved" works, says life's lessons don't come easy.

13. Answers to questions raised earlier
    I understand the essay's title—it's appropriate, "true stories" can be "artful lies." The key here is "artful." Lee says the writer writes out of "obligation" and writes "to write it all down, to transform it, to set it straight" (¶15). The "it" here is experience, and Lee says the writer needs to write but also to "transform" that experience and "set it straight." Transforming requires changing things, perhaps selecting only the key details instead of telling every mundane detail. To select one detail means not to select another, so that's one way the whole story doesn't get told. There's also embellishment by writers (by all of us as we tend to make a good story better?) as they select details. Look at the picture Lee draws of his father—his father ranges over the spectrum from good to bad, positive to negative.

14. Define terms not known
    already did that in both 9 and 11

15. Summary
    In "The True Story of Why I Do What I Do" (Published in *Puerto del Sol,* 1988), Lee K. Abbott talks about a key moment in his growth as a writer, though he realized its importance only sometime after the event. On a Sunday afternoon, Lee's father (a "drinker") takes Lee to their home's utility room and pulls down footlockers and steamer trunks full of memorabilia. He shouts to Lee, "Write it all down!" Lee learns from this incident that the writer's best material lies in himself, in his experience. He was inspired by this and hopes his essay will be "inspirational" to other writers as well. Question for any writers in the class: How true does Abbott's essay ring with you as a writer?

MAKING DIALOGUE NOTES

Another reading strategy is to make dialogue notes. As you keep these notes, you'll create a conversation with yourself about your reading, and you may extend this strategy to include class notes and your responses to them.

To create the conversation, you'll need to keep a dialogue notebook. Divide a page vertically into halves. On the right-hand side of the page, take notes on your reading, using any or all of the strategies listed in the While You Read section above. When you've finished reading, go back through your notes and comment on them in the left-hand column. Raise questions; answer questions; identify curiosities; list points of interest, agreement, disagreement. Take this notebook to class and write additional clarifying notes in the left-hand side as points are discussed. Keeping this notebook will provide a record of your understanding of a text, as well as a record of class discussions of particular points.

An example of dialogue notes follows the next selection, "Vaccine Revolution," an article from *Newsweek* by Geoffrey Cowley.

GEOFFREY COWLEY

VACCINE REVOLUTION

1   Back in the Dark Ages, circa 1981, children all over the world were dying of bacterial meningitis. Hemophilus influenza type b (Hib)—the primary culprit—struck one in 200 kids in the United States alone, and a quarter of those who survived the infection suffered brain damage or hearing loss. Today, thanks to a new generation of vaccines, Hib is a rarity. Infection rates have fallen by more than 90 percent in developed countries, and some have vanquished the microbe entirely. If the story sounds familiar it should. Small pox and polio have followed the same arc, and for the same reason. Vaccines, says Dr. Margaret Liu of the California-based Chiron Corp., have had "the greatest impact on human health of any medical intervention."

2   The revolution isn't over. Armed with new tools for manipulating genes and proteins, scientists are now concocting vaccines to fight everything from food poisoning to cervical cancer. At the same time, they're discovering radical new ways to produce compounds that generate immunity. If the new strategies work, future vaccines won't be manufactured in costly laboratories or doled out through needles. We'll cull them cheaply from genetically altered fruits, vegetables or farm animals—and we'll consume them in pills, ointments and nose sprays. Dozens of new compounds are in the works. And together with existing vaccines, they could prevent 12 million deaths a year worldwide.

3   Scientists realized centuries ago that a benign substance can sometimes rally the body's defenses against a harmful one. The surest way to put a dangerous microbe out of business is simply to infect people with a mild strain of it. Live, weakened pathogens have helped control many diseases, from mumps and measles to polio. Now California-based Aviron Corp. is using one to create a flu vaccine that can be placed in a nasal spray. Unlike conventional flu shots, which rely on killed viruses to rouse the immune system, Aviron's FluMist employs a live virus that thrives in the cool climate of the nose and throat but perishes in warmer regions of the body. The bug provokes a vigorous response in the mucosal tissues that flu viruses invade, but its heat aversion keeps it from

invading other tissues. Studies published this spring confirm that FluMist is effective. If approved by the FDA, it could reach the market as early as this fall.

4   Live microbes are not easy to work with. Some won't grow in test tubes, and those that will grow require special handling and constant refrigeration. Until recently, the only alternative to a live pathogen was a dead one. But scientists can now mass-produce small fragments, or "subunits," of a microbe and use them to attract the immune system's attention. The hepatitis B vaccine, introduced in the early 1980s, is based on a genetically engineered piece of the hep B virus. Now researchers at Maryland's MedImmune Corp. are turning the same technique against human papillomavirus, the nation's most common sexually transmitted infection and a common cause of cervical cancer. HPV won't grow in test tubes, so MedImmune scientists have stitched several of its genes into viruses that infect lab-grown insect cells. Once infected, the insect cells churn out HPV fragments that can be used in vaccines. The company is now starting tests in humans, and hoping to market a vaccine by 2003.

5   Other researchers are pursuing variations on this strategy. If a subunit—or a whole pathogen—doesn't trigger immunity, they fasten it to a molecule that will attract more attention. That's the strategy that yielded the new meningitis vaccines, and it may also be our best hope of controlling *Streptococcus pneumoniae*, the leading cause of childhood ear infections. Some 83 percent of American kids suffer an ear infection by the age of 3. The condition accounts for 35 million doctor visits every year, as well as a flood of antibiotic prescriptions, at a cost of roughly $3.5 billion. Children's immune systems don't respond forcefully to the outer coat of strep pneumoniae, which consists of sugar molecules. So researchers at Wyeth-Lederle have created copies of those sugars and attached them to an easily recognized diphtheria protein. If this "conjugate" vaccine works as intended, kids will respond to both of its elements, and achieve lasting immunity from earaches. Scientists at ImmuLogic of Waltham, Mass., hope to use the same trick to immunize addicts against cocaine. They've designed a vaccine that combines cocaine molecules with proteins that elicit antibodies. In principle, those antibodies should bind with cocaine whenever it enters the body. And the size of the antibodies should keep the drug from entering the brain.

6   For all their sophistication, most vaccines share a common drawback: you can't produce them without costly, elaborate facilities, or administer them without sterile needles. But if the new field of "transgenics" fulfills its promise, subunit vaccines could soon be growing on trees. Agricultural scientists routinely introduce foreign genes into crops to help them resist pests, drought and other hazards. And some are now using the same technique to make plants produce immunologically active proteins. At Cornell University's Boyce Thompson Institute for Plant Research, for example, researchers led by Charles Arntzen are growing potatoes that contain harmless proteins from toxic *E. coli*, a leading cause of diarrheal disease. And they've recently shown that people who eat the spuds generate antibodies to the bacterium (transgenic bananas, tomatoes or corn would presumably have the same effect). To turn such foods into vaccines, researchers will have to identify effective doses and devise reliable ways of delivering them. But edible vaccines could be the key to controlling many global killers. "There are 300 million hepatitis B carriers in the world," says Iain Cubitt of Axis Genetics, a British company, "so you need to produce huge amounts of protein. The only conceivable way of doing that is in plants."

7   Or, in some cases, animals. Scientists at Genzyme Transgenics and the National Institute of Allergy and Infectious Diseases are working to create goats whose milk could be used to vaccinate children against malaria. They have already gotten goats and mice to churn out pieces of MSP-1, a protein displayed on the surface of the malaria parasite. If tests show that the MSP particles protect monkeys from malaria, the scientists will try testing them in humans. Some 500 million people contract malaria every year, and up to 3 million die. Vaccines remain our best hope of reversing such tragedies. And at the moment, there is every reason to think they'll succeed.

DIALOGUE NOTES

Response to Notes	Reading Notes
	Preview: from "Medicine" entry under "Society" section
	7 ¶s, no headers in the text.
rings true—I remember taking polio vaccine orally (on sugar cubes) as a school kid in Ft. Worth key terms: new generation of vaccines	Reading: ¶1—vaccines attacked Hib (causes meningitis), smallpox, polio. Dr. M. Liu: Vaccines have had "the greatest impact on human health of any medical intervention."
much promise—amazing potential key terms: genetically altered	¶2—vaccines now being developed to fight everything from cervical cancer to food poisoning. No needles: "pills, ointments and nose sprays" instead for delivery. Made from genetically altered fruits, veggies, & farm animals. "could prevent 12 million deaths" annually.
seems dangerous, but my kids have all been through the polio & MMR vaccines—no problems key terms: benign substance	¶3—how it works: people infected w. "mild strain" of harmful microbe. Examples: MMR, polio. Now "infection" can be done simply, ex. nose spray for flu. Live vs. dead virus, live more effective.
ain't science amazing? This technology is incredible. key terms: fragments, subunits	¶4—process: live microbes hard to work with. Scientists try to attach "fragments" ("subunits") of microbes to other, hardier cells, which in turn produce fragments that can be used in vaccines.
like gene splicing? cloning? key terms: hitchhiking microbe, conjugate vaccine	¶5—research strategy: weak infectious virus piggybacks on stronger cell. Ex. ear infection in kids; immunize cocaine addicts
delivery through foods. *E. coli* reminds me of kids infected in the kiddie pool of a water park (where?), also food poisoning via fast-food hamburgers. Nasty stuff. key terms: transgenics, edible vaccines	¶6—"transgenics"—name for this "new field." vaccines produced in food, ex. *E. coli* strains grown in potatoes & folks who eat them generate antibodies to this virus. Plants can produce the protein needed.
Animal products, too? Seems a panacea, *if* it works. *Great* promise, probably will make somebody a ton of money. key terms: animals, best hope	¶7—animals, too (protein production). Goat milk to vaccinate against malaria. "Vaccines remain our best hope" for preventing disease.

SUMMARY

In "Vaccine Revolution" (*Newsweek,* July 27, 1998), Geoffrey Cowley reports that new vaccines are being developed that can be delivered through food, pills, ointments, and sprays. Traditionally, vaccines are delivered through injection (via a needle), so there's great potential here for immunizing more people than we can now. Cowley lists various diseases this method could fight against: *E. coli,* HPV (human papillomavirus, most common sexually transmitted disease and cause of cervical cancer), ear infections, even cocaine addiction. These new vaccines could prevent some 12 million deaths annually worldwide, so Cowley concludes that vaccines are our "best hope" of disease prevention.

RESPONSE

The technology at work here is amazing. I wonder what the potential drawbacks or liabilities are? And how much government intervention is there likely to be (e.g., FDA approvals)? And what are the ethical issues involved? It's ethical to try to save lives by immunizing kids against diseases so that they don't die, but then that raises other issues: Who'll feed this increased population? What kind of life can they look forward to? Still, this is something to watch—could make some companies a whole lot of money.

Exercise 4.4

Write a dialogue-notebook entry for an article from a weekly magazine, such as *Newsweek, Time,* or *Sports Illustrated,* that has both text and graphic elements. You may use any of the reading strategies provided here, but be sure to preview the article (strategy 4), looking particularly at its graphic elements. After completing your dialogue entry, write a summary of the article. What do you think of the article? What's your response to it?

Computer Tip

If you want to use your computer for dialogue notes, you may set up the format by using the Table function in either WordPerfect or Microsoft Word. (*Note:* Different versions of these programs may use slightly different procedures from those described here.)

WORDPERFECT

1. Click on Table in the menu bar at the top of the screen.
2. Click on Create. You'll see two boxes in the Table Size box. Set both columns and rows to 2
3. Click on SpeedFormat. On the left-hand side will be a listing of formatting options. Click on No Lines Columns. Click on Apply.

4. Move your cursor on top of the vertical line splitting the two columns until it forms a crosshair icon. Click and drag the line to the left, to the position 2.25 inches.
5. Set the justification in both columns to "left." If the Bold button is on, turn it off.

MICROSOFT WORD

1. Click on Table in the menu bar at the top of the screen.
2. Click on Insert Table. Set the number of columns and rows to 2. (Note: These may already be the default figures.)
3. Click on AutoFormat. On the left-hand side under Format select Grid 6. Click OK twice.
4. Move your cursor on top of the vertical line splitting the two columns until it forms a crosshair icon. Click and drag the line to the left, to the position 2.25 inches.
5. If the Bold button is on, turn it off.

Once you've established the columns, you're ready to begin entering text. Use the wider column on the right for your reading notes and the column on the left for your comments on those notes.

You may also devote part of your dialogue notebook to class notes and your responses to them. In the right-hand column, take notes during discussions, lectures, laboratories, and the like. As you review your notes in preparation for your next class meeting, respond to them in the left-hand column. If there are points you don't understand, formulate a question or two to raise during class, or simply comment on what you found interesting or important. Reviewing your notes in this manner will not only help you prepare for class discussions and other activities (such as tests) but will also help you get a more comprehensive or thorough grasp of the course's material.

WRITING A RESPONSE

You probably noticed that we included a short response to the *Newsweek* article, an element we didn't include as a reading strategy. For each assigned reading, you should write a response, because doing so will take you beyond summarizing to interpreting the material you read. Such interpretation is crucial to critical reading, and it's important that you decide and write about the worth or value of what you read. Responding to a text begins with summary and then continues with a value judgment of some kind about the reading. Why should you summarize a text before responding to it? Writing a summary oftentimes gives you insight that you might not get otherwise, because you have to be engaged with the text to summarize it. And checking your summary against the text by rereading both can help you gauge the accuracy of your summary; it can help you identify portions of the text that you haven't understood clearly and so need to reconsider.

To make a value judgment is to consider the quality of the text you read. This judgment may take the form of a fairly straightforward statement of like or dislike. Or you may want to argue or take issue with the writer on one or more aspects of the reading. Several of the questions based on consequence in the Questions for Analysis (see pp. 24–25) can guide you in writing a response:

> *What did you learn from your reading?* What new information did the writer present to you? Do you count it valuable or not?
>
> *What did you learn by investigating the topic of your reading?* If the reading inspired you to do some reading or other kinds of investigation into the topic, what did you learn? Do you count it valuable or not?
>
> *What problems are inherent in your reading? What are their solutions?* Did the author identify problems to which you might respond? Do you agree or disagree with the author's solutions? Or did the reading raise problems for you? What in the reading is potentially problematic for you?
>
> *What about your reading is good? Bad? Desirable? Undesirable? Necessary?* Would you recommend this reading to a friend? Why or why not? To what extent was the reading helpful to you in the context of any assignment that required you to read it? Why?

Answering such questions as these can help you find a focal point—something about the text that intrigued or angered or irritated or amused you—to use as the center of your response. Once you have a focal point, you may then decide what you want your response to do. It may

1. argue with the text's author—you may find points of agreement or disagreement, and you may write either to support the author's points or to disagree with, perhaps even debunk, them.
2. evaluate the text—you may evaluate the effectiveness of the text as a whole or of some particular aspect of it. How clearly did the author write? How effective was her argument, how effectively supported? How fairly did the author treat her subject?
3. comment on the text's meaning or importance to you—to what extent does the text ring true in your own experience? What did it say that you count important to you personally?

Whether arguing, evaluating, or commenting, you should begin your written response with a summary of the text, so that your reader will have a concise, accurate overview of the text. Next, present your opinion of the text, and then support that opinion with enough detail from the text to let your reader understand your point of view.

The following sample responses are to Denise Knight's "No Hunting Here, Please," which you read at the beginning of this chapter. These samples include dialogue notes, a summary, and three different responses to the essay. How accurately do you think the summary reflects the contents of Knight's essay? How does each response differ from the others? With which response(s) do you agree? Disagree? Why?

DIALOGUE NOTES

Response to Notes	Reading Notes
This place is an Eden	¶1—Knight paints an idyllic picture of her "dream house" and its surroundings—143 acres with lots of wildlife.
	¶2—problem arises because of hunters wanting to hunt on their property; Knights don't grant permission. One neighbor's house shot by stray slug.
some sarcasm in here, a bit reductive about hunter safety courses	¶3—how hunters are "trained" in NY. Knight says they're not trained well or responsibly.
detailed example shows problem. very little penalty for ignoring posted signs	¶4—Knight's property "conspicuously posted." Hunters ignore signs, shoot while standing next to one, run when confronted, picked up later by "environmental-conservation officer" (game warden?), charged with misdemeanors, fined $200.
Aren't they really "anti-hunting"?	¶5—presents crux of conflict: property owners' rights vs. hunters' wanting to hunt. She says she and her husband don't hunt but "are not altogether anti-hunting."
2 more strong examples of abuse by hunters, real danger & disregard for law	¶6—2 more examples, first of an 18-yr-old with a gun and a violent temper, second of a man and a boy ignoring posted signs.
Knight goes well beyond hunters on her property, saying that examples represent an increasingly lawless society. Is this an accurate assessment?	¶7—Knight says signs aren't effective. Moves past immediacy of hunting problems to society as a whole: it's a "manifestation of the same social illness that causes some people to believe that they are above the law." Uses analogy of restraining orders against stalkers and batterers.
pretty strident tone in here, a real contrast to the opening ¶. Knight hits hunters hard.	¶8—final ¶. Knight talks about "hazards" of country life, but they're natural hazards. She contrasts these against "weapon-toting" hunters who ignore posted "No Hunting" signs.

SUMMARY

In "No Hunting Here, Please" (*Newsweek*, Oct. 5, 1998, p. 16), Denise Knight presents a strongly worded persuasive essay attacking hunters who ignore "No Hunting" signs on her and her husband's property. She gives three specific examples of problems with hunters on their land, each one involving hunters who break the law by hunting without permission. Knight describes their 143-acre tract almost as an Eden, with lots of birds and animals. She describes hunters in less admirable terms, e.g., talking about many of them as having "willful disregard" for the law and describing one 18-year-old as having "trouble controlling his temper." Knight then extends her thinking about hunters as being representative of a "social illness that causes some people to believe that they are above the law."

FIRST RESPONSE—AGREEING

Property owners' rights vs. hunters' rights—Knight is right on target. Actually, hunters don't have the right to hunt; it's a privilege, though they think it's a right. Knight details the abuses just on her property very clearly, depicting hunters as out of control and as emblematic of society as a whole. She sees these hunters' disregard for her property rights (as shown in the NO HUNTING signs) as representative of an increasingly lawless society. And she's right. How many drivers nearly always drive 10–20 mph faster than the posted speed limit? Or roll through stop signs without stopping, unless they happen to see somebody coming? How many people think or have said something like, "It's breaking the law only if you get caught"?

SECOND RESPONSE—SKEPTICAL

Okay, Denise, you're right. Hunters who ignore your no hunting signs are wrong. And you're right that there are public lands available for hunting. What bothers me about this piece is the NIMBY approach: Not In My Back Yard. You say you're "not altogether anti-hunting." I'm not so sure. The term "No Hunting" appears four times in your essay, and that sends a pretty clear message. If you aren't "altogether anti-hunting," then what you are is anti-hunting wherever you are. (It's kind of like people who want to help the homeless, so long as they don't have to see them.) This essay is nicely written. The examples Knight gives are clear and strong. The language is slanted to Knight's side, but it's not outright unfair, and the examples of abusive hunters are clear and convincing. It's just the underlying assumption of NIMBY that I don't like.

THIRD RESPONSE—DISAGREEING

I'm offended. I'm a responsible hunter, and I'm offended. Knight paints us all with the same brush. Anybody reading this essay would probably come away thinking that every hunter in the United States is out of control—a bunch of gun totin', mentally troubled, lawless maniacs who want to run around the countryside taking potshots at Bambi, probably with AK-47s. At least one of her statements is unfair. The safety course she refers to is probably one in hunter safety. Yes, first aid is part of it, but the biggest single emphasis is gun safety. Accidents are going to happen, but not in the numbers Knight might be suggesting. Trespassers should be prosecuted—absolutely. But stereotyping all hunters as total gun nuts is unfair.

Exercise 4.5

Read the following essay by Shelby Steele, using various reading strategies listed in this chapter. Then write a summary of it and a response to it. As you work with this essay, particularly as you begin to frame both your summary and response, consider these questions:

1. Steele takes what could be construed as a controversial and unpopular stance on affirmative action. How effectively does he justify his position?
2. Steele says that affirmative action has led to "racial representation" through "racial preference." What, according to Steele, are the effects of such preferences?

3. Steele offers this statement about affirmative action:

> But after 20 years of implementation I think that affirmative action has shown itself to be more bad than good and that blacks—whom I will focus on in this essay—now stand to lose more from it than they gain. (¶4)

How effectively has he supported this assertion? Is it Steele's thesis? If so, how effectively does it guide the essay?

4. What do you think the purpose of this essay is? On what do you base your assessment?

SHELBY STEELE

A NEGATIVE VOTE ON AFFIRMATIVE ACTION

1   In a few short years, when my two children will be applying to college, the affirmative-action policies by which most universities offer black students some form of preferential treatment will present me with a dilemma. I am a middle-class black, a college professor, far from wealthy, but also well removed from the kind of deprivation that would qualify my children for the label "disadvantaged." Both of them have endured racial insensitivity from whites. They have been called names, have suffered slights and have experienced first hand the peculiar malevolence that racism brings out of people. Yet they have never experienced racial discrimination, have never been stopped by their race on any path they have chosen to follow. Still, their society now tells them that if they will only designate themselves as black on their college applications, they will probably do better in the college lottery than if they conceal this fact. I think there is something of a Faustian bargain in this.

2   Of course many blacks and a considerable number of whites would say that I was sanctimoniously making affirmative action into a test of character. They would say that this small preference is the meagerest recompense for centuries of unrelieved oppression. And to these arguments other very obvious facts must be added. In America, many marginally competent or flatly incompetent whites are hired every day—some because their white skin suits the conscious or unconscious racial preference of their employers. The white children of alumni are often grandfathered into elite universities in what can only be seen as a residual benefit of historic white privilege. Worse, white incompetence is always an individual matter, but for blacks it is often confirmation of ugly stereotypes. Given that unfairness cuts both ways, doesn't it only balance the scales of history, doesn't this repay, in a small way, the systematic denial under which my children's grandfather lived out his days?

3   In theory, affirmative action certainly has all the moral symmetry that fairness requires. It is reformist and corrective, even repentant and redemptive. And I would never sneer at these good intentions. Born in the late 1940's in Chicago, I started my education (a charitable term, in this case) in a segregated school, and suffered all the indignities that come to blacks in a segregated society. My father, born in the South, made it only to the third grade before the white man's fields took permanent priority over his formal education. And though he educated himself into an advanced reader with an almost professorial authority, he could only drive a truck for a living, and never earned more than $90 a week in his entire life. So yes, it is crucial to my sense of citizenship, to

my ability to identify with the spirit and the interests of America, to know that this country, however imperfectly, recognizes its past sins and wishes to correct them.

4   Yet good intentions can blind us to the effects they generate when implemented. In our society affirmative action is, among other things, a testament to white good will and to black power, and in the midst of these heavy investments its effects can be hard to see. But after 20 years of implementation I think that affirmative action has shown itself to be more bad than good and that blacks—whom I will focus on in this essay—now stand to lose more from it than they gain.

5   In talking with affirmative-action administrators and with blacks and whites in general, I found that supporters of affirmative action focus on its good intentions and detractors emphasize its negative effects. It was virtually impossible to find people outside either camp. The closest I came was a white male manager at a large computer company who said, "I think it amounts to reverse discrimination, but I'll put up with a little of that for a little more diversity." But this only makes him a half-hearted supporter of affirmative action. I think many people who don't really like affirmative action support it to one degree or another anyway.

6   I believe they do this because of what happened to white and black Americans in the crucible of the 1960's, when whites were confronted with their racial guilt and blacks tasted their first real power. In that stormy time white absolution and black power coalesced into virtual mandates for society. Affirmative action became a meeting ground for those mandates in the law. At first, this meant insuring equal opportunity. The 1964 civil-rights bill was passed on the understanding that equal opportunity would not mean racial preference. But in the late 60's and early 70's, affirmative action underwent a remarkable escalation of its mission from simple anti-discrimination enforcement to social engineering by means of quotas, goals, timetables, set-asides and other forms of preferential treatment.

7   Legally, this was achieved through a series of executive orders and Equal Employment Opportunity Commission guidelines that allowed racial imbalances in the workplace to stand as proof of racial discrimination. Once it could be assumed that discrimination explained racial imbalances, it became easy to justify group remedies to presumed discrimination rather than the normal case-by-case redress.

8   Even though blacks had made great advances during the 60's without quotas, the white mandate to achieve a new racial innocence and the black mandate to gain power, which came to a head in the very late 60's, could no longer be satisfied by anything less than racial preferences. I don't think these mandates, in themselves, were wrong, because whites clearly needed to do better by blacks and blacks needed more real power in society. But as they came together in affirmative action, their effect was to distort our understanding of racial discrimination. By making black the color of preference, these mandates have reburdened society with the very marriage of color and preference (in reverse) that we set out to eradicate.

9   When affirmative action grew into social engineering, diversity became a golden word. Diversity is a term that applies democratic principles to races and cultures rather than to citizens, despite the fact that there is nothing to indicate that real diversity is the same thing as proportionate representation. Too often the result of this, on campuses for example, has been a democracy of colors rather than of people, an artificial diversity that gives the appearance of an educational parity between black and white students that has not yet been achieved in reality. Here again, racial preferences allow society to leapfrog over the difficult problem of developing blacks to parity with whites and into a cosmetic diversity that covers the blemish of disparity—a full six years after admission, only 26 to 28 percent of blacks graduate from college.

10   Racial representation is not the same thing as racial development. Representation can be manufactured; development is always hard earned. But it is the music of innocence and power that we hear in affirmative action that causes us to cling to it and to its distracting emphasis on representation. The fact is that after 20 years of racial preferences the gap between median incomes of black and white families is greater than it was in the 1970's. None of this is to say that blacks don't need policies that insure our right to equal opportunity, but what we need more of is the development that will let us take advantage of society's efforts to include us.

11   I think one of the most troubling effects of racial preferences for blacks is a kind of demoralization. Under affirmative action, the quality that earns us preferential treatment is an implied inferiority. However this inferiority is explained—and it is easily enough explained by the myriad deprivations that grew out of our oppression—it is still inferiority. There are explanations and then there is the fact. And the fact must be borne by the individual as a condition apart from the explanation, apart even from the fact that others like himself also bear this condition. In integrated situations in which blacks must compete with whites who may be better prepared, these explanations may quickly wear thin and expose the individual to racial as well as personal self-doubt. (Of course whites also feel doubt, but only personally, not racially.)

12   What this means in practical terms is that when blacks deliver themselves into integrated situations they encounter a nasty little reflex in whites, a mindless, atavistic reflex that responds to the color black with negative stereotypes, such as intellectual ineptness. I think this reflex embarrasses most whites today and thus it is usually quickly repressed. On an equally atavistic level, the black will be aware of the reflex his color triggers and will feel a stab of horror at seeing himself reflected in this way. He, too, will do a quick repression, but a lifetime of such stabbings is what constitutes his inner realm of racial doubt. Even when the black sees no implication of inferiority in racial preferences, he knows that whites do, so that—consciously or unconsciously—the result is virtually the same. The effect of preferential treatment—the lowering of normal standards to increase black representation—puts blacks at war with an expanded realm of debilitating doubt, so that the doubt itself becomes an unrecognized preoccupation that undermines their ability to perform, especially in integrated situations.

13   I believe another liability of affirmative action comes from the fact that it indirectly encourages blacks to exploit their own past victimization. Like implied inferiority, victimization is what justifies preference, so that to receive the benefits of preferential treatment one must, to some extent, become invested in the view of one's self as a victim. In this way, affirmative action nurtures a victim-focused identity in blacks and sends us the message that there is more power in our past suffering than in our present achievements.

14   When power itself grows out of suffering, blacks are encouraged to expand the boundaries of what qualifies as racial oppression, a situation that can lead us to paint our victimization in vivid colors even as we receive the benefits of preference. The same corporations and institutions that give us preference are also seen as our oppressors. At Stanford University, minority-group students—who receive at least the same financial aid as whites with the same need—recently took over the president's office demanding, among other things, more financial aid.

15   But I think one of the worst prices that blacks pay for preference has to do with an illusion. I saw this illusion at work recently in the mother of a middle-class black student who was going off to his first semester of college: "They owe us this, so don't think for a minute that you don't belong there." This is the logic by which many blacks, and some whites, justify affirmative action—it is something "owed," a form of reparation. But this logic overlooks a much harder and less digestible reality, that it is impossible

to repay blacks living today for the historic suffering of the race. If all blacks were given a million dollars tomorrow it would not amount to a dime on the dollar for three centuries of oppression, nor would it dissolve the residues of that oppression that we still carry today. The concept of historic reparation grows out of man's need to impose on the world a degree of justice that simply does not exist. Suffering can be endured and overcome, it cannot be repaid. To think otherwise is to prolong the suffering.

16   Several blacks I spoke with said they were still in favor of affirmative action because of the "subtle" discrimination blacks were subject to once they were on the job. One photojournalist said, "They have ways of ignoring you." A black female television producer said: "You can't file a lawsuit when your boss doesn't invite you to the insider meetings without ruining your career. So we still need affirmative action." Others mentioned the infamous "glass ceiling" through which blacks can see the top positions of authority but never reach them. But I don't think racial preferences are a protection against this subtle discrimination; I think they contribute to it.

17   In any workplace, racial preferences will always create two-tiered populations composed of preferreds and unpreferred. In the case of blacks and whites, for instance, racial preferences imply that whites are superior just as they imply that blacks are inferior. They not only reinforce America's oldest racial myth but, for blacks, they have the effect of stigmatizing the already stigmatized.

18   I think that much of the "subtle" discrimination that blacks talk about is often (not always) discrimination against the stigma of questionable competence that affirmative action marks blacks with. In this sense, preferences make scapegoats of the very people they seek to help. And it may be that at a certain level employers impose a glass ceiling, but this may not be against the race so much as against the race's reputation for having advanced by color as much as by competence. This ceiling is the point at which corporations shift the emphasis from color to competency and stop playing the affirmative-action game. Here preference backfires for blacks and becomes a taint that holds them back. Of course, one might argue that this taint, which is after all in the minds of whites, becomes nothing more than an excuse to discriminate against blacks. And certainly the result is the same in either case—blacks don't get past the glass ceiling. But this argument does not get around the fact that racial preferences now taint this color with a new theme of suspicion that makes blacks even more vulnerable to discrimination. In this crucial yet gray area of perceived competence, preferences make whites look better than they are and blacks worse, while doing nothing whatever to stop the very real discrimination that blacks may encounter. I don't wish to justify the glass ceiling here, but only suggest the very subtle ways that affirmative action revives rather than extinguishes the old rationalizations for racial discrimination.

19   I believe affirmative action is problematic in our society because we have demanded that it create parity between the races rather than insure equal opportunity. Preferential treatment does not teach skills, or educate, or instill motivation. It only passes out entitlement by color, a situation that in my profession has created an unrealistically high demand for black professors. The social engineer's assumption is that this high demand will inspire more blacks to earn Ph.D's and join the profession. In fact, the number of blacks earning Ph.D's has declined in recent years. Ph.D's must be developed from preschool on. They require family and community support. They must acquire an entire system of values that enables them to work hard while delaying gratification.

20   It now seems clear that the Supreme Court, in a series of recent decisions, is moving away from racial preferences. It has disallowed preferences except in instances of "identified discrimination," eroded the precedent that statistical racial imbalances are prima facie evidence of discrimination, and, in effect, granted white males the right to

challenge consent decrees that use preference to achieve racial balances in the workplace. Referring to this and other Supreme Court decisions, one civil-rights leader said, "Night has fallen . . . as far as civil rights are concerned." But I am not so sure. The effect of these decisions is to protect the constitutional rights of everyone, rather than to take rights away from blacks. Night has fallen on racial preferences, not on the fundamental rights of black Americans. The reason for this shift, I believe, is that the white mandate for absolution from past racial sins has weakened considerably in the 1980's. Whites are now less willing to endure unfairness to themselves in order to grant special entitlements to blacks, even when those entitlements are justified in the name of past suffering. Yet the black mandate for more power in society has remained unchanged. And I think part of the anxiety many blacks feel over these decisions has to do with the loss of black power that they may signal.

21 But the power we've lost by these decisions is really only the power that grows out of our victimization. This is not a very substantial or reliable power, and it is important that we know this so we can focus more exclusively on the kind of development that will bring enduring power. There is talk now that Congress may pass new legislation to compensate for these new limits on affirmative action. If this happens, I hope the focus will be on development and anti-discrimination, rather than entitlement, on achieving racial parity rather than jerry-building racial diversity.

22 But if not preferences, what? The impulse to discriminate *is* subtle and cannot be ferreted out unless its many guises are made clear to people. I think we need social policies that are committed to two goals: the educational and economic development of disadvantaged people regardless of race and the eradication from our society—through close monitoring and severe sanctions—of racial, ethnic or gender discrimination. Preferences will not get us to either of these goals, because they tend to benefit those who are not disadvantaged—middle-class white women and middle-class blacks—and attack one form of discrimination with another. Preferences are inexpensive and carry the glamour of good intentions—change the numbers and the good deed is done. To be against them is to be unkind. But I think the unkindest cut is to bestow on children like my own an undeserved advantage while neglecting the development of those disadvantaged children in the poorer sections of my city who will most likely never be in a position to benefit from a preference. Give my children fairness; give disadvantaged children a better shot at development—better elementary and secondary schools, job training, safer neighborhoods, better financial assistance for college and so on. A smaller percentage of black high school graduates go to college today than 15 years ago; more black males are in prison, jail or in some other way under the control of the criminal-justice system than in college. This despite racial preferences.

23 The mandates of black power and white absolution out of which preferences emerged were not wrong in themselves. What was wrong was that both races focused more on the goals of those mandates than on the means to the goals. Blacks can have no real power without taking responsibility for their own educational and economic development. Whites can have no racial innocence without earning it by eradicating discrimination and helping the disadvantaged to develop. Because we ignored the means, the goals have not been reached and the real work remains to be done.

Exercise 4.6

Locate an essay on the Internet. Read it on-line, and complete a reading log entry for it, including summary and response. How is this experience different from reading and responding to a hard-copy text? Which do you prefer? Why?

Writing Occasions

In this part of the book, we present seven occasions for writing. Of course, there will be thousands of different occasions on which you will write during the course of your life, and they will all differ in certain ways. They will also share similarities. Our seven chapters on writing occasions represent our attempt at very broad categories that capture some of these similarities and differences.

Before we discuss these occasions, however, we need to explain two terms that we use in talking about them: *aims of discourse* and *modes of discourse*.

AIMS OF DISCOURSE

Central to the concept of aims of discourse is the rhetorical triangle. This triangle allows us to analyze any writing situation according to three key elements: a writer, a subject, and a reader. Another way of looking at this is that in any writing situation, someone is saying something to somebody. This is rather basic and obvious. All three elements would have to exist, or there would be no reason for writing. But the elements may be seen as being more or less important in various writing situations—and this is where rhetorical aims come in.

Rhetorical aims allow us to look at the three elements in the rhetorical triangle as if they were rings in a three-ring circus. If you've ever been to a circus, you know that it's virtually impossible to attend to the action occurring in all three rings at once. The ringmaster proudly announces what is in the center ring, for instance, and the circus spotlight shines down on this ring in such a way as to move what is going on in the other two rings to the background. Our attention is captured by the spotlighted act.

This is not to say, of course, that the acts in the other two rings are no longer there or no longer worth paying some attention to. It wouldn't be a three-ring circus without them. And if one of those acts is particularly interesting to you for some reason—perhaps you're learning to juggle and there is a juggling act in the ring on the right—you may resist the pull of the center ring and fasten your attention on the other ring instead. Whether you do or not, it is still there. The same is true with writing. All three rings are always there—writer, subject, and reader—but in some writing situations, the spotlight is on the writer. In other situations, the subject is spotlighted, and in still other situations, the reader is spotlighted.

Think for a minute about three very different types of writing you might do. Have you ever had an experience that was so powerful, exciting, or unusual that you wanted to capture something of that experience in writing? Perhaps you wrote about it in your journal or diary. Or you may have simply written a letter to yourself in which you recounted some of its high points and some of your feelings about it.

Now consider another very different type of writing. Have you ever written a note or a letter telling a friend how to find your house? Perhaps your friend lives in a different city and has never visited your home. You begin with some landmark close to you that you assume your friend will pass, and then you direct your friend point by point to find your home from there.

Finally, consider a situation in which you bought a product, used it for a short time, and found it defective in some way. You attempted to return it to the local store that sold it to you, but because the normal time for returns had passed and you did use the product for a brief time before finding it defective, you were told that you could not return it for the purchase price. The clerk suggested that you check into the warranty and have the product repaired for a reasonably low cost. However, you feel that the product was defective and should be replaced or your money refunded. So you want to write the company and convince its customer service office of your point of view.

What will be the focus in these three types of writing? In the first, in which you try to capture an important experience, you will no doubt focus on what this experience meant to you. Ten or twenty years from now, you may well be able to remember or reconstruct the itinerary of an important trip, but you will probably not be able to remember the specific details of what you did on one particular afternoon or the way a particular sunset affected you. Your focus in writing about this experience is on yourself as experiencer—and writer.

You'll have a different focus in the writing situation in which you offer directions to a friend who intends to visit you. Most likely, you will spend time going over the route in your mind. If Ron were writing these directions for Bill (who has never been to the house Ron now lives in), he might proceed by thinking: "Okay, Bill's going to get to my house by beginning at the intersection of I-85 and Highway 73. So, when he gets off the interstate and turns left, how far will he have to go before he gets to the BP, where he'll turn right? I travel that road every day, but I haven't really measured the distance. What would I guess it to be? And then he turns right onto Trinity Church Road and goes—now how far is that? And then it's a right onto Orphanage Road and about—what? One or two miles, before he turns left onto—what is the name of that little road?" Your focus here is on the subject, on giving accurate directions.

And for the final piece of writing, the one in which you are going to attempt to get a replacement or a refund for a defective product, you'll have yet another focus—this time, on the reader. You may begin by asking for a policy statement from the company so that you can read about the procedures for returns. After studying that document, you may reason along these lines: Technically, you kept the product a bit longer than prescribed in the document. But, after all, you bought the lawn mower at the end of the mowing season, so, although you have had it for six months, you have effectively just bought it. Furthermore, you meet all of the other criteria for returns—you have a sales receipt, you have all the packaging the product came in, and so forth.

How does all this relate to the rhetorical triangle? In the first writing situation—writing about an exciting trip or event—you focus on yourself as writer. In the second situation, writing directions to your friend, your focus is on the subject. And in the third situation, in which you are attempting to get your money back, your focus is on the company representative who will decide on your claim—your reader. Every writing situation will require all three elements of the rhetorical triangle. In writing about your personal experience, you must have a subject to write about—the events of the trip in this case. And there is a reader, even if that reader is only yourself 10 or 20 years from now. But your spotlight is on yourself as experiencer (and writer). As you ponder what word or phrase to use in capturing an exhilarating moment, your focus is on capturing what this trip meant to you.

Similarly, in giving directions to a friend, you still exist as writer and your friend is your reader. But the subject is spotlighted as you sit to write. What are you thinking about? To some degree, you will have to be aware of what your friend knows about the area you live in, but right now, first and foremost, you have to get down what you know about it. In our example, Ron has to ask: How far is it from I-85 to the BP? What is the name of that little street that intersects with Orphanage Road? If he cannot come up with satisfactory answers to these questions, he will find himself making the drive from I-85 to his home and focusing on those things he looks at every day, but never "sees." He is clearly spotlighting the subject—the path he takes from I-85 to his house.

And in the letter about the defective product, you certainly exist as writer, and you have something to say, but the spotlight is on the reader. You want something from this reader—your money back. And if you don't get it, your writing will not have been successful—no matter how well you know your subject. As you sit down to write this letter, you focus on your reader and the rules under which your reader is operating. Your task is to show that the rule you have broken—keeping the product too long before returning it—is a minor technicality and that in all other respects you are operating within the guidelines the company has set down; thus, your reader should refund your money.

These are the aims, then, that form the major divisions within Part Two:

Spotlight on Writer	Chapter 5, Personal Essays
Spotlight on Subject	Chapter 6, Informative Essays
	Chapter 7, Evaluation Essays
	Chapter 8, Essays About and From Literature
Spotlight on Reader	Chapter 9, Position Essays
	Chapter 10, Persuasion Essays
	Chapter 11, Problem/Solution Essays

MODES OF DISCOURSE

You may already know the term *modes of discourse*. In the past, you may have approached modes of discourse as types of papers. If you were asked to write a paper based on modes, you understood that in a narration, you tell a story; in a description, you describe a person, place, or thing; in an exposition, you explain something; and in an argument, you defend an assertion.

Whether or not you have worked with these modes, you can no doubt see the logic here. But the logic does not hold up. If you examine some of the writing in our occasional chapters, you will find that most writing employs more than one mode. In a personal essay, you will no doubt narrate *and* describe, and you may well *explain* certain things. We call an essay "personal" not because it uses narrative, but because the writer's aim is to focus attention on his experiences. We call an informative essay by that name not because it tends to use explanatory modes—such as comparison and causality—but because the writer's aim is to focus attention on the subject about which he is writing. Yet the writer may well tell a story as part of his informative essay.

WEDDING AIM AND MODE

To summarize, then, a writer's aim is determined by which of the elements in the rhetorical triangle he wishes to spotlight. In spotlighting any one element, he may well use several modes to order, or structure, his essay. In a sense, when we know the writer's aim, we know *what* he is writing about. When we examine the various modes he employs, we gain insight into *how* he accomplishes his aim. The following list identifies the key question a writer will ask for each of the expository modes. As the writer answers these questions, the structure of his essay will unfold.

Mode	Key Question That Provides Structure
Narration	What happens next?
Description	How does this person, place, thing, or event look, smell, taste, feel, and/or sound?
Process	How do I do this, or how does this thing work?
Comparison	How are these things alike or different from one another?
Causality	How does one of these things come from or lead to the other?
Classification	How are the things in this group like each other and different from things in similar groups?
Definition	What names will be assigned to any one item (or the various items) in the group(s) I have identified?
Analysis	How do the elements of this thing or event fit together to form the whole?

CLASSIFYING OCCASIONS

We are now ready to return to the writing occasions. There is nothing magic about the seven writing occasions we have chosen to present. Our choice of these occasions is itself an example of the use of classification. Since the criteria by which we have developed this classification are ours—and not those of the writers of these essays—it should be expected that some of the essays seem to fit our categories better than others do. For example, Jerry Z. Muller's essay, "The Conservative Case for Abortion," seems to fit our concept of the position essay very well. Susan Jacoby's essay, "Common Decency," however, fits less well. But we decided that it more nearly fit a position occasion than a persuasion occasion and thus included it in the position essay chapter.

As you work through these chapters and read the various sample essays included in them, remember that we offer our classification to help you analyze and emulate some of the strategies these writers use. Above all else, these essays are examples of people taking the time to share their thoughts on various subjects with their readers. In the end, that should be the goal of your writing.

The personal essay is close to the writer's self. The writer often begins by trying to gain personal insight into a situation or event, but then looks beyond and shapes her writing so that readers can share her experience. Your goal as a writer of a personal essay is to structure your thoughts so that your reader can experience, insofar as possible, what you experienced.

Some personal essays become philosophical, in-depth examinations of a writer's life, detailing such intensely personal topics as faith, religion, and belief in God. A writer uses this kind of writing in an attempt to define who she is. Sometimes such writing becomes a book-length work as the writer probes nearly every aspect of her life to learn about herself.

Your personal essay will probably differ from these philosophical essays, not only in length but in scope as well. Later, we'll offer a writing prompt with three options. The first invites you to write about a significant event that taught you something; the second, about a place that's significant to you; the third, about who you are and what you stand for. Each prompt invites you to focus tightly on important events, places, or people in your life and to probe or explore these to find out what they mean to you.

Why write a personal essay? Such an essay can serve you in a number of ways. It can help you gain perspective on a meaningful time in your life so that you come to understand that time in deeper ways than you had before. It can help you explore an important shaping or defining moment of your life. Or it can

Personal Essays

CHAPTER 5

help you rediscover a significant experience, so that you may relive that experience, albeit from a distance.

Writing this essay can help you with other college courses, because you'll be strengthening your writing skills as you work through this assignment. It will help you practice using details, a skill you'll need in informative and persuasive writing. Whereas other kinds of writing provide practice with other kinds of details (e.g., examples, statistics, or facts), a personal essay will help you get into the habit of providing details to support your thoughts. Writing this essay will also let you hone the narrative and descriptive skills you'll need in many other writing situations.

SAMPLE ESSAYS

Read the following examples of personal essays, and respond to the questions that follow each. As you read, keep in mind that each essay carries significance for its writer. Try to identify that significance, or importance, and decide how the writer presents or reveals it to you.

Our first sample essay was written by Datus Proper, a travel writer with a national reputation. This particular essay, which focuses on an event Proper experienced while he was fishing a favorite stream, appeared in *Field & Stream*.

DATUS PROPER

DARK HOLLOW

1   Fish a place long enough and it becomes a homestead, a personal stretch of boulders and water and trout. I've been proving my claim on Dark Hollow Run for twenty years now, so I wondered about the other car parked on Skyline Drive, right where I always start my hike down to the stream. Maybe the visitor was just the usual refugee from the city, out for a stroll on the Appalachian Trail, but then again I might find a fisherman ahead of me. I hurried down the mountainside with my rod and rucksack.

2   The visitor was easy to catch. "Hill's getting hard to pull," she said. Her hair was more gray than red where it fell over the lace collar of her dress. Her name was Betty Cave and her only burden was a bunch of flowers, but it established a claim 200 years older than mine. I read the names of her family when we got to what used to be the Dark Hollow settlement.

3   There were more headstones in the clearing than Betty had flowers to decorate— rough fieldstones, big ones and little ones, lots of little ones. One of the unmarked stones was for the Cave who brought the family's red hair from Ireland to the Blue Ridge long ago. The oldest legible marker was for John G. Cave of the Virginia Light Artillery, C.S.A. Near it there were stones for Betty's parents and her sister Lula Belle.

4   Not far away was a fireplace, stones chinked with mud, standing lonely in the woods. Betty Cave had stories to go with that old hearth. It had been part of her family's cabin, once, and she remembered the days when her mother tended the fire and her father came home with food.

5   *Daddy used to bring a leather pouch with trout spilling over the top. He caught 'em on worms—big fish, like this—a foot long, some of 'em. They was real pretty.*

Mama cleaned 'em all and kept 'em cool in a stone jar in the springhouse. The meat was pink when she cooked 'em. They tasted awful good.

6   I strung up my rod, tied on a little dark-water fly, and worked upstream making backcasts when I could, but otherwise just pushing the line out. This sounds impossible—like pushing a string—but you get good at pushcasting on Dark Hollow Run. When there is brush behind, you just pile line on the water at your feet, hold the rod straight up, and make half a roll-cast, the forward half. It's not a way to break distance records. The line goes where the rod tip points, though, and the fish are not far away. The little fly rights itself, shimmies its peacock body at the trout, and flashes you a V-for-victory sign with white wings. You hold the rod tip high so that the line does not get caught in the fast water at the tail of the pool. You want the fly to take life easy, like a big trout.

7   Watching a good fly is like watching a bird dog that knows what it's doing. You have faith. Almost every pool has at least a small fish—in the middle, where a trout can hold in slow water and foray into the current for a passing snack, or in the calm patch above a boulder, or in little eddies at the head of the pool. When the fly dallies over just the right spot, the fish responds. A little one is a sparkle, making up its mind and pouncing in the same instant. A big trout is a shadow, a lovely lazy rise without fuss.

8   The oldtimers all say that the fish used to run larger than they do now. Betty Cave tends to understatement, like most of the mountain people, so you must not dismiss her foot-long trout as yarn-spinning. I don't know what has changed the ecology of the stream. Acid rain is probably involved and so are the young oaks and maples, which drink up moisture that used to reach the Run. There was more water for the fish when the Caves lived in Dark Hollow.

9   *We had 400 acres, all grass but for the orchard and the hemlocks around the house. We kept the brush cut down till the government made us leave. We grazed six heifers and a horse and two milk cows, and Mama stored the butter in the springhouse.*

10   *Grandma planted that snowball bush, too. It blooms every June and the apple trees still set fruit, but the pears and peaches are shaded out now. Mama used to can all the fruit. Mama and Daddy worked hard, but we weren't hungry.*

11   I worked hard, too, sneaking up to the tails of pools, sitting on a rock to keep my head below the trout's line of sight, and planning before each cast. The brook trout that took the fly were two-year-olds about 7 inches long. None of the big three-year-olds would rise to my fly. The concentration was tiring, more so than the walk down the mountain. I was relieved to reach the Lunch Pool, sit on a patch of moss, and pull out my food.

12   The Lunch Pool is one of those places that just grew around me over the years. Maybe it was in the middle of my homestead water because I deserved a break, or maybe I staked my claim knowing that the pool was available. The sycamore tree beat me there by a long time, anyhow. It may have been growing even in the days of Great-grandfather Cave. The trunk was as thick as four Dark Hollow girls standing back to back, pale toes wriggling down into the pool.

13   I ate each of my rye crackers with a sardine dripping oil on it and halfway through lunch there was a grumble over the ridge to the south. Dark clouds moved overhead fast but the thunder stayed lazy. A few raindrops made rings in the pool while I rushed through my apple, and then there was another ring made from below the water. I stripped line off the reel and covered the fish with one false cast, not standing up. The trout drifted under the fly and took it and pulled with a strength almost unseemly on such a small battlefield. Then the fish gave up and lay in my left hand. Both its mouth and its girth were big for its length of 9½ inches and its belly was the deep red-orange of a maple tree. This was a three-year-old, survivor of two spawning seasons but pro-grammed by its genes to die before another. It died instead for my wife's dinner.

14   The shower was steady by then, and I wasted no time. Another good fish took my fly in the next pool but the hook lost its grip. I changed to a fly with more clearance between point of hook and fat herl body, and in the two pools upstream I caught two more big fish, which meant that both my wife and I could have dinner. That's how it goes on Dark Hollow Run: you can fish for hours without a venerable trout, but the first shower gives you satisfaction.

15   The old fish hide when the water gets low. Then the rain comes and they move out, chase the small fry away from the best spots in the pools, and lie in wait, tails moving, eyes looking up. Even the first few raindrops revive some genetic recollection of the wetter, colder climate Betty Cave describes.

16   *I let the cat out one time and it froze in the snow before it got back in. I cried and cried. My Daddy hiked down to the old copper mine for work in winter. He didn't have no boots—had to put socks over his shoes and tie them up with tar strings. The snow was so deep that his clothes was froze up to his waist when he got home. We were happy to get the money.*

17   *There was eight cabins in Dark Hollow then, and the church. They was awful good people, good Christian people. Daddy went around with a lantern in the snow when the diphtheria came. He visited the houses of sick people to pray. Two children died the same day. Daddy had to cut up a church bench to make a coffin for them.*

18   The climb back up through the woods to Skyline Drive was slow, my excuse being that I wanted to take an inventory of my homestead. Rain made that easier, too. The violets stood straighter, the wild geraniums glowed pink-purple, and the first white trilliums began to open. In what was left of the orchard at Betty Cave's old place, a mountain pheasant twisted off through gray trunks. We call them ruffed grouse now. I saw no woodcock, but farther along the path a gray squirrel darted to the back side of its tree and I wondered why it was so spooky till a goshawk buzzed me. Its nest must have been nearby, with young hungry for small game.

19   Two bunches of deer, on the other hand, stood watching me tamely. Recently deer have become too abundant for their forage—a problem common in the National Parks. Hunting is not allowed and there are not enough big predators to control populations.

20   *I don't remember deer in the '30s. Never heard Daddy name a deer, but he hunted mountain pheasants here in the hollow and walked to Big Meadow to shoot wood hens. They was funny little birds with long bills and round heads and big eyes.*

21   *We heard a mountain panther screamin' and hollerin' like a baby one time, and our dog was so scared we let him inside. I looked out the window and saw the panther coming closeter and closeter. It had eyes like a piece of fire.*

22   *A bear broke into our smokehouse one night and stole a ham. Daddy tracked the bear down but he told me he didn't kill it, because I didn't like anything to get hurt. We had plenty of ham left, I remember. Wonder if some of it come from that bear.*

23   *Daddy tracked rabbits and squirrels with his little dog, and they did smell good when Mama cooked 'em. I remember she baked raccoons, too, with potatoes and carrots from the garden. We ate the mushrats and sold their hides. We didn't eat 'possums, but some folks did—fattened them up and cooked 'em.*

24   Change would have come to the settlement in time, even if the old families had been allowed to stay in their homes. Somebody would have driven a car to the cabins and the world would have followed, one vehicle at a time. People who had been part of nature would have erected television antennas in the heart of Dark Hollow.

25   With humans gone, the original vegetation returned, and if the young hardwoods drank some of the stream's water, they also protected the watershed from erosion. The trout were not big, but they were doing better here than in most parts of their an-

cestral range. I expected to find the native wildlife waiting for me as long as I could manage the hard pull.

26   Something beautiful had been saved for me—and taken from the Caves.

27   *When they first built Skyline Drive, I would hike up there and sell little paper flowers. Mama made 'em for me. I'd charge a dime, but some of the guests would stop their cars and give me a dollar. I was five years old.*

28   *After awhile, the government pushed us off our land and made it part of Shenandoah National Park. That was before the war started—1939 or the edge of '40, I think. Daddy got a dollar an acre. Friends gave us use of a house outside the Park—they knew we couldn't pay rent. We wanted to go back to Dark Hollow but the government burnt down all eight cabins. Burnt the church, too.*

29   *Daddy didn't have any work. All he knew was farming and hunting and fishing. I remember him sitting outside every evening, cryin' and cryin'.*

Questions for Review

1. What is the point or significance of this essay? How effectively does Proper reveal it to you?

2. How does Proper structure his essay? Identify its beginning, middle, and end.

3. Proper's use of Betty Cave's dialogue with him is a bit unusual. How effective do you think it is? Why does Proper place Cave's words in italics instead of the usual quotation marks? How does Proper ensure that he can juggle what essentially are two narratives—his and Cave's—yet maintain a unified, coherent essay?

4. Identify at least two places in the essay where Proper uses vivid description. How effective are these descriptions?

5. At first, it seems as though the essay's title, "Dark Hollow," simply identifies the locale or scene of the essay. What else does this title suggest to you, now that you've finished the essay?

6. What kind(s) of conflict or tension does Proper create in this essay? How effectively does he use it?

Our second essay is by Steven Barboza, who discusses his reasons for converting to Islam. As you read through the essay, identify the key moments that moved Barboza to embrace Islam.

STEVEN BARBOZA

MY CONVERSION

1   My abandonment of Roman Catholicism was spawned by a premature death, my mother's at age 49, on the day before my 22nd birthday. I prayed like crazy for God to spare her, and when He did not, I established a new line of communication. I called God

Allah and prayed with my palms cupped (to catch blessings) and my eyes wide open (to keep Allah's creations in sight).

2   Given the irony and absurdity of events in racially torn Boston, where I lived, Islam was a godsend. A few months after my mother's death, whites assaulted a black man in front of Boston City Hall, using as one weapon a flagpole with an American flag attached. With that attack and my mother's death, a lifetime of frustrations reached the breaking point.

3   My odyssey 20 years ago was not unlike that of hundreds of thousands of blacks in the United States. The journey became my jihad—literally "struggle"—waged not for political power or economic enfranchisement, but for control over my own soul.

4   Then as now, in the Roxburys and Harlems across America, only liquor stores outnumbered churches in vying for blacks' attention, and in my opinion, both stupefied millions of black Americans.

5   Islam, as I was familiar with it, seemed the perfect way to fight back. As a religion, it offered clear-cut guidelines for living; as a social movement, it stood for a pride born of culture and discipline.

6   Before my mom died, I had dipped into Malcolm X's autobiography. After she passed, I plunged into it. Malcolm had undergone a metamorphosis: from hoodlum to cleaned-up spokesman for the Nation of Islam and finally a convert to orthodox Islam, and through his own transformation he had shown that change, even from the most miserable beginnings, was possible.

7   Of course, Malcolm's life and mine were very different. He had discovered Islam in prison. I discovered it in college. He was the spokesman for a black theocratic visionary. I held down a midlevel white-collar job in a Fortune 500 company. Still, I felt a kinship with Malcolm and the Black Muslims. The color of our skin made us all cargo in a sinking ship, and Islam beckoned, like a life preserver.

8   Two decades ago in Boston and New York, however, there were few orthodox mosques. In black neighborhoods, one institution, the Nation of Islam, dominated in the teaching of Islam, or, rather, a homegrown version of it. Many blacks who converted took to the Nation's teachings—its admonitions to self-love and racial solidarity; its belief in productivity and entrepreneurship. And with equal ardor, they also took to the Nation's other teachings—its racial chauvinism, and belief that white people were genetically inferior, intrinsically evil "blue-eyed devils" who had been created to practice "tricknology" against blacks.

9   Using the twin motivators of myth and pride, Elijah Muhammad built the Nation into one of the largest black economic and religious organizations America had seen. It claimed a heavyweight boxing champion the whole world adored, Muhammad Ali. Its women looked like angels in their veils, crisp jackets and ankle-length skirts; its men cut no-nonsense yet gallant figures in their smart dark suits and trademark bow ties.

10   But sitting in the Nation's Roxbury temple was like being on a jury listening to a closing argument. The defendants (in absentia): white folks. The prosecutor: a dapper minister who practically spat, saying whites were so utterly devilish that their religion was grotesquely symbolized by a "symbol of death and destruction"—the crucifix. The charge: perpetrating dastardly deeds on blacks "in the name of Christianity." The verdict: guilty.

11   I barely lasted my one visit. To me, demonizing the "enemy" as the Nation did hardly seemed the best way to learn to "love thyself." Anyway, I abhorred the idea of colorizing God, or limiting godly attributes to one race. And though Elijah deserved credit for redeeming legions of blacks from dope and crime when all else, including Christianity, had failed them, I didn't believe that earned him the title of Allah's "messenger."

12   So I moved to New York and became an orthodox Muslim in the manner all converts do: I declared before Muslim witnesses my belief in Allah and my faith that the Prophet

Muhammad of Arabia was His very last messenger. I entered a Sunni mosque and prostrated myself on rugs beside people of all ethnicities.

13   Here was what I deemed a truer Islam—the orthodoxy to which Malcolm had switched, the one most of Elijah's followers opted for when the Nation of Islam waned after his death, the Islam to which most of America's 135,000 annual converts, 80 to 90 percent of them black, belong.

14   Questions, however, persisted. For example: Why didn't we blame Arabs for their ancestors' role in slave trading the way we blamed white Americans and Europeans? One answer is that mistreatment of slaves is specifically prohibited by Islamic law, and the vast majority of Muslims living during the slave trade era observed that law. The children of female slaves and free men would assume the social status of the father, unlike the children of American slave owners. And while the children of two slaves remained slaves, Islamic law encouraged manumission.

15   And why did so many black Americans revere the Middle East as if it were their homeland? On a plane to Senegal, sitting next to a black American wearing a traditional Arab robe, I got an inkling of the answer. The man was headed to meet an imam, his spiritual leader, a black African Muslim. I later met other black Americans who had spent years in Africa studying Islam. Through research, I found that up to 35 percent of enslaved blacks brought to the New World were Muslim. In converting, many black Americans may have been simply returning to the religion of their forefathers.

16   Over the years, I have come to understand what should have been obvious long ago—that Jesus had not forsaken my mother. She died because God had willed it, regardless of what form my prayers took.

17   And I hadn't rejected Christianity so much as embraced Islam. Malcolm X's struggle—and Mom's death—had been Allah's instruments for my conversion. After all, Allah, it is said, makes Muslims by whatever means He sees fit.

Questions for Review

1. What is the point or significance of this essay? How effectively does Barboza reveal it to you?
2. How does Barboza structure his essay? Identify its beginning, middle, and end.
3. Barboza uses less description than does Datus Proper. What kind of detail does Barboza provide to support his reasons for converting to Islam? How effective is this detail?
4. Barboza names two key figures in this essay: Malcolm X and Elijah Muhammad. Who were these men? What was their role in Islam in the United States? In the black community in the United States?
5. What role did the Nation of Islam play in Barboza's conversion to orthodox Islam?
6. What tension or conflict is at work in this essay? Is it primarily internal or external; that is, is Barboza reporting a struggle within himself or with someone or something else? How does he resolve this conflict?

Our third sample essay, "Purple Mountains' Majesty," is by Arlene Yusnukis, a writing student at New Mexico State University (NMSU). In Chapter 1, we provided two freewrites by Arlene that led to this essay. Before you read it, review those freewrites (pp. 12 and 13–14).

ARLENE YUSNUKIS

PURPLE MOUNTAINS' MAJESTY

1   I awoke slowly, letting the subdued light in the little two-man tent filter through my eyelids and slowly activate my consciousness. I could not remember where I was or what I was doing in a sleeping bag lying uncomfortably on top of a stick the size of the leg bone of the Christmas turkey. Then snapshots of the last two days sequenced through my mind. I saw the fourteen of us, eleven high school-aged people, the two other chaperones and me, most of us from the church I worked for, hoisting thirty to forty pound packs on our backs. I saw the two bighorn sheep, a ram and a ewe, gracefully leaping down the steep embankment bordering our first night's camp. I visualized the saddle we had to cross that day, and I breathed a sigh of relief at the picture of yesterday's saddle. It had risen nearly vertically from the slight depression we were in, and the switchbacks in the trail were so small, numerous, and tight that the trail resembled a zipper sewn askance on the hillside. I remembered. . . . My stomach rumbled, demanding a hearty breakfast to take me through the day. As I emerged from the tent, the cool, fresh Rocky Mountain air whetted not only my appetite for food but also my appetite for whatever adventure lay on today's trail. With all the gear packed, we finally set off on the third day of our four-day backpacking trip.

2   Around noon we walked down a saddle into a huge, barren, rocky meadow, right into a storm. At a fork in the trail, the group split, with half going on to make camp, the rest waiting until the rain had moved on and then tackling Sante Fe Baldy. A good portion of the upper half of the mountain, which rises to 12,600 feet, is bare of trees, hence the name "Baldy." Up to fifty yards short of the summit, Baldy is green. The ground is covered with miniature (one inch worth of miniature) pine trees which send wiry roots deep into the hard rock and hang on for dear life. From my vantage point, the mountain looked conquerable.

3   I believed that until I was halfway up, too far to turn back, almost too exhausted to go on. Go on we did, though. Up and up we climbed, resting almost every twenty feet. The meadow we started from had an elevation of 11,500 feet, and Baldy rose seemingly straight out of it, making the climb extremely strenuous. But with every step, my range of vision expanded by tens of miles. And with this new vision came a sense of conquering the beast. I found the strength to go on. Upon reaching the uneven line where the little pine trees disappeared and only tiny, fragrant flowers struggled to survive, I realized that I was now above the timberline. Lumbering onward, I finally reached the crown of the mountain. I let out a triumphant but breathless whoop.

4   The view from that elevation was breathtaking, literally. I slowly pivoted, turning round and round trying to absorb all that I saw, smelled, and felt. I wanted to store it all in my memory permanently. I wanted to be able to share this scene with my future grandchildren. To fulfill this dream, I decided to explore this baldy and all that I saw.

5   The baldy itself did not come to a pointed peak; rather the summit formed a large letter "C" of rock. The top provided an excellent viewing platform. Twenty-five hundred feet below, Sante Fe Baldy Lake perched on the east side, a small blue-gray dot of water sparkling up at me. All along the steep east side of the baldy, huge snowbanks melted slowly. With my back to the lake, I faced west to the Jemez Mountains rising from a great flat expanse. In the bosom of the Jemez, my hometown nestled comfortably. To the north, the New Mexico Rockies faded into the Colorado Rockies. To the south, lay Albuquerque, small as a quarter, then Socorro, and off to the left, Las Vegas. All over the east and northeast, the rest of the untamed Pecos Wilderness rose defiantly to the crisp, clear blue sly. On the mottled shades of green that all the mountains and hills blended into were the scars of fires, fields of aspen, and spring-green meadows. Over this vast expanse of wilderness, the sun shone through and around clouds, creating a dappled effect. To the north, jutting above their surroundings, were the baldy's twin equals, Truchas Peaks, lightning forking from the storms surrounding their crowns.

6   Then my eye caught the Sante Fe Ski Basin. There was raw beauty marred for man's pleasure. The basin reminded me that this throne on the top of Sante Fe Baldy was only temporary. When we joined it again, civilization would not seem as tantalizing as it did from such dizzying heights. I could even see, I fancied, the road that would lead us down from the high country and eventually home. Shaking the unwanted thought free, I again whirled round, viewing my kingdom. Then I lay down and joined the overly curious, yet shy, yellow-bellied marmots sunning on the rocks. Their shrill whistles penetrated the keen silence and kept it from overwhelming. I dozed.

7   Jerking awake, I noticed that the air had become ominously heavy, threatening rain. Getting caught in an electrical storm above the timberline was not what any of us wanted. Before running pell-mell down the steep side of the mountain, I slowly revolved three times being sure my memory had the fine tune in focus. With a heavy sigh, I turned to leave. Glancing back I thought, "And God saw everything that He had made, and behold, it was very good" (Genesis 1:31).

Questions for Review

1. Which of the prompts did Arlene respond to?
2. How much of her second freewrite (see pp. 13–14) do you find in the final draft?
3. Identify at least two places where you think the language is particularly effective. What makes it effective?
4. What significance does Arlene convey in this essay? How effectively does she do so?
5. What advice would you offer Arlene, were she to revise this essay?

Daniel Kinken, a first-year writer from the University of North Carolina at Charlotte (UNC–Charlotte), wrote our next sample essay. As you read, think about initial comparisons between this essay and Arlene's.

DANIEL KINKEN

AT THE MAC

1   I sit here in English not believing what the professor has just asked us to do. It is 8:30 in the evening, and he is telling us to close our eyes and take several deep breaths. I hardly know this professor, considering it is only our second class meeting, and I cannot imagine what he wants us to do with our eyes closed. But that is exactly what he wants us to do—imagine a place that we have visited several times before. He speaks in a soft, soothing voice, prompting us to close our eyes and allow our imaginations to overwhelm us. I begin imagining several places that I have been before. I experience what is like a slide show of all the distinctive places that I visited in my life, but one seems to keep reoccurring with greater and greater frequency. This is a place that I have visited very often, so often that it seems like a second home to me. This place that stands out in my mind is the pool where I swam competitively over the past six years. The image seems real, as if I am there.

2   I stand on the deck of the Mecklenburg Aquatic Club, otherwise known as the MAC. The first sound that greets me is the laughter of little children excited about starting their swim lessons. I have seen this many times, though the children do not always laugh and sometimes cry as their mother or father prompts them into the water. For many the water is cold; their lips turn blue as they begin to shiver. The instructor encourages them to take the first step off the underwater platform and begin to swim. Many are scared and need a little help, but most will succeed in learning to swim.

3   The thick smell of chlorine, acrid and pungent, begins to overtake me. I maneuver down the deck, past several awkward piles of kickboards scattered about. It is about 3:45 in the afternoon, and the sun glistens through the window and reflects off the dancing water. I walk carefully past a young group of swimmers who are preparing for their Junior Swim League practice. "Thompson."

4   "Yo, Coach."

5   "Group A today, Thompson."

6   "Williams."

7   "Present, Sir."

8   "Group B, Williams."

9   The coaches call names, organizing the swimmers into groups. I step carefully so as not to slip and fall on the cold, damp concrete. Further down the pool, my team is already in the water warming up.

10   I am late. I am always late. Due to circumstances beyond my control, I am never on time. It is impossible for me to arrive at practice on time because my school gets out too late for me to make the thirty-minute trek across town in time for my team's starting time. I quickly hurry down the deck so I don't waste any more precious practice time. "Hey, Coach, I'm here." I pass my coach with this quick hello and hurry still further down the deck to where my equipment is stored. As I reach the end of the deck, the roar of the fans which bring life to the pool overcomes the sound of the splashing water. The fans supply the swimmers with the precious gift of fresh air necessary to swim their best. I grab my equipment bag and head back up the deck and prepare to swim.

11   This is the place where I should have made my dreams come true or fall apart. It is here that I spent more of my free time than anywhere else. Through hours and hours of practice, sweat and tears this place has shaped me into who I am today. Having to balance a rigorous two-hour daily swim workout with my school work taught me how to use my time wisely, to plan ahead, and to schedule. Swimming daily—no matter the weather, school or personal conflicts, swimming till I was afraid I'd die and then swimming more

until I was afraid I wouldn't—taught me the value of discipline and of working hard, really hard, to achieve a goal I'd set for myself. I learned the hard rule of self-control, one that many people my age have yet to learn. Winning a race, losing a race, my response was to be the same: congratulate my teammates and opponents not on winning or losing but on having competed, having done the best possible that day. Working my way from team member to team co-captain and then captain, I learned what it was like to be a leader and how to handle responsibility, not only for myself but for my teammates.

12   Not only did I learn several life lessons, but I also learned what it is like to compete. Competition is something that I will be faced with all my life, but because of my experiences as a swimmer I think I will be able to handle competition and use it to my advantage. Competition taught me how to set goals and how to handle pressure situations. It taught me to not get excited or worry too soon but to have faith in my abilities and let the hours of practice and preparations come into play.

13   The MAC is the place that seemed to stick in my head. My unconscious thought is trying to tell me something as I sit here, in this English class, miles from the pool that taught me so much, and I miss it. I no longer swim competitively and visit only to say hello to old friends and coaches and to feel the energy that exudes from the cool water. I have lost the adrenaline rush that goes hand in hand with competition and practice. I long for that rush and the feeling of gliding through the water. Most of all, I just miss being in the MAC and hearing the pounding of the water, smelling the stench of chlorine, and seeing the sun glare off the ripples in the water.

14   I never succeeded in achieving all of my goals. Life dealt me a different set of cards than what I had planned for myself. This is not meant to be a sad story, it is a story of success hidden away where you have to look for it. In retrospect I feel like I achieved far more than I had ever expected. No other experience will ever teach me as much as my six years of swimming have.

15   Now the professor is asking us to open our eyes and write down everything we can and be as descriptive as possible. I cannot concentrate enough on the assignment, I am too busy trying to recapture the feelings that I experienced there on the deck of the Mecklenburg Aquatic Club.

Questions for Review

1. Daniel writes about a particular place that's been significant for him. How effectively does he convey to the reader this significance?
2. How does Daniel structure his essay? Identify its beginning, middle, and end.
3. Identify two places where Daniel uses language effectively. What makes these passages effective?
4. What advice would you offer Daniel, were he to revise this essay?

Our final sample essay was written by Ali Duffy, a first-year composition student at the UNC–Charlotte. Ali wrote this essay about her favorite place, turning a freewrite into a polished essay.

ALI DUFFY

THE DANCE

1   My eyes rise slowly and delicately to meet the bright, warm spotlight that I can finally call my own. The stage is my canvas and I am the brush, stroking the wood floor gracefully with my hard, satin shoes. June of 1997 is a month that I will never forget. Besides graduating from high school, I am graduating from myself. Through my experience on stage I am becoming an adult. I look around Spotsylvania High School's vast space of stage and see huddles of elegant, lithe dancers in long, flowing tutus that make a lovely flowing blur when you squint your eyes. With their hair slicked back in perfect buns and their sleek muscles, they look like an army of cloned soldiers ready to pounce on and conquer the enormous stage when the music calls on them. But the sweet resonance of Adam's *Giselle* does not ask them to dance. It asks me. I feel tension in my back that has built up from fifteen years of exhausting, invigorating, inspiring, painful, gratifying . . . joyful performing. I see a good friend, Lee, and am taken back to my freshman year of high school.

2   "I am sixteen going on seventeen," I sang out. I shyly glanced over at Lee, a cute but awkward drama student at my school, knowing that he was about to grace me with my first kiss, and couldn't help but turn away. *The Sound of Music* lyrics, innocent and familiar, poured out faster and faster. Panic racked my body as the moment of doom closed in on me. What if my breath smelled like the pickle I ate at lunch? What if my nose got in the way? My feet slowed as I squeaked out the last syllables of song and came to a halt three inches from his nose. My heart raced and numbness flooded my face and neck. "It's called *acting,* Ali," my drama teacher said. "Lee is such a nice boy," my mom said. "He *is* kind of a nerd," said my friend. "*Extra lasts extra long,*" blared the commercial. "Refraining from sexual activity will prevent STD's and pregnancy," preached my health teacher. Their voices lingered in my head . . . then . . . SMACK! It was over and before I could look up, I was running offstage in a flushed and shaky frenzy.

3   My thoughts skip ahead to my sophomore year. I looked around nervously at the silent bustling of the familiar performers, little honey bees buzzing about their blooming flower, the stage. The eerie silence sent chills down my spine. The curtain regally lifted and the *entr'acte* of *Guys and Dolls* burst from the orchestra pit. Our collection of dancers, singers, and actors retreated from their everyday individualism, and we became a family, all equal in talent, grace, and importance. My fellow dancers caught my eye, and we exchanged warm smiles and hugs. Suddenly it was time. With clammy hands and a prayer still faint on my breath, I clung to one last inhale of stale makeup and dusty costumes and let the stage take me once again. Dancing and belting out song after song, I realized that this was where I belonged. This was my home.

4   Another beat, and I am still on stage, this time in May of 1997. Two years, four boyfriends, and two algebra classes later, I was ready to inherit the world and make it my own. But first, I would perform for my local fans one last time. Although I could not see the crowd, I could tell from the rustling paper and random coughs that the theater was filled to the brim with local royalty and theater fat cats. The mayor, superintendent, and other impressive aristocracy of Spotsylvania were all there to catch a last glimpse of the performers of the class of 1997 and of *Crazy for You,* the biggest show Spotsylvania High School had ever put on. I felt my feet and the stage grip each other as if in a friendly embrace. I knew that I was alone in my quest, but that my brothers and sisters on stage would catch me if I fell. My character, Tess, took over my brain, and I became the sassy, spunky personality that she is. I seemed to black out, but I saw clearly—the panicked ex-

pression on Tom's face when he realized his props were in the wrong place, and the goodbye hugs I received from my theater peers, and my sheer elation as I looked off into the wings from the limelight of the stage and saw my stage family cheering me on. The curtain fell and my chest heaved with deep breaths. I heard both crying and laughing, felt both joy and sorrow. We ran out and took curtain calls and sang at the top of our lungs. "Who could ask . . . for . . . anything . . . MORE!" "Exactly," I thought to myself.

5   I refocus and am back to the present, preparing to finish my performance as the lead in *Giselle*, my final performance on the Spotsylvania High School stage. My hair is perfectly set and my costume perfectly fit. I am unnaturally still. The butterflies that once stalked my stomach are gone, and my meditative state motivates me to perform flawlessly. I hear the slight twinkle of music and glide on stage, a cautious facade masking my face. I have become Giselle. The "mad scene" of *Giselle* is said to be the hardest theatrically in ballet, but I have formed a plan to perfect it. This stage has become my best friend, my shelter, my shrine, the platform of my youth, maturity, courage, and love. There is nothing I love more in the world than the feel of this stage supporting me. I cannot bear to leave it behind, and decide that my mad scene will be a farewell and dedication to my stage as well as my childhood.

6   I do not pretend to be mad. I have gone mad. With a crazed look in my eye, I transfix the audience, my fellow stage members, and my backstage family with a spontaneous, Oscar-worthy mad scene. I feel the tears well up in my eyes as I jolt my body back and forth across the stage, stumbling and falling as if in a drunken stupor. The rage inside me tears my hair from the majestic up sweep that it held, and I feel the floor give way to my passionate stomping, running, and gasping through sobs. All of the years, energy, and love that I gave to the stage return as I fall and earnestly crawl toward the audience, reaching for any sign of fleeting hope. I find the strength to stand again and see the stunned expressions and flowing tears of everyone in the auditorium. We share a common knowledge that the stage has taken over me and I am venting all my anger, frustration, agony, pain, and love through my dancing, as crazy as it appears. With one last rush of adrenaline, I sprint to my dance partner, stop dead in my tracks, and collapse to the floor. I do not feel myself hitting the floor; I feel only its support beneath me. As the curtain slowly retrieves, my eyes see the audience stand in approval, and my stage family rushes toward me. I smile through the tears, for they are now tears of joy. This is the happiest day of my life.

7   That day I reached the conclusion that I have come full circle on the stage. With my mad scene I said goodbye to my favorite place. The stage at Spotsylvania High School gave me confidence and pushed me to explore new and different things; it also served as a crutch for my insecurities. The end is now the beginning, and thanks to my mad scene, I am ready to begin again.

Questions for Review

1. In this essay, Ali recounts events that took place on her high school stage, which she calls her favorite place. What is the significance of this essay?
2. How does Ali structure her essay? Identify its beginning, middle, and end. How, particularly, does she use verb tense to help her reader move through the essay?

3. How effectively does Ali use dialogue in this essay?
4. Identify at least two places where Ali uses vivid description. How effective are these descriptions?
5. What kind of conflict or tension does Ali create in this essay? How effectively does she use it?
6. What advice would you give Ali, were she to revise this essay?

THE RHETORICAL TRIANGLE
WRITER

It's your job to engage in honest exploration of a topic that matters to you, to treat that topic seriously and in depth. You and what you learned from your experience will figure as the most important aspects of a personal essay. As the writer of this essay, you'll work to identify an event that taught you something important. Each of us has such experiences, but we may not realize their importance until much later, when we take the time to reflect on them and try to puzzle out their meaning. Your job, then, will be to consider past events you count meaningful, to select one of them to write about, and then to probe and explore it thoroughly. You'll relive the event through recounting it, first for yourself and then for another reader. Ultimately, your job is to capture the meaning or significance of this event and then, using your language, to help your reader experience the event as you did.

To help your reader understand the significance of the topic for you, you'll work to recreate the topic's scene and events so that you bring them to life. Note that we're not asking you to write a piece of fiction, nor are we asking you simply to tell about something that happened to you. Instead, you'll need to select the most important details and events and then use your language to reveal their importance. You'll focus on these, so that your reader can say, "I understand," after having read your essay.

SUBJECT

As we've said, the subject for your essay will be an event that you count significant, one that taught you something about yourself. Now, significance can sometimes be a troublesome term, because many student writers think they've never had a truly significant experience. The kind of significance we're talking about here may be earth-shattering; then again, it may not. We think an event has significance if it helped you understand something about yourself, if it changed your mind or your actions in some way, or if it helped you see someone else in a different way. For example, if you ran for a student government office while in high school but didn't win, what did that experience teach you about your own feelings and your abilities to cope with disappointment? If you were active in a high school or other organization, how did your experiences in that organization affect you? If you've ever been supported at a critical moment by someone you thought an enemy, how did that affect your opinion of that person? If you've ever been betrayed by a friend in a critical situation, how did that affect your view of that friend? Recognizing that your experience has affected or changed you in some way is the first step in seeing that experience's significance to you.

The topic for your personal essay will involve an event in which you participated, one that affected you more than superficially. Datus Proper's topic—a chance encounter with a former tenant of land he likes to fish—gave him a sense of history of the Cave family and of the land, causing him to see the land in a very different light. Thus, he gained a new, deeper appreciation for Dark Hollow. Steven Barboza's topic—his conversion to Islam—helped him understand that conversion as a complex experience that he cannot attribute to a single event, the death of his mother. Arlene Yusnukis's topic—a backpacking trip in the Pecos Wilderness—enabled her to relive an enjoyable event and to confirm some beliefs she held. Daniel Kinken's topic—the swimming pool (the MAC)—let him range over a six-year span of swimming to consider exactly what those years of his life meant. Finally, Ali Duffy's topic—her performing in her high school's music and dance programs—allowed her to relive and celebrate her high school stage career, something she counted as incredibly valuable. In each of these topics, the writer figured as a participant. As you consider a topic for your writing, focus on events you have participated in that hold very real significance for you, even if you can't articulate that significance at first.

READER

Initially, you'll serve as the primary audience for your personal essay. You'll write to make sense of your experience in the attempt to reach a deeper understanding of your essay's subject and its importance to you. But keep in mind that you'll also shape a final draft for an audience beyond yourself. You should assume that your readers will be sympathetic to you and interested in what you have to say. Your job will be to help your readers relive the experience with you, so you'll have to make sure that the detail you choose captures as exactly as possible what happened and how you felt about it. As you work to make those insights clear for your readers, you'll invite them to come along with you as you reexperience the topic of the essay, to make sense of things just as you did in exploring the topic.

Look again at "Dark Hollow." Proper is not merely capturing his experience of meeting Betty Cave on a fishing trip to the hollow; he is shaping that experience to make it meaningful for his readers. One of the primary themes of this essay is ownership, and Proper raises the question, "Just who owns Dark Hollow; whose property is it?" Early in the essay, he establishes this theme, using the terms "homestead," "personal stretch," and "claim" in the first two sentences. How does his use of "claim" in the second paragraph qualify these terms in the first paragraph? And how do these images of Proper's ownership compare to or contrast with "something beautiful" (paragraph 25) and "our land" (paragraph 27)?

Add to these images of ownership what Betty Cave says about her father as she talks with Proper. In each of the first four episodes, he is seen as a strong man fully capable of taking care of family and community affairs. In paragraph 5, he catches fish to feed his family; in paragraph 10, he works hard (as does her mother), so that his family won't go hungry; in paragraphs 15–16, he hikes to work in the copper mines in winter and offers comfort to the sick and dying in Dark Hollow; in paragraphs 19–22 he hunts game to feed his family. How do these images contrast with the last we see of her father (paragraph 28)? What is the impact of Proper's leaving the reader with the final image of this strong man "sitting outside every evening, cryin' and cryin' "?

We don't know when Betty Cave told Proper of this last image, but we do know that Proper made it serve as the essay's concluding image. Thus, Proper shaped the events of his trip to Dark Hollow to have the greatest possible impact on his readers. He selected the events, the language he used to present them, and their position in the essay to create the meaning he intended his readers to understand.

DISTINGUISHING FEATURES OF PERSONAL ESSAYS

CONFLICT

Writers use narrative to shape events in a fashion that reveals their significance. These events constitute the plot of the narrative. Just as the plot (what happens) in a piece of fiction is based on conflict, so may be the plot of a personal narrative. That narrative often depends on the writer's creating conflict and then resolving it. Think about the structure of a television situation comedy. Characters get themselves into and out of various situations, some comical, some serious, each one marked by conflict of one kind or another. Each conflict comes to a head, usually just before a commercial so that you'll want to keep watching to see how the conflict will be worked out. Right after the commercial, the conflict gets resolved, but then another conflict presents itself, which gets resolved, which is followed by more conflict and more resolution, until the half hour is filled and the plot's major climax is reached. What keeps us absorbed as viewers? If we're interested in the characters, we want to know how things turn out, we want to see how the conflict is resolved.

Writers of nonfiction narratives also may create interest in their writing by creating conflict or tension that the reader wants to see resolved. Ali Duffy creates tension by focusing on her mixed feelings at dancing one last time for a hometown audience, feeling at once happy that she'll soon graduate from high school and sad that she'll soon leave this very comfortable part of her life behind. Steven Barboza begins his conversion to Islam by rejecting Catholicism, but he rejects the Nation of Islam as well before his final acceptance of orthodox Islam. Barboza, then, moves from one conflict through another to his final position. And in "Dark Hollow," at least three kinds of tension are at work. Initially, Datus Proper wonders who is ahead of him on the stream and feels that, in a sense, "his" stream has been usurped by this intruder. At the end of the essay, a more significant tension is at work in the conflict between the Caves and the government that moved them from the land; we may say that this conflict is between people like the Caves and U.S. society at large. Finally, there is the internal tension Proper feels. His empathy for the Caves and others like them is countered by his pleasure at having land like Dark Hollow preserved for people like him.

As you consider various events for your own narrative, look for those marked by conflict (whether real, implied, potential, or threatened). Oftentimes, our experiences teach us their lessons as we struggle with others, our environment, or ourselves; they teach us as we are engaged in conflict. These experiences are the stuff of narrative, the stuff of the personal essay.

DIALOGUE

The more detail you include in a particular scene or event in your paper, the more importance that scene or event will assume for your readers. One way to provide this kind of detail is through dialogue. If you want your readers to remember the specifics of a particular event that involves key characters, try telling the event by means of a conversation between those characters.

Below are two versions of the same event, one a summary, the other a detailed account of the event given in dialogue. How do they differ? In what circumstances would each be appropriate for an essay?

Version 1

Linda had a heated argument with John, her father, that resulted in her being grounded.

Version 2

"I'm tired of always being last!" Linda shouted. Her face started to flush, and she clenched her fists.

John, her father, paused a moment before replying, seeming to weigh his words carefully. "Honey," he began, "I know it can seem that your sister, being the youngest, gets favored, but . . . "

"Seems like? Seems like! Don't patronize me, Dad. It's absolutely true, and you know it!" Linda's words echoed in the spacious den. "You're so unfair," she whined, "You always let Beth do whatever she wants, but not me. Oh, no! I have to do all the work around here—wash the dishes, cut the grass, walk the dog, haul Beth around in my car burning my gas—doesn't matter what it is. Nope, sweet little ol' Bethie just lounges around while I do everything!"

"All right now, Linda," John muttered through clenched teeth, "best you'd be careful. You're pushing it, young lady."

Linda saw her father's set jaw and knew what that meant. She was flirting with disaster, dangerously close to losing her freedom. But that didn't matter; heedless of the consequences, she pressed on. "I'm not your 'young lady'; I'm not a child! I'm 16 years old, Dad, and I'm sick and tired of being treated like I'm 8. It's so unfair!"

"That's it, kiddo." (She hated it when her father called her "kiddo.") Both of them had lost sight of the original bone of contention; both knew what was coming; both knew they'd both lost. "You're grounded." John pronounced the punishment solemnly, like a judge sentencing a criminal. "You're grounded till next Wednesday."

"A whole week!" Linda exploded, outraged. "But, but, but I have a date this weekend!" she sputtered. She stopped, pondering her options. "Aw, come on, Dad, please let me just apologize. Please don't embarrass me like that. I'll just die if I have to break my date. Please, Dad, please?" she begged.

"I'll think about it," John said. "But for now, go to your room."

Linda turned on her heels and stalked down the hallway, slamming her door in reply.

Exercise 5.1

Identify the verbs that report who said what in the conversation between Linda and her father. How many times does "said" appear? Write your own dialogue between two characters, paying particular attention to verbs, especially those used to report who said what and how they said it.

VIVID DETAIL

Details carry freight. "The person entered the room" may be a grammatically correct sentence, but it doesn't reveal anything about the person, the person's actions, or the room. Consider these sentences, each of which involves a person entering a room:

> Exhausted, the junior high teacher stumbled into her principal's office, muttering, "I just can't stand it any longer."

> His coattails flapping in the breeze, little Johnny Wilson, the ten-year-old terror of the neighborhood, wheeled his skateboard to a skidstop just inside the door to Mrs. Smith's kitchen, his wheels marking tracks on the freshly waxed linoleum floor.

> Sgt. Sally Johnson, undercover policewoman extraordinaire, crept stealthily into the crack house, leading her infamous team—The Drugbusters—on yet another raid to rid her town of dope, druggies, drug dealers, and other sundry undesirable elements.

Although somewhat facetious, these examples should illustrate the point that your description—the language you use to detail the events of your writing—is all that is available for the reader to consider. Your job is to bring those events to life, to use your language to ensure your reader's understanding of the significance of those events.

You can also create detail by using lists, sometimes called *catalogs,* that present a string of details, naming things. Here's a passage from Lee K. Abbott's "The True Story of Why I Do What I Do" that shows how cataloging can help create an image in the reader's mind:

> "See this, Kit?" he said. He was standing in the center of the utility room, lawn mower here, gas can there, the walls hung with tools I never got the sense of. Golf clubs were in there, a bucket of practice balls, cans of oil, greasy rags, a hoe, a rake, a cheap hardware store of goodies that smelled old and used and too sweet.

Abbott depicts a cluttered utility room and emphasizes clutter by describing the room's contents as almost a jumble. The detail "lawn mower here, gas can there" in the second sentence emphasizes the random placement of items, with this randomness underscored by the layering of detail in the next sentence. Abbott keeps adding details one by one until the reader sees the scene Abbott wants her to see.

ASSIGNMENT AND GUIDELINES FOR WRITING

ASSIGNMENT

As you begin your personal essay, you may use one of the three writing prompts listed below or a prompt provided by your teacher. Remember that, ultimately, your task is to discover and then reveal the significance in your topic to your readers.

1. Describe an event from which you learned something. Your job is to use your language to recreate the event so that your readers will feel that they have been at least observers of this important event with you, if not participants in it.
2. Describe a favorite place, one that's significant for you. What makes it a favorite? What makes it significant? Your job is to depict this place so that your readers will see clearly its importance to you. Option: Use this place as the setting for an essay about a significant event that occurred there.
3. Who are you? What do you stand for? What have been the strongest shaping elements and events in your life? Using narration and description, write an essay in which you help your readers see and understand these influences, so that they come to know you in ways they otherwise would not.

CHOOSING A TOPIC

If you've already settled on a potential topic for this essay, move to Part B of these instructions. If you're undecided about a topic, try any or all of the activities in Part A.

PART A

1. Take a look again at your responses to the Interest Inventory (pp. 8–9). Look especially for topics about events, places, and people you know well. Pick two or three, and write about each for 10 minutes. Why did you pick these particular potential topics? What's important about them? Why do they stand out or appeal to you?
2. Develop an Important List, a list of people (family, friends, teachers), places (home, favorite places, work, school), ideas (family values, family history, your desires and dreams, your goals), or things (awards, events, personal objects) that are significant or meaningful for you. Write two or three sentences about each entry on your list. Then, select the ones you think are most important, and write three or four more sentences about each of those. Why did you select these particular entries? [We adopted this activity from *Paideia*, edited by Kristina Fury and Kimberly Whitehead

(New York: Forbes Custom, 1998). For an example of its use, see Chris Miller's prewriting, pp. 154–155.]

3. Freewrite for 15 minutes about your memories of events, places, and people. Start with "I remember" and jot down all the events, places, and people that come to mind. Write nonstop for 15 minutes. Don't censor any thoughts that come to mind; don't worry about grammar, mechanics, or sentence structure—just write.

From these writings, select a topic that you think you may want to use as the basis for your essay.

PART B

Now that you've identified a possible topic, freewrite for at least 15 minutes about it. Again, don't stop during the entire period; don't censor any thoughts that come to mind; don't worry about grammar, mechanics, or sentence structure—just write.

After you've finished this 15-minute writing period, look back over what you've written. What is beginning to emerge as the focal point of your topic? If you don't see anything just yet, you may want to continue with another 15-minute freewrite, followed by reflection on what you write. This process may be repeated until you find a topic.

COLLECTING INFORMATION

Reader. You may use your reader as a means of generating details for your writing. Write a short statement describing someone you imagine will want to read your essay. What will make the experience come alive for that person? What details will you need to present to enable your reader to understand the significance of the topic for you?

Visualization. Another way to generate material is to visualize your topic (see the visualization exercise, pp. 18–19). When you've finished your visualization, write down everything you remember about the exercise as quickly as you can. Just as with freewriting, don't worry about anything except writing.

Talking. Talking is another good way of generating information for this assignment. Find a sympathetic listener and tell her your story, or find someone who was part of your topic and reminisce with that person about it. Use a tape recorder; take notes during your conversation, or write down as much of the discussion as you can remember immediately following it.

Freewriting. Return to freewriting. If you get stuck, then freewrite to get started again. Select one aspect of your topic and write about only that aspect for 10 minutes. If you need more information about a certain part of your topic, freewrite about it.

FOCUS STATEMENT

As you generate information for your paper, look back over your freewriting and then write a brief statement about the focal point of your essay. Keep in mind that this will be a tentative statement. You may phrase it something like this:

Significant event. I want to write about the time that _____ happened and show that I learned _____. To do this, I need to include these details: _____, _____, _____, and _____.

Significant place. I want to write about the peacefulness I feel at the _____ campground in the _____ mountains and talk about how it helps me deal with _____.

Who am I? I would describe myself as a person who _____, _____, and _____. I need to show how I got to be this way by talking about _____, _____, and _____.

Use this statement as a very general guide to getting started. It should begin to address the significance you want your writing to carry, and it can point the way toward the kind of details you'll have to present in the essay: In order to fulfill your focus statement, what will you have to do; what details (and in what order) will you have to present?

PLANNING YOUR ESSAY'S STRUCTURE

The primary structuring principle of the personal essay is chronology, which shows the relationship of events and people in time. The significance is revealed gradually through the layering of details the writer presents, so that when the reader finishes, he has a sense of having gradually come to understand the writer's intent.

It's not enough, however, to tell what happened in a "first this, then this, then this" sequence. Instead, you'll need to craft the order so that you move from a beginning through a middle to an end. That is, you'll need to structure your writing so that it's clear how one part of the event leads to the next, and that to the next, and so on until you make your point or show how the events form an important or significant whole.

Typically, the chronology is straightforward, though occasionally a writer will use a flashback, moving backwards in time to tell a part of the story that comments on the story line she is developing. Ali Duffy's "The Dance" opens with Ali on stage, ready to begin her final high school performance in the role of Giselle. Then, in paragraph 2, she begins a flashback that will carry us from her freshman through her senior years:

paragraph 2—freshman year, performing in *The Sound of Music*
paragraph 3—sophomore year, performing in *Guys and Dolls*
paragraph 4—senior year (May 1997), performing in *Crazy for You*

In paragraphs 5–6, Ali returns us to the present, to her final performance as a senior in June 1997, and in paragraph 7, she sums up the significance that performing holds for her. Note that Ali uses the present tense in paragraphs 1 and 5–7 and the past tense in paragraphs 2–4. This shifting of verb tense signals the movement from the present (paragraph 1) to the past (paragraphs 2–4) and then back to the present (paragraphs 5–7).

Datus Proper's narrative takes a different approach to using chronology as a structuring device. Proper takes us through a day's fishing from start to finish, moving from one event to the next in order. At the same time, he weaves Betty Cave's narrative into his, so that they comment on each other. But the point here is that Proper takes us through the events of his day of fishing in the order in which they happened.

Did any of the authors write everything that happened during the events they reported? Clearly not. They couldn't have. But then, they shouldn't have. Their job was to present the most important details to the reader and to shape those details so that the reader would come to understand the significance they wanted the reader to understand. Selecting details is an important consideration for a writer of personal essays.

Exercise 5.2

1. "Dark Hollow" is arranged chronologically, with Proper taking us with him as he walks from his car to the stream, encounters and converses with Betty Cave, and then fishes the stream. He doesn't tell everything that occurs on that trip; instead, he selects events that are important to the significance he's trying to present to his readers. Are there events that don't seem to be important enough to warrant inclusion in the essay, or does each event that Proper reports contribute something to the essay? Which events could, or should, have been deleted? Pick two events or details from this essay that carry special significance for you and explain what they contribute to it.

2. Make a list of the details you think will be important in your essay. Then, create an order for them. Is this order absolutely chronological, or are there reasons to tell things out of sequence in places? Why? Using this ordered list as a guide, write a draft of your essay.

REFINING YOUR WRITING

After you've written your essay and taken some time away from it, revise it, keeping the following principles in mind:

Selection of detail. Select only the key moments, the ones that your paper won't make sense without. Focus on those moments that create conflict or tension.

Amount of detail. Give important moments more space or detail. The more time your reader spends with a given section of your essay, the more importance it will assume.

Quality of detail. Provide sufficient detail to help the reader see the scene you're writing about. The more vivid the image—the more descriptive the language—the more likely your reader will be to grasp its importance to you.

Dialogue. Use dialogue to help bring characters to life. Letting a character speak instead of summarizing or reporting what she said can give that character immediacy and importance in the paper. Two notes: (1) Be sure to pay attention to the conventions of punctuation at work with dialogue (e.g., quotation marks); (2) try to help readers hear how a speaker sounds by describing how he utters his words. It is fine to use "say" or "said" sometimes, but keep in mind that speakers often "reply," "retort," "respond," "exclaim," "utter," "whisper," "whimper," "comment," "cry," and "shout."

Exercise 5.3

1. Look again at the essays by Datus Proper, Steven Barboza, Arlene Yusnukis, Daniel Kinken, and Ali Duffy. How does each writer feature or emphasize the important moments in his or her essay? Identify any parts of each essay that you think are extraneous. Why do you think so? How vivid is the detail each writer provides? Is this detail sufficient to help you see the event? Why or why not? To what extent and how effectively does each writer use dialogue?

2. Identify the key moments in the event you've chosen to write about. How can you feature or emphasize them? Why do they figure as key or important? In what order do you think you should present them to your reader? Which event or events do you think you'll give more space to? Why? What kind of detail will help bring these moments to life? Does any event lend itself to dialogue? If so, what will you have each character say?

SAMPLE STUDENT PROCESS

In this section, we present a student writer at work from start to finish. Chris Miller, a first-year student at NMSU, began his essay by doing several prewriting exercises. He then tried out two potential topics to see which might be the more promising, picked one, changed his mind, and then wrote and revised a draft of his essay. We've reproduced Chris's writings exactly as he wrote them—abbreviations, spelling errors, mechanical errors, and all. These examples make it clear that Chris is following our instructions not to worry about correctness until the final draft.

PREWRITING

Chris began by writing an "I remember" list of places, people, and events (see p. 150). His job was to list everything that came to mind—not to censor anything, simply to list.

I remember . . .

50-miler backpack trip
mountain climbing
my house
Silver Jack
OA Greagor
Key Club convention
State cross-country meet
Oak Grove Elementary
vacations in Washington, Oregon, California
Mexico w/ Habitat for Humanity
working at Kirtland
Amy
Philmont
continuation
Mrs. Woelfel, Mr. Brown, Mrs. Brice, Mrs. Winkler
academic decathlon
White Sands
Montrose
Grand Junction—Beth
Christmas w/ my family
Lassie
He-man
my brother breaking his arm
NJHS trip
BSA Jamboree
50-miler in Utah
Eagle Court of Honor
getting in trouble with police
Game Boy
grandparents
woodcutting
Kayla/Misty
the countryside
getting Gina
my great-grandma
my biology test

The second prewriting exercise Chris completed was an Important List of people, places, and ideas (see p. 149). Again, Chris was not to censor but to name, then to expand his initial list, and then to discuss the expanded list.

Name
People—groups, teachers, family
Places—home, travel, work
Ideas—ethics & morality, goals & desires, self-respect

Expand
People—
    groups: Scouts and Key Club
    teachers: elementary, middle, and high school
    family: mom and dad

Places—
    home: Montrose, Albuquerque
    travel: Scouts, Mexico
    work: fast food, OA Greagor, Kirtland
Ideas—
    ethics & morality: Scouts, importance
    goals & desires: help, happiness, learning
    self-respect: originality, drinking

Discuss
People—
    Many groups have influenced my life. The biggest influence has definitely come from scouts. I've been influenced with scouts since I was about six in Cub Scouts. My mom helped w/ my pack and volunteered at my elementary school. She definitely had a big influence on my life at this time. I feel like I had a good start on life thanks to her. When I joined Boy Scouts, the influence shifted to my father, who soon became scoutmaster. Many experiences that I had in Boy Scouts influenced me, but few changed me as much as being on staff at our council's scout camp, OA Greagor. I learned and changed more from being on staff for two summers than at any other time.
Places—[*Since Chris misplaced this portion of his prewriting, it can't be reproduced here.*]
Ideas—
    If I could narrow down the basis of my life and who I am to one thing, it would be my ethics. I consider them in everything I do. The main source of my ethics was scouts. I learned to value honesty and truth. Today I base my life on these beliefs. I am also very concerned with my self-respect. It is very important to me. My personal code is very strict. I don't smoke or drink. Sometimes it is hard, but it's well worth it. My goals for my life are to be happy, to help others, and to learn as much as I can.

FOCUS STATEMENT

Having chosen to write about a significant place—the OA Greagor Scout Camp—Chris wrote this focus statement designed to give him some direction for his drafting:

My purpose is to educate readers about a favorite place of mine. I will tell about its significance to me, and what I learned from it.

describe the place
tell about experiences
tell about significance
what I learned
who I met
how it affected me
The place is OA Greagor and I worked there for two years.

Chris submitted his focus statement to his peer group (three other students in his first-year composition class), and they raised these questions:

Why is this place so significant to you? How has it influenced your life to make you who you are today?

What is OA Greagor? What did you do while you worked there?

What types of work did you do—fun, strenuous? How does this job mean more to you than perhaps others in the past? What is it that you hope the readers will gain? Experiences, hardships, etc.?

Knowing what his peer-group readers would want to learn from reading the paper, Chris began to write a narrative about his experiences at this camp, producing this draft:

OA Greagor

When I think back on my life before I moved to Albuquerque, age 15, there are many memories. I was a typical kid. I had my friends, with whom I spent a great deal of time <u>playing with</u>. I was involved in a <u>few activities</u>, and I had worked doing babysitting or mowing people's lawns. All these things hold memories for me, but none stand out as much as OA Greagor Boy Scout Camp. The first time I ever rode up the rutted, dirt road leading to the camp, I was 10 and had just joined Boy Scouts. I didn't know any one, and I got my <u>first horrible taste of homesickness</u>. I spent the week either physically ill or depressed, and despite the <u>five merit badges I earned</u>, I swore I would never go back. ~~The next year~~ Early the next year my father ~~took~~ agreed to take over the ~~scoutmaster position~~ troop from our handicapped scoutmaster. He boosted the troop membership and got many younger kids to join.

You'll note that Chris underlined a couple of phrases to remind himself to return to these places later and add detail. He also scratched out some words, substituting others he thought more appropriate. And he stopped very short of producing a first or discovery draft. For whatever reasons, Chris didn't like the way this essay was developing, so he did a very smart thing—he changed topics. He returned to the prewriting he'd done earlier and selected as his new topic a trip to Mexico that he'd mentioned in both prewriting exercises.

Having picked this new topic, Chris made a prewriting list of specific things he recalled from a trip to Nogales, a border town in both Arizona and Mexico, to do volunteer work for Habitat for Humanity.

Mexico
Habitat house
stories—Mexican prison
Nogales—US
Nogales—Mexico
Nogales habitat house
Chano
work sites
Doña Chuy
dinners at houses
marketplace

poverty
factories
pickaxing
moving rocks
hauling & leveling dirt
showers & bathrooms
food
sleeping
Dos X's
strip poker
border crossing
video camera
writing
Tucson
trying to speak Spanish
Bueno, lame, Gringos on Safari
show examples (cheese thing)

Chris then wrote this outline of the points he wanted to make in a draft:

I. Mexicans have little or no money
   A. houses
   B. food
   C. inflation—reason
      2 ~~1.~~) Makiladores—machines
      1 ~~2.~~) cheese & other prices
II. They are happy and kind
   A. family
   B. friends
   C. food—give up what they have
   D. Chano
   E. worksites
   F. house materials

Note that this isn't a traditional outline; it is more a list of things to remember to include than a structure for the paper to come. Chris then wrote part of a draft before stopping for a breather:

It was approaching midnight when Chano, our ~~Mexican~~ translator, finally lead us into what would become our home for the next week. It was a small rectangular ~~concrete~~ building with one half serving as an office and the other as two bedrooms ~~and the~~ divided by the bathroom. ~~Standing in the center of the bathroom I could reach both my hands out and touch the opposing walls.~~ ~~It~~ We piled our bags in the corner and then, to tired to do anything else, stumbled into the bedrooms and ~~went to~~ fell asleep.

Six short hours later, ~~we~~ after some asking, reminding, and finally threatening, ~~by our chaperones,~~ we grudgingly got out of bed. ~~The only food~~ We hadn't been to a grocery store yet, so the only food we had for breakfast was leftover bread and some apples. We ate this while listening to Chano explain what was to happen. "Today we will begin working. We ~~are going to a~~ will be ~~helping with a house~~ working on a house

Chris stopped this draft here but returned to it later and completed it. He submitted the draft that follows for his peer group to review.

ROUGH DRAFT FOR PEER REVIEW

It was approaching midnight when Chano, our translator, finally lead us into what would become our home for the next five days. It was a small rectangular building with one half serving as an office and the other as two bedrooms divided by the bathroom. We piled our bags into the corner and then, too tired to do anything else, stumbled into the bedrooms and fell asleep.

Six short, uncomfortable hours later, after some asking, reminding, and finally threatening, we grudgingly got out of bed. There hadn't been time to go to a grocery yet, so the only food we had for breakfast was leftover bread and some apples. We ate this while listening to Chano.

"Thank you for coming. Habitat for Humanity appreciates your help. We will leave for the first work site in about half an hour." Chano's English was grammatically flawless and had only a slight Spanish accent, the result of working with "gringos" for the last ten years. He was the director of Habitat for Humanity in the Nogales area. Under his guidance the organization had built over one hundred houses and donated thousands of hours to help the local residents. Because our group of teenagers and two chaperones contained only three people who had ever been to Mexico, we had been dubbed "Gringos on Safari" by our friends in Albuquerque, and it stuck, becoming the name of our expedition.

We loaded the van with shovels, picks, rakes, axes, and several other tools that we had been told we would use. It was a thirty minute drive to the work site on the outskirts of Nogales. This drive was my first real introduction to Mexico. I knew it was a poor nation, but I hadn't even imagined this much poverty could exist. The houses we saw were smaller than many of friend's living rooms. They were built with wood, dirt, cardboard, or whatever else was available. It seemed like a strong wide would blow Nogales over. As we advanced further from the city the road became worse. Soon the van had to be put into four wheel drive. Chano explained that the city had not been built for cars, since less than ten percent of the population owned one.

Finally we got to the work site. It consisted of a small, flat plot of dirt that was going to be a house foundation and a large pile of dirt a short distance away. We spent the first five hours moving dirt from the pile to the flat foundation. By about 11:00 the blistering sun had warmed the area to almost 90 degrees and it kept getting hotter. The twelve of us worked along with Chano and the six people that would eventually occupy the house. They had a deal with Habitat, so that they helped build the house in exchange for paying less for it. I couldn't imagine one person living in a house this size much less six. Finally the lunch break arrived. We struggled over to the van and got our lunch out. Then we dropped to the ground in the only shade at the site, provided by a small, dying tree. The break ended far to soon and it was back to work for five more hours. The only comfort came from the fact that it gradually cooled off as the afternoon wore on. Finally we hauled the last load of dirt to the foundation. It was almost six by then and we had added a foot to the entire 20 x 20 foot plot. We celebrated the end of the day by dragging ourselves into the van and collapsing. I had three blisters, a sprained ankle, and a sore back to show for my ten hours of work. When we arrived back at the house the chaperones prepare dinner while the rest of us cleaned up. Their was no water pressure in this part of Nogales, because no one could afford it. To shower, we poured water over our heads and washed off as best we could. We ate a quick dinner and then, to tired to do anything else, went straight to sleep.

Once again we had to be forced out of bed. We devoured a slightly larger breakfast to give us energy for the long day ahead and then piled into the van. The new site was only about ten minutes away, but it lead us to an even worse part of town. Here the houses were sometimes made of tires or even old trash. There were dogs running around the streets and filthy, naked babies playing in trash. The house we were working on was made of wood on the three sides it had. The owner had run out of money after building three sides of it and had been living there with no back wall for two months. He had finally saved enough money to buy the forty tires which he was going to use as a wall since they were cheaper than wood. We started by splitting into two groups. One group started filling dirt into the first layer of tires along the back wall, while the other began picking a hole that would serve as an outhouse. I started out with a pick ax and began working on the outhouse. We worked for about four hours, picking into the rocky, hard ground until we were exhausted, and dug the hole almost three inches deep. During lunch we sat back admiring our accomplishment until Chano informed us that the hole needed to be at least six feet deep. The owner couldn't afford to hire a jackhammer. We switched jobs after lunch and worked for another four hours. Our moral was much better on this day despite the intense heat and new blisters. That evening we had the honor of eating with some local Nogales residents. We divided into three groups and each went to a different house. Our group went to the house of Doña Chuy, a native of Nogales. She was 47 years old and lived in a two room shack with her husband, three kids, and her oldest daughter's boyfriend. They survived on what the husband and son made at the maquilas. Literally translated maquila means machine, but in Nogales it refers to the huge American owned factories. The companies open factories in Mexico because the labor is much cheaper. Over eighty percent of Nogales works in the maquilas, often for incredibly little money and no benefits. Doña Chuy told us about the maquilas as well as she could in broken fragmented English.

"My husband, once he work for Phillips. He work for five years, then one day he go there and there is no on in the maquila. There is a sign says the company close and leave. He lucky one and get a new job but many others have to leave Nogales." Chano later explained that Phillips had a factory in Nogales, but cheaper labor was available in the Philippines, so overnight they closed the factory and left. They used a legal loophole to avoid paying the people their severance pay and it left about 1200 people out of a job. Most of them were forced to move out of Nogales, because they couldn't get another job. Doña Chuy cooked homemade tortillas for us, and then stuffed them with chicken, rice, and cheese. She also gave us some of her homemade pineapple beer, usually reserved only for religious holidays and birthdays. After a long day of work it tasted better than any gourmet meal I've ever had. We later found out that this one diner cost the family more than they usually spend on food in a week. To the people of Mexico it is a huge honor to have guests and they sacrifice a lot of personal comfort for them. This wasn't the first time that Mexico's generosity would impress me. We reluctantly left Doña Chuy's house, filled with her delicious food and the warmth of her kind and generous attitude toward us.

The next day dawned with the promise of a surprise after lunch. We worked hard all morning fueled by anticipation of the surprise and dug the outhouse hole to an impressive seven inches. At twelve thirty we all crowded inside the house and ate while speculating on the surprise. Just as we finished eating Chano came in and told us that since we had worked so hard and had done so well, we were going to take the afternoon off. He also explained that because we had skipped some of the tourist attractions and had saved money on food, we each had ended up with a sixty dollar refund. We took the money and began to drive to the marketplace. About half way there, however, we changed our minds. After seeing the lifestyles of the people of Nogales, we couldn't just rashly waste sixty dollars on some tourist junk. Instead we took the money to Doña Chuy and the women who fed the other two groups. They were speechless and, after some crying, gratefully accepted the money. We talked with them some more and then drove back to the marketplace to buy a few more groceries. (Three weeks after we got back from the trip, we got a postcard from Chano which said, among other things, that the women had used the money to buy clothes for almost twenty families in Nogales.) On the way we saw a schoolhouse with the children playing at recess. The school was too poor to afford playground equipment, so the kids made up games of their own using whatever they could find. That seemed to be a common theme in Mexico—Do the best you can with what you can find. We spent almost two hours in the marketplace comparing prices to American products. By the time a typical Mexico worker had worked enough hours to buy a pound of cheese, it's price was equivalent to $60.00. The outrageous inflation would be intolerable in America, but to the Mexico people it was accepted as a way of life. I had noticed throughout the trip that the people seemed happier and more content than most people I knew in America. They came to rely more on family and less on money. It was not uncommon to see three generations of family living happily together in one house. It was like the poverty and inflation and working conditions and houses didn't matter to them. They didn't let it depress them. I had always been told that money couldn't buy happiness, but I never believe it until I went to Mexico.

Our last day was another work day. We toiled for about nine hours with a short lunch break and then drove back to the house for one last time. We sadly said our good-byes to Chano and his family, and then loaded our van to leave. I spent the drive home thinking about what I had learned and how I had grown. I thought of Doña Chuy and all the other people we met. I also thought about the poverty and all the problems with Nogales, but when I thin back on the trip today what I remember is the generosity and kindness of the people. I saw the actual value of money and the real power of love on the trip and it has made a dramatic difference in my life. I am more content with what I have and less materialistic than before. I also value my friends and family much more. These have all made me a happier person and I can't imagine a better learning experience.

Chris's peer group read, marked, and commented on the draft. They felt that it was an effective first draft but that Chris needed to pay attention to these things:

1. It tells an awful lot. It's over 1,800 words long (too long for the assignment, a max of 1,500 words), so it needs to be cut down and shaped.
2. The paragraphs are too long, need to be split into more logical units.
3. It has some grammatical errors—but it's a draft, so these aren't bad unless you don't fix them in a final draft.

4. The ending is a bit much; it makes too many unsupported assertions.
5. The attempt at humor (digging the pit—1 inch in 1 day?) doesn't quite work, so it needs to be revised or maybe deleted.
6. Some of the paragraphs have choppy sentence structure, so these need to be smoothed out.
7. More dialogue in a place or two would help bring this piece more to life.

Taking into account his group members' comments (and those of Bill, his teacher), Chris then produced the final draft that follows. As you read it, consider the differences between it and the rough draft. Do you think the changes Chris made are effective? Why or why not?

FINAL DRAFT

GRINGOS ON SAFARI

CHRIS MILLER

1   Near midnight, Chano, the Director of Habitat for Humanity for the Nogales area, finally led us into what would become our home for the next five days—a small rectangular building with one half serving as an office and the other as two bedrooms divided by the bathroom. Piling our bags into the corner and then, too tired to do anything else, we stumbled into the bedrooms and fell asleep. For all but three of us, this was a first trip to Mexico, so our friends in Albuquerque had dubbed us "gringos on safari." We were ready for adventure.

2   Six short, uncomfortable hours later, after some asking, reminding, and finally threatening, we grudgingly got out of bed. Because we'd had no time to shop, we munched on leftover bread and some apples while Chano very concisely laid out the day's itinerary. "Thank you for coming. Habitat for Humanity appreciates your help. We will leave for the first work site in about half an hour."

3   We loaded the van with shovels, picks, rakes, and axes, tools that none of us used very often. The half-hour drive to the work site was my first real introduction to Mexico. I knew it was a poor nation, but I hadn't even imagined this much poverty could exist. The flimsy houses we saw, smaller than many of my friends' living rooms, were built with wood, dirt, cardboard, or whatever else was available. A strong wind could blow Nogales over.

4   The work site consisted of a small, flat plot of dirt that would form a house's foundation and a large pile of dirt a short distance away. "Your job is to move this dirt," Chano pointed at the large pile, "to the foundation, spread it out evenly, and pack it tight." My friend John and I looked at each other and rolled our eyes. Some safari. Some adventure.

5   Five hot, grueling hours later, we dropped gratefully to the ground to have lunch in the only shade available, provided by a small, dying tree. Another hot, grueling five hours later, we stood back to admire our handiwork. We had raised the foundation a foot, and we celebrated by dragging ourselves into the van and collapsing. I had three blisters, a sprained ankle, and a sore back to show for my ten hours of work.

6 I also had a new appreciation for the term "sweat equity." Our work crew this day had included the family of six who would occupy the house. We didn't talk with them very much because none of us knew more than a year of textbook Spanish, and they spoke no English. But at the end of the day, we understand their repeated "*Muchas gracias*" well enough. We were bound by blisters, sweat, and dirt.

7 Next morning, our chaperones had to pry us out of the sack. This day's site was a house with only three sides made of wood. The owner had run out of money before he could complete it and had been living there with no back wall for two months. He had finally saved enough money to buy the forty tires to form this wall since they were cheaper than wood. We split into two groups, one to fill the first layer of tires with dirt, the other to pick a hole in what seemed like solid rock that would serve as an outhouse. Outside of Scout camps and portapotties, none of us had much experience with outhouses.

8 We were amazed by the poverty that surrounded us. Dogs ran in packs in the streets; filthy, naked babies played in the trash. A man saved for two months just to buy forty used tires to keep out the weather. Most of us had an allowance that would buy that much in a week. Six people would live in a 400 sq. ft. house. Most of us lived in four-bedroom, 3500 sq. ft. brick homes, palaces by comparison.

9 That evening we had the honor of dining in the homes of some local Nogales, Mexico, residents. My group dined with Doña Chuy, a 47 year old woman who lived in a two-room shack with her husband, three kids, and her oldest daughter's boyfriend. They survived on what the husband and son made at the *maquilas.* Literally translated *maquila* means machine, but in Nogales it refers to the huge American-owned factories. The companies open factories in Mexico, attracted by cheap labor. Over eighty percent of Nogales works in the *maquilas,* often for incredibly little money and no benefits. Doña Chuy told us about the *maquilas* as well as she could in her fragmented English.

10 "My husband, once he work for Phillips. He work for five years, then one day he go there and there is no one in the *maquila.* There is a sign says the company close and leave. He lucky one and get a new job but many others have to leave Nogales." She did not seem angry about this; instead, she seemed to accept it as something that just happened. Chano later explained that Phillips had a factory in Nogales, but cheaper labor was available in the Philippines, so overnight they closed the factory and left. They used a legal loophole to avoid paying the people their severance pay and left about 1200 people out of a job. Most were forced to leave Nogales. No work.

11 Doña Chuy cooked homemade tortillas for us, then stuffed them with chicken, rice, and cheese. She also served homemade pineapple beer, usually reserved only for religious holidays and birthdays. After a long day of work those tortillas tasted better than any seven-course gourmet dinner I've ever had. We later found out that this one meal cost the family more than they usually spent on food in a week. But for the people of Mexico it is a huge honor to have guests, and they sacrifice a lot of personal comfort for them. Reluctantly, we left Doña Chuy's house, filled with her delicious food and the warmth of kindness and generosity.

12 The next day Chano surprised us after lunch. "You've worked hard, and I thank you. So you get the afternoon off. And because you've toured less and worked more, you've saved some money. Each of you gets a $60.00 refund."

13 "Sixty bucks apiece? Wow! Anybody for the *mercado*?"

14 "Yessir! I want a sombrero and maybe some sandals and a sarape to hang on the wall."

15 "Not me. I want about a gallon of Coke."

16 Halfway there, we changed our minds. After seeing the lifestyles of the people of Nogales, we couldn't just rashly waste sixty dollars on some tourist junk. Instead we

took the money to Doña Chuy and her friends. They were speechless but gratefully accepted the money. (Three weeks later, we got a postcard from Chano which said, among other things, that the women had used the money to buy clothes for almost twenty families in Nogales.)

17   We did drive to the *mercado* for groceries and spent almost two hours there comparing prices to American products. By the time a typical Mexican worker had worked enough hours to buy a pound of cheese, its price was equivalent to $60.00 US. Such outrageous inflation would be intolerable in America, but the Mexican people accepted it as a way of life. I had noticed throughout the trip that the people seemed happier and more content than most people I knew in America. They relied more on family and less on money. They had to, to survive. It was not uncommon to see three generations of family living together in one house. The poverty and inflation and working conditions and ramshackle houses didn't seem to matter to them. They didn't let it depress them. I had always been told that money couldn't buy happiness, but I never believed it until I went to Mexico.

18   Our last day was another work day. We toiled another nine hours with a short lunch break and then drove back to our headquarters one last time. We sadly said our good-byes to Chano and his family, then loaded our van to leave. I spent the drive home thinking about Doña Chuy and all the other people we had met, about the poverty and all the problems in Nogales we had seen. But when I think back on the trip today what I remember most is the generosity and kindness of the people. I saw the actual value of money and the real power of love on the trip and it has made a dramatic difference in my life. I am more content with what I have and less materialistic than before. I also value my friends and family much more. Sometimes, when you go on safari, you come back with less but more than you expected.

Checklist: Critiquing a Personal Essay

1. Which of the assignment options does the essay respond to? In a sentence, summarize the significant statement the essay makes.
2. Identify places in the paper you think worked well. What makes these places effective?
3. Identify places in the paper you think need work. What revisions need to be made?
4. How effective is the paper's organization? Consider the beginning, middle, and end. Does the introduction catch the reader's attention? If so, how? If not, what revisions need to be made?
5. Does the paper adhere to conventions of usage, mechanics, and format? Correct any errors you find.

The following are actual instructions found on consumer goods' labels:

On a hair dryer	*Do not use while sleeping.*
On a bar of soap	*Directions: Use like regular soap.*
On a frozen dinner	*Serving suggestion: Defrost.*
On a hotel-provided shower cap in a box	*Fits one head.*
On a box of bread pudding	*Product will be hot after heating.*
On a sleep aid	*Warning: may cause drowsiness.*
On a packet of peanuts	*Warning: contains nuts.*
On an airline-provided packet of nuts	*Instructions: open packet, eat nuts.*
On a chain saw	*Do not attempt to stop with hands.*

How much of this information do we actually need? Probably none of it. What else would a pack of peanuts contain but peanuts? And would you be likely to try to stop a running chain saw with your hands? Manufacturers include such information on their packages and products because of potential liability problems. For example, if someone actually tried to stop a running chain saw with his hands, the manufacturer would be in a better position to fight a liability lawsuit because of the warning "Do not attempt to stop with hands." For most users of these and other products, this type of information isn't necessary; most people simply don't need it in order to use the products properly. On many occasions, however, we do need to be able to impart information to others. The ability to

Informative Essays

C H A P T E R 6

share information is one of the most important skills humans have. All of us give and receive information every day of our lives, as the following exercise may help illustrate.

Exercise 6.1

In how many different situations have you shared information with others during the last week? In how many situations have you received information from others during this week? Can you group these different occasions? How many different groupings do you come up with? What role, if any, did writing—and here we include any type of keyboarding—play in your giving or receiving information?

Although there are many types of informative occasions, you should have found some common characteristics they all share. The key, whether you are offering information or receiving it, is understanding; that is, informative writing must translate ideas into language that will communicate meaning to the intended readers.

SAMPLE ESSAYS

The following sample essays provide readers with various types of information and differ in many ways. But, as pieces of informative writing, they also have important similarities, as we shall see in our discussion of informative occasions.

Our first sample essay was written by Elisabeth Kübler-Ross, a medical doctor who has spent her lifetime dealing with the issues surrounding death and dying. This essay, "On the Fear of Dying," has become a classic in the literature on the subject.

ELISABETH KÜBLER-ROSS

ON THE FEAR OF DYING

1   The ancient Hebrews regarded the body of a dead person as something unclean and not to be touched. The early American Indians talked about the evil spirits and shot arrows in the air to drive the spirits away. Many other cultures have rituals to take care of the "bad" dead person, and they all originate in this feeling of anger which still exists in all of us, though we dislike admitting it. The tradition of the tombstone may originate in this wish to keep the bad spirits deep down in the ground, and the pebbles that many mourners put on the grave are left-over symbols of the same wish. Though we call the firing of guns at military funerals a last salute, it is the same symbolic ritual as the Indian used when he shot his spears and arrows into the skies.

2   I give these examples to emphasize that man has not basically changed. Death is still a fearful, frightening happening, and the fear of death is a universal fear even if we think we have mastered it on many levels.

3   What has changed is our way of coping and dealing with death and dying and our dying patients.

4   Having been raised in a country in Europe where science is not so advanced, where modern techniques have just started to find their way into medicine, and where people still live as they did in this country half a century ago, I may have had an opportunity to study a part of the evolution of mankind in a shorter period.

5   I remember as a child the death of a farmer. He fell from a tree and was not expected to live. He asked simply to die at home, a wish that was granted without questioning. He called his daughters into the bedroom and spoke with each one of them alone for a few minutes. He arranged his affairs quietly, though he was in great pain, and distributed his belongings and his land, none of which was to be split until his wife should follow him in death. He also asked each of his children to share in the work, duties, and tasks that he had carried on until the time of the accident. He asked his friends to visit him once more, to bid good-bye to them. Although I was a small child at the time, he did not exclude me or my siblings. We were allowed to share in the preparations of the family just as we were permitted to grieve with them until he died. When he did die, he was left at home, in his own beloved home which he had built, and among his friends and neighbors who went to take a last look at him where he lay in the midst of flowers in the place he had lived in and loved so much. In that country today there is still no make-believe slumber room, no embalming, no false makeup to pretend sleep. Only the signs of very disfiguring illnesses are covered up with bandages and only infectious cases are removed from the home prior to the burial.

6   Why do I describe such "old-fashioned" customs? I think they are an indication of our acceptance of a fatal outcome, and they help the dying patient as well as his family to accept the loss of a loved one. If a patient is allowed to terminate his life in the familiar and beloved environment, it requires less adjustment for him. His own family knows him well enough to replace a sedative with a glass of his favorite wine; or the smell of a home-cooked soup may give him the appetite to sip a few spoons of fluid which, I think, is still more enjoyable than an infusion. I will not minimize the need for sedatives and infusions and realize full well from my own experience as a country doctor that they are sometimes life-saving and often unavoidable. But I also know that patience and familiar people and foods could replace many a bottle of intravenous fluids given for the simple reason that it fulfills the physiological need without involving too many people and/or individual nursing care.

7   The fact that children are allowed to stay at home where a fatality has stricken and are included in the talk, discussions, and fears gives them the feeling that they are not alone in the grief and gives them the comfort of shared responsibility and shared mourning. It prepares them gradually and helps them view death as part of life, an experience which may help them grow and mature.

8   This is in great contrast to a society in which death is viewed as taboo, discussion of it is regarded as morbid, and children are excluded with the presumption and pretext that it would be "too much" for them. They are then sent off to relatives, often accompanied with some unconvincing lies of "Mother has gone on a long trip" or other unbelievable stories. The child senses that something is wrong, and his distrust in adults will only multiply if other relatives add new variations of the story, avoid his questions or suspicions, shower him with gifts as a meager substitute for a loss he is not permitted to deal with. Sooner or later the child will become aware of the changed family situation and, depending on the age and personality of the child, will have an unresolved grief and regard this incident as a frightening, mysterious, in any case very traumatic experience with untrustworthy grownups, which he has no way to cope with.

9   We would think that our great emancipation, our knowledge of science and of man, has given us better ways and means to prepare ourselves and our families for this inevitable happening. Instead the days are gone when a man was allowed to die in peace and dignity in his own home.

10   The more we are making advancements in science, the more we seem to fear and deny the reality of death. How is this possible?

11   We use euphemisms, we make the dead look as if they were asleep, we ship the children off to protect them from the anxiety and turmoil around the house if the patient is fortunate enough to die at home, we don't allow children to visit their dying parents in the hospitals, we have long and controversial discussions about whether patients should be told the truth—a question that rarely arises when the dying person is tended by the family physician who has known him from delivery to death and who knows the weaknesses and strengths of each member of the family.

12   I think there are many reasons for this flight away from facing death calmly. One of the most important facts is that dying nowadays is more gruesome in many ways, namely, more lonely, mechanical, and dehumanized; at times it is even difficult to determine technically when the time of death has occurred.

13   Dying becomes lonely and impersonal because the patient is often taken out of his familiar environment and rushed to an emergency room. Whoever has been very sick and has required rest and comfort especially may recall his experience of being put on a stretcher and enduring the noise of the ambulance siren and hectic rush until the hospital gates open. Only those who have lived through this may appreciate the discomfort and cold necessity of such transportation which is only the beginning of a long ordeal—hard to endure when you are well, difficult to express in words when noise, light, bumps, and voices are all too much to put up with. It may well be that we might consider more the patient under the sheets and blankets and perhaps stop our well-meant efficiency and rush in order to hold the patient's hand, to smile, or to listen to a question. I include the trip to the hospital as the first episode in dying, as it is for many. I am putting it exaggeratedly in contrast to the sick man who is left at home—not to say that lives should not be saved if they can be saved by a hospitalization but to keep the focus on the patient's experience, his needs and his reactions.

14   When a patient is severely ill, he is often treated like a person with no right to an opinion. It is often someone else who makes the decision if and when and where a patient should be hospitalized. It would take so little to remember that the sick person too has feelings, has wishes and opinions, and has—most important of all—the right to be heard.

15   Well, our presumed patient has now reached the emergency room. He will be surrounded by busy nurses, orderlies, interns, residents, a lab technician perhaps who will take some blood, an electrocardiogram technician who takes the cardiogram. He may be moved to X-ray and he will overhear opinions of his condition and discussions and questions to members of the family. He slowly but surely is beginning to be treated like a thing. He is no longer a person. Decisions are made often without his opinion. If he tries to rebel he will be sedated and after hours of waiting and wondering whether he has the strength, he will be wheeled into the operating room or intensive treatment unit and become an object of great concern and great financial investment.

16   He may cry for rest, peace, and dignity, but he will get infusions, transfusions, a heart machine, or tracheotomy if necessary. He may want one single person to stop for one single minute so that he can ask one single question—but he will get a dozen people around the clock, all busily preoccupied with his heart rate, pulse, electrocardiogram or pulmonary functions, his secretions or excretions but not with him as a human being. He may wish to fight it all but it is going to be a useless fight since all this is done in the fight for his life, and if they can save his life they can consider the person afterwards. Those

who consider the person first may lose precious time to save his life! At least this seems to be the rationale or justification behind all this—or is it? Is the reason for this increasingly mechanical, depersonalized approach our own defensiveness? Is this approach our own way to cope with and repress the anxieties that a terminally or critically ill patient evokes in us? Is our concentration on equipment, on blood pressure our desperate attempt to deny the impending death which is so frightening and discomforting to us that we displace all our knowledge onto machines, since they are less close to us than the suffering face of another human being which would remind us once more of our lack of omnipotence, our own limits and failures, and last but not least perhaps our own mortality?

Questions for Review

1. What is the thesis of Kübler-Ross's essay? Does it appear in the essay? If so, where? How does she develop (or support) her thesis?
2. Divide the essay into beginning, middle, and end. What rhetorical and/or stylistic devices help form these divisions?
3. What audience might Kübler-Ross be writing for? What knowledge does she assume her audience already has about this topic? Is this audience likely to see this as a controversial topic? Are there any indications in her text that Kübler-Ross thinks readers may take an opposing point of view?
4. What did you know about this subject before reading Kübler-Ross's essay? What information in her essay was particularly interesting to you? Were you surprised by any of it? If so, what? Did you find yourself disagreeing with Kübler-Ross on any points? What were they?
5. Kübler-Ross's essay has become a classic. Of course, since it was written thirty years ago, there have been many changes in the treatment of death and of dying in the United States. What specific changes can you cite in today's practices compared with the practices described by Kübler-Ross? What things have remained essentially the same?

In our second sample essay, "Gender Gap in Cyberspace," Deborah Tannen, a well-known linguist and commentator on the role of language in issues of gender, looks at ways in which men and women differ in their use of language in cyberspace.

DEBORAH TANNEN

GENDER GAP IN CYBERSPACE

1   I was a computer pioneer, but I'm still something of a novice. That paradox is telling.

2   I was the second person on my block to get a computer. The first was my colleague, Ralph. It was 1980. Ralph got a Radio Shack TRS-80; I got a used Apple II+. He helped

me get started and went on to become a maven, reading computer magazines, hungering for new technology he read about, and buying and mastering it as quickly as he could afford. I hung on to old equipment far too long because I dislike giving up what I'm used to, fear making the wrong decision about what to buy and resent the time it takes to install and learn a new system.

3   My first Apple came with videogames; I gave them away. Playing games on the computer didn't interest me. If I had free time I'd spend it talking on the telephone to friends.

4   Ralph got hooked. His wife was often annoyed by the hours he spent at his computer and the money he spent upgrading it. My marriage had no such strains—until I discovered e-mail. Then I got hooked. E-mail draws me the same way the phone does: it's a souped-up conversation.

5   E-mail deepened my friendship with Ralph. Though his office was next to mine, we rarely had extended conversations because he is shy. Face to face he mumbled so, I could barely tell he was speaking. But when we both got on e-mail, I started receiving long, self-revealing messages; we poured our hearts out to each other. A friend discovered that e-mail opened up that kind of communication with her father. He would never talk much on the phone (as her mother would), but they have become close since they both got on line.

6   Why, I wondered, would some men find it easier to open up on e-mail? It's a combination of the technology (which they enjoy) and the obliqueness of the written word, just as many men will reveal feelings in dribs and drabs while riding in the car or doing something, which they'd never talk about sitting face to face. It's too intense, too bearing-down on them, and once you start you have to keep going. With a computer in between, it's safer.

7   It was on e-mail, in fact, that I described to Ralph how boys in groups often struggle to get the upper hand whereas girls tend to maintain an appearance of cooperation. And he pointed out that this explained why boys are more likely to be captivated by computers than girls are. Boys are typically motivated by a social structure that says if you don't dominate you will be dominated. Computers, by their nature, balk; you type a perfectly appropriate command and it refuses to do what it should. Many boys and men are incited by this defiance: "I'm going to whip this into line and teach it who's boss! I'll get it to do what I say!" (and if they work hard enough, they always can). Girls and women are more likely to respond, "This thing won't cooperate. Get it away from me!"

8   Although no one wants to think of herself as "typical"—how much nicer to be sui generis—my relationship to my computer is—gulp—fairly typical for a woman. Most women (with plenty of exceptions) aren't excited by tinkering with the technology, grappling with the challenge of eliminating bugs or getting the biggest and best computer. These dynamics appeal to many men's interest in making sure they're on the top side of the inevitable who's-up-who's-down struggle that life is for them. E-mail appeals to my view of life as a contest for connections to others. When I see that I have 15 messages I feel loved.

9   I once posted a technical question on a computer network for linguists and was flooded with long dispositions, some pages long. I was staggered by the generosity and the expertise, but wondered where these guys found the time—and why all the answers I got were from men.

10   Like coed classrooms and meetings, discussions on e-mail networks tend to be dominated by male voices, unless they're specifically women-only, like single-sex schools. On line, women don't have to worry about getting the floor (you just send a message when you feel like it), but, according to linguists Susan Herring and Laurel Sutton, who have studied this, they have the usual problems of having their messages ignored or attacked. The anonymity of public networks frees a small number of men to

send long, vituperative, sarcastic messages that many other men either can tolerate or actually enjoy, but turn most women off.

11   The anonymity of networks leads to another sad part of the e-mail story: there are men who deluge women with questions about their appearance and invitations to sex. On college campuses, as soon as women students log on, they are bombarded by references to sex, like going to work and finding pornographic posters adorning the walls.

12   Taking time: Most women want one thing from a computer—to work. This is significant counterevidence to the claim that men want to focus on information while women are interested in rapport. That claim I found was often true in casual conversation, in which there is no particular information to be conveyed. But with computers, it is often women who are more focused on information, because they don't respond to the challenge of getting equipment to submit.

13   Once I had learned the basics, my interest in computers waned. I use it to write books (though I never mastered having it do bibliographies or tables of contents) and write checks (but not balance my checkbook). Much as I'd like to use it to do more, I begrudge the time it would take to learn.

14   Ralph's computer expertise costs him a lot of time. Chivalry requires that he rescue novices in need, and he is called upon by damsel novices far more often than knaves. More men would rather study the instruction booklet than ask directions, as it were, from another person. "When I do help men," Ralph wrote (on e-mail, of course), "they want to be more involved. I once installed a hard drive for a guy, and he wanted to be there with me, wielding the screwdriver and giving his own advice where he could." Women, he finds, usually are not interested in what he's doing; they just want him to get the computer to the point where they can do what they want.

15   Which pretty much explains how I managed to be a pioneer without becoming an expert.

Questions for Review

1. What is the thesis of Tannen's essay? Does it appear in the essay? If so, where? How does she develop (or support) her thesis?

2. Divide the essay into beginning, middle, and end. What rhetorical and/or stylistic devices help form these divisions?

3. What audience might Tannen's essay be written for? What knowledge, if any, does Tannen assume her audience already has about this topic? Are there any indications in her text that Tannen thinks readers may take an opposing point of view?

4. What did you know about this subject before reading Tannen's essay? What information in her essay did you find particularly interesting? Were you surprised by any of it? If so, what? Did you find yourself disagreeing with Tannen on any points? If so, what were they?

In our next essay, well-known essayist Michael Kinsley offers his observations on the ways in which modern information technology has increased the freedoms of people all over the world.

MICHAEL KINSLEY

ORWELL GOT IT WRONG

1   George Orwell's famous novel *1984* (written in 1948) opens with its hero, Winston Smith, returning to his squalid apartment. Attached to a wall is a "telescreen," described as "an oblong metal plaque like a dulled mirror." It is in essence a two-way television, which watches Smith's every movement while barking government propaganda at him. "Big Brother Is Watching You" is the state's slogan.

2   This was Orwell's vision of the future: technology would become the tool of totalitarian dictatorship. TV and computers would make Big Brother possible.

3   Fortunately, Orwell got it exactly wrong. The high-tech devices that have invaded our lives—home computers, fax machines, VCRs and now the Internet—have *expanded* human freedom.

4   On the Redmond, Wash. campus of the Microsoft Corporation, where I work these days, there is not much doubt that technology is a wonderful thing. It has made many of the software programmers, wandering the halls in jeans and T-shirts, rich men and women while still in their 20s or 30s.

5   But more than that: people in Cyberworld—shorthand for the culture of computers and telecommunications—passionately believe that today's technology revolution is also a revolutionary advance for human liberty. They're right. But most of them also don't remember a time when computers, especially, were thought to be a menace to freedom.

6   Orwell was far from the only doubter of the post–World War II period. During the 1950s and '60s many other seers worried that ever-bigger computers would lead to centralization of information and power. The menace of giant computers was a major theme of popular culture.

7   Then around 1980, computers suddenly got small. The desktop personal computer (PC) came to market and gave enormous power to the individual. Tiny businesses could do what only large ones could before. Even within big businesses, employees had much more autonomy. A symbolic development was the arrival of inexpensive tax-preparation software. Today you can use your home PC to do your income tax quickly and accurately, while the Internal Revenue Service still can't get its own giant computers to work right.

8   INFORMATION POWER   Even more important for political freedom was another development of the 1980s: the fax machine. It is no coincidence that communism collapsed in 1989 just as the fax machine was becoming widespread and fairly inexpensive. The fax made it impossible for the state to control the spread of information. News from outside couldn't be kept out, and information about conditions inside couldn't be kept in. Government lies were exposed, and the truth spread.

9   "Workers of the World, Fax!" was the headline of a *Washington Post* article in late 1990 during the waning days of the Cold War. The author, Michael Dobbs, reported that correspondents in the Soviet Union had gone from having too little information to too much. It was a "revolution by fax," he wrote, which "has made a mockery of attempts by Communist Party bureaucrats to control the flow of news."

10   Then in the 1990s, along came the Internet—and any government's ability to control information was destroyed for good. At the same time, the Internet empowered individuals, compared with big corporations, even more dramatically than had the PC.

11   Now, there's nothing necessarily wrong with big corporations! I work at one. My job at Microsoft is publishing an on-line magazine called *Slate* (www.slate.com on the Internet). By publishing on-line, we have no paper costs, no printing costs, no postage

costs. When we "go to press," our articles are instantly available to anyone with a computer and a modem anywhere in the world.

12   These same people can also use a computer and modem to publish on-line themselves. All it takes is a bit of software and $20 a month or so for Internet access.

13   The press critic A. J. Liebling once remarked sarcastically, "Freedom of the press is guaranteed only to those who own one." Today, thanks to the Internet, almost anyone can, in effect, own a printing press capable of reaching more people than William Randolph Hearst could in his heyday.

14   Meanwhile, the Internet mocks government efforts to control information. *The New York Times* reported last December that Serbian President Slobodan Milosevic—no lover of freedom—was trying to shut down the independent press but was utterly thwarted by the Internet. Serbian journalists and dissidents set up their own Web sites to tell their story both to fellow Serbs and the outside world. And any Serb with Internet access can call up the Web sites of the *New York Times, Reader's Digest* or *Slate* almost as easily as citizens of the freest countries.

15   A government can try to restrict its citizens' access to the Internet, as China is trying. But it will probably fail. For even if it could deny access to computers and modems, such a success would be too costly, since these tools are crucial to economic growth.

16   TOUGH TRADE-OFF   It's true that the democracy of information can be a mixed blessing. Nothing about the Internet guarantees that the information it spreads so easily is true. In fact, the Internet is a caldron of implausible rumors and conspiracy theories, all zapping around the world at the speed of light.

17   More troubling, sexually explicit material can be disseminated on the Internet just as easily and widely as information about political oppression in Serbia. And many people want to stop that, mainly because of children.

18   This year the Supreme Court will rule on the constitutionality of the federal Communications Decency Act, which forbids disseminating "patently offensive" sexual material through computer networks. The dilemma is that laws which make smut harder for children to obtain make it harder for adults as well. Easing those laws increases freedom for adults but reduces protection for children.

19   To tip my own hand, I'm with those who think the decency law is unconstitutional censorship. But honesty requires admitting there's a cost.

20   On balance, most people would concede that the advantages of today's technologies, including the Internet, outweigh the disadvantages. Certainly our freedom has been enhanced on the everyday personal level. (Remember the time before VCRs when you had to watch a TV show or a movie when *they* wanted you to?)

21   On the more profound political level, is there anyone who thinks the world would be a freer place if computers, fax machines and the Internet didn't exist?

22   This is one that Orwell really did get wrong.

Questions for Review

1. What is the thesis of Kinsley's essay? Does it appear in the essay? If so, where? How does he develop (or support) his thesis?

2. Divide the essay into beginning, middle, and end. What rhetorical and/or stylistic devices help form these divisions?
3. What audience might Kinsley's essay be written for? What knowledge, if any, does Kinsley assume his audience already has about this topic? Are there any indications in his text that Kinsley thinks readers may take an opposing point of view?
4. What did you know about this subject before reading Kinsley's essay? What information in his essay did you find particularly interesting? Were you surprised by any of it? If so, what? Did you find yourself disagreeing with Kinsley on any points? If so, what were they?

In our fourth essay, novelist Gloria Naylor explains what the word "nigger" meant to her as a child and reflects on the ways in which words come to have the power to inflict pain.

GLORIA NAYLOR

MOMMY, WHAT DOES "NIGGER" MEAN?

1   Language is the subject. It is the written form with which I've managed to keep the wolf away from the door and, in diaries, to keep my sanity. In spite of this, I consider the written word inferior to the spoken, and much of the frustration experienced by novelists is the awareness that whatever we manage to capture in even the most transcendent passages falls far short of the richness of life. Dialogue achieves its power in the dynamics of a fleeting moment of sight, sound, smell and touch.

2   I'm not going to enter the debate here about whether it is language that shapes reality or vice versa. That battle is doomed to be waged whenever we seek intermittent reprieve from the chicken and egg dispute. I will simply take the position that the spoken word, like the written word, amounts to a nonsensical arrangement of sounds or letters without a consensus that assigns "meaning." And building from the meanings of what we hear, we order reality. Words themselves are innocuous; it is the consensus that gives them true power.

3   I remember the first time I heard the word "nigger." In my third-grade class, our math tests were being passed down the rows, and as I handed the papers to a little boy in back of me, I remarked that once again he had received a much lower mark than I did. He snatched his test from me and spit out that word. Had he called me a nymphomaniac or a necrophiliac, I couldn't have been more puzzled. I didn't know what a nigger was, but I knew that whatever it meant, it was something he shouldn't have called me. This was verified when I raised my hand, and in a loud voice repeated what he had said and watched the teacher scold him for saying a "bad" word. I was later to go home and ask the inevitable question that every black parent must face—"Mommy, what does 'nigger' mean?"

4   And what exactly did it mean? Thinking back, I realize that this could not have been the first time the word was used in my presence. I was part of a large extended family that had migrated from the rural South after World War II and formed a close-knit network that gravitated around my maternal grandparents. Their ground-floor apartment in one of the

buildings they owned in Harlem was a weekend mecca for my immediate family, along with countless aunts, uncles and cousins who brought along assorted friends. It was a bustling and open house with assorted neighbors and tenants popping in and out to exchange bits of gossip, pick up an old quarrel or referee the ongoing checkers game in which my grandmother cheated shamelessly. They were all there to let down their hair and put up their feet after a week of labor in the factories, laundries and shipyards of New York.

5   Amid the clamor, which could reach deafening proportions—two or three conversations going on simultaneously, punctuated by the sound of a baby's crying somewhere in the back rooms or out on the street—there was still a rigid set of rules about what was said and how. Older children were sent out of the living room when it was time to get into the juicy details about "you-know-who" up on the third floor who had gone and gotten herself "p-r-e-g-n-a-n-t!" But my parents, knowing that I could spell well beyond my years, always demanded that I follow the others out to play. Beyond sexual misconduct and death, everything else was considered harmless for our young ears. And so among the anecdotes of the triumphs and disappointments in the various workings of their lives, the word "nigger" was used in my presence, but it was set within contexts and inflections that caused it to register in my mind as something else.

6   In the singular, the word was always applied to a man who had distinguished himself in some situation that brought their approval for his strength, intelligence or drive:

7   "Did Johnny really do that?"

8   "I'm telling you, that nigger pulled in $6,000 of overtime last year. Said he got enough for a down payment on a house."

9   When used with a possessive adjective by a woman—"my nigger"—it became a term of endearment for husband or boyfriend. But it could be more than just a term applied to a man. In their mouths it became the pure essence of manhood—a disembodied force that channeled their past history of struggle and present survival against the odds into a victorious statement of being: "Yeah, that old foreman found out quick enough—you don't mess with a nigger."

10   In the plural, it became a description of some group within the community that had overstepped the bounds of decency as my family defined it: Parents who neglected their children, a drunken couple who fought in public, people who simply refused to look for work, those with excessively dirty mouths or unkempt households were all "trifling niggers." This particular circle could forgive hard times, unemployment, the occasional bout of depression—they had gone through all of that themselves—but the unforgivable sin was lack of self-respect.

11   A woman could never be a "nigger" in the singular, with its connotation of confirming worth. The noun "girl" was its closest equivalent in that sense, but only when used in direct address and regardless of the gender doing the addressing. "Girl" was a token of respect for a woman. The one-syllable word was drawn out to sound like three in recognition of the extra ounce of wit, nerve or daring that the woman had shown in the situation under discussion.

12   "G-i-r-l, stop. You mean you said that to his face?"

13   But if the word was used in a third-person reference or shortened so that it almost snapped out of the mouth, it always involved some element of communal disapproval. And age became an important factor in these exchanges. It was only between individuals of the same generation or from an older person to a younger (but never the other way around) that "girl" would be considered a compliment.

14   I don't agree with the argument that use of the word "nigger" at this social stratum of the black community was an internalization of racism. The dynamics were the exact opposite: the people in my grandmother's living room took a word that whites used to signify worthlessness or degradation and rendered it impotent. Gathering there

together, they transformed "nigger" to signify the varied and complex human beings they knew themselves to be. If the word was to disappear totally from the mouths of even the most liberal of white society, no one in that room was naive enough to believe it would disappear from white minds. Meeting the word head-on, they proved it had absolutely nothing to do with the way they were determined to live their lives.

15   So there must have been dozens of times that the word "nigger" was spoken in front of me before I reached the third grade. But I didn't "hear" it until it was said by a small pair of lips that had already learned it could be a way to humiliate me. That was the word I went home and asked my mother about. And since she knew that I had to grow up in America, she took me in her lap and explained.

Questions for Review

1. What is the thesis of Naylor's essay? Does it appear in the essay? If so, where? How does she develop (or support) her thesis?
2. Divide the essay into beginning, middle, and end. What rhetorical and/or stylistic devices help form these divisions?
3. What audience might Naylor's essay be written for? What knowledge, if any, does Naylor assume her audience already has about this topic? Is this audience likely to see this as a controversial topic? Are there any indications in her text that Naylor thinks readers may take an opposing point of view?
4. What did you know about this subject before reading Naylor's essay? What information in her essay did you find particularly interesting? Were you surprised by any of it? If so, what? Did you find yourself disagreeing with Naylor on any points? If so, what were they?

In our fifth essay, "Rap's Embrace of 'Nigger' Fires Bitter Debate," Michel Marriott explains how the word "nigger" is currently being used in the rap culture and discusses the issues surrounding its use by both blacks and whites.

MICHEL MARRIOTT

RAP'S EMBRACE OF "NIGGER" FIRES BITTER DEBATE

1   One of America's oldest and most searing epithets—"nigger"—is flooding into the nation's popular culture, giving rise to a bitter debate among blacks about its historically ugly power and its increasingly open use in an integrated society.

2   Whether thoughtlessly or by design, large numbers of a post–civil rights generation of blacks have turned to a conspicuous use of "nigger" just as they have gained considerable cultural influence through rap music and related genres.

3   Some blacks, mostly young people, argue that their open use of the word will eventually demystify it, strip it of its racist meaning. They liken it to the way some homosexuals have started referring to themselves as "queers" in a defiant slap at an old slur.

4   But other blacks—most of them older—say that "nigger," no matter who uses it, is such a hideous pejorative that it should be stricken from the national vocabulary. At a time when they perceive a deepening racial estrangement, they say its popular use can only make bigotry more socially acceptable.

5   "Nigger," of course, has long been an element of black vernacular, almost an honorific of the streets, strictly, and still, off limits to whites. But as the word has found voice in black music, dance and film, the role of black culture in popular culture has driven it into the mainstream.

6   For the last several years, rap artists have increasingly used "nigger" in their lyrics, repackaging it and selling it not just to their own inner-city neighborhoods but to the largely white suburbs. In his song "Straight Up Nigga," Ice-T raps, "I'm a nigga in America, and that much I flaunt," and indeed, a large portion of his record sales are in white America.

7   In movies and on television, too, "nigger" is heard with unprecedented regularity these days. In "Trespass," a newly released major-studio film about an inner-city treasure hunt, black rappers portraying gang members call one another "nigger" almost as often as they call one another by their names.

8   And every Friday at midnight, Home Box Office televises "Russell Simmons' Def Comedy Jam," a half-hour featuring many black, cutting-edge comedians who frequently use "nigger" in their acts.

9   Sometimes, the use of the word is simply a flat-out repetition of the street vernacular. In rap and hip-hop music, a genre in which millions of its listeners adopt the artists' style and language, "nigger" is virtually interchangeable with words like "guy," "man" or "brother."

10   But often it is a discussion of the word's various uses and meanings in society, black or white. Not only is black popular culture the focus of the debate, it is often the medium for it.

"MAKES MY TEETH WHITE"

11   Paul Mooney, a veteran black stand-up comic and writer, recently released a comedy tape titled "Race." On the tape, which includes routines called "Nigger Vampire," "1-900-Blame-a-Nigger," "Niggerstein," "Nigger Raisins" and "Nigger History," Mr. Mooney explains why he uses the word so often.

12   "I say nigger all the time," he said. "I say nigger 100 times every morning. It makes my teeth white. Nigger-nigger-nigger-nigger-nigger-nigger-nigger-nigger-nigger. I say it. You think, 'What a small white world.' "

13   Blacks who say they should use the word more openly maintain that its casual use, especially in the company of whites, will shift the word's context and strip "nigger" of its ability to hurt. That is precisely what blacks have been doing for years, say linguists who study black vernacular. By using the word strictly among themselves, the linguists say, they change its context and in doing so dull its edge whenever whites use it.

14   Kris Parker, a leading rap artist known as KRS-One, predicts that through black culture's ability to affect popular American culture through the electronic media, "nigger" will be deracialized by its broader use and become just another word.

15   "In another 5 to 10 years, you're going to see youth in elementary school spelling it out in their vocabulary tests," he said. "It's going to be that accepted by the society."

16   But other blacks, especially members of the generation for whom Malcolm X and the Rev. Dr. Martin Luther King Jr. were living heroes, say no one should ever be permitted to forget what "nigger" has meant, and still means, in America.

17   "That term encapsulates so much of the indignities forced on our people," said the Rev. Benjamin F. Chavis, Jr., a longtime civil-rights leader who is executive director of the United Church of Christ Commission for Racial Justice. "That term made us less than human, and that is why we must reject the usage of that term."

18   "We cannot let that term be trivialized," he said. "We cannot let that term be taken out of its historical context."

19   Some blacks say they are so traumatized by the oppressive legacy of "nigger," that they cannot even bring themselves to say the word. Instead, they choose linguistic dodges like "the N-word" or simply spelling the word out. Other blacks say they are "ambivalent" about the growing public use of "nigger."

20   "Does it signal a new progressive step forward toward a new level of understanding or a regressive step back into self-hate?" asked Christopher Cathcart, a black 29-year-old public relations specialist in New York. "I fear it is the latter."

21   Throughout history, nearly all minority groups have found themselves branded by hateful terms. Early in the century, such seemingly innocent words as "Irish" and "Jew" were considered pejoratives, said Edward Bendix, a professor of linguistic anthropology at the Graduate Center of the City University of New York.

22   In time the groups have used some of the same terms as passwords to the particular groups, which is what happened with "nigger" in the black vernacular. Indeed, Bob Guccione, Jr., editor and publisher of the popular music magazine, *Spin*— which reports extensively on the rap music scene—said that while whites are very reluctant to use "nigger" because it has "such an incredible weight of ugliness to it," blacks often use it in the presence of whites as a verbal demarcation point.

23   "In a sense, It empowers the black community in the white mainstream," said Mr. Guccione, who is white. "They can use a very powerful word like a passkey and whites dare not, or should not, use it."

24   But seldom has a word like "nigger" been pushed into the mainstream while its negative connotations exist, said Dr. Robin Lakoff, a social linguist and author of the book *Talking Power* (Basic Books, 1990). "That's harder with 'nigger,' especially with so many people around who still use it in its racist meaning," said Dr. Lakoff, a professor of linguistics at the University of California at Berkeley.

25   Many of the blacks who defend their open use of the word acknowledge that whites still cannot publicly say "nigger" without stirring up old black-white antagonisms.

26   "Race in America is like herpes because you can never get rid of it," said James Bernard, who is black and senior editor of *The Source,* a magazine that covers the rap and hip-hop scene. "There is still a line."

"A HORRENDOUS WORD"

27   The magazine's multiracial staff recently published a story about Spike Lee and the basketball star Charles Barkley under a headline "NINETIES NIGGERS." Kris Parker, the rapper, said such uses represent progress. But to the white Chicago writer Studs Terkel, whose latest book, *Race* (The New Press, 1992), is a series of interviews with blacks and whites about race in America, the increased use of "nigger" represents anything but progress.

28   "It is a horrendous word," he said, adding that the new permissiveness may have more to do with the "wink and nod" of the Reagan-Bush years of dismantling civil rights gains than with rap artists naming themselves N.W.A., for Niggas With an Attitude.

29　　　Examples abound that "nigger" has not lost its wounding power when used by whites. Whether scratched into a restroom stall or scrawled on the house of a black family in a white neighborhood, "nigger" remains a graffito of hate—the most commonly heard epithet used during anti-black crimes, the authorities say.

30　　　When a black man from New Jersey was abducted and set ablaze by three white men in Florida on New Year's Day, one of the first things they said to him, according to the victim's mother, was "nigger."

BLURRING A LINE

31　　　The changing uses of the word have made for some curious situations on the white side of an increasingly blurred line.

32　　　Alex T. Noble, a white public relations intern in New York, said he has white friends who use "nigger" with one another as a term of endearment. Mr. Noble, who works with rappers, said when a black friend calls him a "nigger," "I feel flattered, like I'm part of something."

33　　　But, he adds, he is extremely reluctant to return the salutation.

34　　　"As a white person I would never go up to a black person and say, 'Yo, nigger,' " Mr. Noble said. "I think it's hard to outrun the legacy of oppression that word signifies. Anytime a white person says that word it is troublesome."

35　　　The attempts to demystify "nigger" are by no means new. One of the more publicized cases came in the early 1970's, when Richard Pryor used "nigger" in his standup comedy act with the express purpose of defanging its racist bite. He titled his seminal comedy album in 1974 "That Nigger's Crazy." Some years later, however, after a trip to Africa, Mr. Pryor told audiences he would never use the word again as a performer. While abroad, he said, he saw black people running governments and businesses. And in a moment of epiphany, he said he realized that he did not see any "niggers."

Questions for Review

1. What is the thesis of Marriott's essay? Does it appear in the essay? If so, where? How does he develop (or support) his thesis?

2. Divide the essay into beginning, middle, and end. What rhetorical and/or stylistic devices help form these divisions?

3. What audience might Marriott's essay be written for? What knowledge, if any, does Marriott assume his audience already has about this topic? Is this audience likely to see this as a controversial topic? Are there any indications in his text that Marriott thinks readers may take an opposing point of view?

4. What did you know about this subject before reading Marriott's essay? What information in his essay did you find particularly interesting? Were you surprised by any of it? If so, what? Did you find yourself disagreeing with Marriott on any points? If so, what were they?

The last two essays in this section were written by our students. In the first of these, Kelly McGinley, a first-year writing student at New Mexico State University (NMSU), explains the various investing options available in the stock market to young investors.

KELLY MCGINLEY

INVESTING IN YOUR FUTURE

1   An inevitable conversation topic of most college students and graduates deals with money or lack of: "My funds are running low." "When is mom's check getting in?" "Did you know Las Cruces Biologicals will give $150 every month in exchange for plasma?" The simple fact that money is on their minds as often as it is should symbolize a flashing neon sign above their heads constantly reminding them of the importance of efficient money management, no matter how large or small the sum. Realizing that it is possible for young people to safely invest in the stock market and earn substantially better interest rates than they would by placing all their money in a bank will be the deciding factor between financially secure middle aged adults and those who are only just learning of the potential their money holds. The simplicity of it all will be a slap in the face to those who realize what they "could have, would have, and should have" done twenty years ago in order to prevent the feelings of stress and heartache associated with worries about financial security.

2   There are many different ways you can store your money, ranging from piggy banks and sock drawers to bank vaults and the stock market. While using a piggy bank method to store a life savings is a very ignorant choice, an equally ignorant choice would be to ignore the myriad of investment options, and instead place all of your money in a bank. Do not misunderstand me, options offered by banks are numerous and in some situations a necessity. For instance, checking and savings accounts give you easy access to your money while earning you very small amounts of interest on your money. They serve their purpose; however, they should never be used to hold large sums of money. To achieve higher interest on your money at the bank, you would usually deal with a money market account or a Certificate of Deposit (CD). A money market account is almost identical to a savings account but generally pays a better rate of interest. In simple terms, a CD allows you to lend your money to the bank for a set term (usually between six months and ten years). Generally, the longer you lock your money in (that is, the longer time you commit to leaving your money in the bank), the higher interest rate you receive. However, you must remember that you cannot take your money out of the CD before the term has matured without being penalized. The chart below shows the various interest rates you can earn on checking accounts and CD's (of varying lengths) at a bank.

Information on Dividend Rates from Fort Bliss Federal Credit Union

Type of Account	Dividend Rate
Savings/Share Account	3.75%
Checking/Share Draft Account	
(Average daily balance < $650)	0.00%
(Average daily balance of $651–$999)	2.25%
(Average daily balance > $1,000)	2.50%

Money Market Account	5.00%
Individual Retirement Account	4.50%
Share Certificates	
91 day	4.40%
6 month	4.90%
1 year	5.30%
2 year	5.60%
3 year	5.70%
4 year	5.80%
5 year	6.00%

But how do these rates compare with what you could earn in the stock market? To find the answer to that question, I compared the rates offered by Fort Bliss to rates supplied by the Merrill Lynch Quarterly Reports. The various rates in the Merrill Lynch Report ranged from 4.00% and 12.00%, but averaged between 5.00% and 9.00%. Most people keep their money in a savings account where it earns approximately 3.75%, when it could be earning an average of 5.00% and probably more (according to the Merrill Lynch Quarterly Report). Currently, you would have to leave your money in a CD for five years in order to earn 6.00% interest; in the stock market, you could make 6.00% interest on a chosen stock and have the option of selling your stocks any time you need to. When you own a stock, you have actually bought a share of ownership in a particular company. Generally, as the economy grows, the company grows, which means the company earns greater profit, thus raising the stock price. This idea is simple, but the challenge comes when researching and choosing a company that will grow steadily vs. a company whose performance will decline. This is where the risk of investing in the market enters the picture. Some companies are very high risk and others are more stable: By doing extensive research on a company as well as talking to a more knowledgeable party, you can personalize a portfolio of stocks to suit your goals and limits. Because banks insure holdings in an account up to $100,000, banks are seen as the safest place to put money. However, you don't want to compromise your money's potential earnings entirely for the security offered by banks.

3   Once you decide to invest in stocks, you will need to spend some time studying the market. The market offers more options for investing than the bank. The first option you should look into is mutual funds. When you invest in a mutual fund, you place your money in the hands of a professional portfolio manager equipped with a research team who then invest the money of many investors. There seems to be an endless sea of mutual funds to choose from. A second option is to buy individual stocks. You can buy stock in almost any company, from Coca-Cola and Wrigley's gum to the gas and oil companies, to computer and technology companies, to Wal-Mart and Kmart. There are varying degrees of risk involved in investing with individual stocks. For example, Coca-Cola involves a lot less risk than would a computer or technology related company. When investing in the market, you should research a company, talk to a broker and decide how muck risk you are willing and able to take. As a young person, new to the market, you will probably want to invest the majority of your money in a "low risk" stable company or mutual fund. If you have the ability to take a slightly higher risk in the market, you might lean a little more toward a computer or technological company. By placing your money in a company with potential you are not just putting money in a savings account but instead adding to the possibilities your future holds. But remember to keep long term growth in mind. By this I mean you should be willing to put money in a stock or mutual fund and let it sit. You can keep a watchful eye on it, but you should not be obsessive. If you are, the constant fluctuation associated with the market will drive you crazy.

4   A few years ago, my grandfather talked with me about the stock market and took me to seminars held by Merrill Lynch. These seminars focused solely on investment education. The guest speakers spoke of different companies and used reports and graphs as teaching aids. My grandfather also introduced me to a broker by the name of John Jacobs who works for him through Merrill Lynch. Not knowing entirely what to expect, I set up an appointment with him to talk about the possibility of investing. Keep in mind I was a sixteen-year-old girl going to talk with a businessman about investing in the stock market. He sat at his desk and first talked to me about stock options he had researched and felt would benefit me as a young investor; then he proceeded to answer questions I had, and finally, we sat there and talked about our lives. I have to admit at first I felt foolish walking into this large business with a check for $500 knowing most investors invest thousands of dollars at a time. However, after talking with John, I was instantly set at ease and was able to stand confidently behind my desire to learn more about the stock market.

5   Since that first meeting, John has become my investment advisor and friend, but also my mentor. He helped me to invest in a company called USX Marathon which after three years has earned 7.50% interest, as well as a mutual growth fund which has earned 6.30% interest. This is not to say all my choices have ended up with high interest rates. One company to date has earned approximately 4.00% interest, and while that is nothing grand, it is slightly higher than what I would be making in my savings account. With every year, I am saving and investing one hundred dollars here and fifty dollars there, thus expanding personal knowledge and money potential.

6   I know, of course, that it is not easy to save money for investing in college, but it is possible. By making small changes in your lifestyle (eat out one day less per week) or using the money from one week's worth of summer employment, you can save a small sum, which is enough to get your portfolio started. What I am trying to say is that every person has the capability of saving money. Where there is a will, there is a way. Usually the only thing stopping us is the excuses we conjure up. Once you put that money into a portfolio, consider it there for the long term. Not only will it have the possibility of making more money for you, but by not having the money sitting in your savings account, you may be less likely to want to spend it.

7   I believe it is beneficial to invest in the stock market; however I do not think it is wise to invest every penny earned into the market. It is good to try new things but remember to keep a secure base. The security a bank offers serves a purpose as well as the slightly riskier stock market. By utilizing all available options, young investors can make small sums of money reach the highest potential. Upon reaching middle age, the individual who invested early and intelligently will not only learn the importance of her decision, but also will have more knowledge and better control of her financial future.

# Questions for Review

1. What is the thesis of Kelly's essay? Does it appear in the essay? If so, where? How does she develop (or support) her thesis?
2. Divide the essay into beginning, middle, and end. What rhetorical and/or stylistic devices help form these divisions?

3. What audience might Kelly's essay be written for? What knowledge, if any, does Kelly assume her audience already has about this topic? Is this audience likely to see this as a controversial topic? Are there any indications in her text that Kelly thinks readers may take an opposing point of view?
4. What did you know about this subject before reading Kelly's essay? What information in her essay did you find particularly interesting? Were you surprised by any of it? If so, what? Did you find yourself disagreeing with Kelly on any points? If so, what were they?

Our final essay, "The Middleton Inn: An Architectural Triumph," was written by Joshua Morris. Although he was a student in Ron's first-year writing course at UNC–Charlotte, this essay was actually written as an assignment for a sophomore course in Joshua's major, architecture.

JOSHUA MORRIS

THE MIDDLETON INN: AN ARCHITECTURAL TRIUMPH

Architecture has graver ends; capable of the sublime, it impresses the most brutal instincts by its objectivity; it calls into play the highest faculties by its very abstraction.

Le Corbusier

1   Architecture has been called the mother of the arts. Born of the basic human need for shelter, architecture has steadily evolved through time. Architecture is more than just where one sleeps, or what keeps one dry and warm; it is humankind's way of negotiating with the earth and the heavens. It is the most powerful expression, capable of stating the profound and the obvious in one subtle gesture, for the primary purpose of architecture is to provide shelter, but it also supplies humans' need for balance by introducing such oppositional themes as "horizontal/vertical, monolithic/articulated, solid/void, static/dynamic, open/closed, inside/outside, architecture/nature, [and] public/private" (McCarter 288).

2   While these and many other themes are involved in architecture, we can center our discussion of this art on three interlocking and interrelated parts: form, space, and site. The effect that form, space, and site have on the finished product can be easily identified in any number of works, a particularly compelling example being Middleton Inn, SC.

3   As a general principle, we can say that form grows from the site, and the resulting form in turn creates space. At Middleton Inn, the architect, W. G. Clark, looked to the site for inspiration. The facts that the inn is on a river, adjacent to a colonial rice plantation, and near Charleston all have a profound impact on what the architect chose to design. The inn takes full advantage of its site, capturing the river front in its elegantly simple, square windows. The L-shape plan frames a natural void in the landscape, artfully creating an implied courtyard, much in the same language that Middleton Plantation's formal gardens do, by literally framing the landscape with a structure, be it building, tree or hedge. Furthermore, the design of the inn echoes the architecture of

the city of Charleston in its structural language (which builds on the contrast between public and private) as well as in details such as the short, round chimney stacks.

4   Still, the importance of the site cannot be realized without the meaning communicated by form and space. The geometric forms of the inn activate both the landscape and the space within which that landscape is situated. It is clear that this inn is designed specifically with this site in mind. This is not to say that the inn could not be placed anywhere and still remain usable, or beautiful. It does mean, though, that the inn's form was extrapolated from that unique combination of factors.

5   Just as the site inspires form, form clarifies and explains architectural space. At Middleton, Clark utilizes simple geometric figures in his design; the cubes which create the framing element of the plan are pure in manifestation. By placing the pure forms on the organic landscape, Clark creates a visual tension between the perfect and the imperfect and thereby sounds a theme for the rest of the design, one in which there will be tension between the liberation of the ideal of pure form and the limits of an individual site. This theme is sounded in a different key with the interplay between public and private space. The enclosed service spaces are made of solid masonry construct; the spaces designed for those being served are open to the light and space outside. The openness of the structure pulls the outside in, and the architect emphasizes this interaction with nature by utilizing wood paneling of a warm, rich color, bringing one's attention to the beauty of nature.

6   A final principle is that site and form coalesce to create space in architecture. The forms that create the Middleton Inn combine with the landscape to create grids (lines of implication projected onto the landscape). These spatial grids are the inn's way of claiming the landscape, and dictating what occurs within the structure—again, we see the contrast between public and private space.

7   The inn is made up of of five separate buildings that are all inter-connected through a concrete over-structure. There are two buildings oriented towards the south, and three facing west, thereby creating the L-shape which creates a grid within their interaction. Furthermore, by elevating the entrance plane of the inn, Clark is able to create a hierarchy that controls how visitors interact with the space. The inn's visitors are prepared for the various levels they will experience in the inn by their initial ascent, via a flight of stairs, to their rooms. Sensitivity to different types of space is evident from this initial hierarchy all the way down to minute details such as the window blinds. Visitors can control their relationship to the site by means of the way in which they orient their window dressings—whether they be opened fully, closed completely, or placed in any state in between.

8   The attention that the architect pays to space helps create a meaningful building. It is clear that much thought was put into every detail of the Middleton Inn. The design of the building is so organic that it is impossible to discuss site, form, or space in isolation. Yet, these elements do not blend completely; one feels the individual power of form, space and site. Once its power is felt, however, each of these elements will lead one back to the other two elements as the overall idea of the architecture emerges. And that is as it should be. These elements are interrelated; one cannot exist without the other in good architecture. Middleton Inn shows a pleasing harmony between the three parts, which, in the end is the measure of its worth as an excellent piece of architecture.

WORKS CITED

Le Corbusier [Charles Édouard Jeanneret]. *Towards a New Architecture*. Trans. Frederick Etchells. New York: Praeger, 1970.

McCarter, Robert. *Frank Lloyd Wright: A Primer on Architectural Principles*. New York: Princeton Architectural, 1991.

Questions for Review

1. What is the thesis of Joshua's essay? Does it appear in the essay? If so, where? How does he develop (or support) his thesis?
2. Divide the essay into beginning, middle, and end. What rhetorical and/or stylistic devices help form these divisions?
3. What audience might Joshua's essay be written for? What knowledge, if any, does Joshua assume his audience already has about this topic? Is this audience likely to see this as a controversial topic? Are there any indications in his text that Joshua thinks readers may take an opposing point of view?
4. What did you know about this subject before reading Joshua's essay? What information in his essay did you find particularly interesting? Were you surprised by any of it? If so, what? Did you find yourself disagreeing with Joshua on any points? If so, what were they?

THE RHETORICAL TRIANGLE

SUBJECT

Almost any subject can be approached from an informative perspective. But some topics are more difficult than others to treat in an essay with an informative aim. Subjects such as gun control and abortion can shade into argumentation almost before you know what has happened, since you're likely to have an opinion on these topics and to allow that opinion to color the information you're attempting to convey. By the same token, most readers approach essays on such topics as these with strong opinions that tend to make them read to see whether the writer agrees or disagrees with them rather than what information the writer may have to share on this subject.

Other topics, however, do not tend to strike an argumentative note with most readers. In writing about these subjects, you may express a point of view that could be called an argument, without actually writing a paper with an argumentative aim. For example, Elisabeth Kübler-Ross ("On the Fear of Dying") asserts that our fear of death is one of the causes of all the attention we give to medical technology in treating the dying; Deborah Tannen ("Gender Gap in Cyberspace") asserts that men and women relate to computers differently and behave differently in using electronic mail. And Joshua Morris ("The Middleton Inn: An Architectural Triumph") asserts that site, form, and space must all work together harmoniously in successful architecture.

Gloria Naylor's "Mommy, What Does 'Nigger' Mean?" and Michel Marriott's "Rap's Embrace of 'Nigger' Fires Bitter Debate" deal with a subject that is potentially very controversial. No one would argue that the word "nigger" should be used in its usual derogatory sense, but, as Marriott's essay makes clear, there is disagreement as to why (and how) the African American community has used this term. Nevertheless, Marriott writes a purely informative paper on the arguments—pro and con—about the use of this term. He is careful not to take a side. Naylor does argue that the use of this term by blacks is a way of diffusing the word's power to hurt. However, she is assuming an audience that wants to be informed about the ways in which language works, not one that will want to resist what she is saying about the way this hateful word has been used.

In summary, we can say that the most likely subjects for informative essays are those that do not lend themselves to controversy. However, if you're careful to focus your essay on information that your audience does not have and if you structure your essay in a nonargumentative fashion, you can write an informative essay on almost any topic.

WRITER

Before writing, you will want to have a solid base of information, whatever topic you choose. For example, Kübler-Ross, a medical doctor and long-time advocate for the rights of patients, has obviously given much thought to the treatment of dying patients in U.S. society. Likewise, Tannen, a linguist and popular writer on issues having to do with gender, writes from a rich background of information.

You may not be able to bring the kind of professional expertise to a topic that these writers have been able to develop over many years. But you do know a great deal about a number of topics. It is clear from his essay, "Middleton Inn: An Architectural Triumph," that Joshua Morris is learning a lot about architecture in his studies at UNC–Charlotte. And Kelly McGinley's essay, "Investing in Your Future," shows that she has given much thought to ways in which she can invest her money to achieve the optimum return. Later in the chapter, you will be presented with another student essay, by Steve Duran, entitled, "The Space between Your Ears." Steve is an avid golfer and, as his essay makes clear, is becoming something of an expert on the game. Like Steve, you may choose to write about a subject you would not ordinarily associate with formal, or academic, writing. Don't limit yourself to academic subjects; write about topics you really know and care about. You may have been a member of the 4-H club for many years, or you may have traveled widely and learned much about different countries and cultures, or you may have developed an interest in some art or craft very early in your life. Any subject that interests you and about which you know a good deal can be suitable for an informative essay.

As a result of their knowledge about their topics, writers of informative prose speak with confidence. They need not, in fact, should not, be arrogant or high-handed, but they approach the reader with the assumption that what they say is worthy of the reader's attention.

How do writers exhibit this confidence and demonstrate their authority? One key characteristic of informative writing is the writer's willingness to generalize. The writer may, and often does, deal in specifics, but she is willing and able to move from those specifics to the general principles they illustrate. An essay that begins with a story, like Tannen's "Gender Gap in Cyberspace," often moves at some point to generality. After narrating her story, Tannen tells her reader that even though she doesn't like to think of herself as "typical," her "relationship to [her] computer is—gulp—fairly typical for a woman" (paragraph 8). In paragraph 10, she gives the reader a great deal of general information about the ways in which men and women use computers:

> Like coed classrooms and meetings, discussions on e-mail networks tend to be dominated by male voices, unless they're specifically women-only, like single-sex schools. On line, women don't have to worry about getting the floor (you just send a message when you feel like it), but, according to linguists Susan Herring and Laurel Sutton, who have studied this, they have the usual problems of having their messages ignored or attacked. [. . .]
> Deborah Tannen, "Gender Gap in Cyberspace"

Gloria Naylor ("Mommy, What Does 'Nigger' Mean?") begins her essay in generalities. She tells her reader that she considers "the written word inferior to the spoken, and much of the frustration experienced by novelists is the awareness that whatever we manage to capture in even the most transcendent passages falls far short of the richness of life." Note that Naylor uses the first person here, but she does not say, or imply, that this is only her opinion. Her experience with and knowledge of the subject have given her information that is generalizable and sharable. We see the same kind of confidence and authority in Joshua's and Kelly's writing. Joshua connects the descriptions of the Middleton Inn to general principles of architecture. For example: "As a general principle, we can say that form grows from the site, and the resulting form in turn creates space." Kelly provides the reader with many general statements about banking and investing, such as: "Generally, the longer you lock your money in (that is, the longer time you commit to leaving your money in the bank), the higher interest rate you receive."

Probably the most authoritative writing in our sample essays is in Kübler-Ross's "On the Fear of Death." In the first paragraph of her essay, she offers historical information that establishes her knowledge about rituals having to do with death and dying. Then, in the first sentence of the second paragraph, she assumes the authority to say that "man has not basically changed," in regard to the fear of death. Near the end of her essay, Kübler-Ross attempts to help her reader see what makes people want to rely so heavily on the technologies of modern medicine:

> [. . .] Those who consider the person first may lose precious time to save his life! At least this seems to be the rationale or justification behind all this—or is it? Is the reason for this increasingly mechanical, depersonalized approach our own defensiveness? Is this approach our own way to cope with and repress the anxieties that a terminally or critically ill patient evokes in us? Is our concentration on equipment, on blood pressure our desperate attempt to deny the impending death which is so frightening and discomforting to us that we displace all our knowledge onto machines, since they are less close to us than the suffering face of another human being which would remind us once more of our lack of omnipotence, our own limits and failures, and last but not least perhaps our own mortality?
> Elisabeth Kübler-Ross, "On the Fear of Dying"

Kübler-Ross structures the preceding passage with a series of questions. In general, asking questions rather than making assertions can make a writer seem less authoritative, but Kübler-Ross's passage is an exception to this rule. Note how she reveals her authority in asking these questions. She labels the modern approach to medicine as one that is "increasingly mechanical, depersonalized"; she calls reliance on this technology a "desperate attempt to deny the impending death" of the patient; and she asserts that modern practice allows us to "displace all our knowledge onto machines." Her authority and confidence come through even when she is asking questions about this very complex issue.

This last point brings us to another characteristic of successful informative writers: They know enough about their subject matter to avoid oversimplifying. As we see here, despite all her misgivings about modern medicine, Kübler-Ross, in the end, asks a series of questions that point to the difficulty of determining exactly why we rely so much on technology. We may well be using this technology to mask our fears of death, but it is clear also that at times this technology saves us from death. Kübler-Ross is much too knowledgeable to suggest a simplistic solution, such as returning to the practices of her childhood.

READER

Readers of informative writing are assumed to be receivers of information. By this, we mean something a bit more specific than being able to read and process the words on a page. Readers of informative writing meet the following minimal criteria:

1. They have some reason for being interested in the topic. That reason may vary considerably—from a real need to know something about the topic to a curiosity about what interests the writer.
2. They are willing and able to assume the position of one being instructed; that is, they do not feel they know more about the topic in question than the writer.
3. They do not take an opposing position on the topic from that of the writer. (It is the writer's responsibility to know his topic and his reader well enough to ensure that this is the case. If it is not, the writer must write a different kind of essay.)

Exercise
6.2

Examine two of the professional essays presented at the beginning of this chapter. Before looking to see where they originally appeared (this information is provided in the Acknowlegments at the end of the book), give some thought to who the writers' intended readers may have been. What cues in the texts help you gain insight into potential readers? How successful will the writers be in getting their points across to the intended readers? Finally, consider whether you are a suitable reader for each of these texts. If you are not, reflect on what elements in the text do not work for you. What might you do to make yourself a suitable reader for the text?

DISTINGUISHING FEATURES OF INFORMATIVE ESSAYS

In an informative essay, the focus is on the information that is transferred from writer to reader. If the reader doesn't receive the information, for whatever reason, the writing is not successful.

READER'S KNOWLEDGE

What is good writing for one reader may well be very bad writing for another. It is essential that the writer have a clear sense of what his reader knows about the topic in question, since the reader's knowledge is the foundation on which the informative essay is built. If the writer assumes a foundation that does not exist, the reader will not understand what the writer is trying to say; to continue our foundation metaphor, the structure will fall in on itself. This passage is from a recent book on linguistics:

> Propositional content conditions or rules are the most textual: they concern reference and predication (the propositional act). A propositional content rule for promises, for example, is the predication of a future act (A) by the speaker. Preparatory conditions or rules are varied; they seem to involve background circumstances and knowledge about S [speaker] and H [hearer] that must hold prior to (and then be altered by) the performance of the act. A preparatory condition for promises, for example, concerns H's preference about S's doing of an act (A).
>
> Deborah Schiffrin, *Approaches to Discourse*

The writer of this text, Deborah Schiffrin, wants to tell us something about "propositional content conditions." She begins by assuming that we will know the linguistic meaning of such terms as "textual," "reference," "predication," "propositional act," and "preparatory condition." By "linguistic meaning," we are referring to what such a term as "preparatory condition" means in linguistics as opposed to what the two words mean in ordinary conversation. Readers not familiar with these terms will have great difficulty in understanding the information the writer wants to give us.

This difficulty should not lead us, however, to think that good informative writing will explain all terms. To do so would be to slow down and bore—and probably irritate—readers who know the terms. The linguistic students for whom Schiffrin intends her text will know these terms; if she attempted to define all of her terms, Schiffrin would slow the pace of instruction far too much to be effective for her student readers. The following text begins as if it may well be going to attempt to define all of its terms:

> Verbs and their subjects must agree in person and number. By "agree," we mean to indicate that there are patterned changes, or correspondences, between these two elements in a sentence. If "I" is the subject, and a form of the verb "be" is the verb, then the pattern will be "I am." If "he" is the subject and a form of the verb "be" is the verb, then the pattern will be "He is." Here we see patterned

agreement in "person." But what about agreement in number? If "I" is the subject and a form of the verb "be" is the verb, then the pattern will be "I am," as we saw above. However, if "we" is the subject and a form of the verb "be" is the verb, then the pattern will be "We are." Here we see patterning in number.

Ron Lunsford

Are you asleep yet? If not, it probably wouldn't take too much more of this kind of writing to induce sleep. Why? You already know everything the writer is attempting to tell you. You may not know everything the writer could tell you about grammar—such as the basic difference between a gerund and a participle or what constitutes an elliptical adverbial clause—but before you get to this material, you are likely to have quit paying attention to the text. In terms of our metaphor, the writer is attempting to build a foundation that already exists.

CLARITY

Clarity is the watchword in informative writing. You may be tempted to ask why we need to say this here. Shouldn't clarity be the aim in all writing? To answer this question, we ask you to imagine a situation in which you, a teenager, must inform your parents that you have wrecked the family car and that you were at fault. Which of the versions of this incident, given as A, B, and C below, would you prefer your parents to receive? Which is clearer? Which is better suited to informative writing?

A. The car in front of me stopped while I wasn't looking at it. When I saw the car, it was too late to avoid hitting it. The police officer gave me a ticket for following too closely.

B. All I can say is that I am glad that no one was hurt, and I am amazed at how simplistically a police report has to treat a very complicated situation. I never speed, and I was not speeding today. I was paying attention to my driving, as I always do, and trying to be alert to the various possible hazards that might endanger my life—and the lives of those in the car with me—when, in the corner of my eye, I saw a car in a parking lot to my left start to dart out in front of me—or so it seemed. The driver must have managed to stop before I got to him—since I never saw him again—but by the time my gaze returned to the road, the car in front of me had screamed to a stop at a caution light that any experienced driver would have gone through. I talked to the police officer afterward, and he agreed with me that inexperienced drivers—and this kid driving the car in front of me had only had his permit for two weeks—do sometimes stop for caution lights that an experienced driver would, and should, go on through. But the police officer was not there and could not document exactly how it had happened. The officer also told me that at times paying attention to what happens in our peripheral vision can save our lives. He said that if he (or anyone else who might serve as an unbiased witness) could verify that a car had nearly pulled out in front of me, he could write this incident up as a "no fault," which it clearly was. However, given the rules he had to work with, he had to give me a ticket for following too close. The good news, of course, is that no one was hurt and that the damage to both cars was minimal.

C. Car B hit car A from behind at the intersection of Fifth Street and Irwin Avenue. Car A was heading east on Irwin and had stopped at a red light at Fifth. The tire marks and damage to cars indicate that car B was traveling at a rate of speed of between 29 and 37 miles per hour before the incident. The driver of car B reported that a car had nearly darted out in front of him—from the parking lot of the business on the southwest corner of the intersection. No corroboration of this claim was possible.

We would guess that you would prefer your parents to receive the account in example B. In this account, the reader finds the basic information—that there was a wreck and that you were found to be at fault; however, the reader also "feels" with you how complicated this situation was and how easy it is for a wreck to happen when a driver is doing everything possible to drive safely. Your purpose in giving your parents this account would be to help them view this event as you view it.

Exercise 6.3

Our example above makes the point that writers can have multiple purposes. The writer of passage C, the police officer, wants to present as factual and as clear an account of this event as possible. The writer of passage B, the young driver of the car, wants to tell what happened but also wants to draw attention to the complexities of the situation. This account has strong leanings toward persuasion; thus, clarity is not as important as is capturing a full accounting of all the factors in this situation. Look back at the sample essays at the beginning of the chapter and analyze them from the standpoint of purpose. Obviously, the writers intend to give their readers information. Can you discern other goals these writers are attempting to achieve in their essays? Are some of them more purely informational than others? How high a priority do the writers give to clarity in their writing?

The preceding exercise is intended to help you explore the fact that no one piece of writing is exactly like another in its purposes, or aims. For that reason, no two pieces of writing will have exactly the same commitment to clarity. When we say, then, that the hallmark of informative writing is clarity, we are mindful of the fact that various writing situations and purposes will call for, or allow, various degrees of clarity. In general, we can say that your informative writing should be as clear as purpose and situation will allow it to be. Four principles may help you achieve this clarity:

1. Strive to draw attention to your subject, rather than to yourself as writer or to your reader's response to the writing.
2. Choose words that express rather than impress. That is, if a simple word will convey the information you wish, then use it. (For more on word choice in informative writing, see Chapter 15.)
3. Make your sentence structures as direct and readable as possible. Avoid overly complicated sentences that the reader will have to reread to understand. (For more on sentence structures, see Chapter 16.)

4. Make your overall organization as clear as possible early in the essay. When possible, choose a thesis sentence that gives the reader insight into the order of your essay. (For an example, look at the thesis sentence—the last sentence in the second paragraph—of Steve Duran's essay, p. 207.) If your essay is long, consider using headings to make the relationship of its parts clear to the reader.

ASSIGNMENT AND GUIDELINES FOR WRITING

ASSIGNMENT

Write a paper sharing information you have with an audience that is receptive to that information. For this essay, you should identify a topic about which you already know a great deal or about which you would like to know more.

CHOOSING A TOPIC

PART A

1. Select three or four subjects about which you know a great deal. If you need help choosing, refer to the information in your Interest Inventory (see pp. 8–9). Then, freewrite on each of these subjects for 10 minutes or so.
2. Select at least two of these topics, and freewrite for another 15 minutes on each. After you have gathered these thoughts, answer the following questions:
   a. What word or phrase best captures each of these topics?
   b. Why are these topics interesting to you?
   c. Do many people know a great deal about these topics? If so, what special knowledge do you have about these topics? If not, why don't people know a lot about these topics? Are they difficult? Are they uninteresting to most people? Or is there some other reason?

PART B

Pick one topic that is most interesting to you. Briefly describe an audience that might be interested in what you have to say about this topic. How would you reach this audience? Where might your essay be published, or where might you speak to this audience? Describe a typical reader's or listener's dealings with, and knowledge about, this topic.

COLLECTING INFORMATION

You probably already know a lot about this topic, as should be clear from your freewrites. However, you may gather more information in the following ways:

Questions for Analysis. Ask the questions of association, opposition, and sequence presented in Chapter 1 (pp. 22–25).

Brainstorming/clustering/mapping. Use any of these strategies (and others introduced in Chapter 1) to generate additional material about which to write.

FOCUS STATEMENT

Compose a focus statement for your essay. Below is the focus statement that Kelly McGinley used in writing her essay, presented at the beginning of this chapter.

> I want to write a paper in which I give college students information about saving money. I know a good bit about this topic, because my grandfather taught me about it and because he introduced me to a broker who has worked with me. I want to explain to students the various types of savings options available to them.

Kelly's focus statement is a workable start. It allowed her to move on to her next draft. It would have been more helpful, though, if Kelly had known that she wanted to write about two things—the options available for saving and the ways students can find monies to save. She could have noted here that she was going to write an informative paper with an argument thesis. The argument would be that even college students can find some ways to cut back spending and can begin a small savings plan; then she would explain various ways in which to invest this money.

PLANNING YOUR ESSAY'S STRUCTURE

One way to think about the shape of your essay is by using one or more of the modes of discourse we discuss here and in Chapter 7.

MODES OF DISCOURSE

One key to the overall shape of your essay will be the mode of discourse you employ in your writing. You will remember from our discussion in the introduction to Part Two that *mode* refers to the structuring devices we use to organize our thoughts about a topic. Although a writer may make use of several different modes in one essay, one will provide the overall structure for any piece of informative writing. The three modes we feature in this chapter—process, comparison, and causality—often figure prominently in informative writing.

PROCESS   *Process* is the word we use for an organizational strategy based on chronology. In Chapter 5, we said that chronological connections are at the heart of narration. So how do we differentiate process from narration? It's not always easy, but as a rule narration sets up a sequence of events that develops a story, whereas process sets up a sequence of events that provides information. In the following excerpt, John Holt uses a sequence of events detailing how we might teach children to learn to speak—if indeed we did teach them—in order to give us information about how children actually do learn language.

Bill Hull once said to me, "If we taught children to speak, they'd never learn." I thought at first he was joking. By now I realize that it was a very important truth. Suppose we decided that we had to "teach" children to speak. How would we go about it? First, some committee of experts would analyze speech and break it down into a number of separate "speech skills." We would probably say that, since speech is made up of sounds, a child must be taught to make all the sounds of his language before he can be taught to speak the language itself. Doubtless we would list these sounds, easiest and commonest ones first, harder and rarer ones next. Then we would begin to teach infants these sounds, working our way down the list. Perhaps, in order not to "confuse" the child—"confuse" is an evil word to many educators—we would not let the child hear much ordinary speech, but would only expose him to the sounds we were trying to teach.

Along with our sound list, we would have a syllable list and a word list.

When the child had learned to make all the sounds on the sound list, we would begin to teach him to combine the sounds into syllables. When he could say all the syllables on the syllable list, we would begin to teach him words on our word list. At the same time, we would teach him the rules of grammar, by means of which he could combine these newly learned words into sentences. Everything would be planned with nothing left to chance; there would be plenty of drill, review, and tests, to make sure that he had not forgotten anything.

Suppose we tried to do this; what would happen? What would happen, quite simply, is that most children, before they got very far, would become baffled, discouraged, humiliated, and fearful, and would quit trying to do what we asked them. If, outside of our classes, they lived a normal infant's life, many of them would probably ignore our "teaching" and learn to speak on their own. If not, if our control of their lives was complete (the dream of too many educators), they would take refuge in deliberate failure and silence, as so many of them do when the subject is reading.

John Holt, *How Children Learn*

If we look closely at this passage, it is clear that chronological connections provide much of its structure. Holt tells us that if we taught children to speak, "*First*, some committee of experts would. . . ." Two sentences later, the chronological connections continue with "*Then* we would begin to teach infants these sounds . . . " until we have the whole story.

We should not, however, be misled into assuming that structuring by means of process is a simple, straightforward task. Just as the writer of a narrative must choose his details consciously and carefully in order to make the story mean what he wants it to, process requires the writer to keep an astute eye on his reader to determine how much and what kind of detail is needed to promote understanding. For example, what if Ron wanted to tell a friend how to get to his home? How would he begin? Depending on the knowledge of the person for whom he was writing, he could begin with either of the following:

1. As you leave the university, turn right onto Highway 49. Stay on 49 until you get to the first stoplight, about two-thirds of a mile. Im-

mediately after going under this light, take a right onto Harris Boulevard West. Travel west on Harris for about a mile and a half until you get to I-85. Take I-85 north and travel 10 miles to Highway 73.

2. Turn right off Interstate 85 at Highway 73.

The first set of directions would be written for someone who knows very little about Charlotte and its surroundings. Ron would be attempting to give this person the detail needed to find Ron's home, starting at the UNC–Charlotte campus. The set of directions that begins with the sentence in 2 would be written for someone who knows something about the northeast section of Charlotte. For a person who knows where Highway 73 intersects with Interstate 85, the four steps Ron wrote telling how to get from the university campus to this intersection would be unnecessary. Thus, even though the writer using process knows that his basic connectors will involve chronology, he is doing more than simply filling in the blanks with what happens next. His choice of how to connect the various parts of the process and, indeed, his sense of what to include in the process are guided by his overall purpose in this writing situation.

Exercise 6.4

Compare the directions on a household product, such as the cooking instructions on a packaged food, with the directions on some prescription medicine. For what type of person are these directions written? For what situations? Is either set insulting to your intelligence? Are the instructions equally clear?

Exercise 6.5

Although many essays use process as a major ordering device, many others make use of process as one means of order. For example, look at the role process plays in Kübler-Ross's essay at the beginning of this chapter. A major part of her essay is the comparison of the process by which we used to handle death and dying with the process by which we handle them now. Reflect for a few minutes on the role process may play in your essay. What, if any, processes will you need to inform your readers about? Sketch these now as a means of generating material for your essay.

COMPARISON   In our discussion below, we will use comparison in the broad sense in which it can refer to both likenesses and differences. In order to see how basic the recognition of similarities and differences is to learning, you need only observe a young child as she attempts to make sense of her world. She sees a small, fur-covered animal that has two eyes, a nose, a mouth, four legs, and a tail—among many other characteristics that might escape the child's notice. Her parents inform her that this strange-looking creature is a "doggie." Then the child sees another small animal and exclaims, "Doggie." Her parents will be pleased, but they may not fully realize what a feat this child has accomplished.

The child recognizes the second dog even though she has never seen it before and even though it is not exactly like anything she has ever seen before. This dog's coat is not exactly the same color as that of the first dog, its weight is not the same, its nose is not the same length, and so forth. But the child has learned to recognize this animal as a dog by means of comparison. Of course, the child may also "recognize" several cats as dogs for a time, but as her ability to make comparisons sharpens, she will reach a point at which she "knows" what a dog is. She could never do so without mastering the comparative mode of thinking.

What exactly does comparison entail? It involves us in sizing up a subject. In some cases, this sizing up is literal. For example, if someone tells you, "There is a very large bug on your foot," the word "large" must be understood in the context of "bug" and "foot." How large can the bug be if it is on your foot? What does the word "large" mean in this context? That is the crucial question, isn't it? When you hear that a bug is large, you automatically assume a comparative context. You think about this bug's size in terms of the usual bug's size. If this bug is big, then it will be larger than that usual size. A big bug is still very small in comparison with an average-sized elephant.

Of course, at times the sizing up that we do is not literal at all. For example, consider the following excerpt from Jonathan Kozol's *Savage Inequalities:*

> New York City's public schools are subdivided into 32 school districts. District 10 encompasses a large part of the Bronx but is, effectively, two separate districts. One of these districts, Riverdale, is in the northwest section of the Bronx. Home to many of the city's most sophisticated and well educated families, its elementary schools have relatively few low-income students. The other section, to the south and east, is poor and heavily nonwhite.
>
> The contrast between public schools in each of these two neighborhoods is obvious to any visitor. At Public School 24 in Riverdale, the principal speaks enthusiastically of his teaching staff. At Public School 79, serving poorer children to the south, the principal says that he is forced to take the "tenth-best" teachers. "I thank God they're still breathing," he remarks of those from whom he must select his teachers. [. . .]
>
> In order to find Public School 261 in District 10, a visitor is told to look for a mortician's office. The funeral home, which faces Jerome Avenue in the North Bronx, is easy to identify by its green awning. The school is next door, in a former roller-skating rink. No sign identifies the building as a school. A metal awning frame without an awning supports a flagpole, but there is no flag.
>
> In the street in front of the school there is an elevated public transit line. Heavy traffic fills the street. The existence of the school is virtually concealed within this crowded city block. [. . .]
>
> Beyond the inner doors a guard is seated. The lobby is long and narrow. The ceiling is low. There are no windows. All the teachers that I see at first are middle-aged white women. The principal, who is also a white woman, tells me that the school's "capacity" is 900 but that there are 1,300 children here. [. . .]
>
> Two months later, on a day in May, I visit an elementary school in Riverdale. The dogwoods and magnolias on the lawn in front of P.S. 24 are in full blossom on the day I visit. There is a well-tended park across the street, another larger park three blocks away. To the left of the school is a playground for small children, with an innovative jungle gym, a slide and several climbing toys.

Behind the school there are two playing fields for older kids. The grass around the school is neatly trimmed. [. . .]

The school serves 825 children in the kindergarten through sixth grade. This is approximately half the student population crowded into P.S. 79, where 1,550 children fill a space intended for 1,000, and a great deal smaller than the 1,300 children packed into the former skating rink; but the principal of P.S. 24, a capable and energetic man named David Rothstein, still regards it as excessive for an elementary school.

Kozol gives us a good deal of insight into the problems of funding of public education by means of this stark comparison. In a sense, he is using comparison to size up those problems.

Comparison is natural. No one has to encourage a child to compare his allowance to a friend's allowance or his curfew to that of his classmates. Of course, if the comparisons do not produce information that is useful—that is, if he finds his allowance is bigger or his curfew is more lenient than that of his friends—he may keep that information to himself. It is instructive, though, that he knows what types of comparisons might prove useful. He does not bother to compare himself with children reared in a distant part of the country or with children whose socioeconomic status is very different from his. It is not likely to be useful to a young child to know that children of extremely wealthy parents have allowances that are three times the amount of his. However, if Andy across the street has an allowance that is 10 percent larger, it may be time to renegotiate.

This brings us to a basic principle of comparison. There must be essential similarities between the subjects we are comparing if our comparisons are to produce useful information. As subjects become more and more similar, we must look closer and closer to discover features that distinguish between them. If you have ever tried to get into the wrong automobile in a large parking lot (and had a burglar alarm scream at you for doing so), you have probably discovered some rather subtle features that allow you to distinguish your car from others of the same make and model. The fact that there are many automobiles very similar to yours has made you look more carefully at yours.

We should note here, however, that in saying that subjects of comparison should be similar, we do not mean to imply that this rule should be followed slavishly. At times, writers break it for specific purposes. For example, consider the following very brief essay, which is structured by means of comparison.

MEIR SHALEV

IF BOSNIANS WERE WHALES

1   Wherever I go, I always visit the zoo. That's where I get my preconceived notions about the human race.

2   Not long ago, I visited a marine zoo, the aquarium of Baltimore. The place was lavish and attractive, full of sharks, octopuses, eels and many other fish and varieties of marine life that I did not recognize at first, since they look so different on the grill. The aquarium's planners had obviously realized that a few of the exhibits would whet

appetites, for despite the adage "no talking of charcoal in the sheep pen," here and there they'd placed mouth-watering gastronomic descriptions of seafoods.

3   Unlike sea bass and flounder, swordfish and lobster, there are some sea creatures whose flesh Americans refuse to consider edible. In the U.S., quoting the recipe for whale steak from "Moby Dick" is like offering ham braised in butter to a Jew on Yom Kippur. A proud Baltimorean (her mouth stuffed with clams) recently told me of a whale that had drifted too close to shore. It was immediately fished out, resuscitated and flown—at taxpayers' expense—to the Baltimore Aquarium, where it underwent extensive medical treatment, including psychological rehabilitation.

4   Anyone who remembers the whale stuck off Alaska a few years back that had to be freed by an icebreaker and several million dollars will find it difficult to shake the feeling that whales have simply learned to know a sucker when they see one.

5   My visit to the aquarium ended with the dolphin pool. The trainers talked to us about the social lives of marine mammals (most complex), about their emotional virtues (they are full of love) and especially about their astonishing intelligence. The brain of the dolphin, for those who don't yet know it, is larger, more complex and, in particular, deeper than the Silly Putty found in the human cranium. Indeed, while we stupid land mammals sat in the bleachers munching popcorn, these gifted marine mammals were performing complex somersaults in midair. Then we were told that dolphins have highly sophisticated "communications systems." As proof, one of them let out a few shrill shrieks for a reward of two mackerel. (The mackerel, as we all know, is not a marine mammal, but a fish and may therefore be eaten.)

6   We next heard a diatribe against the cruel Japanese tuna fishermen who trap and kill innocent dolphins in their nets. We released a collective moan. It seems that the dolphins have better P.R. people than the tuna: No one asked why it's O.K. to kill tuna.

7   At the end of my visit, I made a donation to save the dugong and the rain forests and then hurried back to my host's house to watch a movie about the large primates of Africa on the Discovery Channel. It was nice. Especially the end. As a gorilla vanished into the bush, the narrator said, "We have to make this world a better place for the mountain gorilla."

8   Then he, too, vanished, never realizing that with these words he had articulated the solution to the problem of U.S. intervention in Bosnia. It would, after all, be a bit difficult to convince the public that the Bosnians are marine mammals. But if it were possible to convince them that they are a land species in danger of extinction—a fact not far from the truth—then it might be possible to make this world a better place for the Bosnians, too.

9   News reports haven't helped the Bosnians. Or the Somalians. Americans have no energy for yet more images of murder, suffering and torture. If I were the leader of the Bosnians, I would kick all the news teams out of Sarajevo and invite the guys from "Survival" to make a nature film about my people. A documentary about the domestic habits of the Bosnians, their mating dances, territorial marking practices, the way they hollow out their lairs, would do the trick.

10   For a conclusion, the narrator could read: "Only a short time ago, millions of Bosnians grazed the mountainsides of Yugoslavia. Now, only a scant few remain. We have to make this world a better place for the Bosnians." Then, and only then, would the world awaken.

One does not normally think of Bosnians and whales as similar. Shalev is using their obvious dissimilarities to illustrate the point that we humans have much concern and empathy for certain animals that are very different from us in many respects, while at the same time turning our backs on the suffering of fellow human beings.

Discussion of Shalev's essay brings us to a second basic principle of using comparison—comparison should be purposeful. In comparing your car with other similar cars, you helped ensure that you could find your car in a crowded parking lot. In comparing our treatment of whales with our treatment of suffering Bosnians (the real comparison being made in his essay), Shalev helped raise our awareness of the ongoing crisis in Bosnia and, perhaps, caused us to rethink what the United States is doing to assist in this crisis. Kozol's comparison is also intended to move us to action that would change the dire circumstances of students in inner-city schools.

Exercise 6.6

In Chapter 15 (pp. 559–564) we discuss the differences in the use of metaphor for informative and for personal writing. Read those pages and decide whether Shalev's metaphor (comparing humans in poorer countries to endangered animals, for which we tend to have much sympathy) is more like the metaphors we generally associate with informative writing or more like those we generally associate with personal writing. Or is it different from both? Once you determine how Shalev is using metaphor in this essay, look at your informative essay to see if this type of metaphor would be useful in it.

Exercise 6.7

Comparison is such a basic ingredient in informative writing that you are likely to find it helpful for whatever subject you have chosen for this assignment. Think of several comparisons relevant to your topic and use them to generate material for your essay. After you have done so, reflect on what purposes these comparisons might serve in your essay.

CAUSALITY   When we use causal thinking, we are attempting to see through things, to look in depth at what causes certain phenomena or what effects they have. Causal thinking is fundamental to modern science, of course. But it also pervades our daily existence. We are constantly attempting to figure out the causes for the actions of people in our lives and to determine what the effects of our decisions and actions will be. But causal analysis is not limited to actions and behaviors; we often ponder the causes of our very thoughts and ideas. As an example, in the following exercise, we ask you to reflect on some of the causes for your thinking.

Exercise 6.8

Consider the following passage from Jonathan Kozol's "The Human Cost of an Illiterate Society":

> Illiterates cannot read the menu in a restaurant. They cannot read the cost of items on the menu in the window of the restaurant before they enter. Illiterates cannot read the letters that their children bring home from their teachers. They cannot study school department circulars that tell them of the courses that their children

must be taking if they hope to write a letter to the teacher. They are afraid to visit in the classroom. They do not want to humiliate their child or themselves.

In this sample passage, Jonathan Kozol outlines some of the ways in which illiteracy affects people. Can you think of additional effects illiteracy might have on a person? Brainstorm for a few minutes, noting every possible effect of illiteracy you can think of. After you have written your list, look over the list below, from the rest of Kozol's essay, then answer these questions: How does your list compare with Kozol's? What significant effects did you see that Kozol did not mention? What effects did Kozol mention that you did not imagine? After you have answered these questions, consider the implications of your findings. What caused you to see things that Kozol did not see? What caused you to overlook effects that Kozol saw?

Other things that people who are illiterate cannot do, according to Jonathan Kozol in "The Human Cost of an Illiterate Society":

read instructions on prescription medicine
understand the written details on a health insurance form
read waivers they sign before surgical procedures
read lease agreements
manage checking accounts
use mail
read notices from welfare offices and the IRS
look up numbers in the telephone directory
read the admonition on a pack of cigarettes
identify no-name (and thus cheaper) products, since illiterate people depend on pictures and logos
distinguish between products with similar labels
read instructions for cooking food
travel freely, because they can't read traffic signs, street names, and bus schedules
read TV programming information

In the preceding exercise, we asked you to examine the causes of something very abstract: your thought processes. Why do you suppose you listed the things you listed? Did you leave out what now seem to you to be significant effects? Why? Perhaps you feel that Kozol's analysis of potential causes and effects is problematic. If so, what makes you feel this way? Could Kozol be guilty of exaggerating? What motivations might he have for doing so?

Exercise 6.9

Generate more material for your essay by exploring the role of causality in your thinking. You may want to return to the sequence and consequence questions in our questions for analysis (pp. 24–25). We do not want to confuse chronological relations with causal relations—and hence be guilty of a logical fallacy (see pp. 348–349). However, whenever one event follows another, it is worth asking whether there is a causal relationship between the two events.

MODE AS A TOOL FOR SHAPING   Even though any piece of expository writing will likely contain several modes of discourse, we can usually point to a dominant mode that provides the primary structure of that writing. As we saw in Chapter 5, narration and description often provide the overall structure for essays that spotlight the writer and her experiences. In essays focusing on the subject, the expository modes—process, comparison, causality, analysis, classification, and definition—provide structure.

As an example, let's look at the structure of one of the sample essays from the beginning of this chapter, Deborah Tannen's "Gender Gap in Cyberspace." Tannen uses several modes to structure her essay. She begins with a narrative telling the story of how she and a friend, Ralph, bought computers at about the same time. This narrative continues through the first five paragraphs. However, chronology is not the only structuring device in these five paragraphs. In the second paragraph, Tannen compares her learning strategies with those of her friend, Ralph. Then, in paragraph 6, Tannen employs causal structure, explaining the factors that cause men to to be more open and forthcoming on e-mail than they tend to be in face-to-face conversation.

Which of these several modes dominates and thus accounts for the overall shape of the essay? Narrative certainly plays a major role. Viewed from one perspective, Tannen's piece could be seen as the *story* of what happened to her and her friend as they moved into the computer age. However, just as important, Tannen is *contrasting* the ways in which she and her friend have reacted to the opportunities and challenges of using computers. From this perspective, Tannen's essay is a comparison of the way she and her friend learned to use computers. But there is more. Tannen moves from this comparison to a comparison of the way in which men and women use computers—hence her title. Of course, underlying these comparisons and this narrative are Tannen's explanations of the *causes* for these differences.

What, then, is the overall structuring device of the essay? That would be impossible to say apart from discussion of Tannen's overall purpose, or aim. Given her title, it would seem that she wants to provide information on the differences in how men and women use computers; thus, we see comparison as the controlling mode of this essay.

Exercise 6.10

Now that you have seen our overview of the structure of "Gender Gap in Cyberspace," try your hand at doing such an analysis of one of the other essays presented in this chapter or of some other essay selected by your instructor. What is (are) the controlling mode(s) for this essay? You may want to limit your analysis to the modes we have talked about in this chapter—process, comparison, and causality. However, if your instructor permits, you may also want to look at the discussion of analysis, classification, and definition in Chapter 7.

As you no doubt discovered in the preceding exercise, modal analysis is not an exact science. Our purpose in suggesting that you attempt an analysis is to illustrate that a writer's selection of modes is connected to his aim. There is a sense in which we are always unsure of claims we might make about the purposes of other writers. However, we can be sure of our own purposes. And that is the point of this discussion—to help you connect your sense of purpose to the overall structure of your essay. As you plan your essay, you may find it useful to see which modal structure provides the overall shape of your essay.

THESIS STATEMENT

At this point, you are ready to write a tentative thesis statement for your essay. As we discussed in Chapter 2, your thesis may or may not appear in the final draft of your essay. For now, state your thesis so that it reveals the basic structure of your essay. For example, the following are possible thesis statements for three of the essays presented at the beginning of this chapter.

> The natural human fear of death is part of the *cause* of the dehumanized treatment of patients in modern hospitals.
> Elisabeth Kübler-Ross, "On the Fear of Dying"

> Men and women tend to use computers and technology in very *different* ways.
> Deborah Tannen, "Gender Gap in Cyberspace"

> The meaning (and power) of words *is caused* by the ways in which communities use those words.
> Gloria Naylor, "Mommy, What Does 'Nigger' Mean?"

Of course, none of these sentences actually appear in the essays in question. We have framed the sentences so that they reveal the writers' structuring devices. Kübler-Ross uses cause to structure her essay—the fear of death partly *causes* the impersonal treatment of the dying in our culture. Naylor also relies on cause—the various meanings of words come about as a result of (*are caused by*) the ways in which people use language. There is, of course, much reliance on definition and classification in the body of Naylor's essay where she outlines these various meanings. (See Chapter 7, pp. 235–236, for more information on classification and definition.) Tannen uses comparison as her overriding structuring device—men and women *differ* in their use of computers.

REFINING YOUR WRITING

After you've written a draft of your essay and taken some time away from it, revise it, keeping the following principles in mind.

> *Audience.* How appropriate is your chosen audience for this paper? Check to see that you have not assumed any knowledge this audience will not have and that you have not included material they will already know.
> *Organization.* Which mode provides the overriding organization for your paper? For example, do you rely more heavily on process than on comparison or perhaps more heavily on causality than on process?

Make a list that describes the primary mode at work in each paragraph. How effectively does this structure work with your topic? With your reader?

Thesis. How effectively does your thesis provide insight into the order of your essay; that is, how effectively does your thesis reveal or predict your essay's structure as a guide for your reader?

Clarity. How appropriate is the language for your audience? Identify any jargon you may have used. How clearly will that jargon communicate to a reader who isn't as familiar with the topic as you are? Would headings be helpful in guiding your reader through the essay?

SAMPLE STUDENT PROCESS

The student example below was written by Steve Duran, a first-year writing student at NMSU.

PREWRITING

Steve began with some notes about his topic.

> *Golf*
> The importance of the mental side of golf is often overlooked.
> Golf is primarily a mental game. Secondly physical.
> Anyone can benefit from good mental tactics, not just low handicappers.
> Preshot routines are very important.
> Confidence in swing. . . . Doubt-free swings are usually good swings.
> Mental doubts and flaws show up physically in the swing.
> Tactical terminology is important also.
> Mental rehearsal is a critical part of training the mind to control the body.
> Anger and emotion are both fine as long as they do not carry over to the next shot.
> Accepting bad shots is necessary.
> It's not how good your good shots are, it's how good your bad shots are.
> The proper way of thinking can turn a potentially bad round into a good round.
> Visualization in the mind is another important technique.
> Indecision will kill a good golf swing.
> Mental tactics are very important to other sports and tasks.
> Because golf is a slow moving game, there is more time for doubts and bad thoughts.

FOCUS STATEMENT

After jotting down these thoughts, Steve wrote the following focus statement for his paper:

> I want my reader to understand (1) the importance of the mental side of golf, (2) the effect of confidence on a golfer's game, (3) the bad effects of a negative thought, (4) the different techniques used to achieve a sound metal game.

Steve's first draft follows.

Ninety percent of the golf game is played in the space between your ears. Golfers hear a lot of phrases (insert some here?) and slogans about the mental side of golf, but many golfers fail to recognize the importance of these sayings. It is true, golf is primarily a mental game. The mental aspect is also a huge part of most sports, but because golf is such a slow moving game with no real opponent, it is just the golfer who must compete with the golf course and his own mind. Mental rehearsal, visualization, positive thinking, and confidence all play important roles in the effort to continue to improve your game.

Every great athlete practices all types of game situations, so he will be physically ready when the situation presents itself. Not only is he training his body, but at the same time, he is training his mind. After a lot of practice, in a real game situation, his subconscious mind knows what to do, so it takes over and directs the muscles to perform the desired task. This same concept applies to golf. You should be creative in your practice, visualizing different situations encountered in an actual round of golf. When hitting balls on the practice range, imagine you are on a particular hole of the golf course that calls for a certain type of shot. When practicing putting, take the time to read the break in the green, and line it up just like you would with an important putt to win a tournament. By trying to put (visualizing/imagining) yourself in these situations, you are training your mind how to react to them. When they actually come up, you should be able to react without nervousness and tension, two killers of a good swing.

Another important technique that directly ties in with mental rehearsal is visualization. Many good golfers see a "mental movie" of the exact ball flight of the shot they want to hit, from impact to the time it stops rolling. This visualization performs two important functions. First, this tells the mind exactly what you want to do. The mind then takes over and tells your muscles what to do to produce the desired shot. Second, this concentration on the shot at hand prevents you from thinking about the bunkers surrounding the green, your score, or what you're going to do after the round.

Another important part of visualization is being able to see the path you want your ball to take to the hole. This is most helpful when putting. After reading your putt, picture a string or a two-inch wide road leading from your ball to the hole. Then picture the ball rolling along the path to the hole. This kind of visualization is mainly to build confidence. You will make a better putting stroke if you are sure of the path you want your ball to take. All you need to do now is get your ball rolling on that path, and if you read your putt correctly, you have a pretty good chance of making the putt.

Another important aspect of the mental game is positive thinking. Positive thinking is simply being able to look at your situation in a positive way instead of a negative way. The main lesson in positive thinking is concentration on what you want to accomplish, not on what you *don't* want to happen. If you are standing over a 150 yard shot to a green with water on the right side, and you are thinking about how much you don't want to go to the right, chances are you will hit to the right and in the water. The reason for this is simple. While thinking about the water on the right, you are subconsciously picturing a shot that goes to the right, splashing down in the water. Instead, you should be consciously picturing the shot you want to hit, a safe shot to the left side of the green.

A second aspect of positive thinking has to do with emotions. Many golfers may start a round with a bad hole, get extremely angry with themselves, and instantly ruin their round. They forget about the next 17 holes in front of them. They see the next 17 holes as seventeen more chances to play terribly, instead of 17 more birdie opportunities. This doesn't have to ruin the whole round. Good golfers have the ability to forget their mistakes and concentrate on the next shot. The key is to accept the fact that you will not hit every shot perfectly every time. This is not easy to do, especially on one of those days when it seems nothing is going right. But you will not help your game by dwelling on the bonehead shot you hit on the last hole. The shot you just hit never matters; the only shot that matters is your next shot.

All of the mental techniques described so far lead directly to the most important part of the mental game: confidence. Confidence allows you to make a smooth, tension free swing because you are not ever thinking about what you might do wrong in your swing. You are positive that you are going to hit the exact shot you just visualized a minute ago while preparing to hit the shot. So there's no need for swing adjustments or distractions, you just go through your pre-shot routine, step-up to the ball, and swing (exactly where you planned) your golf club. It's this type of confidence that leads to (creates?) the best shots. When your mind is not cluttered with too much information, it is free to guide your muscles to a relaxed, smooth swing.

Indecision will kill your confidence, which will kill a good golf swing. Club selection is a problem in this area. Imagine you are about to hit your approach shot to a hole 155 yards away. This is an in-between distance for you, and you don't know if you should hit a 6-iron or a 7-iron. You finally decide on the 6-iron. At the top of your backswing, an evil thought creeps into your head and says that you're going to hit it too far. So what do you do, you try to slow down your swing (big no-no) and so slam your club into the ground 3 inches behind the ball, propelling your ball forward about 10 yards (if you're lucky). Now, you are angry with yourself and now doubt your ability to make a good swing. This is not good for your confidence.

Now imagine this situation again. This time, when the thought that you'll hit the ball too far creeps into your head, you step back from the ball, and go through your pre-shot routine all over again. You convince yourself that the 6-iron is exactly the right club for this shot, and visualize your shot pattern. You address the ball and make a smooth, confident swing. The ball takes off in exactly the path you visualized. It flies right at the hole (and you know it's going to be close) then lands softly—ten yards past the hole! You were wrong. You should have used the 7-iron. But you had the right swing, a confident, smooth swing. You hit a great, solid shot because you did not doubt it. For your error in club selection, you have a thirty foot birdie putt as punishment. That's a lot better than facing another full shot from 140 yards away. And you are still confident and trust your swing, because you know you just hit a great shot, unfortunately with the wrong club.

The idea here is simple. Never even start your backswing until you are absolutely positive that the club in your hands will take your ball to the target just like you visualized. You may be wrong but the confidence you have in your swing will allow you to make the best possible swing for the shot at hand. Even if you don't make the best swing, your shot will probably not be too bad. In golf, your score is not determined by how good your good shots are, it's how good your bad shots are.

The mental game is incredibly important to good golf. Anyone can benefit from a good mental game, not just top amateurs and professionals. Good golfers are good not because they have a consistent, mechanically perfect swing, because the fact is, most don't. But they have swings that are consistent and easily repeatable. The basis for these consistent repeatable reliable swings is a good mental game. They trust their swing to stand up under pressure. Most of the time this works. A good golfer should work hard on his swing during practice time, and build trust in it. Then, during a round of golf, he does not need to think about his swing, he just relaxes and lets his brain do the work. He simply surveys the situation, tells his mind what type of shot the situation needs, and then trusts his swing to get the ball to the target. This trust in their swing and sound mental game is what separates professional golfers from the rest of us. While we can't all have the swings of professionals, we can learn to copy their mental game. By using the techniques of mental rehearsal, visualization, positive thinking, and confidence, we can make sure that the 90% of the game played in the space between our ears, won't be played in empty space.

Steve's draft was read by two classmates, who offered the following advice:

Reviewer 1

Your thesis is clear and your examples are good. I like the way you compare the mental aspect of golf with the mental aspects of other sports. I also liked what you said about visualization.

One part that I thought was just a little confusing was the second paragraph on indecision. You are talking about indecision and then you stress the importance of the clubs and it kind of takes away from the point on indecision. Since you are writing for a general audience you might want to say something about the fun that golf can be. People develop more confidence when they are having fun. You might want to think about cutting some of your longer sentences in half, so you can have shorter sentences that make key points. I think your essay was very well written and I found it interesting even though I don't play golf myself.

Reviewer 2

Steve, It was a perfectly balanced essay, and the essay itself is interesting. The paper is well organized. I like your humor. Your examples are effective. My only suggestion for improvement is that you do more to show us how we can accomplish the things you say we should. It is one thing to know that we should remain calm and visualize good shots. But how does one make such things happen? Maybe there's nothing more you can say, but I felt a little unsatisfied in places. For example, you say that one should not dwell on bonehead shots. But how do we keep from doing that? Good paper.

Following is Steve's final draft.

THE SPACE BETWEEN YOUR EARS

STEVE DURAN

1 Ninety percent of the golf game is played in the space between your ears. We hear a lot of phrases and sayings about the mental side of golf, but many of us brush these

words aside and insist that practicing until your hands bleed is the only way to improve. There is nothing wrong with practice, but no matter how good your swing or how bloody your hands, you cannot score well without a solid mental game.

2   The mental aspect is a huge part of most sports, but thinking plays a unique role in golf. In golf, your opponent is seldom another player. Your goal in golf is not to do better than someone else, but to make yourself a better golfer. Another factor in the mental part of golf is the tempo of the game. Golf is a slow moving game, with a couple of minutes between shots, leaving plenty of time for demons and negative thoughts to enter your mind. The human mind is a funny thing. It can remember to perform all the necessary functions in your body to keep you alive, but step onto a golf course and your mind can become your worst enemy. Cluttered with too much of the wrong information or doubts, your brain can destroy your game. Fortunately, this evil fiend can be stopped. With the right techniques of mental rehearsal, visualization, positive thinking and confidence, you can train your mind to work for you, not against you.

3   Every great athlete practices all types of game situations, so he will be physically ready for any situation. Not only is he training his body, but at the same time he is training his mind to react to the situation and make the right decisions. In football, an offense will run plays over and over again so that everyone knows where he should be at on every play. The goal of these drills is to make players' responses automatic. On each play, the players' subconscious minds know what to do, and tell their bodies how to do it. This same concept applies to golf. Fortunately, no one is trying to tackle you during the average round of golf, so you don't have to make split-second decisions. You have more time to decide what you need to do, so relax and use your head.

4   When you are practicing, create different situations encountered in a round of golf. When hitting balls on the practice range, imagine you are on a certain hole on the golf course. Picture the entire fairway and where you want to hit your ball. Then play this shot exactly as you would if you were playing this hole. When practicing putting, take the time to read the break in the green, and line the putt up just as you would for an important putt to win a tournament. The key is to make practice as much like actual play as possible. The more you can do this, the less tension and nervousness you will feel when you are playing—and the more successful shots you will hit.

5   An important technique that directly ties in with mental rehearsal is visualization. Many good golfers see a "mental movie" of the exact ball flight of the shot they want to hit, from impact to the time it stops rolling. This visualization does two important things that will help your game. First, it lets your mind know exactly what you want to do so that your subconscious mind can take over and tell your muscles what to do to produce the desired shot. Second, by concentrating on the shot at hand, you avoid thinking about the huge bunkers surrounding the green, your ugly shots in the past, or what you're going to be doing after the round. This "mental movie" comes naturally to some golfers, but most of us will have to do some work to start the projector running. And when we do, we will have to be careful that it has the right film in it. The movies in most of our heads might be found in the "horror" section of the movie house. In order to rid yourself of the sights and sounds of balls careening into the woods or splashing into various water hazards, hit some warm-up shots on the practice range before you play. After you hit a pretty solid shot, watch it from the time it takes off until it stops rolling, and note exactly how it felt. When you are on the course and have trouble visualizing your next shot, just remember how that practice shot felt. Picture its flight and how it would look on this particular hole. Now just imagine you are on the range and try to duplicate that shot.

6   Another important part of visualization is being able to see the path you want your ball to take to the hole. This is most helpful when putting. After reading your putt, picture a string or a two-inch wide road leading from your ball to the hole. Then imagine

the ball rolling along that path and dropping into the hole. This kind of visualization will build confidence. You will make a better putting stroke if you are sure of the path you want your ball to take. All you need to do now is start your ball rolling on that path, and if you read your putt correctly, you have a pretty good chance of making the putt.

7   A subtle but important part of the mental game is positive thinking. The first lesson in positive thinking has already been touched on above. We want to concentrate entirely on the shots we want to hit rather than on the shots we do not want to hit. If you are standing over a 150 yard shot to a green, with water on the right side, and you are thinking about how much you don't want to hit your ball to the right and into the water, chances are you will hit your ball to the right and into the water. The reason for this is simple. While thinking about the water on the right, you are subconsciously picturing a shot that goes to the right, splashing down in the water. So your brain, in one of its dumb golfing moments, tells your muscles to hit that very shot. Instead, you should consciously visualize a high, drawing shot to the left side of the green. Picture this shot as vividly as possible, in order to keep your mind focused on exactly what you want to do. This keeps you from worrying that your shiny white Titleist will be laid to rest in a watery grave before its time.

8   A second aspect of positive thinking has to do with emotions. Many golfers may start a round with a bad hole, get extremely angry with themselves, and instantly ruin their round. They focus their anger on that one bad hole and forget about the next seventeen holes in front of them. They see the next seventeen holes as useless after their terrible first hole, instead of as seventeen more birdie opportunities. A bad hole doesn't have to ruin a round. Good golfers have the ability to forget their mistakes and concentrate on the next shot. The key is to accept that you will not hit every shot perfectly every time. Accepting your bad shots as part of the game is hard to do, especially on one of those days when it seems nothing is going right. But you will not help your game by dwelling on that bonehead shot you hit three holes ago. The shot you just hit never matters; the only shot that ever matters is the next one.

9   This sounds good in theory, but it is extremely difficult to learn to accept your bad shots. There are some things you can do, however, to help you achieve this goal. The key is to relax and stay focused on the strategy of this game—and after all, unless you are playing for money, it is just that, a game. After a bad shot, look over the situation, and decide what you need to do to get safely to the hole in the least amount of strokes from that point. The objective of golf is to get the ball from point A to point B in the fewest number of strokes. So once you've made a bad shot, don't focus on the total number of strokes you may have on this hole, but on the total number of strokes it will take from where you are. Also, don't worry about shots that do not look good. So you hit one that looked like a dying duck. It may still have traveled two-thirds as far as it would have had it been beautiful. You can still save par on a par four after hitting two bad shots, if your third and fourth shots are very good. Your four counts exactly the same as the four made by your opponent, who hit four beautiful shots.

10   Watch any professional golf tournament and you will understand how important it is to accept your bad shots. Try to watch the leader through an entire round. If he is well-prepared mentally, you won't see a lot of ups and downs in his behavior. He will not get extremely angry over a bad shot or do a dance of joy after every good shot. He knows that no matter how good or bad his last shot was, he still has to hit one more good shot, followed by another, and then another if he wants to play well. So he concentrates on hitting one good shot at a time, and keeps his emotions in check. He might show a little emotion, and that is fine, as long as it doesn't carry over to the next shot.

11   The most important part of the mental game is confidence. A high level of confidence allows you to make a smooth, tension-free swing because you are not even thinking about any problems in your swing. You are positive that you are going to hit the exact shot you just visualized while preparing to hit the shot. There is no need for swing adjustments or distractions, so you just go through your pre-shot routine, step up to the ball, and swing your golf club. It's this type of confidence that creates the best shots. When your mind is clear of all distracting thoughts or doubts, it is free to guide your muscles to a relaxed, smooth swing.

12   Indecision will kill your golf swing, and in turn, a killed golf swing will kill your confidence. To avoid this vicious cycle of murder, pay close attention to your club selection decisions. Imagine you are about to hit your approach shot to a hole 155 yards away. This is an in-between distance for you, so you can't decide if you should hit a six-iron or a seven-iron. You finally decide on the six-iron and step up to the ball. As you take the club back, an evil thought creeps into your head and informs you that you're going to hit the ball too far. So what do you do? You try to slow down your downswing (big no-no) and thus slam your club into the ground three inches behind the ball, propelling your stupid little white ball forward about ten yards (if you're lucky). Now, you are angry with yourself and anything else in your general area and doubt your ability to make a good swing. This is not good—for your score, for your confidence, or for the worms you just sliced in half with your six-iron.

13   Now imagine this situation again. This time, when that wretched thought that you'll hit your ball too far creeps into your head, you are ready for it. You step back from the ball, and go through your pre-shot routine all over again. You convince yourself that the six-iron is exactly the right club for this shot and visualize your shot pattern. You relax and take a deep breath and make a smooth, confident swing. The ball takes off in exactly the path you visualized. It flies right at the hole and lands softly—ten yards *past* the hole! You were wrong. You didn't have the right club. But you had the right swing, a confident, doubt-free swing. You hit a great solid shot because you did not doubt your ability or decisions. For your error in club selection, you have a thirty foot birdie putt as punishment. You know you hit a great, solid shot; unfortunately you had the wrong club in your hand. The outcome of this shot was bad, but the result for your game was good, since a good golf score is determined not by how good your good shots are but by how good your bad shots are.

14   The mental game is incredibly important to good golf. Anyone who understands the fundamentals of the golf swing can benefit from a good mental game, not just top amateurs and professionals. Many people believe that great golfers are great because they possess "the perfect swing." They are terribly mistaken, because, sadly, "the perfect swing" just does not exist. It is merely a marketing ploy used to sell instructional videotapes. What makes good golfers good is that they have swings that are consistent and easily repeatable. The basis for these consistent, reliable swings is a good grasp of the mental game. They trust their swings to stand up under pressure. They concentrate only on the process of hitting good shots, and leave the technical stuff to their subconscious mind. After hundreds of hours of practice, their subconscious mind has been trained how to swing a golf club, so they don't need to consciously think about swing mechanics. All they need to do is trust their swing, relax, and let their brain do the work. This trust in their swing and sound mental game is what separates PGA pros from the rest of us. While we can't all have the swings of the pros, we can learn to copy their biggest strength, their mental game.

15   Using the techniques of mental rehearsal, visualization, positive thinking, and confidence does not come easily. It takes dedication to concentrate for the four hours of a

round of golf. Every round you play should be a learning experience. You will make mental mistakes, but the key is to learn from them. If you keep working on it, you will be able to reduce the number of mental mistakes in a round, and reduce your scores. By learning to improve our mental game, we make sure that the ninety percent of the game we play in the space between our ears won't be played in empty space.

Checklist: Critiquing an Informative Essay

1. What is the essay's topic?
2. What assertion does the writer make about this topic; what is the essay's thesis? Summarize the thesis in your own words. How effectively does the thesis make its assertion? Make specific suggestions for revision.
3. How clear is the essay's organization? What mode provides the overall structure for the essay? Are transitions clear and effective? Are paragraphs unified and cohesive? Are the introduction and conclusion effective? Make specific suggestions for revision.
4. Who is the audience for the essay? Will the essay's information be interesting to and/or needed by this audience? Is the language of the essay appropriate for this audience? Make specific suggestions for revision.
5. Identify two places in the paper you think are particularly strong. What makes them effective?
6. Identify two places in the paper you think need work. Make specific suggestions for revision.
7. Does the paper adhere to conventions of usage, mechanics, and format? Correct any errors you find.

We evaluate things, events, and ideas every day, making judgments about them. At times, we seem to reach a judgment almost instantaneously. How long, for example, does it take you to decide that a particular blouse or tie looks good? Probably not very long at all. At other times, a judgment may take longer to reach, and we deliberate carefully before making a choice.

Evaluation essays present the writer's opinion about her topic and support for that opinion, so that the reader sees something of the process the writer went through to reach her judgment about the topic. The following exercise clarifies this point.

Exercise 7.1

List as many traits or characteristics of a good teacher as you can. Then think about the teachers you have had. Which of these were good teachers? List two or three of them by name; then decide how many of the traits you listed these teachers had. For each trait give one or two specific examples of how each teacher exemplified that trait.

This exercise offers a fairly concise overview of one way to make and support an evaluation:

1. *Decide what to evaluate*. In the exercise, we gave you a topic or subject to evaluate—a good teacher. If the topic for your writing isn't specified, pick a

Evaluation Essays

C H A P T E R 7

topic that interests you—something about which you'd like to know more, or something you like or dislike and want to justify to someone else.

2. *Establish criteria for your evaluation.* The paper you'll write as you work through this chapter is often called a criterion-based evaluation. How will you determine the worth of the subject of your evaluation? In the exercise, we asked you to develop a list of traits or characteristics of a good teacher. In essence, we asked you to develop a way to measure the quality of a teacher. Once you've listed the criteria for evaluating your topic, you'll be able to compare your topic with the list to see how well it matches up. The criteria that you develop will enable you to formulate and support a carefully deliberated judgment, so that when a reader has finished reading your paper, he will understand why you hold the opinion you hold about your topic.

3. *Make a value judgment.* How well does your topic match with or fit the criteria you established? In the exercise, we asked you to name two or three teachers who matched up well with the criteria you established. In your paper, you'll frame your judgment as an assertion about the value of your topic. This value may be characterized as good or bad, effective or ineffective, beneficial or detrimental, important or unimportant, worthy or unworthy, successful or unsuccessful, best or worst. You're not limited to these terms, by any means, but your judgment should begin with them.

4. *Offer specific support for your judgment.* What details can you provide to help your reader understand how you arrived at your evaluation and whether it's valid? In the exercise, we asked you to give a specific example of how each teacher you evaluated as a good teacher exemplified a particular trait.

If Bill were to evaluate the writer Jean Shepherd, one of his favorite humorists, he would follow the procedure outlined here and produce this prewriting:

1. Decide what to evaluate.
Jean Shepherd, one of my favorite short story writers. Shepherd absolutely cracks me up, and I've used one of his books in a humor course I've taught.

2. Establish criteria.
What makes for a good short story writer? More specifically, what makes for good funny short stories?
a. exaggeration—one of the humorist's stock devices
b. dialogue—vivid, at times ironic
c. humorous situations
d. universality—serious humor is humor I can identify with. Characters aren't so different from me, however exaggerated their situations and actions may be.

3. Make a value judgment.
Jean Shepherd is absolutely one of the funniest short story writers I've ever read. [*Note:* "Funniest" is a superlative, and we assume that this is a positive (good) judgment.]

4. Offer specific support for judgment.
Criterion 1—exaggeration: The exaggeration Shepherd uses brings characters and situations to always funny and sometimes painful life.

(stories to draw details from: "The Grandstand Passion Play of Delbert and the Bumpus Hounds" and "Daphne Bigelow")

Criterion 2—Shepherd's use of dialogue is superb. (stories: "Bumpus" and "The Star-crossed Romance of Josephine Kosznowski")

Criterion 3—Shepherd puts his characters in hilarious conflicts and then lets them squirm their way out. (stories: "County Fair" and "Duel in the Snow" or "Red Ryder Meets the Cleveland Street Kid")

Criterion 4—Shepherd's characters and the events of their lives seem not so far removed from me. (stories: "Wanda Hickey's Night of Golden Memories" and "Daphne Bigelow")

By drawing specific examples from specific stories, Bill would support the assertions he derived from his initial listing of criteria, so that the criteria would actually become topic sentences of paragraphs designed to support the evaluation's thesis, the value judgment Bill makes about Shepherd as "one of the funniest" short story writers he's read.

SAMPLE ESSAYS

The following sample essays involve evaluations of a writer, a book, a legal program, and a CD. As you read through each, consider first what judgment the writer presents and then the criteria the writer used as the basis for his or her evaluation. The first of these samples is by Mark Twain, and it evaluates the writing of James Fenimore Cooper, author of, among other novels, *The Last of the Mohicans*.

MARK TWAIN

FENIMORE COOPER'S LITERARY OFFENSES

The Pathfinder and *The Deerslayer* stand at the head of Cooper's novels as artistic creations. There are others of his works which contain parts as perfect as are to be found in these, and scenes even more thrilling. Not one can be compared with either of them as a finished whole.

The defects in both of these tales are comparatively slight. They were pure works of art.

—*Prof. Lounsbury*

The five tales reveal an extraordinary fulness of invention. . . . One of the very greatest characters in fiction, Natty Bumppo. . . . The craft of the woodsman, the tricks of the trapper, all the delicate art of the forest, were familiar to Cooper from his youth up.

—*Prof. Brander Matthews*

Cooper is the greatest artist in the domain of romantic fiction yet produced by America.

—*Wilkie Collins*

1   It seems to me that it was far from right for the Professor of English Literature in Yale, the Professor of English Literature in Columbia, and Wilkie Collins to deliver opinions on Cooper's literature without having read some of it. It would have been much more decorous to keep silent and let persons talk who have read Cooper.

2   Cooper's art has some defects. In one place in *Deerslayer,* and in the restricted space of two-thirds of a page, Cooper has scored 114 offenses against literary art out of a possible 115. It breaks the record.

3   There are nineteen rules governing literary art in the domain of romantic fiction—some say twenty-two. In *Deerslayer* Cooper violated eighteen of them. These eighteen require:

1. That a tale shall accomplish something and arrive somewhere. But the *Deerslayer* tale accomplishes nothing and arrives in the air.
2. They require that the episodes of a tale shall be necessary parts of the tale, and shall help to develop it. But as the *Deerslayer* tale is not a tale, and accomplishes nothing and arrives nowhere, the episodes have no rightful place in the work, since there was nothing for them to develop.
3. They require that the personages in a tale shall be alive, except in the case of corpses, and that always the reader shall be able to tell the corpses from the others. But this detail has often been overlooked in the *Deerslayer* tale.
4. They require that the personages in a tale, both dead and alive, shall exhibit a sufficient excuse for being there. But this detail also has been overlooked in the *Deerslayer* tale.
5. They require that when the personages of a tale deal in conversation, the talk shall sound like human talk, and be talk such as human beings would be likely to talk in the given circumstances, and have a discoverable meaning, also a discoverable purpose, and a show of relevancy, and remain in the neighborhood of the subject in hand, and be interesting to the reader, and help out the tale, and stop when the people cannot think of anything more to say. But this requirement has been ignored from the beginning of the *Deerslayer* tale to the end of it.
6. They require that when the author describes the character of a personage in his tale, the conduct and conversation of that personage shall justify said description. But this law gets little or no attention in the *Deerslayer* tale, as Natty Bumppo's case will amply prove.
7. They require that when a personage talks like an illustrated, gilt-edged, tree-calf, hand-tooled, seven-dollar Friendship's Offering in the beginning of a paragraph, he shall not talk like a negro minstrel in the end of it. But this rule is flung down and danced upon in the *Deerslayer* tale.
8. They require that crass stupidities shall not be played upon the reader as "the craft of the woodsman, the delicate art of the forest," by either the author or the people in the tale. But this rule is persistently violated in the *Deerslayer* tale.
9. They require that the personages of a tale shall confine themselves to possibilities and let miracles alone; or, if they venture a miracle, the author must so plausibly set it forth as to make it look possible and reasonable. But these rules are not respected in the *Deerslayer* tale.
10. They require that the author shall make the reader feel a deep interest in the personages of his tale and in their fate; and that he shall make the reader love the good people in the tale and hate the bad ones. But the reader of the *Deerslayer* tale dislikes the good people in it, is indifferent to the others, and wishes they would all get drowned together.

11. They require that the characters in a tale shall be so clearly defined that the reader can tell beforehand what each will do in a given emergency. But in the *Deerslayer* tale this rule is vacated.

4   In addition to these large rules there are some little ones. These require that the author shall

12. Say what he is proposing to say, not merely come near it.
13. Use the right word, not its second cousin.
14. Eschew surplusage.
15. Not omit necessary details.
16. Avoid slovenliness of form.
17. Use good grammar.
18. Employ a simple and straightforward style.

5   Even these seven are coldly and persistently violated in the *Deerslayer* tale.

6   Cooper's gift in the way of invention was not a rich endowment; but such as it was he liked to work it, he was pleased with the effects, and indeed he did some quite sweet things with it. In his little box of stage-properties he kept six or eight cunning devices, tricks, artifices for his savages and woodsmen to deceive and circumvent each other with, and he was never so happy as when he was working these innocent things and seeing them go. A favorite one was to make a moccasined person tread in the tracks of the moccasined enemy, and thus hide his own trail. Cooper wore out barrels and barrels of moccasins in working that trick. Another stage-property that he pulled out of his box pretty frequently was his broken twig. He prized his broken twig above all the rest of his effects, and worked it the hardest. It is a restful chapter in any book of his when somebody doesn't step on a dry twig and alarm all the reds and whites for two hundred yards around. Every time a Cooper person is in peril, and absolute silence is worth four dollars a minute, he is sure to step on a dry twig. There may be a hundred handier things to step on, but that wouldn't satisfy Cooper. Cooper requires him to turn out and find a dry twig; and if he must do it, go and borrow one. In fact, the Leather Stocking Series ought to have been called the Broken Twig Series.

7   I am sorry there is not room to put in a few dozen instances of the delicate art of the forest, as practiced by Natty Bumppo and some of the other Cooperian experts. Perhaps we may venture two or three samples. Cooper was a sailor—a naval officer; yet he gravely tells us how a vessel, driving toward a lee shore in a gale, is steered for a particular spot by her skipper because he knows of an undertow there which will hold her back against the gale and save her. For just pure woodcraft, or sailorcraft, or whatever it is, isn't that neat? For several years Cooper was daily in the society of artillery, and he ought to have noticed that when a cannonball strikes the ground it either buries itself or skips a hundred feet or so; skips again a hundred feet or so and so on, till finally it gets tired and rolls. Now in one place he loses some "females"—as he always calls women—in the edge of a wood near a plain at night in a fog, on purpose to give Bumppo a chance to show off the delicate art of the forest before the reader. These mislaid people are hunting for a fort. They hear a cannon-blast and a cannonball presently comes rolling into the wood and stops at their feet. To the females this suggests nothing. The case is very different with the admirable Bumppo. I wish I may never know peace again if he doesn't strike out promptly and *follow the track* of that cannonball across the plain through the dense fog and find the fort. Isn't it a daisy? If Cooper had any real knowledge of Nature's ways of doing things, he had a most delicate art in concealing the fact. For instance: one of his acute Indian experts, Chingachgook (pronounced Chicago, I think), has lost the trail of a person he is tracking through

the forest. Apparently that trail is hopelessly lost. Neither you nor I could ever have guessed out the way to find it. It was very different with Chicago. Chicago was not stumped for long. He turned a running stream out of its course, and there, in the slush in its old bed, were that person's moccasin-tracks. The current did not wash them away, as it would have done in all other cases—no, even the eternal laws of Nature have to vacate when Cooper wants to put up a delicate job of woodcraft on the reader.

8 We must be a little wary when Brander Matthews tells us that Cooper's books "reveal an extraordinary fulness of invention." As a rule, I am quite willing to accept Brander Matthews's literary judgments and applaud his lucid and graceful phrasing of them; but that particular statement needs to be taken with a few tons of salt. Bless your heart, Cooper hadn't any more invention than a horse; and I don't mean a high-class horse, either; I mean a clothes-horse. It would be very difficult to find a really clever "situation" in Cooper's books, and still more difficult to find one of any kind which he has failed to render absurd by his handling of it. Look at the episodes of "the caves"; and at the celebrated scuffle between Maqua and those others on the table-land a few days later; and at Hurry Harry's queer water-transit from the castle to the ark; and at Deerslayer's half-hour with his first corpse; and at the quarrel between Hurry Harry and Deerslayer later; and at—but choose for yourself; you can't go amiss.

9 If Cooper had been an observer his inventive faculty would have worked better; not more interestingly, but more rationally, more plausibly. Cooper's proudest creations in the way of "situations" suffer noticeably from the absence of the observer's protecting gift. Cooper's eye was splendidly inaccurate. Cooper seldom saw anything correctly. He saw nearly all things as through a glass eye, darkly. Of course a man who cannot see the commonest little every-day matters accurately is working at a disadvantage when he is constructing a "situation." In the *Deerslayer* tale Cooper has a stream which is fifty feet wide where it flows out of a lake; it presently narrows to twenty as it meanders along for no given reason, and yet when a stream acts like that it ought to be required to explain itself. Fourteen pages later the width of the brook's outlet from the lake has suddenly shrunk thirty feet, and become "the narrowest part of the stream." This shrinkage is not accounted for. The stream has bends in it, a sure indication that it has alluvial banks and cuts them; yet these bends are only thirty and fifty feet long. If Cooper had been a nice and punctilious observer he would have noticed that the bends were oftener nine hundred feet long than short of it.

10 Cooper made the exit of that stream fifty feet wide, in the first place, for no particular reason; in the second place, he narrowed it to less than twenty to accommodate some Indians. He bends a "sapling" to the form of an arch over this narrow passage, and conceals six Indians in its foliage. They are "laying" for a settler's scow or ark which is coming up the stream on its way to the lake; it is being hauled against the stiff current by a rope whose stationary end is anchored in the lake; its rate of progress cannot be more than a mile an hour. Cooper describes the ark, but pretty obscurely. In the matter of dimensions "it was little more than a modern canal-boat." Let us guess, then, that it was about one hundred and forty feet long. It was of "greater breadth than common." Let us guess, then, that it was about sixteen feet wide. This leviathan had been prowling down bends which were but a third as long as itself, and scraping between banks where it had only two feet of space to spare on each side. We cannot too much admire this miracle. A low-roofed log dwelling occupies "two-thirds of the ark's length"—a dwelling ninety feet long and sixteen feet wide, let us say—a kind of vestibule train. The dwelling has two rooms—each forty-five feet long and sixteen feet wide, let us guess. One of them is the bedroom of the Hutter girls, Judith and Hetty; the other is the parlor in the daytime, at night it is papa's bedchamber. The ark is ar-

riving at the stream's exit now, whose width has been reduced to less than twenty feet to accommodate the Indians—say to eighteen. There is a foot to spare on each side of the boat. Did the Indians notice that there was going to be a tight squeeze there? Did they notice that they could make money by climbing down out of that arched sapling and just stepping aboard when the ark scraped by? No, other Indians would have noticed these things, but Cooper's Indians never notice anything. Cooper thinks they are marvelous creatures for noticing, but he was almost always in error about his Indians. There was seldom a sane one among them.

11   The ark is one hundred and forty feet long; the dwelling is ninety feet long. The idea of the Indians is to drop softly and secretly from the arched sapling to the dwelling as the ark creeps along under it at the rate of a mile an hour, and butcher the family. It will take the ark a minute and a half to pass under. It will take the ninety-foot dwelling a minute to pass under. Now, then, what did the six Indians do? It would take you thirty years to guess, and even then you would have to give it up, I believe. Therefore, I will tell you what the Indians did. Their chief, a person of quite extraordinary intellect for a Cooper Indian, warily watched the canal-boat as it squeezed along under him, and when he had got his calculations fined down to exactly the right shade, as he judged, he let go and dropped. And *missed the house!* That is actually what he did. He missed the house, and landed in the stem of the scow. It was not much of a fall yet it knocked him silly. He lay there unconscious. If the house had been ninety-seven feet long he would have made the trip. The fault was Cooper's, not his. The error lay in the construction of the house. Cooper was no architect.

12   There still remained in the roost five Indians. The boat has passed under and is now out of their reach. Let me explain what the five did—you would not be able to reason it out for yourself. No. 1 jumped for the boat, but fell in the water astern of it. Then No. 2 jumped for the boat, but fell in the water still farther astern of it. Then No. 3 jumped for the boat, and fell a good way astern of it. Then No. 4 jumped for the boat, and fell in the water away astern. Then even No. 5 made a jump for the boat—for he was a Cooper Indian. In the matter of intellect, the difference between a Cooper Indian and the Indian that stands in front of the cigar-shop is not spacious. The scow episode is really a sublime burst of invention; but it does not thrill, because the inaccuracy of the details throws a sort of air of fictitiousness and general improbability over it. This comes of Cooper's inadequacy as an observer.

13   The reader will find some examples of Cooper's high talent for inaccurate observation in the account of the shooting-match in *The Pathfinder.*

"A common wrought nail was driven lightly into the target, its head having been first touched with paint."

14   The color of the paint is not stated—an important omission, but Cooper deals freely in important omissions. No, after all, it was not an important omission; for this nailhead *is a hundred yards from* the marksmen, and could not be seen by them at that distance, no matter what its color might be. How far can the best eyes see a common house-fly? A hundred yards? It is quite impossible. Very well; eyes that cannot see a house-fly that is a hundred yards away cannot see an ordinary nail head at that distance, for the size of the two objects is the same. It takes a keen eye to see a fly or a nail-head at fifty yards—one hundred and fifty feet. Can the reader do it?

15   The nail was lightly driven, its head painted, and game called. Then the Cooper miracles began. The bullet of the first marksman chipped an edge of the nail-head; the next man's bullet drove the nail a little way into the target—and removed all the paint. Haven't the miracles gone far enough now? Not to suit Cooper; for the purpose of this

whole scheme is to show off his prodigy, Deerslayer-Hawkeye-Long-Rifle-Leather-Stocking-Pathfinder-Bumppo before the ladies.

"Be all ready to clench it, boys!" cried out Pathfinder, stepping into his friend's tracks the instant they were vacant. "Never mind a new nail; I can see that, though the paint is gone, and what I can see I can hit at a hundred yards, though it were only a mosquito's eye. Be ready to clench!"

The rifle cracked, the bullet sped its way, and the head of the nail was buried in the wood, covered by the piece of flattened lead.

16   There, you see, is a man who could hunt flies with a rifle, and command a ducal salary in a Wild West show today if we had him back with us.

17   The recorded feat is certainly surprising just as it stands; but it is not surprising enough for Cooper. Cooper adds a touch. He has made Pathfinder do this miracle with another man's rifle; and not only that, but Pathfinder did not have even the advantage of loading it himself. He had everything against him, and yet he made that impossible shot; and not only made it, but did it with absolute confidence, saying, "Be ready to clench." Now a person like that would have undertaken that same feat with a brick-bat, and with Cooper to help he would have achieved it, too.

18   Pathfinder showed off handsomely that day before the ladies. His very first feat was a thing which no Wild West show can touch. He was standing with the group of marksmen, observing—a hundred yards from the target, mind; one Jasper raised his rifle and drove the center of the bull's-eye. Then the Quartermaster fired. The target exhibited no result this time. There was a laugh. "It's a dead miss," said Major Lundie. Pathfinder waited an impressive moment or two; then said, in that calm, indifferent, know-it-all way of his, "No, Major, he has covered Jasper's bullet as will be seen if any-one will take the trouble to examine the target."

19   Wasn't it remarkable! How *could* he see that little pellet fly through the air and enter that distant bullet-hole? Yet that is what he did; for nothing is impossible to a Cooper person. Did any of those people have any deep-seated doubts about this thing? No; for that would imply sanity, and these were all Cooper people.

The respect for Pathfinder's skill and for his *quickness and accuracy of sight* (the italics are mine) was so profound and general, that the instant he made this declaration the spectators began to distrust their own opinions, and a dozen rushed to the target in order to ascertain the fact. There, sure enough, it was found that the Quartermaster's bullet had gone through the hole made by Jasper's, and that, too so accurately as to require a minute examination to be certain of the circumstance, which, however, was soon clearly established by discovering one bullet over the other in the stump against which the target was placed.

They made a "minute" examination; but never mind, how could they know that there were two bullets in that hole without digging the latest one out? for neither probe nor eyesight could prove the presence of any more than one bullet. Did they dig? No; as we shall see. It is the Pathfinder's turn now; he steps out before the ladies, takes aim, and fires.

20   But, alas! here is a disappointment; an incredible, an unimaginable disappointment—for the target's aspect is unchanged; there is nothing there but that same old bullet-hole!

"If one dared to hint at such a thing," cried Major Duncan, "I should say that the Pathfinder has also missed the target!"

21   As nobody had missed it yet, the "also" was not necessary; but never mind about that, for the Pathfinder is going to speak.

> "No, no, Major," said he, confidently, "that would be a risky declaration. I didn't load the piece, and can't say what was in it; but if it was lead, you will find the bullet driving down those of the Quartermaster and Jasper, else is not my name Pathfinder."
> A shout from the target announced the truth of this assertion.

22   Is the miracle sufficient as it stands? Not for Cooper. The Pathfinder speaks again, as he "now slowly advances towards the stage occupied by the females":

> "That's not all, boys, that's not all; if you find the target touched at all, I'll own to a miss. The Quartermaster cut the wood, but you'll find no wood cut by that last messenger."

23   The miracle is at last complete. He knew—doubtless *saw*—at the distance of a hundred yards—that his bullet had passed into the hole *without fraying the edges*. There were now three bullets in that one hole—three bullets embedded processionally in the body of the stump back of the target. Everybody knew this—somehow or other—and yet nobody had dug any of them out to make sure. Cooper is not a close observer, but he is interesting. He is certainly always that, no matter what happens. And he is more interesting when he is not noticing what he is about than when he is. This is a considerable merit.

24   The conversations in the Cooper books have a curious sound in our modern ears. To believe that such talk really ever came out of people's mouths would be to believe that there was a time when time was of no value to a person who thought he had something to say; when it was the custom to spread a two minute remark out to ten; when a man's mouth was a rolling-mill, and busied itself all day long in turning four-foot pigs of thought into thirty-foot bars of conversational railroad iron by attenuation; when subjects were seldom faithfully stuck to, but the talk wandered all around and arrived nowhere; when conversations consisted mainly of irrelevancies, with here and there a relevancy, a relevancy with an embarrassed look, as not being able to explain how it got there.

25   Cooper was certainly not a master in the construction of dialogue. Inaccurate observation defeated him here as it defeated him in so many other enterprises of his. He even failed to notice that the man who talks corrupt English six days in the week must and will talk it on the seventh, and can't help himself. In the *Deerslayer* story he lets Deerslayer talk the showiest kind of book-talk sometimes, and at other times the basest of base dialects. For instance, when someone asks him if he has a sweetheart, and if so, where she abides, this is his majestic answer:

> "She's in the forest—hanging from the boughs of the trees, in a soft rain—in the dew on the open grass—the clouds that float about in the blue heavens—the birds that sing in the woods—the sweet springs where I slake my thirst—and in all the other glorious gifts that come from God's Providence!"

26   And he preceded that, a little before, with this:

> "It consarns me as all things that touches a frind consarns a frind."

27   And this is another of his remarks:

> "If I was Injin born, now, I might tell of this, or carry in the scalp and boast of the expl'ite afore the whole tribe; or if my inimy had only been a bear"

—and so on.

28   We cannot imagine such a thing as a veteran Scotch Commander-in-Chief comporting himself in the field like a windy melodramatic actor, but Cooper could. On one occasion Alice and Cora were being chased by the French through a fog in the neighborhood of their father's fort:

> *"Point de quartier aux coquins!"* cried an eager pursuer, who seemed to direct the operations of the enemy.
>
> "Stand firm and be ready, my gallant 60ths!" suddenly exclaimed a voice above them; "wait to see the enemy; fire low, and sweep the glacis."
>
> "Father! father!" exclaimed a piercing cry from out the mist; "it is I! Alice! thy own Elsie! spare, O! save your daughters!"
>
> "Hold!" shouted the former speaker, in the awful tones of parental agony, the sound reaching even to the woods, and rolling back in solemn echo. "'Tis she! God has restored me my children! Throw open the sally-port, to the field, 60ths, to the field! Pull not a trigger, lest ye kill my lambs! Drive off these dogs of France with your steel!"

29   Cooper's word-sense was singularly dull. When a person has a poor ear for music he will flat and sharp right along without knowing it. He keeps near the tune, but it is not the tune. When a person has a poor ear for words, the result is a literary flatting and sharping; you perceive what he is intending to say, but you also perceive that he doesn't say it. This is Cooper. He was not a word-musician. His ear was satisfied with the approximate word. I will furnish some circumstantial evidence in support of this charge. My instances are gathered from half a dozen pages of the tale called *Deerslayer*. He uses "verbal," for "oral"; "precision," for "facility"; "phenomena," for "marvels"; "necessary," for "predetermined"; "unsophisticated," for "primitive"; "preparation," for "expectancy"; "rebuked," for "subdued"; "dependent on," for "resulting from"; "fact," for "condition"; "fact," for "conjecture"; "precaution," for "caution"; "explain," for "determine"; "mortified," for "disappointed"; "meretricious," for "factitious"; "materially," for "considerably"; "decreasing," for "deepening"; "increasing," for "disappearing"; "embedded," for "enclosed"; "treacherous," for "hostile"; "stood," for "stooped"; "softened," for "replaced"; "rejoined," for "remarked"; "situation," for "conditions"; "different," for "differing"; "insensible," for "unsentient"; "brevity," for "celerity"; "distrusted," for "suspicious"; "mental imbecility," for "imbecility"; "eyes," for "sight"; "counteracting," for "opposing"; "funeral obsequies," for "obsequies."

30   There have been daring people in the world who claimed that Cooper could write English, but they are all dead now—all dead but Lounsbury. I don't remember that Lounsbury makes the claim in so many words, still he makes it, for he says that *Deerslayer* is a "pure work of art." Pure, in that connection, means faultless—faultless in all details—and language is a detail. If Mr. Lounsbury had only compared Cooper's English with the English which he writes himself—but it is plain that he didn't; and so it is likely that he imagines until this day that Cooper's is as clean and compact as his own. Now I feel sure, deep down in my heart, that Cooper wrote about the poorest English that exists in our language, and that the English of *Deerslayer* is the very worst that even Cooper ever wrote.

31   I may be mistaken, but it does seem to me that *Deerslayer* is not a work of art in any sense; it does seem to me that it is destitute of every detail that goes to the making of a work of art; in truth, it seems to me that *Deerslayer* is just simply a literary delirium tremens.

32   A work of art? It has no invention; it has no order, system, sequence, or result; it has no lifelikeness, no thrill, no stir, no seeming of reality; its characters are confusedly

drawn, and by their acts and words they prove that they are not the sort of people the author claims that they are; its humor is pathetic; its pathos is funny; its conversations are—oh! indescribable; its love-scenes odious; its English a crime against the language.

33   Counting these out, what is left is Art. I think we must all admit that.

Questions for Review

1. What is Twain's judgment of Cooper's writing? On what criteria does he base his judgment? How does he support this judgment; what examples does he offer that develop the criteria?
2. Divide Twain's essay into its beginning, middle, and end. How many subsections are there in the middle of this essay, the portion in which Twain presents examples from Cooper's writings?
3. A writer of evaluation essays needs to be fair and thorough in considering the topic. How fair and thorough does Twain appear to be? On what do you base your assessment?
4. To what extent does Twain's use of humor lessen the impact of his criticism?
5. Are you convinced that Cooper is as bad a writer as Twain says he is, or has Twain perhaps inspired you to read some of *The Deerslayer* tales to see for yourself?

The second sample essay is a newspaper column by Ellen Goodman, who writes a syndicated column. In it, Goodman evaluates the importance of a new book about girls in the United States.

ELLEN GOODMAN

BEAUTY INDUSTRY ON RAMPAGE

1   There are times when I wonder if the female body isn't part of some vast evolutionary speedup. In less than a generation, the girls I know seem to have acquired all these new body parts to worry about.

2   A glance at any teen magazine is a new anatomy lesson. Eyes are now subdivided into half a dozen distinct areas from brow to lash, each of which needs to be thinned or thickened, shaved or shaded. Teeth demand brightening as well as straightening. Thighs have grown cellulite. Lips require "plumping." Arms bulge for biceps. And every unmentionable inch of the body seems to need perfume of one kind or another.

3   Of course it is not our bodies but the beauty industry on this evolutionary rampage. It's rather like the trend in medicine. As general practitioners splintered into an array

of subspecialists, the beauty market splintered into products for every inch from scalp to toenail, acne to elbow.

4   The difference of course is that medicine changed to make their patients feel better. The beauty industry changed to make their customers feel worse.

5   Anyone who spends time with teen-age girls knows that they aren't narcissists. Narcissus, after all, wasted away before a pool of water while constantly admiring his image. Teen-age girls are drowning in words like "I hate my body; I hate my looks. I hate myself."

6   It is this despairing mantra that Joan Jacobs Brumberg explores in *The Body Project.* Her book, subtitled *An Intimate History of American Girls,* is the third in a triumvirate of works about the crisis in the lives of adolescent girls.

7   First, Carol Gilligan identified the moment when girls in our culture lose their authentic "voice" and self-confidence. Next Mary Pipher explored this psychological reality of female adolescence in *Reviving Ophelia.* Now Brumberg has filled in the blank, saying that a girl's relationship to her body is "at the heart of the crisis of confidence."

8   Her delightful and painful history ranges from the days when girls were tied into corsets to the days when girls are corseted by internal voices demanding model-thin perfection. It crosses the century from an era when girls rarely mentioned their bodies at all to an era when the body has become their "project."

9   Allowing us to eavesdrop on a wonderful assortment of teen-age diaries, she compares the self-improvement plans of a late 19th-century adolescent to a later 20th-century girl. The first girl resolves "not to talk about myself or feelings. . . . To think before speaking. To work seriously. To be self-restrained in conversation and actions. . . . To be dignified. Interest myself more in others."

10   The second girl resolves to "try to make myself better in any way I possibly can with the help of my budget and baby-sitting money. I will lose weight, get new lenses, already got a new haircut, good makeup, new clothes and accessories."

11   In barely a hundred years, a girl's identity had attached like Velcro to her appearance.

12   *The Body Project* is not a lament for the good old days. Brumberg tells the history of everything from menstruation to virginity, from mirrors to training bras, from petting to eating disorders. But she has no nostalgia for the era when 60 percent of high school students in Boston were totally unprepared for menstruation.

13   Nevertheless she is aware of the trade-offs we've made. Girls who once were held under the Victorian umbrella of protection are "freed" into "a consumer culture that seduces them into thinking that the body and sexual expression are their most important projects." Girls once repressed and chaperoned to adulthood are now more independent and vulnerable in a society sexualizing them at a younger age.

14   While enlivening the history, *The Body Project* draws the crucial connection between bad body images and bad choices, between how girls feel about their bodies and what they do with them.

15   "Girls who do not feel good about themselves need the affirmation of others," Brumberg writes, "and that need, unfortunately, almost always empowers male desire. In other words, girls who hate their bodies do not make good decisions about partners or about the kind of sexual activity that is in their best interest."

16   What is missing today, after a century of change, says Brumberg, is "an intergenerational dialogue" between women and girls. Her book is a fine text for such a conversation. It makes us think seriously about a world in which teen-age misery is described all too seriously as a bad hair day.

1. Goodman's essay is not a simple book review; that is, Goodman does not simply present a summary of the book's contents and then say that she liked or didn't like the book. What is Goodman's evaluation of *The Body Project*? How important or effective a book does she think it is?
2. Identify Goodman's thesis sentence, the one in which she presents her evaluation of this book. Where does it appear in the essay? Is this an effective placement? Why or why not?
3. What does Goodman offer to support her evaluation of *The Body Project*?

In our third sample essay, Stacy Birch, a first-year composition student at New Mexico State University (NMSU), speculates about the potential benefit of a program designed to attack the problem of deadbeat parents in New Mexico.

STACY BIRCH

WHAT A CHILD DESERVES

1   On October fifteenth of this year [1997] a new project, called Project Amnesty, was adopted throughout the state of New Mexico. Project Amnesty has been specifically designed to decrease the number of parents, especially fathers, who do not pay child support or provide medical insurance for their children. These parents who are not currently financially supporting their sons and daughters have now been given a forty-five day amnesty period to make child support payments, or at least provide health care insurance. If no action is taken during this amnesty period, penalties, including heavy fines and even arrest, could and will be levied. Project Amnesty will be an overall benefit to the children of New Mexico because it will force deadbeat parents to provide money and insurance that rightfully belong to their children.

2   Everyday people are in contact with single parents struggling to provide for their children. A good friend of mine, Elizabeth, is one of these parents. Elizabeth was a freshman in college when she learned that she and her boyfriend Andrew, a sophomore, were going to have a baby. She was excited at first but became horrified when Andrew said that he wanted nothing to do with a child or with Elizabeth, if she decided to keep the baby. Weighing her choices, Elizabeth decided to keep her child and so gave birth to a boy, Darren Michael. She vowed that Darren would receive all of the love and support that she could offer, and that would include court-ordered support payments from Andrew. Elizabeth dropped out of college in order to support herself and her young son. Not once has she asked for help from any of the different welfare programs that she is eligible for, though she has expected help from Andrew, and rightfully so.

3   Darren is now two. Andrew has done nothing to support his son. Not once has he accepted his responsibility for Darren; not once has he offered to help Elizabeth with her

financial struggle; not once has he made a single child support payment. Under Project Amnesty all of that would change. As Darren's biological father, Andrew now has forty-five days to begin to make child support payments and so assume his share of responsibility for his child.

4   In New Mexico, one of five children who are separated from a parent has not seen or heard from that mother or father in the past five years. As parents, it is their rightful job to support their children, if not being there themselves and supporting them physically and emotionally, then by supporting them financially. Yet, of all the single parent families in New Mexico, only half of the children receive some sort of support from an absent mother or father. Only twenty-two percent of these young people have health insurance. It makes me wonder if the children of these people mean anything to them at all. Do they not care about the well-being of their offspring?

5   Last year, the state of New Mexico spent over forty-two million dollars in taxpayers' money to pay for Medicaid costs of children who do not have medical insurance and who are not receiving child support. Forty-two million dollars is a lot of money, but that amount could easily have been covered if every parent separated from his or her child supplied the financial support they legally owe. If it takes throwing these people in jail to help them see the error of their ways, then so be it.

6   Many programs in today's society have been set up to help single parents, mostly single mothers, provide for their children. These programs and services really do help families, but in turn a lot of people abuse them. Because of this, beneficial services for children are in danger of being terminated. That would leave a lot of parents between a rock and a hard spot. Also, because of newly-passed government policies, a person can now rely on welfare for only a limited time while trying to find a job. Often jobs don't completely solve the problem; single mothers (or fathers) need financial support to help pay for babysitters while they work. Unpaid child support could be used to take care of such problems as this.

7   In the book *Chicken Soup for the Soul,* I read about Hanoch McCarty, a recently-divorced man with full custody of his two small children. Mr. McCarty is just one of many single parents who know how important a child support payment is. "After work it all crowded in on me: the fatigue, the weight of responsibility, the worry about bills I wasn't sure I could pay that month. The endless details of running a house. Only a short time before, I'd been married and had a partner to share these chores, these bills, these worries with" (126). It is a scary reality to a mother or father when there just isn't enough money to provide for their children. Support payments give that single parent a sense of security, a knowledge that at least their children will have some money available for what they need. Even if that parent works and has a steady income, for emergency's sake it is good to know that that money will be there. Child support payments provide this safety net.

8   Since Project Amnesty has only begun, we cannot gauge its final outcome. It is Project Amnesty's goal to at least double the amount of child support payments currently being paid in New Mexico. I believe that the amount of child support payments will increase, maybe even meet that goal, because of this program. If payments do increase, if children do benefit from this program, then the effort to push the program forward will have been worth it, even if some deadbeat parents are fined or jailed for not supporting their children.

WORK CITED

McCarty, Hanoch. "Permission to Cry." *A 4th Course of Chicken Soup for the Soul.* Ed. Jack Canfield et al. Deerfield Beach, FL: Health Communications, 1997. 125–27.

1. What is Stacy's thesis? What is her judgment about the potential effectiveness of Project Amnesty?
2. What reasons does Stacy offer in support of her judgment?
3. What kinds of support does she provide for her position? How effective are these different supporting details?
4. Divide Stacy's essay into its beginning, middle, and end. What does she do to introduce you to the topic (the beginning)? How effective is this introduction? How effectively does she end this essay?

In the fourth essay, Michelle Lebsock, a first-year writing student at NMSU, evaluates *Revival*, a CD by Gillian Welch, who is one of Michelle's favorite artists.

MICHELLE LEBSOCK

GILLIAN WELCH: MUSIC'S "NEXT BIG THING"

1   *Revival* is a little known CD by Gillian Welch that has been described as everything from a folk CD tinged with blues, western, and gospel influences to alternative country. Welch herself admits that it's hard to categorize, because there are so many different, easily recognizable influences on the CD. However, even in the music world of folk hybrids with such talented and recognizable artists as Jewel and Lori Carson at the forefront, Gillian Welch is a musical force to be reckoned with. *Revival* is an excellent new-folk CD because it encompasses strong vocals and lyrics and varies between songs without losing continuity throughout the CD as a whole.

2   The musical content of *Revival* is refreshingly original in comparison to the majority of CD's being released on the market today, and Welch's voice is critical in delivering the songs the way they are meant to be heard. Powerful and versatile, her voice commands your attention, and she has a good range and impressive control. But her voice also has a hardened quality that makes you believe she has experienced at least some of the hardships endured by the characters in the songs, an essential feature of folk music. Layered harmony tracks are nonexistent on this CD: Welch's voice either stands on its own, or when harmony is called for in a song it is provided very low-key by her song-writing partner David Rawlings. In fact, the recording of the entire CD was very low-fi—to complement the sparse, simple beauty and tone of the songs, it was recorded entirely in mono (not stereo) sound, and a few of the songs such as "Pass You By" were good enough to be put on the album after the first take. For a song to be of album quality on a live take is rare, and is a testament to the exceptional musicianship of Welch and her collaborators.

3   Not only are the vocals impressive, but the lyrics play a large part in the overall impact of the CD. *Revival* follows like a page taken from a history book—it paints an

unmistakable picture of the hardship and perseverance that composed the human experience of a simpler time. There is a storytelling quality to each song Welch writes, which ranges from specific detail in "One More Dollar," a song that chronicles the events that changed the course of one person's life, to just relaying a small event in order to set the tone and mood of a song, such as in "Pass You By." "Pass You By" is a song that especially stands out, even on a CD of excellent songs. The stark imagery of the lyrics is set to a sparse bluesy melody that almost makes you want to be cruising down a deserted highway (think Thelma and Louise) or in a smoky bar with the song playing on the jukebox in the corner and filling up the room almost as thickly as smoke. "Pass You By" starts out seemingly as a simple song about a car:

> I've got an old V-8 from the year I was born
> Don't look like much, just a flat black Ford
> But the engine's clean. I could paint her some day,
> But most of the time I think I like her this way.

But then it blossoms into a song more about independence—"I'm just a wind on the road, gonna pass you by"—with a hint of lawless rebellion:

> I got a brand new plan, gonna help myself
> 'Cause it's the fat man's turn, gonna share the wealth,
> Put the money in the bag, and keep your hands in sight,
> Turn around, count to ten, I'll go back into the night.

4   The songs on *Revival* vary in style, but never outreach their capabilities or disrupt the overall feeling of continuity. "Paper Wings" is a slow, retrospective song about a relationship that failed to meet all expectations, and a commentary on how love can be blind. Layered in reverb and taking full advantage of the sustain pedal, it brings to mind the hazy overtones of a dream. Embodying the opposite mood of "Paper Wings" is "Tear My Stillhouse Down." A spirited account of the evils associated with moonshine—

> When I was a child way back in the hills
> I laughed at the men who tended those stills
> But that old mountain shine, it caught me somehow
> When I die tear my stillhouse down.
> Oh, tear my stillhouse down, let it go to rust
> Don't leave no trace of the hiding place where I made that evil stuff.
> For all my time and money no profit did I see—

it transports you into a world and a time that no longer exists. "Annabelle" also recalls another era, but this time from the perspective of a hardworking farming family, and how the death of their daughter affected their lives:

> When I'm dead and buried I'll take a hard life of tears
> From every day I've ever known
> Anna's in the churchyard, she got no life at all
> She only got these words on a stone.

However, not all the songs have such a defined story line. "Acony Bell" uses the example of a small flower to lend hope in troubled times:

> Well, it makes its home 'mid the rocks and rills,
> Where the snow lies deep on the windy hills,
> And it tells the world "Why should I wait
> This ice and snow is gonna melt away."

And so I'll sing that yellow bird's song
For the troubled times will soon be gone.

The timelessness of the writing ties all the songs together. Welch does not rely on using temporary music fads or jump on the "new trend in music" bandwagon like so many artists do to make a CD, and that is why the songs sound so different from each other, yet still make perfect sense when combined on a CD.

5   Gillian Welch is one of contemporary music's most promising artists, and while *Revival* might not have been as commercially profitable as other CD's, it makes a fan out of almost everyone who listens to it. *Revival* has not only won the admiration of those who own the CD, it was also nominated in 1995 for a Grammy in the best new-folk category. The fact that Gillian Welch is a talented musician is evident on *Revival*, through its professional yet earthy vocals, imaginative lyrics, and overall musical quality.

WORK CITED

Welch, Gillian. *Revival*. UNI/Almo Sounds, 1996.

Questions for Review

1. What is the thesis of this essay? What judgment does Michelle offer of *Revival*?
2. What reasons does Michelle offer to support her judgment?
3. What kinds of support does she provide for her position? How effective are these supporting details?
4. Divide Michelle's essay into its beginning, middle, and end. What does she do to introduce you to the topic (the beginning)? How effective is this introduction? How effectively does Michelle end her essay?
5. How does the title work with the essay? Does it promise more than the essay delivers? Why or why not?

THE RHETORICAL TRIANGLE
SUBJECT

What kinds of topics lend themselves to evaluation? Although we can (and do) evaluate nearly everything in our lives, not all subjects lend themselves readily to evaluation essays. The most suitable topics for evaluation essays are those that, for whatever reasons, may be characterized by some degree of controversy or may be open to debate.

Writing an evaluation will require you to judge whether the topic of your essay is good or bad, effective or ineffective, beneficial or detrimental, important or unimportant, and so on. These descriptors can apply to a number of topics, although not equally well to all. When you look in the mirror just before you leave on a date, you probably think "Lookin' good!" but not "Lookin' effective" or "Lookin' beneficial." Were you to consider a change in policy in your university, you probably would think in terms of effectiveness, benefit, or importance. Here's a list of potential topics for an evaluation essay:

a performance (play, movie, CD, television show, concert, fiction or poetry reading)

a policy (campus housing, affirmative action, university admissions, nongraded courses)

a one-time event (a football, basketball, soccer, volleyball game; a school or political rally)

a piece of literature (novel, short story, drama, poem, autobiography, nonfiction essay)

a bureaucracy (campus housing office, juvenile court system)

a law (concerning drunk driving, underage drinking, education, the environment, child and/or spouse abuse)

a program (date-rape prevention, drug education, child advocacy)

a proposal (to institute a flat income tax, to change a program or implement a new one on campus, to allow or deny high school students off-campus lunch privileges, to add or drop a varsity-level sports program)

a campaign (political, advertising, fund-raising)

a public or professional person (politician, teacher, athlete, writer, artist, performer)

As you can see from this list, topics for evaluation essays can range widely.

WRITER

As an evaluator, you'll need to impress your reader with your fairness and with the thoroughness with which you consider your topic. Because you'll eventually present your opinion about the topic, you cannot avoid your biases, but you must take care not to let any preconceived ideas about your topic go unsupported. That is, if you're evaluating a CD by one of your favorite artists, you may well assume that this CD will be every bit as good as previous ones by this same star. It may be; then again, it may not be. Your job will be to evaluate the new CD as fairly and completely as possible, to proceed as a fan of the artist, but to be willing to criticize when necessary. To convince your reader that your evaluation is worth considering, you'll need to show that you've given serious thought to the topic.

READER

In thinking about the readers for your evaluation essay, you may find it helpful to contrast them with readers of an information essay (discussed in Chapter 6) and with those of a position (or argumentative) essay (which we discuss in Chapter 9). Readers of an information essay generally assume that the writer knows more than they do, and they are receptive to the information being given. Readers of an evaluation essay are likely to be receptive to the writer's opinion but won't necessarily defer to his or her knowledge or expertise. When you write an evaluation essay, you must earn the right to be believed by offering support for the assertions you make. And your readers should be prepared to be convinced, that is, to accept your judgments, if you offer and develop that support.

The readers of a position, or argumentative, essay are more likely to be skeptical about your purpose. They may, in fact, be on the opposite side of the issue; they may disagree with you from the outset. So your job is to help readers on the other side of the issue understand why you think as you do.

In argumentative writing, then, you may assume some resistance or opposition from your readers, but this is not the case in evaluative writing. Instead, you may assume that your audience will approach your essay needing (and willing) to be convinced of the validity of the evaluative assertion it makes.

DISTINGUISHING FEATURES OF EVALUATION ESSAYS
EVALUATION CRITERIA

Sometimes criteria are referred to as the standards against which you'll judge your topic. Look again at your responses to Exercise 7.1 (p. 211). What traits of a good teacher did you list? Those traits form the criteria you used to decide whether Ms. Smith and Mr. Jones fit into the category "good teacher"; they represent the standards you think a good teacher should meet.

If you do not establish criteria, or standards, for your evaluation, you are dealing in a matter of personal taste rather than evaluation. For example, Ron recently attended a movie (*Face/Off*) with his son Christopher. After the movie, when Christopher asked his opinion of it, Ron said that he thought the acting was very good, the musical score exciting, the plot full of twists and turns and surprises, and the cinematography of very high quality. Now, Ron and Christopher don't actually talk like this, but we're giving the gist of what was said.

After this listing, Christopher said, "So you thought it was a good movie." Ron responded, only half in jest, "No." In fact, he thought it worked as an action/suspense movie; he just doesn't happen to like action/suspense movies. Ron doesn't think that there is any action/suspense movie that he would evaluate as a good film. This is a matter of personal taste. Ron would not seriously attempt to write an essay supporting this evaluation. To do so, he would have to come up with a list of criteria for all movies that he and his readers could agree on, and the project would certainly falter at the outset. However, people who like action/suspense movies could probably agree on a listing of criteria (something like those Ron offered) that would characterize good action/suspense movies.

As you explore your topic, you'll need to establish criteria by which to evaluate it. And you may be called on to justify your criteria, to defend them as appropriate and effective in evaluating your topic. To help you think about criteria, complete the following exercise.

Exercise 7.2

1. List the traits or characteristics of two or three of the following: a good restaurant; a good romance novel or technothriller; an effective writing class; an important political announcement; a beneficial self-improvement program (e.g., an exercise or weight-loss program); high-quality children's television programming. After making your lists, name two or three examples that exemplify the traits in each category.

2. Are some of the traits you listed more important or essential than others? For one of the categories, rank your criteria from most to least important. Compare your ranked list with that of one of your classmates for the same category. On what points do you agree? Disagree? Other than personal taste, how can you justify the differences between your list and that of your classmate?

WRITER'S JUDGMENT

Your essay should present a value judgement about the worthiness of your topic. Once you've made this judgment, your job is to marshal support for it. The criteria you established for evaluating your topic can guide you here, because you can state the criteria as reasons, and reasons must be supported.

As an example, look at Michelle Lebsock's essay again (pp. 225–227). In evaluating Gillian Welch's CD *Revival*, Michelle makes a value judgment and presents three criteria in her thesis: "*Revival* is an excellent new-folk CD because it encompasses strong vocals and lyrics and varies between songs without losing continuity throughout the CD as a whole." Michelle then casts these criteria—"strong vocals," "[strong] lyrics," and variety—as topic sentences that she must support.

> *Paragraph 2:* The musical content of *Revival* is refreshingly original in comparison to the majority of CD's being released on the market today, and Welch's voice is critical in delivering the songs the way they are meant to be heard.
>
> *Paragraph 3:* Not only are the vocals impressive, but the lyrics play a large part in the overall impact of the CD.
>
> *Paragraph 4:* The songs on *Revival* vary in style, but never outreach their capabilities or disrupt the overall feeling of continuity.

With a clearly stated thesis that presents her evaluation of *Revival* and then with topic sentences that reflect the criteria she brought to bear on the CD, Michelle wrote a tightly structured essay.

1. Look at the sample essays earlier in this chapter and identify the thesis of each. How did the writer structure his or her thesis? What key evaluative terms (such as "good" or "bad") did the writer use? How effectively does the thesis serve to guide the paper? What criteria does each writer use to develop the thesis? What kind of information does the writer use to support each criterion? How effective are the criteria and their support? Why?

2. Below are several thesis statements. How effective do you think each thesis would be in guiding an evaluation essay? Why? What criteria could be developed in support of each thesis?
   a. The NMSU Department of English is an exceptionally good academic department.
   b. Skateboards should not have been banned from the NMSU campus.
   c. The campus libraries are not open enough hours to meet student needs.
   d. Drug-education programs aimed at educating elementary students are clearly not working.
   e. Mark Twain was a great American novelist.
   f. Despite having been first published over a century ago, *Little Women* succeeds today as a girls' book.
   g. In making cartoon versions of fairy tales, Disney Studios has not been faithful to the original versions.

"BECAUSE" SUPPORT

To support your evaluation, you'll provide details to develop or support the criteria you've chosen. Try framing these details as "because" statements, as in this example:

> Mr. Jones is an effective teacher *because* he makes sure his students understand the subject.

Whether this sentence actually appears in the final paper doesn't matter. What does matter is that you develop such sentences and then add support for them. Each "because" statement may serve as a topic sentence for a paragraph in an essay or as the basis for a given paragraph's topic sentence, as in this example:

> *"Because" statement:* Mr. Jones is an effective teacher *because* he makes sure his students understand the subject.
>
> Mr. Jones amazes his students by the amount of energy he puts into their understanding algebra, the great love of his life. If he needs to explain a concept three or four times before his students get it, he does so. If he needs to work extra sample problems on the board to ensure that his class can successfully complete their homework, he works them. If he needs to establish study groups to give students extra help, he does so, even if it means meeting with them before and after school. Whatever it takes to help his students master algebra, that's what Mr. Jones gives.

ASSIGNMENT AND GUIDELINES FOR WRITING

ASSIGNMENT

Write an evaluation of something with which you're familiar. Your job is to pick a topic, decide on its worth (i.e., whether it's good or bad, effective or ineffective, and so on), state your value judgment, and then offer detailed support for your judgment.

CHOOSING A TOPIC

To find a topic for this essay, think initially about things you like and things you don't like. Draw a vertical line down the middle of a sheet of paper, and label one side with a plus (+) and the other with a minus (−). Then, list things you like or feel positively about on the plus side and things you don't like or feel negatively about on the minus side.

Another source of potential topics is the list we presented on page 228. Pick one of the broader general categories given there, and brainstorm a list of memorable examples (positive or negative) for the various entries following the category. Here's a list of specific examples Bill came up with for the "performance" category:

> drama—*Equus, Children of a Lesser God, Kringle's Window, The Grapes of Wrath*
> movie—*Crossing Delancey, The Pelican Brief, Patriot Games*
> CD—*Now That I've Found You: A Collection* (Alison Krause), *Other Voices/Other Rooms* (Nanci Griffith)
> TV show—*Friends, JAG, Nash Bridges, Suddenly Susan, The Simpsons, Married with Children*
> concert—Matt's spring choir concert, NMSU's production of *Carmen*, St. Paul's Christmas music
> fiction reading—Antonya Nelson's "In the Land of Men," Kevin McIlvoy's excerpt from *The Fifth Station*
> poetry reading—Kathleen West's interview colloquium

Some of Bill's examples are national in scope; others (those in the last three categories) are local. But all are potential topics for an evaluation essay.

Once you settle on a topic, spend at least 15 minutes freewriting about it. Try to focus on what you like or don't like about the topic so that you begin to develop an opinion or prepare to make a value judgment.

COLLECTING INFORMATION

A good beginning point is to brainstorm a list of criteria that may be appropriate to use in judging the quality of the selected topic. For a movie, the criteria may be obvious. But for something like a political campaign, arriving at the criteria for judging may well be the most difficult part of the process—assuming that you won't settle for "winning the election" as the sole means of evaluating the campaign.

Once you've made a value judgment and established the criteria for evaluating your topic, think in terms of "because" and then of "why." For example, someone could say of New Mexico, "The state truly lives up to its reputation as the Land of Enchantment." This writer could then offer the following statements as points in support of the assertion:

> New Mexico is the Land of Enchantment because of its unique azure skies.
>
> New Mexico is the Land of Enchantment because of the quality of light on the mountains as the sun sets each day.
>
> New Mexico is the Land of Enchantment because of its official state question: "Red or green?"
>
> New Mexico is the Land of Enchantment because of the stark contrasts its landscape offers.

Each of the phrases completing the "because" points to a reason that supports the particular assertion. The third sentence, for example, focuses on the official state question. How does this sentence show enchantment? New Mexicans take their chiles seriously. When ordering a plate of enchiladas or any of numerous other entrees, they will be asked whether they want red chiles or green chiles as the basis for the dish. It's rare for a diner to answer "Either" or "It doesn't matter." It's also rare for a diner who prefers green chiles to switch to red chiles or vice-versa. Chile lovers have their preferences, and they hold to them steadfastly. Because of this seriousness, New Mexico's 1999 legislature adopted the question "Red or green?" as the official state question, to go along with the official state mammal (the black bear), and so on. But the state question is also tongue in cheek—just how serious can the decision between red or green chiles be? The combination of seriousness and whimsy would need to be explained by the writer in supporting the assertion that "the state truly lives up to its reputation as the Land of Enchantment." Providing such an explanation involves offering reasons that answer the question "Why?"

FOCUS STATEMENT

Include at least a tentative value judgment in your focus statement. Then provide a brief overview of how you plan to proceed; be sure to present the criteria you'll use in evaluating your topic. Here's the focus statement from Bridget McCollam's essay on the *Spawn* cartoons:

> My topic is an evaluation of the Spawn cartoons, a set of 6 episodes that can be considered controversial due to the extreme violence & crudeness involved. I will defend the cartoons, claiming that they are good, trying to refute the violence. I will also give a brief description and history.

Criteria
plot
money/success
morals
fans
character development & depth

In this statement, Bridget's value judgment is clear; she wants to defend the cartoons against criticism based on their violence. Bridget also lists the criteria she'll use to evaluate *Spawn*, but she would have been better served had she written more about each criterion. (Bridget's essay is featured in the "Sample Student Process" section, pp. 238–243.)

PLANNING YOUR ESSAY'S STRUCTURE

It's a good idea to state your evaluation in a thesis sentence near the beginning of your essay. The body of your essay may be structured by the criteria you use in evaluating your topic. Thus, in an evaluation of a movie, a paragraph (or a block of paragraphs) might be given to acting, a paragraph (or block) to cinematography, and a paragraph (or block) to special effects. Your conclusion may make clear once again what your evaluation is and briefly summarize the evidence you have offered that makes you think your reader should share that evaluation.

MODES OF DISCOURSE

You may find modes of discourse useful in planning the structure of your essay. The following three modes often figure prominently in evaluative writing.

ANALYSIS   Analysis is a process by which we break something into components, or parts, to see how they fit together to form the whole. For example, we can divide a personal computer (PC) system into CPU (central processing unit), monitor, printer, and peripherals (e.g., scanner, modem, fax). To analyze these components further, we can look at the makeup of each. What kind of "brain" does the CPU have—a 286, 386, 486, or Pentium chip of whatever speed? How much memory does it have? How much RAM? Once we begin to break a subject into its parts, we can examine each in detail based on the criteria we have established for this scrutiny.

If you're in the market for a PC, you need to determine what features you want. How fast do you want it to be? How much storage space do you want in the hard drive? How many different disk drives do you need? The PC system you configure will depend on these criteria, and the quality of the parts you put together to form your new system and how effectively they mesh will determine whether it meets the needs you defined.

Breaking a topic into its parts—the basis for analysis—works well in evaluative writing, because the parts work together to create the topic. For example, Michelle Lebsock looks at the various elements of a favorite CD—Gillian Welch's

Revival—talking in detail about Welch's vocals, the lyrics, and the variety as well as continuity of the different songs. None of these elements, by itself, would be strong enough to carry an entire CD, but when all three elements are of high quality, the result is excellent, which is precisely what Michelle claims.

Exercise 7.4

Pick two of the sample essays from the beginning of this chapter and decide whether they use analysis in talking about their subjects. If so, how effective is the analysis? Once you find an analysis, identify the components, or parts, of the subject the writer discusses. How does each writer develop or support his or her analysis of the subject?

CLASSIFICATION   Classification requires grouping like things with like to determine in which class a particular thing belongs. The following are classes into which students in your college may be placed:

> major
> college or school (e.g., College of Arts and Sciences, School of Business and Economics, graduate school)
> gender
> ethnicity
> class (e.g., freshman, graduate student)
> residence status (in-state, out-of-state, foreign)
> admission status (e.g., provisional, probationary, regular)

A given student could fit in any of these classes; for example, a student could be described as an in-state female Hispanic junior English major with regular status in the College of Arts and Sciences.

We form classes by looking at several different things and finding certain ones that share important traits or characteristics. Once we have enough items sharing important attributes, we can form a class and say that all items possessing these attributes belong in that class. As an example, consider the following lists. Which elements of each list are similar enough to be grouped together? What is the basis of your decision; that is, what is the principle on which you based your classification?

> marlin, sailfish, shark, manta ray, largemouth bass
> Chevrolet, Cadillac, Ford, Pontiac, GMC, Saturn, Buick

The first list consists of fish. The largemouth bass is a freshwater fish, but all of the others are saltwater fishes. So, all but the bass can be grouped together, with the basis of the grouping being where the fish reside—in salt water. The second list consists of automobile brands. All except Ford are produced by General Motors Corporation; thus, these items can be grouped together on the basis of parent company.

A powerful process, classification helps us create order by enabling us to identify some new aspect of our experience as being like something we've already experienced. For example, you were able to get started in your college classes because you'd been a student for a number of years already. Although college classes differ from high school classes, there are enough similarities (e.g., a teacher, textbooks, homework, and classmates) that you could feel at least some comfort in knowing that a new course would be like other courses you had taken.

In his essay, Mark Twain uses classification to present several instances of what are, in his opinion, Fenimore Cooper's literary deficiencies. Specifically, Twain classifies Cooper's shortcomings in the areas of "invention," "observation," and "construction of dialogue." To create each section, Twain looked at the various examples and grouped like with like; for each section, he created a basis for sorting or classifying the examples he wanted to use, which enabled him to write a more unified essay than he might otherwise have written. Grouping several examples under the same heading can help you avoid moving from one example to the next in a seemingly random fashion; it can help you maintain order in your essay.

DEFINITION   In defining, we often make use of both classification and comparison (discussed in Chapter 6). Classical definition is a natural process we use when we try to give a concise statement of what a particular thing or concept is. We first place the term to be defined in a class and then modify it with some type of phrase or clause, usually an implied comparison or contrast between the item to be defined and other items in the class. For example, we might define a peninsula (term to be defined) as a body of land (class) surrounded by water on three sides (modifying phrase, which contrasts peninsulas with other bodies of land, such as islands and continents).

Such definition can play an important role in structuring an evaluation, as we see in Michelle's essay. Her thesis sentence follows the classical definition format:

> *Revival* [term to be defined] is an excellent new-folk CD [class] because it encompasses strong vocals and lyrics and varies between songs without losing continuity throughout the CD as a whole [contrastive modifiers].

Michelle uses this structure to guide the rest of the paper, offering detailed support for each element of the modifiers, with a section given in turn to vocals, lyrics, and variety.

Exercise 7.5

Review the sample essays in this chapter. Which make use of definition; which define important terms for the reader? Why do you think it was necessary for the writer to define terms? How effective are the definitions?

Using analysis, classification, and definition can help you while writing an evaluation essay. If your essay is to be more than a simple statement of personal taste, then it must be a criterion-based evaluation. And in order to develop the necessary criteria, you'll have to place your topic in a class and analyze that class to see what criteria help determine membership in it. Once you have established these criteria, you have the basis for evaluation.

THESIS STATEMENT

The thesis sentence for an evaluation essay will make a value judgment couched in such terms as: "good" or "bad," "effective" or "ineffective," "necessary" or "unnecessary," "beneficial" or "detrimental," "important" or "unimportant." When you develop this particular focal point, this value judgment, your job becomes one of marshalling support for it. The criteria you establish for evaluating your topic can guide you here. As you look at your reasons for thinking that something is good or bad, effective or ineffective, and so on, keep asking yourself, "Why?" Answering this question can help you generate the detail you'll need to support your thesis.

SAMPLE STRUCTURE

Below is a structure you may wish to use. Each entry in this outline may be developed into more than a single paragraph.

1. Introduction—identifies the topic of your evaluation and its importance; contains the thesis asserting the quality of the topic; sometimes summarizes the topic's contents or describes the topic
2. Presentation of evaluation
   a. first criterion, supported by detail, examples, and reasons
   b. second criterion, supported by detail, examples, and reasons
   c. *n*th criterion, supported by detail, examples, and reasons
3. Conclusion—summary or restatement of your evaluation, restatement of its importance

Exercise 7.6

Apply this structure to the sample essays by Stacy Birch and Michelle Lebsock. How well do these essays follow this structure? How effective is this plan for structuring an essay?

REFINING YOUR WRITING

After you've written your essay and (ideally) taken some time away from it, your next step is revision. To begin honing and polishing your evaluation, keep these principles in mind:

Evaluative criteria. What is the basis of your evaluation? How did you decide that the topic you've evaluated is good or bad, effective or ineffective, and so on? Be sure that the traits or characteristics you've discussed are the most important or telling ones for your topic.

Writer's judgment. Give your judgment in clear terms, letting this judgment stand as your thesis sentence. Include the evaluative criteria in or near your thesis statement to guide your reader through the essay.

Support. Provide details to develop, explain, or support the criteria you've chosen. Think in terms of "because," as in this example:

"Drug-education programs in elementary schools aimed at decreasing drug use by children and teens clearly are not working *because*...." Listing reasons to complete a "because" statement can help you generate support for your thesis. (Look again at Michelle Lebsock's thesis for her essay evaluating Gillian Welch's CD *Revival*. Michelle words her thesis using "because" to set up the criteria for the evaluation.)

Exercise 7.7

1. Look again at the essays presented earlier in this chapter. For each essay, restate the writer's judgment of the topic and the evaluative criteria on which the judgment is based. How clearly stated is each judgment? How effectively do the criteria support it?
2. How detailed is the support each writer uses to develop his or her essay? How effectively does the support develop "because" statements?

SAMPLE STUDENT PROCESS

This example essay was written by Bridget McCollam, a first-year writing student at NMSU. Bridget began her writing with her topic—HBO's *Spawn* cartoons—already in mind. So her job was to explore that topic, to see whether it would actually serve her as the basis for this paper.

PREWRITING

Here's Bridget's prewriting:

comic book—so popular, movie deal and cartoon deal—HBO
6 cartoons depending on how popular, depending on popularity
making more now
HBO midnight audience he wanted appeal to, Friday nights—violence

Are the Spawn cartoons good, or does the violence & nudity make them
    unvaluable?
Are the Spawn cartoons worthy of the airtime they receive, or should they be
    taken off?
Is the violence & nudity necessary for the Spawn cartoons to give the right
    effect?

controversial—
good   *bad*
plot   extreme violence
interesting   nudity—xx—dirty
good characters   graphic detail

watched it on good night—fun—with Jim—so liked it
now becoming stressed

The Spawn cartoons are exciting, with a plot that captures the attention of the viewer, characters that one can feel empathy for and detail that must be seen, the Spawn cartoons are definitely worth watching.

detail of red cloak, green eyes, clinking of chains, mostly dark burned face
description of clown—repulsive, fat, stomach hanging out, teeth yellow &
    misshapen.
Wanda—beautiful, in charge, nice
good guy—long white beard, respectable
history must be in there
dance bar—naked women—somewhat crude
general plot—many little
war between heaven & hell
character development as Spawn begins to understand
countdown of energy 9:9:9:9

disgusting—nudity—bar
lesbians & fat guy
audience can't relate
detail such as finger ripping off, blood not necessary

CONTINUED PREWRITING

The next bit of writing we see from Bridget continues her prewriting and consists of notes she took while watching these cartoons:

"The following program is recommended for mature audiences only. It contains adult situations, adult language, graphic violence, and nudity."

created by Todd McFarlane
9:9:9:9
narrator/good guy from heaven
every 400 years (?)
begin with graphic death, ruthless
born as clean slate—instincts all drain from past
first image of Spawn—huge, flowing red cloak, chains, then just glowing
    green eyes in a dark face, *voice* "what the hell are you?"
naked lady—"I love you Al"
from hell—"proper escort" from hell—ugly clown, repulsive
Spawn—sad green (glowing) eyes & pool of red cloak
hell spawn—instinct, killer, act upon violence
Spawn confused, desperate
takes off mask—burned face, images of fire in alley, homeless help him
narrator in story gives advice "home—war getting these"
COP & TWITCH
images (black & jumbled) of past happiness with Wanda
Spawn watches as Wanda is married happily with best friend
Spawn has no idea how long
narrator—hell tries to keep him (warrior) confused
clown comes—disgusting
dead 5 years

Al Simmons—govt assassin—really good
where you been all this time
went to hell, back for Wanda who has child *Al couldn't give her*

Bridget's notes continue along these lines for another two or three pages. But these should be enough to give you a good idea of her strategy.

PLANNING PAGE

Bridget then reviewed her notes and wrote this planning page:

My topic is an evaluation of the Spawn cartoons, a set of 6 episodes that can be considered controversial due to the extreme violence & crudeness involved. I will defend the cartoons, claiming that they are good. trying to refute the violence. I will also give a brief description and history.

Criteria

plot
money/success
morals
fans
character development & depth

ROUGH DRAFT FOR PEER REVIEW

Using her planning page as a very rough guide, Bridget wrote a draft of her essay, revised it, and then submitted the following rough draft for peer review.

Adult Audiences Only

1   Every Friday night at midnight millions of viewers tuned in to HBO to watch the Spawn cartoons, a unique creation by Todd McFarlane. These cartoons began as comic books and were so popular that McFarlane was offered both a movie deal and a cartoon deal. HBO was the company to offer the cartoon deal, which was the following: They would make six episodes, and depending on the success of these, more might be made later. These new episodes are in the making right now.

2   The opening warning sums up the problem of the Spawn cartoons when it flashes on the scene: "The following program is recommended for mature audiences only. It contains adult situations, adult language, graphic violence, and nudity." The Spawn cartoons are extremely violent and involve nudity that may very well be considered crude and disgusting. There is almost an unbelievable amount of blood, including one scene where the viewer actually watches the bullet rip through a man's skin. There may be a question of whether all this blood and gore is necessary. Perhaps it is not, but the other factors of these cartoons are so well done that it makes up for the disgusting bloody parts. With plot that captures the attention of the viewer, characters that one can feel empathy for, and detail that must be seen, the Spawn cartoons are definitely worth watching.

3   A government assassin who is rather good at his job is murdered, but his love for his wife leads him to make a deal with the devil. The deal: Al Simmons

can see his wife, but for the price of his soul, which means he must be a warrior for the devil in the eternal battle between heaven and hell, of which "Earth is the battlefield, and human souls are the prize." Al Simmons returns as a Spawn from hell. There is a war within him between good and bad. There are representatives from heaven and hell to lead him whichever way. An evil clown from hell turns into an insectlike demon periodically, and the story is narrated by a respectable man with the long white beard from heaven. Al, now known as Spawn, realizes his beloved wife, Wanda, is now married to his best friend and has a child; a child that for whatever reasons, Al could not give her. He now lives in an alley with a group of homeless people. Spawn must choose between this evil and the good inside of him, but is confused about what is happening to him. There are political issues, crime scenes, child rape and murder, and everything manages to tie in together at the end. The plot has so many twists and turns that it is impossible to not watch, as it sucks the viewer in, catching his attention time and again.

4   In a story so crude and violent, it is hard to imagine deep, complex characters, yet McFarlane manages. Viewers can watch the development of spawn as he "grows" in his understanding of this new world he has been thrown into so violently. He starts out angry at everything around him and scared of what is happening to him. However, by the end of the six episodes, he has matured slightly in his understanding of this new world. He has learned some control of these strange powers he has been granted and has come to terms with the changes in the world he left. Although there is little development in other characters, they are never the less quite complex. Viewers get a full picture of many of the characters personalities, making them more than merely a single-minded image with only one purpose. Wanda is a good example of this. She appears to actually love her new husband, although she misses Al still, and of course mourns his death. Viewers get a real idea of why Al Simmons was so in love with this woman.

5   The detail in these cartoons is almost unbelievable. Spawn is amazingly striking. The first image presented of him is a huge red cloak that he always wears. There are spikes on his knuckles, with red gloves, he wears a red and black mask. The second time Spawn is pictured, it is his face, in darkness except for his glowing green eyes. Spawn's cloak can do many neat tricks, such as reach out and grab someone, strangling them. Spawn also has chains that he can use to grab an enemy and injure them. These chains make a trademark clinking noise to warn viewers of what will happen next. When Spawn takes off his mask, his shriveled, disgusting face is revealed from his death in a fire. The detail is evident in other places. Sound is often important, such as the beating of a fan giving a man flashbacks of a war he once fought. The detail makes it impossible to look away, as viewers get pulled in to watching what will happen next, not wanting to miss anything.

6   I have to admit, I went into the theater to watch these cartoons only because my male friends dragged me, and I stressed that I was going to leave if I did not enjoy them. The first scene I saw was absolutely repulsive, too much to describe here. But needless to say, the cartoons redeemed themselves, and I walked out of the theater impressed.

Bridget's peer group thought she had done a good job with this draft, and they noted that the criteria she had established for her evaluation worked. Bridget evaluated *Spawn* on the basis of its effective plot, depth of characters, and graphic detail. But they suggested that she consider

1. restructuring the paragraph (3) about the plot. It seemed to jump around a little bit, probably because the topic sentence comes at the end of the paragraph.
2. redoing the description of Spawn in ¶ 5. That paragraph also seemed to lack coherence, as Bridget presented details describing Spawn's dress, then his face, then more about his dress, then back to his face. So they suggested that this paragraph be restructured.
3. thinking about smoothing out the writing in several places to eliminate unnecessary words and to create a stronger sense of style in the essay.

Following the peer group's suggestions, Bridget rewrote the essay and submitted a revised draft.

REVISED DRAFT

ADULT AUDIENCES ONLY

BRIDGET MCCOLLAM

1   Every Friday night at midnight millions of viewers tune in to HBO to watch the *Spawn* cartoons, a unique creation by Todd McFarlane. These cartoons began as comic books and were so popular that McFarlane was offered both a movie deal and a cartoon deal. Looking for something offbeat that might appeal to a late night adult audience, HBO offered to make six cartoon episodes, and depending on their success, possibly more. These new episodes are in the making right now.

2   The opening warning sums up the problem of the *Spawn* cartoons when it flashes on the screen: "The following program is recommended for mature audiences only. It contains adult situations, adult language, graphic violence, and nudity." These cartoons are extremely violent and involve nudity that may very well be considered crude and disgusting. There is almost an unbelievable amount of blood, including one scene in which the viewer actually watches a bullet rip through a man's skin. Is all this blood and gore necessary? Perhaps not. But the other factors of these cartoons are so well done that they make up for the disgusting bloody parts. With plot that captures the attention of the viewer, characters that one can feel empathy for, and detail that must be seen to be believed, the *Spawn* cartoons are definitely worth watching.

3   At first, the plot of *Spawn* seems simple enough. Al Simmons, a government assassin who is rather good at his job, is murdered, but his love for his wife leads him to make a deal with the devil. The deal: Al can see his wife, but for the price of his soul, which means he must become a warrior for the devil in the eternal battle between heaven and hell, where "Earth is the battlefield, and human souls are the prize." Al returns as a spawn from hell, but despite his pact with the devil, within him rages a war between good and evil. This battle is sometimes waged by representatives from hell and heaven who attempt to sway Al. An evil clown from hell turns into an insect-like demon periodically and tries to make Al respond, to do evil and so condemn himself to hell. As counterpoint, the story is narrated by a respectable man from heaven with the long

white beard, who advises Al to control himself and to fight against the evil within. But the struggle is difficult. Al realizes his beloved wife, Wanda, is now married to his best friend and has a child, a child that for whatever reasons, Al could not give her. Confused about what is happening to him, Spawn must choose to give in to the evil he sees all around him or to resist it as best he can. His first instinct is to kill his friend, who has replaced him in Wanda's life. Complicating this plot line are political issues and such crimes as child rape and murder. Eventually, these lines manage to tie together at the end. The plot has so many twists and turns that it is impossible to not watch, and it sucks the viewer in, catching his attention time and again.

4   In a story so crude and violent, it is hard to imagine deep, complex characters, yet McFarlane manages. Viewers can watch the development of Spawn as he "grows" in his understanding of this new world he has been thrown into so violently. He starts out angry at everything around him and scared of what is happening to him. However, by the end of the six episodes, he has matured slightly in his understanding of this new world. He has learned some control of these strange powers he has been granted and has come to terms with the changes in the world he left. Although there is little development in other characters, they are nevertheless quite complex. Viewers get a full picture of many of the characters' personalities, making them more than merely single-faceted images with only one purpose. Wanda is a good example of this. While she appears to actually love her new husband, she misses Al still and of course mourns his death. Viewers get a real idea of why Al Simmons was so in love with this woman.

5   The detail in these cartoons is almost unbelievable, and Spawn himself is particularly striking. The first image seen of Spawn is a huge red cloak that he always wears, a cloak that can do many neat tricks, such as reach out and strangle a victim. He wears red gloves, with spikes on his knuckles, and a red and black mask. Spawn also has chains that he can use to seize and injure an enemy. These chains make a trademark clanking noise to warn viewers of what will happen next, so sound reinforces the detail of the Spawn's costume and weapons. The second time Spawn is pictured, the viewer sees his face, obscured in darkness except for his glowing green eyes. When Spawn takes off his mask, his shriveled, disgusting face is revealed, charred from his death in a fire. The detail is evident in other places. Sound is often important, such as the beating of a fan that gives a man flashbacks of a war he once fought. The detail makes it impossible to look away, as viewers get pulled in to watching what will happen next, not wanting to miss anything.

6   I have to admit, I went into the theater to watch these cartoons only because my male friends dragged me, and I stressed that I was going to leave if I did not enjoy them. The first scene I saw contained some of the worst of the gore and nudity, and I very nearly left. Yet as I stayed and watched, I saw the plot unfold in all its complexity. I felt for Spawn and hated the evil clown. I was hooked. Needless to say, the cartoons redeemed themselves, and I walked out of the theater impressed.

Checklist: Critiquing an Evaluation Essay

1. What is the subject of the evaluation?
2. Identify the thesis statement. What evaluation does it make? How effectively is it worded? How should it be strengthened?

3. What criteria and reasons are offered for the evaluation?
4. What support is offered for the reasons? How effective is this support?
5. How effective are the introduction and conclusion? Why?
6. Does the paper adhere to conventions of usage, mechanics, and format? Correct any errors you find.

Why do we read literature? What does it do for us? We may read for pleasure—for the adventure of a technothriller, for the love story of a popular romance, for the humor in an intentionally funny story. We may read to learn, to gain insight into the life and times the writer depicts. And we may read to wonder, to ponder what the writer may be trying to tell us about how we should be. When we read serious literature, our task is to attempt to understand what the writer is saying to us.

Exercise 8.1

In the title essay of *The Philosophy of Literary Form,* 3rd edition (Berkeley: University of California Press, 1973), Kenneth Burke uses the word "poetry" to stand for all types of literature. He defines poetry as "any work of a critical or imaginative cast" (p. 1). Poetry in this broad sense encompasses not only poems, but also short stories, novels, plays, and even nonfiction prose. Later in his essay, Burke says that poetry is "produced for purposes of comfort," that it is "equipment for living," and that it "would protect us" (p. 61). In a short response, explain what Burke might have meant in saying that literature might "comfort" us. How might it "protect us"?

What pieces of literature have you read that you might think of as "equipment for living"? How did they "comfort" or "protect" you?

Essays About and From Literature

CHAPTER 8

Burke's definition of literature as "equipment for living" embraces writing that invites interpretation and that deals with important issues people face. In this sense, his definition would not encompass such escapist writing as a technothriller or a romance. In using Burke's definition as our guide, we don't mean to say that we always know where to draw the line between serious literature and escapist writing; it's probably better to think of works as arranged on a continuum than to think of discrete categories. We also don't mean to say that escapist works aren't worth reading. However, literature that we would deem worthy of study in the classroom tends to require more (rather than less) interpretation and tends to deal with important issues humans face. A detective novel may hold you spellbound, but in reading it, you're engaged in trying to figure out "who done it." Once you solve the mystery, you've satisfied your curiosity and been entertained, but you haven't necessarily learned anything about your life or the lives of other people. On the other hand, a poem by Robert Frost, a short story by Joyce Carol Oates, or a novel by Rudolfo Anaya is more likely to engage you in trying to figure out what the writer meant or what that piece of literature means to you. By writing in response to such works, you'll be engaged in this process of determining their meaning and thus in equipping yourself with knowledge that can help you live your life.

How do we respond to literary texts? As the title of this chapter reveals, we'll consider two primary ways of responding: writing *about* literature and writing *from* literature. Writing *about* literature results in an interpretive essay, a formal paper in which the writer presents her supported opinion of what a work means to her. Writing *from* a piece of literature is a different kind of response. Writing an essay *from* a piece of literature uses the literary text as a springboard. The text figures prominently in the essay as a presence or a context in which the essay is grounded. Yet although it refers to the text, the essay's primary focus is on a topic beyond the text.

"Literature as equipment for living"—keep this principle firmly in mind as you write *from* literature. Your essay should begin with your reading and interpreting a piece of literature, and it should show clearly your understanding of the text. What shape will this paper take? It will be informed by the skills you develop and strengthen in completing pieces for any of our writing occasions.

One kind of essay *from* literature is akin to the personal essay we discussed in Chapter 5. Have you ever read a poem or story and thought you had an experience similar to that of one of the characters? Have you found any help from a poem or story in solving a problem? Have you applied some aspect of a poem or story to your dealings with other people? An essay written from a piece of literature would explore the experience, talk about the problem situation and how it worked out, or offer a narrative account of your dealings with others, and it would tie your experience to that piece of literature.

Other kinds of essays *from* literature are possible as well. If a literary text correlates with a situation in your community, for example, you could write an essay in which evaluation would figure. Or your response, your essay, could be informed by your work with problems and solutions.

Let's assume that one of your favorite teachers is under attack because his teaching style is quirky, unorthodox, or even radical. If you've read Louanne

Johnson's *My Posse Don't Do Homework* (the book on which the movie *Dangerous Minds* was based), then you might point to Johnson's experiences as evidence that out-of-the-ordinary teaching and unusual responses to student needs sometimes work better than do more traditional methods of instruction. And you could draw on this book as a resource in writing a defense of your teacher as

1. a personal essay, in which you recount and then assess his influence on you,
2. an essay evaluating the quality of his teaching, or
3. an essay that examines the problems he confronts (e.g., a lawsuit-wary school board or an unimaginative principal or department chair) and then offers a solution (e.g., comprehensive evaluation of teaching by a committee of teachers instead of a single administrator).

Although you will most often write *about* literature during your college career, both types of responses are valid. Whether writing from or about, your written response begins with your understanding of the piece of literature, which develops from your reading the text closely and then working with it to see what it means to you. At the end of this chapter, we'll offer two options for a formal essay: one writing about literature, the other writing from literature. Whichever option you choose, you'll begin by reading a piece of literature carefully and then analyzing it to see what it says or means to you.

SAMPLE STORIES AND POEMS

In this section, we first present selections of literary texts. Specifically, we have included three short stories and four poems. (In addition, you may review Lorna Dee Cervantes's "Freeway 280," a poem presented in Chapter 4.) These pieces of literature represent a range of good writing, and you may use them not only for practice in interpreting literature but also as the subject of an interpretive essay. Next, we present three student essays, two written *about* short stories and one written *from* a poem. As you read the short stories and poems, you may apply any or all of the reading strategies you have worked with thus far. As you read the sample student essays, you should consider how and how effectively their writers treat the texts that are the subjects of their essays.

Our first story, "Shopping," is by Joyce Carol Oates, a noted American fiction writer.

JOYCE CAROL OATES

SHOPPING

1   An old ritual, Saturday morning shopping. Mother and daughter. Mrs. Dietrich and Nola. Shops in the village, stores and boutiques at the splendid Livingstone Mall on Route 12. Bloomingdale's, Saks, Lord & Taylor, Bonwit's, Neiman-Marcus: and the

rest. Mrs. Dietrich would know her way around the stores blindfolded but there is always the surprise of lavish seasonal displays, extraordinary holiday sales, the openings of new stores at the Mall like Laura Ashley, Paraphernalia. On one of their Mall days Mrs. Dietrich and Nola would try to get there at midmorning, have lunch around 1 P.M. at one or another of their favorite restaurants, shop for perhaps an hour after lunch, then come home. Sometimes the shopping trips were more successful than at other times but you have to have faith, Mrs. Dietrich tells herself. Her interior voice is calm, neutral, free of irony. Ever since her divorce her interior voice has been free of irony. You have to have faith.

2   Tomorrow morning Nola returns to school in Maine; today will be a day at the Mall. Mrs. Dietrich has planned it for days. At the Mall, in such crowds of shoppers, moments of intimacy are possible as they rarely are at home. (Seventeen-year-old Nola, home on spring break for a brief eight days, seems always to be *busy*, always out with her *friends*—the trip to the Mall has been postponed twice.) But Saturday, 10:30 A.M. they are in the car at last headed south on Route 12, a bleak March morning following a night of freezing rain, there's a metallic cast to the sky and no sun anywhere in the sky but the light hurts Mrs. Dietrich's eyes just the same. "Does it seem as if spring will ever come?—it must be twenty degrees colder up in Maine," she says. Driving in heavy traffic always makes Mrs. Dietrich nervous and she is overly sensitive to her daughter's silence, which seems deliberate, perverse, when they have so little time remaining together—not even a full day.

3   Nola asks politely if Mrs. Dietrich would like her to drive and Mrs. Dietrich says no, of course not, she's fine, it's only a few more miles and maybe traffic will lighten. Nola seems about to say something more, then thinks better of it. So much between them that is precarious, chancy—but they've been kind to each other these past seven days. Mrs. Dietrich loves Nola with a fierce unreasoned passion stronger than any she felt for the man who had been her husband for thirteen years, certainly far stronger than any she ever felt for her own mother. Sometimes in weak despondent moods, alone, lonely, self-pitying, when she has had too much to drink, Mrs. Dietrich thinks she is in love with her daughter—but this is a thought she can't contemplate for long. And how Nola would snort in amused contempt, incredulous, mocking—"Oh *Mother!*"—if she were told.

4   Mrs. Dietrich tries to engage her daughter in conversation of a harmless sort but Nola answers in monosyllables, Nola is rather tired from so many nights of partying with her friends, some of whom attend the local high school, some of whom are home for spring break from prep schools—Exeter, Lawrenceville, Concord, Andover, Portland. Late nights, but Mrs. Dietrich doesn't consciously lie awake waiting for Nola to come home: they've been through all that before. Now Nola sits beside her mother looking wan, subdued, rather melancholy. Thinking her private thoughts. She is wearing a bulky quilted jacket Mrs. Dietrich has never liked, the usual blue jeans, black calfskin boots zippered tightly to mid-calf. Mrs. Dietrich must resist the temptation to ask, "Why are you so quiet, Nola? What are you thinking?" They've been through all that before.

5   Route 12 has become a jumble of small industrial parks, high-rise office and apartment buildings, torn-up landscapes—mountains of raw earth, uprooted trees, ruts and ditches filled with muddy water. There is no natural sequence to what you see—buildings, construction work, leveled woods, the lavish grounds owned by Squibb. Though she has driven this route countless times, Mrs. Dietrich is never quite certain where the Mall is and must be prepared for a sudden exit. She remembers getting lost the first several times, remembers the excitement she and her friends felt about the grand opening of the Mall, stores worthy of serious shopping at last. Today is much the same. No, today

is worse. Like Christmas when she was a small child, Mrs. Dietrich thinks. She'd hoped so badly to be happy she'd felt actual pain, a constriction in her throat like crying.

6   "*Are* you all right, Nola?—you've been so quiet all morning," Mrs. Dietrich asks, half-scolding. Nola stirs from her reverie, says she's fine, a just perceptible edge to her reply, and for the remainder of the drive there's some stiffness between them. Mrs. Dietrich chooses to ignore it. In any case she is fully absorbed in driving—negotiating a tricky exit across two lanes of traffic, then the hairpin curve of the ramp, the numerous looping drives of the Mall. Then the enormous parking lot, daunting to the inexperienced, but Mrs. Dietrich always heads for the area behind Lord & Taylor on the far side of the Mall, Lot D; her luck holds and she finds a space close in. "Well—we made it," she says, smiling happily at Nola. Nola laughs in reply—what does a seventeen-year-old's laughter *mean*?—but she remembers, getting out, to lock both doors on her side of the car. The smile Nola gives Mrs. Dietrich across the car's roof is careless and beautiful and takes Mrs. Dietrich's breath away.

7   The March morning tastes of grit with an undercurrent of something acrid, chemical; inside the Mall beneath the first of the elegant brass-buttressed glass domes, the air is fresh and tonic, circulating from invisible vents. The Mall is crowded, rather noisy—it *is* Saturday morning—but a feast for the eyes after that long trip on Route 12. Tall slender trees grow out of the mosaic-tiled pavement, there are beds of Easter lilies, daffodils, jonquils, tulips of all colors. Mrs. Dietrich smiles with relief. She senses that Nola too is relieved, cheered. It's like coming home.

8   The shopping excursions began when Nola was a small child but did not acquire their special significance until she was twelve or thirteen years old and capable of serious, sustained shopping with her mother. This was about the time when Mr. Dietrich moved out of the house and back into their old apartment in the city—a separation, he'd called it initially, to give them perspective—though Mrs. Dietrich had no illusions about what "perspective" would turn out to entail—so the shopping trips were all the more significant. Not that Mrs. Dietrich and Nola spent very much money—they really didn't, *really* they didn't, when when compared to friends and neighbors.

9   At seventeen Nola is shrewd and discerning as a shopper, not easy to please, knowledgeable as a mature woman about certain aspects of fashion, quality merchandise, good stores. Her closets, like Mrs. Dietrich's, are crammed, but she rarely buys anything that Mrs. Dietrich thinks shoddy or merely faddish. Up in Portland, at the Academy, she hasn't as much time to shop but when she is home in Livingstone it isn't unusual for her and her girlfriends to shop nearly every day. Like all her friends she has charge accounts at the better stores, her own credit cards, a reasonable allowance. At the time of their settlement Mr. Dietrich said guiltily that it was the least he could do for them—if Mrs. Dietrich wanted to work part-time, she could (she was trained, more or less, in public relations of a small-scale sort); if not, not. Mrs. Dietrich thought, It's the most you can do for us too.

10   Near Bloomingdale's entrance mother and daughter see a disheveled woman sitting by herself on one of the benches. Without seeming to look at her, shoppers are making a discreet berth around her, a stream following a natural course. Nola, taken by surprise, stares. Mrs. Dietrich has seen the woman from time to time at the Mall, always alone, smirking and talking to herself, frizzed gray hair in a tangle, puckered mouth. Always wearing the same black wool coat, a garment of fairly good quality but shapeless, rumpled, stained, as if she sleeps in it. She might be anywhere from forty to sixty years of age. Once Mrs. Dietrich saw her make menacing gestures at children who

were teasing her, another time she'd seen the woman staring belligerently at *her*. A white paste had gathered in the corners of her mouth. . . . "My God, that poor woman," Nola says. "I didn't think there were people like her here—I mean, I didn't think they would allow it."

11   "She doesn't seem to cause any disturbance," Mrs. Dietrich says. "She just sits—Don't stare, Nola. She'll see you."

12   "You've seen her here before? Here?"

13   "A few times this winter."

14   "Is she always like that?"

15   "I'm sure she's harmless, Nola. She just *sits.*"

16   Nola is incensed, her pale blue eyes like washed glass. "I'm sure *she's* harmless, Mother. It's the harm the poor woman has to endure that is the tragedy."

17   Mrs. Dietrich is surprised and a little offended by her daughter's passionate tone but she knows enough not to argue. They enter Bloomingdale's, taking their habitual route. So many shoppers!—so much merchandise! Nola speaks of the tragedy of women like that woman—the tragedy of the homeless, the mentally disturbed—bag ladies out on the street—outcasts of an affluent society—but she's soon distracted by the busyness on all sides, the attractive items for sale. They take the escalator up to the third floor, to the Juniors department where Nola often buys things. From there they will move on to Young Collector, then to New Impressions, then to Petites, then one or another boutique and designer—Liz Claiborne, Christian Dior, Calvin Klein, Carlos Falci, and the rest. And after Bloomingdale's the other stores await, to be visited each in turn. Mrs. Dietrich checks her watch and sees with satisfaction that there's just enough time before lunch but not *too* much time. She gets ravenously hungry, shopping at the Mall.

18   Nola is efficient and matter-of-fact about shopping, though she acts solely upon instinct. Mrs. Dietrich likes to watch her at a short distance—holding items of clothing up to herself in the three-way mirrors, modeling things she thinks especially promising. A twill blazer with rounded shoulders and blouson jacket, a funky zippered jumpsuit in white sailcloth, a pair of straight-leg Evan-Picone pants, a green leather vest. Mrs. Dietrich watches her covertly. At such times Nola is perfectly content, fully absorbed in the task at hand; Mrs. Dietrich knows she isn't thinking about anything that would distress her. (Like Mr. Dietrich's betrayal. Like Nola's difficulties with her friends. Like her difficulties at school—as much as Mrs. Dietrich knows of them.) Once, at the Mall, perhaps in this very store in this very department, Nola saw Mrs. Dietrich watching her and walked away and when Mrs. Dietrich caught up with her she said, "I can't stand it, Mother." Her voice was choked and harsh, a vein prominent in her forehead. "Let me go. For Christ's sake will you let me go." Mrs. Dietrich didn't dare touch her though she could see Nola was trembling. For a long terrible moment mother and daughter stood side by side near a display of bright brash beachwear while Nola whispered, "Let me go. *Let me go.*"

19   Difficult to believe that girl standing so poised and self-assured in front of the three-way mirror was once a plain, rather chunky, unhappy child. She'd been unpopular at school. Overly serious. Anxious. Quick to tears. Aged eleven she hid herself away in her room for hours at a time, reading, drawing pictures, writing little stories she could sometimes be prevailed upon to read aloud to her mother, sometimes even to her father, though she dreaded his judgment. She went through a "scientific" phase a while later—Mrs. Dietrich remembers an ambitious bas-relief map of North America, meticulous illustrations for "photosynthesis," a pastel drawing of an eerie ball of fire labeled "Red Giant" (a dying star?) which won a prize in a state competition for junior high stu-

dents. Then for a season it was stray facts Nola confronted them with, often at the dinner table. Interrupting her parents' conversation to say brightly: "Did you know that Nero's favorite color was green?—he carried a giant emerald and held it up to his eye to watch Christians being devoured by lions." And once at a large family gathering: "Did you know that last week downtown a little baby's nose was chewed off by rats in his crib?—a little *black* baby?" Nola meant only to call attention to herself but you couldn't blame her listeners for being offended. They stared at her, not knowing what to say. What a strange child! What queer glassy-pale eyes! Mr. Dietrich told her curtly to leave the table—he'd had enough of the game she was playing and so had everyone else.

20   Nola stared at him, her eyes filling with tears. Game?

21   When they were alone Mr. Dietrich said angrily to Mrs. Dietrich: "Can't you control her in front of other people. at least?" Mrs. Dietrich was angry too, and frightened. She said: "I *try.*"

22   They sent her off aged fourteen to the Portland Academy up in Maine and without their help she matured into a girl of considerable beauty. A heart-shaped face, delicate features, glossy red-brown hair scissor-cut to her shoulders. Five feet seven inches weighing less than one hundred pounds—the result of constant savage dieting. (Mrs. Dietrich, who has weight problems herself, doesn't dare to inquire as to details. They've been through that already.) Thirty days after they'd left her at the Portland Academy Nola telephoned home at 11 P.M. one Sunday giggly and high telling Mrs. Dietrich she adored the school she adored her suite mates she adored most of her teachers particularly her riding instructor Terri, Terri the Terrier they called the woman because she was so fierce, such a character, eyes that bore right through your skull, wore belts with the most amazing silver buckles! Nola loved Terri but she wasn't *in* love—there's a difference!

23   Mrs. Dietrich broke down weeping, *that* time.

24   Now of course Nola has boyfriends. Mrs. Dietrich has long since given up trying to keep track of their names. There is even one "boy"—or young man—who seems to be married: who seems to be, in fact, one of the junior instructors at the school. (Mrs. Dietrich does not eavesdrop on her daughter's telephone conversations but there are things she cannot help overhearing.) Is your daughter on the Pill? the women in Mrs. Dietrich's circle asked one another for a while, guiltily, surreptitiously. Now they no longer ask.

25   But Nola has announced recently that she loathes boys—she's fed up.

26   She's never going to get married. She'll study languages in college, French, Italian, something exotic like Arabic, go to work for the American foreign service. Unless she drops out of school altogether to become a model.

27   "Do you think I'm fat, Mother?" she asks frequently, worriedly, standing in front of the mirror twisted at the waist to reveal her small round belly which, it seems, can't help being round. She bloats herself on diet Cokes all day long. "Do you think it

28   *shows*?"

When Mrs. Dietrich was pregnant with Nola she'd been twenty-nine years old and she and Mr. Dietrich had tried to have a baby for nearly five years. She'd lost hope, begun to despise herself, then suddenly it happened: like grace. Like happiness swelling so powerfully it can barely be contained. I can hear its heartbeat! her husband exclaimed. He'd been her lover then, young, vigorous, dreamy. Caressing the rock-hard belly, splendid white tight-stretched skin. Mr. Dietrich gave Mrs. Dietrich a reproduction on stiff glossy paper of Dante Gabriel Rossetti's *Beata Beatrix,* embarrassed, apologetic, knowing it was sentimental and perhaps a little silly but that was how he thought of her—so beautiful, rapturous, pregnant with their child. She told no one but she knew the baby was to be a girl. It would be herself again, reborn and this time perfect.

29   "Oh, Mother—isn't it *beautiful?*" Nola exclaims.

30   It is past noon. Past twelve-thirty. Mrs. Dietrich and Nola have made the rounds of a half-dozen stores, traveled countless escalators, one clothing department has blended into the next and the chic smiling saleswomen have become indistinguishable and Mrs. Dietrich is beginning to feel the urgent need for a glass of white wine. Just a glass. "Isn't it beautiful?—it's *perfect,*" Nola says. Her eyes glow with pleasure, her smooth skin is radiant. As Nola models in the three-way mirror a queer little yellow-and-black striped sweater with a ribbed waist. Punk style, mock-cheap, Mrs. Dietrich feels the motherly obligation to register a mild protest, knowing that Nola will not hear. She must have it and will have it. She'll wear it a few times, then retire it to the bottom of a drawer with so many other novelty sweaters, accumulated since sixth grade. (She's like her mother in that regard—can't bear to throw anything away.)

31   "*Isn't* it beautiful?" Nola demands, studying her reflection in the mirror.

32   Mrs. Dietrich pays for the sweater on her charge account.

33   Next, they buy Nola a good pair of shoes. And a handbag to go with them. In Paraphernalia, where rock music blasts overhead and Mrs. Dietrich stands to one side, rather miserable, Nola chats companionably with two girls—tall, pretty, cutely made up—she'd gone to public school in Livingstone with, says afterward with an upward roll of her eyes, "God, I was afraid they'd latch on to us!" Mrs. Dietrich has seen women friends and acquaintances of her own in the Mall this morning but has shrunk from being noticed, not wanting to share her daughter with anyone. She has a sense of time passing ever more swiftly, cruelly.

34   She watches Nola preening in a mirror, watches other shoppers watching her. My daughter. Mine. But of course there is no connection between them—they don't even resemble each other. A seventeen-year-old, a forty-seven-year-old. When Nola is away she seems to forget her mother entirely—doesn't telephone, certainly doesn't write. It's the way all their daughters are, Mrs. Dietrich's friends tell her. It doesn't *mean* anything. Mrs. Dietrich thinks how when she was carrying Nola, those nine long months, they'd been completely happy—not an instant's doubt or hesitation. The singular weight of the body. A trancelike state you are tempted to mistake for happiness because the body is incapable of thinking, therefore incapable of anticipating change. Hot rhythmic blood, organs packed tight and moist, the baby upside down in her sac in her mother's belly, always present tense, always *now.* It was a shock when the end came so abruptly but everyone told Mrs. Dietrich she was a natural mother, praised and pampered her. For a while. Then of course she'd had her baby, her Nola. Even now Mrs. Dietrich can't really comprehend the experience. *Giving birth. Had a baby. Was born.* Mere words, absurdly inadequate. She knows no more of how love ends than she knew as a child, she knows only of how love begins—in the belly, in the womb, where it is always present tense.

35   The morning's shopping has been quite successful but lunch at La Crêperie doesn't go well for some reason. La Crêperie is Nola's favorite Mall restaurant—always amiably crowded, bustling, a simulated sidewalk café with red-striped umbrellas, wrought-iron tables and chairs, menus in French, music piped in overhead. Mrs. Dietrich's nerves are chafed by the pretense of gaiety, the noise, the openness onto one of the Mall's busy promenades where at any minute a familiar face might emerge, but she is grateful for her glass of chilled white wine. She orders a small tossed salad and a creamed-chicken crepe and devours it hungrily—she *is* hungry. While Nola picks at her

seafood crepe with a disdainful look. A familiar scene: mother watching while daughter pushes food around on her plate. Suddenly Nola is tense, moody, corners of her mouth downturned. Mrs. Dietrich wants to ask, What's wrong? She wants to ask, Why are you unhappy? She wants to smooth Nola's hair back from her forehead, check to see if her forehead is overly warm, wants to hug her close, hard. Why, why? What did I do wrong? Why do you hate me?

36   Calling the Portland Academy a few weeks ago Mrs. Dietrich suddenly lost control, began crying. She hadn't been drinking and she hadn't known she was upset. A girl unknown to her, one of Nola's suite mates, was saying, "Please, Mrs. Dietrich, it's all right, I'm sure Nola will call you back later tonight, or tomorrow, Mrs. Dietrich?—I'll tell her you called, all right?—Mrs. Dietrich?" as embarrassed as if Mrs. Dietrich had been her own mother.

37   How love begins. How love ends.

38   Mrs. Dietrich orders a third glass of wine. This is a celebration of sorts isn't it? Their last shopping trip for a long time. But Nola resists, Nola isn't sentimental. In casual defiance of Mrs. Dietrich she lights up a cigarette—yes, Mother, Nola has said ironically, since *you* stopped smoking *everybody* is supposed to stop—and sits with her arms crossed, watching streams of shoppers pass. Mrs. Dietrich speaks lightly of practical matters, tomorrow morning's drive to the airport, and will Nola telephone when she gets to Portland to let Mrs. Dietrich know she has arrived safely?

39   Then with no warning—though of course she'd been planning this all along—Nola brings up the subject of a semester in France, in Paris and Rouen, the fall semester of her senior year it would be; she has put in her application, she says, and is waiting to hear if she's been accepted. She smokes her cigarette calmly, expelling smoke from her nostrils in a way Mrs. Dietrich thinks particularly coarse. Mrs. Dietrich, who believed that particular topic was finished, takes care to speak without emotion. "I just don't think it's a very practical idea right now, Nola," she says. "We've been through it haven't we? I—"

40   "I'm going," Nola says.

41   "The extra expense, for one thing. Your father—"

42   "If I get accepted, I'm going."

43   "Your father—"

44   "The hell with him too."

45   Mrs. Dietrich would like to slap her daughter's face. Bring tears to those steely eyes. But she sits stiff, turning her wine glass between her fingers, patient, calm, she's heard all this before; she says, "Surely this isn't the best time to discuss it, Nola."

46   Mrs. Dietrich is afraid her daughter will leave the restaurant, simply walk away, that has happened before and if it happens today she doesn't know what she will do. But Nola sits unmoving; her face closed, impassive. Mrs. Dietrich feels her quickened heartbeat. Once after one of their quarrels Mrs. Dietrich told a friend of hers, the mother too of a teenage daughter, "I just don't know her any longer, how can you keep living with someone you don't know?" and the woman said, "Eventually you can't."

47   Nola says, not looking at Mrs. Dietrich: "Why don't we talk about it, Mother?"

48   "Talk about what?" Mrs. Dietrich asks.

49   "You know."

50   "The semester in France? Again?"

51   "No."

52   "What, then?"

53   "You *know*."

54   "I don't know, really. Really!" Mrs. Dietrich smiles, baffled. She feels the corners of her eyes pucker white with strain.

55   Nola says, sighing, "How exhausting it is."

56   "How *what*?"

57   "How exhausting it is."

58   "What is?"

59   "You and me—"

60   "What?"

61   "Being together—"

62   "Being together how—?"

63   "The two of us, like this—"

64   "But we're hardly ever together, Nola," Mrs. Dietrich says.

65   Her expression is calm but her voice is shaking. Nola turns away, covering her face with a hand, for a moment she looks years older than her age—in fact exhausted. Mrs. Dietrich sees with pity that her daughter's skin is fair and thin and dry—unlike her own, which tends to be oily—it will wear out before she's forty. Mrs. Dietrich reaches over to squeeze her hand. The fingers are limp, ungiving. "You're going back to school tomorrow, Nola," she says. "You won't come home again until June 12. And you probably will go to France—if your father consents."

66   Nola gets to her feet, drops her cigarette to the flagstone terrace and grinds it out beneath her boot. A dirty thing to do, Mrs. Dietrich thinks, considering there's an ashtray right on the table, but she says nothing. She dislikes La Crêperie anyway.

67   Nola laughs, showing her lovely white teeth. "Oh, the hell with him," she says. "Fuck Daddy, right?"

68   They separate for an hour, Mrs. Dietrich to Neiman-Marcus to buy a birthday gift for her elderly aunt, Nola to the trendy new boutique Pour Vous. By the time Mrs. Dietrich rejoins her daughter she's quite angry, blood beating hot and hard and measured in resentment, she has had time to relive old quarrels between them, old exchanges, stray humiliating memories of her marriage as well, these last-hour disagreements are the cruelest and they are Nola's specialty. She locates Nola in the rear of the boutique amid blaring rock music, flashing neon lights, chrome-edged mirrors, her face still hard, closed, prim, pale. She stands beside another teenage girl looking in a desultory way through a rack of blouses, shoving the hangers roughly along, taking no care when a blouse falls to the floor. As Nola glances up, startled, not prepared to see her mother in front of her, their eyes lock for an instant and Mrs. Dietrich stares at her with hatred. Cold calm clear unmistakable hatred. She is thinking, Who are *you*? What have I to do with *you*? I don't know *you*, I don't love *you*, why should I?

69   Has Nola seen, heard?—she turns aside as if wincing, gives the blouses a final dismissive shove. Her eyes look tired, the corners of her mouth downturned. Anxious, immediately repentant, Mrs. Dietrich asks if she has found anything worth trying on. Nola says with a shrug, "Not a thing, Mother."

70   On their way out of the Mall Mrs. Dietrich and Nola see the disheveled woman in the black coat again, this time sitting prominently on a concrete ledge in front of Lord & Taylor's busy main entrance. Shopping bag at her feet, shabby purse on the ledge beside her. She is shaking her head in a series of annoyed switches as if arguing with someone but her hands are loose, palms up, in her lap. Her posture is unfortunate— she sits with her knees parted, inner thighs revealed, fatty, dead white, the tops of cotton stockings rolled tight cutting into the flesh. Again, streams of shoppers are making a careful berth around her. Alone among them Nola hesitates, seems about to approach the woman—Please don't, Nola! please! Mrs. Dietrich thinks—then changes her mind and keeps on walking. Mrs. Dietrich murmurs isn't it a pity, poor thing, don't you won-

der where she lives, who her family is, but Nola doesn't reply. Her pace through the first door of Lord & Taylor is so rapid that Mrs. Dietrich can barely keep up.

71   But Nola's upset. Strangely upset. As soon as they are in the car, packages and bags in the backseat, she begins crying.

72   It's childish helpless crying, as though her heart is broken. But Mrs. Dietrich knows it isn't broken, she has heard these very sobs before. Many times before. Still she comforts her daughter, embraces her, hugs her hard, hard. A sudden fierce passion. Vehemence. "Nola honey. Nola dear, what's wrong, dear, everything will be all right, dear," she says, close to weeping herself. She would embrace Nola even more tightly except for the girl's quilted jacket, that bulky L. L. Bean thing she has never liked, and Nola's stubborn lowered head. Nola has always been ashamed, crying, frantic to hide her face. Strangers are passing close by the car, curious, staring. Mrs. Dietrich wishes she had a cloak to draw over her daughter and herself, so that no one else would see.

Questions for Review

1. Oates presents a mother and daughter who are very much at odds with each other. What is the source of their conflict? Do you like either of these characters? Why or why not?
2. The physical setting for this story is the Livingstone Mall, which we may assume is a typical suburban U.S. mall. What does it represent (or symbolize), other than a place to go shopping?
3. What does this story say about the Dietrich family? How might this family represent others in our society?
4. Identify two or three places where Oates's use of language is particularly effective. What makes these passages effective?
5. What is your overall assessment of this story? Did you like it? Why or why not?

"In the Land of Men," our second story, is the title story of *In the Land of Men*, a collection of short fiction by Antonya Nelson. An associate professor of English at New Mexico State University (NMSU), Nelson won the Flannery O'Connor Prize for Short Fiction in 1989.

ANTONYA NELSON

IN THE LAND OF MEN

1   Since my attack last year, when I get off work at night one of my brothers is always waiting for me in our family car, the rusted boat, engine idling, double-parked on Halsted right outside Mizzi's, where I wait tables. No one asked them to do this and we don't talk about it, but when I emerge from the steamy restaurant into the biting,

steel cold of Chicago, my heart offers up a grateful sigh at the presence of one or the other of my brothers' placid, safe faces.

2   Tonight they all three show. Sam, nineteen, the oldest boy but four years younger than me, sits on the hood with his pointed black ankle boots wedged between bumper and car. An inch of bare skin is exposed where the boots and pants cuffs don't quite meet, which is Sam's style. It is zero degrees out, according to the radio, factoring in wind chill, but Sam doesn't wear a coat.

3   "Too cool to feel cold?" I say.

4   He shells out a pittance of a smile. "Let's go." He hops off the hood to hold open the front door and presses my back with his palm. Sensing his eyes casting about protectively behind me, I catch my first whiff of something gone awry.

5   "I love a warm car," I say, settling in the passenger seat with my hands in front of the blowing heat vents. My other two brothers sit in the back the way the youngest always do. I say to them, "Hey."

6   Sam slams the driver's door and jerks us out of park. He drives as if our transmission is not automatic, shifting into low or neutral frequently, keeping one hand active on the thin metal stick. Even as his older sister, I stay a certain nervous distance from Sam. Beneath his meticulously maintained smooth surface is a rage that can erupt and break windows or punch walls.

7   For a time I just ride along in the warmth, quietly losing my waitress aches. Lately I've found real comfort in these pocketlike moments of heat and peace, which can be as refreshing as deep, unconscious sleep. I breathe out, at last, hating to end it, but knowing I must. "So, what's the occasion?"

8   Sam grimly says nothing, flicking his eyes to the rearview. I turn, catty-corner, to Donald. Seventeen, the worrier, he looks alarmingly pale in the passing streetlights. His hand is in a fist under his nose as he bites a fingernail, staring desperately at the sidewalk and storefronts like a trapped dog. Donald has ulcers, migraines, all the ailments symptomatic of early adulthood. Beside him, Les, the family baby, seems more rosy-cheeked than usual, as if he's siphoning off Donald's color to top his own. But even happy Les has an uncertain smile on his face and watches Sam for cues. His teeth chatter, despite the car's abundant warmth.

9   Without taking his eyes off the panel van in front of him, Sam says tightly, "You got any plans tonight?"

10   I point at my chest. "Me? You're talking to me?"

11   "That's right. Anything you were going to do?"

12   "Is something wrong?" I ask, simultaneously anxious and annoyed that they are protecting me by withholding. "Is it Dad? Has something happened to Dad?"

13   "No," Donald says, looking at his watch. "Time for *WBN News at Nine.* Pistachios and beer."

14   From behind me, Les pats my arm soothingly. "Dad's cool," he assures me.

15   Sam catches my eye and we share an older siblings' smile, as if over Les's head. "He's fine," Sam says.

16   "And here you guys are. So what could it be?" I sit back, relieved: My family is alive. Lesser scenarios occur to me. A surprise party. An unexpected friend waiting at the airport. A trip to the police to clear up some minor infraction before my father discovers the offense. But here we are, enclosed and fine and balanced. I enjoy, for a second, suspense's tantalizing luxury. "So when do you tell me, guys?"

17   Sam stops uncharacteristically at a yellow light. We rock forward with inertia, rock back. Pedestrians, loaded down with afterwork, early Christmas shopping, plunge into the crosswalks, heads ducked in irritation against the cold. Telltale forest-green Marshall Field's sacks swing from their gloved fingers. It's late and they're homeward

bound. A man carries a paper funnel of flowers, shielding it with his chest, turning his back to protect this gift for some woman. Ashy snow blows up in the six-way intersection, sings along the cracks in our car doors, and the taxi in front of us decides to turn left; a signal begins flashing. Generally, this draws a heavy lean on Sam's horn, but tonight he simply waits.

18 "You have a decision to make," he says.

19 Les adds excitedly, "A very *important* decision. Mega-important. Man, it's big, really big. Life and death, you could say."

20 Sam frowns into the rearview mirror at Les, his profile so sharp and grown-up I have a sudden moment of wonder: My brother's a man. I quickly look at Donald—has he, too, crossed the line? But no, Donald has no beard, no jutting jaw, no buried rage. He shakes his young head pessimistically, eyes still glued in appeal to the passing world.

21 The light changes.

22 "We got your perp," Sam says to me as we take off again and slide around the taxi. He shifts his eyes momentarily from the road to my face. He's a dangerously handsome man, the family heartbreaker, and his direct gaze has a life—volition, power—of its own.

23 "My perp?"

24 "Perpetrator!" Les shouts gleefully. "We got your perpetrator! That guy! He's in our trunk."

25 Last year on a night not unlike tonight—that is, a night in which one instant knifed the odds of my otherwise fair life—a man looped his bright red wool scarf over my head lasso-style and pulled me to his chest. Fast and easy. He was right behind me and I could feel the serious metal cylinder of a gun at my back.

26 "Let's walk," he suggested, "and not make too much racket."

27 We'd been the only two people waiting for the bus and I hadn't looked closely at him. His red scarf had been woven around his neck, and his hair stood up comically in the back as a result. A cane hooked over his forearm. That's all I remembered. Innocuous. Maybe he wore a long camel's hair coat. Behind me, he matched his footsteps to mine so exactly that if I looked down I could see his right galoshes toe coming forward just behind my own. There weren't many people on Fullerton Avenue that night and those who were seemed to misread my frantic blinking eyes. What could our peculiar closeness have appeared to be? He took me as quickly as possible to an alley. I heard our bus pass without stopping, its upward-shifting gears, feeling furious with the driver, who knew my name, who knew I always rode home with him. . . .

28 "Got any money, baby?" the man asked as we hastened down the alley, leaning near enough to my ear for me to feel his eyelashes kiss it. I stumbled, but he led me through my clumsiness like an expert dancer. We were approaching the back of Mizzi's, and I prayed for one of the busboys, Danbo or Rudy, to be outside smoking a j. But it was too cold; they would be up above the walk-in refrigerator, in the airspace between floors. There wasn't a soul in the alley. I heard the muffled clatter of dishes and the motor of the Hobart, could easily imagine that lively, hot kitchen only a few crucial feet of space away from me.

29 "Money, babe?" he reminded me.

30 I nodded in my scarf sling. "I do. Take it, please, in my bag." I lifted my right shoulder carefully to draw attention to my purse hanging there.

31 He said, "Good girl. You a good girl? It would be in your interest to be a very good girl, you know." He had a precise British accent, cheerful and civilized-sounding. Could I have felt relief? We'd stopped and he positioned me face first against the rear wall of the empty storefront down the block from Mizzi's. It would be open in a month, its front windows claimed. A comedy club. I'd passed the sign a hundred times. Open mike

on Wednesdays, no cover, two-drink minimum. He pushed me gently to the wall, nose to brick, and told me to grab on to the black window bars on either side.

32   "You hang on for dear life, do you hear me?"

33   I certainly did.

34   His gun, that metal erection, pressed into my lower spine, sending its insinuations to every part of me. Without lowering the gun, he dropped his cane to the ground and told me to put a foot on either end of it. I concentrated on the rubber tip and the curve of its worn handle. The worst thing that *could* happen, I told myself, was not going to. Then he drew my head back by the hair and slammed my forehead against the bricks. I tasted red wool.

35   Donald says, "He can probably hear us, you know. The trunk is right here." He pats the seat behind him, leaning away from it. Les looks startled and also tips forward.

36   Even the remotest possibility of this man's presence has made me queasy and I clutch the door handle, as if waiting for the right moment to escape. "You can't be serious," I say hopefully.

37   "Serious as a heart attack, sweetheart," Sam says.

38   We're heading west on the Eisenhower. Magnificent, colorful Michigan Avenue has given way to gloomy industrial warehouses. Traffic is light and, for the second time in my city life, I wish it otherwise. Cars, humanity, witnesses—but to what?

39   I say, "How can you be positive it's him? I mean, did you ask him?"

40   "We didn't *talk* to him," Les says. "God, it was hard enough to find him. We've been watching him for a long time. We knew it was him. He had that England accent. Plus the cane."

41   My feet arch reflexively at the mention of the cane, the dry texture of scarf once more in my mouth. "What do you mean, you've been watching him? What are you talking about?"

42   Donald says, "*They.* These two have been staking out this guy since last winter. Not me. I was ready to let the police do it."

43   "The police," Sam scoffs. He shakes his head once.

44   "That's right!" Donald says. "The cops. You can't just go around being above the law."

45   Sam says, "Says who?"

46   "I thought about dressing up like a girl," Les tells me, and new images unreel before my eyes at a dizzying speed. "A decoy. But I would have looked like Bride of Frankenstein, and I kept thinking, what would Mom have thought?"

47   "Mom," Donald says, "would have wondered where you guys were all those nights. Mothers know where their kids are. With Dad, it's like, 'Oh, Sam and Les? Huh. Studying in their rooms, I guess.' Mom would never have let you out the door."

48   I say, "What are you saying?"

49   "They chased the guy," Donald explains.

50   "We *tailed* him," Les corrects. "There was no chasing. Chasing means running."

51   "Whatever. They *tailed* him. They—"

52   "We waited until he was alone," Les says. "We saw him at that same bus stop, you know. . . ." He clears his throat to indicate discretion in alluding to my rape.

53   "And?" I say.

54   "And we followed him home."

55   "On foot," Sam says pointedly. Since he's had his driver's license he's hardly walked anywhere.

56   Les bounces on the seat as he talks, "We know where he lives!"

57   "Pricey," Sam adds. "Yuppie."

58   "After we found out, we watched his walk-up, we saw him through the curtains. He's got those see-through kind, the ones Mom always said was a bad idea on the first floor. But we couldn't get him alone. He would walk out the door, and we'd start to get out of the car—here comes some people. Man, it was frustrating. I don't see how you could make a living doing it."

59   Sam says to me, "It *is* weird how hard it was to find him by himself."

60   The car is silent for a moment, all of us meditating on my rapist's extended good fortune. Then Donald says, "These two have been out asking for it, just asking for—"

61   "We had a gun," Les protests. "*He* didn't have a gun—"

62   "Luckily for you," Donald interrupts.

63   "—but we *did,* see, that's the whole point. We were in charge. Once we got some privacy, the rest was so easy you couldn't believe it. He comes out to get the paper, nobody around, and bang, Sam's there with the gun."

64   "Bang?" I ask. "Bang? Oh guys, you didn't shoot him?"

65   "Not bang like that, just bang, like, get in the car, bud, let's go for a cruise. We didn't even have to tie him up."

66   "But he had a gun," I say. "Last year, he had a gun."

67   Sam turns to me. "Nuh-uh. Piece of pipe. We've been watching, like Les said. We saw asswipe's weapon. Carries it in his coat. Jesus. Little six-inch pipe."

68   Donald, relinquishing his role as the voice of reason for a moment, giggles and says, "Saturday night plumber's special." They all three laugh, a frightening expulsion of breath.

69   "Please tell me you don't have a man in the trunk of this car."

70   "Sorry," Sam says. "No can do." His coldness, his assuredness—the way the thrust of his strong, righteous jaw seems to drive the very car—these things let me know they not only have a man in the trunk, but the right man. I now feel his weight, as if the back end of the automobile were notably lower to the road.

71   "Please," I say weakly, "could we think for a minute about going to the cops with this?"

72   "They'll turn him free," Sam says. "Right now we have him, he's ours, but they'll set him free."

73   "You know what the problem is?" Donald says speculatively. "The problem is over-crowding in jails. I've been thinking that they should just stick the smaller-crime guys in the army. You know how the army always needs recruits? Two birds with one—"

74   "Dumb," Sam says. "Put *that* guy in the army?"

75   "Not him. He's in prison for life. I said, *small*-crime guys get in the army."

76   "Dumb," Sam repeats.

77   "Why? It could work," Donald says, then adds, "But now it's too late to go to the cops. Now we'd be in trouble, even me, accessory after the fact. This is a no-win situation."

78   "We followed him on a date." Les leans against my seat, elbows on either side of me. "Movie at the Biograph, coffee at the French place. We could see him through one window, and you waiting tables right across the street through another window. Was that bizarre, or what?"

79   "We thought about getting him *and* his date," Sam says. "See how he'd feel about that."

80   "I can't believe we finally got him!" Les says in awe. "We waxed his ass. We showed him!"

81   Donald shakes his head at the sorriness of Les's logic. "Right. Let's talk counting chickens before they're hatched. He's still here." He indicates the trunk with his thumb. "We haven't shown him thing one."

82   For two weeks after the rape, I didn't go back to work. I didn't often leave the house, and, if I did, I was escorted to and from like a politician or criminal. I read the *Trib* every morning looking for other attacks. They seemed to be epidemic, but what doesn't, once it's happened to you? The cops told me my assailant sounded like one they'd been after for months. They liked to name their rapists; this one was Big Ben. He *did* have a British accent. He *did* speak in complete sentences. I saw a counselor. She'd been raped before, too. It was like a club. I prepared myself for nightmares, as instructed, but never had any directly related to that night. The signs in my dreams were more oblique. I would be pursuing a seemingly safe course on a road, then suddenly I would look around—where were the landmarks of civilization? Billboards, buildings, traffic lights? Surrounding me would be blank, cool air. High as an airplane, I would suddenly realize even my vehicle was gone. Nothing kept me from plummeting. The road, my world—all of it snatched out from under me, and it was then that horror would return.

83   I took sedatives. I slept like something dead.

84   And then two weeks later I was back at work. I'd been emptied but other things began inevitably to fill my life again, so that the attack was, soon enough, supplanted. Or, at least, shuffled into the deck. Still, it was the marked card, the one dividing before and after.

85   "I could kill him," Sam admits calmly, and I realize he's speaking the truth. He could. "If it was me, I'd kill him, but you decide." He turns to his brothers. "We'll do what she decides." We're parked a few yards from an off ramp, in front of the boarded windows of the Five Cents Germ-Free Cleaners. Inland from Lake Michigan, the snow falls more heavily and soon the car is its own late-model Ford igloo of isolation.

86   "I thought we were going to definitely kill him," Les whines. "I thought we had a plan. We had a lot of plans. Tell her about the Dumpster plan, Sam."

87   "Shut up," Donald says. "Really, just shut up. The right thing to do is turn around and go back to his house. We have to let him go. Otherwise we're all in trouble. Doesn't that make sense, Sam? He doesn't know us."

88   "'We pull up, dump him, say, 'Hey, sorry, pal, just a joyride'?" Sam says this snidely, whirling in his seat to face Donald, behind him. "Who do you think is going to press charges at that point? We kidnapped him, basically."

89   Donald puts his finger to his lips. "He might be listening," he whispers. "You're giving him ideas."

90   "What about the drive-the-car-into-the-lake plan?" Les goes on. "That was good. We get a new car out of it, too, so it's a double good plan." His teeth, crooked and spotted with minuscule notches from his braces, chatter loud enough for us to hear over the sound of the wind. "Or castrating him. We talked about that."

91   "Jesus," Donald says.

92   "What if he's dead?" Les says suddenly, his teeth still. "What if he suffocated back there?"

93   Sam nods solemnly. "Back to the Dumpster plan. Dead, we don't have a problem."

94   "Man, if he's dead we have about ten million problems," Donald says, forgetting to whisper.

95   "But alive," Sam continues, "alive, I'm not sure what to do with him." He turns to me. "Like I said, it should be up to you. What do *you* want?"

96   "Shoot him," Les pleads. "Choose shooting."

97   "Shut *up!*" Donald orders. They all three look at me. The car has grown so cold I can see their breath. It would be colder still in the trunk. I review my options: Turn him

loose, maim him, kill him, variations thereof. The moment I say the word, we all move into the future. For now, however, we're in one of those pockets.

98   Of course I have wanted this man punished, but I never went further than hoping he would *get what he deserved,* a concrete wish with only abstract underpinnings, one I would have been happy to let someone else make real. I never saw the man's face—maybe if I had I could have declared the correct retribution, hollowed the perfect scar—but as it was, he might have been any man, and any man might have been him.

99   "Maybe I should look at him," I say, stalling.

100   "Yeah?" Sam takes the keys from the ignition and spins them on his forefinger. "Yeah?"

101   "I want to see him," I decide.

102   Sam reaches across me and pokes the glove compartment open. A gun spills into his waiting hand. "Okey-doke," he says. "You want it, you got it."

103   "He's ugly," Les warns me as he clambers out.

104   From the outside, our car looks like one abandoned, the four swung-open doors leaving gaping holes in the storm. Feeling a curious and appealing sense of dèjá vu, I imagine our walking away, four children on a long winter trek. But, of course, passive as it is, even walking away is doing something.

105   Les whisks the snow off the trunk with his bare hand and raps on the metal. "Anyone home?"

106   "Listen," Donald says. "Okay, we don't let him go, that won't work. But . . . " He ticks off steps on his fingers. "We drive to the police station, we say Les and I got the guy—we're under eighteen, so it's a juvenile crime—we know he's the one, the cane, et cetera, and she"—he nods at me—"she identifies his voice. She makes him say what he said to her last year, he sounds like Prince Charles, they book him. It can happen. Okay?" He moves his head up and down as if he can coach us into agreement.

107   "Finished?" Sam asks.

108   Donald sighs. "You all are crazy, I swear."

109   Sam tries to hand me the gun.

110   "I don't want that."

111   "Yes," he says, "you do." He nudges my fingertips with the cold handle.

112   "I'll hold it," Les volunteers. "Let me hold it. I haven't gotten to hold it yet." This from my fourteen-year-old brother, the one who, until he was at least twelve, cried when he saw dead animals in the road.

113   "Give me that," I tell Sam. I use both hands and find myself with my knees bent like a TV cop.

114   "Ready?" he says, key to the lock.

115   I shake my head no. It's funny, but even with a gun in my hands and the lid locked I don't feel at all invulnerable. Donald turns and begins walking away from us.

116   Sam yells to his back, "Keep a look out for cars."

117   Donald stops at the street, his shoulders drawn, as if trying to decide whether to step off the curb and keep on going.

118   "You watching?" Sam calls to him. A horn blows in the distance.

119   When Donald turns our way, I admire his loyalty to his brothers' bad cause. He nods to Sam. I aim the gun at the back of our car, quaking.

120   Then I say, "Now." Without taking my eyes off the bumper, I blink rapidly so I won't have to when the lid flies up.

121   The man lies fetuslike, filling our trunk, back to us. Expensive camel's hair coat. A cane thrown on top of him like an afterthought. The little light inside shows half his face, one closed eye, which, while I stare, opens.

122   "Shut it!" I yell at Sam. "Shut it! Shut it!"

123   Our mother died three years ago. We worried all along about the wrong things. We fretted about her recovery from cancer, chemotherapy, and the fluctuating number of months her doctors had thrown around as her life expectancy. But those things never turned out to be relevant. Some percentage of people slip away under anesthesia. It's a risk of every operation, a posted figure, like car accidents, like crimes. After my mother was gone, with only my brothers and my father and me, I thought, *Here you are in the land of men.* I never missed her more, I never felt more outnumbered, than when I came home from the police station last year. I told myself growing up meant losing things, but then it didn't feel so much like loss as it did theft.

124   "What do you want us to do?" my brother Sam asks me patiently. He must know that patience, or its illusion, is a grown-up virtue. Back in the driver's seat, he is tired, his duties in this territory of his own kind so mercilessly neverending.

125   "We can't just leave him there," Donald says. "'For one thing, this is our car. What if we want to go somewhere? For another, it's cruel and unusual punishment.'"

126   Les, brave and savagely young, proclaims, "He could rot in there, for what he did to our sister!"

127   "That's true," Sam agrees. "He could rot . . . and he could not. You want him to rot?" he asks me.

128   I look out at the blanketed and beautified ugly buildings around us. Is there any wish made more often than the one for time to stop? But the snowdrift forming around our car has gotten deeper, and soon, if we let it, it will trap us, all five of us. What I want is for him to disappear, but I consider my real choices and also the misnomer *justice* in an unjust world. Soon I will insist on driving the car back into the city, back to the lights and signs and authorities created by mankind to keep us civilized.

129   Meanwhile, my brothers wait.

130   "I'm thinking," I tell them.

Questions for Review

1. What kinds of external and internal conflict are at work in this story? What is the primary conflict? On what do you base your response?
2. Who is the narrator of this story? How reliable is the narrator? On what do you base your assessment?
3. How appropriately titled is this story? Why?
4. Identify two or three passages in which Nelson's use of language is particularly effective. What makes these passages effective?
5. At the end of this story, the narrator has a choice to make, but we don't know what she'll decide. What are her options? What would you advise her to do? Why?
6. What is your overall assessment of this story? Did you like it? Why or why not?

Our third story, "El Tonto del Barrio," is by José Armas, a writer from Albuquerque, New Mexico. It appeared in *Cuentos Chicanos* (Albuquerque: University of New Mexico Press, 1984), a collection of short fiction edited by Rudolfo A. Anaya and Antonio Marquez. The story's title translates as "The Fool of the Neighborhood."

JOSÉ ARMAS

EL TONTO DEL BARRIO

1   Romero Estrado was called "El Cotoro" because he was always whistling and singing. He made nice music even though his songs were spontaneous compositions made up of words with sounds that he liked but which seldom made any sense. But that didn't seem to bother either Romero or anyone else in the Golden Heights Centro where he lived. Not even the kids made fun of him. It just was not permitted.

2   Romero had a ritual that he followed almost every day. After breakfast he would get his broom and go up and down the main street of the Golden Heights Centro whistling and singing and sweeping the sidewalks for all the businesses. He would sweep in front of the Tortilleria America, the XXX Liquor Store, the Tres Milpas Bar run by Tino Gabaldon, Barelas' Barber Shop, the used furniture store owned by Goldstein, El Centro Market of the Avila family, the Model Cities Office, and Lourdes Printing Store. Then, in the afternoons, he would come back and sit in Barelas' Barber Shop and spend the day looking at magazines and watching and waving to the passing people as he sang and composed his songs without a care in the world.

3   When business was slow, Barelas would let him sit in the barber's chair. Romero loved it. It was a routine that Romero kept every day except Sundays and Mondays when Barelas' Barber Shop was closed. After a period of years, people in the barrio got used to seeing Romero do his little task of sweeping the sidewalks and sitting in Barelas' Barber Shop. If he didn't show up one day someone assumed the responsibility to go to his house to see if he was ill. People would stop to say hello to Romero on the street and although he never initiated a conversation while he was sober, he always smiled and responded cheerfully to everyone. People passing the barber shop in the afternoons made it a point to wave even though they couldn't see him; they knew he was in there and was expecting some salutation.

4   When he was feeling real good, Romero would sweep in front of the houses on both sides of the block also. He took his job seriously and took great care to sweep cleanly, between the cracks and even between the sides of buildings. The dirt and small scraps went into the gutter. The bottles and bigger pieces of litter were put carefully in cardboard boxes, ready for the garbage man.

5   If he did it the way he wanted, the work took him the whole morning. And always cheerful—always with some song.

6   Only once did someone call attention to his work. Frank Avila told him in jest that Romero had forgotten to pick up an empty bottle of wine from his door. Romero was so offended and made such a commotion that it got around very quickly that no one should criticize his work. There was, in fact, no reason to.

7   Although it had been long acknowledged that Romero was a little "touched," he fit very well into the community. He was a respected citizen.

8   He could be found at the Tres Milpas Bar drinking his occasional beer in the evenings. Romero had a rivalry going with the Ranchera songs on the jukebox. He would try to outsing the songs using the same melody but inserting his own selection of random words. Sometimes, like all people, he would "bust out" and get drunk.

9   One could always tell when Romero was getting drunk because he would begin telling everyone that he loved them.

10   "I looov youuu," he would sing to someone and offer to compose them a song.

11   "Ta bueno, Romero. Ta bueno, ya bete," they would tell him.

12   Sometimes when he got too drunk he would crap in his pants and then Tino would make him go home.

13   Romero received some money from Social Security but it wasn't much. None of the merchants gave him any credit because he would always forget to pay his bills. He didn't do it on purpose, he just forgot and spent his money on something else. So instead, the businessmen preferred to do little things for him occasionally. Barelas would trim his hair when things were slow. The Tortilleria America would give him menudo and freshmade tortillas at noon when he was finished with his sweeping. El Centro Market would give him the overripe fruit and broken boxes of food that no one else would buy. Although it was unspoken and unwritten, there was an agreement that existed between Romero and the Golden Heights Centro. Romero kept the sidewalks clean and the barrio looked after him. It was a contract that worked well for a long time.

14   Then, when Seferino, Barelas' oldest son, graduated from high school he went to work in the barber shop for the summer. Seferino was a conscientious and sensitive young man and it wasn't long before he took notice of Romero and came to feel sorry for him.

15   One day when Romero was in the shop Seferino decided to act.

16   "Mira, Romero. Yo te doy 50 centavos por cada dia que me barres la banqueta. Fifty cents for every day you sweep the sidewalk for us. Qué te parece?"

17   Romero thought about it carefully.

18   "Hecho! Done!" he exclaimed. He started for home right away to get his broom.

19   "Why did you do that for, m'ijo?" asked Barelas.

20   "It don't seem right, Dad. The man works and no one pays him for his work. Everyone should get paid for what they do."

21   "He don't need no pay. Romero has everything he needs."

22   "It's not the same, Dad. How would you like to do what he does and be treated the same way? It's degrading the way he has to go around getting scraps and handouts."

23   "I'm not Romero. Besides you don't know about these things, m'ijo. Romero would be unhappy if his schedule was upset. Right now everyone likes him and takes care of him. He sweeps the sidewalks because he wants something to do, not because he wants money."

24   "I'll pay him out of my money, don't worry about it then."

25   "The money is not the point. The point is that money will not help Romero. Don't you understand that?"

26   "Look, Dad. just put yourself in his place. Would you do it? Would you cut hair for nothing?"

27   Barelas just knew his son was putting something over on him but he didn't know how to answer. It seemed to make sense the way Seferino explained it. But it still went against his "instinct." On the other hand, Seferino had gone and finished high school. He must know something. There were few kids who had finished high school in the barrio, and fewer who had gone to college. Barelas knew them all. He noted (with some pride) that Seferino was going to be enrolled at Harvard University this year. That must count for something, he thought. Barelas himself had never gone to school. So maybe his son had something there. On the other hand . . . it upset Barelas that he wasn't able to get Seferino to see the issue. How can we be so far apart on something so simple, he thought. But he decided not to say anything else about it.

28   Romero came back right away and swept the front of Barelas' shop again and put what little dirt he found into the curb. He swept up the gutter, put the trash in a shoe box and threw it in a garbage can.

29   Seferino watched with pride as Romero went about his job and when he was finished he went outside and shook Romero's hand. Seferino told him he had done a good job. Romero beamed.

30   Manolo was coming into the shop to get his hair cut as Seferino was giving Romero his wages. He noticed Romero with his broom.

31   "What's going on?" he asked. Barelas shrugged his shoulders. "Que tiene Romero? Is he sick or something?"

32   "No, he's not sick," explained Seferino, who had now come inside. He told Manolo the story.

33   "We're going to make Romero a businessman," said Seferino. "Do you realize how much money Romero would make if everyone paid him just fifty cents a day? Like my dad says, 'Everyone should be able to keep his dignity, no matter how poor.' And he does a job, you know."

34   "Well, it makes sense," said Manolo.

35   "Hey. Maybe I'll ask people to do that," said Seferino. "That way the poor old man could make a decent wage. Do you want to help, Manolo? You can go with me to ask people to pay him."

36   "Well," said Manolo as he glanced at Barelas, "I'm not too good at asking people for money."

37   This did not discourage Seferino. He went out and contacted all the businesses on his own, but no one else wanted to contribute. This didn't discourage Seferino either. He went on giving Romero fifty cents a day.

38   After a while, Seferino heard that Romero had asked for credit at the grocery store. "See, Dad. What did I tell you? Things are getting better for him already. He's becoming his own man. And look. It's only been a couple of weeks." Barelas did not reply.

39   But then the next week Romero did not show up to sweep any sidewalks. He was around but he didn't do any work for anybody the entire week. He walked around Golden Heights Centro in his best gray work pants and his slouch hat, looking important and making it a point to walk right past the barber shop every little while.

40   Of course, the people in the Golden Heights Centro noticed the change immediately, and since they saw Romero in the street, they knew he wasn't ill. But the change was clearly disturbing the community. They discussed him in the Tortilleria America where people got together for coffee, and at the Tres Milpas Bar. Everywhere the topic of conversation was the great change that had come over Romero. Only Barelas did not talk about it.

41   The following week Romero came into the barber shop and asked to talk with Seferino in private. Barelas knew immediately something was wrong. Romero never initiated a conversation unless he was drunk.

42   They went into the back room where Barelas could not hear and then Romero informed Seferino, "I want a raise."

43   "What? What do you mean, a raise? You haven't been around for a week. You only worked a few weeks and now you want a raise?" Seferino was clearly angry but Romero was calm and insistent.

44   Romero correctly pointed out that he had been sweeping the sidewalks for a long time. Even before Seferino finished high school.

45   "I deserve a raise," he repeated after an eloquent presentation.

46   Seferino looked coldly at Romero. It was clearly a stand-off.

47   Then Seferino said, "Look, maybe we should forget the whole thing. I was just trying to help you out and look at what you do."

48   Romero held his ground. "I helped you out too. No one told me to do it and I did it
anyway. I helped you many years."

49   "Well, let's forget about the whole thing then," said Seferino.

50   "I quit then," said Romero.

51   "Quit?" exclaimed Seferino as he laughed at Romero.

52   "Quit! I quit!" said Romero as he walked out the front of the shop past Barelas who
was cutting a customer's hair.

53   Seferino came out shaking his head and laughing.

54   "Can you imagine that old guy?"

55   Barelas did not seem too amused. He felt he could have predicted that something
bad like this would happen.

56   Romero began sweeping the sidewalks again the next day with the exception that
when he came to the barber shop he would go around it and continue sweeping the rest
of the sidewalks. He did this for the rest of the week. And the following Tuesday he began sweeping the sidewalk all the way up to the shop and then pushing the trash to the
sidewalk in front of the barber shop. Romero then stopped coming to the barber shop
in the afternoon.

57   The barrio buzzed with fact and rumor about Romero. Tino commented that
Romero was not singing anymore. Even if someone offered to buy him a beer he
wouldn't sing. Frank Avila said the neighbors were complaining because he was leaving
his TV on loud the whole day and night. He still greeted people but seldom smiled. He
had run up a big bill at the liquor store and when the manager stopped his credit, he
caught Romero stealing bottles of whiskey. He was also getting careless about his
dress. He didn't shave and clean like he used to. Women complained that he walked
around in soiled pants, that he smelled bad. Even one of the little kids complained that
Romero had kicked his puppy, but that seemed hard to believe.

58   Barelas felt terrible. He felt responsible. But he couldn't convince Seferino that
what he had done was wrong. Barelas himself stopped going to the Tres Milpas Bar after work to avoid hearing about Romero. Once he came across Romero on the street
and Barelas said hello but with a sense of guilt. Romero responded, avoiding Barelas'
eyes and moving past him awkwardly and quickly. Romero's behavior continued to get
erratic and some people started talking about having Romero committed.

59   "You can't do that," said Barelas when he was presented with a petition.

60   "He's flipped," said Tino, who made up part of the delegation circulating the petition. "No one likes Romero more than I do, you know that, Barelas."

61   "But he's really crazy," said Frank Avila.

62   "He was crazy before. No one noticed," pleaded Barelas.

63   "But it was a crazy we could depend on. Now he just wants to sit on the curb and
pull up the women's skirts. It's terrible. The women are going crazy. He's also running
into the street stopping the traffic. You see how he is. What choice do we have?"

64   "It's for his own good," put in one of the workers from the Model Cities Office.
Barelas dismissed them as outsiders. Seferino was there and wanted to say something
but a look from Barelas stopped him.

65   "We just can't do that," insisted Barelas. "Let's wait. Maybe he's just going
through a cycle. Look. We've had a full moon recently, que no? That must be it. You
know how the moon affects people in his condition."

66   "I don't know," said Tino. "What if he hurts . . . "

67 "He's not going to hurt anyone," cut in Barelas.

68 "No, Barelas. I was going to say, what if he hurts himself. He has no one at home. I'd say, let him come home with me for a while but you know how stubborn he is. You can't even talk to him any more."

69 "He gives everyone the finger when they try to pull him out of the traffic," said Frank Avila. "The cops have missed him, but it won't be long before they see him doing some of his antics and arrest him. Then what? Then the poor guy is in real trouble."

70 "Well, look," said Barelas. "How many names you got on the list?"

71 Tino responded slowly, "Well, we sort of wanted you to start off the list."

72 "Let's wait a while longer," said Barelas. "I just know that Romero will come around. Let's wait just a while, okay?"

73 No one had the heart to fight the issue and so they postponed the petition.

74 There was no dramatic change in Romero even though the full moon had completed its cycle. Still, no one initiated the petition again and then in the middle of August Seferino left for Cambridge to look for housing and to register early for school. Suddenly everything began to change again. One day Romero began sweeping the entire sidewalk again. His spirits began to pick up and his strange antics began to disappear.

75 At the Tortilleria America the original committee met for coffee and the talk turned to Romero.

76 "He's going to be all right now," said a jubilant Barelas. "I guarantee it."

77 "Well, don't hold your breath yet," said Tino. "The full moon is coming up again."

78 "Yeah," said Frank Avila dejectedly.

79 When the next full moon was in force the group was together again drinking coffee and Tino asked, "Well, how's Romero doing?"

80 Barelas smiled and said, "Well. Singing songs like crazy."

Questions for Review

1. In this story, Seferino tries to do what he thinks is the right thing to do. What is his motivation? How and why does it not work out as he expects?

2. To what extent are you prepared for the story's ending? Is it a satisfying resolution for you? Why or why not?

3. What conflicts are at work in this story? Begin by identifying conflicts between characters (e.g., between Seferino and Romero and between Seferino and his father). Are there any conflicts at work beyond those between characters? Consider how the community responds to Romero.

4. What is the tone of this story? Do you find elements of humor in it? If so, identify them. How do such elements affect the story's tone?

5. Identify two or three passages in which Armas's use of langauge is particularly effective. What makes these passages effective?

6. What is your overall assessment of this story? Did you like it? Why or why not?

Our final story was written by Kate Chopin and published in 1894 as "The Dream of an Hour." It was later retitled "The Story of an Hour." As you read, consider what this story has to say to readers today.

KATE CHOPIN

THE STORY OF AN HOUR

1   Knowing that Mrs. Mallard was afflicted with a heart trouble, great care was taken to break to her as gently as possible the news of her husband's death.

2   It was her sister Josephine who told her, in broken sentences; veiled hints that revealed in half concealing. Her husband's friend Richards was there, too, near her. It was he who had been in the newspaper office when intelligence of the railroad disaster was received, with Brently Mallard's name leading the list of "killed." He had only taken the time to assure himself of its truth by a second telegram, and had hastened to forestall any less careful, less tender friend in bearing the sad message.

3   She did not bear the story as many women have heard the same, with a paralyzed inability to accept its significance. She wept at once, with sudden, wild abandonment, in her sister's arms. When the storm of grief had spent itself she went away to her room alone. She would have no one follow her.

4   There stood, facing the open window, a comfortable, roomy armchair. Into this she sank, pressed down by a physical exhaustion that haunted her body and seemed to reach into her soul.

5   She could see in the open square before her house the tops of trees that were all aquiver with the new spring life. The delicious breath of rain was in the air. In the street below a peddler was crying his wares. The notes of a distant song which some one was singing reached her faintly, and countless sparrows were twittering in the eaves.

6   There were patches of blue sky showing here and there through the clouds that had met and piled one above the other in the west facing her window.

7   She sat with her head thrown back upon the cushion of the chair, quite motionless, except when a sob came up into her throat and shook her, as a child who has cried itself to sleep continues to sob in its dreams.

8   She was young, with a fair, calm face, whose lines bespoke repression and even a certain strength. But now there was a dull stare in her eyes, whose gaze was fixed away off yonder on one of those patches of blue sky. It was not a glance of reflection, but rather indicated a suspension of intelligent thought.

9   There was something coming to her and she was waiting for it, fearfully. What was it? She did not know; it was too subtle and elusive to name. But she felt it, creeping out of the sky, reaching toward her through the sounds, the scents, the color that filled the air.

10   Now her bosom rose and fell tumultuously. She was beginning to recognize this thing that was approaching to possess her, and she was striving to beat it back with her will—as powerless as her two white slender hands would have been.

11   When she abandoned herself a little whispered word escaped her slightly parted lips. She said it over and over under her breath: "free, free, free!" The vacant stare and the look of terror that had followed it went from her eyes. They stayed keen and bright. Her pulses beat fast, and the coursing blood warmed and relaxed every inch of her body.

12   She did not stop to ask if it were or were not a monstrous joy that held her. A clear and exalted perception enabled her to dismiss the suggestion as trivial.

13   She knew that she would weep again when she saw the kind, tender hands folded in death; the face that had never looked save with love upon her, fixed and gray and dead. But she saw beyond that bitter moment a long procession of years to come that would belong to her absolutely. And she opened and spread her arms out to them in welcome.

14   There would be no one to live for during those coming years; she would live for herself. There would be no powerful will bending hers in that blind persistence with which men and women believe they have a right to impose a private will upon a fellow-creature. A kind intention or a cruel intention made the act seem no less a crime as she looked upon it in that brief moment of illumination.

15   And yet she had loved him—sometimes. Often she had not. What did it matter! What could love, the unsolved mystery, count for in face of this possession of self-assertion which she suddenly recognized as the strongest impulse of her being!

16   "Free! Body and soul free!" she kept whispering.

17   Josephine was kneeling before the closed door with her lips to the keyhole, imploring for admission. "Louise, open the door! I beg; open the door—you will make yourself ill. What are you doing, Louise? For heaven's sake open the door."

18   "Go away. I am not making myself ill." No; she was drinking in a very elixir of life through that open window.

19   Her fancy was running riot along those days ahead of her. Spring days, and summer days, and all sorts of days that would be her own. She breathed a quick prayer that life might be long. It was only yesterday she had thought with a shudder that life might be long.

20   She arose at length and opened the door to her sister's importunities. There was a feverish triumph in her eyes, and she carried herself unwittingly like a goddess of Victory. She clasped her sister's waist, and together they descended the stairs. Richards stood waiting for them at the bottom.

21   Some one was opening the front door with a latchkey. It was Brently Mallard who entered, a little travel-stained, composedly carrying his grip-sack and umbrella. He had been far from the scene of accident, and did not even know there had been one. He stood amazed at Josephine's piercing cry; at Richards' quick motion to screen him from the view of his wife.

22   But Richards was too late.

23   When the doctors came they said she had died of heart disease—of joy that kills.

Questions for Review

1. Kate Chopin published this story over a hundred years ago. How current or contemporary do you think it is; that is, how effectively does this story speak to you as a reader today?

2. What does this story say about the relationships between men and women? Between husbands and wives?

3. Identify two or three passages in which you think Chopin's language is particularly effective. What makes these passages effective?

4. What is your overall assessment of this story? Did you like it? Why or why not?

The first poem we present is by Robert Frost, one of the most famous and best-liked of American poets.

ROBERT FROST

FOR ONCE, THEN, SOMETHING

1   Others taunt me with having knelt at well-curbs
        Always wrong to the light, so never seeing
        Deeper down in the well than where the water
        Gives me back in a shining surface picture
5   Me myself in the summer heaven, godlike,
        Looking out of a wreath of fern and cloud puffs.
        Once, when trying with chin against a well-curb,
        I discerned, as I thought, beyond the picture,
        Through the picture, a something white, uncertain,
10   Something more of the depths—and then I lost it.
        Water came to rebuke the too clear water.
        One drop fell from a fern, and lo, a ripple
        Shook whatever it was lay there at bottom,
        Blurred it, blotted it out. What was that whiteness?
15   Truth? A pebble of quartz? For once, then, something.

Questions for Review

1. How much of Frost's poetry have you read? Do you like his poetry? Why or why not?
2. How does this poem compare with others by Frost that you have read?
3. What questions does this poem raise for you? (For example, who are the "Others" Frost opens the poem with? Why is "Once" italicized in line 7)?
4. Is there a conflict at work in this poem? If so, what is it? How does Frost resolve it?
5. Mark the poem's key terms. Why did you select these terms as important?
6. What point or points do you think Frost is trying to make in this poem? What is Frost trying to say? What is the poem's theme?
7. What is your overall assessment of this poem? Did you like it? Why or why not?

The next two poems are by Sherman Alexie, a member of the Spokane/ Coeur d'Alene tribe. Alexie is the author of several volumes of poetry (including *The Business of Fancydancing* and *Old Shirts & New Skins*) and fiction (including *The Lone Ranger and Tonto Fistfight in Heaven* and *Reservation Blues*). In addition, Alexie's movie, *Smoke Signals*, was released during the summer of 1998. The two poems that follow are from Alexie's collection of poems and short stories, *The Summer of Black Widows*. After you've read them, decide how well each poem succeeds individually and then how effectively the two poems complement or provide a comment on each other.

SHERMAN ALEXIE

THAT PLACE WHERE GHOSTS OF SALMON JUMP

1   Coyote was alone and angry because he could not find love.
Coyote was alone and angry because he demanded a wife

from the Spokane, the Coeur d'Alene, the Palouse, all those tribes
camped on the edge of the Spokane River, and received only laughter.

5   So Coyote rose up with his powerful and senseless magic
and smashed a paw across the water, which broke the river bottom

in two, which created rain that lasted for forty days and nights,
which created Spokane Falls, that place where salmon traveled

more suddenly than Coyote imagined, that place where salmon swam
10   larger than any white man dreamed. Coyote, I know you broke

the river because of love, and pretended it was all done by your design.
Coyote, you're a liar and I don't trust you. I never have

but I do trust all the stories the grandmothers told me.
They said the Falls were built because of your unrequited love

15   and I can understand that rage, Coyote. We can all understand
but look at the Falls now and tell me what you see. Look

at the Falls now, if you can see beyond all of the concrete
the white man has built here. Look at all of this

and tell me that concrete ever equals love. Coyote,
20   these white men sometimes forget to love their own mothers

so how could they love this river which gave birth
to a thousand lifetimes of salmon? How could they love

these Falls, which have fallen farther, which sit dry
and quiet as a graveyard now? These Falls are that place

25   where ghosts of salmon jump, where ghosts of women mourn
their children who will never find their way back home,

where I stand now and search for any kind of love,
where I sing softly, under my breath, alone and angry.

1. This poem has strong narrative elements in it. Identify those elements and comment on their effectiveness.
2. Identify two or three places where Alexie's use of language is particularly effective. What makes these passages effective?
3. What is the tone at the beginning of this poem? At what point does it change and to what effect?
4. The poem's narrator addresses "Coyote." Who is Coyote? Why does the narrator call him a liar? Why does the narrator not trust Coyote? How important is Coyote's role in the poem?
5. What is the theme of this poem? What comment does the poem seem to make about contemporary society? About the place of Native Americans in that society?
6. What is your overall assessment of the poem? Did you like it? Why or why not?

SHERMAN ALEXIE

THE POWWOW AT THE END OF THE WORLD

1   I am told by many of you that I must forgive and so I shall
           after an Indian woman puts her shoulder to the Grand Coulee Dam
           and topples it. I am told by many of you that I must forgive
           and so I shall after the floodwaters burst each successive dam
5   downriver from the Grand Coulee. I am told by many of you
           that I must forgive and so I shall after the floodwaters find
           their way to the mouth of the Columbia River as it enters the Pacific
           and causes all of it to rise. I am told by many of you that I must forgive
           and so I shall after the first drop of floodwater is swallowed by that salmon
10   waiting in the Pacific. I am told by many of you that I must forgive and so I shall
           after that salmon swims upstream, through the mouth of the Columbia
           and then past the flooded cities, broken dams and abandoned reactors
           of Hanford. I am told by many of you that I must forgive and so I shall
           after that salmon swims through the mouth of the Spokane River
15   as it meets the Columbia, then upstream, until it arrives
           in the shallows of a secret bay on the reservation where I wait alone.
           I am told by many of you that I must forgive and so I shall after
           that salmon leaps into the night air above the water, throws
           a lightning bolt at the brush near my feet, and starts the fire
20   which will lead all of the lost Indians home. I am told
           by many of you that I must forgive and so I shall
           after we Indians have gathered around the fire with that salmon
           who has three stories it must tell before sunrise: one story will teach us

25   how to pray; another story will make us laugh for hours;
the third story will give us reason to dance. I am told by many
of you that I must forgive and so I shall when I am dancing
with my tribe during the powwow at the end of the world.

 # Questions for Review

1. This poem has strong narrative elements in it. Identify those elements and comment on their effectiveness.
2. Identify two or three places where Alexie's use of language is particularly effective. What makes these passages effective?
3. What is the theme of this poem? What do you think Alexie is saying in it? How does this theme compare with that of "That Place Where Ghosts of Salmon Jump"?
4. What is the tone of the poem? How effectively does the tone support Alexie's theme? How does the tone of this poem compare with that of "That Place Where Ghosts of Salmon Jump"?
5. Images of water, food, and life clearly conflict with the dams Alexie mentions in this poem. How might "The Powwow at the End of the World" work with Julie Titone's essay "Balance of Power" (see pp. 415–418) to form a comprehensive comment about dams and salmon fisheries in the Northwest?
6. What is your overall assessment of "The Powwow at the End of the World"? Did you like it? Why or why not?

SAMPLE STUDENT ESSAYS

The first student essay is *about* Joyce Carol Oates's story, "Shopping," which you read at the beginning of this chapter. As you read "The Shopping Ritual" by Kelly McGinley, a first-year writing student at New Mexico State University (NMSU), look for places where you agree or disagree with her reading of Oates's story.

KELLY MCGINLEY

THE SHOPPING RITUAL

1   "Shopping" by Joyce Carol Oates is a melancholy narrative that deals with a strained relationship between a daughter and her mother who spend the afternoon together shopping despite their differences. Nola, the daughter, reveals her spoiled nature through picky fashion purchases and a refusal to compromise. Only seventeen years old, but with a purse full of charge cards and spending accounts, she is nevertheless

unhappy, spending much of her time complaining to her mother about not being able to go abroad for a semester. All of Nola's actions are seen from the point of view of Mrs. Dietrich, the mother, who regrets how their relationship has turned out but does not know how to correct the situation. Mrs. Dietrich has feelings of guilt for having sent Nola away, unwillingly and unhappily, to boarding school, and Nola's barely suppressed hostility towards her mother makes genuine communication between the two difficult.

2   "An old ritual, Saturday morning shopping" (Oates, 50). Oates begins the story with this statement to focus you on the shopping Nola and Mrs. Dietrich do as ritual. It is familiar and comfortable because they have done it the same way since Nola was "twelve or thirteen years old and capable of serious, sustained shopping with her mother" (52). Now, the shopping ritual that they participate in can be seen as an attempt by both of them to bridge the gap that has developed between them. Mrs. Dietrich alleviates some of her feelings of guilt by overindulging Nola: buying her anything she wants and allowing her to be disrespectful.

3   Their journey to the mall is set in a barren landscape, "[. . .] a bleak March morning following a night of freezing rain [with] a metallic cast to the sky and no sun anywhere in the sky [. . .]" (50). This description in particular foreshadows the events of the day and simultaneously illustrates the nature of the Dietrich women's relationship. When they first set out to the mall, few words are exchanged between them even though it is their last day together before Nola returns to school. The few words that are spoken are abrupt and lack sincerity. Soon they both retreat into their own thoughts. Mrs. Dietrich reminisces about when the mall first opened. Her thoughts are of Christmas and of hope for some form of reconciliation: "She hoped so badly to be happy she'd felt actual pain, a constriction in her throat like crying" (52). It seems both strange and sad to her that happiness should be so hard to attain, and that she and her daughter found it necessary to venture out to the artificial setting of the mall in order to spend time together.

4   The reader does not know what Nola is actually thinking, only what Mrs. Dietrich believes her to be thinking, and it is through the mother's observations of her daughter that the reader comes to see Mrs. Dietrich's flaws. She is bothered by Nola's spoiled ways and wonders how and why Nola lives her life the way she does, yet she offers little to no guidance. Oates says the Dietriches "sent her off aged fourteen to the Portland Academy up in Maine and without their help she matured into a girl of considerable beauty" (53). The act of sending her child to boarding school is itself a distancing mechanism that leaves most of the job of raising Nola to what appears to be a cold and indifferent system of education.

5   All of this raises the question that if Mrs. Dietrich is barely present in Nola's life anymore, how can she claim to know her daughter's feelings? How can she know if she is happy, or sad, or even indifferent? The reality of the situation is that Mrs. Dietrich has seen to it that her daughter is making the transition into womanhood without the benefit of an intimate parent-child relationship.

6   By the end of the story, Mrs. Dietrich's understanding of her daughter becomes seriously questionable, because she seems to misunderstand Nola's reaction to a disheveled (possibly homeless) woman who is sitting in the mall. In conversation with her mother, Nola speaks of the woman compassionately:

"My God, that poor woman," Nola says. "I didn't think there were people like her here—I mean, I didn't think they would allow it."

"She doesn't seem to cause any disturbance," Mrs. Dietrich says. "She just sits—Don't stare, Nola, she'll see you."

"You've seen her here before? Here?"

"A few times this winter."

"Is she always like that?"

"I'm sure she's harmless, Nola. She just *sits*."

Nola is incensed, her pale blue eyes like washed glass. "I'm sure *she's* harmless, Mother. It's the harm the poor woman has to endure that is the tragedy." (52)

7   Perhaps Nola subconsciously identifies with the woman, who is being picked on and made unhappy even in the flat, impersonal environment of the mall—a place that Nola very likely sees as a refuge from her own sad existence. It is ironic that Mrs. Dietrich, who is so critical of her daughter's trivial nature, is not moved by the passion of her words. Instead, they offend Mrs. Dietrich because they remind her of her own pettiness. One would think a mother would be proud to hear her daughter express concern for the less fortunate, but in Mrs. Dietrich's case, she seems unable to comprehend this reaching out to someone from a lower class. It isn't long, though, before both women forget the plight of the homeless woman to reenter their own tortured and self-centered world until the story's end as they make their way to the parking lot, Mrs. Dietrich trying to shield her daughter, and Nola crying out of what we can only presume to be frustration.

8   Nola's crying at the end of the story reveals that she seems to be more knowledgeable about the futility of their situation than Mrs. Dietrich. At one point Nola exclaims, "How exhausting it is" (73). She of course is referring to their strained relationship. Mrs. Dietrich doesn't seem to grasp it, though. She only replies, "But we're hardly ever together, Nola" (73). She misses the point completely that it is this lack of contact that has caused the strain in the first place.

9   The strain has reached a point where it causes Dietrich to admit that she hates her daughter:

She is thinking, Who are *you*? What have I to do with *you*? I don't know *you*, I don't love *you*, why should I? (73)

Whether the hatred has always been a part of their relationship or whether it has developed over the years is unknown, but we know by the end of the story that there seems little hope of the two ever establishing a loving relationship. It is through shopping and only shopping that they will ever be able to connect.

WORK CITED

Oates, Joyce Carol. "Shopping." *Ms.* Mar. 1986: 50+.

Questions for Review

1. How does Kelly's reading of "Shopping" square with your own? On what points do you agree with her? Disagree? Why?
2. How does Kelly's essay compare or contrast with that by Kristina Geray at the end of this chapter?
3. Identify Kelly's thesis statement. How effectively does she support it?

4. How much of Kelly's discussion of the story is given to plot summary? Is it enough; that is, do you feel that you have a fair sense of the story? Why or why not?

5. According to Kelly, what is this story's theme? How effectively does she support her interpretation of the story?

6. How effective is the essay's introduction? Conclusion? Why?

7. How well does Kelly use passages from the story to support her points?

8. Write Kelly a note assessing her essay. What are its strengths? What parts might need revision? Why?

Jessica Edwards, a first-year writing student at NMSU, wrote the second of our student essays, about Kate Chopin's "The Story of an Hour."

JESSICA LYNN EDWARDS

THE PRICE OF FREEDOM

1   "I don't get it," I told my sister who had just read the ending of the story aloud to me. She laughed, having already assumed my reaction. "Her husband was still alive," she explained. "Well, then why did she still die?" I asked, becoming even more confused. "You must not have been paying attention to the story, then," my sister replied. Realizing that I should have listened better instead of flipping through an art book while she was reading, I silently agreed with her.

2   Until then I had never read anything by Kate Chopin. I had only heard of her from my sister, an English major. To me, Chopin's writing seemed like it would be boring. Perhaps it was because of her plain name. "Chopin" was exotic enough, but it just didn't fit with "Kate." And, as my sister sat down to read the story I had already decided that I did not like it. I tried to act interested and involved, but actually I wished that the story would be short so it would end soon. When she began to read her voice was not hers; she had changed it to fit the story, and it was driving me crazy! I almost got claustrophobic just listening to her speak; her voice made me nervous and antsy. I wanted to get up and leave, but that would have only hurt her feelings. So, I endured her annoying voice and seemingly pointless story, trying not to let it get to me.

3   I wondered why my sister liked this stuff. She was only twenty-one; could she already be so into this boring literature? Why does she have to be so dramatic, I wondered, as I heard her voice drop. I turned my head to roll my eyes. The situation seemed so silly to me that I almost laughed—my sister sitting in a chair in the middle of the room, her boyfriend and I quietly listening on the couch, both of us trying to seem enthralled by the story. I knew that this was not the first time he had been forced to listen to this story. How could he stand it?

4   Her voice startled me, so I looked up. "When the doctors came," she read, "they said she died of heart disease—of joy that kills." When she looked up to see my reaction, I could not believe that the story was over! That could not have been the last line! The woman died? I knew then that I was going to have to read the story on my own.

5   Alone in my room I reread "The Story of an Hour." I read it through fast at first, trying to understand its plot. Then I read it through again, more slowly this time, trying to catch all the little things that I had missed before. Each time I read it I understood a little more my sister's reasons for liking this thought-provoking story about a woman who, while grieving over her husband who supposedly has just died in a train wreck, realizes the control that he had had over her life. And she begins to see how her life would be if she lived it purely for herself and for no one else. She is filled with joy at the thought of a life driven only by self-satisfaction. But in all her joy she does not realize that her husband has walked in through the front door. Upon seeing him all her dreams are crushed, and she dies on the spot.

6   My sister appreciated the story not only because of Chopin's captivating writing style, which seizes the reader's attention and does not let go, but also because of the story itself. It is a story not just about one woman, but about all women. In it, Chopin says that the oppression that marriage sometimes brings to women is wrong and that a woman's freedom is just as important to her as a man's is to him.

7   Looking deeper into "The Story of an Hour," one can see that it is not just a story about a woman grieving over her dead husband. Instead, it is a story about a woman freed by the death of her husband. Chopin tells us that, alone in her room after hearing the news, the woman, Mrs. Mallard, reacted with joy: " 'Free! Body and soul free!' she kept whispering" (Chopin, 360). Mr. Mallard's death brought her a new will to live, to live her own life: "Her fancy was running riot along those days ahead of her. Spring days, and summer days, and all sorts of days that would be her own" (360). She would no longer have her husband's "powerful will bending her" (360). Rather, she could live each day as she, and no one else, dictated. She could now see the inhumanity in marriages in which "men and women believe they have a right to impose a private will upon a fellow-creature. A kind intention or a cruel intention made the act seem no less a crime as she looked upon it in that brief moment of illumination" (360).

8   Mrs. Mallard "had loved him—sometimes. Often she had not" (360). She knew, however, that she would mourn for him. But it did not matter, for "what could love, the unsolved mystery, count for in face of this possession of self-assertion which she suddenly recognized as the strongest impulse of her being!" (360). How could one not see that imposing oneself upon another, no matter how kind an intention, was wrong? She realized that her personal freedom was priceless.

9   Mrs. Mallard is described as a woman "afflicted with a heart trouble," so "great care was taken to break to her as gently as possible the news of her husband's death" (360). In her response, she had exceeded all friends' and family's expectations in accepting her husband's death. She had embraced it, welcoming the prospects of the solitary life before her. Joy instead of dread filled her when looking at the future. She was happy, and in all her joy Mrs. Mallard did not notice the man who entered through the front door. It was Mr. Mallard who "had been far from the scene of accident, and did not even know there had been one" (360). She did not realize that her husband had not died in that fatal train wreck, as everyone had thought, but had been far from it.

10   Just as family and friends had attempted to shield her from the news of Mr. Mallard's death, they now attempted to shield Mrs. Mallard from being surprised by her husband. They failed. Seeing him smothered all her hopes for the future. She knew then that all of the things she had just seconds before anticipated so joyfully were no longer attainable; she knew that there was nothing left to live for. So she collapsed and died. "When the doctors came they said she had died of heart disease—of joy that kills" (360).

11   How ironic this last statement is. It is true that she died of heart disease, but more from a broken heart at having lost her freedom once again. The doctors, probably men,

decided she died because her heart could not stand the strain of the joy of seeing her husband alive. Instead, she died sorrowfully, and death became her way out of the stifling relationship of her marriage. "The Story of an Hour" could be titled "The Story of a Lifetime," because during the hour when she contemplated life after her husband's death, Mrs. Mallard truly lived.

WORK CITED

Chopin, Kate. "The Dream of an Hour." *Vogue* 6 Dec. 1894: 360.

Questions for Review

1. Identify Jessica's thesis statement. How effectively does she support it?
2. How much of Jessica's discussion of the story is given to plot summary? Is it enough; that is, do you feel that you have a fair sense of the story? Why or why not?
3. According to Jessica, what is this story's theme? How effectively does she support her interpretation of the story?
4. How effective is the essay's introduction? Conclusion? Why?
5. How well does Jessica use passages from the story to support her points?
6. Write Jessica a note assessing her essay. What are its strengths? What parts might need revision? Why?

The third student essay is an example of writing *from* literature. In it, Kacey Atwood, a first-year writing student at NMSU, relates Robert Frost's "The Road Not Taken" to aspects of her high school days.

KACEY ATWOOD

ONE ROAD TAKEN

1   In 1916, Robert Frost published one of his most famous poems, "The Road Not Taken," in a collection of poetry, *Mountain Interval*:

Two roads diverged in a yellow wood,
And sorry I could not travel both
And be one traveler, long I stood
And looked down one as far as I could
To where it bent in the undergrowth;

Then took the other, as just as fair,
and having perhaps the better claim,
Because it was grassy and wanted wear;
Though as for that the passing there
Had worn them really about the same,

And both that morning equally lay
In leaves no step had trodden back.
Oh, I kept the first for another day!
Yet knowing how way leads on to way,
I doubted if I should ever come back.

I shall be telling this with a sigh
Somewhere ages and ages hence:
Two roads diverged in a wood, and I—
I took the one less traveled by,
And that has made all the difference.

This poem is about making choices and, if we take Frost literally, it talks in particular about a decision Frost made as a younger man. What was the specific nature of the decision? We don't know. What we do know is that Frost decided to take the path "less traveled by," so he chose to follow the path that most others chose not to.

2   There are countless moments in life when we must choose which road to travel, the interstate or the country road. One particular period in my life that will affect me for the rest of my days consisted of the four years that involve the most peer pressure I will probably ever encounter: high school. It starts out as a competition as to which group you will fit into. Everyone tries to impress everyone else. You watch your best friends fail in your expectations as they change right before your eyes. At the same time, you yourself change a little more each day.

3   Once I got into the groove of high school, I found myself involved in various clubs, organizations and athletics. As far as role models and pressures go, the most important for me were athletics, National Honor Society, Student Council and Fellowship of Christian Athletes. As a member of these organizations, I was seen as an outstanding student-athlete by my teachers. I could feel the pressures on every aspect of my life. I had to perform well in my athletic outings, I had to keep my grades up, and I had to keep my nose clean and stay out of trouble. If it were ever discovered that I attended a kegger or any other kind of unchaperoned party, I would have been disgraced, because all of the organizations I belonged to strongly disapproved of this type of activity. I had to set the "right" example, not become "the" example.

4   I grew up in a very small town: Reserve, New Mexico. With a population of less than 500, the whole town knew what you were going to do before you did it. And it didn't help that my family was somewhat respected in the community. My mother was my basketball coach; one of my grandfathers was the municipal judge, and the other was a retired superintendent everyone respected very much. In addition, I had a few relatives in law enforcement. As you can imagine, if I had been caught with the party crowd, plenty of people were ready to jump down my throat.

5   I also had a lot of friends, and partying was prominent. At times it was extremely hard for me to take the road "less traveled by." There were instances when the pressure from my friends to party was almost overwhelming. But I had seen firsthand what the result would be if I gave in to it. My sister hung out with the party crowd while she

was in high school, and I can recall countless times when she and my father engaged in heated, angry arguments about who her friends were and what she was doing with her life. Since we had family involved with law enforcement, they were constantly watching my sister and me. If we did anything wrong, they let our parents know before we had a chance to confess. I was labeled a "good kid," so I was expected to go down the road that "was grassy and wanted wear."

6   One specific instance stands out in my mind in which the peer pressure almost got the best of me. Over Christmas break of my senior year, which was also the middle of basketball season, we didn't have school, just practice, so everyone was looking for something to do in their spare time. One night, my cousin's parents went out of town to do some last-minute shopping. Within about an hour, the whole town knew her parents were gone. And, of course, the first thing on everyone's mind was: PARTY! I had nothing to do either, so I decided to go to her house and see what was going on. I figured that it didn't matter if I went to her house—she wouldn't tell on me, because she would get in just as much trouble as I would, if not more.

7   When I arrived, quite a few people were already there, along with an ample amount of alcohol. Everyone I walked by had a drink in their hand, and they looked as if they were having so much fun. One of my friends handed me a beer. "I don't want this," I said and tried to hand the bottle back to him. "Aw, come on, Kacey," he whined. "Don't be a wuss. Nobody's gonna rat you out." For a moment I faltered. I raised the bottle toward my mouth, and then it hit me. "What am I doing?" I thought to myself. Everything I feared losing flashed through my head—basketball, college scholarships, my freedom, my reputation, my self-respect—and I realized I had the rest of my life to drink. I couldn't put myself at risk of losing the things that I had worked so hard for, especially since I was a senior and had only half a year of high school to go. Besides, I was having enough fun laughing at how stupid everyone else was acting.

8   I didn't consume any alcohol while I was in high school. There were many instances that influenced my decision. I had seen too many of those close to me lose out because they got caught breaking the rule of NO ALCOHOL. Athletics were extremely important to my friends and me. There were a few times that someone got caught drinking and ended up suspended or even kicked off the team. I saw how it devastated the whole team as well as the individuals who had been caught and disciplined. NHS had a large effect also. Keeping my grades up and not doing anything to embarrass the organization helped me to get college scholarships. If I had been kicked out of NHS because I'd given in to these peer pressures, I would not be at NMSU right now. I knew there was no way my parents could afford to pay for me to attend college, so I had to keep my work up.

9   As you can see, I had many pressures and influences that helped me make up my mind. Even though the decision was tough at the time, I am thankful that I chose to travel down the country road. Like Frost,

> I shall be telling this with a sigh
> Somewhere ages and ages hence:
> Two roads diverged in a wood, and I—
> I took the one less traveled by,
> And that has made all the difference.

WORK CITED

Frost, Robert. "The Road Not Taken." *Mountain Interval.* New York: Holt, 1916. 3.

Questions for Review

1. How does Kacey's essay differ from those by Jessica Edwards and Kelly McGinley?
2. How has Kacey shown you that she has understood Frost's poem?
3. Kacey incorporates phrases from Frost's poem. How effectively has she done so?
4. Identify any use Kacey makes of language that you find effective. What makes it effective?
5. Write a note to Kacey assessing her essay. What are its strengths? What parts might need revision? Why?

THE RHETORICAL TRIANGLE

SUBJECT

The most prominent point of the rhetorical triangle in an interpretive essay is the subject—the piece of literature about which the essay is written—thus, the primary focus is on the literary text and what it means. Your written response begins with your understanding of that piece of literature, an understanding you may develop from reading the text closely and then working with it to see what it means to you. To illustrate some of the ways in which you can read, examine, and then respond to a literary text, we'll work with the poem by Robert Frost presented earlier, "For Once, Then, Something," first published in 1923. Try this procedure (which should remind you of several of the reading strategies in Chapter 4):

1. First, read the poem silently. Then, read it again, this time aloud, and listen for the language—that is, listen for natural points of emphasis.
2. Read the poem a third time, marking key terms (words or phrases) as you go. Also mark those passages that you emphasized while reading aloud. Jot a quick note about why these seem important or warrant emphasis.

At times, it's tempting to mark nearly every word in a poem as a key term, because poetry can be so compact and intense that nearly every image seems to figure as important. In looking at key terms in Frost's poem, Bill identified four sets of terms and then clustered other words and images that related to those terms to try to bring some kind of order to his investigation. In addition, Bill raised some questions about some terms and jotted comments on others. He also commented briefly on each set of terms and on the sets as a whole; these comments are underlined.

Conflict
   Others taunt (who are these others? why do they taunt Frost?)
   Taunting speaks of opposition, teasing.

Others' view of Frost as poet
>   *Always wrong to the light* (light = illumination = insight—but he's always wrong)
>   *shining surface picture* (superficial, no insight?)
>   *Me myself…godlike* (Narcissus imagery?)
>   Frost says taunters see him as superficial and, perhaps, narcissistic.

Nature imagery
>   *well-curbs* ⎤
>   *well*   ⎬ (water as life-giving, life-sustaining, place to look for insight?)
>   *water*   ⎦
>   Frost, known for his poetry dealing with nature, creates images of water and wells as suitable places to look for insight. These images say that nature is a place to look for insight.
>   *Water…rebuke the too clear water* (nature won't give up secrets easily?)
>   *Blurred … blotted*
>   But nature doesn't always cooperate; it's not easy to find whatever it is that Frost's detractors want him to find and write about.

Something seen
>   *a something white* (symbolic value of white?)
>   *uncertain* (why uncertain?)
>   *Something more of the depths* (literal or symbolic depths? both?)
>   *What was that…Truth? A pebble of quartz?*
>   *something*
>   Okay, this is what Frost says his detractors want him to see. But it's not always available—it's uncertain, and Frost doesn't really know what he glimpsed at the bottom of the well. But at least it was something.

Taken together, what these terms show is a conflict between Frost and his taunters—critics of his early poetry? They also suggest that seeing deeply into the well isn't always easy. And even when a poet does see something, he's not always sure of what he's seen. So it's a "maybe" kind of deal—maybe he'll see something insightful, maybe he won't. But at least he tries.

3. Divide the poem into a beginning, middle, and end. Think about why you made the divisions you made. What happens in each part?

beginning—lines 1–6. Frost talks about being criticized for being superficial or shallow.

middle—lines 7–14. Story of trying to catch a glimpse of that elusive "something more of the depths." Note that *"Once"* is the only word in the poem that's italicized.

end—lines 14–15. Frost draws (or at least implies) a conclusion based on his experience of trying to reveal deeper insights in his poetry.

4. Apply the Questions for Analysis (see Chapter 1, pp. 24–25).

a. What goes with what? (association)

associations with Frost as poet—
Frost (1874–1963), a beloved and popular American poet, many poems dealt with nature but many also explored psychological aspects of

people (see "An Old Man's Winter's Night" and "Tree at My Window," to name but two), read at JFK's inaugural in 1960.

associations with key terms—

In lines 1–6, the terms associated with Frost as poet suggest superficiality, Narcissism. There's an image that reminds me of Pan (the Roman god of the forest), which doesn't suggest seriousness at all. Frost reports that "Others" (critics?) say that he sees only himself and reports only that in his poetry.

In lines 7–14, Frost reports a time when he was "trying" to see deeper into a well-curb. The terms here suggest that it's really not possible, that nature just won't give up its secrets very readily.

In lines 14–15, Frost presents a conclusion of sorts that may figure as the poem's theme—Truth isn't knowable in any final sense, but whatever Frost saw was enough for him.

b. What opposes what? (opposition)

There is opposition at work in the poem—the "Others" Frost mentions in the poem's first line. Who are these others? Why do they taunt Frost? What have they said about his poetry? Why does Frost feel it necessary to respond to them? (*Note:* Answering these questions will take some research. Were you to research this, you'd find that Frost was criticized early in his career. For example, an anonymous review published in 1913 said that "many of his verses do not rise above the ordinary [. . .]" [Greiner 71]. Another anonymous review, published in the January 1915 issue of the *Bulletin of the Poetry Society of America,* said, "Mr. Frost has been greatly acclaimed by prophets of new poetic cults in England, but his work could hardly be said to have found sympathizers in the Poetry Society" [Greiner 85]. And in 1917, Amy Lowell closed a critical essay on Frost "with the questionable suggestion that his art, while surely brilliant, is painted on a canvas so 'exceedingly small' that he can never equal the achievement of a man with a wider vision" [Greiner 89]. For a thorough discussion of Frost's reception by such critics as these, see Donald J. Greiner's *Robert Frost: The Poet and His Critics* [Chicago: American Library Association, 1974].)

Because the opening clearly reveals conflict—taunting is hardly conciliatory—there is tension at work in the poem. How is it resolved?

c. What follows what? (sequence)

Although we've already divided the poem into three parts—beginning, middle, and end—we can talk a bit more about its structure by looking at sequence. First, we can examine where the poem divides, where its breaks are, by considering how various lines relate to one another. How do lines 1–6 work to form a unit, lines 7–14 another, and lines 14–15 yet another?

Second, we can examine how individual images follow one another, so that the separate images join to form larger or more comprehensive images. For example, we identified these key terms in lines 1–6 that are associated with Frost as a poet, images he attributes to the "Others" mentioned in line 1: always wrong to the light, shining surface picture, me myself, godlike, [framed by a] wreath of fern and cloud puffs. Individually, each image suggests a bit of the nature of criticism of Frost by the "Others," but as a whole they paint a complete picture of a poet who is so self-centered as to be Narcissistic. Further, the Pan image (which derives from "god-like" and the framing wreath) suggests that Frost is not a serious nature poet but one who sees only himself and celebrates only his own assumed divinity.

    d. What follows from what? (consequence)

What results from the taunting, from the conflict and tension Frost reports? Obviously, the poem. Frost wants to respond to his critics, not only to defend himself as a poet but also to present his view about the nature of truth. Ultimately, Frost says that truth is elusive at best, that it's difficult to know truth, even more difficult to present it in a poem. Such a view would probably run counter to Frost's critics in the Poetry Society of America.

5. Write (a) a sentence (or two) summarizing or paraphrasing the poem, (b) a sentence (or two) speculating about Frost's purpose in writing the poem, and (c) a sentence (or two) saying whether you think he achieved his purpose. Identify specific elements from the poem to support the sentences you wrote for (b) and (c).

    a. "For Once, Then, Something" details Frost's conflict with his critics and reveals his idea that you can't fix truth with a capital "T."

    b. Frost's purpose seems to have been (1) to tell his critics (the "Others" who "taunt" him about their perception of shallowness in his poetry) that they're wrong and (2) to present his own view about discovering and then presenting insights or truth in his poetry.

    c. Yes, he succeeds. In the first section of the poem, he presents the nature of the criticism of his poetry (he's shallow and Narcissistic); in the second, he shows how difficult it is to discern truth (or insights) from nature (water imagery); in the third, he gives his own vision of what's discernible (it's uncertain, but whatever he saw was enough for the moment). On one level, this poem shows Frost taunting his critics. On another, it suggests that Frost felt that poetry either couldn't or shouldn't fix truth in ways that his critics called for.

    At times, there's an indeterminancy at work in poetry, something that leaves the reader great leeway to read a poem in a highly personal way. This is actually one of the strengths of poetry and speaks to the fact that people read literature from an individual perspective and take from that literature what it says to them. As we'll point out below, serious literature is open to interpretation, and because we read as individuals, each reader is privileged to develop her own interpretation of a piece of literature.

Apply this reading procedure to Alexie's and Cervantes's poetry and to at least one of the three short stories presented at the beginning of this chapter. How did your applications enhance your reading and understanding of the poetry? The story?

ELEMENTS OF LITERATURE

Interpreting a piece of literature, whether novel, short story, play, or poem, often requires you to consider particular aspects or elements of the text. What follows is a brief look at some of the major elements of literature, with questions you may answer as you consider each element. Throughout this discussion, we refer to stories, but keep in mind that much of what we say will apply not only to fiction but also to drama and poetry, especially narrative poetry.

PLOT   The sequence of events in a piece of literature, sometimes known as the *story line,* is the *plot.* To examine the plot, we have to look at what happens, and we can do so by considering these questions: "What follows what?" (sequence) and "What follows from what?" (consequence). Events in a story follow other events, sometimes because they come later in time (a matter of sequence), but at other times because one event causes another to occur (a matter of consequence, or cause and effect). Looking at the questions "What follows what?" and "What follows from what?" provides a starting point for considering the quality of the action of a literary text. For Frost's poem, answering these questions gives us this summary and initial interpretation:

> Critics (the "Others" mentioned in line 1) taunt Frost for not finding deeper insights into life than he seems to find in his poetry. This taunting causes Frost to try to see deeper into nature (the "well-curb," lines 1, 7) so as to find deeper insights. And, sure enough, he seems to catch sight of something just by trying to glimpse it. But a brief glimpse is all he gets, for nature won't give up its secrets readily and, taking on human attributes, uses a drop of water from a fern to keep Frost from finding that ultimate insight his critics want him to find (line 12). This teaches Frost that, as far as he's concerned, we can't realize the kinds of insights his critics call for. He tells us this by trying to name the thing he saw: "What was that whiteness? / Truth? A pebble of quartz?" (lines 14–15). He doesn't really know whether he saw a piece of rock or some kind of insight. He knows only that he looked for it and that it was "For once, then, something" (line 15). This realization causes Frost to write the poem, so that he offers an answer to his critics.

Another way of considering the plot, or story line, is to trace (and perhaps even chart or map) its development as we proceed through the story. Consider how the story opens (begins), how that opening leads to and through the action of the story (its middle), and how the conclusion (end) of the story derives from that action. And consider all of this with an eye toward the eventfulness or significance or quality of the story's parts (i.e., its beginning, middle, and end) and its various events. That is, as you trace the story's sequence of events, you should note the quality of the events, not only what happens but also why it happens and then what it causes.

To begin considering plot, ask questions like these: What happens? How does the story begin? What happens in the story's middle? How does the story end? How does the beginning lead to the middle and the middle to the end? Which events are important or significant? Why?

CONFLICT   Plot proceeds on the conflict between characters and its resolution. Think about how the action in a situation comedy proceeds. There's an opening situation (a beginning) that at least suggests the sequence of events to follow. Then, as the action unfolds (as it moves through the sitcom's middle), it builds conflict. Most often, two characters (or groups of characters) are at odds with or oppose each other, and their conflict comes to a head right before a commercial, so as to keep viewer interest. After the commercial, that conflict is either resolved or complicated further. This pattern of conflict followed by resolution or further complication continues until the end of the program, when some sort of final resolution is reached. This final resolution is often called the *climax,* the most important moment of the program. In serious literature, the climax often strongly suggests the theme of the piece of literature.

Questions to help you consider conflict include these: What is the conflict? What tension is there at work in the story? What is the quality of that tension? How does it get resolved? Who resolves it? Are you satisfied with the resolution? Is the resolution consistent with the story itself?

Exercise 8.3

Describe or summarize the plot of any of the short stories or poems you've read in this text. Then describe any conflict you may find in the piece of literature you're working with. How does the conflict drive or advance the plot?

CHARACTER   We may define a story's characters in several ways:

Major. Major characters are the primary characters in the story.

Minor. Minor characters are characters on the story's periphery who work to further the plot, oftentimes by serving as foils for the major characters. A *foil* is a character whose interaction with a major character serves primarily to develop or reflect some important trait of the major character.

Protagonist. The protagonist is the main character in a story, the one about whom the story revolves. At times, the protagonist is called the *hero* of the story, but that doesn't mean she always acts heroically (in the idealistic sense of that term). Sometimes, we may not like a protagonist, but like her or not, she still serves as the story's main character.

Antagonist. An antagonist is a character in conflict with the protagonist. At times, this antagonist is a foil, but at other times, an antagonist is a major character who greatly influences the actions of the protagonist and so the outcome of the story.

Questions for thinking about characters include these: Who is the major or primary character? Is there more than one? How would you describe each character physically? Ethically? Emotionally? What kind of turmoil is a character in? What causes it? Is the character's reaction believable? Do you like a given character? Why or why not? What action is each character involved in throughout the story? What is the quality of this action? How do the characters interact with one another? What is the result of this interaction?

Exercise 8.4

For at least one of the short stories in this chapter, make a list of characters. Which are major? Minor? Who is the protagonist? The antagonist? How do the protagonist and the antagonist work against each other? To what effect?

SETTING   Setting is the background in which the story takes place. Think about the set for a movie or television show. Much of *Friends,* a situation comedy, is set in the apartments of this show's six major characters. But the setting expands to include various places of work (e.g., the coffeehouse in which one of them worked and where the six friends often meet) and places in New York City. It also extends beyond these physical scenes to embrace the United States in the 1990s and the social scene of young, urban professionals in this era. So the setting of a story involves not only its physical scene but also its social or political climate.

Consider such questions as these in looking at setting: Where is the story set—time (e.g., season of the year, time of day, particular year, decade, century), place (e.g., specific town or country)? What influences the setting (e.g., weather, terrain, construction, political or social climate)? How does the setting influence or support the characters' actions? How does the setting comment on the characters' actions? What is the meaning of the setting?

Exercise 8.5

In "Shopping," how does the wealth implicit in the mall as the physical setting work with the bag lady, the reactions of other shoppers to her, and Nola's reactions to her? What does the mall represent or symbolize? How does this aspect of "Shopping" reflect U.S. culture?

POINT OF VIEW   What vantage point does the writer take in the story? Through whose eyes do we see the action? Here's a list of possible points of view:

Objective. The narrator (the story's teller) simply describes the action without going into any character's mind; also called *camera eye.*

First person. The narrator of the story is also a character in the story and uses "I" as the focal point. The narrator can tell the reader only what he sees and thinks. ("In the Land of Men" is told from this perspective.)

Third person limited omniscience. The narrator of the story tells the tale from the perspective of one character in the story and may enter into the thoughts of only that character. It's as though the narrator sits on the shoulder of that character, telling the reader what that character sees and thinks. ("Shopping" is told from this perspective.)

Third person omniscience. The narrator of the story is free to roam. The narrator may report the thinking of any character and may tell what each character sees. ("El Tonto del Barrio" is told from this perspective.)

One thing to keep in mind when considering point of view is the reliability of the narrator. A first-person narrator may not be the most reliable of story-tellers, because her perspective is necessarily skewed. Consider the first-person narrator of "In the Land of Men," a 23-year-old woman who is a rape victim. In this story, her brothers have captured the man whom they think is her rapist, and they offer her the opportunity to decide his fate. Although her narration suggests that she has come to terms with being a rape victim, the last statement she makes could suggest otherwise. Just how reliable a narrator is she? Can we as readers take everything she tells us at face value? Why or why not? Answering such questions as these provides a starting point in considering a story's point of view.

SYMBOLS   A *symbol* is a word or image that represents something more than its literal meaning. Writers use symbols to direct the reader's attention toward the meaning they intended. The reader's job is to identify and examine symbols, considering the attitudes implicit in each and how they support or develop the story's theme. Like a rock thrown into a pool of water, symbols create a ripple effect, and their importance spreads beyond their immediate, literal meaning as the reader connects a particular symbol to his experience. Symbols resonate or reverberate within the reader.

In "That Place Where Ghosts of Salmon Jump," Sherman Alexie presents Coyote (note the capital C) as a major character. But Coyote also has symbolic value, assuming mythic proportions. Alexie alludes to what may be a flood myth taken from his tribe's lore. Given Alexie's statement that the rain Coyote created "lasted for forty days and nights," there are clear, immediate connections to the biblical story of Noah and the ark. Later, Alexie tells Coyote, "you're a liar and I don't trust you." In the lore of many tribes, Coyote is a trickster, a shifty, untrustworthy figure. For anyone familiar with such lore, Coyote brings these associations to mind. The coyote is also a popular motif for jewelry and house decorations in the Southwest. Usually, it's a stylized coyote, benign, almost cute, as it sits back on its haunches, head thrown back, yipping and howling at the moon. Yet another dimension to the coyote is the actual four-legged animal *(Canis latrans),* a cousin of the wolf. A fair number of ranchers in the West consider the coyote a pest to be eradicated, because coyotes are reputed to kill lambs and calves, not to mention pet cats and dogs. Alexie evokes all of these aspects just by writing "Coyote." Do you have to understand or be familiar with all of them to understand or interpret or enjoy the poem? No. But as a reader, you must be alert to what such symbols may embody.

1. What symbols (including colors, objects, and gestures) might represent these concepts?

innocence	purity	anger	evil
life	growth	death	solidarity

2. What might these terms symbolize?

eagle	skyscraper	hawk	open arms
dove	snake	river	apple
ocean	baseball	rain	water
house	mountain	hearth	

TRADITIONAL THEMES AND PATTERNS   Many pieces of literature rely on themes and structural patterns that have been employed throughout the history of literature. The quest motif, for example, is important: A character goes in search of self, so that gaining self-knowledge figures as the story's theme. Another major motif, initiation, involves a character's moving from one stage of life to another. And how many stories have been written about the conflict between men and women, between parent and child, between one group or culture and another? Look also for conflict generated by reality versus illusion, nature versus technology, justice versus injustice, or the individual versus society, to name but a few possibilities.

How does a story or poem develop any of these themes and structural patterns? How, for example, does the conflict between mother and daughter play out in "Shopping"? Is this a generational conflict, or is it some other kind of conflict? What conflict is at work in "El Tonto del Barrio"? Generational? Cultural? In either of Alexie's poems, what is the conflict? What is its source?

WRITER

To write *about* literature, you need to be actively engaged with the text. This means that you should approach a literary text with an inquisitive mind-set; you should treat the text as a puzzle that will speak to you if you'll only take the time to play with it, to tease it into giving up its secrets. To engage actively means to read aggressively. You can use the various reading strategies we discussed in Chapter 4. In particular, though, you should ask questions about the text that you want your reading to answer and preview the various parts of the work, especially if it's a longer piece of literature. Asking questions and previewing the text before you read can help give you a focus, so that the time you spend actually reading will be more productive than it might otherwise be.

What questions might you ask about "For Once, Then, Something"? What is the tone of the title? Does it suggest exasperation? What is the "something" the title names? How is it important to this poem? To preview this poem, you may begin by asking how long it is and why Frost italicizes "Once" at the beginning of line 7.

Exercise 8.7

Write several questions raised by the titles of Sherman Alexie's poems, questions you would want your reading of the poems to help you answer.

A final note about your role as the writer of an interpretive essay—many times, students tend to adopt the pose of expert critic because that's the model they have seen for literary criticism. However, in this essay, your voice as writer should be that of an interested explorer, someone engaged with puzzling out meaning from a text, but not a seasoned, experienced literary critic writing *the* definitive critical analysis of that text. One of your goals as a reader of literature should be to enjoy the experience of reading, hence the explorative nature of your work with the text.

READER

You should assume that your reader will be interested in what you have to say, will be receptive to your thinking, and won't offer resistance to your ideas. Your job, then, is to prove your point, to support the assertion you make about the text. Although an interpretive essay will have an argumentative edge to it—you will, after all, make a case for the validity of your thesis—it will not be a position or persuasion essay (as we define them in Chapters 9 and 10), because you may assume that your reader isn't predisposed to be hostile or resistant to your interpretation.

Nonetheless, you need to consider your reader carefully as you write and revise. For one thing, your understanding of who your reader is will determine how much background information you need to present. If you're writing about "For Once, Then, Something," the amount of attention you give to specific statements critical of Frost will depend on how knowledgeable your reader is about Frost and his reception as a poet. Likewise, if you assume your reader is well-read, you may not need to explain the Pan image implicit in lines 5–6, for simply mentioning Pan will be enough to evoke this image in your reader's mind. Although your primary focus in an interpretive essay will be the literary text (the subject corner of the rhetorical triangle), you'll still need to take your reader into account.

DISTINGUISHING FEATURES OF INTERPRETIVE ESSAYS
INTERPRETATION

Interpreting involves offering your supported opinion of the meaning of a story—so you're actually writing an argument. You'll need to make an assertion about the story's meaning in a thesis sentence and then support it with detail from the story itself so that you convince your reader that your interpretation is plausible. What we're after here is not the one and only valid interpretation, because that really doesn't exist. Different people may read the same text and derive differing understandings of it. Your job, then, is to use information from the story to support your thinking about the story, so that you give your reader insight into your thinking—what you think and why you think that way.

THEME

What the writer is trying to say is the story's theme, and part of your job in interpreting a piece of literature is to make an assertion about the story's theme. What is the story really about? What insight into life or people or human actions does the writer seem to want you to gain?

THESIS AND SUPPORT

As we have noted several times, an interpretive essay makes an argument. You'll write a thesis sentence that makes an assertion about your understanding of the text, and then you'll offer support from the text for that assertion. Look again at Jessica Edwards's essay about "The Story of an Hour." Jessica presents a thesis that makes an assertion about the story's meaning, or theme, and then supports it with details from the story. Here's a brief overview of the parts of Jessica's essay:

¶s 1–6: beginning (the introduction). ¶s 1–4 are a personal narrative detailing Jessica's introduction to Chopin's story. ¶5 provides a very brief plot summary; it tells very quickly what happens in the story. The thesis sentence comes at the end of ¶6—"In it, Chopin shows that the oppression that marriage sometimes brings to women is wrong and that a woman's freedom is just as important to her as a man's is to him."

¶s 7–10: middle (the body). ¶7 talks about Mrs. Mallard's freedom and the joy that this thought brings her. ¶8 talks about love (an assumed cornerstone of any marriage) and what it could not counter for Mrs. Mallard (love was not as important as her freedom). In ¶9, Jessica tells a bit more about the plot, preparing the reader of her essay for Mrs. Mallard's death and her (Jessica's) interpretation of that death's meaning. ¶10 continues this summary, and Jessica recounts the story's climax for her readers.

¶11: end (the conclusion). Jessica returns to interpretation by focusing on the irony of Mrs. Mallard's death and of the doctors' diagnosis of the cause of death.

BEYOND SUMMARY

Although interpreting a story may involve writing a summary of part or all of the story, interpreting is not summarizing. A plot summary is a simple retelling of what happens in a story. An interpretive essay has to move well beyond summary; it has to move past the "what" to the "why." Why does Robert Frost "try" to find "something more of the depths"? Why does Nola cry at the end of "Shopping"? How hopeful or affirmative is "Freeway 280"? What is José Armas saying in "El Tonto del Barrio"? Working to consider the "why" of a story and of its key moments or important parts means working to understand its theme, what it means to you as a reader. And it is precisely your understanding of theme that will form the core of any essay you write about a piece of literature.

In their essays, both Kelly and Jessica summarize the plot of the story they write about. Take a look again at their essays. How much plot summary do they give? How do they move beyond summary in writing their essays?

CITING SOURCES

As the writer of an interpretive essay, you'll need to cite or document any sources you use for your essay. In the student essays at the start of this chapter, each writer uses only a primary source for her essay. A *primary source* is the particular text that is the subject of the interpretation and so of the essay. We'll have more to say about documenting sources in Part Three. For now, we'll simply note the format our student writers chose for documenting their use of passages from the texts on which they based their essays. Look at the end of any of the essays—Jessica's, Kelly's, or Kacey's—and you'll find a "Work Cited" listing, which could just as easily have been titled "Bibliography." Each writer listed the source of the text she read and used in her essay. Here's Kelly's listing:

Oates, Joyce Carol. "Shopping." *Ms.* Mar. 1986: 50+.

Note that Kelly begins with the author's name (last name first) and then gives the story's title, the magazine she read it in, the magazine's publication information (when published), and finally, the page numbers of the story. Then, in the text of her essay, Kelly gives parenthetical references to the page numbers from which she took the passages or quotations she used in her essay, for example, (72). Why cite a source? Why list the various sources used in an essay and why list individual page references? For one thing, it's a courtesy to the story's writer to do so; it recognizes the story's status as a publication. For another thing, it's a courtesy to the reader of your interpretive essay. It enables your reader to pursue the story further by reading it himself: The publication data (where and when published) help the reader locate the original text, and the page references guide him quickly to the particular passages you've quoted. Finally, citing sources is required by copyright law.

For more specific information about quoting from and documenting sources, see Chapter 12.

ASSIGNMENT AND GUIDELINES FOR WRITING

ASSIGNMENT

Write an essay based on a piece of literature using one of the following prompts as a starting point:

1. Write *about* a piece of literature; that is, write an essay interpreting a piece of literature. For example, write about a short story or poem, presenting your interpretation of the story or poem and using information from that piece of literature to support your interpretation. You may, of course, use sources other than the piece you're dealing with, but you must document them correctly. In presenting your interpretation, focus on any of the following elements of literature, talking about how the author uses them to reveal theme:

   plot
   conflict

characters (major and minor)
imagery
symbolism

2. Write *from* a piece of literature; that is, write about an event you experienced that was informed by your work with a piece of literature or that was similar to an experience described in a piece of literature. The following are examples of topics that derive from stories and poems presented in this text:

   a. "Shopping"—write about a conflict you've had with a member of your family or a close friend. What was its source? Its resolution? How might you apply this story to your situation?

   b. "In the Land of Men"—write about a crisis you or a friend experienced. How did the crisis occur? What was its outcome? How do you view it now? How might you apply this story to your or your friend's situation?

   c. "El Tonto del Barrio"—have you, like Seferino, ever tried to do what you thought was the right thing? What was the situation? What happened? Did your efforts get the results you wanted, or did they backfire on you? What was the outcome? How might you apply this story to your situation?

   d. "The Road Not Taken" (see pp. 278–279)—write about a choice you've made that you count as significant. What was the choice? Was it the right choice? What factors went into your decision? What resulted from it? How might your experience parallel that of Robert Frost, as expressed in this poem?

   e. "That Place Where Ghosts of Salmon Jump"—write about a clash between society and your family's lore or cultural traditions. Describe the lore or traditions and the conflict you felt. What was the outcome? How might you apply this poem to your situation?

   f. "The Powwow at the End of the World"—in one sense, this poem is about the negative impact of progress on society. What questionable instances of progress have you seen? What was their impact? Whom or what did they affect? What was the outcome? Read Julie Titone's essay "Balance of Power" (pp. 415–418). In what ways do Sherman Alexie's poem and Titone's essay speak with a unified voice? Write an essay exploring this issue and bring both Alexie's poem and Titone's essay to bear on it.

   g. "Freeway 280"—write about a change you've seen in your community. Has this change been for better or worse? What was its outcome? How might you apply this poem to this situation?

WRITING ABOUT LITERATURE
COLLECTING INFORMATION

If you're writing *about* a piece of literature, you may follow this procedure in your prewriting:

1. Select a piece of literature—one presented in this text or one assigned by or approved by your teacher. Read your selection using the reading strategies presented in this chapter and in Chapter 4.

2. As you read and after you've read, focus on questions the text raises. Look for questions beginning with "why": Why did Mrs. Mallard die at the end of "The Story of an Hour"? Why was Nola crying at the end of "Shopping"? Why did Romero resume his normal daily activities after Seferino left for college? Why did the narrator of "In the Land of Men"? keep her brothers waiting at the end of the story, saying "I'm thinking"?
3. Relate these questions to theme, because the focus of an interpretive essay (an essay *about* literature) is the story's theme. Define the story's theme, stating it in a single sentence.

FOCUS STATEMENT

Develop a focus statement based on your theme sentence by writing at least an initial statement of theme. Then make a list of details from the story that reveal or support the theme.

Here's the focus statement written by Kristina Geray, whose essay we present at the end of this chapter:

Nola and Mrs. Dietrich use each other and use Mr. Dietrich. And both are too much concerned with appearances.

Support:
1. reactions to the bag lady—meet her, talk about her on their way into the mall, see her again at the end, Nola cries (why?)
2. Nola's vanity and concern for her weight—her mother's obsessed with her physical appearance also.

Note that Kristina gives her initial interpretation of the story in two sentences. Then she lists very briefly the elements of the story that she'll use to support her assertion that both Mrs. Dietrich and Nola are overly concerned with appearances. Although she would have been better served by writing a more fully developed focus statement, Kristina used this statement effectively as an initial focus for her writing.

PLANNING YOUR ESSAY'S STRUCTURE

An interpretative essay—an essay *about* literature—is argumentative in nature; you'll make and then support an assertion about what the text means. This assertion will be your thesis statement, so you should think of this essay in terms of thesis and support. Here's one structure you might use:

Beginning. Present a brief summary of the text that builds to the thesis statement.
Middle. Present detailed support for your thesis that comes from the text itself. Identify key passages that illustrate some aspect of your thesis, and either summarize or quote them. Each time you cite a passage from the text, be sure to tell what it means and how it supports or develops your thesis.

End. Return to the main idea of your thesis. Define the theme, what the writer has said to you.

Kristina Geray's final draft (pp. 305–307) follows this suggested shape.

Beginning—¶1 characterizes Nola and Mrs. Dietrich as unhappy and lonely. The thesis statement is the next-to-the-last sentence, and Kristina then had to support her assertion about these characters' preoccupation with appearances.

Middle—¶s 2–7 offer support. ¶2 focuses on physical appearances. ¶3 shows their inability to communicate. ¶s 4–7 focus on the meaning of the woman in black. In each paragraph, Kristina offers support for her thesis by summarizing or quoting passages from Oates's story and noting their importance. Look at the topic sentence for ¶4: "The most glaring example of this concern over appearances is shown by Nola's and Mrs. Dietrich's reactions to the woman in black, a 'disheveled woman' (52) who is probably a bag lady." This sentence signals support for the thesis, and it makes an assertion Kristina must support, which she does throughout ¶s 4–7.

End—¶8 is a short paragraph that restates ideas from the introduction and then says very clearly the effect of their obsession with appearances on Nola and Mrs. Dietrich.

REFINING YOUR WRITING

As you begin sharpening your essay's focus, make sure that you've paid attention to these aspects of writing about literature:

Interpretation and theme. Does your thesis statement present your interpretation of the story? Does it speak to the story's theme? What details from the story have you discussed to support your interpretation? Are these details the most telling or important elements of the story?

Beyond summary. Remember that although a plot summary may be an essential part of your essay, your job is to interpret the story, to give your view of its theme and then to offer support for that view. Simply retelling the story is not interpreting, so be sure to go beyond summarizing the story. Be sure to focus tightly on why something happens or why a character says something or behaves in a particular way and then on what these events, statements, and actions mean. Writing about what things mean is interpreting.

Citing sources. You must cite all sources you use in writing about a piece of literature. One citation will be for the story itself, the primary source. But you'll also list all secondary sources that you use. These sources include reviews of the story and essays of criticism about the story. Use the documentation and citation formats specified by either the Modern Language Association (MLA) or the American Psychological Association (APA), unless your instructor specifies a different format. (For more information about documenting and citing sources, see Chapter 12.)

WRITING FROM LITERATURE
COLLECTING INFORMATION

Begin by thinking about your favorite stories, those that you count as important or that have had an impact on your life. Remember the comments we made at the start of this chapter about this kind of essay: Have you ever read a poem or story and thought you had an experience similar to that of one of the characters? Have you found any help from a poem or story in solving a problem that you encountered? Have you applied some aspect of a poem or story to your dealings with other people? An essay written *from* a piece of literature would explore the experience, talk about the problem situation and how it worked out, or offer a narrative account of your dealings with others, and it would tie your experience to that piece of literature.

Try this procedure as you begin to work on your essay:

1. Pick a favorite piece of literature, one that fairly sings to you. In completing the first exercise in this chapter, did you write about such a piece of literature as this, one that protected or consoled you? If so, that story just might be a good one for you to base your essay on.
2. Reread the story, using the reading strategies presented in this chapter and in Chapter 4. From your reading, write a short interpretation of the story.
3. Freewrite about the story and its importance to you. Consider such questions as these: When did you read it? In what context, in what circumstances? How did it reflect or help you through a particular period or event, positive or negative, in your life? How does the experience of one of the characters parallel your own experience during this event or period? How did the story influence your dealings with other people?

FOCUS STATEMENT

Based on your interpretation and your freewriting, write a focus statement. What do you want your reader to understand about the experience that's the topic of your essay? How did the piece of literature relate to that experience? What details will you have to present about the experience and from the story in order for your reader to understand these things? Responding to these questions will help you develop a focus statement for your writing *from* literature.

PLANNING YOUR ESSAY'S STRUCTURE

An essay *from* literature may be informed by one or more of the writing occasions we presented in Part Two of this text, so it's difficult to offer a single structure for this particular kind of essay. We can say, however, that your essay from literature must show that you've read and interpreted the text. You can show this by featuring the text prominently at the beginning and end of your essay so that you establish its relevance to your topic.

Look at Kacey Atwood's essay (pp. 278–280), written *from* Robert Frost's "The Road Not Taken." Kacey begins by quoting the entire poem and presenting a brief interpretation of it. Then (in paragraph 2) she provides transition from the poem to the subject of her essay—peer pressure and decisions. In the middle of the essay (paragraphs 3–7) Kacey presents a personal narrative of various instances of peer pressure and its implications. In paragraph 8, Kacey talks about the impact of the choices she made in high school, and then in paragraph 9 she concludes the essay by returning to the poem.

REFINING YOUR WRITING

Although an essay *from* literature will focus more on your experience than on the story itself, working with the traits of an interpretive essay can help you sharpen your writing from literature.

Interpretation and theme. An essay from literature begins in interpretation, whether you actually give your interpretation as part of your final essay or not. Even if you don't include interpretation in your final draft, you should be sure to work with interpretation and theme as important elements of your prewriting. Look again at Kacey's introduction (pp. 278–279). Because the poem is relatively short, Kacey presents it in its entirety and then follows it with a brief statement about what it means to her.

Application to experience. What event forms the core of your essay, and how does the piece of literature square with or apply to it? Be sure that your essay makes explicit connections between the story and the event. In "One Road Taken," Kacey alludes to Robert Frost's "The Road Not Taken" in the body (see paragraph 5) and then quotes five lines in the last paragraph. In each instance, she sets a context for the material; she incorporates it smoothly.

SAMPLE STUDENT PROCESS

The interpretive essay that follows was written by Kristina Geray, a first-year writing student at NMSU who took Joyce Carol Oates's "Shopping" as her subject. As you work through this essay, compare and contrast it with Kelly McGinley's essay on the same story and with your own interpretation of Oates's story.

READING

"Shopping" was assigned for class reading and discussion. In an e-mail to Bill, her instructor, Kristina asked whether the class could talk about why Nola cried at the story's end. During that discussion, Kristina decided to explore this story in depth and so began her writing process by reading "Shopping" a second time, making the following dialogue notes as she read.

Response to Notes	Reading Notes
	Preview-- title: "Shopping" author: Joyce Carol Oates pub.: *Ms.* (March '86) narrator: 3rd pers. ltd (perspective)
What happens to change the positive mood to negative? 2nd ¶ shows potential danger.	Beginning--Mother/daughter to go to "splendid Livingstone Mall." It's an "old ritual." Seems positive--Mrs. D's "interior voice" is "calm, free of irony."
Why N's tears and Mrs. D's skepticism that they're real?	Ending--not positive. Nola's upset & crying. Very different feeling, mood from 1st ¶. Story breaks into 9 shorter parts by extra spacing between parts. Questions--why does mood change, start to finish? Why does Nola lose control? Why the "ritual" of shopping? Why so many breaks in such a short story?
key terms: old ritual *busy, friends* (why italics?) Harmless conversation monosyllables Nola's smile	1st part--¶s 1-6 conflict between Mrs. D & N--lots of tension. Mrs. D divorced, holds tight to N. ritual elements--trip, parking place (always the same). Mrs. D seems ditzy--bad driver.
why "significant"? Began at time of divorce--Mrs. D holding on to N to keep sense of family?	part 2--¶s 7-8 contrasts mall (bright) with outdoor setting (gritty, acrid air). mall a place of sanctuary ("It's like coming home."). shopping trips "significant."
significance of "disheveled woman"? key terms: disheveled woman surprise N's content, absorbed "Let me go"	3rd part--¶s 9-18 "disheveled woman" enters story Nola's social conscience emerges, but as soon as she gets in the mall she gets "distracted" and forgets the homeless woman. tension again--N tells Mrs. D, "Let me go. Let me go."
family's dysfunctional key terms: considerable beauty savage dieting fat herself again reborn perfect ironic--N's hardly perfect	4th part--¶s 19-21 background on N as child, normally weird kid--tries to constantly "call attention to herself." father upset, yells at Mrs. D. part 5--¶s 22-28 more background--Nola sent away to boarding school. grew to become "a girl of considerable beauty." diets. (signs of anorexia?) Shows N's concern w. body appearance--vanity? Also shows Mrs. D's vision of who N would be: "herself again, reborn and this time perfect."

Response to Notes	Reading Notes
key terms: time passing no connection present tense how love ends how love begins	6th part--¶s 29-34 back to shopping at mall. N finds "beautiful" "perfect" sweater. Mrs. D thinks it's ugly. real tension--Mrs. D fears time passing, realizes there's no connection between her and Nola. But she can't let go.
key terms: N's tense, moody hate Mrs. D alcoholic? rationalizes 3rd glass of wine away as "celebration"	7th part--¶s 35-67 lunch--things fall apart. They argue. N wants to go to school in France. Mrs. D--3rd glass of wine. N--smokes to defy her mother. father castigated--N's got a trash mouth.
appearances again--Mrs. D notices N's skin--"fair and thin and dry" "wear out before she's 40" (during conversation)	important conversation between N & Mrs. D--Mrs. D doesn't understand "How exhausting it is" (N says this). no real relationship--Nola's hand "limp, ungiving" when Mrs. D squeezes it.
very strong section. Mrs. D understands how hopeless it is. But she's "anxious, immediately repentant"--dependent on N for meaning to her life?	8th part--¶s 68-69 more shopping. Mrs. D feels hatred for N--"cold calm clear unmistakable hatred." Mrs. D thinks she doesn't know Nola, doesn't love Nola.
key terms: disheveled woman N's upset, strangely upset crying cloak	last part--¶s 70-72 leaving mall--shopping's over. see homeless woman again. N may approach her but then doesn't. Mrs. D's condescending. Nola's upset, cries. Mrs. D wants a cloak to hide them--mask reality? keep up appearances? no public embarrassment? Important elements--appearances throughout. no relationship between N and Mrs. D, only conflict. Mrs. D just doesn't get it.

PREWRITING

Kristina decided to work with the two primary characters in Oates's story, Nola and Mrs. Dietrich. She continued her prewriting by writing a set of notes in which she listed various attributes of each character, at times contrasting one of Nola's traits with one of her mother's.

Nola	Mrs. Dietrich
young	old
never married	divorced
dry skin	oily skin
underweight	overweight
smokes	alcoholic
prep school	thinks she loves Nola
hates father	was happiest when pregnant with Nola
hates to throw things away	feels lonely
spends late nights partying with friends	wants to keep Nola for herself
wants to talk to lady in black	thinks Mr. Dietrich owes her something
liked reciting misc. facts	wants to ignore the lady in black
father disliked her	is a lousy driver
acts coarsely (i.e., putting cigarette butt out on floor)	worries about appearances
wants to confront mother	

FOCUS STATEMENT

Nola and Mrs. Dietrich use each other and use Mr. Dietrich. And both are too much concerned with appearances.

Support:
1. reactions to the bag lady—meet her, talk about her on their way into the mall, see her again at the end, Nola cries (why?)
2. Nola's vanity and concern for her weight—her mother's obsessed with her physical appearance also.

Based on this statement, Kristina wrote a rough draft for peer review. But as she wrote, the focus shifted, moving away from the initial statement about both Nola and Mrs. Dietrich using Mr. Dietrich, so that the essay takes the concern for appearances as its primary focal point.

ROUGH DRAFT FOR PEER REVIEW

Joyce Carol Oates short story "Shopping" centers around two characters, Mrs. Dietrich and her daughter Nola, and their obsession with shopping. As the story develops so does the readers understanding of Nola and her mother who seem as different as night and day. Nola is a weight-obsessed, prep school brat, smart-mouthed and confrontational. Her mother on the other hand is an alcoholic divorcee, desperately trying to cling to the one thing in life that truly made her happy, Nola. All of these differences are on the surface, however. Underneath it all Nola and Mrs. Dietrich are as alike as two peas in a pod. They are both very lonely people, unwilling or incapable of taking the right steps to make themselves happy. Nola and Mrs. Dietrich are much more concerned with the way things appear to be bothered with actually trying to change things. This preoccupation with appearance is shown time and time again throughout the short story "Shopping."

The most glaring example of this concern over appearances is shown by Nola's and Mrs. Dietrich's reactions to the woman in black. Mrs. Dietrich seems to see the woman in black as nothing more than an eyesore. She is content to simply ignore her, as the other shoppers do, by walking past her without even acknowledging her presence. She defends her actions by saying, when questioned, that the woman is "harmless . . . She just sits." As far as Mrs. Dietrich is concerned, the lady in black is simply a flaw in the mall scenery. As long as the lady continues to "just sit" Mrs. Dietrich can keep up the pretense that people such as the lady in black don't exist. In her world of luxury, Mrs. Dietrich's pretense is an important way to keep up appearances and keep from standing out in the crowd.

Nola's reaction to the lady in black is a bit more complex than her mother's. Upon first seeing the lady in black, Nola is horrified that "people like her" are allowed in the mall. At this point, Nola seems more upset that the beautiful and blemish-free interior of her second home has been tarnished, rather than with the idea that the lady in black may be suffering any harm. It is only after speaking with her mother about the lady in black that Nola seems to care about the woman as a person. She bemoans the fact that the lady in black may somehow be harmed by the actions of those who choose not to acknowledge her prescence. It is possible that Nola is honestly concerned about the well-being of the woman in black, however, it is more likely that she is simply paying lip-service to the "tragedy of women like that." By speaking of such things Nola may hope to appear more caring and concerned for the outcasts of an affluent society than she really is. Her concern, real or otherwise, is fleeting and she quickly forgets, moving on to the important business of the day: shopping. It is not until Nola and Mrs. Dietrich are preparing to leave the mall that Nola is reminded of the wretched lady in black. Mrs. Dietrich and the other shoppers continue to file past the woman as if she weren't there. Nola, on the other hand, seems to be getting ready to approach her. This is not because of any real concern on Nola's part. It is more out of a desire to appear as a caring person. It almost seems as if Nola is thinking, "If I were to approach this woman and offer her my help, wouldn't it look good to everyone else? Perhaps they'd all comment on what a lovely young woman I am for helping this wretch out." In the end, though, Nola does not approach the woman in black. Helping her out would mean standing out in the crowd. Even though it is important to appear concerned, it is even more important to fit in and not to stand out.

The story ends with Nola sobbing in her mother's car "as though her heart is broken." It would be easy to assume that Nola is crying out of sorrow for the woman in black or out of shame for not having approached her. Neither is the case, however. Nola's tears are very likely a continuation of her act as a genuinely caring person. The idea that these are crocodile tears is supported by the fact that Mrs. Dietrich has "heard these very sobs before." On the other hand, if Nola's tears are real, they most certainly are not for the woman in black. Nola is much too self-centered and spoiled to truly feel that strongly for anyone else. Nola is crying because she came to the mall to forget how isolated she feels. By choosing not to approach the woman in black Nola only served to reinforce her loneliness. In this way, the woman in black has sabotaged Nola's escape from her self-imposed solitary confinement. If Nola's tears are real, Nola is crying for herself, not for the woman in black.

Another example of Nola's and Mrs. Dietrich's concern over appearances is the way they both seem to obsess over Nola's physical appearance. As they prepare to enter the mall Mrs. Dietrich's breath is taken away by Nola's beautiful smile. Mrs. Dietrich's memories of Nola as a child center around the fact that Nola was "plain, rather chunky . . . (and) . . . unpopular at school." When trying to draw attention to herself as a child, it was Nola's physical appearance that came under fire as her relatives began to criticize her "queer, glassy-pale eyes." After being sent away to school it is stated that Nola "matured into a girl of considerable beauty." From this statement it seems pretty evident that Nola's academic progress and character development mean little when compared to Nola's blossoming into an attractive young woman. When Mrs. Dietrich and Nola argue in La Créperie Mrs. Dietrich puts little effort into understanding what her daughter is trying to say and more effort into noticing her daughter's physical attributes. At this point, Mrs. Dietrich "sees with pity that her daughter's skin is fair and thin and dry . . . it will wear out before she's forty." Nola and Mrs. Dietrich both seem tremendously concerned with Nola's weight. Nola is 5 foot 7 and weighs less than 100 lbs, "the result of constant savage dieting.' Despite her slenderness (which, in my opinion, is unhealthy) Nola constantly obsesses about her weight. This is well illustrated in a paragraph on p. 53: "Do you think I'm fat, mother?" The last sentence of this paragraph is especially interesting. "Do you think it shows?" she asks her mother as if it would be acceptable for her to be fat as long as it didn't show. This seems to be Nola's & Mrs. Dietrich's entire philosophy on life. It's okay to feel miserable and hopelessly alone as long as it doesn't show.

Kristina's review group members felt that her essay was a good start, that Kristina had done a good job of wrestling with the meaning of the story. One reviewer told her that the paragraphs making up the body of the essay had "great detail; even more would make the essay better." Another reviewer offered mostly positive comments about the essay, but noted two areas that needed revision:

> I think your introduction is a little too long. Maybe use the contrast & comparisons in a paragraph after the introduction. Rather than having them lead up to the thesis have them support it.

> I think you need to work on the intro. You need to shorten it so that your point is more clear. I don't know if this is a completed essay, but the end leaves you hanging.

Although this draft did form a good start, it was not quite the quality her group thought Kristina capable of. Kristina didn't receive as much help from her group as she had wanted, but, given deadlines and due dates, she had to produce a second draft.

SECOND ROUGH DRAFT

An Interpretation of Joyce Carol Oates "Shopping"

1   Joyce Carol Oates short story "Shopping" centers around two characters, Mrs. Dietrich and her daughter Nola, and their obsession with shopping. As the story develops so does the readers understanding of Nola and her mother who seem as different as night and day. Nola is a weight-obsessed, smart-mouthed,

confrontational, prep-school brat. Her mother, on the other hand, is an alcoholic divorcee, desperately trying to hold on to the only thing in her life that ever came close to making her happy, Nola. All these differences are on the surface, however. Underneath it all, Nola and Mrs. Dietrich are as alike as two peas in a pod. They are both very lonely people, unwilling or incapable of taking the right steps to make themselves happy. Nola and Mrs. Dietrich are much more concerned with the way things appear to really bother with actually trying to change things. This preoccupation with appearance is shown time and time again throughout the short story "Shopping."

2   The most glaring example of this concern over appearances is shown by Nola's and Mrs. Dietrich's reactions to the woman in black. Mrs. Dietrich seems to see the woman as nothing more than an eyesore. She is content to simply ignore her, as the other shoppers do, by walking past her without even acknowledging her presence. She defends her actions by saying, when questioned, that the woman is "harmless . . . she just sits." As far as Mrs. Dietrich is concerned, the lady in black is simply a flaw in the mall scenery. As long as the lady continues to "just sit," Mrs. Dietrich can keep up the pretense that people such as the lady in black don't exist. In her world of luxury, Mrs. Dietrich's pretense is an important way to keep from standing out in the crowd.

3   Nola's reaction to the lady in black is a bit more complex than her mother's. Upon first seeing her, Nola is horrified that "people like her" are allowed in the mall. At this point, Nola seems more upset that the beautiful and blemish-free interior of her second home has been tarnished rather than with the idea that the lady in black may be suffering any harm. It is only after speaking with her mother about the lady in black that Nola expresses any concern for the woman. She bemoans the fact that the lady in black may somehow be harmed by the actions of those who choose not to acknowledge her presence. There is a *slight* chance that Nola is honestly concerned about the welfare of the woman in black, however, it is more likely that she is simply paying lip-service to the "tragedy of women like that." By speaking of such "tragedy," Nola may hope to appear more caring and concerned for "the outcasts of an affluent society" than she really is.

4   Despite her passionate words, Nola's concern is fleeting and she quickly forgets, moving on to the important business of the day: shopping. It is not until Nola and Mrs. Dietrich are preparing to leave the mall that Nola is reminded of the wretched lady in black. Mrs. Dietrich and the other shoppers continue to file past the woman as if she weren't there. Nola, on the other hand, seems to be getting ready to approach her. This is not because of any real concern on Nola's part. It is more out of a desire to appear as a caring person. It almost seems as if Nola is thinking "If I were to approach this woman and offer her my help wouldn't it look good to everyone else? Perhaps they'd all comment on what a lovely young woman I am for helping this wretch." In the end though, Nola does not approach the woman in black. Nola's offer of help would cause her to stand out in the crowd. Despite the fact that Nola seems to feel it is important to appear concerned, it is even more important not to stand out.

5   The story ends with Nola sobbing in her mother's car "as though her heart is broken." It would be easy to assume that Nola is crying out of sorrow for the woman in black or out of shame for not having approached her. Both of these reactions are unlikely, though. Nola's tears are more likely a continuation of her act as a genuinely caring person. The idea that these are crocodile tears is supported by the fact that Mrs. Dietrich has "heard these very sobs before." On the other hand, if Nola's tears are real the reader should assume that she is not

crying for the woman in black. Nola is much too self-centered and spoiled to truly feel that strongly for anyone else. Nola is crying because she came to the mall to forget how isolated she feels. By choosing not to approach the woman in black Nola only served to reinforce her loneliness. In this way, the woman in black has sabotaged Nola's escape from her self-imposed solitary confinement. If Nola's tears are real, she is crying for herself, not the woman in black.

6   Another example of Nola's and Mrs. Dietrich's concern over appearances is the way they both seem to obsess over Nola's physical appearance. Mrs. Dietrich's memories of Nola as a child center around the fact that Nola was "plain, rather chunky . . . (and) . . . unpopular at school." When Nola tried to draw attention to herself it was her appearance that came under fire as her relative's began criticizing on "her queer glassy-pale eyes." After being sent away to school it is stated that Nola "matured into a girl of considerable beauty." From this statement is seems pretty evident that Nola's academic progress and character development mean little when compared to Nola's blossoming into an attractive young woman. When Nola and Mrs. Dietrich argue in La Crêperie, Mrs. Dietrich puts little effort into understanding what her daughter is trying to say and more effort into noticing her daughter's physical attributes. At this point, Mrs. Dietrich "sees with pity that her daughter's skin is fair and thin and dry . . . it will wear out before she is forty."

7   Finally, Nola and Mrs. Dietrich both seem tremendously concerned with Nola's weight. Nola is 5'7" and weighs less than a hundred pounds, "the result of constant savage dieting." Despite her slenderness Nola obsesses about her weight. This is well illustrated in a paragraph on page 53:

> "Do you think I'm fat, Mother?" she ask frequently, worriedly, standing in front of the mirror twisted at the waist to reveal her small round belly which, it seems, can't help being round: she bloats herself on diet Cokes all day long. "Do you think it shows?"

The last sentence of this paragraph is especially interesting. "Do you think it shows?" Nola asks her mother as if it would be acceptable for her to be fat as long as it didn't show. This seems to be Nola's and Mrs. Dietrich's entire philosophy on life. It's okay to be miserable and hopelessly alone as long as it doesn't show.

8   Nola and Mrs. Dietrich, the characters in Joyce Carol Oates short story "Shopping" seem very different. However, their almost all-consuming obsession with appearances makes them, underneath it all, nearly identical and, despite being surrounded by people, very much alone.

Because Kristina wanted to write a strong essay, she scheduled a conference with Bill. After reading this draft, he offered this advice:

Kristina—your focus on the theme of appearance versus reality (and its relation to loneliness) works, so what's here is a very good start. I especially like the way you set up the rest of the paper with the last 2 sentences of ¶1. You got some good advice from your group, especially the comment about your needing to provide a conclusion. Now, you still have some work to do on this, so let's start with the conclusion and go from there:

1. conclusion—it's a little flat; it's more a summary or restatement than a clincher. One way to strengthen it is to talk about Mrs. D's disappointment in Nola not being her reincarnation (see the end of the paragraph about Mrs. D's pregnancy).

2. what's the best order of your paragraphs—you say "most glaring example" to open ¶2, so should you save this example for last? It's an important event—their seeing the homeless woman—so think about leaving your readers with that as most important.

3. Should you expand discussion of their argument in the restaurant (now in ¶6)?—sets up the fact that Mrs. D doesn't really know who Nola is, which can point to the conclusion.

4. Nola's eyes—did anyone really criticize her for these or just notice that they seemed strange?

5. Nola's crying—in the paragraph in which you talk about this (¶5) you give 2 reasons for her tears. Should you give 2 or 1?

6. gotta use proper documentation of sources. Follow the guidelines from the Writing Center, the ones we talked about in class.

7. Can you find some fresher wordings for "as different as night and day," "as alike as two peas in a pod," and "time and time again" (all in ¶1)?

8. mechanics—check possessives, e.g., "Oates's short story" v. "Oates short story" (1st sentence).

One thing more—can you provide a more colorful title? I suspect the one you have above wouldn't be very competitive for Title of the Week. And one more "one thing more"—how many times do you say either "woman in black" or "lady in black"?

After this conference, Kristina wrote her final draft. How does it compare with the other drafts she wrote for this assignment? How much of her group's and Bill's advice did she take? To what effect?

FINAL DRAFT

"HOW EXHAUSTING IT IS" TO KEEP UP APPEARANCES

KRISTINA GERAY

1   Joyce Carol Oates's short story "Shopping" centers around two characters, Mrs. Dietrich and her daughter Nola, and their obsession with shopping. As the story develops so does the reader's understanding of Nola and her mother who seem to be complete opposites. Nola is a weight-obsessed, smart-mouthed, confrontational, prepschool brat. Her mother, on the other hand, is an alcoholic divorcee, desperately trying to hold on to the only thing in her life that ever came close to making her happy, Nola. All these differences are on the surface, however. Underneath it all, Nola and Mrs. Dietrich are very much alike. Both are very lonely people, unwilling or incapable of taking the right steps to make themselves happy. Nola and Mrs. Dietrich are much too concerned with the way things appear to really bother with actually trying to change things. This preoccupation with appearance is shown time and time again throughout the short story "Shopping."

2   Nola and Mrs. Dietrich obsess over Nola's physical appearance. Mrs. Dietrich's memories of Nola as a child center around the fact that Nola was "plain, rather chunky [. . . and . . .] unpopular at school" (Oates, 53. All other references are to this source.). When Nola tries to draw attention to herself, her relatives focus on her appearance: "What a strange child! What queer glassy-pale eyes!" (53). Rather than seeing a lonely child who craved attention, her family sees only her strangeness and her eyes. But after being sent away to school Nola "matured into a girl of considerable beauty" (53). From this statement it seems pretty evident that Nola's academic progress and character development mean little when compared to her blossoming into an attractive young woman. Finally, Nola and Mrs. Dietrich both seem tremendously concerned with Nola's weight. Nola is 5'7" and weighs less than a hundred pounds, "the result of constant savage dieting" (53). Despite her slenderness Nola obsesses about her weight. This is well illustrated in a paragraph on page 53:

> "Do you think I'm fat, Mother?" she asks frequently, worriedly, standing in front of the mirror twisted at the waist to reveal her small round belly which, it seems, can't help being round: she bloats herself on diet Cokes all day long. "Do you think it shows?"

The last sentence of this paragraph is especially interesting. "Do you think it shows?" Nola asks her mother as if it would be acceptable for her to be fat as long as it didn't show. This seems to be Nola's and Mrs. Dietrich's entire philosophy on life. It's okay to be miserable and hopelessly alone as long as it doesn't show.

3   What does show is that Nola and Mrs. Dietrich are miserable. Mrs. Dietrich makes no effort to understand Nola, and Nola resents it. When they argue in La Crêperie, Mrs. Dietrich puts little effort into understanding what her daughter is trying to say and more effort into noticing her daughter's physical attributes. The argument is important. Nola, not looking at her mother, asks, "Why don't we just talk about it, Mother?" (73). Mrs. Dietrich claims not to know what Nola means by "it," and that frustrates Nola. Eventually, this conversation occurs:

> Nola says, sighing, "How exhausting it is."
> "How *what?*"
> "How exhausting it is."
> "What is?"
> "You and me—"
> "What?"
> "Being together—"
> "Being together how—?"
> "The two of us, like this—"
> "But we're hardly ever together, Nola," Mrs. Dietrich says. (73)

Either Mrs. Dietrich does not know that Nola means their strained relationship is the exhausting "it," or she pretends not to know because she cannot talk about it. At this point, Nola turns away, and Mrs. Dietrich's only response is to silently pity Nola. She "sees with pity that her daughter's skin is fair and thin and dry [. . .] it will wear out before she is forty" (73). Appearance means everything to Mrs. Dietrich.

4   The most glaring example of this concern over appearances is shown by Nola's and Mrs. Dietrich's reactions to the woman in black, a "disheveled woman" (52) who is probably a bag lady. Mrs. Dietrich seems to see the woman as nothing more than an eyesore. She is content to simply ignore her, as the other shoppers do, by walking past

her without even acknowledging her presence. She defends her actions by saying, when questioned, that the woman is "harmless [. . .] she just *sits*" (52). As far as Mrs. Dietrich is concerned, the lady in black is simply a flaw in the mall scenery. As long as the lady continues to "just sit," Mrs. Dietrich can keep up the pretense that people such as the lady in black don't exist. In her world of luxury, Mrs. Dietrich's pretense is an important way to keep from standing out in the crowd.

5   Nola's reaction to the bag lady is a bit more complex than her mother's. Upon first seeing her, Nola is horrified that "people like her" are allowed in the mall. At this point, Nola seems more upset that the beautiful and blemish-free interior of her second home has been tarnished rather than with the idea that this woman may be suffering any harm. It is only after speaking with her mother about the lady in black that Nola expresses any concern for the woman. She bemoans the fact that the bag lady may somehow be harmed by the actions of those who choose not to acknowledge her presence. There is a *slight* chance that Nola is honestly concerned about the welfare of the woman in black; however, it is more likely that she is simply paying lip-service to the "tragedy of women like that" (52). By speaking of such "tragedy," Nola appears to be more caring and concerned for "the outcasts of an affluent society" (52) than she really is.

6   Despite her passionate words, Nola's concern is fleeting and she quickly forgets, moving on to the important business of the day: shopping. It is not until Nola and Mrs. Dietrich are preparing to leave the mall that Nola is reminded of the wretched lady in black. Mrs. Dietrich and the other shoppers continue to file past the woman as if she weren't there. Nola, on the other hand, seems to be getting ready to approach her. This is not because of any real concern on Nola's part. It is more out of a desire to appear as a caring person. It almost seems as if Nola is thinking "If I were to approach this woman and offer her my help wouldn't it look good to everyone else? Perhaps they'd all comment on what a lovely young woman I am for helping this wretch." In the end though, Nola does not approach the bag lady. Nola's offer of help would cause her to stand out in the crowd. Despite the fact that Nola seems to feel it is important to appear concerned, it is even more important not to stand out.

7   The story ends with Nola sobbing in her mother's car "as though her heart is broken" (73). It would be easy to assume that Nola is crying out of sorrow for the woman in black or out of shame for not having approached her. Both of these reactions are unlikely, though. Nola's tears are more likely a continuation of her act as a genuinely caring person. The idea that these are crocodile tears is supported by the fact that Mrs. Dietrich has "heard these very sobs before" (73). On the other hand, if Nola's tears are real the reader should assume that she is not crying for the woman in black. Nola is much too self-centered and spoiled to truly feel that strongly for anyone else. Nola is crying because she came to the mall to forget how isolated she feels. By choosing not to approach the woman Nola only served to reinforce her loneliness. In this way, the bag lady has sabotaged Nola's escape from her self-imposed solitary confinement. If Nola's tears are real, she is crying for herself, not the woman in black.

8   Nola and Mrs. Dietrich, the characters in Joyce Carol Oates's short story "Shopping" seem very different. However, their almost all-consuming obsession with appearances makes them, underneath it all, nearly identical and, despite being surrounded by people, very much alone.

WORK CITED

Oates, Joyce Carol. "Shopping." *Ms.* March 1986: 50+.

Checklist: Critiquing an Essay About Literature

1. What piece of literature is the essay about? (*Note:* Hereafter, we'll refer to *story,* whether the piece of literature is a short story, poem, novel, or drama.)
2. Identify the essay's thesis. What interpretation does it carry about the story? What is the basic point of interpretation? How clearly is it stated?
3. How effectively are the topic sentences developed? What kinds of detail support the interpretation? How effectively does the detail from the story itself support the thesis?
4. How has the writer introduced and concluded the essay? How effective are these parts of the essay?
5. Is the documentation and citation of primary and secondary sources correct? (For discussion of proper documentation, see Chapter 12.)
6. Does the paper adhere to conventions of usage, mechanics, and format? Correct any errors you find.

Checklist: Critiquing an Essay From Literature

1. What event forms the basis for the essay? What story has the writer chosen as relating to the event?
2. What is the writer's interpretation of the story? How clearly does the interpretation come through in the essay, even if the writer doesn't explicitly state it?
3. How has the writer developed the paper—for example, as a personal, argumentative, or problem/solution essay? How effectively has the writer followed the conventions for the selected development? (See other chapters in Part Two for help here.)
4. How clearly has the writer related the story to the essay's primary event? That is, how effectively does the writer show how the story related to or informed her actions or her response to the event?
5. Is the documentation and citation of primary and secondary sources correct? (For discussion of proper documentation, see Chapter 12.)
6. Does the paper adhere to conventions of usage, mechanics, and format? Correct any errors you find.

In this chapter, we will ask you to take a stance on an issue, to be ready to qualify your position by considering the opinions of others, and then to write an essay that presents your informed stance or opinion—your position—on that issue.

What does it mean to take a position on an issue? And what is the relationship between taking a position and having an argument? A position essay involves argument in the best sense of that term. What comes to mind when you hear the words "argue" and "argument"? You may think about the last time you stood toe to toe with someone verbally duking it out over something that mattered to you both. In such a situation, you (and your opponent) were probably much more interested in winning the argument than in being sure that you stated your position clearly. You probably didn't pay a great deal of attention to stating your argument in such a way as to avoid misrepresenting your opponent's position. That kind of argument is precisely what this chapter is not about.

Instead, we want you to think of argument in terms of developing an informed position. Such development will involve you in exploring a topic to find out what you think about it and why, but it will also involve you in seriously considering what someone opposed to your stance thinks about the topic and why. You'll use that opponent's thinking as a means of sharpening your own focus. To do this, you'll have to keep an open mind from the outset. You'll have to be

Position Essays

CHAPTER 9

willing to modify your stance if you cannot show why you do not accept the arguments your reader is making.

Ultimately, writing a position paper will help you hone your critical-thinking skills. As you explore your topic to discover a stance and ways to support it and then as you consider why and in what ways someone might oppose your stance, you should become a stronger, more logical, and more critical thinker.

SAMPLE ESSAYS

The following sample essays include arguments about drug laws, abortion, date rape, and the legal age for driving.

The first essay, by Phil Gramm, a senator from Texas, is a call for stricter laws regarding the use and sale of illegal drugs.

PHIL GRAMM

DON'T LET JUDGES SET CROOKS FREE

1   Two Federal judges recently announced that they would refuse to take drug cases because they oppose mandatory minimum sentences. One judge, Jack Weinstein of Brooklyn, confessed to a "sense of depression about much of the cruelty I have been party to in connection with the war on drugs." The other, Whitman Knapp of Manhattan, heartened that President Clinton "has not committed himself to the war on drugs in such a way as the Republican Administration had," hoped his action would influence the President to abandon tough mandatory sentencing.

2   If the Clinton Administration listens to these voices, and their echoes, and tries to roll back minimum mandatory sentences, it will certainly win applause from some criminal defense lawyers, judges and the media—and no doubt many criminals—but it will betray millions of Americans who took the President at his word when he promised to be tough on crime.

3   Contrary to conventional wisdom, most criminals are perfectly rational men and women. They don't commit crimes because they're in the grip of some irresistible impulse. They commit crimes because they think it pays. Unfortunately, in most cases they are right: In America today, crime does pay.

4   Morgan Reynolds, an economist at Texas A&M University, has calculated the amount of time that a person committing a serious crime in 1990—the last year for which we have complete statistics—could reasonably expect to spend in prison. By analyzing the probability of arrest, prosecution, conviction, imprisonment and the average actual sentence served by convicts for particular crimes, Professor Reynolds has reached some shocking conclusions.

5   On average, a person committing murder in the United States today can expect to spend only 1.8 years in prison. For rape, the expected punishment is 60 days. Expected time in prison is 23 days for robbery, 6.7 days for arson and 6.4 days for aggravated assault. And for stealing a car, a person can reasonably expect to spend just a day and a half in prison.

6   Given this extremely low rate of expected punishment, is it any wonder that our nation is deluged by a tidal wave of crime? In trying to account for the six million violent crimes committed annually, analysts point to the breakdown of the family, the effects of television violence and the failure to teach moral values in our schools. While these factors have an impact, they overlook the main culprit: a criminal justice system in which the cost of committing crimes is so shamelessly cheap that it fails to deter potential criminals.

7   Mandatory minimum sentences deal with this problem directly. When a potential criminal knows that if he is convicted he is certain to be sentenced, and his sentence is certain to be stiff, his cost-benefit calculus changes dramatically and his willingness to engage in criminal activity takes a nose dive.

8   Again, Professor Reynolds's statistics are revealing. He found that since 1950, the expected punishment for a serious criminal has declined by two-thirds, while the annual number of crimes has risen seven-fold. In 1950, each perpetrator of a serious crime risked, on average, 24 days in prison. By 1988, the amount of risked time was 8.5 days. Over 38 years, soft sentencing—treating criminals as victims of dysfunctional families, of predatory capitalism, of society at large—has brought a dramatic decline in the cost of committing a crime and a dramatic increase in crime.

9   Critics of mandatory minimum sentences point out, often with considerable indignation, that mandatory sentencing denies judges discretion in imposing sentences. And they are perfectly right. That's what we want.

10   Americans have lost faith in our criminal justice system. Too many violent criminals have walked away with light or even no prison sentences. Mandatory minimum sentencing is a massive no-confidence vote by the American people in the discretionary powers of our judges. If judges and parole boards were legally liable for the actions of convicted felons who walk the streets due to their decisions, I would have more confidence in their judgment. But they are not.

11   "But what about fairness?" critics of mandatory minimum sentencing ask. "Is it fair that someone who has never committed a crime in his life should go to prison for 10 years because one day he sold drugs to some kid? Shouldn't we distinguish between a major drug dealer and a minor drug offense?"

12   Once again, the critics are right: There is a distinction between major and minor drug offenses. A minor drug offense takes place when a pusher sells drugs to somebody else's child; a major drug offense takes place when he pushes drugs on yours. Only when our nation's elites are as outraged about what happens to someone else's child as they would be were it happening to their own will we deal with crime effectively.

13   Of course, there is the cost issue to be considered. At a time when we are desperately trying to reduce the Federal deficit, can we really afford to sentence more criminals to jail for lengthier periods of time?

14   Of course we can. In 1990, the Department of Justice's bureau of statistics found that it costs from $15,000 to $30,000 to keep a felon in prison for a year. A Rand Corporation study calculated that the active street criminal imposes a financial cost of $430,000 a year on the general public—not to mention such immeasurable but very real costs as grief, fear and anger. By Washington standards (or anybody's, for that matter), spending $30,000 a year to save $430,000 a year is a brilliant allocation of resources.

15   In dealing with our nation's crime problem, cost is not the fundamental issue. Indifference is. I am appalled by the shoulder-shrugging approach some Americans take to the issue of crime in this country. Americans saw the pictures of starving children in Somalia and were outraged; we saw "ethnic cleansing" in Bosnia and were furious. But our outrage and fury evaporate when American children are the victims of criminals.

16   Like Judge Weinstein, all too many are ready to agonize over the "cruelty" that mandatory sentencing inflicts on drug pushers, and to overlook the cruelty that mandatory sentencing avoids by keeping these criminals off the streets and preventing them from brutalizing your children, mine or even Judge Weinstein's.

17   With the end of the cold war, domestic crime is now the greatest threat to the safety and well being of Americans. And just as the U.S. developed a military strategy—"containment"—to deter Soviet aggression by raising its costs, so today we need a legal strategy to contain, and reverse, the growth of violent crime.

18   That is why, along with many other Americans, I am a strong supporter of mandatory minimum sentences. In fact, I will go so far as to say that as long as I am in the Senate, we will be imposing more minimum sentences, not repealing them.

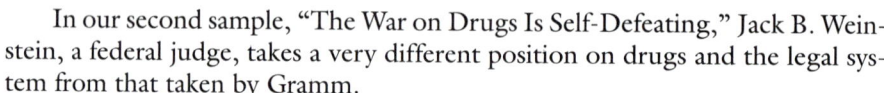

Questions for Review

1. What is the thesis of Gramm's essay? Does it appear in the essay? If so, where? What reasons does he give for accepting his position?
2. Divide the essay into beginning, middle, and end. What rhetorical and/or stylistic devices help form these divisions?
3. What audience might Gramm's essay be written for? Is that audience likely to resist his argument? Does Gramm show respect for those who might disagree with him? Explain.
4. Does this essay take opposing points of view into consideration? If so, are they represented fairly? Are they effectively countered?
5. How would you characterize your attitude toward this subject before reading Gramm's essay? What effect did this essay have on your thinking?

In our second sample, "The War on Drugs Is Self-Defeating," Jack B. Weinstein, a federal judge, takes a very different position on drugs and the legal system from that taken by Gramm.

JACK B. WEINSTEIN

THE WAR ON DRUGS IS SELF-DEFEATING

1   In the debate over national drug policy, too many policy makers, unsure of what might work or why, appear to rely upon what seems politically safe: harsher law enforcement based on more prison time.

2   A nonpartisan Federal Commission on Drugs needs to be formed. Its object should be to report candidly on the costs, benefits, risks and advantages of present and potential national drug policies. Such a commission could provide the fact-finding and serious analysis lacking in the political climate surrounding drugs.

3   The nation can look for guidance to the Wickersham Commission, appointed by President Hoover in 1929, whose report led to a full debate on Prohibition laws and a constitutional amendment returning responsibility to the states for control of alcohol. Also instructive is the National Commission on Marijuana and Drug Abuse, appointed by President Nixon in 1971, which recommended ending prosecution for possession of marijuana for private use.

4   So urgent is the issue that Chief Justice William H. Rehnquist in a speech in June said, "The law by itself is not going to solve the problems of drugs and violence," raising "questions of public policy which must be decided, not by lawyers, judges or other experts, but by the popularly elected branches of government"—and ultimately, I think, by a well-informed electorate.

5   Attorney General Janet Reno, confronting the problem of drug crime immediately upon assuming office, emphasized the importance of reconsidering the existing policy.

6   America has had three national drug policies. Before 1914, a freedom model reigned. Opiates were sold as over-the-counter household remedies and marijuana was a legal crop. In 1914, we began to tax narcotics to control them, but we, like Britain, relied primarily on a medical model of treatment and prescriptions.

7   In the 1930's, we embarked upon a strict punitive model, and the medical profession was largely pushed out of the field. The drug supplier–law enforcement complex was enormously expanded by the war on drugs in the 1980's at an annual cost of tens of billions of dollars.

8   Meanwhile, in my judicial district, the Federal probation service has had to radically cut its drug-testing and medical treatment program; many parents have no place to send their children for help; educational and other nonpenal controls are ineffective, and, too frequently, ghetto youths seek to emulate sellers and thugs who brazenly walk city streets.

9   Largely because of drug prosecutions, our justice system is in crisis. Nationally, over one-third of all new inmates are drug offenders. Over 60 percent of those in Federal prisons have been convicted of drug offenses.

10   In the Eastern District of New York, we sentence about 400 drug "mules" each year. These are usually poor people who smuggle drugs, primarily heroin from Nigeria and cocaine and heroin from Colombia. They are cheaply hired for one trip. Before the adoption of guideline sentencing, they were sentenced to 30 months and paroled in about one year.

11   Now they must serve an average of two additional years, and sometimes a 10-year minimum, leading to at least 800 more penal years, at millions of dollars of added expense for incarceration in our district alone.

12   Largely because of mandated and unnecessarily harsh sentences for minor drug offenders, which fail to deter, I have exercised my option as a senior Federal judge not to try minor drug cases.

13   When I wrote a report on drug laws for the City Bar Association in the early 1950's and then served as chairman of the lay board of the North Brothers Island Hospital— the first for teen-age narcotics users—I believed a modified medical model was desirable. In the 60's, as a father I supported some form of criminal model because I thought that it might discourage drug use by young people. As a judge, in the 80's and 90's, I have become increasingly despondent over the cruelties and self-defeating character of our war on drugs.

14   A national commission could address the difficult questions. How should marijuana be treated? Has it become such a large and widely available cash crop that prohibition is neither attainable nor affordable? (In some districts Federal prosecutors decline cases involving less than a ton, while in other places people are sent to prison for years when they possess a few plants for their own use.)

15   How dangerous is marijuana? Does it have useful therapeutic values? How much money could be saved in law enforcement by decriminalizing its use? Would savings be offset by an increase in health and other costs attributable to a rise in consumption? Or would we find that noncriminal social controls—ranging from taxation and bans on smoking in public places to peer pressure—would reduce use, as they have for cigarette smoking?

16   For hard drugs, a national commission should consider the tradeoffs between medical controls and education, and our current punitive approach. Our investments in increased law enforcement are no longer providing adequate returns. If we reduce our criminal-penal efforts, how much of the savings could be better utilized for education and medical efforts to decrease demand? What is the optimal balance?

17   We must also consider moral and religious issues. Would decriminalization imply society's approval? Is there an overlooked moral dilemma in our penal approach that results, for example, in one in four black males in their 20's being under the control of the criminal justice system?

18   Different strategies might be required in dealing with different sectors of society. An airplane mechanic testified before me that he stopped using cocaine and marijuana when random drug testing was imposed, for fear of losing his job. Should we take greater advantage of alternative forms of control? Would such forms of control help those who may have lost hope for better lives?

19   Many such questions require analysis by economists, scientists, law enforcement specialists, sociologists, ethicists, religious leaders and others.

20   In considering loosening legal controls on narcotics, we must weigh the claim that our inner cities would be devastated against the price we now pay in daily body counts from gunfire. Unthinking acceptance of the current policy is unreasonable. It is time to compile the likely results of different drug policies. Only a national commission can do this. If we are fortunate, a national debate would follow. Perhaps then we could reduce the violence, moral degradation and waste associated with drugs in a more humane, effective and cost-efficient way.

Questions for Review

1. What is the thesis of Weinstein's essay? Does it appear in the essay? If so, where? Is Weinstein's position diametrically opposed to Gramm's? What reasons does Weinstein give for accepting his position?

2. Divide the essay into beginning, middle, and end. What rhetorical and/or stylistic devices help form these divisions?

3. What audience might Weinstein's essay be written for? Is that audience likely to resist his argument? Does Weinstein show respect for those who might disagree with him? Explain.

4. Does this essay take opposing points of view into consideration? If so, are they represented fairly? Are they effectively countered?

5. How would you characterize your attitude toward this subject before reading Weinstein's essay? What effect did this essay have on your thinking?

In our third essay, Jerry Z. Muller writes on the controversial topic of abortion.

JERRY Z. MULLER

THE CONSERVATIVE CASE FOR ABORTION

1   In contemporary American political debate, struggles over abortion are usually treated as conflicts between rival interpretations of individual rights. Those who favor abortion most often invoke the "right to choose" of the woman who has conceived the fetus. Those who oppose abortion focus on the "right to life" of the fetus. But there is a third position that is largely overlooked. Essentially conservative and "pro-family," it favors abortion as the right choice to promote healthy family life under certain circumstances.

2   This argument, which emphasizes the social function of the family over the rights of the individual, begins with the assumption that the possibility of choice matters less than the choices made. It argues that the choice to give birth to a child isn't always the right one. In fact, under some conditions, choosing to give birth may be socially dysfunctional, morally irresponsible or even cruel: inimical to the forces of stability and bourgeois responsibility conservatives cherish.

3   Supporters of middle-class family values may agree with many Christian Coalition positions. They may advocate raising the income-tax deduction for dependent children, question the legitimation of homosexuality and condemn violence and sex in the cultural marketplace. But the right-to-life position undermines their fundamentally conservative effort to strengthen purposeful families. For the right-to-life position requires massive government intrusion into the most intimate of realms, removes decisions about whether to bear children from those who are to raise them and threatens what many conservatives regard as the most significant mediating institution in modern capitalist society, the family. The success of the right-to-life position would lead almost inevitably to an increase in the number of children born into socially dysfunctional settings.

4   The prime obstacle to the right-to-life movement is not feminism. It is the millions of more or less conservative middle-class parents who know that, if their teenage daughters were to become pregnant, they would advise her to get an abortion rather than marry out of necessity or go through the trauma of giving birth and then placing the child up for adoption. Many people—young, unmarried, pregnant women loath to bring a child into a family-less environment; parents of a fetus known to be afflicted by a disease such as Tay-Sachs that will make its life painful and short; parents whose children are likely to be born with severe genetic defects, who know that the birth of the fetus will mean pain for them and for their other children—all choose abortion, not because they fetishize choice but because they value the family. Many couples who know that their offspring will be at risk for genetic diseases and other birth defects owe their actual families to abortion: were it not for the possibility of detecting these diseases in utero and of aborting stricken fetuses, such couples would not risk having children at all.

5   The right-to-life movement regards human "life" as a good—a claim most of us are broadly inclined to accept. But the right-to-life movement goes further. It regards *all* human life as a good, regardless of the mental, emotional or intellectual capacities of the individual. To right-to-lifers, keeping alive anencephalic infants (children missing all or most of their brains) is a moral imperative. The right-to-life movement regards

every degree of human life as equal to the most complete development of human life: that is why the moral status of a fetus two weeks into its development is the same as that of children and adults.

6   For the right-to-life movement, then, human life is not only a good, it is the highest good, and it is always the highest good. The movement's strategic aim is to extend state power to preserve and protect every fetus that is conceived, regardless of the circumstances under which it is conceived, regardless of the condition of the fetus and regardless of the will of the fetus's parents.

7   The right-to-life movement has done our society a service by insisting upon the humanity and moral worth of the unborn child. But opponents of abortion have turned a legitimate moral concern into a moral absolute. They have made biological life not one good to be fought for, but the only good, to which all others must be subordinated. For this reason, anti-abortion activists insist that abortion be forbidden in cases of rape or incest; to suggest there are moral considerations other than those of the life of the fetus is to question the fundamental premises of the right-to-life movement.

8   One of those considerations is the creation and preservation of families. The pro-life movement is at odds with the assumptions of middle-class family formation. These families believe that the bearing and rearing of children is not an inexorable fate but a voluntary vocation, and that, like any other vocation, it is to be pursued methodically using the most effective means available. Such a conception of the family includes planning when children are to be born and how many are to be born. It seeks to increase the chances of successfully socializing and educating children in order to help them find fulfilling work and spiritual lives. The number of children is kept low in part because the amount of parental time and resources devoted to raising them is expected to be high.

9   This depiction of the middle-class family as a vocation borrows from the characterization of economic activity as a vocation in Weber's *The Protestant Ethic and the Spirit of Capitalism.* Weber argued that a key element in the rise of capitalism was a notion of economic activity as purposeful. This notion motivated those most active in capitalist economic activity, providing an alternative to traditional, fatalistic conceptions of economic life. Just as older patterns of economic traditionalism and fatalism persist within advanced industrial societies, fatalistic conceptions of family life remain as well, in which families are not consciously "made" but "happen" because fate has so decreed.

10   Declining fertility is universal among advanced industrial societies. Beginning in the European bourgeois family, fertility was consciously curtailed by contraception or abortion when the desired and limited number of children was reached. By the late nineteenth century, marriage in Europe was increasingly postponed until a decade or more after puberty, and one or another form of contraception allowed greater control over the timing and spacing of births.

11   The technological repertoire of today's family planning includes abortion to prevent out-of-wedlock childbirth, artificial contraception within marriage and voluntary sterilization when families have reached their desired size. This activist conception of family formation also suggests that artificial reproductive technology should be used to reverse infertility. Prenatal screening is part of the package: potential children known to carry debilitating diseases may be aborted to make possible the birth of children more likely to grow into healthy, productive adulthood. Given the assumptions of middle-class family formation, ignoring such technological possibilities can even be regarded as a form of child neglect.

12   This middle-class vision of the family is linked to other elements of modern life. It is a conception that those who seek to conserve modern society ought to fortify rather than undermine. It is under attack from many quarters, including the individualism and

hedonism of much of our popular and elite culture and the emphasis on career advancement among both men and women. But it is also threatened from another direction by the right-to-life movement.

13   The struggle between the ideals of middle-class family formation and more fatalistic conceptions of family life is in part a struggle between groups in our society with divergent conceptions of rational, purposeful behavior. Members of the upper middle class are usually either the product of families with a rational, purposeful, planned view of domestic life or have adopted such behavior on their own. It is no coincidence that the Evangelical Protestant denominations that most vociferously oppose abortion draw disproportionately from the lower middle and working classes, emphasize faith as the antidote to fate and stress redemption through divine grace rather than through a lifetime of purposeful activity.

14   The ideology of middle-class family formation maintains that families are not just another lifestyle option but an essential part of a modern society. Illegitimacy is stigmatized because it is socially dysfunctional. Conservatives have long assured that government should promote those social norms that encourage the creation of decent men and women and discourage those that experience has shown to be harmful. This logic lies at the heart of conservative debates on public policy, including recent proposals to reform welfare to discourage out-of-wedlock births.

15   The right-to-life movement stands as a barrier to such reform. The removal of government subsidies for the bearing of out-of-wedlock children, it is said, will create an incentive for pregnant teenagers and other pregnant unmarried women to resort more frequently to abortion. Though the claim is most often articulated by pro-life opponents of welfare reform, it is also an unarticulated premise of many who favor the elimination of welfare payments to unwed mothers.

16   Is it more important to minimize abortion or to minimize the birth of children to women who are unprepared to provide the familial structure needed for children to become stable and responsible adults? A growing consensus holds that unsocialized children are at the heart of our social deterioration, not only because they are more likely to engage in violent and criminal activity, but because they lack the discipline needed to learn in school and to function in the workplace. The socializing influence of the family—comprising husbands and wives in ongoing union and with a commitment to child-rearing—appears to be an essential element of any solution. If these assumptions are correct, as conservatives and many liberals now believe, the trade-off is more biological lives at the cost of more unsocialized children—making people versus making people moral.

17   Opposition to the elimination of welfare payments of out-of-wedlock children comes from two quarters: the pro-choice movement and the right-to-life movement. The former condemns "welfare caps" because they reduce the choices facing women, and all choices are to be protected. In the words of liberal feminist Iris Young, "A liberal society that claims to respect the autonomy of all its citizens equally should affirm the freedom of all its citizens to bear and rear children, whether they are married or not, whether they have high incomes or not." For the right-to-life movement, of course, no fact about the potentially miserable outcome of the fetus's birth affects the imperative that it be born. Beginning from different commitments, therefore, feminists and pro-lifers converge in rejecting the conservative assumption that the troubling social effects of out-of-wedlock births justify government attempts to limit them.

18   The current right-to-life strategy calls for "chipping away" at the liberal abortion culture to "save" as many babies as possible under the political circumstances. Because pro-lifers can have the greatest impact on legislation affecting the poor, the socially marginal

and those dependent on governmental funding for medical procedures, among their first targets have been, for example, Medicaid recipients. As a result, the success of the pro-life movement is now measured in the lives of poor children born out of wedlock. Most abortions in the U.S. occur to avoid the birth of children out of wedlock. Of the roughly 1.5 million abortions in 1991, only 271,000 were performed upon married women. Among married women, there were eight abortions for every ninety births; among unmarried women, there were forty-eight abortions for every forty-five births. All else being equal, then, eliminating the possibility of abortion would hike the number of out-of-wedlock births from its already disastrous level of 30 percent to 49 percent.

19   Indeed, the anti-abortion movement may already have helped increase the number of children born out of wedlock. The percentage of out-of-wedlock births in the United States rose from 18.4 percent in 1980 to 30.1 percent of all births in 1992, according to recent reports from the National Center for Health Statistics. During the same period, the proportion of non-marital pregnancies ending in abortion declined, from 60 percent in 1980 to 46 percent in 1991, and the abortion rate among married women fell by 12 percent. Thirty percent of these mothers were teenagers. The statistics on all potential mothers aged 15 to 17, those least able to care adequately for their children, are more alarming still. In the years from 1986 to 1991 the pregnancy rate for this group rose by 7 percent, but the abortion rate dropped by 19 percent, so that the rate of out-of-wedlock births among these very young mothers increased by 27 percent. This trend toward out-of-wedlock births rather than abortion may be due either to the increased difficulty of obtaining abortions or to increased preference for carrying babies to term. Either way, it marks a partial victory for the pro-life movement.

20   The second thrust of the current right-to-life strategy is the prohibition of abortion late in pregnancy, on the plausible assumption that even those with doubts about prohibiting abortion entirely regard the fetus as subject to ever greater respect as it develops. Here, too, the effect is tragic. Late-term abortions are rare, and, when they do occur, it is frequently because the parents have discovered late that their prospective child suffers from a serious birth defect or malformation. Yet it is these fetuses whom the pro-life movement now aims to "save." A bill now before Congress tries to force women to give birth to such babies. Titled the Partial-Birth Abortion Ban Act by its sponsors, it would be better dubbed the Cruelty to Families Act.

21   The public is genuinely ambivalent on the question of abortion. It adheres to the tenets of middle-class family life, yet without hearing those tenets articulated. To focus on the conflict between the right-to-life movement and middle-class family values is to call into question the terms in which the abortion debate is usually cast in our political culture. The abortion struggle should be understood as a three-way debate: among liberals, who believe that to let each of us do as we like will work out for the best; pro-lifers, who cling to one ultimate good at the expense of all others; and those committed to conserving middle-class families, sometimes at the expense of "choice," sometimes at the expense of "life." The third group lays best claim to the title "conservative."

Questions for Review

1. What is the thesis of Muller's essay? Does it appear in the essay? If so, where? What reasons does Muller give for accepting his position?

2. Divide the essay into beginning, middle, and end. What rhetorical and/or stylistic devices help form these divisions?

3. What audience might Muller's essay be written for? Is that audience likely to resist his argument? Does Muller show respect for those who might disagree with him? Explain.

4. Does this essay take opposing points of view into consideration? If so, are they represented fairly? Are they effectively countered?

5. How would you characterize your attitude toward this subject before reading Muller's essay? What effect did this essay have on your thinking?

In our fourth sample essay, Susan Jacoby deals with some of the difficult issues surrounding what has come to be called date rape.

SUSAN JACOBY

COMMON DECENCY

1   She was deeply in love with a man who was treating her badly. To assuage her wounded ego (and to prove to herself that she could get along nicely without him), she invited another man, an old boyfriend, to a dinner *à deux* in her apartment. They were on their way to the bedroom when, having realized that she wanted only the man who wasn't there, she changed her mind. Her ex-boyfriend was understandably angry. He left her apartment with a not-so-politely phrased request that she leave him out of any future plans.

2   And that is the end of the story—except for the fact that he was eventually kind enough to accept her apology for what was surely a classic case of "mixed signals."

3   I often recall this incident, in which I was the embarrassed female participant, as the controversy over "date rape" . . . heats up across the nation. What seems clear to me is that those who place acquaintance rape in a different category from "stranger rape"—those who excuse friendly social rapists on grounds that they are too dumb to understand when no means no—are being even more insulting to men than to women.

4   These apologists for date rape—and some of them are women—are really saying that the average man cannot be trusted to exercise any impulse control. Men are nasty and men are brutes—and a woman must be constantly on her guard to avoid giving a man any excuse to give way to his baser instincts.

5   If this view were accurate, few women would manage to get through life without being raped, and few men would fail to commit rape. For the reality is that all of us, men as well as women, send and receive innumerable mixed signals in the course of our sexual lives—and that is as true in marital beds at age 50 as in the back seats of cars at age 15.

6   Most men somehow manage to decode these signals without using superior physical strength to force themselves on their partners. And most women manage to handle conflicting male signals without, say, picking up carving knives to demonstrate their displeasure at sexual rejection. This is called civilization.

7   Civilized is exactly what my old boyfriend was being when he didn't use my mud-dleheaded emotional distress as an excuse to rape me. But I don't owe him excessive gratitude for his decent behavior—any more than he would have owed me special thanks for not stabbing him through the heart if our situations had been reversed. Most date rapes do not happen because a man honestly mistakes a woman's "no" for a "yes" or a "maybe." They occur because a minority of men—an ugly minority, to be sure—can't stand to take "no" for an answer.

8   This minority behavior—and a culture that excuses it on grounds that boys will be boys—is the target of the movement against date rape that has surfaced on many campuses during the past year.

9   It's not surprising that date rape is an issue of particular importance to college-age women. The campus concentration of large numbers of young people, in an unsu-pervised environment that encourages drinking and partying, tends to promote sexual aggression and discourage inhibition. Drunken young men who rape a woman at a party can always claim they didn't know what they were doing—and a great many people will blame the victim for having been there in the first place.

10   That is the line adopted by antifeminists like Camille Paglia, author of the contro-versial *Sexual Personae: Art and Decadence from Nefertiti to Emily Dickinson.* Paglia, whose views strongly resemble those expounded 20 years ago by Norman Mailer in *The Prisoner of Sex,* argues that feminists have deluded women by telling them they can go anywhere and do anything without fear of rape. Feminism, in this view, is both naive and antisexual because it ignores the power of women to incite uncontrollable male passions.

11   Just to make sure there is no doubt about a woman's place, Paglia also links the male sexual aggression that leads to rape with the creative energy of art. "There is no female Mozart," she has declared, "because there is no female Jack the Ripper." Ac-cording to this "logic," one might expect to discover the next generation of composers in fraternity houses and dorms that have been singled out as sites of brutal gang rapes.

12   This type of unsubtle analysis makes no distinction between sex as an expression of the will to power and sex as a source of pleasure. When domination is seen as an in-evitable component of sex, the act of rape is defined not by a man's actions but by a woman's signals.

13   It is true, of course, that some women (especially the young) initially resist sex not out of real conviction but as part of the elaborate persuasion and seduction rituals ac-companying what was once called courtship. And it is true that many men (again, es-pecially the young) take pride in the ability to coax a woman a step further than she intended to go.

14   But these mating rituals do not justify or even explain date rape. Even the most callow youth is capable of understanding the difference between resistance and gen-uine fear; between a halfhearted "no, we shouldn't" and tears or screams; between a woman who is physically free to leave a room and one who is being physically restrained.

15   The immorality and absurdity of using mixed signals as an excuse for rape is cast in high relief when the assault involves one woman and a group of men. In cases of gang rape in a social setting (usually during or after a party), the defendants and their lawyers frequently claim that group sex took place but no force was involved. These up-right young men, so the defense invariably contends, were confused because the girl had voluntarily gone to a party with them. Why, she may have even displayed sexual in-terest in *one* of them. How could they have been expected to understand that she didn't wish to have sex with the whole group?

16   The very existence of the term "date rape" attests to a slow change in women's consciousness that began with the feminist movement of the late 1960's. Implicit in this consciousness is the conviction that a woman has the right to say no at any point

in the process leading to sexual intercourse—and that a man who fails to respect her wishes should incur serious legal and social consequences.

17   The other, equally important half of the equation is respect for men. If mixed signals are the real cause of sexual assault, it behooves every woman to regard every man as a potential rapist.

18   In such a benighted universe, it would be impossible for a woman (and, let us not forget, for a man) to engage in the tentative emotional and physical exploration that eventually produces a mature erotic life. She would have to make up her mind right from the start in order to prevent a rampaging male from misreading her intentions.

19   Fortunately for everyone, neither the character of men nor the general quality of relations between the sexes is that crude. By censuring the minority of men who use ordinary socializing as an excuse for rape, feminists insist on sex as a source of pure pleasure rather than as a means of social control. Real men want an eager sexual partner—not a woman who is quaking with fear or even one who is ambivalent. Real men don't rape.

Questions for Review

1. What is the thesis of Jacoby's essay? Does it appear in the essay? If so, where? What reasons does she give for accepting her position?
2. Divide the essay into beginning, middle, and end. What rhetorical and/or stylistic devices help form these divisions?
3. What audience might Jacoby's essay be written for? Is that audience likely to resist her argument? Does Jacoby show respect for those who might disagree with her? Explain.
4. Does this essay take opposing points of view into consideration? If so, are they represented fairly? Are they effectively countered?
5. How would you characterize your attitude toward this subject before reading Jacoby's essay? What effect did this essay have on your thinking?

Our last sample essay was written by Heather Cully, a first-year student at the University of North Carolina at Charlotte (UNC–Charlotte). Her essay deals with an issue that has been the cause of much debate in North Carolina—the law, passed in 1997, that raised the legal driving age in the state.

HEATHER CULLY

THE AGE REQUIREMENT FOR TEEN DRIVERS

1   Wham! Boom! These were the sounds that I heard as I glanced at my rearview mirror, only to see two cars piled on top of each other. One of the cars was driven by an

older woman and the other car was driven by a young teenager. It looked as though the teen driver was not paying attention and ran into the stopped vehicle in front of him.

2   This accident is only one of the thousands that are caused by teen drivers each year. Until very recently, our procedures for granting drivers licenses have been partly responsible for these deaths. In the past, North Carolina has allowed teens to apply for a learner's permit at the age of fifteen. They could then apply for an unrestricted driver's license on their sixteenth birthdays. In order to qualify for this right, teens only had to complete a state approved drivers' education course, usually offered at their high schools. However, effective December, 1997, teens must hold a learner's permit for a full year. Then they can be granted a day-time driver's license, which they must keep for six months. Then, and only then, are they permitted to obtain an unrestricted driver's license. Theoretically, teens can apply for a learner's permit at the age of fifteen, in which case the new procedure would result in only an additional six months to obtain an unrestricted license. However, since it is necessary to complete a driver's education course before obtaining a learner's permit and since the schools are unable to provide this course to most teens before they are fifteen, the effect is to push back the time when teens can be fully licensed; in many cases, teens are at or near their seventeenth birthdays before being eligible for an unrestricted driver's license. Many teens and some parents have objected loudly to this change. However, I feel we should all support this new law. It is an excellent policy that will make our roads safer.

3   Driving an automobile is an inherently dangerous activity. According to the National Highway Traffic Safety Administration, in 1997, automobile crashes took the lives of 41,967 people in the United States (*Traffic* par. 5). As a licensed driver, you must take the responsibility for the actions and decisions that you make while driving. Otherwise you could be one of far too many teens responsible for a highway death. NHTSA statistics for 1996 show that while teenagers (15–20) "make up only seven percent of the driving population, they are involved in 14 percent of all traffic fatalities" (*Saving* par. 2). The statistics for 1997 are equally tragic: "Compared with the fatality rate for drivers 25 through 69 years old, the rate for teenage drivers is about 4 times as high, . . . " (*Traffic* par. 54). What accounts for these deaths? According to the NHTSA report issued in 1997, teenagers are deadly drivers because of their inexperience and their tendency to take risks (*Saving* par. 3).

4   In my experience, teen drivers see driving as fun and do not take it seriously enough. At sixteen, they don't have the necessary maturity to do so. Maturity is a key to safe driving. Mature drivers are cautious and abide by the rules of the road. Many young teens, however, get caught up in playing practical jokes and racing each other while they are driving. For example, some teens in South Carolina recently thought that it would be fun to steal a stop sign in their neighborhood. That "fun" cost another driver's life when he was hit going through the intersection where the sign had been stolen. Those teens are now having to face imprisonment and just as importantly, they have to face the fact that their joke caused an innocent person to die.

5   Experience makes a good driver. The more experience you have, the more you come into contact with different situations and know how to handle them. Experience allows the driver to be prepared for situations that may occur. It keeps the driver "on his toes" and allows him to be aware of not only the mistakes he might make but also those that other drivers may make. Young teens do not have this experience, and thus they are at greater risk for accident, injury, and death. The increased age requirement will allow teen drivers more time for much needed experience since they will be required to spend a longer time driving with a learner's permit. This will give teens the opportunity to practice their driving skills with adult supervision before they are allowed to drive on their own. In Ontario, Canada and in New Zealand, where gradu-

ated licensing systems have been employed, injuries and deaths to teen drivers have decreased. In the U.S. both Maryland and California have introduced new restrictions on drivers and have already seen declines in the numbers of deaths and injuries for teen drivers (National Highway Traffic Safety Administration, *Saving* par. 5).

6 There will be an additional benefit from this new law. Our current high insurance rates reflect the high number of accidents we now have. If the accident rate drops, then our insurance rates will drop. Some of us who may not have been in an accident also have to pay high rates because of the high number of accidents that happen on a daily basis. As a teen, I've had to pay a high insurance rate because I am labeled as an "inexperienced driver." When the percentage of accidents caused by teens goes down, then insurance rates for teens will go down accordingly.

7 Teens who will be turning sixteen after December of 1997 may feel that this new requirement is unfair. They may feel that this will cut into their social lives and their dating lives. However, they should not look at this change with a negative attitude. Teens need to realize that there are more and more drivers on these busy roads every day. With dramatic increases in population, more and more experience is needed to drive safely. The bottom line is that the state is trying to save the lives of these teens so that they can continue to have social lives for many years to come.

8 Parents of teens may also feel that this new age requirement will be an inconvenience to them. Parents will have to find more time in their busy schedules to make sure that their teens get from one place to another. However, parents should take comfort in the fact that their teens will be in the hands of an experienced driver, like themselves, rather than in the hands of an inexperienced teen driver who is at high risk of an accident. It's worth a little inconvenience to have this peace of mind.

9 This, then, is a law that we can all live with. We can live with it because it will produce more experienced, mature, and responsible drivers. We can live with it because it will save us money. But most of all, more of us *will* live with it.

WORKS CITED

National Highway Traffic Safety Administration. *Saving Teenage Lives.* 25 Oct. 1998. <http://www.nhtsa.dot.gov/people/injury/newdriver/SaveTeens/sect1.html>.

---. *Traffic Safety Facts.* 25 Oct. 1998. <http://www.nhtsa.dot.gov/people/ncsa/ovrfacts.html>.

Questions for Review

1. What is the thesis of Heather's essay? Does it appear in the essay? If so, where? What reasons does she give for accepting her position?
2. Divide the essay into beginning, middle, and end. What rhetorical and/or stylistic devices help form these divisions?
3. What audience might Heather's essay be written for? Is that audience likely to resist her argument? Does Heather show respect for those who might disagree with her? Explain.

4. Does this essay take opposing points of view into consideration? If so, are they represented fairly? Are they effectively countered?
5. How would you characterize your attitude toward this subject before reading Heather's essay? What effect did this essay have on your thinking?

THE RHETORICAL TRIANGLE

READER

A position essay addresses readers who take the other side of the argument. The writer's goal is to show these readers how a reasonable person could take the position the writer is arguing for. Note that we are not suggesting that a writer should aim to convince readers to change their minds and accept the writer's position on an issue. No one changes anybody else's mind, at least not by means of one brief piece of writing. The writer can provide information that may be helpful if the reader is interested in examining a position. In the final analysis, however, any change of mind will take place over a long period of time and will involve the reader's will and emotion; it will not occur as the direct result of the power of any arguments a writer may make in one paper. Still, if arguments are couched in such a way as to seem fair and reasonable, they may play a role in the evolution of a reader's thinking. If they seem illogical or strident, they will likely be rejected out of hand—if they are read at all.

We may seem to be undervaluing the power of reason and logic, but there is logic to what we are saying. If reason and logic were sufficient to make people form and change beliefs, then—assuming that all of us are reasonable people—reason would lead us all to the same set of beliefs. Since eminently reasonable and intelligent people disagree about many issues, there must be more involved than reason. Otherwise, we could all reduce our thinking to the kind of formulaic principles used by the famous Spock character in the *Star Trek* movies.

READER AS OPPOSITION

Your task in writing a position essay is to lay out your thinking in such a way as to help your readers see how a sensible person could take a point of view different from theirs. In this situation, your readers' role is to resist you and thereby help sharpen your argument. Just as a knife is sharpened by rubbing it against a sharpener, your argument can be strengthened if you make every effort to counter the points you think opposing readers would make against it. In the end, all you ask of readers is that they hear you out and attempt to understand your reasoning.

SUBJECT

The subject for a position paper should be one about which sensible people can disagree. It would not be worthwhile to write a position paper arguing that human life is precious or that the use of addictive drugs such as cocaine or heroin is harmful. Most of us can readily agree to these assertions; in fact, most of us would not consider it sensible for a person to disagree with these positions.

However, a close look at these issues will reveal ways in which you can frame arguable topics dealing with them. For example, you could take the position that in certain cases the lives of those already born must take precedence over the lives of those not yet born. This is essentially the position that Jerry Z. Muller takes in his essay, "The Conservative Case for Abortion." Similarly, you could take the position that we should consider decriminalizing certain drugs, an argument made by Jack B. Weinstein in "The War on Drugs Is Self-Defeating."

Exercise 9.1

As you saw in the first two sample essays of this chapter, Phil Gramm and Jack B. Weinstein take very different positions on the issue of how we should go about combating the use of drugs in society. Despite their differences, these writers would agree on a number of issues relating to drugs. For example, both would probably agree that hard drugs, such as cocaine, are bad for the individuals who use them and for society in general.

Keeping this observation in mind, read three other essays that defend an argument (essays you choose or essays provided by your teacher), and respond to the questions below for each essay:

1. What would be the thesis of an essay written in opposition to this essay?
2. What points might the writer of this essay and the writer of an opposing argument agree on?

One final note about topic selection: You do not have to write about a subject of national importance, such as abortion or drug laws. You may well choose a topic of local interest. For example, you may care about campus issues, such as raising the tuition at your school, increasing the number of parking spaces for students, or increasing (decreasing) support for athletic teams. Other issues may be regional: Your state may be considering whether to institute a lottery or to remove unenforced laws (having to do with adultery, homosexuality, or the like). Heather Cully's essay, "The Age Requirement for Teen Drivers," is a good example of a regional essay, since North Carolina recently passed a law raising the legal age for obtaining a driver's license.

The benefits of dealing with a local or regional issue are obvious: You will no doubt be interested in such issues if they affect you directly, and you should not have much difficulty finding information on them. Be careful, however, to choose issues that are indeed arguable—that is, that sensible people can disagree about. Also, be aware that many local issues, such as traffic problems on campus, lend themselves more readily to problem/solution essays than to position essays. (If you are considering writing about a local matter, you may want to read Chapter 11 to determine whether your topic is better suited to a problem/solution format.)

WRITER

According to Aristotle, there are three basic means of persuading. He labeled them ethos, logos, and pathos. *Ethos,* or ethical appeal, is the writer's credibility; *logos,* or logical appeal, is reasoned argument; *pathos,* or pathetic appeal, is emotional argument. In practice, it is often impossible to separate these types of persuasion. For example, if a writer offers an argument that is seriously flawed in its logic, he at once undermines his rational argument and his credibility. But for purposes of discussion, we will consider these as three different avenues of persuasion.

As we envision the position essay, the writer's credibility (ethical appeal) is very important. It is important because the writer's goal in this type of essay is to help the reader gain respect for someone who holds a position diametrically opposed to his. As we will see, the writer's logic is important, but logos without ethos will not be successful in this assignment. To achieve ethos, the writer must prove that he is knowledgeable, engaged, and fair.

KNOWLEDGE

The writer of a position essay must know a great deal about his topic. It helps, of course, if he is a U.S. senator (such as Gramm) or a state supreme court judge (such as Weinstein). Readers are likely to assume that people in such positions bring a certain amount of knowledge to the topics they write about, especially if those topics are related to their professional expertise. However, you do not need to hold such a position of authority to speak with authority about the topic you have chosen. Look, for example, at the essay written by Emily Weast, "Learning about Sex" (pp. 360–362). Emily makes no claims to expertise in matters of school curriculum, but her obvious interest in the subject of sex education in the schools allows her to write from a position of knowledge and authority. Likewise, Heather Cully ("The Age Requirement for Teen Drivers") took the time to make herself knowledgeable about her topic.

In argumentative writing, it is assumed that the writer will get the facts right. Of course, facts do not convince readers by themselves. Two people can agree on the number of people in the United States who are addicted to hard drugs without agreeing on the steps government should take to combat drugs. However, a writer completely undermines himself if he is not in possession of relevant facts or if he presents as fact information with which the reader will disagree.

Exercise 9.2

Look back to three of the essays at the beginning of this chapter (or essays that your instructor chooses). Identify any instances in which the writer presents as fact information with which someone opposing his or her argument might disagree. Also identify instances in which these authors could have used more facts to support their arguments. How would their arguments be strengthened by the use of more facts?

ENGAGEMENT

An engaged writer has a much better chance of drawing readers into her topic. To be engaged in her writing, the writer must care about her subject. Much of the writing that lacks this quality treats subjects we have all seen over and over again. There is nothing wrong with writing about these subjects; but, if writers aren't really interested in their topics, they tend to speak in general terms, saying the same things so many other people have said. There is no specific detail and no personal experience.

Such essays present a stark contrast to the kind of writing represented in the essays in this chapter. It is clear that Heather and Emily have a genuine interest in their topics. Heather is a new driver who has given much thought to the issue of what makes for safety in driving. Emily is a young person who sees the dangers ignorance about human sexuality poses for young people. As the daughter of two teachers, she is also knowledgeable about the system of public education in the United States. We do not mean to suggest that engagement requires that you have personal experience with the subject, but you must find a way to engage yourself with and get below the surface of your subject. This is precisely what Emily has done in the various revisions of her paper. When she started, she had an opinion on her topic, but she did not have a great deal of information about it. Her research both confirmed parts of her original opinion and modified her thinking on this complicated issue.

FAIRNESS

The writer of a position essay must be sure that his involvement with the topic does not impair his ability to see the issue from the perspective of the reader. That is, the writer's interest must not blind him to the work that has to be done in writing about this topic. For example, a writer's interest in affirmative action could grow out of a personal experience of having been denied a certain job. If the pain the writer experienced in that situation makes it impossible for him to imagine why anyone would be in favor of affirmative action, then he is too close to this topic to write about it. To examine your feelings about a possible topic for a position paper, try to sketch what an argument for your opposition might look like. It will be crucial that you counter the arguments the other side is likely to make. If you find that it's impossible to imagine how that side would argue, you may have difficulty writing about the topic.

In countering the arguments of the opposition, it is neither necessary nor desirable to show disdain for either the arguments or those who would offer them. Rather, the writer should let the reader know that he understands that a sensible person could hold a position on this topic that is different from his. Finally, however, the writer has to show why the opposing argument does not convince him.

Two essays in this book illustrate the point we are making. Earlier in this chapter, in "The Conservative Case for Abortion," Jerry Z. Muller notes that the "right-to-life movement regards human 'life' as a good—a claim most of us are broadly inclined to accept" (paragraph 5). Later, he says that "the right-to-life movement has done our society a service by insisting upon the humanity and moral worth of the unborn child" (paragraph 7). Muller indicates that he understands the claim made by his opponents that human life is a treasure that should be protected and guarded carefully. But then he counters that there are other treasures that might, in certain circumstances, take precedence over the human life of an unborn child—namely, "the creation and preservation of families" (paragraph 8).

Those who disagree with Muller will likely counter that he doesn't fully understand the worth of human life or that he doesn't understand the moral imperatives against taking any human life. But they are not likely to feel that he has misstated their argument or that he has labeled them as irrational or evil. When Muller says, in paragraph 6, that members of the right-to-life movement see human life as "the highest good, and [. . .] always the highest good," he is saying what they would say of themselves. Even in his harshest criticism of right-to-lifers (paragraph 7), Muller does not say anything that seems untrue from their perspective. If we had to imagine how they might respond to the statements made there, we would guess that they would say that it is not they, but rather God, who has made "biological life not one good to be fought for, but the only good, to which all others must be subordinated" (paragraph 7). Perhaps they would also suggest that the second "only good" be changed to "overriding good."

Our point here is that Muller has started a conversation with those opposed to his point of view. They will want to counter what he is saying, but they do not have to begin by showing how he has completely missed or willfully ignored their arguments.

This is not the case with a second essay dealing with this topic, "Dismemberment and Choice," by Michael R. Heaphy (see Chapter 10, pp. 364–366). In his essay, Heaphy completely undermines any chance of real conversation with those who take an opposing view to his by referring to a physician who performs abortions as "an expert at killing human fetuses at five and six months' gestation" (paragraph 5). He continues to assault those who take an opposing point of view, ending with this caustic statement in his conclusion: "At present, good people in America are working to undo a decree that has transformed an entire class of human beings into constitutional outlaws suitable for discretionary killing."

Heaphy's essay is very powerful and likely to be quite effective in achieving the purpose he has in mind. But it is clear that he does not intend to have a conversation with those who would disagree with him. Heaphy has decided that the issue of abortion is not one on which sensible people can disagree—at least, not if they know the facts. Thus, he is not worried about the loss of ethical appeal that will result in calling those who perform abortions "killers," because his essay is not intended for such an audience—or if it is, it is intended as an attack rather than an attempt at conversation.

Exercise 9.3

In talking about fairness, we compared an essay presented at the beginning of this chapter, "The Conservative Case for Abortion," with an essay presented at the beginning of Chapter 10, "Dismemberment and Choice." Two other essays in these two chapters also deal with a common topic—date rape. Compare the attitude that Susan Jacoby ("Common Decency," pp. 319–321) exhibits toward those who would disagree with her with the attitude that Camille Paglia ("Rape and Modern Sex War," pp. 367–370) takes toward those who would disagree with her. Do these writers seem to indicate that a sensible person could disagree with them? Point to specific passages that support your answer.

DISTINGUISHING FEATURES OF POSITION ESSAYS
LOGICAL ARGUMENTS

The primary distinguishing feature of a position essay is the writer's logical argumentation. Although you may well write persuasively (in ways we will discuss in Chapter 10), the thrust of your essay will be to offer readers logical support for your point of view. You will make your thesis clear and then offer your readers ample support for your position.

Given an argumentative thesis, there are two basic means of supporting a position: You can link the thesis to a key value you espouse, or you can offer an analysis of causes. For example, given the thesis that the United States should not consider legalizing any drugs, how could you proceed? You could offer readers a statement of value, something like "Drugs are an inherent evil that any self-respecting society should oppose." Or you could focus on causality, as in the assertion "Legalizing drugs would cause more people to abuse drugs, thereby hurting themselves and, by extension, the entire society."

Figures 9.1 and 9.2 illustrate these two possible foundations of a position essay.

FIGURE 9.1   Argumentative Thesis Supported by a Value Statement

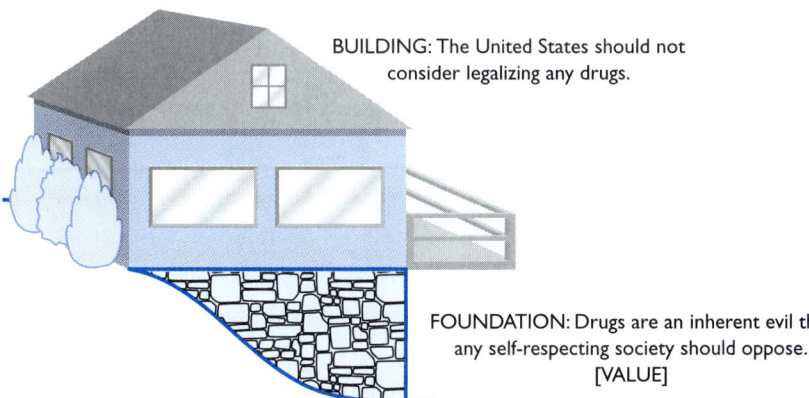

BUILDING: The United States should not consider legalizing any drugs.

FOUNDATION: Drugs are an inherent evil that any self-respecting society should oppose. [VALUE]

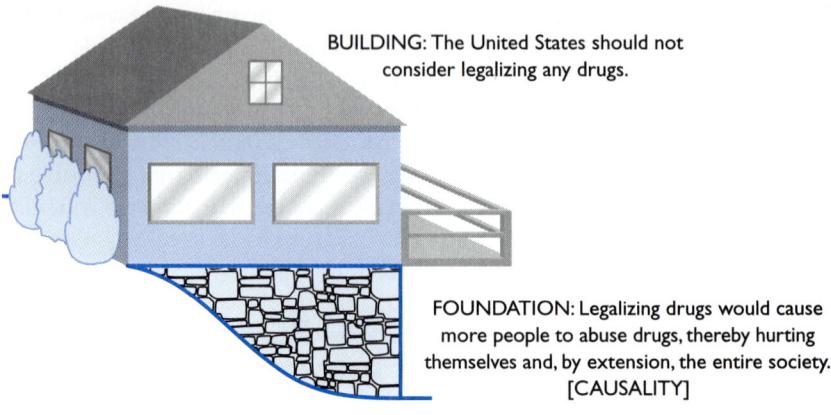

FIGURE 9.2   Argumentative Thesis Supported by an Analysis of Causes

Exercise 9.4

Examine three of the sample essays from the beginning of this chapter (or essays chosen by your teacher). What is the thesis of each essay? What claim(s) does each thesis rest on? Explain.

If we wanted to argue that we should have stronger gun-control laws, we could support our thesis with a claim such as (1) individual safety is a *good* to be chosen over other *goods* (such as individual freedom) or (2) stricter gun-control laws will *cause* an increase in the safety of individuals in this society. Of course, neither statement is a self-evident truth; both need support if the reader is to understand why the writer offers them as reasons for stronger gun-control laws.

TYPES OF LOGICAL SUPPORTS

APPEALS TO AUTHORITY   As children, when we wanted our siblings to understand why they should do what we told them to do, we often resorted to authority: "Mommy said you'd better . . . ." We knew it would mean something to our siblings if we could convince them that what we were saying carried the authority of a parent.

Appeals to authority are also a mainstay of adult argumentation. To support claims that the city council should spend tax dollars on a sports team, proponents offer testimony by an expert economist who explains the potential benefits to the city in terms of increased revenues from fans coming to see the team play. To support claims that drugs should remain illegal, advocates offer testimony of leading religious leaders or quotations from holy books that indicate that these substances are inherently immoral.

Appeals to authority are different from the other types of support we will discuss because they focus not on *why* one is making a claim but on *who* is making this claim. If someone says, for instance, that drugs are immoral and we ask why, that person may well answer with a *who* response: "Because my minister (or spiritual teacher or church or synagogue or holy book) says that drugs are immoral." We entrust a lot of our lives to the assumptions that come with our religious, moral, or ethical heritages. We accept the truths that come to us in this way without empirical or scientific proofs; we do not attempt to move beyond these authorities to ask why.

Of course, such reasoning will not be convincing to those who have a different set of religious teachers and values. So, arguments resting on competing authoritative assertions of value and opinion often grind to a halt when these authorities clash with one another.

Arguments in which authority figures are used to establish the accuracy of facts and figures and causal analyses are in danger of suffering the same fate. In what has come to be a cliché, the defense attorney brings in an expert witness to say that the defendant is not responsible for the criminal action because the defendant had a horrible childhood, which led to a type of insanity that ultimately led to the crime's being committed. But the prosecutor brings in an expert witness who says that even though the defendant's childhood was indeed horrible, this childhood was not the *cause* of the criminal action, and thus the defendant should be held responsible for that action.

Will the two lawyers leave it at that? Probably not. Often, when two authorities present differing views of what caused a defendant to behave in a certain way, each side will attempt to show that its authority is more of an expert in these matters than the other. Perhaps one authority teaches at a more prestigious university, has a national following of psychologists who can testify to her expertise, or has been an expert witness in hundreds of similar court cases. In other words, the attorneys can argue over which authority is more likely to assess the situation correctly.

Exercise 9.5

Examine the supports for the two sample essays dealing with drug laws: "Don't Let Judges Set Crooks Free" and "The War on Drugs Is Self-Defeating" (see pp. 310–314). What kinds of authorities do these two essays appeal to? Which essay makes more use of appeals to authority? Why do you think it does? Is this an effective strategy?

It should be clear that appeals to authority have their limitations. They are most effective when they are used in combination with other types of supporting evidence, such as facts and figures, opinions, examples, and personal experience.

FACTS AND FIGURES   By *facts*, we mean events or actions that are verifiable. When we say, "It's a fact," we should be able to offer proof that is undeniable. It is a fact that water boils at 212 degrees Fahrenheit. How do we know? We heat water to 212 degrees Fahrenheit and watch it. In this case, the statement of fact lends itself to what we call *empirical* verification; we can see—or, to use a more scientific term, *observe*—its truth. Other facts have to be verified by means of historical record or statements from authorities. Thus, you can "prove" that there were inhabitants in North America before Columbus arrived by researching the historical record. You can establish the fact that light travels at a speed of 186,000 miles per second by resorting to the testimony of experts who have the resources to do the empirical tests that establish this fact.

Figures, or statistics, are a bit more complicated than facts. The truism that just about anything can be proved with statistics points to the difficulty involved in connecting statistics to the claims you want to make. You must remember that statistics do not prove anything by themselves. However, with other supports, they can be an important ingredient in argumentative writing. Statistics may be as simple as a listing of the numbers of men and women enrolled in a given college or as complicated as the data given in support of DNA testing in a court of law. But simple statistics are often more effective than complicated statistics. The writer has enough of a burden in helping his readers understand the relevance of statistics to his claim without also having to explain how the statistics were obtained and to convince readers of their correctness.

Nevertheless, statistics can be very useful tools in argumentation. For example, if you know that a new law has resulted in 800 additional penal years for a certain class of drug offenders ("The War on Drugs Is Self-Defeating"), you have valuable statistical support for your claim that current drug laws are leading to intolerable crowding in the penal system.

OPINION STATEMENTS   Although there are various types of opinion statements, as we will see, in general, opinion statements are assertions that cannot be tested empirically or established as fact by reference to historical documentation. It may seem that a position essay should contain only one opinion statement and a host of facts, statistics, and examples in support of that opinion. But that is not the way we argue—or think, for that matter.

As a simple example, imagine that we want to argue that Alfred should be elected class president. We might offer as support for our claim the opinion that Alfred is a disciplined person. If we think it necessary—as it probably is—we can offer facts in support of this opinion: Alfred made the honor role; he established a record for the mile run at the school; and so forth. Our opinion statement (that he is a disciplined person) connects our facts about his performance in academics and athletics to our predictions about his performance as class president: We predict that the same discipline that led to his achievements in these areas will lead to achievements as class president.

Since opinion statements are crucial in argumentation, it is important that we dispel the myth that one opinion is as good as another. You may hear friends and acquaintances offer their opinions in such a way as to imply that in calling something an opinion, they immediately remove any need or possibility of evaluating that statement. In certain cases, this is true. There are at least three different kinds of opinions, represented by these three statements:

1. Murder is bad.
2. Milk tastes good.
3. Alfred is a disciplined person.

Sentence 1 is the type of opinion statement that needs no support. Anyone who would not accept this statement at face value would likely reject any supports we might offer for it. Such a person would not be the kind of sensible reader we would be writing for. Sentence 2 is difficult to support. Even though many people like milk, that fact is support only for the assertion that many people think milk tastes good. This is a matter of personal taste—literally—and as such is the type of opinion you will do well to avoid in your arguments.

Sentence 3, about Alfred, is the type of opinion statement that will prove most useful in argumentative writing. It is not a truism, and it is a statement that lends itself to support. If we think Alfred would make a good class president, we may well think it useful to offer the opinion that he is a disciplined person. As noted, we can then offer our supports for this opinion and the reader is free to evaluate that opinion, to see whether it seems valid or not.

Exercise 9.6

Choose a paragraph from two of the sample essays at the beginning of this chapter. List every opinion you find in these two paragraphs. Then, label them as one of the three types of opinion statements we discussed. What kinds of support for the third type of opinion statements—those needing support—are offered? What insights into these essays do you get from of this analysis?

EXAMPLES   We are all familiar with examples, perhaps so familiar as to sometimes overlook their power. We reason with them all the time. Most of our parents reared us on examples. They told us of horrible things that happened to little boys or girls who didn't do what their parents said. (There was one little boy—remember Pinocchio?—whose proboscis became extremely elongated because he was factually challenged. But that's another story.)

Sometimes facts and examples overlap. For instance, a person arguing for capital punishment may use as an example (and a fact) a state in which capital punishment was reinstated and the violent crime rate went down. We tend to think of something as an example rather than a fact when we view it in some detail. Many examples are stories, or we can make them into stories if we choose to do so. Stories are powerful. For example, look at the story Heather Cully tells (in "The Age Requirement for Teen Drivers") about the teenage drivers who stole a stop sign and thus contributed to the death of a person at that intersection.

PERSONAL EXPERIENCE   A specific type of example you may use in your position essay is the personal experience. In the past, you may have been reluctant to use personal experiences in expository or argumentative writing, relegating them to personal writing. It is certainly true that your arguments cannot rest entirely on personal experience; however, personal experience can be a powerful tool in argumentation. Look, for example, at the beginning of Heather's essay, in which she tells of a personal experience that occurred while she was driving, and at Weinstein's essay, in which he uses many personal experiences he had as a federal judge. One of the most effective (and persuasive) argumentative essays we know of, Martin Luther King, Jr.'s "Letter from Birmingham Jail," contains the following powerful passage, built on personal experience:

> [. . .] Perhaps it is easy for those who have never felt the stinging darts of segregation to say, "Wait." But when you have seen vicious mobs lynch your mothers and fathers at will and drown your sisters and brothers at whim; when you have seen hate-filled policemen curse, kick, and even kill your black brothers and sisters; when you see the vast majority of your twenty million Negro brothers smothering in an airtight cage of poverty in the midst of an affluent society; when you suddenly find your tongue twisted and your speech stammering as you seek to explain to your six-year-old daughter why she can't go to the public amusement park that has just been advertised on television, and see tears welling up in her eyes when she is told that Funtown is closed to colored children, and see ominous clouds of inferiority beginning to form in her little mental sky, and see her beginning to distort her personality by developing an unconscious bitterness toward white people, [. . .] then you will understand why we find it difficult to wait.

(This entire essay is reprinted in Chapter 10, beginning on page 371.)

ETHICAL STANCE

We said that the primary distinguishing feature of a position essay is logical argumentation. A second, and very important, characteristic of a successful position essay is the writer's ethical stance. A key to that is her fairness. She must make it clear that she knows, and respects, arguments on the other side.

An analogy that comes to mind in thinking about the stance of the writer of a position essay involves the art of fencing. In fencing, the two combatants begin with a ceremonial touching of swords, in which they symbolize respect for the sharpness of their blades and for each other's skill in the art of fencing. They proceed to thrust and parry, each attempting to gain advantage over the other. Unlike a street brawl, however, in which any means of conquering the opponent would be used—kicking, throwing sand in the face, or pulling hair—the fencing contest is carried out under the strictest rules of fairness. The hand not holding the sword is held behind the back to symbolize the contestant's commitment to fair play and honest competition. Each combatant wishes to win the day, but also wants to be sure that in doing so neither she nor her opponent is demeaned.

ASSIGNMENT AND GUIDELINES FOR WRITING

ASSIGNMENT

Write a paper in which you state and support your position on an issue about which reasonable people can disagree.

CHOOSING A TOPIC

The exercises in Part A should help you find and begin to examine your topic. If you think you already know what topic you want to write about, skip to Part B.

PART A

1. Begin your search for a topic by thinking of two or three issues you feel strongly about. If issues do not come to mind immediately, consult your responses to the Interest Inventory (p. 9), looking especially at the sections dealing with school, work, and society. For each potential topic you uncover, freewrite for 10 minutes or so.
2. After you have written about your potential topics, answer the following questions about each one:
   a. What is the topic?
   b. What is your stance on it? What opinion do you hold about it?
   c. How did you come to think this way? How did you develop this stance?

PART B

Pick one topic that you feel strongly about. Think of someone you know and respect who might take an opposing point of view on this topic. Spend a few minutes describing this person, including his or her political leanings, home life (the neighborhood in which the person lives, for example), job, and so on. Then spend 15 minutes freewriting on your topic from this person's perspective. After you have finished writing, answer these two questions:

1. Are you sufficiently interested in this topic to write about it?
2. Are you able to look at the topic from the perspective of your opponent?

If you can answer both questions affirmatively, this is probably a good topic for you to write about. You are ready to move on to consider what about the topic interests you most and what the best arguments for the opposing position are. Otherwise, go through this exercise again, using a different potential topic.

COLLECTING INFORMATION

QUESTIONS FOR ANALYSIS   If you have selected a topic that you care about, chances are you already know a good deal about it. However, in order to have the credibility you are going to need for this writing situation, you may want to learn more. To see what you already know about your topic, it may be helpful to ask the questions of association, opposition, sequence, and consequence presented in Chapter 1 (pp. 24–25); in particular, it may be helpful to focus on issues of definition and cause as they relate to your position.

KEY VALUES   One way to provide a foundation for your argument is to appeal to key values. You should determine which of your key values are relevant to your argument and what your reader's response will be to those values. In most cases, your reader will not completely dismiss the values you believe in—just as you will not dismiss your reader's values—but he probably will assign different priorities to those values. For example, if you are writing in favor of gun control, those on the other side will agree with you that safety is important. However, their commitment to freedom and living in a free country will take precedence over their concern for safety. Once you have determined the differences between the two sides by analyzing key values, you will have a better sense of how to proceed in your argument. Below is an analysis of key values for the gun-control example. In this case, you will have to either convince those holding a different position to change their priorities—a very difficult thing to do—or redefine gun control so that they no longer see it as a challenge to freedom.

Topic: Gun Control

Thesis: U.S. citizens should not be allowed to own guns unless they have a need for them in their professions (such as law enforcement) or in hunting activities.

Values Relevant to My Argument

My key values:

Freedom—one of many good things that we should strive for. It can be a bad thing when it endangers other individuals.

Government control—a good thing when it promotes the good of a society. A bad thing when it takes away citizens' rights for no reason

Safety and protection—a very desirable goal worth sacrificing for

My reader's key values:

Freedom—a basic human right that is to be guarded with great diligence

Government control—inherently evil because governments are inherently evil. They take freedoms away from individuals.

Safety and protection—one of many good things we should strive for. It cannot be allowed to take precedence over freedom.

KEY CAUSAL ASSERTIONS   Another major foundation for arguments is causal reasoning. You can generate material for your essay by exploring the types of causal statements you might want to use as your foundation and predicting your reader's responses to these causal assertions. Because it is extremely hard to prove that one thing causes another, agreement about causes and effects is difficult to achieve. Still, it is very important to gain insight into disagreements between you and your reader about causes. You may argue that more controls should be placed on the sale of guns because you believe that such controls will cause a decrease in gunshot injuries and deaths. Your reader may disagree. How, you may wonder. It seems almost obvious that fewer guns would result in fewer accidents and more guns would result in more accidents, right? Well, not as far as your reader is concerned. Your reader does not agree with a causal claim that you haven't even asserted because it seems so obvious to you. You believe that stricter gun laws will surely result in fewer guns. But your reader may disagree, arguing that guns will always be available to those who want them and that making something illegal only makes people want it more. Once you realize how you and your reader differ on the causal claims you associate with this thesis, you can begin to plan your strategy for supporting your claims.

Topic: Gun Control

My beliefs about causes of (reasons for) gun control:

- a desire by those in authority to find ways to protect citizens

My reader's beliefs about causes of (reasons for) gun control:

- government's desire to control our lives in general
- government's attempt to be sure citizens have no arms with which to re-sist the government

My beliefs about effects of gun control:

- fewer accidental deaths
- less violence in streets
- fewer armed robberies

My reader's beliefs about effects of gun control:

- no real reduction in accidental deaths
- no real reduction in street violence
- no real reduction in armed robberies

or

- a police state in which the reduction in these bad things is gained at tremendous cost of individual freedoms

IMAGINARY DIALOGUE   Another useful strategy in generating information for a position essay is an *imaginary dialogue*, a conversation you create between two people who disagree about an arguable topic. Below is such a conversation that Ron wrote, imagining what he and his reader might say to each other about gun-control laws.

Topic: Gun Control

Imaginary dialogue:

Me: We certainly need stronger gun laws in this country.

Counterpart: We already have way too many laws about too many things, and the laws don't do anything but restrict the freedoms of those people who are willing to abide by laws.

Me: I don't see how you can say that, given the increase in crimes in which guns are used. In this city alone, we have had a tremendous increase in armed robberies in the last few years.

Counterpart: What makes you think that controlling guns will lower the num-ber of armed robberies? People who are going to rob are not worried about laws against owning guns.

Me: But the laws will make it harder for them to get guns. It's not that they are trying to obey laws, but laws do control the flow of any product. So laws would make it harder for them to get guns in the first place. And the laws would also make it easier to trace guns used by criminals.

Counterpart: Why? Given the fact that our borders are absolutely porous and given the fact that making guns illegal will increase the profits to be made on selling guns, why should we think that making guns illegal will make it harder for people to get them? If anything, it might increase the supply of guns. Look at what is happening with drugs. Does anyone think that our laws are keeping drugs out of the hands of those who really want them? And for that matter, look back at the Prohibition saga. All these laws do is to restrict the rights of law-abiding citizens, increase profits for those who want to traffic in illegal goods, and, perhaps, create a nuisance for those who want the contraband. But if they want the contraband badly enough, they will find a way to get it.

Me: So you are arguing that the government shouldn't control any substance, or good, at all—that the citizens should be able to get anything they want?

Counterpart: Well, I would say there are some things that should be controlled by governments, but not many. I don't like the government protecting me where I don't need protecting.

Me: So where would you say the government should protect citizens?

Counterpart: I'd say that harmful products should be regulated when it comes to children. Children should not be able to buy pornography, to buy drugs that might harm them, and so forth.

Me: So that's all? Governments should not protect us from ourselves otherwise?

Counterpart: No, it's more complicated than that. I'd say that the government should protect us from such things as nuclear devices. The ordinary citizen should not be able to get his hands on a nuclear device that could destroy thousands or millions of people.

Me: So the government should protect us from nuclear destruction, but it should not protect us from a maniac down the street walking into a store and buying a handgun that he can use to kill me the next time he cuts me off in traffic and I object. Won't I be just as dead whether I'm killed by a nuclear device or by a handgun owned by someone who has no business having one? Where do we draw the line? If governments are in the business of protecting citizens, why should they not try to protect me from the idiot down the street?

Counterpart: There are several ways to answer you here. We can start by saying that I am not absolutely sure where to draw this line between what governments should try to accomplish and what they should not try to accomplish. However, that does not mean that there is no such line or that I should not continue to try to find it. I'm reminded of the logical rule of thumb called the argument of the beard. A person asks how many hairs it takes to make a beard. The answer comes back, "I don't know." The questioner then asks, "So you don't know the difference between a man with a beard and a man without one?" To which the second person responds, "The fact that I don't know where exactly to draw a line doesn't mean there is no line." Let me move on to another answer. Surely it would be a good thing to protect your life from both, from the person who would attempt to blow up your whole city with a nuclear device and from the person who would kill you for a traffic disagreement. However, it is much harder to protect you from the kind of random violence represented by the latter case than from the terrorist groups that might try to steal nuclear weapons. The government may be able to keep tabs on certain groups, but it cannot control the behavior of every individual citizen—not and maintain a free country. And that brings me to a third point. The more authority we give governments to protect us, the more of our lives we have to give them in return. If we have a law that says that someone cannot own a gun, how do we enforce it? Do we undertake routine checks like the routine license checks we now have? Would you be willing to submit to an unwarranted search of your car any time you go out for a Sunday afternoon drive?

Me: Well, I might. But I'm not sure. You have given me a good deal to think about. We'll have to continue this conversation later on, since I have to finish writing this chapter. Thanks.

FOCUS STATEMENT

As you begin to generate information for your essay, look back over your freewriting and write a brief statement about the focal point of your essay. It should include a tentative thesis statement, which simply states the issue and the side you are taking on the issue. It should also suggest the claims you will use as the foundation for your thesis and how you will counter major objections to your position. Here is a sample focus statement for a paper on the issue of putting a basketball arena in uptown Charlotte:

> I am in favor of a basketball arena in uptown Charlotte. I believe that cities are healthier when they have a clearly defined center. Since Charlotte already has a major football stadium in its uptown, the addition of the basketball arena will help to solidify the uptown as the center of a major city. I am aware that this project will require some tax dollars and that many people will object to raises in taxes to support this project. I am not sure that we will have to raise taxes, if our priorities are clear—I will look into this question in my paper and see what I think. Even if we do have to raise taxes, I think the benefits in terms of the local economy will offset that—I will look into this matter in some detail. The benefits to the average citizen can be many. A vibrant uptown will make this a much more desirable city to live in—I may want to talk about some cities that have such uptowns and describe them a bit. In addition, the traffic flow of the outerbelt can be designed with this center city in mind, and the positive effect on the daily commute of all commuting citizens will be payoff enough for this project.

PLANNING YOUR ESSAY'S STRUCTURE

In a position essay, you will assume a reader who takes an opposing point of view. Thus, the overall structure of your essay will be provided by the argument mode. It is based on thesis and support: You make an assertion (which will be the essay's thesis) and then spend the rest of the essay showing *why* that thesis should be accepted or believed. This is very general, of course. As you think about the overall shape of your essay, you may find it useful to look at the argument structure in more detail. To help you do so, we will explore two separate structures—one informal, the other formal.

INFORMAL ARGUMENT STRUCTURE

The informal argument structure includes a thesis, support for that thesis, and answers to the arguments that are put forward by the other side. The following plan for a position essay in favor of raising taxes on tobacco uses this informal argument structure:

I. A *thesis statement* (with "should"): Taxes should be raised on tobacco products.
II. A list of reasons (or claims) that indicate why one should accept this thesis
    A. *Cause:* Raising taxes will decrease smoking.
    B. *Value:* Taxing "sins" is a good thing.
III. Supporting information for those reasons
    A. 1. Statistics about drops in smoking in other countries that have increased taxes on tobacco, such as Canada
       2. Statements of opinion from authority figures: psychologists, on failure of health concerns to make people modify behavior
       3. Statistics about the role money plays in causing people to take action
       4. Personal experience as to why the writer quit smoking
    B. 1. Statistics on amount of money the government spends on health problems caused by cigarettes
       2. Statistics on numbers of underage people currently smoking
IV. Counterarguments to the reasons your counterpart will offer for her position
    A. 1. *Argument:* This is another case of the government running our lives.
       2. *Counter:* We run our lives, but if we run them in such a way that the government has to pay for our mistakes, the government has a right to charge us.
    B. 1. *Argument:* This is another tax aimed at the poor.
       2. *Counter:* This is not aimed at the poor, but admittedly will hit them harder—since a larger percentage of their paycheck will be required to keep smoking. It would be good if this did not have to happen. But to put the financial burden on the well-off would not be fair. And if this were done, some would say it is just another example of society's lack of concern for the poor—let them kill themselves if they want to. So, there is no winning this kind of debate. But if lives are saved—as they will be—it is worth it.

THE "SHOULD" THESIS It is important that you include the word "should" when you state your thesis. In doing so, you separate the argument you want to make from the claims you are offering in support of that argument. Many times, writers begin with a specific claim, ignoring this need for a "should" thesis. For example, a writer could assert that professional sports teams are a financial drain on most cities. She could develop an argument in support of this claim, but why would she do so? We will know why if she provides us with a "should" thesis that this claim might support. We can think of several thesis statements that could be connected to this claim:

Professional sports teams are a drain on a city's finances; thus,

1. our city should not attempt to obtain a professional sports team.
2. our city planners should raise taxes to support a professional sports team.
3. our city planners should not build the new stadium that our current sports team wants.

As you can see, one claim may be used in support of several different "should" theses. It is important for you, and your reader, to have a clear understanding of what your argument is. Even if your "should" thesis does not appear in your paper, be sure that you know how you would phrase it if you were asked to do so.

Exercise 9.7

Write two or three "should" theses for each of the following claims:

1. Lowering taxes in this city will cause an increase in the number of businesses locating here.
2. Gambling is wrong.
3. Killing is immoral.
4. A good system of higher education will improve the economy in this state.
5. Car telephones cause more accidents than alcohol does.

REASONS (CLAIMS) Next, you give reasons, the claims that underlie and provide a foundation for your thesis. These reasons will be either claims of value or claims about causes and effects. For example, you might argue in favor of increasing efforts to rid a city of prostitution because

prostitution is wrong (evil, or immoral) (*value*)
and/or
prostitution has other undesirable consequences (such as increased traffic in drugs or loss of business for uptown merchants) (*cause*)

Of course, these claims will be made in various ways, and it will be important to make your readers understand when claims of value and cause are being made. In many cases, you will have to be able to translate these claims into sentences that have a specific value or a causal assertion. For example, you might say that prostitution should not be tolerated because laws should protect us from such things as prostitution. In doing so, you are likely making a claim based on a value that assumes that paying for sex is evil by definition. You could have written, "Prostitution should be banned because it is inherently evil." This is a very clear claim of value. Unfortunately, such clear statements are the exception rather than the rule.

Another possible argument would be that prostitution should not be tolerated because sexually transmitted diseases are on the rise in the community. In this case, you would be making a claim based on a causal argument; your assumption is that prostitution is responsible, at least in part, for the rise in sexually transmitted diseases.

Below we offer several claims that might be given in support of "should" theses. In each case, explain whether the claim is based on value or causality. Are there cases in which both cause and value are implicit in one claim?

1. *Thesis:* Citizens of this state should not vote for Senator X.
   Claim: He is the pawn of special interests such as the tobacco lobby.
2. *Thesis:* We should abolish capital punishment.
   Claim: We do not have the right to play God.
3. *Thesis:* Euthanasia should be legal.
   Claim: It is inhumane to make individuals continue to exist when there is no quality to their lives.
4. *Thesis:* You should support the school bond issue.
   Claim: Education is crucial if society is going to make the progress necessary for the survival of the human race.
5. *Thesis:* The referendum on a state lottery should be defeated.
   Claim: The state should not encourage gambling.

SUPPORT   Claims of value and cause may be supported by appeals to authority, facts and statistics, opinion statements, examples, and personal experience. For example, the last claim in Exercise 9.8 is based on causality. The claim is that state lotteries cause people to gamble more than they would if there were no lottery. This is a debatable claim. Those who oppose this argument may believe that gamblers will find a means to gamble, whether they live in a state with a lottery or not. So, how will the writer support her claim? She could search for data on gambling in states with lotteries. She might cite the amount of money collected in lotteries and ask readers to assume that not all of this money would have been spent on gambling had there been no lottery. She could also search to see whether there have been in-depth studies on the matter. If she could find surveys about gambling habits suggesting that people gamble more when states have lotteries, she could bolster her argument greatly. Finally, she might relate any personal information she has on gambling and the influence that lotteries have on gambling.

Here is an overview of the types of support Jack B. Weinstein offers in his essay, "The War on Drugs Is Self-Defeating," (pp. 312–314).

I.   *Thesis:* A nonpartisan federal commission on drugs should be formed to study the cost, benefits, risks, and advantages of present and potential drug policies.
II. *Claim:* Current drug policies aren't causing the reduction in drug use we desire.
     Support:
     A. *Opinion*
        1. Chief Justice Rehnquist: "The law by itself is not going to solve the problems of drugs and violence."
        2. Attorney General Reno believes we should reconsider current drug policy.

B. *Factual history:* The United States has had three different drug policies since 1914.

C. *Factual history/personal experience*

1. In his district, 400 "drug mules" are sentenced each year; guideline sentencing has raised their jail time from 1 to 3 years—adding up to 800 more penal years.

2. Federal probation service had to cut drug-testing and medical-treatment programs.

D. *Personal history:* He has moved in his thinking from medical model, to penal model, to despair with the system.

E. *Fact:* Some federal prosecutors decline to prosecute cases involving less than a ton of marijuana; in other places people are sent to prison for years for possessing plants they grew.

F. *Fact:* One in four black males in their 20s is under the control of the criminal justice system.

G. *Statistics*

1. Judicial system overwhelmed and paralyzed with drug cases.

2. One-third of new inmates are drug offenders.

3. Over 60 percent of those in federal prisons have been convicted for use of drugs.

III. *Claim:* Federal commissions have helped find solutions to difficult problems in the past.

   Examples:

A. Wickersham Commission, appointed by President Hoover in 1929, wrote report that led to full debate on Prohibition laws.

B. National Commission on Marijuana and Drug Abuse, appointed by President Nixon in 1971, recommended ending prosecution for possession of marijuana for private use.

Exercise 9.9

Using as a model our analysis of the types of support offered in Weinstein's essay, choose one of the other essays in this chapter (or one selected by your instructor) and analyze the types of support the writer uses.

COUNTERARGUMENTS   In successful arguing, it is crucial to understand how your reader would structure her argument. If you are arguing that your city should not support a major sports team ("should" thesis) because doing so would cost the city a lot of money and thus cause an increase in taxes (claim), what will your counterpart say? We know what her thesis will be, since it will be the direct opposite of yours: The city *should* support a major sports team. Now, what kind of reasons can she offer? She can, and in most cases will, disagree with your causal claim. She may believe that although the team will require money from the city, it will also generate increased revenues for the city, which will offset those costs; thus, the team will not cause an increase in taxes—in the most optimistic case, it will allow for a reduction in taxes. Your task is to anticipate the supports your reader will offer for her claim (in this case, that increased revenues will offset the costs). Perhaps you know that she is likely to refer to another city where the acquisition of a new sports team did not cause an increase in taxes for the citizens. Your task in this situation is to show why your city is not like that other city.

However, your reader is not obligated to disagree with your causal claim. She could agree with your assessment that this sports team will cause an increase in taxes but argue that taxes are relatively low at present and that the other benefits that a team will bring—such as more jobs, more recreational opportunities for citizens, and a sense of pride and identity—will offset this increase in taxes. In a case such as this, your reader is accepting your analysis of cause but is shifting the ground (the foundation) on which the argument is being waged. You want to ground your argument on cost, but your reader is looking to other grounds, such as city pride and increased jobs.

Your argument will be strengthened if you can anticipate such shifts in ground and be prepared to counter them. You may show why cost *is* the crucial ground for the argument. How much do citizens in your city pay in taxes, and how does their tax rate compare with rates in comparable cities? You may also want to counter the claims your reader makes in her counterargument. For example, if she claims that sports teams bring about a feeling of pride and unity, you might refer to riots that have broken out when a sports team has won a championship and suggest that your city can do without such "pride."

Exercise 9.10

Choose one of the essays in this chapter or an essay selected by your instructor, and analyze the way in which the writer anticipates and responds to the counterarguments of the other side.

FORMAL ARGUMENT STRUCTURE

The more formal argument structure we will examine is often called *classical argument*. It comes to us from the classical rhetoricians, who divided argument into six parts:

> *exordium*—the writer captures the reader's attention
> *narratio*—the writer offers background information
> *partitio*—the writer states the argument
> *confirmatio*—the writer makes the case for his position
> *confutatio*—the writer offers refutation of major arguments against his position
> *peroratio*—the writer concludes the argument

In practice, very few writers follow this formal, classical structure completely. The attention they give to the various parts varies greatly, and at times certain parts are left out. We can see this variety in two of the arguments presented at the beginning of this chapter. In his argument for stricter drug laws, Gramm introduces the problem very quickly, dedicating only one part of paragraph 2 to *narratio*. In his argument that we should seriously question current drug policies, Weinstein dedicates eleven paragraphs (paragraphs 2–13) to the history (*narratio*) of this very complicated problem. This difference is very telling. Gramm takes the position that the problem is clear-cut, so he dedicates his essay to arguments about what should be done and why. Weinstein argues that the issue is very complicated, and he dedicates a large part of his essay to providing background about how we arrived at the current situation. As our analysis of these two arguments indicates (see below), your overall purpose will help you determine how much time to devote to each part of a classical argument.

Gramm, "Don't Let Judges Set Crooks Free"

exordium—in paragraph 1, the writer uses shocking statements from two federal judges to capture the attention of readers

narratio—in paragraph 2, the writer offers a very brief discussion of the debate going on in the Clinton administration over this issue

partitio—in paragraph 2, last sentence, the writer lets readers know he will oppose any lessening of the war on drugs

confirmatio—in paragraphs 3–8, the writer makes his argument detailing what he sees as light punishments for crime and stating his logic that light sentences result in more crime

confutatio—in paragraphs 9–16, the writer offers refutation of major arguments against him

peroratio—in paragraphs 17–18, the writer concludes his argument, intensifying his point by including an analogy with the struggle between the United States and the Soviet Union and a promise to continue to fight against drugs

Weinstein, "The War on Drugs Is Self-Defeating"

exordium—in paragraph 1, the writer makes a claim that too many people take the politically safe road when it comes to drugs, as opposed to thinking carefully about what might work

narratio—in paragraphs 2–13, the writer offers background about how the United States has dealt with drugs

partitio—in paragraph 2, sentence 1, and paragraph 14, sentence 1, the writer states his argument that a national commission should be formed to study U.S. drug policies

confirmatio—in paragraph 14, the writer makes his argument for establishing a commission to study the problem and, from sentence 2 to the end of the paragraph, offers a series of questions that he feels must be answered

confutatio—in paragraph 15, sentence 1, the writer offers refutation to those who would say this matter is clear-cut

peroratio—in paragraph 15, from sentence 2 to the end, the writer emphasizes the need for this study

Exercise 9.11

After examining the structure of the two essays outlined above, use the formal argument structure as a means of analyzing one of the other sample essays or an essay selected by your instructor. Then discuss how the writer's purpose dictates the way she or he structures the argument.

THESIS STATEMENT

Since it is crucial to know your thesis early in the argument process, you should have decided on it by this time. Be sure you have included "should" as a part of your formal thesis statement.

CHECKING FOR LOGICAL FALLACIES

Your opponents can challenge your argument in many ways. It isn't possible to write an irrefutable argument if you are dealing with a debatable topic. However, you can avoid discrediting yourself and your position by making sure your argument is valid. Your argument will be valid if you do two things: (1) offer support for claims that need support and (2) connect your claims logically to your thesis. If you say that a new stadium should be built because it will enhance the economy of the uptown, you must support this claim. Your reader will see the logical connection between the claim (that the new stadium will enhance the economy of the uptown) and your thesis (that the stadium should be built). If, however, you argue that a new stadium should be built because professional sports do many good things for a city, you have a problem of validity—of connection between claim and thesis. Opponents may argue that even though this is true, it is not reason enough to pay the money that such teams will require. Arguments can go wrong in many ways, but the overriding problem for the writer is a failure to look at arguments from the perspective of the reader. You may think that the only way to have a major sports team in the city is to build a new stadium, but if your reader does not see the connection between a new stadium and getting a sports team, she may well reject your argument that the city should build a new stadium.

Offering an argument that is worthy of your reader's consideration means constructing an argument free of logical fallacies. As you refine your essay, be sure you aren't guilty of any reasoning errors. There are many different ways to categorize such logical fallacies. We choose to group them into three types: fallacies of irrelevance, causal fallacies, and fallacies of definition.

FALLACIES OF IRRELEVANCE

As we've noted, you may support your claims by reference to authority, facts and figures, examples, opinion statements, and personal experience. However, if these supports are to be effective, they must be clearly connected to the claims you are making. Failure to make this connection will result in one or more of the following logical fallacies: argumentum ad hominem, stereotyping, bandwagon fallacy, argumentum ad ignorantiam, or hasty generalization.

ARGUMENTUM AD HOMINEM   The fallacy of *argumentum ad hominem* involves name-calling, or arguing by attacking a person instead of an issue. When a speaker attacks a person rather than speaking to the issue at hand, the attack is irrelevant. For example, a politician may argue that her opponent should not be elected because he has been divorced, but if the politician fails to show how this "fact" is related to the thesis—that one should not vote for her opponent—she is making an error of relevance and reducing her chances of convincing her audience.

This is not to suggest that facts concerning a politician are never relevant to questions of whether that politician should serve in an office; the fact that a candidate for county treasurer has been convicted of embezzlement is certainly relevant. Our point is that in writing an argument, you must be sure that your audience sees how the facts you present are relevant to the question at hand.

STEREOTYPING   We are guilty of stereotyping when we attempt to attribute certain characteristics to an individual by placing her in a certain group—often, but not always, a racial, ethnic, or religious group. Examples of stereotypical thinking include the following: Girls do well in English, whereas boys do well in mathematics; civil servants are plodding, bureaucratic types who do not really care for people. An example of reasoning by stereotype is "I wouldn't hire her; she belongs to some strange religious group." The assumption underlying such a statement is that this person's membership in the group will have some bearing on the way she performs the job. Of course, if the person offering this argument can show that the religious group in question believes that employees should undermine their capitalistic employers, he can show the relevance of this fact. Otherwise, it is irrelevant.

BANDWAGON FALLACY   We often see the bandwagon fallacy in advertisements: "Kangaroos have outsold the competition for two consecutive years. When are you going to drive a Kangaroo?" The argument offers no relevant reason for buying this type of car. It could be that many people are buying Kangaroos because they are well-built cars. However, it could also be that many people are buying Kangaroos because they have been convinced that many people are buying Kangaroos. The advertisement asks us to do something without giving us a good reason for doing it.

ARGUMENTUM AD IGNORANTIAM   The phrase *argumentum ad ignorantiam* can be translated as "argument from ignorance." The error occurs when the writer fails to take responsibility for his supporting assertions. Children are noted for this type of reasoning: "My dad is Superman; you can't prove he isn't." The U.S. court system has declared that a defendant's failure to prove his innocence is irrelevant to the question of whether he is in fact innocent—thus the maxim "innocent until proven guilty." When arguing, the one who asserts is responsible for supporting those assertions with relevant information.

HASTY GENERALIZATION   The fallacy of hasty generalization results when a writer moves too quickly from specific information—such as facts, figures, and personal experience—to conclusion. For example, consider a person who has never seen a cat. If that person then sees three black cats and generalizes from this personal experience that all cats are black, she will be guilty of hasty generalization. The fact that cats A, B, and C are black does not give the necessary support for the conclusion that all cats are black. That one person happened upon three black cats is irrelevant to the color of cats.

Similarly, consider the argument "Boxing is safer than football, because each year twice as many football players as boxers are injured." A close examination of these statistics would show that they are irrelevant to the question of safety in the two sports because the number of people who play football is much larger than the number of people who box.

It is important to note here that generalizing is indispensable to learning; if we could not generalize, we would not be able to learn anything new. Furthermore, there is no way to be absolutely sure that we always make correct predictions. Consider again the person who has never seen a cat. What if the person now sees a hundred cats and all of them have four legs? Wouldn't she be in a position to generalize that all nondeformed cats are born with four legs? She can't be sure (absolutely) of this generalization, but she would feel relatively confident in making it. Of course, it is conceivable, though highly unlikely, that the first hundred cats this person sees will be black. In this case, although her generalization that all cats are black will still not be correct, at least she will not have made the leap from one or two specific instances to the generalization.

Exercise 9.12

The following is the first paragraph of "For Pollsters, 'More' Doesn't Always Mean 'Better'" by John Shelton Reed:

> Just before the election of 1936, *The Literary Digest,* a widely read and influential magazine, announced the results of its presidential preference poll. The New Deal was going to be repudiated; FDR would be swept out of office. Alf Landon would be the next president, taking nearly 60 percent of the two-party popular vote. The announcement was made with a great deal of hoopla. The *Digest* quoted a reference to itself as an "oracle, which, since 1920, has foretold with almost uncanny accuracy the choice of the nation's voters. . . ." And, after all, hadn't they mailed out over 10 million "secret ballots" to voters all over the nation, after ransacking tax rolls, telephone directories, automobile registration and magazine subscription lists for names? And hadn't they heard from more than 20 percent of the nation's voters in return?

Of course, President Roosevelt won by a large margin. Explain in a paragraph any logical fallacies you see in the reasoning of those who conducted the poll.

CAUSAL FALLACIES

Given how difficult it is to prove that one thing causes another, it is little wonder that many arguments fail because readers cannot accept the causal statements that are offered. When working with causality, you must be careful to give your readers insight into the reasoning that underlies your causal assertions. If you say that Alfred will be a good class president because he earns good grades, you should be aware of the assumptions that led you to accept this causal statement. A spokesperson for another candidate may well argue that Alfred's good grades are a sign that he will work too hard at being a good student to pay the proper attention to his role as president. You could support your statement by providing examples of individuals who have been good presidents (in the opinions of students and faculty) and who have had good grades, by offering your opinion that the same intelligence and discipline that cause Alfred to earn good grades will cause him to be a good president, or, perhaps, by presenting the opinions of authority figures. You cannot simply make this causal statement and expect your audience to accept it at face value.

As this example illustrates, a writer can fall prey to faulty causal reasoning by assuming a cause-and-effect relationship when his audience is unwilling to make such an assumption. Two other causal errors, oversimplification and the either/or dilemma, are also frequent culprits in faulty causal reasoning.

OVERSIMPLIFICATION   The writer who focuses on one of several causes of a phenomenon as *the* cause of that phenomenon is oversimplifying. A classic example of this error in reasoning occurs when a motorist claims that the motorist in front caused an accident by failing to signal for a turn before she stopped to wait for oncoming traffic. Certainly, failure to signal could be a contributing cause of such an accident. However, would the accident have occurred if the following motorist had been traveling at a proper speed and distance from the first car, had been paying careful attention to his driving, and had been operating a car with no mechanical defects? Probably not. In these circumstances, the following motorist would likely have been able to stop in time even though the leading motorist failed to signal. The person who blames the high price of petroleum on the greed of large oil companies, on conflicts in the Middle East, on the policies of a particular administration, or on any other *one* cause is guilty of the same type of oversimplified causal reasoning.

When framing arguments, you will do well to resist the temptation to find *the* cause of any complicated event or human situation. Things are not usually so simple. We are not suggesting, however, that you must account for all the potential causes of any one event. For example, there is a sense in which the invention of the automobile is a cause for any auto accident, but that cause is so far removed from the effect as not to be a valid factor. How, then, do you decide which causes are appropriate to an analysis? There is no easy way to answer this question, but there are three distinctions among causes that may help you make the decision concerning their relevance. A cause may be seen as necessary, sufficient, or contributory.

A *necessary cause* is one that is essential to produce the effect. In the hypothetical car accident, negligence on the part of the following driver is a necessary cause for the accident. He was driving too fast or too close to the car in front, was not paying proper attention to the situation, or had failed to maintain his car properly. In a more literal sense, both cars are necessary causes for the accident. In this sense, of course, it is also necessary for the car in front to come to a stop.

A *sufficient cause* is one capable of producing the effect. In our example, any of several errors on the part of the following driver is sufficient to cause the accident. No matter what other factors are present—no matter how carefully the first driver signals or how carefully the second driver is watching the situation—if the second car is too close to the first car, the crash is going to occur. Thus, following too closely is a sufficient cause for the accident. (Of course, there is a sense in which this cause is not sufficient without a stop on the part of the driver in front; however, we are treating the stop of the first car as a given here, because at some time a stop must occur.)

In addition to the necessary and sufficient causes we have examined for our hypothetical accident, there may be *contributing causes*. The brakes of the following car may not be as effective as they were when the car was new, and these less than optimal brakes may be a contributing cause to the accident. If they are not severely deficient, however, they are not a sufficient cause for the accident, because they would have stopped the car if the driver had been thoroughly attentive and driving at a safe speed and at a proper distance.

In sum, you would be well advised not to say what *the* cause of an event or a situation is unless you can show that that cause is necessary for the effect. You must also be aware that any effect will have many more contributing causes than you can possibly treat; thus, you should devote most of your energies to necessary and sufficient causes.

THE EITHER/OR DILEMMA   A specific type of oversimplification, the either/or dilemma, occurs when a writer pretends that only two causes or two effects exist when multiple causes or effects exist. For example, consider the statement "Either the allocation for education in the state budget must be held at its present level, or the taxpayers are going to have to pay more taxes in the future." This either/or statement is based on the following assumed causal relations: Allocating more money for education causes taxes to be raised to pay for that education budget; not allocating more money for education requires no higher taxes. However, these are not the only possible causes of these effects. Taxes could be raised even if the amount of money spent on education were not increased. Other factors, such as increased expenditures for welfare and unemployment compensation, could cause a need for increased taxation. There may also be other effects of these causes. For example, an increased budget for education will not necessarily increase the overall tax burden of citizens. If the increased expenditure on education produces more people who are capable of assuming jobs and, thus, more people who are paying taxes, individual taxpayers may end up paying lower taxes at some time in the future. Also, if the increased expenditure on education ultimately causes fewer people to need welfare or unemployment compensation, this increase in funds could be balanced by a decrease in the amount of money needed for these services.

Our purpose here is not to prove that the statement given as our example is patently false; it could be that increased monies spent on education will require increases in taxation. Rather, our point is to demonstrate the oversimplification found in either/or statements. Sophisticated readers will not find them convincing.

Exercise 9.13

Find and explain the errors in causal reasoning in the statements below.

> *Example:* Detroit automakers say they are building better cars, and it must be so, for since 1973 the number of highway deaths has decreased significantly.

Explanation: This is a rather obvious case of oversimplification. Automakers may be building better cars, but many other factors may be contributing to the decrease in highway deaths. A very important factor that must be taken into account is the reduction of the maximum highway speed to 55 miles per hour, which occurred in 1974 and continued in most states until 1987. Other factors, such as safe-driving campaigns and reductions in travel due to increased fuel costs, may also have been causes.

1. The spouses of successful business executives wear expensive clothing, so the best way to help your spouse be successful in business is to buy expensive clothing.
2. Mr. Smith will surely support the ERA. After all, he has been active in civil rights work for twenty years.
3. Either you are for an increase in teachers' pay or you prefer your own pocketbook to the welfare of the youth of our society.
4. It was obvious when Jimmy Carter became president that the Soviet Union would become more aggressive in such countries as Poland. A U.S. president just could not afford to give any indication of weakness to the USSR.
5. The federal government should never cut taxes again. It cut them in 1981, and unemployment rose immediately.
6. You were bound to be mugged sooner or later. A person cannot continually be part of crowds the size of those at baseball games without being mugged.
7. If I were you, I would take German from a native German. After all, you do want the best instruction for your money.
8. If I were you, I would take German from a nonnative speaker. After all, you do want to pass the course, don't you?

Exercise 9.14

When we label an assertion as an example of faulty reasoning, we do not mean to imply that it is impossible to treat the topic of that assertion in a reasonable and convincing fashion. For example, there is quite a bit of difference in the basic reasoning at work in statements 1 and 2 in the preceding exercise. Whereas statement 1 is unreasonable to the point of being humorous, there is some degree of reason involved in statement 2, even though we cannot accept the assertion as it stands. If you were going to argue that Smith will back the ERA, how would you develop your argument? Write a paragraph in which you plan a strategy for such an argument.

FALLACIES OF DEFINITION

Fallacies of definition occur when arguments are supported by opinion statements. We call them fallacies of definition because all opinion statements hinge on definitions. If a writer asserts that Joe fought with Bill, readers will probably see little point in arguing the fact. They may not believe the statement; indeed, they may decide to investigate to see whether it is true, but they will not argue it. However, if the speaker goes on to offer the opinion that Joe is brave, readers may be inclined to disagree and to question the speaker's definition of "brave." Opinion statements are so labeled because they include one or more such arguable terms.

To be successful, the writer of an argumentative paper must be sure that the definitions of terms in his opinion statements are clear and that he offers support for those definitions that need support. If he fails in either of these tasks, his argument will be less effective. A failure in clarity is called *equivocation,* and a failure in support is called *begging the question.*

EQUIVOCATION   Equivocation is the stuff of the slick advertising slogan. For example, consider the following slogan: "When guns are outlawed, only outlaws will have guns." Here there is a shift in meaning of the word "outlaw." In its verb form, it means simply "to declare illegal or against the law." However, in its noun form, it has come to mean "a habitual criminal," the kind of person who can be shot on sight in some states. Although it is true that when guns are outlawed only people who are going against that law will have guns, it is not true that when guns are outlawed only habitual criminals will have guns.

For another example, suppose a person offers as a supporting premise the assertion that anyone who would commit a premeditated murder is insane and then moves from this premise to the conclusion that such a person should be found "not guilty by reason of insanity." The equivocation here involves the word "insane." In the conclusion, the word must mean "mentally deranged to the point of not knowing the difference between right or wrong and/or not being in sufficient control of oneself to keep from doing wrong things." However, if readers accept the premise, they are probably ascribing a less technical meaning to "insane": "disturbed in thinking, not normal." They might accept the premise that a person who would kill is "disturbed," but they would not necessarily believe that a person who kills lacks the ability to control his actions.

BEGGING THE QUESTION   The fallacy of begging the question occurs when a conclusion is deduced from a premise that masks the same assertion made in the conclusion. For example, the sentence "You should not major in a liberal arts field because it will do you little good" has a pair of assertions that are actually saying the same thing: A liberal arts major is not *good* because it does one little *good.* Both assertions claim that a liberal arts major is not good, but neither helps a reader understand what the writer means by "good."

In many cases, the writer who falls into the trap of begging the question could frame a workable argument by carefully defining terms. For example, the preceding argument could be structured as follows:

A college education should provide one with marketable skills.
A liberal arts major does not provide one with marketable skills.
One should not choose a liberal arts major in college.

Of course, the writer has much work to do in helping her readers accept the two supporting premises, but she is no longer begging the question.

Label the fallacies of definition in the following examples, and explain which word or phrase causes the difficulty.

> *Example:* That film should be given the Academy Award because it was the best picture of the year.
>
> *Explanation:* This is a simple case of begging the question. There is really only one assertion that is stated twice. The film is the best because it is the best. The writer offers no insight into what "best picture" means or why he considers this the best film.

1. We all agree that each company should be free to set its own price. Therefore, how can we deny companies the freedom to set prices as a group?
2. I wouldn't choose only children to be camp counselors because they are not good in group situations.
3. Dad, how can you say I'm not dependable enough to have the car? Yesterday, you said you could depend on me to ask for the car every weekend.
4. I can't believe you voted for a Democrat.
5. The West wasn't won with a registered gun.

By this time, it should be clear that these three types of reasoning errors remain mutually exclusive only so long as they are viewed from the perspectives we offer. By changing our perspective, we can see the same error as a definitional fallacy, a causal fallacy, or a fallacy of irrelevance. To illustrate the point, consider the fourth statement in the previous exercise: I can't believe you voted for a Democrat. Because this exercise followed our discussion of fallacies of definition, you probably found a definitional problem in it. To reveal the problem, you may have phrased the argument as follows: One should not vote for a Democrat; she is a Democrat; thus, you should not vote for her. Or, to make the question begging even more obvious, the argument could be phrased as follows: Democrats are bad (should not be voted for) because they are Democrats. This makes it clear that no premise is given in support of the assumption that Democrats are bad.

But if this particular example had followed the section on causal fallacies, you could well have discussed its problems in the terminologies we developed there. In order to do so you might have phrased the underlying assumption as follows: The fact that she is a Democrat will cause her to do a bad job in office. Of course, the writer offers no support for this implicit causal assertion.

From a third perspective, the error may be seen as a fallacy of irrelevance—specifically, as a stereotype. The writer is attempting to determine the worth of a certain individual by placing her in a class. No support is offered for the assumption that all Democrats are unworthy candidates. Thus, the sophisticated reader is likely to see the implied premise—the candidate is a Democrat—as irrelevant to the conclusion—you should not vote for her.

Although the three categories of problematic arguments we have devised may be helpful to you, the preceding discussion should make the point that the basic principles of logical argument are much more important than any classification system for fallacious arguments. *The* basic principle is that disagreements arise because of differences in the perceptions of those who are arguing. A corollary to this principle is that whenever there is a real argument, the short, albeit witty, statement will not suffice. Arguments such as "When guns are outlawed, only outlaws will have guns" and "The West wasn't won with a registered gun" will work only for people who already share the point of view of the writer or for people who are not sophisticated enough to see the problems in these statements.

REFINING YOUR WRITING

After you've written a draft of your essay and taken some time away from it, revise it, keeping the following principles in mind:

> *Thesis sentence.* Be sure that you (and your reader) know what your "should" thesis sentence is. Check that you have not allowed yourself to argue for foundational claims without making it clear what thesis they are supporting.
>
> *Logical argument.* Be sure that your thesis is clearly connected to foundational claims of cause and/or value and that these claims are adequately supported. Be sure that you have countered the major arguments that your counterpart would offer. Check to see that you are not guilty of any logical fallacies.
>
> *Ethical appeal.* Be sure that you have not misrepresented your counterpart's argument and that you have treated those on the other side fairly.

SAMPLE STUDENT PROCESS

The student example below was written by Emily Weast, a first-year writing student at UNC–Charlotte.

PREWRITING

Emily began her writing by listing various issues she might be interested in writing a position paper about. After completing her list, Emily simply thought about the topics on the list for a few days and then decided on sex education as a potential topic because of her interest in the topic, because some other topics in her list had already been treated by essays read by the class, and because she thought she could find information on this topic. She then went to the library and read articles on the topic. Her next step was to use the Questions for Analysis to generate a starting place for her paper.

> *What do I associate with sex education?*
> sensible people
> public education
>
> *What goes with sex education?*
> not helpful
>
> *What opposes sex education?*
> religious groups
> uneducated people

This was not particularly helpful to Emily. Next, she attempted to explore the foundational claims of cause and value.

Value

What are my key values?

Safety from disease (This is very important to me—worth giving up a lot)

Freedom from burden of abortion and/or unwanted children (Very important to me—I do not like the thought of a person's entire future being endangered by one mistake)

Morality (Very important to me—but I don't think as important as to my opponents)

What are key values for my opponents?

Morality (At the top of their list)

Religious freedom (It is very important that schools do not force things on them that they do not believe in)

Cause

What do I see as the cause for sex education?

The need to prevent disease and pregnancy

What does my opponent see as the cause of sex education?

Society's desire to control the lives (and morals) of individuals—government is behind this, and my opponent does not trust the government.

What do I see as the effects of sex education?

More knowledgeable teens, who will make safer decisions.

I don't really think there will be less sexual activity, but I don't think there will be more—and what happens will be safer.

What does my opponent see as the effects of sex education?

Teens will lose all moral inhibitions and will think they are being encouraged to have more sex. As a result, there will be an increase in teenage sex.

After generating this information, Emily was ready to move on to a focus statement.

FOCUS STATEMENT

My position is that sex education classes should be taught in the schools. I will show how ignorance about sex is causing a tremendous rise in the number of unwanted pregnancies and STD's. I will show how much misinformation in the media is contributing to these problems. I will state the objections that those against sex education have—especially the Catholic church—and show why their objections should not prevent sex education in the schools.

Emily was now ready to write her discovery draft.

DISCOVERY DRAFT

Sex education should be included in the curriculum at all middle schools and high schools. Only through the process of acquiring knowledge can students learn to make rational decisions based on fact instead of fiction. Despite the many attacks on sex education, education is the only way our country and the rest of the world are ever going to decrease the number of young people giving birth at early ages, contracting STD's, and dieing of AIDS (Dority, p. 36).

The increasing number of people with HIV/AIDS has ended any possibility of continuing the conservative and moral approach to educating our adolescents (Moore, p. 106). Our youth have difficulty personalizing the dangers of AIDS and other STD's due to their lack of knowledge about how these diseases are transmitted and the "can't happen to me" theory (Moore, p. 114). Sex education aims to teach adolescents how their bodies work, the consequences of irresponsible behavior, and to reveal the truth about sexual freedom and diversity. Teenagers need an unbiased source of knowledge on sex so they will be able to protect themselves in their sexual activities.

Another important aspect of sex education is the portion concerning the different sexual preferences and orientations. The different ways in which the sexual act can be performed (anal, oral, vaginal) and discussion on homosexual, heterosexual, and bisexual orientations are important aspects that are covered in sex education curriculums. Students should be aware of the freedom they have with sex and that there is not one correct choice. Without a focus on all sexual orientations many young people who do not fit into the life style choice covered will be left ignorant and their choice will seem wrong and immoral based on it's omission from the curriculum. Students who are taught that only heterosexuality is correct will be harmed because they will develop, or have reinforced, prejudices against bisexual or homosexual individuals. This lack of knowledge is largely responsible for the risky experimentation of teenagers and global prejudice against anyone with a differing sexual preference. Youths need an environment of support as they are trying to establish their sexual identity (Moore, p. 121).

The media has great influence over adolescents today and the often misleading, incorrect, and biased information given out is partly responsible for the sexual problems they encounter. TV, radio, and magazines are common sources of knowledge for confused teenagers. Although some call in radio or TV shows offer sound advice from doctors and privacy, the fact that these shows are so popular emphasizes the demand for more sex education (Moore, p. 116–117). Soap operas promote sexual promiscuity, give unrealistic representations of sex, and often neglect to mention contraception and the risk of STD's and AIDS associated with such risky behavior. Talk shows are another important example of media that confuses and distorts sex. Some talk show audiences give support and acceptance to people of every sexual persuasion while others are dominated with audiences that denounce any variation of heterosexual activity. These contradicting opinions confuse youths about what is right and acceptable behavior.

An important point made by those against sex education is the assumption that teenagers are going to have sex so a strong focus should be on contraception. They feel abstinence should be taught as the best protection from disease and pregnancy (p. 21). Many parents question sex programs where homosexuality and other life styles different from heterosexuality are discussed as equally correct choices for sexual preferences. These same parents are concerned with the amount of graphic information their children are given and it's appropriateness for youth (Garber, p. 57).

In response to the religious concerns over sex education, I would like to mention that parent's have the right to withdraw their children from such a class according to the 1st Amendment. Also, not all Americans are Christians and therefore to require that all sex education courses support the Christian religion would not please everyone with children. Abstinence is given as an option and is clearly shown to be the safest option but the objective of sex educa-tion is not to force a certain choice on students but show all the options so they can make an informed choice. Parents can still teach their teenagers their fam-ily values and what their particular religion believes is right, but whether they agree with other life styles is not relevant. There is also an important problem with relying solely on parents for informing their children about sex. An im-portant barrier is embarrassment for both the youth and parent. Adolescents need an increasing amount of privacy and an invasion by a parent on such a sen-sitive subject is likely to hinder communication. Some parent's also assume that there children must already know everything they need to know and so do not approach them about sex. The most important barrier are the parents' own val-ues and bias' that may only give a one sided view of sexual behavior. Some par-ent's may not know all the accurate facts themselves and so their adolescents may receive false information (Moore, pp. 107–108).

CONCLUSION

PEER REVIEW

Emily's draft was read by a classmate, who asked the following questions:

1. Can you define more clearly what you mean by sex education?
2. Who would teach sex education and what qualifications would these teachers need?
3. Can you say more about what parents can do if they want to take their children out of sex education courses?

Emily then wrote the following draft, which she submitted to her instructor.

SECOND DRAFT

Sex education should be included in the curriculum at all middle and high schools. The type of sex education that needs to be taught in schools would teach contraception to reduce unwanted pregnancy, sexual orientation, how the reproductive system works, and how STD's are spread and can be prevented. Only through the process of acquiring knowledge can students learn to make rational decisions based on fact instead of fiction. Despite the many attacks on sex education, education is the only way our country and the rest of the world are ever going to decrease the number of young people giving birth at early ages, contracting STD's, and dieing of AIDS.

The increasing number of people with HIV/AIDS has ended any possibil-ity of continuing the conservative and moral approach to educating our adoles-cents (Moore 106). Abstinence should be covered as the only completely safe choice regarding sex, but the classroom's function is to give information, not dictate what a student should choose. Contraception should also be covered for those student's who may choose to have sex so they can protect themselves from disease and pregnancy. Susan Moore, one of the authors of *Youth, AIDS and Sexually Transmitted Diseases,* feels our youth have difficulty personalizing the dangers of AIDS and other STD's due to their lack of knowledge about how these diseases are transmitted (114). Sex education aims to teach adolescents how their bodies work, the consequences of irresponsible behavior, and to reveal the truth about sexual freedom and diversity. Teachers specifically trained to deliver factual and unbiased information should be hired at every school to inform the student body about sex. Teenagers need this source of knowledge about sex so they will be able to protect themselves in their sexual activities.

Another important aspect of sex education is the portion concerning the different sexual preferences or orientations. Discussion on homosexual, heterosexual, and bisexual orientations are important aspects that should be covered in sex education curriculums. Students should be aware of the freedom they have with sex and that there is not one correct choice. Without covering all sexual orientations, many young people who do not fit into the life style choice covered will be left ignorant, and their choice will seem wrong and immoral based on it's omission from the curriculum. Students who are taught that only heterosexuality is correct will be harmed because they will develop, or have reinforced, prejudices against bisexual or homosexual individuals. Lack of knowledge is largely responsible for the risky experimentation of teenagers and global prejudice against anyone with a differing sexual preference. Youths need an environment of support as they struggle to establish their sexual identity (Moore 121).

The media has great influence over adolescents today and the often misleading, incorrect, and biased information given out is partly responsible for the sexual problems they encounter. TV, radio, and magazines are common sources of knowledge for confused teenagers. Although some call in radio or TV shows offer sound advice from doctors and privacy, the fact that these shows are so popular emphasizes the demand for more sex education (Moore 116, 117). Soap operas promote sexual promiscuity, give unrealistic representations of sex, and often neglect to mention contraception and the risk of STD's and AIDS associated with such risky behavior. Talk shows are another important example of media that confuses and distorts sex. Some talk show audiences give support and acceptance to people of every sexual persuasion while others are dominated with audiences that denounce any variation of heterosexual activity. These contradicting opinions confuse youths about what is right and acceptable behavior.

There are many statistics that show the dire need to inform youth about the consequences of sexual activity. The US in 1966 reported 50,000 cases of genital warts, but by 1989 that number had risen to a staggering 300,000. It is estimated that over half of the world's HIV infections occur in 15–24 year olds, and the most deaths from AIDS are among those in the 20–40 age range. AIDS is the sixth leading cause of death for individuals between the ages of 15 and 24 in the US. The number of teenagers infected between 1990 and 1992 has increased by seventy percent. In 1993 eighty-six percent of all STD's in the US occurred in young people ages 15–29 years old. Infection rates for chlamydia in that year were as high as thirty-seven percent for adolescents. In 1989 thirty percent of new gonorrhea cases were accounted for by youth ages 10–19 years of age. The report concludes that one in five adolescents will have acquired a sexually transmitted disease by age 21 (Moore 12, 13).

The controversy over sex education is strongly debated by both sides. One important advocate against sex education is the Roman Catholic Church. Pope John Paul II, "favors sexual abstinence outside of marriage, opposes contraception and abortion and declares homosexual practices and masturbation to be 'disorders'." (Williams A23) The Vatican "urges parents to remove their children from sex-education classes that teach such practices as 'safe sex' or that deal with sex purely as a health issue outside the realm of Christian values." (Williams A23) Many people feel that by teaching 'anti-birth' and 'family planning' ideas, the family value framework is being destroyed. Others feel sex education is destroying the parent-child educational relationship. Advocates feel that to control problems like AIDS, parents should teach their children to abstain from sex until marriage and refuse to promote safe sex as an alternative to abstinence. These individuals feel that despite the information given in a sex education class, it will be ineffective without family values (Williams A23).

Another important point made by those against sex education is that the school systems assume that teenagers are going to have sex, therefore, a strong focus should be on contraception. They feel that only abstinence should be taught as the best protection from disease and pregnancy. Many parents question sex programs where homosexuality, and other life styles different from heterosexuality, are discussed as equally correct choices for sexual preferences. Much of this controversy comes from Christians who view homosexuality as immoral, therefore, they feel that it should not be covered at all in the classroom. These same parents are concerned with the amount of graphic information their children are given and it's appropriateness for youth.

In response to the religious concerns over sex education, I would like to mention that parent's have the right to withdraw their children from such a class according to the 1st Amendment. Parents should be able to remove their children from sex education as long as they can offer the school an alternative for the child at home. Also, not all Americans are Christians and therefore to require that all sex education courses support the Christian religion would not please everyone with children. Abstinence is given as an option, and is clearly shown to be the safest choice, but the objective of sex education is not to force a certain choice on students but show all the options so they can make an informed choice. Parents can still teach their teenagers their family values and what their particular religion believes is right, but whether they agree with other life styles is not relevant. There is also an important problem with relying solely on parents for informing their children about sex. An important barrier is embarrassment for both the youth and parent (Moore 107). Adolescents need an increasing amount of privacy and an invasion by a parent on such a sensitive subject is likely to hinder communication (Moore 107). Some parent's also assume that there children must already know everything they need to know and so do not approach them about sex (Moore 108). The most important barrier are the parents' own values and bias' that may only give a one-sided view of sexual behavior (Moore 108). Some parent's may not know all the accurate facts themselves and so their adolescents may receive false information.

The young people of this generation are obviously not being adequately informed at home about sex, due to the large number of teenage pregnancies and STD's in this country. Sex education is the optimum way in which to inform all adolescents about the importance of responsible and safe behavior. Parent's wish for their children safe and healthy lives, and with the help of mandatory sex education classes, this goal can be reached.

INSTRUCTOR'S REVIEW

Emily's teacher, Ron, wrote the following comment on the second draft:

Emily, this is an excellent treatment of a very difficult topic. I think you are one draft away from a great essay—and I would very much like to see you revise. Should you revise, I would suggest two things: (1) Be careful early on not to state things in such a way as to draw needless attacks from the other side—I've given you some marginal notes about this, and I can explain more in person. And (2) drop the sexual orientation part of the paper. That's a separable argument. By telling the other side that they have to let you (and people who think like you) teach homosexuality as an acceptable sexual behavior, you are guaranteeing that many people in your audience will not hear anything you have to say about premarital sex, AIDS, and STD's.

Let's talk about this paper at your earliest convenience.

Emily and Ron did talk, and Emily revised her essay to produce a final draft.

FINAL DRAFT

LEARNING ABOUT SEX

EMILY WEAST

1   Sex education should be included in the curriculum at all middle and high schools. The type of sex education that needs to be taught in schools would include information about contraception, sexually transmitted diseases (STD's), and the reproductive system. Only through the process of acquiring knowledge can students learn to make rational decisions based on fact instead of fiction. Despite the many attacks on sex education, education is the only way our country and the rest of the world are ever going to decrease the number of young people giving birth at early ages, contracting STD's, and dying of AIDS.

2   The increasing number of people with HIV/AIDS has ended any possibility of continuing the passive approach to educating our adolescents. The kind of program I propose would teach abstinence as the only completely safe choice regarding sex, but the public school's function is to give information, not dictate what a student should choose. Contraception should also be covered for those students who may choose to have sex so they can protect themselves from disease and pregnancy. The authors of *Youth, AIDS and Sexually Transmitted Diseases*, Susan Moore, Doreen Rosenthal, and Anne Mitchell, feel our youth have difficulty personalizing the dangers of AIDS and other STD's because of their lack of knowledge about how these diseases are transmitted (114). Sex education aims to inform adolescents about their bodies and about the consequences of having sex, such as STD's and pregnancy.

3   This program would require teachers specifically trained to deliver factual and unbiased information. Oftentimes, the teachers appointed to teach sex education (if the school teaches it) have no training in the health field. Any teacher with a free period during the school day, regardless of qualification, can be given the responsibility of informing our youth about a very serious subject. Teachers of sex education classes should have a college degree in health education, and most importantly be trained on how to respond to students' questions in an unbiased way and teach the curriculum untainted by personal opinions. Teenagers need this source of knowledge about sex so they can make educated decisions and protect themselves if they choose to be sexually active.

4   There may have been a time when parents could have taken a passive approach to their child's sex education, but they cannot do so any more, in part because they as parents have less and less influence on their children. Conversely, the media and society have more and more influence over adolescents. The information in the media is often misleading, incorrect, and biased. Teenagers are prone to do what others do. This is a dangerous tendency when the media portray risky lifestyles as the accepted behavior. TV, radio, and magazines are common sources of knowledge for confused teenagers. Al-

though some call-in radio or TV shows offer sound advice from doctors in an anonymous situation, the fact that these shows are so popular emphasizes the demand for more sex education (Moore 116–117). Soap operas promote sexual promiscuity, give unrealistic representations of sex, and often neglect to mention contraception and the risk of STD's and AIDS associated with such risky behavior. Talk shows also confuse and distort sex. Some talk show audiences give support and acceptance to people who engage in dangerous sexual behavior. Most talk shows discuss sex in some way during every airing on television. The issues seem to focus more on who is cheating on whom and with how many people rather than on the extreme risk of disease from such behavior. These dangerous opinions mislead youths about the seriousness of choosing to have sex.

5   There are many statistics that show the dire need to inform youth about the consequences of sexual activity. The following data are taken from the book mentioned above, *Youth, AIDS and Sexually Transmitted Diseases.* In 1966, 50,000 cases of genital warts were reported in the U.S., but by 1989 that number had risen to a staggering 300,000; by 1989, thirty percent of new gonorrhea cases were accounted for by youth 10–19 years of age (12). It is estimated that over half the world's HIV infections occur in 15–24 year olds, and the most deaths from AIDS are among those in the 20–40 age range (13). Between 1990 and 1992, the number of teenagers infected with AIDS increased by seventy percent; by 1996, AIDS had become the sixth leading cause of death for individuals between the ages of 15 and 24 in the U.S. (13). In 1993, eighty-six percent of all STD's in the U.S. occurred in young people ages 15–29 years old, and infection rates for chlamydia in that year were as high as thirty-seven percent for adolescents (12). Moore, Rosenthal, and Mitchell conclude that one in five adolescents will have acquired a sexually transmitted disease by age 21 (12).

6   The controversy over sex education is strongly debated by both sides. One important opponent of sex education in public schools is the Roman Catholic Church. Pope John Paul II "favors sexual abstinence outside of marriage, opposes contraception and abortion and declares homosexual practices and masturbation to be 'disorders'" (Williams A23). The Vatican "urges parents to remove their children from sex-education classes that teach such practices as 'safe sex' or that deal with sex purely as a health issue outside the realm of Christian values" (Williams A23). Many people feel that family values are destroyed by instruction in family planning. They believe that in order to control problems like AIDS, parents should teach their children to abstain from sex until marriage and refuse to promote safe sex as an alternative to abstinence. These individuals feel that information given in sex education classes will be ineffective and even harmful without instruction in family values (Williams A23).

7   Another important argument is that by focusing on contraception, the schools seem to assume that teenagers are going to have sex. Those who oppose sex education classes feel that abstinence should be taught as the only protection from disease and pregnancy. This viewpoint is strongly held by conservative Christians who view premarital sex as immoral and feel the topic should not be covered at all in the classroom. These same people feel that sex education classes tend to transmit graphic information that is often inappropriate for the children it is being given to.

8   I understand why these people would find a problem with the kind of sex education I propose; however, I would like to mention that parents have the right to withdraw their children from such a class according to the 1st Amendment. In order to do so, they have only to offer the school an alternative for the child at home. This may be a hardship on those individuals, but we cannot allow a minority to prevent us from educating the vast majority of students whose parents do not find sex education objectionable. To incorporate the Christian religion into education would be disregarding a fundamental rule of this country to separate church and state.

9   In public school sex education, abstinence should be advocated as the safest choice, but the objective of sex education is not to force a certain choice on students but rather to show all the options so students can make an informed choice. Parents can still teach their teenagers their family values and the tenets of their religion. But, there is an important problem with relying solely on parents to inform their children about sex. An important barrier is embarrassment for both the youth and parent (Moore 107). Adolescents need an increasing amount of privacy and an invasion by a parent on such a sensitive subject could hinder communication. Some parents also assume that their children must already know everything they need to know and so do not approach them about sex. The most important problem is caused by the fact that parents' own values and biases may only give a one-sided view of sexual behavior (Moore 107, 108). Some parents may not know all the accurate facts themselves and so their adolescents may receive false information.

10   The large number of teenage pregnancies and the spread of STD's indicate that the young people of this generation are not being adequately informed about sex at home. Sex education is the optimum way in which to inform all adolescents about the importance of responsible and safe behavior. Parents wish for their children safe and healthy lives, and with the help of mandatory sex education classes, this goal can be reached.

WORKS CITED

Moore, Susan, Doreen Rosenthal, and Anne Mitchell. *Youth, AIDS and Sexually Transmitted Diseases.* Chatham: Mackays of Chatham, 1996.

Williams, Daniel. "Vatican Cautions on Sex Education; Panel Says Classes Should Promote Morality." *Washington Post* 22 Dec. 1995: A23.

Checklist: Critiquing a Position Essay

1. State the essay's thesis, being sure to include the word "should." Is this a thesis about which reasonable people will disagree? State the foundational (value and/or causal) assertions that support this sentence. Are they logically connected to the thesis?

2. List the types of support that the writer uses for each causal or value claim made in the argument. Are all claims clearly supported?

3. Briefly sketch the organization of the paper. Does the writer use an informal or a formal structure? Is the organization effective?

4. What is the thesis of those who would oppose this argument? Does the writer present the opposition's point of view fairly, without distortion? What counterarguments would be made against this argument? Does the writer acknowledge and respond to these counterarguments?

5. Does the paper adhere to conventions of usage, mechanics, and format? Correct any errors you find.

In this chapter, we turn to persuasive writing. How does persuasive writing differ from the argumentative writing we discussed in Chapter 9? Your goal in writing a position paper was to make your position clear to someone who disagreed with you on the issue in question. Your goal in this chapter will be to move readers to action.

As we explained in Chapter 9, persuasion is not possible in many situations. Some of our beliefs are central to our concept of self. Thus, when we enter into a discussion about these beliefs, we are not likely to change them. When both sides in an argument are operating from such fixed beliefs, persuasion is not possible. The best that can be hoped for in such situations is a meeting of the minds in which the two sides present their arguments as clearly and cogently as possible, with the modest hope that each will understand the logic behind the other's position—hence the position essay.

The goal in a persuasion essay is, in one sense, more ambitious and, in another sense, less ambitious than the goal in a position essay. It is more ambitious in that the goal in persuasion is to cause readers to take some action. It is less ambitious in that the writer assumes an audience that is already sympathetic to her argument. The writer's purpose, then, is not to change the mind of the reader, but to energize and move the reader who already shares (or at least leans toward) the writer's viewpoint.

Persuasion Essays

C H A P T E R 10

The key component in persuasive writing is pathos, or emotion. Whereas reason may help us formulate and solidify our beliefs, emotion acts as the catalyst that brings our actions and our beliefs together. We tend to act because we are moved to do what we have come to understand to be the right course of action—or at least that is the way it should be. Of course, this isn't always the case. We are sometimes moved to do things even though we can give no good reasons for doing them. When an advertiser persuades us to buy a product that costs more money than we can really afford to spend or one that harms our health, we have been moved to take an action without having been convinced logically that the action is good for us. In such a situation, the advertiser's ability to separate reason and emotion makes his writing effective, even though what he is doing is not ethical.

In analyzing the sample essays in this chapter, we will differentiate between effective writing and good writing. In order to be *good*, writing must be both effective and ethical. Each of the sample essays presented here is effective. However, we have included writing that we see as problematic from an ethical standpoint. We have done so because much of the persuasive writing we face on a daily basis is designed to use emotion as a tool to achieve the writer's ends—sometimes with little or no attempt to connect reason and emotion. In the writing you do in this chapter, you should focus on emotion as a way of moving your readers to take action. However, you will be advocating actions that you believe will be good for you and your readers. And even though you may not spend as much time developing a logical argument as you would if you were writing for an audience that would resist your reasons, you will argue your case logically and avoid oversimplifications and distortions of your opponents' arguments that would amount to an abuse of logic.

SAMPLE ESSAYS

The following sample essays attempt to persuade readers to take actions on beliefs they hold about abortion, date rape, race and poverty, domestic violence, and capital punishment. The first essay, by Michael R. Heaphy, is aimed at convincing readers to take action to make abortion illegal.

MICHAEL R. HEAPHY

DISMEMBERMENT AND CHOICE

1   For the last few years, it has been commonplace to hear conventionally enlightened people soberly and confidently announce that they are not pro-abortion but, rather, pro-choice. Because of the generality that is implicit in the unqualified word "choice," it is logical to examine the pro-choice argument from a broad perspective.

2   To make a *pro-choice* argument is to assert a liberty to perform an action, X, without bothering to explain why X should be legal, without acknowledging the nature of X, and, sometimes, without permitting the name for X to cross one's lips. Illogically, "choice" is both the premise and the conclusion. The pro-choice argument for abortion is that abortion should be legal because women have a *right to choose.* The problem with this argument is that an unqualified right purely and simply to *choose* could be used to advocate legal status for drunk driving, cannibalism, insider trading, or anything else. Unless one believes that all conceivable actions should be legal, it is not reasonable to base advocacy of legality for a particular action on *unqualified* choice.

3   To understand what abortion is all about, it is useful to re-direct our attention from the abstract plane down to a more practical level. Such a real-world viewpoint can be achieved by considering the day-to-day work of a physician who does little else with his professional life except abortions. For example, in my own state of Ohio, there is the practice of W. Martin Haskell, M. D.

4   Depending on the size of the unborn child (or should I use one of the sanitized terms—like the "conceptus"?), Dr. Haskell employs various techniques. If the fetus isn't too far along, Haskell can probably use the suction curettage method in which a sharp curette is used to reduce the fetus into chunks small enough to be sucked out of the uterus.

5   Later in pregnancy the fetus is too large for this method. Such cases provide Dr. Haskell with many of his referrals. He is an expert at killing human fetuses at five and six months' gestation. He uses laminaria to dilate the cervix in a three-day procedure, then simply goes in, makes a direct instrument attack on the fetus, kills it, and takes it out.

6   Of course, the head is usually crushed in this D&E (dilation and evacuation) procedure. An unripened cervix just doesn't expand enough to pass a five- or six-month head. If the unborn baby is big enough, then the arms and legs may have to go too. The fetus is typically dismembered and removed piece by piece in a D&E abortion. The parts are often inspected to make sure an arm or a leg hasn't been left in the mother.

7   The news organizations' reticence about mentioning the actual nature of abortion may arise in part from a chink in the gleaming semantic armor that otherwise encases the subject: The abortion advocates forgot to re-name the body parts encountered in abortion.

8   Presumably the "conscientious practitioners" of abortion (as the AMA now calls them—in slight departure from its own earlier description of them as "modern day Herods"), would be loath to admit to killing unborn children. They would rather say that they *terminate pregnancies,* an odd assistance for a process that invariably terminates itself.

9   As long as the discussion is couched in such genteel terms, there isn't much room for primitive, natural words like "arm" and "leg." They are gaucheries. On the other hand, if we could simply introduce a few Choice words into the vocabulary, then our mass media would no longer need to shy away from the topic of abortion techniques. The unborn child won't be called a child but just a "fetus" (Latin for "offspring"), and the arm is only a "potential arm" or, say, a "brachium."

10   Dr. Haskell operates abortion facilities in Cincinnati and suburban Dayton. When Yvonne Brower, a University of Cincinnati student, called to enquire if she could observe abortions to gather information for a term paper, the clinic manager was magnanimous. On September 21, 1989, Miss Brower observed Dr. Haskell killing fetuses at the Women's Med Center, which he owns, in Kettering, Ohio. The events of that morning prompted Miss Brower to file a complaint with the police.

11   The following excerpt from the police report is of interest:

> She stated that by 11 o'clock she had already observed two "D&E" three-day procedures on two patients. She stated on the third patient, however, the abortion was different. . . . The patient's water was already broken and she spontaneously gave birth prematurely before the proper D&E procedure could be done. She stated that the baby was delivered feet first very quickly through the birth canal. The head was on its way out when Dr. Haskell reached over and got his scissors and snipped the right side of the baby's common carotid artery.

12   Even then, Miss Brower stated, the newborn infant was not exactly dead. The police report again:

> The complainant stated that the baby was still moving when she looked at it once again. . . . it was breathing shallow breaths, as was evidenced by the chest moving up and down. She stated that she could also observe the baby's hand having slow, controlled, muscular movements, unlike the short jerky twitchy motions she had seen and learned to expect when the baby was already dead before it came out of the birth canal.

13   The *Dayton Daily News* reported this story on Sunday, December 10, 1989. In the *Daily News* Dr. Haskell described the event in question in this way: "it came out very quickly after I put the scissors up in the cervical canal and pierced the skull and spread the scissors apart. It popped right on out. . . . the previous two, I had to use the suction to collapse the skull."

14   Haskell also said Miss Brower "quite possibly" misinterpreted what happened in the abortion. Miss Brower, however, said she saw Dr. Haskell perform 15 abortions the day before and two others that morning. "So it's not like I hadn't seen any before," she said.

15   Dr. Haskell was questioned by the police. He maintains that when he does abortions he always causes the death of the fetus to occur just before delivery rather than after. The prosecutor did not bring charges.

16   Of course, if killing the unborn, at the moment when Haskell *openly admits* to the act, is not merely *not illegal* but rather a "fundamental right," it would be remarkable for virtually the same act to constitute legal homicide a few seconds later. *Legal* homicide or not, however, it would seem clear that a direct, intentional, and lethal assault on a human fetus must constitute a *homicide-in-fact* in that old-fashioned, as-long-as-words-have-meanings sense that even our federal judges are not quite able to change. It would be rather surprising if, here or there, some abortionist did not proceed to act on the logical basis that the result is the same whether one kills the fetus and then takes it out or takes it out and then kills it.

17   At present, good people in America are working to undo a decree that has transformed an entire class of human beings into constitutional outlaws suitable for discretionary killing. The idea that something so grandiose and Platonic as "choice" will be lost to our people if this killing is prohibited is as ludicrous as suggesting that the American people are already deprived of the same ideal by the prohibition of burglary or rape. The abortion struggle is of pivotal importance for humanity because it is about the value of human life and the value of truth. If that seems too abstract, then consider a more concrete approach: Recall that it is also about crushing unborn babies' skulls and ask whether or not it is OK to do that.

1. What is the thesis of Heaphy's essay? Does it appear in the essay? If so, where? What reasons does he give for accepting his position?
2. Divide the essay into beginning, middle, and end. What rhetorical and/or stylistic devices help form these divisions?
3. What audience might Heaphy's essay be written for? Is that audience likely to resist his argument? Explain.
4. Does Heaphy offer counterarguments to those who would disagree with him? If so, does he represent the opposition's argument fairly? Explain. What counterarguments are offered?
5. In addition to (or instead of) logical argumentation, what kinds of persuasive appeals does Heaphy use in this essay? Would these appeals be likely to work for his intended audience? Why or why not?
6. How would you characterize your attitude toward this subject before reading Heaphy's essay? What effect did this essay have on your thinking?

In our second essay, "Rape and Modern Sex War," Camille Paglia seeks to persuade women that feminism has been responsible for promoting ideas that will ultimately lead women to put themselves in dangerous situations.

CAMILLE PAGLIA

RAPE AND MODERN SEX WAR

1   Rape is an outrage that cannot be tolerated in civilized society. Yet feminism, which has waged a crusade for rape to be taken more seriously, has put young women in danger by hiding the truth about sex from them.

2   In dramatizing the pervasiveness of rape, feminists have told young women that before they have sex with a man, they must give consent as explicit as a legal contract's. In this way, young women have been convinced that they have been the victims of rape. On elite campuses in the Northeast and on the West Coast, they have held consciousness-raising sessions, petitioned administrations, demanded inquests. At Brown University, outraged, panicky "victims" have scrawled the names of alleged attackers on the walls of women's rest rooms. What marital rape was to the '70s, "date rape" is to the '90s.

3   The incidence and seriousness of rape do not require this kind of exaggeration. Real acquaintance rape is nothing new. It has been a horrible problem for women for all of recorded history. Once fathers and brothers protected women from rape. Once the penalty for rape was death. I come from a fierce Italian tradition where, not so long ago in the motherland, a rapist would end up knifed, castrated, and hung out to dry.

4   But the old clans and small rural communities have broken down. In our cities, on our campuses far from home, young women are vulnerable and defenseless. Feminism has not prepared them for this. Feminism keeps saying the sexes are the same. It keeps telling women they can do anything, go anywhere, say anything, wear anything. No, they can't. Women will always be in sexual danger.

5   One of my male students recently slept overnight with a friend in a passageway of the Great Pyramid in Egypt. He described the moon and sand, the ancient silence and eerie echoes. I will never experience that. I am a woman. I am not stupid enough to believe I could ever be safe there. There is a world of solitary adventure I will never have. Women have always known these somber truths. But feminism, with its pie-in-the-sky fantasies about the perfect world, keeps young women from seeing life as it is.

6   We must remedy social injustice whenever we can. But there are some things we cannot change. There are sexual differences that are based in biology. Academic feminism is lost in a fog of social constructionism. It believes we are totally the product of our environment. This idea was invented by Rousseau. He was wrong. Emboldened by dumb French language theory, academic feminists repeat the same hollow slogans over and over to each other. Their view of sex is naive and prudish. Leaving sex to the feminists is like letting your dog vacation at the taxidermist's.

7   The sexes are at war. Men must struggle for identity against the overwhelming power of their mothers. Women have menstruation to tell them they are women. Men must do or risk something to be men. Men become masculine only when other men say they are. Having sex with a woman is one way a boy becomes a man.

8   College men are at their hormonal peak. They have just left their mothers and are questing for their male identity. In groups, they are dangerous. A woman going to a fraternity party is walking into Testosterone Flats, full of prickly cacti and blazing guns. If she goes, she should be armed with resolute alertness. She should arrive with girlfriends and leave with them. A girl who lets herself get dead drunk at a fraternity party is a fool. A girl who goes upstairs alone with a brother at a fraternity party is an idiot. Feminists call this "blaming the victim." I call it common sense.

9   For a decade, feminists have drilled their disciples to say, "Rape is a crime of violence but not of sex." This sugar-coated Shirley Temple nonsense has exposed young women to disaster. Misled by feminism, they do not expect rape from the nice boys from good homes who sit next to them in class.

10   Aggression and eroticism are deeply intertwined. Hunt, pursuit, and capture are biologically programmed into male sexuality. Generation after generation, men must be educated, refined, and ethically persuaded away from their tendency toward anarchy and brutishness. Society is not the enemy, as feminism ignorantly claims. Society is woman's protection against rape. Feminism, with its solemn Carry Nation repressiveness, does not see what is for men the eroticism or fun element in rape, especially the wild, infectious delirium of gang rape. Women who do not understand rape cannot defend themselves against it.

11   The date-rape controversy shows feminism hitting the wall of its own broken promises. The women of my '60s generation were the first respectable girls in history to swear like sailors, get drunk, stay out all night—in short, to act like men. We sought total sexual freedom and equality. But as time passed, we woke up to cold reality. The old double standard protected women. When anything goes, it's women who lose.

12   Today's young women don't know what they want. They see that feminism has not brought sexual happiness. The theatrics of public rage over date rape are their way of restoring the old sexual rules that were shattered by my generation. Because nothing about the sexes has really changed. The comic film *Where the Boys Are* (1960), the ultimate expression of '50s man-chasing, still speaks directly to our time. It shows smart,

lively women skillfully anticipating and fending off the dozens of strategies with which horny men try to get them into bed. The agonizing date-rape subplot and climax are brilliantly done. The victim, Yvette Mimieux, makes mistake after mistake, obvious to the other girls. She allows herself to be lured away from her girlfriends and into isolation with boys whose character and intentions she misreads. *Where the Boys Are* tells the truth. It shows courtship as a dangerous game in which the signals are not verbal but subliminal.

13   Neither militant feminism, which is obsessed with politically correct language, nor academic feminism, which believes that knowledge and experience are "constituted by" language, can understand pre-verbal or non-verbal communication. Feminism, focusing on sexual politics, cannot see that sex exists in and through the body. Sexual desire and arousal cannot be fully translated into verbal terms. This is why men and women misunderstand each other.

14   Trying to remake the future, feminism cut itself off from sexual history. It discarded and suppressed the sexual myths of literature, art, and religion. Those myths show us the turbulence, the mysteries and passions of sex. In mythology we see men's sexual anxiety, their fear of women's dominance. Much sexual violence is rooted in men's sense of psychological weakness toward women. It takes many men to deal with one woman. Woman's voracity is a persistent motif. Clara Bow, it was rumored, took on the USC football team on weekends. Marilyn Monroe, singing "Diamonds Are a Girl's Best Friend," rules a conga line of men in tuxes. Half-clad Cher, in the video for "If I Could Turn Back Time," deranges a battleship of screaming sailors and straddles a pink-lit cannon. Feminism, coveting social power, is blind to woman's cosmic sexual power.

15   To understand rape, you must study the past. There never was and never will be sexual harmony. Every woman must take personal responsibility for her sexuality, which is nature's red flame. She must be prudent and cautious about where she goes and with whom. When she makes a mistake, she must accept the consequences and, through self-criticism, resolve never to make that mistake again. Running to Mommy and Daddy or the campus grievance committee is unworthy of strong women. Posting lists of guilty men in the toilet is cowardly, infantile stuff.

16   The Italian philosophy of life espouses high-energy confrontation. A male student makes a vulgar remark about your breasts? Don't slink off to whimper and simper with the campus shrinking violets. Deal with it. On the spot. Say, "Shut up, you jerk! And crawl back to the barnyard where you belong!" In general, women who project this take-charge attitude toward life get harassed less often. I see too many dopey, immature, self-pitying women walking around like melting sticks of butter. It's the Yvette Mimieux syndrome: Make me happy. And listen to me weep when I'm not.

17   The date-rape debate is already smothering in propaganda churned out by the expensive Northeastern colleges and universities, with their overconcentration of boring, uptight academic feminists and spoiled, affluent students. Beware of the deep manipulativeness of rich students who were neglected by their parents. They love to turn the campus into hysterical psychodramas of sexual transgression, followed by assertions of parental authority and concern. And don't look for sexual enlightenment from academe, which spews out mountains of books but never looks at life directly.

18   As a fan of football and rock music, I see in the simple, swaggering masculinity of the jock and in the noisy posturing of the heavy-metal guitarist certain fundamental, unchanging truths about sex. Masculinity is aggressive, unstable, combustible. It is also the most creative cultural force in history. Women must reorient themselves toward the elemental powers of sex, which can strengthen or destroy.

19   The only solution to date rape is female self-awareness and self-control. A woman's number one line of defense is herself. When a real rape occurs, she should report it to the police. Complaining to college committees because the courts "take too long" is ridiculous.

College administrations are not a branch of the judiciary. They are not equipped or trained for legal inquiry. Colleges must alert incoming students to the problems and dangers of adulthood. Then colleges must stand back and get out of the sex game.

Questions for Review

1. What is the thesis of Paglia's essay? Does it appear in the essay? If so, where? What reasons does she give for accepting her position?
2. Divide the essay into beginning, middle, and end. What rhetorical and/or stylistic devices help form these divisions?
3. What audience might Paglia's essay be written for? Is that audience likely to resist her argument? Explain.
4. Does Paglia offer counterarguments to those who would disagree with her? If so, does she represent the opposition's argument fairly? Explain. What counterarguments are offered?
5. In addition to (or instead of) logical argumentation, what kinds of persuasive appeals does Paglia use in this essay? Would these appeals be likely to work for her intended audience? Why or why not?
6. How would you characterize your attitude toward this subject before reading Paglia's essay? What effect did this essay have on your thinking?

In our third essay, "Letter from Birmingham Jail," Martin Luther King, Jr., writes an "open" letter to eight clergymen who had written a published statement (also reprinted here) calling for citizens in Alabama to obey the law while working for peaceful changes in what they termed "racial matters."

PUBLIC STATEMENT BY
EIGHT ALABAMA CLERGYMEN

April 12, 1963

1   We the undersigned clergymen are among those who, in January, issued "An Appeal for Law and Order and Common Sense," in dealing with racial problems in Alabama. We expressed understanding that honest conviction in racial matters could properly be pursued in the courts, but urged that decisions of those courts should in the meantime be peacefully obeyed.

2   Since that time there had been some evidence of increased forbearance and a willingness to face facts. Responsible citizens have undertaken to work on various problems which cause racial friction and unrest. In Birmingham, recent public events had given indication that we all have opportunity for a new constructive and realistic approach to racial problems.

3   However, we are now confronted by a series of demonstrations by some of our Negro citizens, directed and led in part by outsiders. We recognize the natural impatience of people who feel that their hopes are slow in being realized. But we are convinced that these demonstrations are unwise and untimely.

4   We agree rather with certain local Negro leadership which has called for honest and open negotiation of racial issues in our area. And we believe this kind of facing of issues can best be accomplished by citizens of our own metropolitan area, white and Negro, meeting with their knowledge and experience of the local situation. All of us need to face that responsibility and find proper channels for its accomplishment.

5   Just as we formerly pointed out that "hatred and violence have no sanction in our religious and political tradition," we also point out that such actions as incite to hatred and violence, however technically peaceful those actions may be, have not contributed to the resolution of our local problems. We do not believe that these days of new hope are days when extreme measures are justified in Birmingham.

6   We commend the community as a whole, and the local news media and law enforcement officials in particular, on the calm manner in which these demonstrations have been handled. We urge the public to continue to show restraint should the demonstrations continue, and the law enforcement officials to remain calm and continue to protect our city from violence.

7   We further stongly urge our own Negro community to withdraw support from these demonstrations, and to unite locally in working peacefully for a better Birmingham. When rights are consistently denied, a cause should be pressed in the courts, and in negotiation among local leaders, and not in the streets. We appeal to both our white and Negro citizenry to observe the principles of law and order and common sense. Signed by:

C. C. J. Carpenter, D.D., LL.D., *Bishop of Alabama*

Joseph A. Durick, D.D., *Auxiliary Bishop, Diocese of Mobile, Birmingham*

Rabbi Milton L. Grafman, *Temple Emanu-El, Birmingham, Alabama*

Bishop Paul Hardin, *Bishop of the Alabama-West Florida Conference of the Methodist Church*

Bishop Nolan B. Harmon, *Bishop of the North Alabama Conference of the Methodist Church*

George M. Murray, D.D, LL.D., *Bishop Coadjutor, Episcopal Diocese of Alabama*

Edward V. Ramage, *Moderator, Synod of the Alabama Presbyterian Church in the United States*

Earl Stallings, *Pastor, First Baptist Church, Birmingham, Alabama*

MARTIN LUTHER KING, JR.

LETTER FROM BIRMINGHAM JAIL

April 16, 1963

My Dear Fellow Clergymen:

1   While confined here in the Birmingham city jail, I came across your recent statement calling my present activities "unwise and untimely." Seldom do I pause to answer

criticism of my work and ideas. If I sought to answer all the criticisms that cross my desk, my secretaries would have little time for anything other than such correspondence in the course of the day, and I would have no time for constructive work. But since I feel that you are men of genuine good will and that your criticisms are sincerely set forth, I want to try to answer your statement in what I hope will be patient and reasonable terms.

2 I think I should indicate why I am here in Birmingham, since you have been influenced by the view which argues against "outsiders coming in." I have the honor of serving as president of the Southern Christian Leadership Conference, an organization operating in every southern state, with headquarters in Atlanta, Georgia. We have some eighty-five affiliated organizations across the South, and one of them is the Alabama Christian Movement for Human Rights. Frequently we share staff, educational and financial resources with our affiliates. Several months ago the affiliate here in Birmingham asked us to be on call to engage in a nonviolent direct-action program if such were deemed necessary. We readily consented, and when the hour came we lived up to our promise. So I, along with several members of my staff, am here because I was invited here. I am here because I have organizational ties here.

3 But more basically, I am in Birmingham because injustice is here. Just as the prophets of the eighth century B.C. left their villages and carried their "thus saith the Lord" far beyond the boundaries of their home towns, and just as the Apostle Paul left his village of Tarsus and carried the gospel of Jesus Christ to the far corners of the Greco-Roman world, so am I compelled to carry the gospel of freedom beyond my own home town. Like Paul, I must constantly respond to the Macedonian call for aid.

4 Moreover, I am cognizant of the interrelatedness of all communities and states. I cannot sit idly by in Atlanta and not be concerned about what happens in Birmingham. Injustice anywhere is a threat to justice everywhere. We are caught in an inescapable network of mutuality, tied in a single garment of destiny. Whatever affects one directly, affects all indirectly. Never again can we afford to live with the narrow, provincial "outside agitator" idea. Anyone who lives inside the United States can never be considered an outsider anywhere within its bounds.

5 You deplore the demonstrations taking place in Birmingham. But your statement, I am sorry to say, fails to express a similar concern for the conditions that brought about the demonstrations. I am sure that none of you would want to rest content with the superficial kind of social analysis that deals merely with effects and does not grapple with underlying causes. It is unfortunate that demonstrations are taking place in Birmingham, but it is even more unfortunate that the city's white power structure left the Negro community with no alternative.

6 In any nonviolent campaign there are four basic steps: collection of the facts to determine whether injustices exist; negotiation; self-purification; and direct action. We have gone through all these steps in Birmingham. There can be no gainsaying the fact that racial injustice engulfs this community. Birmingham is probably the most thoroughly segregated city in the United States. Its ugly record of brutality is widely known. Negroes have experienced grossly unjust treatment in the courts. There have been more unsolved bombings of Negro homes and churches in Birmingham than in any other city in the nation. These are the hard, brutal facts of the case. On the basis of these conditions, Negro leaders sought to negotiate with the city fathers. But the latter consistently refused to engage in good-faith negotiation.

7 Then, last September, came the opportunity to talk with leaders of Birmingham's economic community. In the course of the negotiations, certain promises were made by the merchants—for example, to remove the stores' humiliating racial signs. On the basis of these promises, the Reverend Fred Shuttlesworth and the leaders of the Alabama

Christian Movement for Human Rights agreed to a moratorium on all demonstrations. As the weeks and months went by, we realized that we were the victims of a broken promise. A few signs, briefly removed, returned; the others remained.

8   As in so many past experiences, our hopes had been blasted, and the shadow of deep disappointment settled upon us. We had no alternative except to prepare for direct action, whereby we would present our very bodies as a means of laying our case before the conscience of the local and the national community. Mindful of the difficulties involved, we decided to undertake a process of self-purification. We began a series of workshops on nonviolence, and repeatedly asked ourselves: "Are you able to accept blows without retaliating?" "Are you able to endure the ordeal of jail?" We decided to schedule our direct-action program for the Easter season, realizing that except for Christmas, this is the main shopping period of the year. Knowing that a strong economic-withdrawal program would be the by-product of direct action, we felt that this would be the best time to bring pressure to bear on the merchants for the needed change.

9   Then it occurred to us that Birmingham's mayoral election was coming up in March, and we speedily decided to postpone action until after election day. When we discovered that the Commissioner of Public Safety, Eugene "Bull" Connor, had piled up enough votes to be in the run-off, we decided again to postpone action until the day after the run-off so that the demonstrations could not be used to cloud the issues. Like many others, we waited to see Mr. Connor defeated, and to this end we endured postponement after postponement. Having aided in this community need, we felt that our direct action program could be delayed no longer.

10   You may well ask: "Why direct action? Why sit-ins, marches and so forth? Isn't negotiation a better path?" You are quite right in calling for negotiation. Indeed, this is the very purpose of direct action. Nonviolent direct action seeks to create such a crisis and foster such a tension that a community which has constantly refused to negotiate is forced to confront the issue. It seeks so to dramatize the issue that it can no longer be ignored. My citing the creation of tension as part of the work of the nonviolent-resister may sound rather shocking. But I must confess that I am not afraid of the word "tension." I have earnestly opposed violent tension, but there is a type of constructive, nonviolent tension which is necessary for growth. Just as Socrates felt that it was necessary to create a tension in the mind so that individuals could rise from the bondage of myths and half-truths to the unfettered realm of creative analysis and objective appraisal, so must we see the need for nonviolent gadflies to create the kind of tension in society that will help men rise from the dark depths of prejudice and racism to the majestic heights of understanding and brotherhood.

11   The purpose of our direct-action program is to create a situation so crisis-packed that it will inevitably open the door to negotiation. I therefore concur with you in your call for negotiation. Too long has our beloved Southland been bogged down in a tragic effort to live in monologue rather than dialogue.

12   One of the basic points in your statement is that the action that I and my associates have taken in Birmingham is untimely. Some have asked: "Why didn't you give the new city administration time to act?" The only answer that I can give to this query is that the new Birmingham administration must be prodded about as much as the outgoing one, before it will act. We are sadly mistaken if we feel that the election of Albert Boutwell as mayor will bring the millennium to Birmingham. While Mr. Boutwell is a much more gentle person than Mr. Connor, they are both segregationists, dedicated to maintenance of the status quo. I have hope that Mr. Boutwell will be reasonable enough to see the futility of massive resistance to desegregation. But he will not see this without pressure from devotees of civil rights. My friends, I must say to you that we have not made a single gain in civil rights without determined legal and nonviolent pressure. Lamentably, it is an

historical fact that privileged groups seldom give up their privileges voluntarily. Individuals may see the moral light and voluntarily give up their unjust posture; but, as Reinhold Niebuhr has reminded us, groups tend to be more immoral than individuals.

13   We know through painful experience that freedom is never voluntarily given by the oppressor; it must be demanded by the oppressed. Frankly, I have yet to engage in a direct-action campaign that was "well timed" in the view of those who have not suffered unduly from the disease of segregation. For years now I have heard the word "Wait!" It rings in the ear of every Negro with piercing familiarity. This "Wait" has almost always meant "Never." We must come to see, with one of our distinguished jurists, that "justice too long delayed is justice denied."

14   We have waited for more than 340 years for our constitutional and God-given rights. The nations of Asia and Africa are moving with jetlike speed toward gaining political independence, but we still creep at horse-and-buggy pace toward gaining a cup of coffee at a lunch counter. Perhaps it is easy for those who have never felt the stinging darts of segregation to say, "Wait." But when you have seen vicious mobs lynch your mothers and fathers at will and drown your sisters and brothers at whim; when you have seen hate-filled policemen curse, kick and even kill your black brothers and sisters; when you see the vast majority of your twenty million Negro brothers smothering in an airtight cage of poverty in the midst of an affluent society; when you suddenly find your tongue twisted and your speech stammering as you seek to explain to your six-year-old daughter why she can't go to the public amusement park that has just been advertised on television, and see tears welling up in her eyes when she is told that Funtown is closed to colored children, and see ominous clouds of inferiority beginning to form in her little mental sky, and see her beginning to distort her personality by developing an unconscious bitterness toward white people; when you have to concoct an answer for a five-year-old son who is asking: "Daddy, why do white people treat colored people so mean?"; when you take a cross-country drive and find it necessary to sleep night after night in the uncomfortable corners of your automobile because no motel will accept you; when you are humiliated day in and day out by nagging signs reading "white" and "colored"; when your first name becomes "nigger," your middle name becomes "boy" (however old you are) and your last name becomes "John," and your wife and mother are never given the respected title "Mrs."; when you are harried by day and haunted by night by the fact that you are a Negro, living constantly at tiptoe stance, never quite knowing what to expect next, and are plagued with inner fears and outer resentments; when you are forever fighting a degenerating sense of "nobodiness"— then you will understand why we find it difficult to wait. There comes a time when the cup of endurance runs over, and men are no longer willing to be plunged into the abyss of despair. I hope, sirs, you can understand our legitimate and unavoidable impatience.

15   You express a great deal of anxiety over our willingness to break laws. This is certainly a legitimate concern. Since we so diligently urge people to obey the Supreme Court's decision of 1954 outlawing segregation in the public schools, at first glance it may seem rather paradoxical for us consciously to break laws. One may well ask: "How can you advocate breaking some laws and obeying others?" The answer lies in the fact that there are two types of laws: just and unjust. I would be the first to advocate obeying just laws. One has not only a legal but a moral responsibility to obey just laws. Conversely, one has a moral responsibility to disobey unjust laws. I would agree with St. Augustine that "an unjust law is no law at all."

16   Now, what is the difference between the two? How does one determine whether a law is just or unjust? A just law is a man-made code that squares with the moral law or the law of God. An unjust law is a code that is out of harmony with the moral law. To put it in the terms of St. Thomas Aquinas: An unjust law is a human law that is not

rooted in eternal law and natural law. Any law that uplifts human personality is just. Any law that degrades human personality is unjust. All segregation statutes are unjust because segregation distorts the soul and damages the personality. It gives the segregator a false sense of superiority and the segregated a false sense of inferiority. Segregation, to use the terminology of the Jewish philosopher Martin Buber, substitutes an "I–it" relationship for an "I–thou" relationship and ends up relegating persons to the status of things. Hence segregation is not only politically, economically and sociologically unsound, it is morally wrong and sinful. Paul Tillich has said that sin is separation. Is not segregation an existential expression of man's tragic separation, his awful estrangement, his terrible sinfulness? Thus it is that I can urge men to obey the 1954 decision of the Supreme Court, for it is morally right; and I can urge them to disobey segregation ordinances, for they are morally wrong.

17   Let us consider a more concrete example of just and unjust laws. An unjust law is a code that a numerical or power majority group compels a minority group to obey but does not make binding on itself. This is *difference* made legal. By the same token, a just law is a code that a majority compels a minority to follow and that it is willing to follow itself. This is *sameness* made legal.

18   Let me give another explanation. A law is unjust if it is inflicted on a minority that, as a result of being denied the right to vote, had no part in enacting or devising the law. Who can say that the legislature of Alabama which set up that state's segregation laws was democratically elected? Throughout Alabama all sorts of devious methods are used to prevent Negroes from becoming registered voters, and there are some counties in which, even though Negroes constitute a majority of the population, not a single Negro is registered. Can any law enacted under such circumstances be considered democratically structured?

19   Sometimes a law is just on its face and unjust in its application. For instance, I have been arrested on a charge of parading without a permit. Now, there is nothing wrong in having an ordinance which requires a permit for a parade. But such an ordinance becomes unjust when it is used to maintain segregation and to deny citizens the First-Amendment privilege of peaceful assembly and protest.

20   I hope you are able to see the distinction I am trying to point out. In no sense do I advocate evading or defying the law, as would the rabid segregationist. That would lead to anarchy. One who breaks an unjust law must do so openly, lovingly, and with a willingness to accept the penalty. I submit that an individual who breaks a law that conscience tells him is unjust, and who willingly accepts the penalty of imprisonment in order to arouse the conscience of the community over its injustice, is in reality expressing the highest respect for law.

21   Of course, there is nothing new about this kind of civil disobedience. It was evidenced sublimely in the refusal of Shadrach, Meshach and Abednego to obey the laws of Nebuchadnezzar, on the ground that a higher moral law was at stake. It was practiced superbly by the early Christians, who were willing to face hungry lions and the excruciating pain of chopping blocks rather than submit to certain unjust laws of the Roman Empire. To a degree, academic freedom is a reality today because Socrates practiced civil disobedience. In our own nation, the Boston Tea Party represented a massive act of civil disobedience.

22   We should never forget that everything Adolf Hitler did in Germany was "legal" and everything the Hungarian freedom fighters did in Hungary was "illegal." It was "illegal" to aid and comfort a Jew in Hitler's Germany. Even so, I am sure that, had I lived in Germany at the time, I would have aided and comforted my Jewish brothers. If today I lived in a Communist country where certain principles dear to the Christian faith are suppressed, I would openly advocate disobeying that country's antireligious laws.

23 I must make two honest confessions to you, my Christian and Jewish brothers. First, I must confess that over the past few years I have been gravely disappointed with the white moderate. I have almost reached the regrettable conclusion that the Negro's great stumbling block in his stride toward freedom is not the White Citizen's Counciler or the Ku Klux Klanner, but the white moderate, who is more devoted to "order" than to justice; who prefers a negative peace which is the absence of tension to a positive peace which is the presence of justice; who constantly says: "I agree with you in the goal you seek, but I cannot agree with your methods of direct action"; who paternalistically believes he can set the timetable for another man's freedom; who lives by a mythical concept of time and who constantly advises the Negro to wait for a "more convenient season." Shallow understanding from people of good will is more frustrating than absolute misunderstanding from people of ill will. Lukewarm acceptance is much more bewildering than outright rejection.

24 I had hoped that the white moderate would understand that law and order exist for the purpose of establishing justice and that when they fail in this purpose they become the dangerously structured dams that block the flow of social progress. I had hoped that the white moderate would understand that the present tension in the South is a necessary phase of the transition from an obnoxious negative peace, in which the Negro passively accepted his unjust plight, to a substantive and positive peace, in which all men will respect the dignity and worth of human personality. Actually, we who engage in nonviolent direct action are not the creators of tension. We merely bring to the surface the hidden tension that is already alive. We bring it out in the open, where it can be seen and dealt with. Like a boil that can never be cured so long as it is covered up but must be opened with all its ugliness to the natural medicines of air and light, injustice must be exposed, with all the tension its exposure creates, to the light of human conscience and the air of national opinion before it can be cured.

25 In your statement you assert that our actions, even though peaceful, must be condemned because they precipitate violence. But is this a logical assertion? Isn't this like condemning a robbed man because his possession of money precipitated the evil act of robbery? Isn't this like condemning Socrates because his unswerving commitment to truth and his philosophical inquiries precipitated the act by the misguided populace in which they made him drink hemlock? Isn't this like condemning Jesus because his unique God-consciousness and never-ceasing devotion to God's will precipitated the evil act of crucifixion? We must come to see that, as the federal courts have consistently affirmed, it is wrong to urge an individual to cease his efforts to gain his basic constitutional rights because the quest may precipitate violence. Society must protect the robbed and punish the robber.

26 I had also hoped that the white moderate would reject the myth concerning time in relation to the struggle for freedom. I have just received a letter from a white brother in Texas. He writes: "All Christians know that the colored people will receive equal rights eventually, but it is possible that you are in too great a religious hurry. It has taken Christianity almost two thousand years to accomplish what it has. The teachings of Christ take time to come to earth." Such an attitude stems from a tragic misconception of time, from the strangely irrational notion that there is something in the very flow of time that will inevitably cure all ills. Actually, time itself is neutral; it can be used either destructively or constructively. More and more I feel that the people of ill will have used time much more effectively than have the people of good will. We will have to repent in this generation not merely for the hateful words and actions of the bad people but for the appalling silence of the good people. Human progress never rolls in on wheels of inevitability; it comes through the tireless efforts of men willing to be coworkers with God,

and without this hard work, time itself becomes an ally of the forces of social stagnation. We must use time creatively, in the knowledge that the time is always ripe to do right. Now is the time to make real the promise of democracy and transform our pending national elegy into a creative psalm of brotherhood. Now is the time to lift our national policy from the quicksand of racial injustice to the solid rock of human dignity.

27   You speak of our activity in Birmingham as extreme. At first I was rather disappointed that fellow clergymen would see my nonviolent efforts as those of an extremist. I began thinking about the fact that I stand in the middle of two opposing forces in the Negro community. One is a force of complacency, made up in part of Negroes who, as a result of long years of oppression, are so drained of self-respect and a sense of "somebodiness" that they have adjusted to segregation; and in part of a few middle-class Negroes who, because of a degree of academic and economic security and because in some ways they profit by segregation, have become insensitive to the problems of the masses. The other force is one of bitterness and hatred, and it comes perilously close to advocating violence. It is expressed in the various black nationalist groups that are springing up across the nation, the largest and best-known being Elijah Muhammad's Muslim movement. Nourished by the Negro's frustration over the continued existence of racial discrimination, this movement is made up of people who have lost faith in America, who have absolutely repudiated Christianity, and who have concluded that the white man is an incorrigible "devil."

28   I have tried to stand between these two forces, saying that we need emulate neither the "do-nothingism" of the complacent nor the hatred and despair of the black nationalist. For there is the more excellent way of love and nonviolent protest. I am grateful to God that, through the influence of the Negro church, the way of nonviolence became an integral part of our struggle.

29   If this philosophy had not emerged, by now many streets of the South would, I am convinced, be flowing with blood. And I am further convinced that if our white brothers dismiss as "rabble-rousers" and "outside agitators" those of us who employ nonviolent direct action, and if they refuse to support our nonviolent efforts, millions of Negroes will, out of frustration and despair, seek solace and security in black-nationalist ideologies—a development that would inevitably lead to a frightening racial nightmare.

30   Oppressed people cannot remain oppressed forever. The yearning for freedom eventually manifests itself, and that is what has happened to the American Negro. Something within has reminded him of his birthright of freedom, and something without has reminded him that it can be gained. Consciously or unconsciously, he has been caught up by the *Zeitgeist,* and with his black brothers of Africa and his brown and yellow brothers of Asia, South America and the Caribbean, the United States Negro is moving with a sense of great urgency toward the promised land of racial justice. If one recognizes this vital urge that has engulfed the Negro community, one should readily understand why public demonstrations are taking place. The Negro has many pent-up resentments and latent frustrations, and he must release them. So let him march; let him make prayer pilgrimages to the city hall; let him go on freedom rides—and try to understand why he must do so. If his repressed emotions are not released in nonviolent ways, they will seek expression through violence; this is not a threat but a fact of history. So I have not said to my people: "Get rid of your discontent." Rather, I have tried to say that this normal and healthy discontent can be channeled into the creative outlet of nonviolent direct action. And now this approach is being termed extremist.

31   But though I was initially disappointed at being categorized as an extremist, as I continued to think about the matter I gradually gained a measure of satisfaction from the label. Was not Jesus an extremist for love: "Love your enemies, bless them that

curse you, do good to them that hate you, and pray for them which despitefully use you, and persecute you." Was not Amos an extremist for justice: "Let justice roll down like waters and righteousness like an ever-flowing stream." Was not Paul an extremist for the Christian gospel: "I bear in my body the marks of the Lord Jesus." Was not Martin Luther an extremist: "Here I stand; I cannot do otherwise, so help me God." And John Bunyan: "I will stay in jail to the end of my days before I make a butchery of my conscience." Abraham Lincoln: "This nation cannot survive half slave and half free." And Thomas Jefferson: "We hold these truths to be self-evident, that all men are created equal . . . " So the question is not whether we will be extremists, but what kind of extremists we will be. Will we be extremists for hate or for love? Will we be extremists for the preservation of injustice or for the extension of justice? In that dramatic scene on Calvary's hill three men were crucified. We must never forgot that all three were crucified for the same crime—the crime of extremism. Two were extremists for immorality, and thus fell below their environment. The other, Jesus Christ, was an extremist for love, truth and goodness, and thereby rose above his environment. Perhaps the South, the nation and the world are in dire need of creative extremists.

32   I had hoped that the white moderate would see this need. Perhaps I was too optimistic; perhaps I expected too much. I suppose I should have realized that few members of the oppressor race can understand the deep groans and passionate yearnings of the oppressed race, and still fewer have the vision to see that injustice must be rooted out by strong, persistent and determined action. I am thankful, however, that some of our white brothers in the South have grasped the meaning of this social revolution and committed themselves to it. They are still all too few in quantity, but they are big in quality. Some—such as Ralph McGill, Lillian Smith, Harry Golden, James McBride Dabbs, Ann Braden and Sarah Patton Boyle—have written about our struggle in eloquent and prophetic terms. Others have marched with us down nameless streets of the South. They have languished in filthy, roach-infested jails, suffering the abuse and brutality of policemen who view them as "dirty nigger-lovers." Unlike so many of their moderate brothers and sisters, they have recognized the urgency of the moment and sensed the need for powerful "action" antidotes to combat the disease of segregation.

33   Let me take note of my other major disappointment. I have been so greatly disappointed with the white church and its leadership. Of course, there are some notable exceptions. I am not unmindful of the fact that each of you has taken some significant stands on this issue. I commend you, Reverend Stallings, for your Christian stand on this past Sunday, in welcoming Negroes to your worship service on a nonsegregated basis. I commend the Catholic leaders of this state for integrating Spring Hill College several years ago.

34   But despite these notable exceptions, I must honestly reiterate that I have been disappointed with the church. I do not say this as one of those negative critics who can always find something wrong with the church. I say this as a minister of the gospel, who loves the church; who was nurtured in its bosom; who has been sustained by its spiritual blessings and who will remain true to it as long as the cord of life shall lengthen.

35   When I was suddenly catapulted into the leadership of the bus protest in Montgomery, Alabama, a few years ago, I felt we would be supported by the white church. I felt that the white ministers, priests and rabbis of the South would be among our strongest allies. Instead, some have been outright opponents, refusing to understand the freedom movement and misrepresenting its leaders; all too many others have been more cautious than courageous and have remained silent behind the anesthetizing security of stained-glass windows.

36   In spite of my shattered dreams, I came to Birmingham with the hope that the white religious leadership of this community would see the justice of our cause and,

with deep moral concern, would serve as the channel through which our just grievances could reach the power structure. I had hoped that each of you would understand. But again I have been disappointed.

37   I have heard numerous southern religious leaders admonish their worshipers to comply with a desegregation decision because it is the law; but I have longed to hear white ministers declare: "Follow this decree because integration is morally right and because the Negro is your brother." In the midst of blatant injustices inflicted upon the Negro, I have watched white churchmen stand on the sideline and mouth pious irrelevancies and sanctimonious trivialities. In the midst of a mighty struggle to rid our nation of racial and economic injustice, I have heard many ministers say: "Those are social issues, with which the gospel has no real concern." And I have watched many churches commit themselves to a completely otherworldly religion which makes a strange, un-Biblical distinction between body and soul, between the sacred and the secular.

38   I have traveled the length and breadth of Alabama, Mississippi and all the other southern states. On sweltering summer days and crisp autumn mornings I have looked at the South's beautiful churches with their lofty spires pointing heavenward. I have beheld the impressive outlines of her massive religious-education buildings. Over and over I have found myself asking: "What kind of people worship here? Who is their God? Where were their voices when the lips of Governor Barnett dripped with words of interposition and nullification? Where were they when Governor Wallace gave a clarion call for defiance and hatred? Where were their voices of support when bruised and weary Negro men and women decided to rise from the dark dungeons of complacency to the bright hills of creative protest?"

39   Yes, these questions are still in my mind. In deep disappointment I have wept over the laxity of the church. But be assured that my tears have been tears of love. There can be no deep disappointment where there is not deep love. Yes, I love the church. How could I do otherwise? I am in the rather unique position of being the son, the grandson and the great-grandson of preachers. Yes, I see the church as the body of Christ. But, oh! How we have blemished and scarred that body through social neglect and through fear of being nonconformists.

40   There was a time when the church was very powerful—in the time when the early Christians rejoiced at being deemed worthy to suffer for what they believed. In those days the church was not merely a thermometer that recorded the ideas and principles of popular opinion; it was a thermostat that transformed the mores of society. Whenever the early Christians entered a town, the people in power became disturbed and immediately sought to convict the Christians for being "disturbers of the peace" and "outside agitators." But the Christians pressed on, in the conviction that they were "a colony of heaven," called to obey God rather than man. Small in number, they were big in commitment. They were too God-intoxicated to be "astronomically intimidated." By their effort and example they brought an end to such ancient evils as infanticide and gladiatorial contests.

41   Things are different now. So often the contemporary church is a weak, ineffectual voice with an uncertain sound. So often it is an arch-defender of the status quo. Far from being disturbed by the presence of the church, the power structure of the average community is consoled by the church's silent—and often even vocal—sanction of things as they are.

42   But the judgment of God is upon the church as never before. If today's church does not recapture the sacrificial spirit of the early church, it will lose its authenticity, forfeit the loyalty of millions, and be dismissed as an irrelevant social club with no meaning for the twentieth century. Every day I meet young people whose disappointment with the church has turned into outright disgust.

43   Perhaps I have once again been too optimistic. Is organized religion too inextricably bound to the status quo to save our nation and the world? Perhaps I must turn my faith to the inner spiritual church, the church within the church, as the true *ekklesia* and the hope of the world. But again I am thankful to God that some noble souls from the ranks of organized religion have broken loose from the paralyzing chains of conformity and joined us as active partners in the struggle for freedom. They have left their secure congregations and walked the streets of Albany, Georgia, with us. They have gone down the highways of the South on tortuous rides for freedom. Yes, they have gone to jail with us. Some have been dismissed from their churches, have lost the support of their bishops and fellow ministers. But they have acted in the faith that right defeated is stronger than evil triumphant. Their witness has been the spiritual salt that has preserved the true meaning of the gospel in these troubled times. They have carved a tunnel of hope through the dark mountain of disappointment.

44   I hope the church as a whole will meet the challenge of this decisive hour. But even if the church does not come to the aid of justice, I have no despair about the future. I have no fear about the outcome of our struggle in Birmingham, even if our motives are at present misunderstood. We will reach the goal of freedom in Birmingham and all over the nation, because the goal of America is freedom. Abused and scorned though we may be, our destiny is tied up with America's destiny. Before the pilgrims landed at Plymouth, we were here. Before the pen of Jefferson etched the majestic words of the Declaration of Independence across the pages of history, we were here. For more than two centuries our forebears labored in this country without wages; they made cotton king; they built the homes of their masters while suffering gross injustice and shameful humiliation—and yet out of a bottomless vitality they continued to thrive and develop. If the inexpressible cruelties of slavery could not stop us, the opposition we now face will surely fail. We will win our freedom because the sacred heritage of our nation and the eternal will of God are embodied in our echoing demands.

45   Before closing I feel impelled to mention one other point in your statement that has troubled me profoundly. You warmly commended the Birmingham police force for keeping "order" and "preventing violence." I doubt that you would have so warmly commended the police force if you had seen its dogs sinking their teeth into unarmed, nonviolent Negroes. I doubt that you would so quickly commend the policemen if you were to observe their ugly and inhumane treatment of Negroes here in the city jail; if you were to watch them push and curse old Negro women and young Negro girls; if you were to see them slap and kick old Negro men and young boys; if you were to observe them, as they did on two occasions, refuse to give us food because we wanted to sing our grace together. I cannot join you in your praise of the Birmingham Police Department.

46   It is true that the police have exercised a degree of discipline in handling the demonstrators. In this sense they have conducted themselves rather "nonviolently" in public. But for what purpose? To preserve the evil system of segregation. Over the past few years I have consistently preached that nonviolence demands that the means we use must be as pure as the ends we seek. I have tried to make clear that it is wrong to use immoral means to attain moral ends. But now I must affirm that it is just as wrong, or perhaps even more so, to use moral means to preserve immoral ends. Perhaps Mr. Connor and his policemen have been rather nonviolent in public, as was Chief Pritchett in Albany, Georgia, but they have used the moral means of nonviolence to maintain the immoral end of racial injustice. As T. S. Eliot has said: "The last temptation is the greatest treason: To do the right deed for the wrong reason."

47   I wish you had commended the Negro sit-inners and demonstrators of Birmingham for their sublime courage, their willingness to suffer and their amazing discipline in the midst of great provocation. One day the South will recognize its real heroes. They

will be the James Merediths, with the noble sense of purpose that enables them to face jeering and hostile mobs, and with the agonizing loneliness that characterizes the life of the pioneer. They will be old, oppressed, battered Negro women, symbolized in a seventy-two-year-old woman in Montgomery, Alabama, who rose up with a sense of dignity and with her people decided not to ride segregated buses, and who responded with ungrammatical profundity to one who inquired about her weariness: "My feets is tired, but my soul is at rest." They will be the young high school and college students, the young ministers of the gospel and a host of their elders, courageously and nonviolently sitting in at lunch counters and willingly going to jail for conscience sake. One day the South will know that when these disinherited children of God sat down at lunch counters, they were in reality standing up for what is best in the American dream and for the most sacred values in our Judaeo-Christian heritage, thereby bringing our nation back to those great wells of democracy which were dug deep by the founding fathers in their formulation of the Constitution and the Declaration of Independence.

48   Never before have I written so long a letter. I'm afraid it is much too long to take your precious time. I can assure you that it would have been much shorter if I had been writing from a comfortable desk, but what else can one do when he is alone in a narrow jail cell, other than write long letters, think long thoughts and pray long prayers?

49   If I have said anything in this letter that overstates the truth and indicates an unreasonable impatience, I beg you to forgive me. If I have said anything that understates the truth and indicates my having a patience that allows me to settle for anything less than brotherhood, I beg God to forgive me.

50   I hope this letter finds you strong in the faith. I also hope that circumstances will soon make it possible for me to meet each of you, not as an integrationist or a civil-rights leader but as a fellow clergyman and a Christian brother. Let us all hope that the dark clouds of racial prejudice will soon pass away and the deep fog of misunderstanding will be lifted from our fear-drenched communities, and in some not too distant tomorrow the radiant stars of love and brotherhood will shine over our great nation with all their scintillating beauty.

> Yours for the cause of Peace and Brotherhood,
> Martin Luther King, Jr.

Questions for Review

1. What is the thesis of King's essay? Does it appear in the essay? If so, where? What reasons does he give for accepting his position?
2. Divide the essay into beginning, middle, and end. What rhetorical and/or stylistic devices help form these divisions?
3. What audience might King's essay be written for? Is that audience likely to resist his argument? Explain. In answering this question, you will want to consider what we meant in calling King's piece an "open" letter.
4. Does King offer counterarguments to those who would disagree with him? If so, does he represent the opposition's argument fairly? Explain. What counterarguments are offered?

5. In addition to (or instead of) logical argumentation, what kinds of persuasive appeals does King use in this essay? Would these appeals be likely to work for his intended audience? Why or why not?
6. How would you characterize your attitude toward this subject before reading King's essay? What effect did this essay have on your thinking?

Our fourth sample essay, "Zero Tolerance for Abuse," was written by Jaime Sherrill, a first-year writing student at the University of North Carolina at Charlotte (UNC–Charlotte). In her essay, Jaime attempts to persuade readers to take action against men who physically abuse women.

JAIME SHERRILL

ZERO TOLERANCE FOR ABUSE

Most injuries were to the head and neck and, in addition to bruises, strangle marks, black eyes, and split lips, resulted in eye damage, fractured jaws, broken noses and permanent hearing loss. Assaults to the trunk of the body were almost as common and produced a broken collarbone, bruised and broken ribs, a fractured tail bone, internal hemorrhaging, and a lacerated liver.

1   Unfortunately these injuries were not inflicted upon a boxer at a boxing match; these were injuries to women as a result of domestic violence. According to Natalie Jaffe's pamphlet, "Assaults on Women: Rape and Wife Beating," this description is typical of the kind of physical harm suffered by battered women surveyed in shelters and treatment centers in California. The fact that men can inflict such physical and emotional harm upon a woman infuriates me.

2   Many women get trapped in abusive relationships that are oftentimes too difficult to get out of. Children are sometimes trapped in these vicious cycles, watching their mothers helpless at the fist of an all too overpowering man. Why are there not more regulations against domestic violence? It seems to me that we are only turning our heads to a problem that will never disappear unless we stand up as women and say, "We are too strong to allow this to happen, and we will not tolerate it under any circumstances."

3   Many times, abuse in relationships goes unacknowledged. The abused may think it is a one-time thing and that it will never happen again. History, however, is destined to repeat itself unless we rally together and tell men we will no longer allow them to get away with this intolerable act. We need stricter laws for the abusers. They should be behind bars just like any other criminal. They have committed larceny by robbing a woman of her dignity and self-esteem. They have committed murder by killing the hopes and dreams of a woman. They have committed assault, and have left physical and emotional bruises on their victims. They have been labeled repeat offenders and always seem to make bail with simply an apology or a dozen roses.

4   A woman should be able to wear make-up to make herself feel more beautiful, instead of having to wear make-up to cover up the black eye she received because her

husband's or lover's "hand slipped." Make-up can cover up the temporary scars, but permanent scars run much deeper. It takes more than make-up to conceal them. A woman who has been abused is frightened. She is frightened of her partner, and this is a fear that she shares with many other women in all social classes and backgrounds that are abused. An abused woman often times feels guilty. She feels as if she is to blame for her partner's violence and that she has provoked him in some way. She then puts the blame on herself instead of the abuser and thinks of herself as a failure.

5 A 15-year-old girl lay motionless on the concrete unable to stand. Her boyfriend, who was about to become a new father, had just violently beaten her in a heated argument. The young female almost nine months pregnant lay crying at the hands of a man who supposedly loved her and her unborn child. After this episode the girl and her parents decided that some sort of action must be taken against the man and they decided to press criminal charges. Several weeks later the unwed mother gave birth to a beautiful healthy baby boy and decided after much emotional and physical trauma to list the baby's father "unknown" on the birth certificate and give the baby her last name. Two years later the father of the child is still a part of her life even though they are no longer in a relationship. He has supervised visitation with the child once a week and is now seeking joint custody. Why did the court even allow this violent man supervised visitation with his record? Unfortunately, this is the story of a very close friend of mine and she is still struggling with the issue that she was once in this very unhealthy relationship and now this abuser wants to take this child from her. Anyone can see that this man is an unfit father and does not deserve to be with a child he abused while it was still in the womb. Yet, the judicial system is allowing him visitation with the child and considering joint custody. Is this a sign that society is now almost condoning violence?

6 Why do men abuse their partners? Many factors may play a role in this behavior. It could be that we live in a society that condones violence. Violence is everywhere, especially in movies, television, and newspapers. Sadly, violence is almost accepted as a part of life. Many of those responsible for this violence grew up watching their fathers abuse their mothers; they are only acting out what was part of their environments as young children. Although these situations are a part of the cause of this violence, there still can be no excuse for this kind of behavior.

7 The behavior I am talking about is all too predictable. Domestic abuse most of the time follows one specific pattern. There are three phases: the tension-building phase, the explosion or actual beating, and the loving phase. The tension-building phase often occurs or builds as a result of small incidents, such as a woman's failure to comply with her partner's request. The tension is followed by the explosion in which the abuser unfairly takes out all of his anger on his partner, and she becomes the object of his rage. He may violently punch, choke, kick, or even stab his partner. When the beating is complete, the abuser usually feels guilty and apologizes saying it will never happen again. Foolishly, the woman often believes him, and this is one major reason a woman remains in an abusive relationship.

8 We must find a way to prevent this horrifying pattern. But unless society as a whole refuses to tolerate violence any longer, meaningful changes will not occur. We cannot sit in the dark and let the violence continue; no one deserves to be beaten or threatened with physical harm. There is absolutely no excuse for this type of behavior and society should not tolerate such senseless violence. If the problem continues, it will only get worse. But women must have help to get out of these abusive relationships. We have already begun by opening many shelters and organizations devoted to helping these unfortunate victims seek refuge from abusers. This, however, is not nearly enough; it is only a small step on a long path towards a permanent solution.

WORKS CONSULTED

Fleming, Jennifer Baker. *Stopping Wife Abuse: A Guide to the Emotional, Psychological, and Legal Implications for the Abused Woman and Those Helping Her.* New York: Anchor/Doubleday, 1979.

Jaffe, Natalie. *Assaults on Women: Rape and Wife Beating.* New York: Public Affairs Committee, pamphlet no. 579, n.d.

Questions for Review

1. What is the thesis of Jaime's essay? Does it appear in the essay? If so, where? What reasons does she give for accepting her position?
2. Divide the essay into beginning, middle, and end. What rhetorical and/or stylistic devices help form these divisions?
3. What audience might Jaime's essay be written for? Is that audience likely to resist her argument? Explain.
4. Does Jamie offer counterarguments to those who would disagree with her? If so, does she represent the opposition's argument fairly? Explain. What counterarguments are offered?
5. In addition to (or instead of) logical argumentation, what kinds of persuasive appeals does Jaime use in this essay? Would these appeals be likely to work for her intended audience? Why or why not?
6. How would you characterize your attitude toward this subject before reading Jaime's essay? What effect did this essay have on your thinking?

Our last essay in this section was written by Jaclyn Talbert, a first-year writing student at UNC–Charlotte. In her essay, "Justice for Those Who Have Shown Us No Mercy," Jaclyn wants to persuade readers to support efforts to keep capital punishment in the U.S. legal system.

JACLYN TALBERT

JUSTICE FOR THOSE WHO HAVE SHOWN US NO MERCY

1   What do we dream of as children? Some girls dream about their weddings and what they will name their children, and some boys dream about the fame their pro football careers will bring them. Of course the dreams differ from person to person, but there is one milestone in life that all children cannot wait to reach. They can't wait to get their drivers' licenses so that they can cut the cord and experience some freedom from their parents. After reaching this milestone, my cousin had only two more days to dream. She

went to the grocery store for her mom one day, and she never returned. A nicely dressed average looking guy was standing in the middle of a country road a few blocks from her house waving his arms as if he needed help, so she stopped. She rolled down her window, and before she could ask how she could help, he shot her six times in the head and neck. She was the sixth of seven people that he killed that night. The sixth lifeless body he pushed aside so that he could pull her car behind a barn and await his last victim.

2   He was caught. And my aunt and uncle, and the families of six other victims, sat and listened to him explain the events of that awful night. He explained how each one of these innocent people looked like a demon and how he murdered each one in cold blood. After that day, he went to live in a home for the mentally ill, where he continues to live in peace and quiet. He was diagnosed as insane.

3   There is no peace for my aunt and uncle. Their lives have been shattered, ripped apart. Not a day goes by when my aunt does not blame herself for sending her daughter to the store that night. Hardly a night passes without her wondering if she could have warned her more clearly about strangers. Driving continues to be a nightmare for my aunt and uncle even now that nine years have passed, and they check and double check their doors to be sure they are locked. Anger and fear fills their hearts because the man who murdered their baby sits in a state supported hotel with his parole date inching closer and closer.

4   My cousin's death is but one example. There are many more. A young woman named Susan Smith sits comfortably in a North Carolina jail after drowning her two young sons. I still remember the shock and sorrow I felt as I heard about their deaths. At first it appeared that someone had kidnaped the children from Susan and murdered them—that was Susan's story. But then we learned the truth. I can still remember hearing the news as I was riding in the back seat, in busy Charlotte traffic, headed to the funeral of my friend, Brian, a twenty-year-old victim of cancer. The announcer said, "I never dreamed I would be announcing this, but there has been a confession in the Smith case. She did it. She killed her children." The news paralyzed me. How was it possible? What had caused her to lose her senses? Was there some mistake? We all know there was no mistake. Susan killed those precious little boys. The world watched as the car was pulled out of the lake, and as she excused what she had done because her boyfriend did not want to be a father and was going to leave her.

5   Another example involves a couple, Richard and Dawn Heikkia, who adopted Matthew and loved him as their son. This son murdered Richard and Dawn in cold blood, after planning the murder for months. Police found shotgun shells labeled "mom" and "dad." And in one of many letters written from prison, Matthew told the prosecutor about planning the crime. "My parents loved me, but I still wanted them dead because they pissed me off. . . . I did kill my parents for money and the car. I know they loved me. My mother told me that she loved me right before I put the slug through her head." The letters he wrote to his girlfriend included a gruesome, detailed story of the murders, and but one regret: "I am not sorry for what I have done. I just wish that I killed you when I had the chance" (Lang 136–145).

6   Unfortunately, Matthew was familiar with our system of justice. He mocked the prosecutor, telling him: "I'll cop an insanity plea, be out in twenty or so years, still young and smart enough to find you and Linda [his girlfriend]." He was right—at least about the verdict. He was deemed insane and is now living in a psychiatric hospital (Lang 145).

7   Does the state not have the right to rid itself of these killers—of people who would stand on the side of the road and methodically murder six strangers, of people who would kill their children because they were an "inconvenience," of people who would kill their parents in cold blood and boast of their intentions to kill others while awaiting

trial? Many people argue against capital punishment, but those who would do so are concerned over the rights of the wrong person. When it comes time to deal with these murderers, the innocent victim is already dead. The murderer is not the one who deserves our pity. The victim and the victim's family should be our primary concern.

8   The murderer should die. It is not we, as a society, who are deciding his fate; he did that himself when he decided to murder, to rape—to torment a fellow human being. A person responsible for stealing someone else's life hardly deserves the chance to live his own. I know there are those who consider it inhumane to take the lives of killers—even confessed killers. They give us arguments full of contortions and misplaced human concern. They argue that our methods of execution are inhumane because the murderer may feel pain. I agree that we should attempt to remove these killers from our society with as little pain as possible; we should not try to make them suffer, since we do not wish to stoop to their level. However, we cannot stop enforcing punishment simply because the killer might feel some pain.

9   Pain abounds in this situation. Someone has died; someone has lost his daughter, grand-daughter, sister, or mother—and someone is responsible. The murderer did not stop to think, or care, how this person would be missed. The murderer did not bother to wonder whether she had reached her goals in life! It is amazing that anyone would speak for these killers. But Nicholas Jenkins argues, in "Dirty Needle," that since it is against the law to electrocute chinchilla in America, we are being inhumane in electrocuting human beings. There is one vital difference between the chinchilla and the murderer, however: the chinchilla has not forfeited its right to live.

10   The murderer can blame no one but himself for his seat on death row. The person who has no say in this matter is the victim. He did not ask to be murdered. Why should our justice system take the side of the accused? Is it not our duty to punish those who have stolen innocence from our children and the last beat of our hearts?

11   We have lost touch with the value of human life when we are more concerned for the rights of murderers than the rights of their victims. But this is what has happened. Criminals know that the chances are slim that they will be truly punished for their crimes. In 1987, the Bureau of Justice records indicated that a murderer sentenced to life in prison with a chance of parole would serve an average of 85.3 months (Baird and Rosenbaum 108). We cannot judge just how effective execution is as a deterrent to other criminals, but we do know that it prevents that murderer from being free to murder again in slightly more than seven years.

WORKS CITED

Baird, Robert M., and Stuart E. Rosenbaum. *Punishment and the Death Penalty: The Current Debate.* New York: Prometheus, 1995.

Jenkins, Nicholas. "Dirty Needle." *New Yorker* 19 Dec. 1994: 5+.

Lang, Denise. *The Dark Son.* New York: Avon, 1995.

 *Questions for Review*

1. What is the thesis of Jaclyn's essay? Does it appear in the essay? If so, where? What reasons does she give for accepting her position?

2. Divide the essay into beginning, middle, and end. What rhetorical and/or stylistic devices help form these divisions?

3. What audience might Jaclyn's essay be written for? Is that audience likely to resist her argument? Explain.

4. Does Jaclyn offer counterarguments to those who would disagree with her? If so, does she represent the opposition's argument fairly? Explain. What counterarguments are offered?

5. In addition to (or instead of) logical argumentation, what kinds of persuasive appeals does Jaclyn use in this essay? Would these appeals be likely to work for her intended audience? Why or why not?

6. How would you characterize your attitude toward this subject before reading Jaclyn's essay? What effect did this essay have on your thinking?

THE RHETORICAL TRIANGLE

READER

The reader of a persuasion essay is not someone who is opposed to the writer's thesis. At first glance, this seems wrong. Why would a writer attempt to persuade someone who already agrees with him? When we look more carefully, however, we see that the writer is not attempting to persuade the reader to believe something, but rather to act on his beliefs. Think for a moment about situations in which an author might present an essay like those at the beginning of this chapter. For example, where might one hear such an essay as "Dismemberment and Choice"? It would be much more likely to be heard at a gathering of people with conservative leanings than at one of people with more liberal views. Liberal thinkers would dismiss Michael Heaphy's essay immediately because of the name calling and distortion he engages in. Those predisposed toward an anti-abortion position might well pass over these issues and respond emotionally to the details Heaphy provides about how abortions take place.

You might be tempted to wonder whether Heaphy is wasting his time in speaking to such an audience. He may be said to be "preaching to the choir"—addressing readers who already subscribe to his basic position. But as a preacher in Ron's past once explained, the choir is the perfect audience for most sermons. Those who do not come to church will not heed the preacher's message even if they are somehow exposed to his sermon. But if those who *are* coming to church aren't doing what the preacher is exhorting them to do, they are well-suited to hear this message; they know what they should do—they just don't always do as they should.

Exercise 10.1

We discussed what kind of readers Heaphy's "Dismemberment and Choice" might have been intended for and speculated on a situation in which the essay might be read. Choose two or three other essays from the beginning of this chapter, and discuss the audiences that would be appropriate for them. Then, think of specific occasions on which these essays might be read aloud to a particular audience. What new insights can you gain into the relationships of the rhetorical triangle by imagining such situations?

SUBJECT

The subject of a persuasion essay should be something that elicits an emotional response. Such essays often deal with the same types of debatable issues that position essays treat. However, the subject for a persuasion essay does not have to be debatable. Four of our five sample essays treat subjects that are clearly controversial. However, in "Zero Tolerance for Abuse," Jaime Sherrill seeks to impress on readers how much spousal abuse there is in the United States and to make readers feel the awful pain that is inflicted by this abuse in the hope of causing these readers to take actions to help solve this problem. Alysia Tucker's "No More," the student essay featured at the end of this chapter, also treats this noncontroversial topic. No one is likely to oppose Jaime and Alysia's basic thesis and speak in favor of spousal abuse. (For another example of a persuasion essay that deals with a noncontroversial subject, see "No Hunting Here, Please," pp. 90–92.)

In saying that a subject isn't debatable, we are not suggesting that the issues involved in and around it do not allow for disagreements. Humans can, and will, disagree about the details and nuances of any subject. We are suggesting, rather, that with subjects such as spousal abuse, sensible people will likely agree on the basic issues at hand. How could we not agree with Jaime and Alysia that we should do more to protect women from abuse? Of course, there are reasons we don't do more, ranging from selfishness over money (that we might donate to treatment programs dealing with abusers) to lethargy. But no one is likely to speak up in favor of selfishness or lethargy. The writer's task, then, is not to argue against another point of view, but rather to appeal to readers to do what they would agree they should do.

Exercise 10.2

Most readers would certainly agree with Jaime Sherrill (in "Zero Tolerance for Abuse") and Alysia Tucker (in "No More") that more should be done to protect women from violence, but they may not agree with all the claims these writers use to build their cases. Find one or two statements in each essay with which reasonable people may disagree. Do the writers offer support in favor of their points of view on these matters? Explain. Do they acknowledge potential disagreements?

WRITER

As the discussion in Chapter 9 indicated, there is a sense in which a writer of a position essay may want to draw attention to herself. The writer wants to be seen as a clear thinker (someone capable of mounting a logical argument for her case) and as ethical (someone who can be trusted to be honest and fair in dealing with the issue). The writer of a persuasive paper is not as likely to draw this kind of attention to herself. She takes the stance that anyone who is thinking clearly on an issue would see things the way they are being presented in her paper. Whereas the writer of a position essay may tend to focus on her beliefs as opposed to the beliefs of potential readers, the writer of a persuasion essay focuses on aspects of the subject on which she and her readers agree, thereby taking attention away from herself.

As we noted earlier, persuasive writing often deals with issues that are not arguable in the way that topics of position papers are. Thus, writers of persuasion essays often do not need to deal with the possibility that they hold opinions differing from those held by others. Writers such as Jaime are free to emphasize the pain and suffering caused by abuse. Even when they deal with topics that are controversial, writers of persuasion essays do not focus on the controversial nature of their topics. For example, Heaphy ("Dismemberment and Choice") writes about abortion as if there were really only one correct point of view on this subject. These kinds of essays are most successful when the reader has the feeling that any right-thinking person would see things in the way this writer sees them.

Exercise 10.3 We mentioned Heaphy's essay as an example of a persuasion essay in which the writer seems to assume that his is the only point of view on a controversial issue. Compare Heaphy's tactics in this essay with those of two or three of the other writers whose essays are featured at the beginning of this chapter. Rank these essays in terms of the degree to which they show awareness of an opposing point of view.

DISTINGUISHING FEATURES OF PERSUASION ESSAYS
EMOTIONAL APPEAL

The key distinguishing feature of a persuasion essay is emotional appeal. The writer wants to move his readers to action; humans seldom act on the basis of reason alone. How many former smokers can trace their "conversion" from smoking to not smoking to a presentation of the statistics on the health risks of smoking? Argumentation may have been helpful in laying the groundwork for the change, of course. Most smokers know, and accept, the argument that smoking is bad for them. Most of those who have quit, however, were moved to action by some emotional appeal or event, such as an appeal from a loved one or the death of someone close to them from a smoking-related illness. Those who wage campaigns against smoking are aware of this fact, as you can see by looking at their campaigns. Although they may offer statistics to show the harmful effects of smoking, the focus of antismoking advertisements is usually on an emotional appeal of some sort.

It is telling that those who would have us smoke also rely on persuasion and emotion as opposed to reason and argument. No cigarette advertiser lists the health benefits of smoking or attempts any other kind of rational argument in favor of smoking. Rather, the advertisements appeal to our emotions—our appetite for the pleasure of a relaxed smoke; our desire to be "sexy," "cool," and "popular"; or, if that won't do it, our desire to be seen as daring and defiant, as going our own way, as disdainful of the fears and cautions of the less strong among us.

Exercise
10.4

1. One of the mainstays of cigarette advertising for years has been the "Marlboro Man." Find two or three examples of advertisements (from magazines in your library) using this theme. Who is the Marlboro Man? What emotions are being appealed to by the use of this theme?
2. Another long-standing and controversial advertising campaign involved the mascot for Camel cigarettes, Joe Camel. Find two or three advertisements using this theme. What emotions do these advertisements appeal to? What readers would most likely be attracted to these advertisements?
3. Find two or three other advertisements for cigarettes. Analyze the components of these advertisements: the pictures, the words, and the overall composition—that is, the way in which the words and pictures are combined. What emotions do the advertisements arouse in readers? What types of people are likely to be most affected by this type of appeal?

ETHICAL PERSUASION

It may seem that we are picking on cigarette advertisers. We are. They provide us with a clear example of the distinction between effective persuasion and good persuasive writing. We think it is unethical to attempt to persuade people to take actions for which it is impossible to offer logical arguments. All of the issues we present in this chapter could be argued logically. Jaime could have made a logical argument for doing more to combat domestic abuse, though she didn't need to; Heaphy could have made a logical argument against abortion, though he did not choose to do so; and so on. However, it would not be possible, at least from the moral foundations on which we build, to argue in favor of smoking or in favor of refinancing one's house at a higher interest rate to buy a vacation or luxury consumer item.

Exercise
10.5

Examine three or four persuasive arguments you encounter in advertisements—in magazines, on radio or television, or in some other medium, such as the Internet. What do the advertisements seek to persuade you to do? What methods of persuasion are employed? How effective are they in persuading you to take the desired action? Given our discussion here, how ethical are these attempts at persuasion—that is, how effectively could the advertisers argue their cases logically?

We noted that each of the essays at the beginning of this chapter deals with a topic that could be argued logically. However, when writers decide to dismiss their opposition, they often write in ways that will discredit them with anyone who takes the opposing side. Such is the case with two of the essays in this chapter. In his diatribe against those who perform abortion, Michael Heaphy ("Dismemberment and Choice") indicates that all those who would disagree with him on this issue are assisting those who commit murder. Similarly, Camille Paglia ("Rape and Modern Sex War") dismisses "academic feminism [as] lost in a fog of social constructionism" and goes on to assert that "It [academic feminism] believes we are totally the product of our environment." According to Paglia, these feminists espouse a "dumb" theory of language, and their conversation consists of the repetition of "hollow slogans." The tactics Heaphy and Paglia use are diametrically opposed to the strategies of ethical argumentation we discussed in Chapter 9. But does that make them "unethical"? We choose to reserve that term for persuasion that encourages actions that could not be argued for logically. You should be aware, however, that the question of what is, and what is not, ethical persuasion is itself an arguable topic. What is not arguable is whether these types of emotional appeals are effective—they most certainly are.

Exercise 10.6

It should be clear from our discussion that there is no clear-cut line between ethical and unethical persuasion. It is probably best to think of a continuum, from most ethical to least ethical, on which individual pieces of writing may be placed. Examine three of the essays from this chapter (excepting Heaphy's, which we have discussed) or three essays selected by your instructor, and rank them from most ethical to least ethical. Use as your criteria for this ranking the fairness with which they represent the arguments of those who oppose them and the tendency to insult those who oppose them or to call them names.

PERSUASIVE LANGUAGE

Once you decide to write persuasively—that is, to concentrate on engaging the emotions of your readers—what tools are available to you to accomplish your task? Put simply, the basic tool of persuasion in writing is the force of your language. Next, we discuss three ways of achieving this forceful language: description, narrative, and prose style. (For more information on the language of persuasion, see Chapters 15 and 16.)

DESCRIPTION

In Chapter 5, we talked about the powerful role that description plays in personal writing. The following passage makes it clear that description is also effective in persuasive writing:

> Maudlin viewers of the death penalty call the most wanton slayer a "Child of God" who should not be executed regardless of how heinous his crime may be because "God created man in his own image, in the image of God created he him." (Genesis 1:27) Was not this small, blonde six-year-old girl a child of God? She was choked, beaten, and raped by a sex fiend whose pregnant wife

reportedly helped him lure the innocent child into his car and who sat and watched the assault on the screaming youngster. And when he completed his inhumane deed, the wife, herself bringing a life into the world, allegedly killed the child with several savage blows with a tire iron. The husband has been sentenced to death. Words and words and words may be written, but no pleas in favor of the death penalty can be more horribly eloquent than the sight of the battered, sexually assaulted body of this child, truly a "child of God."

J. Edgar Hoover, *Law Enforcement Bulletin.*

In this passage, J. Edgar Hoover, former director of the Federal Bureau of Investigation, illustrates and explains the role that description can play in persuasive writing. Hoover is aware that those who oppose capital punishment appeal to our emotional reaction to the killing of any human being, even one who has taken someone else's life. He counters this appeal to emotion with one of his own—the description of the horrible death of a beautiful and innocent child. Hoover then explains what he is doing, by stating ironically that words cannot be as effective as the sight of a child who has been killed in such an awful fashion. We say "ironically" because words are all that Hoover has at his disposal to create this image for us. The more effective his description, the more effective his argument for the death penalty.

Exercise 10.7

Examine two or three of the sample essays at the beginning of this chapter to determine how they use description to persuade their readers. Select two or three especially effective passages, and explain how they engage the reader's emotions.

NARRATIVE

It is easy to see why narrative is so effective in persuasion. Our emotions are engaged when we react personally to the issue at hand, and what better way to engage readers personally than by telling stories that they can relate to? In the following passage from "Crack and the Box," Pete Hamill uses a story of a brief visit with a woman addicted to drugs to introduce his readers to the horrors of addiction:

One sad, rainy morning last winter, I talked to a woman who was addicted to crack cocaine. She was 22, stiletto-thin, with eyes as old as tombs. She was living in two rooms in a welfare hotel with her children, who were two, three, and five years of age. Her story was the usual tangle of human woe: early pregnancy, dropping out of school, vanished men, smack and then crack, tricks with johns in parked cars to pay for the dope. I asked her why she did drugs. She shrugged in an empty way and couldn't really answer beyond "makes me feel good." While we talked and she told her tale of squalor, the children ignored us. They were watching television.

Walking back to my office in the rain, I brooded about the woman, her zombie-like children, and my own callous indifference. I'd heard so many versions of the same story that I almost never wrote them anymore; the sons of similar women, glimpsed a dozen years ago, are now in Dannemora or Soledad or Joliet; in a hundred cities, their daughters are moving into the same loveless rooms. As I walked, a series of homeless men approached me for change, most of them junkies. Others sat in doorways, staring at nothing. They were additional casualties of our time of plague, demoralized reminders that although this country holds only two percent of the world's population, it consumes 65 percent of the world's supply of hard drugs.

Hamill's story is an attempt to persuade readers not to be indifferent in the face of the tragedy of drug addiction. He tells us about a visit to a specific woman, all the while pointing out that this woman—and her faceless children—are representative of the thousands of people whose lives have been ruined by drugs. If we feel sympathy for this woman, "stiletto-thin, with eyes as old as tombs," and her innocent children forced to live in "squalor" through no fault of their own, we may well be moved to take the action that Hamill proposes later in his essay.

Exercise 10.8

Several of the sample essays at the beginning of this chapter make use of narratives. Choose two or three of those narratives, and discuss the role they play in their respective essays. What is the writer attempting to persuade her or his readers of? What emotions do these narratives appeal to? How effective do you imagine they will be in helping the writers achieve their purposes?

PROSE STYLE

A final tool for persuasion is much easier to illustrate than to explain. We see it at work in the following excerpt from the powerful essay that Jaime Sherrill wrote against the abuse of women:

> Many times, abuse in relationships goes unacknowledged. The abused may think it is a one time thing and that it will never happen again. History, however, is destined to repeat itself unless we rally together and tell men we will no longer allow them to get away with this intolerable act. We need stricter laws for the abusers. They should be behind bars just like any other criminal. They have committed larceny by robbing a woman of her dignity and self-esteem. They have committed murder by killing the hopes and dreams of a woman. They have committed assault, and have left physical and emotional bruises on their victims. They have been labeled repeat offenders and always seem to make bail with simply an apology or a dozen roses.
>
> A woman should be able to wear make-up to make herself feel more beautiful, instead of having to wear make-up to cover up the black eye she received because her husband's or lover's "hand slipped." Make-up can cover up the temporary scars, but permanent scars run much deeper. It takes more than make-up to conceal them.

We also see a wonderful illustration of prose style in the following excerpt from Martin Luther King, Jr.'s "Letter from Birmingham Jail."

We have waited for more than 340 years for our constitutional and God-given rights. The nations of Asia and Africa are moving with jetlike speed toward gaining political independence, but we still creep at horse-and-buggy pace toward gaining a cup of coffee at a lunch counter. Perhaps it is easy for those who have never felt the stinging darts of segregation to say, "Wait." But when you have seen vicious mobs lynch your mothers and fathers at will and drown your sisters and brothers at whim; when you have seen hate-filled policemen curse, kick and even kill your black brothers and sisters; when you see the vast majority of your twenty million Negro brothers smothering in an airtight cage of poverty in the midst of an affluent society; when you suddenly find your tongue twisted and your speech stammering as you seek to explain to your six-year-old daughter why she can't go to the public amusement park that has just been advertised on television, and see tears welling up in her eyes when she is told that Funtown is closed to colored children, and see ominous clouds of inferiority beginning to form in her little mental sky, and see her beginning to distort her personality by developing an unconscious bitterness toward white people; when you have to concoct an answer for a five-year-old son who is asking: "Daddy, why do white people treat colored people so mean?"; when you take a cross-country drive and find it necessary to sleep night after night in the uncomfortable corners of your automobile because no motel will accept you; when you are humiliated day in and day out by nagging signs reading "white" and "colored"; when your first name becomes "nigger," your middle name becomes "boy" (however old you are) and your last name becomes "John," and your wife and mother are never given the respected title "Mrs."; when you are harried by day and haunted by night by the fact that you are a Negro, living constantly at tiptoe stance, never quite knowing what to expect next, and are plagued with inner fears and outer resentments; when you are forever fighting a degenerating sense of "nobodiness"—then you will understand why we find it difficult to wait. [. . .]

In both these essays, one by a student writer and one by an acknowledged master of prose style, we find examples of powerful language that makes writing persuasive. Note the use of sentence repetition for effect in both pieces. Jaime Sherrill begins four consecutive sentences with the same pronoun and verb: "they have." Martin Luther King uses the repetition of an adverbial clause beginning with "when you" to introduce each indignity that blacks have had to suffer. In the passage from Jaime's essay, she is consciously using repetition to drive home her point that women have suffered far too often at the hands of violent men; King is consciously repeating an adverbial clause structure to reinforce his point that the indignities suffered by blacks have been more numerous and constant than human endurance can be expected to tolerate. These repetitions add power to both pieces of writing.

These are not the only elements that make for effective prose style in these two excerpts. Note the turns of phrase Jaime uses in the second paragraph when she talks about what make-up should be used for as contrasted with what it is used for by battered women. Also note the contrast between the "temporary scars" that make-up can cover and the "permanent scars" that run too deep to be covered over by anything. Note the contrast King draws between the "jetlike speed" at which African nations are moving toward "political independence" and the "horse-and-buggy pace" at which blacks in the United States are moving toward "gaining a cup of coffee at a lunch counter." Note also the way in which King uses figurative language to picture the "clouds of inferiority beginning to form in [his daughter's] little mental sky."

As we said, it is much easier to illustrate this prose style than to analyze its parts. Explaining why it is so effective is even more difficult. We have more to say about these matters in Chapters 15 and 16. Here we say simply that in persuasive writing, you want to use all of the tools of language at your disposal to help readers identify with your subject emotionally and remember what you are asking from them. Humans respond to the way something is said as well as to what is said. That is why we remember President Kennedy's famous admonition, "Ask not what your country can do for you; ask what you can do for your country." How much less effective would his speech have been had he said, "Don't be selfish when it comes to civic matters; see what you can do to make this a better country"? The power and much of the persuasive effect of this part of his speech would be missing.

Exercise 10.9

We have discussed description, narrative, and prose style separately. In practice, the three often work together to make persuasive writing. Our discussion of the passage from King's essay, "Letter from Birmingham Jail," focused on his prose style. However, the passage also makes use of descriptive detail and narrative. Find examples of each, and discuss how they add power to King's argument.

ASSIGNMENT AND GUIDELINES FOR WRITING

ASSIGNMENT

Write a paper in which you persuade readers to take action on a belief you hold. Your readers may already share this belief with you. Assume that, if they do not, they are at least favorably disposed to the arguments supporting this belief.

CHOOSING A TOPIC

If you have written a position essay, you have already uncovered one or more topics that you feel strongly about. If so, consider writing a persuasion essay about one of these topics. If you're undecided about a topic, try any or all of the activities in Part A.

PART A

1. Take a look again at your responses to the Interest Inventory (p. 9). Look especially for topics that you feel strongly about, topics that make

you angry or frightened. Pick two or three, and freewrite about each for 10 minutes. Why did you pick these particular potential topics? Why do they arouse such strong feelings?

2. Make a "Bug List," as described by James L. Adam in *Conceptual Block-busting* (Reading, MA: Perseus, 1986). Develop a list of things that bug you about your school, your community, your friends, your educational system, and the world. Write two or three sentences about each entry on your list. Then, select those you think are most interesting, and write three or four more sentences about each of these. Why did you select these particular entries as more interesting than the others?

PART B

Choose two potential topics, and freewrite for 15 minutes about each. Then, determine which topic is more interesting to you. Which involves you more emotionally? Select it as your subject for this essay, or if you do not feel ready to do so, return to some of the activities above.

COLLECTING INFORMATION

Questions for Analysis.   Apply the Questions for Analysis (pp. 24–25) to your topic. Write a detailed response to each question that seems pertinent to your topic.

Logic.   Examine your topic to see whether it lends itself to logical support. To do so, state your position tentatively, and then determine whether it is possible for a reasonable person to take an opposing point of view. If you find that yours is a debatable topic, sketch briefly the argument that you would offer in favor of your point of view. It may be helpful to construct an imaginary dialogue of the type presented in Chapter 9 (pp. 337–339).

Emotional appeals.   List key emotional appeals you would use in support of your topic. You may want to list key values that you and your reader share (see Chapter 9, pp. 335–336) so that you can determine what emotions may be associated with those values. For example, if "fairness" is a key value, then you may well find that appeals to anger (over unfair treatment) are effective. Or, if a key value is "family," then appeals to fear (that something may harm a member of one's family) may be effective.

Reader.   Use your reader as a means of generating information. Decide what specific occasion you will use to present your appeal to your reader. Analyze your reader in terms of his knowledge and feelings about your topic. Also reflect on what will be most successful in helping make your reader take the action you propose.

FOCUS STATEMENT

As you begin to generate information for your essay, look back over your freewriting and write a focus statement. The following focus statement was written by Jaime Sherrill for her essay "Zero Tolerance for Abuse":

> I want to convince women to take action against men who are constantly abusing women. I will not need to offer a logical argument, since this isn't a debatable topic. I want to help make my audience, women who care about the world they live in, start doing something about this problem. I will attempt to stir their emotions by telling stories about women who have been beaten.

Jaime's focus statement provided her with a starting place: She did mount an effective emotional appeal by telling the stories of abused women. She probably did not know when she wrote this statement that she would also use prose style effectively to engage the emotions of her reader. Had she known this, she could have listed it as a strategy here in her statement.

PLANNING YOUR ESSAY'S STRUCTURE

Persuasion essays may be organized by either of the argument structures (formal or informal) introduced in Chapter 9 (pp. 340, 344–345). However, they are more likely to assume the informal structure, with relatively little attention given to logical supports and more attention devoted to emotional supports. Michael Heaphy's essay, "Dismemberment and Choice," makes use of an informal argument structure that may be analyzed as follows:

   I. *Thesis* (implicit): The pro-choice position on abortion is not defensible (paragraph 1).
  II. *Logical support for thesis:* Arguments as to the meaning of pro-choice (paragraph 2)
 III. *Emotional support for thesis:*
     A. Description of abortion practices of Dr. Haskell (paragraphs 3–6)
     B. Discussion of euphemisms used in renaming parts of murdered babies (paragraphs 7–9)
     C. Detail from Ms. Brown's charges against Dr. Haskell (paragraphs 10–14)
 IV. *Refutation of counterargument:* There is no distinction—as the other side would attempt to make—between killing that takes place just before birth and killing immediately after birth (paragraph 15).
  V. *Concluding statements* (paragraph 16)

THESIS STATEMENT

The thesis statement for a persuasion essay is often implied rather than stated. For example, Heaphy does not say anywhere in his essay exactly what he wants readers to do. If he were to do so, his thesis might be something like the following:

> You should do all within your power to cause our government to make abortion illegal and to discourage anyone from having an abortion.

Note the difference between what we envision as a thesis sentence for a persuasion essay, such as Heaphy's, and a thesis sentence for a position essay on the same topic, which might be stated as follows:

> Abortion should be illegal.

To arrive at a possible thesis sentence for your persuasion essay, begin with a thesis for a companion argument. For example, Jaime Sherrill might have begun with this argumentative thesis:

> Spousal abuse should never occur.

To move to a persuasive thesis, she needs to involve her readers:

> You should take actions to help decrease spousal abuse.

It is good to specify what the actions should be, but it is not necessary. In "Rape and Modern Sex War" (pp. 367–370), Camille Paglia does give her readers some specifics: Because human sexuality is genetically encoded and because young men are sometimes controlled by their testosterone, young women should never go to fraternity parties alone, should not drink while there, and should never go upstairs in a fraternity house. At another level, she argues that people should take responsibility for their own mistakes and not whine when their behavior causes them to get into trouble. However, in a persuasion essay, such as "No Hunting Here, Please" (pp. 90–92), we are never given specifics as to what the readers should do. Reading between the lines, we can see that Denise K. Knight wants her readers to take actions to help bring about stiffer penalties for hunters who lack respect for private property.

REFINING YOUR WRITING

After you've written a draft of your essay and taken some time away from it, revise it, keeping the following principles in mind:

> *Emotional appeal.* Be sure that you have given your readers a way to identify emotionally with your subject. Explore ways to strengthen the emotional impact of your essay.
>
> *Effectiveness of language.* Review your essay to determine whether its prose style plays an important role in its overall effectiveness. Consider the role that narration and description play in your essay, and determine whether additional narratives or more descriptive language would add to the overall effectiveness of your essay. Review the sections on powerful language in Chapters 15 and 16, to determine how to make your

word choice and sentence structure as effective as possible.

Ethical persuasion. Examine your treatment of those who would oppose your position to be sure that your essay is both effective and ethical—making for what we consider *good* writing.

SAMPLE STUDENT PROCESS

Our example student essay was written by Alysia Tucker, a first-year writing student at New Mexico State University (NMSU). Alysia knew very early on that she wanted to write about battered women, so her prewriting begins with some responses to the Questions for Analysis.

PREWRITING

What do I associate with battering?

- anger, pity, suffering in general
- people who will not help themselves
- frustration

What goes with battering?

- poverty, lack of education
- suffering children

What opposes battering?

- my life and that of most of the people I know (in the sense of being opposite to?)
- legal system (in the sense of being intended to stop battering)

What causes battering?

- power difference between men and women (men are stronger than women)
- poverty of women who can't leave batterers
- weak men who take out frustrations on weaker people
- court system that allows batterers to go free
- women who stay with batterers

What does battering cause?

- suffering for all
- children scared for life
- death of many women
- shame in our society

FOCUS STATEMENT

I want my audience to understand abuse and how dangerous it is. I want them to know they can help put a stop to it.

This is a good statement of what Alysia wants to do, but it provides little insight into how she might go about accomplishing her goals. Her discovery draft allows her to experiment with how to develop her paper and leads to an audience analysis.

DISCOVERY DRAFT

Battering is the establishment of control and fear in a relationship through violence and other forms of abuse. Millions of women were physically abused by their husbands or boyfriends within the last year. Battery is a crime that *often* ~~sometimes~~ goes *unnoticed and* unreported. It results in severe harm and death among our countrys women. (Add stats here.) We must take a stand for victims by encouraging them. (Put in article from Standard Times here.) One woman I know was abused *by her husband*. She had a little girl and he would make her *sit and* watch him beat her mom. He would come home drunk and abuse her until she finally escaped. She is now married to a man who loves her and has never beat her. (Add Stephanie Rodriguez's story here.)

It is never easy *for a battered woman* to leave a batterer. (Add stat here.) They are afraid of reprisal. Authorities should interfere and take action. Some women are afraid of homelessness. (Add stat.) A woman and child shouldn't have to be afraid to leave (Add stat about 1st shelter here.)

(Add stat about murdered women here.) Police think that strangers will do more harm than intimates. But they need to understand that they can do more damage than strangers. Some people say they just "lost it." But then they would be beating other people who angered them.

There are signs you can look for in a battered woman. Low self-esteem and denial is one of them. Another one is taking responsibility of the abuser's actions. She may be very family-oriented in a traditional way and may be over-protected. If you see these signs, take action and help them or she may stay, allowing it to continue.

AUDIENCE ANALYSIS

After writing her discovery draft, Alysia wrote the following audience analysis to help her move to a second draft of her essay:

> The projected reader of my essay is people who know abused victims. They probably already know a little about abuse but are unwilling to take the steps necessary to prevent it. The reader is likely to ignore the essay. The reader will most likely respond to the sources and facts. I will try to use shocking facts to get my message across.

SECOND AUDIENCE ANALYSIS

Next, Alysia produced a second audience analysis from a list of questions provided by her teacher, Bill.

1. What should this paper do for (or to) your readers?

I want my readers to gain knowledge of what they can do for abuse victims.

2. What will the readers' initial reaction to your thesis be?

They will probably ignore the essay but hopefully read it and understand.

3. What do your readers know about the topic at this point?

They probably know a little but aren't ready to involve themselves.

4. What question(s) should your essay raise for readers?

How can they take actions, how can they be involved, especially if they are younger?

5. Ultimately, what do you want your readers to do?

I want my readers to speak up for battered women. If they know someone being abused, help her out of the situation.

6. How will the readers respond to the information you give them?

I think all the sources will surprise the reader because they were very shocking to me.

Alysia then wrote her second draft.

SECOND DRAFT

1   Battering—the establishment of control and fear in a relationship through violence and other forms of abuse. The batterer uses acts of violence and a series of behaviors, including, intimidation, threats, psychological abuse, isolation, etc. to coerce and to control the other person. Battery is a crime that often goes unnoticed, unreported, and ignored, resulting in severe bodily harm and death among our country's woman today.

2   Our communities allow violence to occur in homes and families too often. People may not think we should interfere in the lives of other people, but in this

case we must take a stand for victims of violence. An article from *The Standard Times* reported examples of beaten women:

> Kathy was beaten when there were dirty dishes in the sink. She was beaten when her live-in boyfriend was drunk. She was beaten when he was sober. Janine's eye was blackened when her fiance disagreed with their wedding plans. Doris was punched when she was pregnant. She was slapped when dinner was a minute late. She was shoved and beaten when dinner was on time. Laura was kicked in the stomach when she tried to breakup. She was slapped around when she tried make up. And all were hit at least once because the man in their lives claimed they "pushed their buttons"—brought abuse on themselves by not seeing how stressed their mates were. (1)

3   One woman I know was abused by her husband repeatedly. She had a little girl and her husband would make the child sit and watch him beat her. He would come home drunk and punch her in the face until it was black and blue with bruises. He would shove her violently against the walls, then kick her in the stomach, enabling her to breath. He would slap her around, while her child cried in the background. This continued for two years. Then she developed the courage to leave him. Now she is remarried to a man who loves her and would never consider hitting her. This woman was lucky to have left her husband before she was severely injured or killed. But leaving isn't always the best alternative.

4   It is never easy for a battered woman to leave her husband. They are often afraid of reprisal from the offender and so they stay, allowing the abuse to proceed. They also fear the thought of being homeless. There are nearly 3 times as many animal shelters in the United States as there are shelters for battered women and their children (Senate Judiciary Hearings, 1990). Do we put more value on the lives of animals or do we just refuse to think there is a problem with domestic violence? We need to wake up and get back to reality, and realize that the women in our country are being savagely beaten and killed by husbands and boyfriends. The victims need our encouragement and support. They should know they will have a decent shelter to live in if they choose to leave their offenders. A woman and her child should never be homeless because they are beaten. They should be welcomed with open arms to homes that are run with caring people. Although some women are afraid to speak up, those who publicly report their abuse can help women in their situation.

5   Stephanie Rodriguez, a woman battered by her father and her ex-husband, wrote a powerfully worded book about her survival through her abusive situations. In her book, she retold a story used by her friend, a train engineer, about abuse: One night on a long stretch of track, he noticed a figure far ahead. On the tracks, he thought. For a long time the distance between the train and the figure appeared to remain the same. He wondered if it wasn't some sort of optical illusion. After awhile, however, the train began to gain on the figure, and soon my friend was close enough to see the terrified and exhausted dog, running for all he was worth, looking back over first one shoulder, then the other at the tremendous monster bearing down on him. He blew the whistle. The dog increased his speed, but was unable to maintain his pace. Finally the train ran over him. She stated that she hated that story but came to realize what it meant. That the dog was so involved in the business of staying ahead of the monster on his tail that he couldn't possibly conceive of another thing. He

didn't have time to reason that a single step in either direction would save him. It was just like being a victim of abuse. She was so caught up in violence that she couldn't hear her friends and a family calling from the other side. When she was a child, her mother committed suicide as a result of years of abuse, thinking it was her only way out. She married an abusive husband but managed to escape from him before she was faced with the same situation. Many abused women are faced with options such as suicide or killing in self-defense.

6   Currently there are 2,000 battered women in America who are serving prison time for defending their lives against their batterers. (source) These women who killed their aggressors did not kill in cold blood—they were defending themselves and sometimes the children involved in the abusive position. So why did the court system incarcerate them? If women cannot protect themselves from being murdered, the number of female homicide victims will increase. The average prison sentence of men who kill their women partners is 2 to 6 years, Women who kill their partners are sentenced on average to 15 years, despite the fact that most women who kill do so in self-defense. (Source).

7   Of the 5,745 women murdered in 1991, 6 out of 10 were killed by someone they knew. Half were murdered by a spouse or someone with whom they had been intimate (source). One memorial on an Internet home page tells one woman's story: Linda M. Ponder, a 27 year old, was killed by her ex-boyfriend in a mad rage. He had previously been arrested for beating her and the police had confiscated a gun from him after he threatened her with it. After she was killed, the police wanted the case closed concerning the person who supplied him with both guns (one they took away and one the boyfriend was given before he murdered his girlfriend). The police claimed they didn't have enough evidence. It is a shame that this woman died because the police and those around her, stood by and watched. Police were more likely to respond within 5 minutes if the offender was a stranger than if an offender was known to the female victim (Bachman 1994). Authorities need to understand that husbands and boyfriends can do just as much damage to females than strangers can.

REVIEWS

After Alysia completed this draft, she presented it to a classmate, with a list of questions for review. Here are the questions and the reviewer's answers to them:

1. Does the story in ¶ 5 fit or should I leave it out?

I like the story—it fits very well—maybe elaborate some more on the meaning of the dog not getting off the tracks.

2. I think I use "should" too many times at the end of ¶ 4. Can you help with sentences and give ideas on how I can change that?

I would definitely switch up ¶ 3 so that the reader does not encounter so many "should's."

3. I still need a conclusion para. Any ideas?

Well—I like the idea of maybe presenting a case where an institution has been up and running and helping women. Present the idea that it can be done. Your last paragraph is a little weak—sentence structure is not quite there. Maybe use that paragraph with your example and a lead into what can be done (conclusion).

4. Some of my paragraphs are lacking and I'm still looking up sources to use.

No comment on this.

Alysia also sent a copy (by e-mail) to Ron Lunsford, who offered the following comments, along with some marks in the margins of her draft:

> Hi Alysia, thanks for your paper. You're on your way to writing a very good one, I think—the basic material is here. Below I am using the system that Bill and I use. That is, we make comments in each other's texts in capital letters. Some of the comments just tell what we think about a word, sentence, or section. Other times, we rewrite for each other. So what I've done is to point out some places where I think you might work on your paper.
>
> As I said above, I think your materials are strong. I would suggest, however, that your overall organization can be stronger in general. In particular, you need something at the beginning to capture your reader. I would suggest seeing if you can't bring the story of the dog running from the train to the beginning. That gives me chills just to think about it—the fear and torment of the animal as the train slowly overtakes it. I think you could move from that to another case or two of battered women and then go into your discussion of just how bad this problem is and what should be done about it.
>
> Speaking of which, it would be good if you could make it clearer to your readers what you would like them to do (or what anyone can do) about this situation. That brings us to the question of whom you are writing for. I don't think you are writing to battered women. If you are, I take back my suggestion about starting with the dog and the train—that makes them look too helpless. However, if you are talking to others, then that story works as a beginning. But what can (should) your readers do about this situation? Think about what group of people you would like to speak to about this topic; that might help.
>
> Well, I won't say more now. I'm copying these comments to Bill—he might have something to say about them, and I suspect he'll have some of his own.
>
> Good luck. It's going to be a good paper.

Alysia then produced the following final draft.

FINAL DRAFT

NO MORE

ALYSIA TUCKER

1   Stephanie Rodriguez tells a story about an incident that happened to a friend of hers, who had been an engineer at one time. Rodriguez recounts this story of the engineer's encounter with a lone figure on the tracks in front of his train:

> For a long time the distance between the train and the figure appeared to remain the same. He wondered if it wasn't some sort of optical illusion. After

awhile, however, the train began to gain on the figure, and soon my friend was close enough to see the terrified and exhausted dog, running for all he was worth, looking back over first one shoulder, then the other at the tremendous monster bearing down on him. He blew the whistle. The dog increased his speed, but was unable to maintain the pace. Finally the train ran him over. (4, 5)

2   Rodriguez tells this frightening story as a way of dramatizing the plight of battered women. According to Rodriguez, the dog "was so involved in the business of staying ahead of the monster on his tail that he couldn't possibly conceive of another thing. He didn't have time to reason that a single step in either direction would save him" (5).

3   What is domestic violence? In broad terms, it may be defined as "violent acts carried out by persons in a marital, sexual, parental, or caregiving role toward others" (Stith, Williams, and Rosen 1). In this paper, I will concern myself with abuse that men inflict on women they are (or have been) living with. This type of spousal violence is responsible for an unbelievable number of injuries to women each year. In his book *Family Violence,* Henry Wallace estimates that 8.7 million couples experienced some form of spousal abuse (or battering) in 1985 (165). These cases lead to the deaths of thousands of women each year, and these deaths occur in homes where there are other family members and in communities where other people know there is abuse. These people may not think we should interfere in the lives of others, but we must take a stand for the victims of violence by encouraging them to be courageous and leave their abusers before serious injuries occur.

4   An article from *The Standard Times* reported examples of beaten women.

    Kathy was beaten when there were dirty dishes in the sink. She was beaten when her live-in boyfriend was drunk. She was beaten when he was sober. Janine's eye was blackened when her fiancé disagreed with their wedding plans. Doris was punched when she was pregnant. She was slapped when dinner was a minute late. She was shoved and beaten when dinner was on time. Laura was kicked in the stomach when she tried to break up. She was slapped around when she tried make up. And all were hit at least once because the man in their lives claimed they "pushed their buttons"—brought abuse on themselves by not seeing how stressed their mates were. (par. 1)

5   There are stories closer to home. One woman I know was abused by her husband repeatedly. She had a little girl and her husband would make the child sit and watch him beat her. He would come home drunk and punch his wife in the face until it was black and blue with bruises. He would shove her violently against the walls, then kick her in the stomach, making it difficult for her to breathe. He would slap her around, while her child cried in the background. This continued for two years. Then she developed the courage to leave him. Now she is remarried to a man who loves her and would never consider hitting her. This woman was lucky to have left her husband before she was severely injured or killed.

6   But it is never easy for a battered woman to leave her husband. These women are often afraid of reprisal from the offender and so they stay, allowing the abuse to continue. When this is the case, the authorities should act without hesitation for the safety of the victim. Other cases are even more difficult to deal with, however. Many women do not even seem to want to leave their terrible situations. Such women were often abused as children and grow up thinking that abuse is natural in a home. Or, they may depend on their abusive spouses economically. The husband brings in the money that allows the wife to live and have a home, constantly showing the power and control he

has over her. This leads the battered women to fear the thought of being homeless, and they have a right to do so. There are nearly three times as many animal shelters in the United States as there are shelters for battered women and their children (Senate Judiciary Hearings, 1990). Do we put more value on the lives of animals than on those of these women, or do we just refuse to think there is a problem with domestic violence? Regardless, we need to realize that the women in our country are being savagely beaten and killed by husbands and boyfriends. These victims need our encouragement and support. They should know they will have a decent shelter to live in if they choose to leave their offenders. A battered woman and her child should never be homeless. They should be welcomed with open arms in homes run by caring people.

7   But in many cases intervention is needed while women are still living with violent abusers. Yet it is very hard for women to get the protection they need. Police are more likely to respond within five minutes if the offender is a stranger than if an offender is known to the female victim (Bachman 1). Authorities need to understand that husbands and boyfriends can do just as much damage to females as strangers can. And we need to stop excusing the violent behavior of these killers. Some batterers excuse their behavior by saying that they just "lost it." If this were true, wouldn't they be hitting and beating on bosses and clients who repeatedly anger them? But they don't. They always find the easy victim, someone who loves, honors, and cherishes them, someone who will accept their apology if given.

8   We must find a way to help these innocent victims. We can start by learning how to identify them. There are many signs you can look for in a battered woman. The victim will have low self-esteem and will deny the fact that she is being abused. She will often take responsibility for the offender's actions and accept them as right, thinking she was wrong for angering him. The woman may also be very family-oriented in a traditional way, staying close to home, being overly protective of her children. A battered woman may believe that no one can help her situation because they do not understand and that their attempts to help will only cause more problems. If you see any of these signs in a loved one or in someone you know, take action! Get her help! If nothing is done, the problems will only continue. She may claim to love her husband or boyfriend, and show her love by staying, but he will only return this love with a slap in the face or a punch in the stomach, possibly escalating through the years.

9   The horrible reality is that many women in our country are being hurt and killed by people they love and trust. Innocent women feel alienated and abandoned by their friends and family when they call for help and nobody responds. The call may be a silent pleading in their eyes or bruises on their bodies, but it is there. Unless abuse is stopped, the only change we will see is an increase in the number of injuries and deaths occurring among battered women every year. If someone is calling out to you for help, take action. Like the frightened dog losing ground to the monster locomotive, these women are too tired and weary to think clearly for themselves. You would help that dog. Won't you help these innocent women?

WORKS CITED

Bachman, Ronet. *Response from the Criminal Justice System.* US Dept. of Justice. Bureau of Justice. Rept. 0717-R-01. Washington: GPO, 1994.

Rodriguez, Stephanie. *Time to Stop Pretending.* Middlebury, VT: Eriksson, 1994.

Stith, Sandra, Mary Beth Williams, and Karen Rosen. *Violence Hits Home.* New York: Springer, 1990.

Wallace, Harvey. *Family Violence.* Boston: Allyn, 1996.

United States. Senate Committee on the Judiciary. *The Violence against Women Act of 1990.* Rept. 1008-C. Washington: GPO, 1990.

"Why Does Society Allow This to Happen?" *Standard Times.* 4 June 1995. 9 Oct. 1998 <http://www.s-t.com/projects/DomVio/dvwhydoessoc.html>.

Exercise 10.10

You will note that two of the essays in this chapter—Jaime Sherrill's "Zero Tolerance for Abuse" and Alysia Tucker's "No More"—treat the same general topic. Although the topics are the same, the essays are very different. We would argue that both are very effective, however. Analyze these two essays in terms of the criteria for successful persuasion we have developed in this chapter. What makes each essay successful? Then, choose a topic that is treated by one of the other writers in this chapter, and sketch a plan for how an essay you might write on this topic would differ from the one that writer has written.

Checklist: Critiquing a Persuasion Essay

1. State the action the writer of the essay would like her audience to take. What "should" thesis is this action connected to? Is that argument debatable?
2. State the audience for the essay. Is this audience likely to be favorably disposed—or at least neutral—to the underlying "should" thesis?
3. If the "should" thesis is debatable, does the writer offer logical arguments in favor of her position? Are they effective?
4. List the types of persuasive arguments the writer uses in the essay. How effective are they?
5. Sketch the basic organization of the essay. Is it effective? Does the introduction capture the reader's attention and draw him into the topic? Does the conclusion leave the reader with a sense of completeness?
6. Does the paper adhere to conventions of usage, mechanics, and format? Correct any errors you find.

Writing is one of the best means we have for solving problems, especially when we take the time to write through a problem, exploring it thoroughly, speculating about potential solutions, and then selecting and justifying what seems the best of those solutions. Problem solving is something of an art, requiring a willingness on the part of the investigator (the problem solver) to range widely and freely over the whole terrain or scene of the problem, giving serious consideration to every solution that occurs, no matter how frivolous, difficult, obvious, or fantastic it may seem. At times, the solution selected may not be the best or most efficient, even though it works.

The following story offers an example of an elegant, yet seemingly overdone, solution to a problem. As part of research and development efforts for the U.S. space program, NASA scientists wanted to develop a reliable pen for astronauts to use for recording data and observations while in space. Ordinary pens won't work in outer space, because they need gravity to make ink flow onto the page. So NASA created a pen with a pressurized ink cartridge, at a cost of $1 million. And it worked in outer space; U.S. astronauts had reliable pens for making permanent records. Facing the same problem, Soviet scientists provided their cosmonauts with pencils.

Now, the purpose of this example isn't to denigrate NASA and its efforts to provide U.S. astronauts with the best, most efficient equipment. Ink *is* more permanent and therefore more legible in the long run; pencil tips break and wear

Problem/Solution Essays

CHAPTER 11

down, so pencils have to be sharpened periodically, raising the question of what to do with the shavings. The point is that you may well find more than one solution to a problem. A more elaborate solution isn't always the best; then again, that more elaborate solution may be, depending on the investigator's exploration of the problem and evaluation of all the possible solutions that arise.

Writing an essay that presents a problem and then offers a viable solution to it will in many ways be the most comprehensive writing task you'll undertake, for it brings together the skills of evaluation, interpretation, argument, and persuasion. As you work through this assignment, keep in mind that your goal is to convince your audience that you've considered the problem thoroughly and that the solution you propose is the most workable and efficient—the best—solution to it.

SAMPLE ESSAYS

The following sample essays focus on problems and solutions to them. As you read each, try to identify those places where each writer clearly defines a problem and then a solution to it.

In "Clean Up or Pay Up," Louis Barbash presents his concerns for college athletes. Focusing on academic and financial problems, Barbash labels collegiate athletics a "mess."

LOUIS BARBASH

CLEAN UP OR PAY UP

1   Tom Scates is one of the lucky ones. He has a bachelor's degree from Georgetown University, where he played basketball under the fabled John Thompson, one of the best college basketball coaches in the country, and one of the few who insist that their players go to class. Ninety percent of Thompson's players at Georgetown receive degrees, about three times the national average.

2   More than a decade after Tom Scates received his diploma, he has managed to parlay his Georgetown degree and education, his athletic skills, and the character he developed during his career in intercollegiate athletics into a job as a doorman at a downtown Washington hotel.

3   Still, Scates *is* one of the lucky ones. He played for a good team at a good school, under a moral coach, and under a president, Father Timothy Healy, who believed that Georgetown was a school with a basketball team, not a basketball team with a school. He was not implicated in drug deals, shoplifting, violence, grade altering, point shaving, or under-the-table money scandals. He didn't have his scholarship yanked. He didn't emerge from school functionally illiterate. He got a job.

4   Many of the men Scates played against when he was at Georgetown, and their basketball and football counterparts at major colleges and universities, have not been so fortunate. Less than half the football and basketball scholarship athletes will graduate

from college. And what education athletes do get is often so poor that it may be irrelevant whether they graduate or not.

5   In addition to corrupting the university's basic academic mission, big-time sports have been a lightning rod for financial corruption. College athletes are cash-poor celebrities. Although their performance on the field or court produces millions in revenue for the university, they receive in return only their scholarships—tuition, room, and board—and no spending money. They are forbidden from working part-time during the season. Athletes have been caught trying to make money by getting loans from coaches and advisers, selling the shoes and other gear they get as team members, taking allowances from agents, and getting paid for no-show summer jobs provided by jock-sniffing alumni—all violations of National Collegiate Athletic Association (NCAA) rules.

6   Things might be different if the NCAA would show some real inclination to clean up the college sports mess. But that organization has a well-developed instinct for the capillaries: instead of attacking the large-scale academic, financial, and criminal corruption in college sports, too often the investigators from Mission, Kansas, put their energies into busting athletes for selling their complimentary tickets and coaches for starting their practices a few weeks ahead of schedule. Meanwhile, the real problems of college athletics continue to fester.

7   Will the NCAA change? And if so, would that matter? Earlier this year, NCAA Executive Director Dick Schultz proposed new rules to stem college sports corruption. Schultz's reforms included "quality academic advising and career-counseling programs," restriction of recruiting, long-term contracts for coaches, reduced pressure and time demands on athletes, and the elimination of athletic dormitories to "make the athlete as indistinguishable from the rest of the student body as is humanly possible."

8   It's illegal to bet on sports except in Nevada, so bet on this instead: Schultz's proposals will not pass an NCAA dominated by college sports officials whose careers rest on winning games. Recall what has happened to much weaker suggestions. Even Georgetown's Coach Thompson boycotted his own team's games to protest as too severe the timid requirements of the NCAA's Proposition 48, which would have barred entering freshmen from athletic scholarships and competition if they did not have a 2.0 high school GPA and SAT scores totaling 700 points. Interested in even better odds? Take this to the bank: Even if Schultz gets every one of his proposals put in exactly as he outlined them, they—like everything else the NCAA has tried—will not work.

9   Well then, is there any way out of this mess? Yes. Actually, there are *two* ways out. Because the NCAA has so utterly failed, because in the present system the big-money pressures to cheat are so enormous, and because, like it or not, sports have such a widespread impact on the country's moral climate, there should be a federal law that requires schools *either* to return to the Ivy League ideal in which players are legitimate members of the student body, judged by the same standards as everybody else, *or* to let players on their teams be non-student professionals. All the trouble comes from trying to mix these two alternatives—from trying to achieve big revenues while retaining the veneer of purity.

10   The pure alternative doesn't have to ignore athletic ability among prospective students—there were plenty of good teams before today's double-standard disaster got firmly entrenched. You want to consider the athletic ability of college applicants for the same reason you want to consider musical or theatrical ability: a university should be a wonderfully diverse collection of talents that together stimulate people to develop in all sorts of positive ways. Athletic skill is one such talent—one that even academic purists ought to look at. But the key is that universities must consider athletic ability as only *part* of what they take into account when they accept a student. The fundamental

mistake of today's college sports system is that it supposes a student could be at a university *solely* because of his athletic skill.

11   While the purely amateur option is probably the more desirable of the two, the professional one isn't nearly as horrible as it might seem at first. After all, coaches were originally volunteers, and now they're paid. (Army's first head coach, Dennis Michie, received no pay. Jess Hawley coached for free at Dartmouth from 1923–28. His 1925 team went undefeated and was the national champion.) So why not players?

SWEAT EQUITY

12   How much would a salaried college athlete make? If the example of minor league baseball is anything to go on—and such authorities as Roger Meiners, a Clemson University economist who specializes in the economics of college sports, and Ed Garvey, the former head of the NFL Players Association, think that it is—college salaries would be enough for a young athlete to live on, but not so much as to bust college budgets. Minor league baseball players start at around $11,000 for their first full professional season and range upward to the neighborhood of $26,000 for players on AAA teams under major league option. So it seems fair to estimate a salary of about $13,000 for an average player on an average team.

13   The professional option's chief virtue is honesty. The current student-athlete system requires both students and universities to pretend that the young athletes are not full-time professionals, but rather full-time students who play sports in their spare time. But does anyone suppose that high school athletes reading four and five years below grade level would be considered for college admission, much less recruited and given full scholarships, if they were not football or basketball stars? Can the abuses of NCAA rules that have been uncovered at almost half of its biggest schools have any other meaning than that giving these athletes a real education is not what universities are trying to do?

14   The hypocrisy begins with the fundamental relationship between the players and the university: 18- to 20-year-olds, many of them poorly educated, inner-city blacks, coerced and deceived into playing four years of football or basketball without pay so that the university can sell tickets and television rights.

15   The coercion comes from the colleges' control of access to professional football or basketball: It is virtually impossible to go to the pros without playing college ball first. Colleges open that opportunity only to athletes who will agree to perform for the college for four years without getting a salary or even holding an outside part-time job. The athlete does receive a four-year scholarship and room and board while he is enrolled, a package the NCAA values at about $40,000. The deception lies in the fact that the inducements held out to athletes by colleges—the chance to play pro ball and getting a college education—are essentially worthless, and the schools know it.

16   The athlete's first priority is to play pro ball. Forty-four percent of all black scholarship athletes, and 22 percent of white athletes entertain hopes of playing in the pros. That's why they will play four years for nothing. But in fact, the lure of sports that keeps kids in school is a false hope and a cruel hoax. "The dream in the head of so many youngsters that they will achieve fame and riches in professional sports is touching, but it is also overwhelmingly unrealistic," says Robert Atwell, president of the American Council on Education. The would-be pro faces odds as high as 400–1: of the 20,000 "students" who play college basketball, for example, only 50 will make it to the NBA. The other 19,950 won't. Many of them will wind up like Tom Scates, in minimum wage jobs, or like Reggie Ford, who lost his football scholarship to Northwest Oklahoma State after he injured his knee and now collects unemployment compensation in South Carolina.

17   The scholarships and promises of education are also worthless currency. Of every 10 young men who accept scholarships to play football at major schools, according to NCAA statistics, just 4 will graduate. Only 3 of every 10 basketball players receive degrees.

18   Not only are these athletes being cheated out of a promised education, but they and their universities are forced to erect elaborate, meretricious curricula to satisfy the student-athlete requirement, so of those who do get degrees, many receive diplomas that are barely worth the parchment they're printed on. Running back Ronnie Harmon majored in computer science at the University of Iowa, but took only one computer course in his three years of college. Another Iowa football player also majored in computer science, but in his senior year took only courses in billiards, bowling, and football; he followed up by getting a D in a summer school watercolor class. Transcripts of the members of the basketball team at Ohio University list credit for something called "International Studies 69B"—a course composed of a 14-day/10-game trip to Europe.

19   As things stand now, athletically gifted students who genuinely want an education are often steered away by eligibility-conscious advisers. Jan Kemp, the University of Georgia academic adviser for athletes who won a lawsuit after the university fired her for insisting on the athletes' right to be educated, recalls how a Georgia athlete was always placed in "dummy" classes despite his efforts to take "real" ones. "There's nothing wrong with his mind," says Kemp. "But the situation is magnified for athletes because there is so much money involved. There is too much control over who gets in and who takes what courses."

20   No case illustrates the cynicism that poisons big-time college sports better than that of former Washington Raiders star defensive end Dexter Manley. Manley spent four years as a "student athlete" at Oklahoma State University only to emerge, as he admitted years later, functionally illiterate. But OSU President John Campbell was not embarrassed: "There would be those who would argue that Dexter Manley got exactly what he wanted out of OSU. He was able to develop his athletic skills and ability; he was noticed by the pros, he got a pro contract. So maybe we did him a favor by letting him go through the program."

21   One scarcely knows where to start in on a statement like that. It's appalling that an accredited state university would admit a functional illiterate, even recruit him, and leave him illiterate after four years as a student. It's shocking that it would do all this in order to make money from his unpaid performance as an athlete. And it is little short of grotesque that an educator, entrusted with the education of 20,000 young men and women, would argue that the cynical arrangement between an institution of higher learning and an uneducated high school boy was, after all, a fair bargain.

22   The infection of hypocrisy spreads from the president's office to the athletic department and coaching staff. This may be the saddest betrayal in the system. These are 17-year-olds, dreaming of a lucrative career in sports. They have placed their faith in the coaches who have visited their homes, solicited their trust, and gotten to know their parents. But those coaches, as Robert Atwell points out, "may have a vested interest in perpetuating the myth rather than pointing out its inherent fallacy." That vested interest, of course, is that if they do not produce winning teams, at whatever cost, they will lose their jobs.

23   So instead, to recruit highly sought-after high-school athletes, coaches promise playing time, education, and exposure to national TV audiences and professional scouts. But once the player arrives on campus, coaches are under strong pressure to treat him like what he is: an employee, whose needs must be subordinated to the needs of the enterprise, i.e., winning.

24   Gary Ruble, a former scholarship football player at the University of North Carolina, told a House subcommittee investigating college athletics that North Carolina "came to me and offered me, basically, the world. They came to me and said come to our school. Be a student athlete. We will guarantee that you graduate. We will promise you to be a star, et cetera, et cetera, et cetera." But once in Chapel Hill, Ruble found himself riding the bench. "You go in as an offensive lineman, which I was, at 240 pounds, and you go into a system where you have offensive linemen who are 285 and they are telling you that you are going to play. That's an impossibility," Ruble told the subcommittee. After three years, "my position coach called me into his office and stated that I should consider either transferring to another school or dropping out gracefully. I was no longer to be considered in their plans for our team," Ruble says. When he reported back to school anyway, he was told "I had no option of whether to stay or go. They were not allowing me to retain my scholarship."

25   A system of sports without strings—releasing college athletes and their universities from the pretense that they are students, and instead paying them for their services—would cure the student-athlete system's chief vices: its duplicity and its exploitiveness.

26   Athletes who want to get started on careers in sports, including those whose only way out of the ghetto may be the slam dunk and the 4.4–40, would find paying jobs in their chosen field. Overnight, thousands of new jobs as professional football and basketball players would be created. Players with the ability to get to the NFL and NBA would get paid during their years of apprenticeship. For those of lesser abilities, playing for college teams would be a career in itself, a career they could start right out of high school and continue as long as skills and bodies allowed. And as they matured and their playing careers drew to a close, the prospect of a real college education might seem more inviting than it did at 17.

27   Releasing athletes from having to be students would, ironically, make it easier for those who want an education to get it. Even with the best intentions, today's college athletes have little hope of being serious students. Basketball practice, for instance, begins October 13, and the season does not end for the most successful teams until after the NCAA championships in early April; in other words, the season starts one month after school begins and ends one month before school is out. During the season, athletes spend six or more hours a day, 30 to 40 hours a week, on practice, viewing game-films, at chalk talks, weight training, conditioning, and attending team meetings. The best-prepared students would have difficulty attending to their studies while working 34 hours a week—and these are not the best-prepared students.

28   But under no-strings sports, athletes who want educations will fare better than they do now, because the pace of their education need not be governed by their eligibility for athletic competition. A football player could play the fall semester and study in the spring. Basketball players, whose season spans the two semesters, might enroll at schools with quarter or trimester systems, or study summers and after their sports careers are over. Instead of being corralled into courses rigged to provide high grades like "Theory of Volleyball," "Recreation and Leisure," "Jogging," and "Leisure Alternatives," athletes would be in a position to take only the courses they want and need. This would be even more likely if, as part of the pro option, universities were still required to offer full scholarships to athletes, to be redeemed whenever the athletes wanted to use them.

29   Under these changes, those athletes who end up going to college would be doing so because they were pursuing their own educational goals. This reform would replace today's phony jock curriculum with the kind of mature academic choices that made the G.I. Bill such a success.

30   Such considerations make it clear that it's time for schools to choose between real amateurism and real professionalism. They can't have a little of both. From now on, in college sports, it's got to be either poetry or pros.

Questions for Review

1. In a sentence, state the problem Barbash addresses. Does he offer a single sentence that states this problem, or did you have to infer it?
2. What is Barbash's thesis? Where does it appear in the essay? How is it worded? What point will Barbash support, given this thesis?
3. How effective is the essay's introduction?
4. What are the main points of Barbash's argument as he explores the problem in paragraphs 12–23? How effectively does he show that the problem truly is a problem?
5. Barbash offers an either/or solution—athletes should either be pure amateurs or be professionals. Which of these solutions do you think Barbash thinks the more workable? Why?
6. Identify several key terms that Barbash uses in exploring the problem (e.g., "hypocrisy" in paragraph 14 and "worthless currency" in paragraph 17). How effectively does he use such terms in presenting his thoughts? Do they seem fair and accurate? Why?
7. What opposition is there likely to be to Barbash's proposal? How does Barbash's knowledge of this opposition help him shape his argument?

In "Balance of Power: Can Endangered Salmon and Hydroelectric Plants Share the Same Rivers?" Julie Titone discusses the alarming decline of the salmon population in the Pacific Northwest.

JULIE TITONE

BALANCE OF POWER: CAN ENDANGERED SALMON AND HYDROELECTRIC PLANTS SHARE THE SAME RIVERS?

1   At the turn of the century, thousands of sockeye salmon swam back to their central Idaho spawning grounds at Redfish Lake every year. So many crowded the creek that drains the lake, in fact, that they spooked the mounts of riders trying to cross. By last year, however, their numbers had shrunk dramatically: only four sockeye salmon made it to Redfish Lake, only one of them a female.

2   The sockeye earned the dubious distinction of becoming a federal endangered species last November. They are far from alone in their predicament. This spring, the Snake River stocks of spring, summer, and fall chinook salmon were listed as endangered, and biologists have identified 214 Northwest populations of wild-spawning salmonids threatened with extinction.

3   In the early 1900s, as many as 16 million wild salmon traveled up the Columbia River and its tributaries each year. Today, there are only 2 million, all but 300,000 of which are from hatcheries. As salmon sport-fishing declined in recent decades, many Idaho riverside communities lost an important source of income. Now the misery is flowing downstream, as fishing communities on the Lower Columbia and along the Pacific coast face up to rough new harvest restrictions. The fish just aren't there anymore.

4   Genetically weaker hatchery fish, overharvesting, and degraded spawning habitat share some of the blame for the dwindling runs. But biologists say the biggest culprits are the dams, which are blamed for up to 95 percent of the deaths of young making their way from their spawning beds to their adult homes in the Pacific Ocean.

5   There are 30 major dams in the Columbia Basin. Some of them, such as Grand Coulee Dam, have no fish passage facilities at all, and have blocked entire drainages to oceangoing fish. Eight of them—four on the Lower Snake, four on the Columbia—provide a 460-kilometer obstacle course for such fish as the Snake River sockeye. The turbines in each of these dams kill up to 15 percent of the young fish that pass through them.

6   Young salmon, or smolts, are particularly vulnerable during their journey from spawning grounds to the ocean because the transformation from freshwater fish into saltwater creatures, "smoltification," appears to make them lethargic. Without natural spring freshets to push them downstream, the young salmon must find their way through a series of slack-water reservoirs. The journey from spawning grounds to ocean, which once took a week before the dams were built, now takes up to six weeks.

7   To help juvenile salmon through the slow, predator-filled reservoirs, since 1977 the U.S. Army Corps of Engineers has collected millions of fish at the first of the eight dams, then barged or trucked them downstream. Critics of that elaborate transportation system note that it has not resulted in an increase in the number of adults coming back upstream to spawn. Quite the opposite has happened.

8   The Endangered Species Act gives the National Marine Fisheries Service final say in recovering the wild salmon. But the Northwest Power Planning Council has significant authority in managing the Columbia River system, thanks to the Northwest Power Act of 1980. That Act required that fish and wildlife get equal attention with hydropower and other industrial uses of the Columbia. After more than a decade that hasn't happened. The Power Council set a goal of doubling the total salmon population. Instead, the total numbers dropped and numbers of wild species plummeted.

9   Balancing the loss of these fish against the costs of modifying dozens of dams has put the Pacific Northwest into an all-too-familiar predicament. In 1990, when conservation groups first petitioned for endangered status for some salmon species, the region was already deadlocked over spotted owl protection. Comparisons between the salmon and owl were inevitable and frightening. Protecting the spotted owl and its ancient forest habitat has dealt a major blow to the timber industry, which will have a ripple effect on the economics of Oregon, Washington, and northern California.

10   Salmon protection will involve tampering with the very lifeblood of the four-state region: the Columbia River and its tributaries. Improving fish passage could mean blasting new fish tunnels through the dams. It means changing the amount of water that goes through hydropower turbines, and the timing of that water's release from reservoirs.

For example, allowing spring "drawdowns" will turn reservoirs into rivers and flush the fish to the ocean. Such changes could have a dramatic impact on reservoir levels, which would drop as much as 11 meters during the drawdowns. That eliminates barge traffic, leaves marina docks high and dry, and can cause embankments to slough and crack.

11   Salmon protection would thus raise utility rates for residents and industries, such as aluminum factories, grown reliant upon cheap hydropower. It would affect inland ports and the businesses that depend on them, because the reservoirs would no longer be high enough year-round to float barges. It would force irrigators to lengthen pipes they use to suck water from the rivers.

12   At first glance, the salmon may seem to have even more sociopolitical cards stacked against it than the spotted owl.

13   But unlike the spotted owl, the salmon has economic value. More than one far-reaching law protects it, and no one says salmon are expendable. There's no fish equivalent of the bumper sticker "Save a logger. Eat an owl."

14   Efforts to recover the endangered salmon would boost all salmon and steelhead populations, both in the wild and in hatcheries (wild populations supply the varied genetic stock that keeps hatchery populations healthy). Therefore, salmon protection could actually be an enormous boon to the economy. Furthermore, the impact of more salmon for canning or as a lure for tourists has not been calculated. The focus has been on the short-term costs of recovering the endangered populations, not the long-term benefits of bolstering all the salmon runs. According to the Northwest Resource Information Center, one conservative 1992 estimate held that 44 million adult salmon and steelhead trout were lost to Northwest fisheries in the years 1960–1980. The estimated commercial and recreational loss to the region: $6.5 billion.

15   Annual drawdowns could well be part of the Snake River sockeye recovery plan currently being written by a team of biologists for the National Marine Fisheries Service. The team is building upon work done by the Northwest Power Planning Council. Last December the Power Council gave a qualified endorsement to drawdowns as part of its own complex plan for reestablishing salmon runs.

16   Officials of the Bonneville Power Administration, which markets most of the region's hydropower, often note that the effort to restore salmon runs has cost its ratepayers a billion dollars in lost power sales and physical improvements to the river system. But they no longer contend that annual drawdowns to help the fish would increase consumers' power costs by a third; that estimate is down to about 4 percent. The Northwest would still have some of the cheapest electricity in the country.

17   This March the U.S. Army Corps of Engineers took its first reluctant but well-orchestrated step toward changing river operations. The corps conducted a month-long experiment to see how the reservoir system would respond to lower, faster flows. It dramatically dropped the reservoirs behind Lower Granite and Little Goose dams, the first ones that young Idaho salmon confront on their way down the Snake River. Official results of the drawdown test are still being written, but no major physical failures were observed. The dams' turbines didn't vibrate wildly when their power generation was cut in half; the levees protecting the upstream city of Lewiston, Idaho, didn't collapse.

18   Hydropower interests and communities that would suffer most from drawdowns demand proof that drawdowns, by pushing the juvenile salmon downstream, will result in more adults coming up to spawn. Biologists have no proof, only strong evidence.

19   Unfortunately, because the dams haven't been reconstructed to pass fish through at low water levels, the test had to be done before juvenile fish were actually traveling to the sea. So the March experiment does not prove that drawdowns would actually move fish quickly through the reservoirs.

20   According to a new report prepared for Idaho Governor Cecil Andrus, drawdowns would be 5 to 20 times cheaper than the other salmon protection plans that have been proposed. Although there is no guarantee that drawdowns will save any of the Columbia Basin's wild salmon, they remain an expensive gamble worth taking. Without help, the Northwest's remaining wild salmon—and eventually the hatchery fish that depend on those wild stocks for genetic diversity—will surely swim to extinction.

Questions for Review

1. Titone writes about the decline of the salmon population. How does she help her readers understand the scale of this problem?
2. What causes of this decline does Titone acknowledge as contributing to the problem? What does she identify as the major causes of the problem?
3. How effectively does Titone discuss the effect of dams on the salmon population? What details does she provide that you think are effective?
4. What solution does Titone offer? How effectively does she support it?
5. How effectively does Titone address such concerns as the economic impact of dam restructuring, the effects of drawdowns, and the protection of the spotted owl?
6. How effective is the title of this piece? How does Titone use the term "power" in it? Identify and comment on other instances of word play that you think particularly effective.
7. What is the thesis of this essay? Where does it appear? How does it compare to that of Barbash's essay?

In "The War against Witnesses," Randy Fitzgerald discusses a serious problem—the intimidation of witnesses by the criminals they're to testify against.

RANDY FITZGERALD

THE WAR AGAINST WITNESSES

1   Heavy rain fell as Alberta Burden, 60, parked her car at the mental-health center in Palm Beach County, Florida, where for two decades she had cared for elderly patients. As she reached for her umbrella, a man in his 20s walked up to her car and fired five shots through the window. Burden slumped over, covered by shattered glass, and died. It was shortly after 7 a.m.

2   "They shot Bertie," a frantic co-worker told Terry Allen, the center's executive director. Allen did not need to ask who "they" were. Two months earlier, on July 9, 1994, Burden had witnessed the murder of her goddaughter, Tannis Parson. Burden identified the killer as Dumas Parson, Tannis's husband—a leader of a gang of crack-cocaine dealers called the Parson Posse.

3   Parson warned Burden not to cooperate with the police. Gang members began staking out her home and job. At first Burden listened to her friends and stayed in hiding and away from her job. But Burden, a deaconess in her church, was determined to testify and see justice done. "We have to stand up to those people," she told Allen.

4   Soon after she returned to work, she was murdered. The shooter, police say, was one of a two-man hit team from Tallahassee hired by another leader of the Parson Posse for $3000 each. All three men were caught and await trial.

5   Alberta Burden's death is part of a growing trend of violence against witnesses that has often paralyzed American justice over the past decade. "Witness intimidation is widespread, increasing and having a serious impact on the prosecution of crime across the entire country," concludes a 1996 study by the National Institute of Justice, a research arm of the U.S. Department of Justice.

6   Philadelphia prosecutors say that one in five of that city's homicides remain unsolved because of witness fear. In Washington, D.C., one drug gang on trial in early 1994 had nine witnesses and potential witnesses slaughtered. Observes Michael Mansfield, assistant district attorney for Queens County, New York, "A decade ago there were threats against witnesses. Now threats are being carried out."

SEE NO EVIL

7   In Des Moines at least 40 patrons were in the Café Divang when seven gang members arrived to settle a grudge. Four waited outside while the others went in and began shooting. One man was killed and two others wounded.

8   For two weeks after the August 6, 1995, shooting rampage, police interviewed witnesses. But gang members had gone door-to-door warning people against providing information. "No one would cooperate," says police investigator Blaine Tellis. "The gang had everyone scared."

9   With one 20-year-old witness, however, the gang went too far. After being threatened with a gun jammed against his head, the man sought police protection. He became their first big break in the case. Police eventually coaxed two more witnesses to come forward.

10   Yet during the February 1996 trial of five gang members, defense attorneys scored with the jury by pointing to the shortage of witnesses and the fact that on the witness stand, one had contradicted what she earlier told police. It apparently worked: three defendants were freed, one was convicted of a lesser charge, and the jury hung on the fifth defendant's guilt. (Ultimately, four of the seven gang members were convicted or pleaded guilty to murder or other charges.)

11   In similar incidents across America, communities have been cowed into silence, and justice is delayed or prevented. Some 250 people at a May 1993 softball game in Pittsburgh watched a local gang charge onto the field and attack rivals—shooting one dead and beating a second to death with baseball bats.

12   "It took us a year to move forward on the case," says Cmdr. Ronald Freeman of the Pittsburgh police. "Players on the field claimed they saw nothing. We had to go before a grand jury and force people to testify." Seven persons were eventually convicted or pleaded guilty.

13   In February 1994 Lawrence Manuel, 24, was talking with friends at a concert in San Francisco when a gang member walked up, shot Manuel in the head, then casually strolled out. "He killed Manuel in front of at least 50 witnesses," says assistant police chief Prentice Sanders. "Another 100 people saw him pass through the crowd with the gun still smoking. But to this day, witnesses are afraid to talk. That's what we are running up against time and time again."

STALKING WITNESSES

14   According to the National Institute of Justice, criminals are able to intimidate entire communities by engaging in the "execution, assault or public humiliation of victims, witnesses or their families." Gangs have damaged witnesses' property or parked conspicuously outside their homes. In court they have worn "gang colors," packed the public seats and stared down witnesses. Washington, D.C. drug gangs hung posters in the street naming prospective witnesses and warning that those who cooperate with police will be killed.

15   Criminals will often go far to track down witnesses. Philadelphia and New York prosecutors have known drug gangs to hire private eyes. Under a credo of "snitches die," Los Angeles gangs have used friends and relatives working for the Department of Motor Vehicles and other public agencies to trace, intimidate and attack witnesses.

16   "Gangs have infiltrated every informational system," says L.A. prosecutor Snyder. "They would sometimes know when people were going to court before we knew."

17   As a result of such harassment, says Charles F. Gallagher, a deputy district attorney of Philadelphia, scared witnesses will sometimes "go south"—a term prosecutors use to describe memory lapses or altered testimony—and the case must be dropped.

18   Consider what happened in Palm Beach County, Florida, where three witnesses had identified Ronald Knight, 25, as the man who robbed and killed bartender Richard Kunkel. Before the trial could begin on January 3, 1995, each witness, claiming to fear for his life, had retracted his statement or refused to attend the trial. "Knight had intimidated them while out on bond," says State Attorney Barry Krischer. "We had no choice but to drop the charges."

19   When the case's dismissal was announced in court, the prosecutor says, a smiling Knight turned to her, curled his fingers into a the shape of a gun, pointed it and cocked his trigger finger.

20   Five months later, on May 8, 1995, Brendan Meehan, a 22-year-old substance abuse counselor, was shot and killed, then robbed. Police investigators quickly noted similarities with the Kunkel murder and arrested Knight five days later.

21   In county jail Knight began intimidating witnesses again. Thanks to Florida's open-discovery law, which gives defendants access to the names and addresses of witnesses after their grand jury testimony, he learned the identity of his accusers and began calling them from the prisoners' telephone, threatening them. Only after prosecutors obtained a judge's order to revoke Knight's phone privileges did the harassment stop.

22   This time Knight was convicted of murder. He was then tried for Kunkel's murder, found guilty and given the death penalty.

23   "Our state's open-discovery process enables killers like Knight to get to the very people who could put them away," says State Attorney spokesman Michael Edmondson. "Victims refuse to come forward because they're not willing to have their names and addresses published."

FIGHTING BACK

24   After Alberta Burden's murder in 1994, authorities built a federal case against the Parson gang for distributing cocaine. Arresting the entire gang, rather than individual members, helped avoid the witness intimidation problem. And defendants in federal courts, unlike Florida state courts, are not entitled to the names, addresses and depositions of the prosecution witnesses. In 1996 eight of the principal gang members were

convicted; seven of them received life sentences, and the eighth was sentenced to nearly 25 years in prison.

25   "We got the whole gang because of Alberta Burden," says Krischer. "But we still had no program where we could truthfully tell a witness, 'We will protect you.' "

26   To solve that problem, he and other Palm Beach County officials decided to write state legislation creating a witness-protection program. It pays for protection and relocation of witnesses identified as targets of intimidation. State Rep. Addie Greene of Palm Beach County, a member of Alberta Burden's church, introduced the bill before the Florida legislature, where it passed unopposed and was signed into law in 1997.

27   California has also adopted a witness-protection program, which took effect this year. Otherwise, few states or localities have any witness-protection programs.

28   In interviews with *Reader's Digest,* police, prosecutors and legal authorities urged these additional steps:

- State laws permitting dangerous criminals to learn the names and addresses of witnesses long before trial must be changed. Where retaliation seems imminent, judges should have the authority to seal the identities of key witnesses until trial.
- Dangerous prisoners should not have access to unmonitored phones.
- At trial, witnesses should have a separate waiting area. In special cases witnesses should be allowed to testify from remote locations over closed-circuit TV.
- Penalties for witness intimidation should be toughened.
- Finally, state and federal agencies should cooperate on speedier identity changes for witnesses needing protection, such as new driver's licenses and Social Security numbers.

29   "People have got to understand that it's safer to cooperate with law enforcement than to keep criminals in their communities," says San Francisco assistant police chief Sanders. "When we all stand together against criminals, the law of the streets cannot triumph over the rule of law."

Questions for Review

1. The problem Fitzgerald takes on is a very important one. How does he help his readers understand the scale of this problem?
2. What does he identify as the major causes of the problem?
3. How effectively does Fitzgerald discuss the problem? What details does he provide that you think are effective?
4. What solution does Fitzgerald offer? How effectively does he support it?
5. What is the thesis of this essay? Where does it appear? How does it compare to that of Barbash's essay? Of Titone's essay?

Andrew Overton, a first-year writing student at New Mexico State University (NMSU), wrote the following problem/solution essay, which shows that not all problems addressed in an essay need to be as serious as athletic scandals, the extinction of a species, or the intimidation of witnesses through violence.

ANDREW OVERTON

CHANGE

1   Pepsi. Not Coke, but Pepsi. No other selection of soda will do for Jay Burmac. Everyone at the factory in which he works knows his preference; his wife knows what brand to buy on shopping day, and most importantly all the vendors in Baltimore's metro area know what kind to stock in their machines. Every Friday at 2:00 in the afternoon, the Pepsi guy can be seen pulling his truck in and unloading fresh cases of Pepsis to stock in the vending machine. And every Friday at 2:05, Jay can be seen leaving his office for his Pepsi break.

2   This Friday has been especially hard on Jay, and nothing would ease his tension like a cold Pepsi. Silently walking up to the machine, not to disturb the sanctity of his shrine, Jay checks his front pockets of his Dockers khakis for change. Finding only thirty-some-odd cents, he checks his wallet. Whew, one last dollar. It's not like him to be without the necessary change at hand. Not the greatest dollar bill, either. It seems to have changed hands a thousand, no, a million times, and each time someone hastily crammed it in a billfold, he folded and creased the corners, or he worked off some nervous tension by tearing it a couple of times. Making it as flat as he can, Jay attempts to slide it into the vending machine's bill acceptor. Nope, rejected. "I knew that was going to happen," Jay mutters as he begins rubbing it on the corner of the machine to make the bill smooth and even. He feeds the bill in again. It slides right back out. Much like feeding an infant applesauce, time and time again Jay slides in the bill only to have it spat back at him, his anger increasing with each rejection. Realizing it won't work, his frustration gives him only one option, to go man-to-man or, in this case, man-to-machine. Pounding his adversary with his fists, he demands his Pepsi. "Give it up, give it up!" he yells. "Please just give me my Pepsi!" Two of his coworkers hastily drag Jay off the machine, consoling him all the way, "You'll get him next time, Jay, wait till next time."

3   An epidemic of inconvenience grips our nation. Its signs can be found everywhere, in wallets and purses, in the clenched fists of little children. The dollar bill, the most inconvenient convenience around. Many do not see the problem the dollar bill poses, because the problem is not what it is or what its value is, but what it is made of. Using paper for a one-dollar amount is no longer necessary or prudent. Too many problems arise from the fact that it is made of paper, problems that will be solved, for "on December 1, 1997 President Clinton signed legislation calling for a new $1 coin, which will be placed into circulation during the year 2000" (Coin Coalition, 1998, par. 1).

4   Who has not come across the problem of putting a dollar bill into a vending machine? It is an inconvenience to not receive the candy bar from the machine despite having the cash. All of these crumpled problems could be solved if the dollar were in the form of a coin instead of paper. It would be as easy as inserting a quarter into the coin slot, something most machines will gracefully take. Imagine reaching into your pocket and pulling out a single coin that more than covers the cost of your snack of choice. No more fumbling in your pockets to find one more nickel, no more hassle with a paper dol-

lar the machine will not take. Your favorite snack would only be a drop and not a shove, grumble, and pound away.

5   Not only would the dollar coin save vending machine customers a lot of grief, but it would also save vending machine companies a lot of money. Vending machines are equipped with dollar changers that can cost $300 dollars each. Additional costs include service calls and repairing machines with jammed bill changers. According to a 1991 University of Chicago study, the vending industry would save an estimated $142 million dollars a year (Kapner, 1995). Saving this much money a year could then be translated into greater savings for the consumer, possibly curbing rising vending costs.

6   Vending machine companies are not the only ones who would save money using the dollar coin. Other businesses, which don't necessarily make as many transactions involving the dollar bill, would save money if the dollar coin were implemented. Using a coin instead of a cumbersome bill would speed up transactions and would reduce the number of bills employees would have to count at the end of the work shifts. According to a study performed by the Walgreen's Drug Store chain, changing from the bill to the coin would save the company $500,000 a year (Kapner, 1995).

7   Switching from the dollar bill to the dollar coin would not only improve profit margins of businesses, but it would save the government money, too. Dollar bills last on average only 17 months; coins, on the other hand, can remain in circulation for 30 years. Although cheaper to produce (four cents compared to eight cents), the dollar bill costs more to maintain in circulation because of its short life span. According to estimates made by the Federal Reserve and General Accounting Office, if the dollar coin replaced the dollar bill it would mean a savings to the United States government of $2.28 billion dollars over the first five years (Coin Coalition, 1998, par. 2). Just one more way for the Federal government to curb unnecessary spending of taxpayer dollars.

8   A loud whistle blows. Startled by the sudden noise, Jay looks up from his desk at the old circular clock hanging on his wall. Five o'clock. "The best time in the world," Jay points out as he gathers a loose bundle of papers into a somewhat manageable pile to be stuffed into his briefcase. With his mind set on reaching the bus stop on time, Jay doesn't hesitate as he exits the large red brick building. He has little time between five o'clock closing and the bus that delivers him home. Shuffling quickly, he entertains the same thoughts he has a thousand times before while making the walk—never understanding why his wife must be so Earth conscious, disallowing an automobile. Arriving at the stop he looks at his watch, noticing he has made better time than usual. Pulling a one out of his wallet, he slides it into a vending machine, hesitating slightly at the remembrance of the earlier events of the day. Right as the bus pulls up to the stop, the machine finally accepts his cash and gives him a Susan B. Anthony dollar coin to be used as the token allowing him to ride.

9   Today's destination isn't like others, because instead of riding straight home Jay is on a mission, charged by his wife to buy a new shirt she saw in a shop downtown for their infant. Stepping onto the bus, handing over the coin he just received, Jay finds just the right seat. The bus goes from stop to stop, leaving people behind at each one, until it reaches Jay's stop. He steps onto the curb and heads straight into the Baby Gap. Browsing for just the right shirt (anything different and he would catch hell at home), Jay notices the sickly condition of the sales clerk. He picks up the little shirt his wife had in mind and lines up at the cash register. As he stands in line, he notices the woman in front of him is carrying a white cane. "That will be 75 cents, Ma'am," the cashier announces to the lady in between several sneezes. She fumbles in her purse, and Jay sees that she has handed the clerk a ten dollar bill. The cashier deposits it in the cash tray and returns only a quarter in change. Assuming nothing is wrong, the lady replaces the

quarter into her purse, takes the baby shoe laces she bought, and makes her way tapping side to side out the door of the store.

10   Jay steps forward, ready to come to the woman's aid. He clears his throat. "You want something, Jack?" the clerk asks. "You got a problem or something?" Jay hears menace in the voice and steps back. "Uh, no. No, I don't at all. Nope, not me." Bad neighborhood, bad neighborhood, he thinks, best to not get involved.

11   The clerk sneezes, then asks for $17.93. Jay hands him a twenty. The clerk stifles another sneeze with his hand and reaches into the cash register, pulling out $2.07 in change. Stuffing the moist bills into his wallet, Jay grabs his bag and briefcase and leaves the store, mumbling under his breath the whole way, "Filthy, filthy town."

12   Every day in several large cities around the country, mass transit systems use the Susan B. Anthony dollar coin as their tokens. Dollar bills are expensive to process and count for the large mass transit systems that must carry thousands of people a day. Since the dollar coin is already used by several systems, it would be much easier to just use a new dollar coin. Rather than having to exchange a dollar bill for a dollar coin and to put up with all the hassle of making that exchange, people would already have dollar coins. Having coins instead of bills would also save money; making the switch would save an estimated $124 million dollars annually for nationwide mass transit systems (Feulner, 1995, par. 8). How? Processing dollar bills is expensive. Edwin Feulner, President of the Heritage Foundation, gives Chicago as an example of how money could be saved: "The Chicago Transit Authority (CTA) handles about 410,000 dollar bills a day. The cost of sorting these bills is about $22 per thousand. But coins can be counted for just $2. Switching to a dollar coin could save the CTA $2.4 million per year in bill-processing costs" (par. 10).

13   Coins are also healthier than currency. How many times have those old dollar bills been handled by a guy with a bad cold, who probably has blown his nose several times? How disease ridden are those dollar bills? A paper dollar bill is very susceptible to collecting dirt, filth, or anything else that touches it, compared to its coin counterparts. In a recent examination of two twenty dollar bills, a one dollar bill, and one quarter performed by *Discover* magazine, the dollar bill was found to be the most bacteria ridden of the bunch. The one with least bacteria was the quarter ("On the money," 1998, p. 78).

14   By now you may be thinking that the legislation President Clinton signed into law will fail. After all, the government tried to replace paper dollars with the Susan B. Anthony dollar coin in the 1970s. They failed to catch on with the public then; why should they gain approval now? Opponents of the legislation flatly state that "coins are cumbersome, inconvenient, and . . . tend to get lost" (Poulson, par. 3). Rep. Thomas Davis of Virginia said, "About the only people who benefit are the tailors as we wear out our pockets with more coins" (Geier, 1995, p. 14). Not gaining popularity would lead a new dollar coin towards the same outcome as the Anthonys—sitting in vaults at the U.S. mint.

15   One of the biggest reasons for the failure of the 1979 Susan B. Anthony dollar coin was its close resemblance to the quarter. Not only in its silver color, but its ridged edge was very similar, too. Having similar characteristics can make it confusing for the blind which coin to choose when attempting to make a transaction. Despite this earlier botched attempt, switching to a coin from a bill can make it easier on the blind. Bills can be indistinguishable from each other. This shouldn't matter because if a blind person hands a higher denomination bill to someone, the correct change should be returned, but because dishonest people exist the system is very unfair for them. Switching to a different colored, smooth edged dollar coin would make it easy on all. People with sight could quickly distinguish the coin from others in their pocket, and those without wouldn't be taken advantage of in smaller exchanges.

16   Ultimately, the problem to be solved is how to gain public acceptance of the new coin. One way to do this is by publicizing Canada's success with its own coin. In 1987 despite initial public resistance, Canada introduced a dollar coin that has become so popular there are now calls for a two-dollar coin (Geier, 1995). A second step is just to stop making paper bills, so that eventually the dollar bill would become an increasingly rare collector's item, too valuable to spend on candy or gum. Finally, the government will have to mount an advertising campaign to help the public get used to the idea. Infomercials are everywhere on late night TV, and Americans are used to having as much as one-third of their favorite sitcom taken up by commercials. Some smart ad agency is bound to be able to sell the public on the convenience of the new coin.

17   And that's what switching from a bill to a coin is about—convenience. Convenience for the vendor when accepting money for their goods. Convenience for the businesses that must employ people to deal with counting. Convenience for the blind who decide which is the right amount to give. Convenience for every individual involved in making one dollar transactions. Switching to a dollar coin would make life much more convenient and easier for everyone; it just makes sense.

REFERENCES

Coin Coalition. (1998). Why a $1 coin? Retrieved November 16, 1998 from the World Wide Web: http://www.coincoalition.org/why/htm

Feulner, E. (1995, November 30). Time to say goodbye to dollar bill. *Heritage Foundation Commentary.* Retrieved November 19, 1998 from the World Wide Web: http://www.townhall.com/heritage/commentary/op-ef8.html

Geier, T. (1995, May 1). The buck's farewell? *U.S. News & World Report,* 14.

Kapner, S. (1995, May 1). To coin or not to coin: Chains, vendors debate dollar's fate. *Nation's Restaurant News,* 4.

On the money. (1998, October). *Discover,* 78–80.

Poulson, B. (1997, June 18). The one dollar coin act. *Independence Institute Opinion-Editorial.* Retrieved November 19, 1998 from the World Wide Web: http://i2i.org/SuptDocs/OpEdArcv/op970618.htm

Questions for Review

1. Andrew begins his essay with a narrative and then returns to it about halfway through the paper. What do you think is the purpose of this narrative? How effective is it?

2. What is Andrew's problem statement? His thesis? Where does each come in the essay? How effectively is each worded?

3. What solution does Andrew offer? How effectively does he support it?

4. What opposition is there likely to be to Andrew's solution? How effectively has he considered such opposition?

5. How effective is the title of this essay? In how many contexts does this one-word title work?

THE RHETORICAL TRIANGLE
READER

The primary audience for a problem/solution essay is someone who can solve the problem, and your task is to encourage that person to take the action you think will solve the problem. In order to ascertain just who this reader is and what you need to do to convince him to accept your position, answer such questions as these:

1. Who can solve the problem? Who has the power or authority to change things?
2. What is this person's role in the problem? Did he create the problem? Is his role one of oversight—of being responsible for, say, enforcing a policy that you may argue against? Or is he a concerned individual who has no particular official involvement with the problem, but who might be able to influence the eventual outcome—for example, a taxpayer and voter who is living in a city that is in the process of deciding how to solve the problem of traffic congestion?
3. What does he already know about the problem? Is he likely to see it as a problem?
4. What does he need to know to take the action you think he should?
5. How opposed is he likely to be to your solution? Why?

Determining a specific audience for your paper can help you sharpen its focus from the outset, and you may use your responses to such questions as those above to guide you in exploring the problem and then in writing a discovery draft and subsequent drafts of your essay.

Exercise 11.1

Speculate about the intended readers of Barbash's "Clean Up or Pay Up," Titone's "Balance of Power," Fitzgerald's "The War against Witnesses," and Andrew's "Change." How effectively did these writers seem to have considered their respective audiences? Identify any details that you think are particularly effective for their readers. Why do think they are effective?

SUBJECT

What topics are appropriate for an essay that explores a problem and then poses a solution to it? Problems range widely, from the very personal to the global, and some are not solvable in the kind of argumentative essay this chapter presents. In the list of problems that follows, identify those for which you think you could offer a workable or feasible solution.

world hunger
financial aid snafus on your campus
the U.S. budget deficit
mudslinging political campaigns
a dangerous intersection near your home

lighting on your campus
gangs
racism
sexism
your study habits
your less-than-ideal grades
favorable or unfavorable treatment of one of the following groups on your
     campus: women, minorities, students with disabilities, athletes
inner-city unemployment rates
clear-cutting in national forests
environmentalists' interference with legal logging operations in national
     forests

Although each of these problems could be solved, at least theoretically, the problems that are closer to your immediate world are often easier for you to think about solving in tangible ways. As you seek a topic for this paper, consider those that are closer to you and your interests and that lend themselves to argument. For example, a topic such as sexism would be too broad for the scope of this essay. But you could narrow that topic to sexism on your campus so that you deal with specific instances of sexist behavior, with your essay offering specific solutions for the situation at your school.

WRITER

Your voice as a writer should be strong in this essay, so take care that you represent yourself well. You'll need to be engaged, informed, and fair.

A writer's passion often shows her depth of engagement with a topic. Writing passionately—with emotion—can be very persuasive, but you have to be careful not to let your emotions lead you into shrillness. This aspect of writing—passion for a topic, being intense without being shrill—shows your engagement with your topic, one of the elements of a writer's ethos we talked about in Chapter 9.

Your ethos is also marked by the knowledge and fairness you show on the page. To convince your reader to accept your solution to a problem he may actually have caused or be responsible for, you'll need to demonstrate that you have in-depth knowledge of your topic, that you have explored the topic thoroughly and considered both the problem and your proposed solution carefully. Fairness is also tied to thoroughness of treatment. If you seem to understand the complexity of a situation, you are much more likely to be perceived as fair. Thus, it is important that you show that you have explored the topic thoroughly, examining such aspects as why the problem truly is a problem, how it came to be a problem, what it causes or creates, and whether major causes of the problem may actually provide benefits for certain people. For example, were you to write about the pollution caused by a particular industry, you would consider such questions as these: What is beneficial about this industry? What product does it produce? How many people does it employ? If your solution would negate these benefits, what could you offer as an alternative, so that, for example, workers would not lose jobs?

What is your ethos as the writer of this essay? Who are you as the writer of this piece? What is your involvement with the topic? What do you know about the topic? How do you feel about it? Answering such questions can help you develop a strong argument for your solution to the problem.

Exercise 11.2

Look again at the essays presented at the beginning of this chapter. How engaged, knowledgeable, and fair does the writer of each seem to be? Point to specific places in each essay that demonstrate these three elements of the writer's ethos. What do those examples show you about the writer?

DISTINGUISHING FEATURES OF PROBLEM/SOLUTION ESSAYS
WELL-DEFINED PROBLEM

Problems may be defined in any number of ways; how we define a problem helps shape the solution. Here's an example that illustrates this point:

> Oftentimes, patients in hospitals or nursing homes are physically restrained as a means of protecting workers and the patients themselves. These restraints most often take the form of tie-downs, with a patient strapped into a bed by ties around his wrists and ankles, and occasionally around his chest. But many times, patients do not need such restraints to be applied.

Below are four possible problem statements dealing with this issue. Which seems most accurate, most clearly defined?

1. Restraints are unnecessary for many patients; thus, their use should be banned.
2. The problem is restraints.
3. Indiscriminate use of physical restraints is unnecessary and oftentimes detrimental to a patient's well-being.
4. The use of restraints is unnecessary and harmful.

Of these, the third forms the best problem statement. It details the writer's value judgment about the use of restraints and points to indiscriminate use as the primary problem. The problem is not with the restraints themselves, but with how they're used.

The first statement offers a blanket indictment of restraints, saying that all use of restraints should be banned no matter the circumstances. But at times, restraints are called for. An emergency-room patient who is violent because of drug-induced hallucinations, for example, may need to be physically restrained. The second statement is too broad to be of much help. Does the problem with restraints lie in their design and construction, allowing patients to slip out of them easily? Or are they too constrictive, again a design and construction problem? The fourth statement, like the first, offers a judgment about using restraints but, like the second, is too broad to be of much help.

Developing a detailed problem statement is important, because in defining the problem specifically, you may point toward a solution and, subsequently, to the development of the paper as a whole. Were you to select the third statement to use in a paper, you would give examples of instances when physical restraints should be used and when they were used but weren't necessary. Such development is at least implied by the problem statement.

We must point out that, however important the problem statement will be in guiding your investigation of the problem and potential solutions, it will not stand as your essay's thesis. Instead, your thesis will carry a call to action on the part of your reader, or it will present your stance on the topic. (We'll have more to say on this matter in the section on structuring your essay.)

Exercise 11.3

For each of the essays presented at the beginning of this chapter, identify the problem statement. How effectively does the problem statement for a particular essay help shape that essay's structure? If you don't find a specific problem statement, write one. How might such a statement as the one you wrote have helped the writer during prewriting and drafting?

THOROUGH EXPLORATION OF THE PROBLEM

To explore the problem, consider each aspect of it, answering such questions as these:

1. What is your definition of the problem? How specifically have you defined it? Is this definition the most accurate? How would changing the definition refocus the problem statement?
2. What caused or causes the problem? What are its effects? For example, what does it cost? How damaging is it?
3. Who is affected by the problem? Why is it a problem for them? To what extent are they affected?
4. Who or what is responsible for the problem?
5. What changes need to be made? Why?

Exercise 11.4

In "Balance of Power," Julie Titone discusses the potential economic impact of saving the salmon, contrasting that with the feared negative impact on local and regional economies. Why did she spend several paragraphs talking about economic matters? How effectively does her speculation about economic benefits counter the fears that an economic downturn would result if her plan were adopted?

BEST SOLUTION

As the example of the space pen at the beginning of this chapter illustrates, a problem may well have more than one solution. Part of your work with this essay will involve your considering as many solutions as seem feasible. You may consider three or even four possible solutions, each of which may solve the problem. If such is the case, then you'll need to pick the best solution, the one that seems most effective or fair or cost-efficient. Making this selection will require you to evaluate the various solutions you've developed, so you need to establish criteria for evaluating them. Whatever your criteria, the solution you pick will fit those criteria best. (For a discussion of using criteria to evaluate a topic, see Chapter 7.)

In "Clean Up or Pay Up," Louis Barbash offers two solutions to the problem of student athletes, academics, and money, knowing which of these solutions is the more likely to gain acceptance. Barbash knows full well that college athletics is big business, with schools raking in millions of dollars from appearances in the year-end bowls (e.g., the Rose Bowl, Orange Bowl, and Sugar Bowl) or in March Madness, the NCAA's annual basketball championship play-offs. Although he presents his "pure alternative" as a potential solution, he gives much greater attention to the nonstudent professional athlete solution, which suggests that he feels this is the more feasible solution of the two.

SOLUTION THAT ADDRESSES THE AUDIENCE

As the discussion about the audience for problem/solution essays suggests, you must select the most appropriate reader to consider your solution, and you must make sure that your solution effectively addresses that reader. What objections or concerns is your reader likely to have? How may you counter them? What examples or details or statistics are most likely to convince your reader to accept your view that the problem is a problem and then to accept your solution as the best course of action to take?

ASSIGNMENT AND GUIDELINES FOR WRITING

ASSIGNMENT

Identify a problem, something that bothers you. Explore it, and pose a solution you think is workable or feasible. The first part of your job is to identify a specific problem, define it clearly, and explore its implications. The second part is to consider potential solutions, evaluate those solutions, and then make an argument for what you think is the best, most workable, or most feasible solution. The third part is to ensure that your essay addresses your intended reader as effectively as possible.

CHOOSING A TOPIC

What bothers you? What problems can you identify that irritate you or that make you shake your head in dismay or that give you cause for real concern? To select a topic, try writing a "Bug List" (as described in James L. Adams's, *Conceptual Blockbusting*). This list is just what its name implies—a list of things that disturb, anger, irritate, vex, or rankle you, no matter how big or small. As an example, here are the first several entries of a list that Bill wrote:

> soccer refs who don't
> attitude
> "Little League" parents (whatever the level)
> no stoplights where Stern Drive and Sam Steel Way intersect Union Ave.
> students who don't study
> wooden-headed administrators
> irresponsible parents
> child and spouse abuse
> treatment of divorced women in our legal system
> weeds forever in my lawn
> my golf swing
> the apparent idiocy of too many elected officials

As these entries indicate, a Bug List is a list of whatever bothers you, whatever you think is problematic. Some of the issues Bill listed are personal and fairly solvable. For example, the problem of his golf swing could be solved by a few lessons, so that really wouldn't be a topic with enough depth for this paper. Nor would this problem lend itself to argument. On the other end of the spectrum, can we expect to solve a problem like "attitude"? What is "attitude," and what tangible solutions might we find to solve it? Such a topic is too broad and too vague to be the topic for a problem/solution essay. Another problem that Bill can't solve is that of child and spouse abuse. But this topic could be narrowed to something like this: the inadequacy of efforts in the United States to make deadbeat parents pay child support. This revised topic is more workable because it focuses on a specific problem—what is and is not being done to make deadbeat parents pay up—and could lead to an argument for specific actions to be taken by officials with the power to enforce court-decreed child support.

Exercise 11.5

Respond to at least one of these options:

1. Write a Bug List. Spend at least 15 minutes making a list of anything that irritates you, no matter how big or small or serious or frivolous it may seem. Pick two of your entries and freewrite about each for 10 minutes.
2. What problems do you confront or know about that you'd like to see solved? Spend at least 15 minutes developing a list of all such problems that come to mind. Then pick two of your entries and freewrite about each for 10 minutes.

3. Look at your Interest Inventory for less-than-ideal situations that could be potential topics. Although any section could hold potential topics for this essay, take a close look at the "education," "jobs," and "attitudes and issues" sections. Pick two topics and freewrite about each for 10 minutes.

After you've completed this exercise, look over what you wrote, and identify two or three topics that you think have potential. Continue freewriting about just these topics, focusing on why you think each is a problem and how it might be solved. If one of these problems seems to be one you want to write an essay about, then proceed to the next step (collecting information). If not, keep freewriting about the problems you uncovered in any of the lists you generated.

COLLECTING INFORMATION

As you begin to collect information, look back to the assignment, which lists three parts to your job as a writer. What kinds of questions does each part bring to mind? Consider responding to such questions as the following:

Defining and exploring the problem. What is the problem? Why is it a problem? Just how dire or big is this problem? How did it come to be; what or who caused it? What are its effects, consequences, or ramifications? What will happen if it isn't solved? Whom does it affect, to what extent, how positively or negatively? Why hasn't this problem been solved yet; what obstacles stand in the way?

Finding a solution. What are possible solutions? What aspect(s) of the problem would each potential solution solve? How effectively? What benefits does each solution hold? Which seems the best or most workable or most feasible solution? Why?

Defining an audience. Who can solve the problem; who has the power, authority, or funding necessary to solve it? What opposition is your audience likely to have to your solution? How can you most effectively counter those points of opposition? (Once you've defined your reader, write a dialogue between you and the reader about the problem.)

In addition to considering these questions, look again at the Questions for Analysis (pp. 24–25) and ask those that seem most applicable. Look particularly at questions of sequence and consequence and at those involving both support for and opposition to the problem you're working with.

Gathering information may also involve you in research, interviews, or observation.

RESEARCH If your topic is one that's been in the news, that's been written about in professional or popular journals, or that involves questions of legality, you may need to conduct research in your library or on the Internet. Just remember that you must document any sources you use. (For more discussion of researching and documenting sources, see Chapter 12.)

INTERVIEWS   Are there people you know or can identify who are involved in some way with this problem? Which side of the problem are they on—have they created the problem or are they affected by it? In considering interviews, you'll need to establish a set of questions to ask each person so that you get the information you need. Your job is not to challenge but to gather information. (For more discussion of interviewing, see Chapter 12.)

OBSERVATION   It may be helpful for you to spend time observing some part of the problem. For example, if Bill decided to write about the lack of stoplights at the two intersections he named in his Bug List, he could gather some information by observing traffic patterns during peak-use hours, counting cars, accidents, near accidents, and so on. What aspects of your problem are observable? What might you gain by spending some time on-site, seeing what goes on as part of the problem? (For more discussion of observing to gather information, see Chapter 12.)

FOCUS STATEMENT

Your focus statement for this essay should consist of two parts: (1) a statement of the problem and (2) a statement of the solution you think best or most effective. Then, for each of these statements, you should list the kinds of supporting information you can or will need to offer to convince your reader that the problem truly is a problem and that your proposed solution is the best. Here's a template you could use for your focus statement:

> *Problem*. Support: statistics? examples? impact on people, environment, animals?
> *Solution*. Alternative solutions: why not the best? Support: statistics? examples? effectiveness?
> *Audience*. Write at least an initial definition of your intended audience. How will you convince its members that your assessments of the problem and the proposed solution are accurate?

Use these categories as headings and then list support under each category. If you find that you don't have any support listed in a particular category, that may point you toward the necessity of conducting some research into the topic.

PLANNING YOUR ESSAY'S STRUCTURE

This particular essay readily lends itself to blocking (see p. 42); that is, the essay form can divide fairly neatly into a problem block and a solution block. Think of these blocks as bins into which you can put the information you generated while exploring the problem and possible solutions. Or look back over that information, and mark various entries with a "P" for "problem" and an "S" for "solution." These bins or blocks can form the two major sections of your paper.

> *Problem block—defining the problem.* In presenting the problem section, you'll need to define the problem clearly and explore it in depth so that you convince your reader that it really is a problem. This section of the essay will contain the problem statement (the definition of the problem), followed by discussion of the problem's importance, significance, costs, harm, and so on.
>
> *Solution block—finding a solution.* In presenting the solution section, you have a number of options. If your solution is detailed, you should make it the focal point of the entire section, discussing thoroughly the implications of the solution and why it's workable or feasible. If several solutions occur to you or seem workable, you may want to treat each solution in turn, considering its strengths and weaknesses, and then settle on the one you think best. From there, your job is to argue the merits of this best solution so that you convince your reader of its worth.

Julie Titone's "Balance of Power" offers a good look at both problem and solution blocks. We can divide this essay into the following sections:

I. Beginning—¶s 1–3
Here, Titone uses some startling statistics to alert the reader to the problem of salmon population decline, and she focuses on the impact of this decline, labeling it a "misery."

II. Problem block—¶s 4–13
In this section, Titone explores the impact of dams as the primary reason for the decline. Specifically, these paragraphs do the following:
¶4—acknowledges various causes for decline, naming dams as biggest problem
¶s 5–7—show how dams impede the migration of salmon
¶8—shows legal aspects of the power struggle
¶9—offers spotted owl comparison
¶10—shows impact of salmon protection on reservoirs
¶11—shows impact of salmon protection on economy
¶s 12–13—debunk spotted owl comparison

III. Solution block—¶s 14–19
In this section, Titone discusses the potential benefits of restructuring dams and salmon runs:
¶14—potential positive economic impact
¶15—plan for study to be conducted
¶16—revised estimates of costliness to power companies and their customers
¶s 17–19—Corps of Engineers experiment, potential positive results

IV. Ending—¶20
This paragraph forms an effective conclusion for Titone's essay, focusing on potential benefits and the need to protect the salmon.

THESIS STATEMENT

Earlier we said that the problem statement would not stand as the thesis for this essay. Essentially, you're writing an argument, and your thesis should therefore be one that urges your reader to take a particular action or takes a particular stance on your topic. Where may a thesis occur in a problem/solution essay? As with other types of essays, it may appear anywhere. Generally, however, a problem/solution thesis appears in one of two places: at the beginning of the solution section, so that the writer outlines the direction the rest of the essay will take, or at the end of the essay, so that the thesis functions to drive the writer's point home. The essays by Louis Barbash and Julie Titone illustrate well how a writer may structure and then place an essay's thesis sentence.

In "Clean Up or Pay Up," Barbash provides this thesis in paragraph 9, where he moves from his definition of the problem to discussion of his proposed solution:

> [. . .] Because the NCAA has so utterly failed, because in the present system the big-money pressures to cheat are so enormous, and because, like it or not, sports have such a widespread impact on the country's moral climate, there should be a federal law that requires schools *either* to return to the Ivy League ideal in which players are legitimate members of the student body, judged by the same standards as everybody else, *or* to let players on their teams be non-student professionals. [. . .]

The stance Barbash takes here is clear—college athletics are in sore need of reform, and there are, in his opinion, two routes to that reform, only one of which can be selected. As to an action, he says that a "federal law" should be enacted to require such reform. Barbash returns to this either/or idea in the concluding paragraph of his essay, so he uses this idea presented first in his thesis as a unifying device for the entire essay.

Titone takes a different tack, presenting her thesis in the final paragraph of her essay. That thesis—"Although there is no guarantee that drawdowns will save any of the Columbia Basin's wild salmon, they remain an expensive gamble worth taking"—presents Titone's stance on the topic. She spends the first nineteen paragraphs of her essay discussing the problem thoroughly and then speculating about the potential benefits of her proposed solution. But it isn't until the final paragraph that we see her definitive stance on the issue.

REFINING YOUR WRITING

As you begin revising your essay, consider once again the distinguishing features of problem/solution essays.

> *Well-defined problem.* Define the problem as clearly and specifically as you can. Keep in mind that your definition of the problem may well point toward a solution—inherent in the problem is the solution.
> *Thorough exploration of the problem.* What is the problem? Why is it a problem? Whom does it affect? What are its costs? Who caused it?

Remember that part of your job is to convince your reader that the problem truly is a problem.

Best solution. Not all solutions are created equal. In exploring and selecting the best solution, you should consider alternative solutions; generally, a problem will have more than one possible solution. As you reconsider how effectively you've presented your solution, use such questions as these to sharpen your response to the problem: What is your solution? What are its elements? Which aspects of the problem will it solve? What alternative solutions exist? Why are these not as good as the one you've selected as best?

Solution that addresses the audience. In your prewriting, you should have written at least an initial audience analysis, and you may well have written a second, more detailed analysis of your intended reader. Who is your reader? Why did you select this reader; that is, what is the reader's relation to or involvement with the problem? How effectively have you considered your reader's possible objections to or doubts about your solution?

SAMPLE STUDENT PROCESS

The sample student essay is by Kristina Geray, a first-year writing student at NMSU, who decided to write about a problem with some immediacy for her—unwanted stray pets. Kristina's interest in the topic derives from her personal experience. As she notes in the essay's introduction, a lot of stray dogs wander by her home, but she can't take every one in.

PREWRITING

I'm so tired of this—another dog dropped off, pretty reddish color. She'll probably grow up to be a big dog, if she lives. That's—how many? At least 4 or 5 since December. Can we keep her? I doubt it. We have too many now as it is. Can't afford another one. It's hard. If she leaves, she'll just get run over if she gets on the highway. Or maybe coyotes will get her if she tries to run in the desert. Or she'll get picked up. Maybe she'll get to Arthur's house—he takes in every stray that comes along. I wonder what his feed bills are. I really admire him for trying to save every animal that comes his way.

FOCUS STATEMENT

I want to write about the problem of stray pets (mostly dogs and cats).

Problem. We have an overpopulation of pets. There are too many strays that nobody wants, so they end up living a short, lousy life. Strays get euthanized by county agents or humane society—how many? What's the cost?

Solution. What solutions will work? Euthanization is not humane, and it does not work anyway, not if the number of strays at my house means anything. Sterilization makes more sense, but that would be like legislating morality—how do you get pet owners to neuter their pets?

Audience. My audience would be those people affected most by the problem of pet overpopulation. The people most affected would be pet owners since they are most directly impacted by anything involving their pets. Any solution to this problem would involve pet owners since it would be up to them to actually start using the solution.

RESEARCH STRATEGIES

Kristina knew that she would need statistics to illustrate the magnitude of the problem with strays, so she searched the Internet, using such key terms as "American Society for the Prevention of Cruelty to Animals (ASPCA)," "spaying," and "neutering" as a start. She quickly found three sites that carried information she could use. At <http://www.aspca.org>, she found two documents: "Why Spay or Neuter?" at <http://www.aspca.org/spay.htm> and "New York State Animal Population Control Program" at <http://www.aspca.org/apcp.htm>. At an environmental site—<http://www.geocities.com/CollegePark/6280>—she found a link to a site covering a number of issues, including animal abuse. One article she found there, titled "Have You Ever Tortured an Animal?" included information about strays.

To gather still more information, Kristina interviewed two people directly involved with pet care in Doña Ana County: Pamela Angell, director of the Doña Ana Humane Society Animal Shelter, and Alice Lewis, an employee of a local veterinary clinic. Further, while at the animal shelter Kristina picked up a Humane Society pamphlet, which figured as another source. During her conversations with both Angell and Lewis, Kristina took these few notes that show the severity of the problem of too many strays in the county, focusing on the number of animals and the costs associated with them:

> *Personal communication—Pamela Angell, May 7, 1998*
> numbers are incredible—13K+ dogs & cats in county (13,157)
> 10,208 euthanized—killed
> 1,554 adopted
> 1,359 back to owners
> cost—$321,762 (½ from taxes, rest from adoption charges and donations)
> numbers on the rise—23% increase, last 10 years
> Angell says 1 female dog & girl pups produce min. of 13,120 puppies in
>   6-year span
> spaying best—county humane society sponsors low cost neutering & spaying,
>   available to pet owners with low income

> *Personal communication, Alice Lewis, May 14, 1998*
> male cat $35 under 5
> kidney & blood work is more expensive after 5
> test kidneys liver, red & white blood cells
> male dog 90 lbs. $90
> girl cat $65
> $120 for heavy female, $75 for lighter female
> c-section $350 for *small* dog
> uterus 5–10 times larger—blood supplied is greater
> $200–300 for pyemetra
> male prostate—requires extra blood work, EKG & possibly X-rays

Having taken notes and thought through her topic, Kristina began writing a discovery draft. When you read the final draft, note which information in this initial draft appears in that final draft and which does not.

~~He is the poster~~   ~~He can't save the world but he tries~~.

As I write this I'm contemplating a problem. She's a very pretty, red-haired problem with a muscular body and big, warm, brown eyes. She's also the ~~sixth~~ seventh stray dog to wander by my home in fourteen months. She's the fourth one ~~I've decided~~ my mother and I have decided we can't keep. She'll have to go to the pound. She <u>might</u> be adopted. More likely she'll be euthanized. └ With 5 dogs allready in our care we can't afford to take on another one.

She's an example of a problem faced by every person in this nation at one point or another, the problem of pet overpopulation. It is estimated that seven to thirteen hundred animals are abandoned <u>per county</u> per year in the U.S. In 1997 in Dona Ana county alone over 13000 dogs and cats ~~are abandoned~~ are picked up by or given into the care of the Doña Ana County Humane society.

Some people may argue that it is not their problem ~~if~~ that the number of unwanted pets has reached such high levels. They are sadly mistaken. The pet overpopulation problem affects everyone which makes it everyone's problem. Aside from the obvious annoyances that stray animals cause, such as fighting with wanted animals and knocking over trash containers in pursuit of a meal, they are a health hazard and an economic drain. Stray animals do not recieve shots or any other type of veterinary care. As a result of this stray animals can carry *fleas, ticks,* rabies, parvo, ~~and~~ heartworm ~~Stray cats~~ and distemper. They ~~defecate~~ in public places and on private lawns. ~~They live in~~ and obtaining their meals by rummaging in dumps and trash cans. These ~~del~~ problems *have adverse* affects on both wanted animals and humans ~~as well~~. └ spread these diseases by biting humans & animals, defecating

The economic drain these animals cause is absorbed by individuals as well as by the taxpayers. Some individuals, such as Father Lon Ashley, an Episcopalian preacher *living in Chaparral*, take it upon themselves to care for the numerous strays that ~~find their way to the homes of these caring people every day~~ roam New Mexico streets. At this point in time Father Ashley cares for over 70 dogs and many more cats, goats, and horses. He pays about $? a day to feed all the animals that have been abandoned on his doorstep.

More often than not, however, stray ~~animals~~ and abandoned animals end up in the local Humane Society where the tax payers pick up the tab for their care and eventual euthanization. In 1997, 13157 cats and dogs ~~wound up~~ were left in the care of the Doña Ana County Humane Society. Of these 78%, 10208 animals, were euthanized, 12%, 1554 animals, were adopted, and 10%, 1395 were returned to their owners. The total cost ~~to the taxpayers~~ for care of these animals was $321,762, *about* half of which was payed by the taxpayers. The other half was made up by donations and service charges.

ROUGH DRAFT FOR PEER REVIEW

Kristina stopped writing before completing an initial draft; in fact, she had written only about the problem. But she had started. A day or two later, she returned to her writing and produced this draft. Other than the obvious one of length, what differences do you see between this draft and her discovery draft?

1   As I write this I am contemplating a problem. She's a very pretty, red-haired problem with a muscular body and big, warm, brown eyes. She's also the seventh stray dog to wander by my home in the last fourteen months. She's the fourth dog my mother and I have decided we can't keep. With five dogs already in our care, we cannot afford to take another into our home. She will have to go to the pound. Hopefully, she'll be adopted. More likely, though, she will be euthanized.

2   This pretty, rust-colored pup is an example of a problem faced by every person in this country at one time or another: pet overpopulation. It is estimated that seven to thirteen hundred animals are abandoned per county per year in the United States (Berthiaume et al., 1996). In 1997 in Doña Ana County alone over 13,000 dogs and cats were picked up by or given into the care of the Doña Ana County Humane Society (P. Angell, Animal Shelter Director DACHS, personal communication, May 7, 1998).

3   Some people may argue that it is not their problem that the number of un-wanted pets has reached such disastrously high levels. They are sadly mistaken. The problem of pet overpopulation affects everyone. It is *everyone's* problem.

4   Aside from the obvious annoyances that stray animals cause, fighting with wanted animals, for example, they are a health hazard and an economic drain. Stray animals do not receive shots or any other form of veterinary care. As a result, stray pets may carry fleas, ticks, rabies, parvo, heartworm, and/or distemper. They spread these diseases by biting humans and other animals, by defecating in public places as well as on private lawns, and by rummaging in dumps and trash cans (Be a PAL, 1989). The health of strays has an adverse effect on the health of both humans and wanted animals.

5   The economic drain these animals cause is, more often than not, absorbed by taxpayers. Humane Societies, where most strays and abandoned animals end up, use tax money to defray the expense of caring for and eventually euthanizing these pets. In 1997, 13,157 dogs and cats were left in the care of the Doña Ana County Humane Society. Of these 78 percent, 10,208 animals, were euthanized. Twelve percent, 1,554 animals, were adopted and ten percent, 1,395 animals, were returned to their owners. The total cost for the care of these animals was $321,762, half of which was paid by taxpayers. The other half was made up by donations and service charges.

6   The most popular method of solving the problem of pet overpopulation, the euthanization of strays, has proved inefficient. Over the past ten years there has been a 23 percent increase in the number of animals impounded by the Doña Ana County Humane Society (P. Angell, 1998). It can be assumed that this increase reflects a trend in the overall population of pets in Doña Ana County as well as throughout the nation. Euthanization has only served to slow the rate of growth of the pet population, not to keep it down. Another, more successful method is greatly needed.

7   The best solution to this problem is prevention. It is estimated that in six years one female dog and her female offspring can produce 13,120 puppies. (This is a low estimate). This number is nearly equivalent to the number of animals (cats and dogs) taken care of by the Doña Ana County Humane Society in 1997 (P. Angell, 1998).

8   Others make the claim that 70,000 puppies and kittens are born every day in the United States (Be a PAL, 1989). At this rate an estimated 25.5 million puppies and kittens are born in the United States in a year. Only 7.5 million animals are destroyed, nationwide, by Humane Societies every year (Be a PAL, 1989). Assuming that in one year Humane Societies euthanized only those animals born in that same year, there would still be a *whopping 18 million puppies and kittens* needing loving homes in our nation. Even if half of these animals die from disease or neglect during the first few months of their lives, taxpayers will still be responsible for the care of *nine million animals*. Let's make a few more assumptions here. Let's assume that half (4.5 million) of these animals were kept from breeding and the other half were allowed to breed at the rate mentioned earlier in this paper (13,120 animals produced by one female pet and her female offspring in six years). Only half of the breeding animals would be female so we need only concern ourselves with 2.25 million animals, less than one-tenth of the original 25.5 million dogs and cats born in one year. If this small fraction of all the animals born in a single year and their offspring are allowed to breed unchecked for six years, our nation will be faced with the responsibility of caring for *over 29.5 billion (mostly unwanted) pets!*

9   These numbers show how important it is to find some way of preventing these animals from breeding as soon as *possible!*

10   The most obvious and effective of these methods of accomplishing this goal is the sterilization of pets. Two operations are involved in the sterilization of animals. The first of these is spaying in which the ovaries are removed from a female dog or cat. The second is castration, or neutering, in which a male animal's testes are removed.

11   The chief objection most people have to this form of population control is the expense, which can run from $35 for a small male cat to $120 for a very large female dog. The cost goes even higher if the female animal is in heat at the time of the operation. However, this cost is nothing when compared to the amount the owner may pay if complications arise during a beloved female pet's pregnancy. An emergency cesarean section for a small dog costs about $350. This price increases for larger animals. Treatment for prostate cancer, a condition that may affect unsterilized male dogs or cats, also costs several hundreds of dollars (A. Lewis, Solano Animal Clinic employee, personal communication, May 14, 1998).

12   In addition to these high veterinary costs, numerous incentive programs exist to encourage people to sterilize their pets. Many animal welfare programs offer spay/neuter operations at a reduced price. The Doña Ana County Humane Society has a financial aid program set up to assist low income families who want to have their pets sterilized (P. Angell, 1998). Many states also offer reduced licensing fees to owners of spayed or neutered animals (ASPCA Government Affairs, 1998). For these reasons, cost is not a legitimate excuse for anyone to avoid sterilizing their animals.

13   Another reason people often refuse to have their female pets spayed is the myth that a female dog or cat must have at least one litter in order to lead a healthy life. Nothing could be further from the truth. The earlier a female pet is spayed, the healthier she will be as she ages. A female pet spayed before the age of sexual maturity, at about six to nine months, faces only one-seventh the risk that a full female faces of developing mammary cancer. Spaying a pet also reduces the animals risk of developing other expensive to treat and potentially fatal conditions such as breast cancer and pyometra (a pus-filled uterus) (ASPCA, 1998).

14   Other popular myths that prevent people from sterilizing their pets are that the operation will be dangerous and painful for the pet, that after the surgery the animal will become fat and lazy, and that the operation will cause the animal's personality to change.

15   The first of these should be taken with a grain of salt. There is only a very slight risk to any animal undergoing this common procedure, and it takes only two to three days for a dog or cat to recover if given proper care (ASPCA, 1998).

16   Second, sterilization cannot make an animal fat or lazy. Only lack of exercise and an unhealthy diet can cause that. Responsible owners can prevent a pet from becoming obese by monitoring food intake and exercising the pet regularly (ASPCA, 1998).

17   Finally, any changes that take place in an animal's personality after sterilization will be to the owner's benefit. Spaying or neutering a pet destroys its desire to mate, causing it to wander from home less frequently. The animal will be less territorial, making it less eager to fight or to mark its territory (the owner's home and yard) with urine. Also, a sterilized cat or dog is less likely to attack a person without provocation and is just as loyal as an animal that has not been spayed or neutered (ASPCA, 1998).

18   Despite the euthanization of large numbers of dogs and cats every year by Humane Societies across the nation, the pet population continues to grow at an alarming rate. This increase creates health and economic problems for every person in this country and can best be controlled by one method: the sterilization of pets by responsible owners. Despite the many objections pet owners may find to this operation, there is no reason not to spay or neuter a pet. The benefits of sterilization, for dogs and cats as well as for owners, far outweigh any risk or inconvenience the pet or owner may experience.

References

ASPCA. (1998). Why spay or neuter?: This low cost surgery offers you and your pet many, many advantages. Retrieved May 8, 1998 from the World Wide Web: http://www.aspca.org/spay.htm

ASPCA Government Affairs. (1998). New York State Animal Population Control Program. Retrieved May 8, 1998 from the World Wide Web: http://www.aspca.org/apcp.htm

Berthiaume, B., Cornielle, C., Forrest, K., Funai, D., Nachmann, M., Shrugrue, T., & Tisdale, C. (1996). Have you ever tortured an animal?: Are you sure? There are many ways in which we indirectly abuse animals. Retrieved May 8, 1998 from the World Wide Web: http://www.geocities.com/College Park/6280

Humane Society of the United States. (1989). *Be a PAL: Pet Overpopulation Fact Sheet.* [Brochure]. Washington, DC: Author.

REVIEWS

Kristina's essay was reviewed by a classmate in a one-on-one reading session. The reviewer thought that the essay worked, in the main. Among her comments to Kristina about the draft were these:

1. The problem is very clearly stated and gives very good reasons for why animal overpopulation is such a big problem.
2. By talking about how spaying/neutering animals will help decrease the problems people face as well as the benefits to the animals' well-being, the writer's solution is convincing.
3. The use of statistics throughout is very good. The writer did the math, and the number of animals and the cost to us all really worked.
4. The thesis is stated at the end of the essay and is effective in relating the problem and solution clearly.
5. By addressing concerns as taxpayers (which we all are), the writer relates to her readers that the problem does indeed involve everyone.

The reviewer also offered some suggestions for revision:

1. I like the introduction, but it could hit harder. At the end of ¶1, the writer says the dog "will be euthanized." Why not just say "killed"? "Euthanized" doesn't carry as much impact as "killed."
2. Can you incorporate some sources more smoothly? On p. 1, that long reference to "P. Angell" gets in the way. What does the "P" stand for? Same with "A. Lewis."

3. At the end of ¶6 I was a little confused by the idea that euthanization has slowed the rate of growth. Most of what the writer said
about euthanization so far is that it doesn't work.
4. In the next ¶ (7), I don't think the first sentence fits with the other 2.

Before she began her final draft, Kristina asked Bill, her instructor, to look
over her rough draft. Bill found the reviewer's comments to be on target, but he
did make two suggestions dealing with format:

1. Your reviewer is right about the topic sentence of ¶7. Why not
delete that sentence and write a new one? You could also inset
the statistical information and use either numbers or bullets of
some kind to feature or emphasize the numbers here.
2. Near the end, you talk about myths that some pet owners believe.
That section has a fair number of short, choppy paragraphs. How
might you put them together to smooth things out?

With advice, then, from two readers, Kristina reviewed her essay and produced a final draft. What differences do you see between this draft and the review rough draft? How much of her readers' advice did she take? To what effect?

FINAL DRAFT

THE PET OVERPOPULATION PROBLEM

KRISTINA GERAY

1 As I write this I am contemplating a problem. She's a very pretty, red-haired problem with a muscular body and big, warm, brown eyes. She's also the seventh stray dog
to wander by my home in the last fourteen months. She's the fourth dog my mother
and I have decided we can't keep. With five dogs already in our care, we cannot afford
to take another into our home. She will have to go to the pound. Hopefully, she'll be
adopted. More likely, though, she will be killed. She'll be picked up by a dog catcher,
taken to an animal shelter, and put up for adoption. Odds are she won't be adopted
and, after a short period—only three days—she'll be euthanized. She'll be killed.

2 This pretty, rust-colored pup is an example of a problem faced by every person in
this country at one time or another: pet overpopulation. So many dogs and cats are running loose that they simply cannot be controlled. Many of these strays once were pets
but are abandoned by their owners. And they are abandoned in alarming numbers. It
is estimated that seven to thirteen hundred animals are abandoned per county, per
year in the U.S. (Berthiaume et al., 1996). The problem locally is even worse. According
to Pamela Angell, Animal Shelter Director for the Doña Ana County Humane Society,
over 13,000 dogs and cats were picked up by or given into the care of the Doña Ana
County Humane Society (personal communication, May 7, 1998).

3 Why are so many pets abandoned? For one, people move and either can't take
their pet with them or just don't want the hassle of moving Rover with them. For another, Fluffy, that cuddly little furball somebody's child brought home, became a walking allergen. And then there's always that litter of puppies somebody intends to find
homes for but somehow never does (Berthiaume et al., 1996). In each of these instances, abandonment provides an easy way out.

4   Some people may argue that it is not their problem that the number of unwanted pets has reached such disastrously high levels. They are sadly mistaken. The problem of pet overpopulation affects everyone. It is *everyone's* problem.

5   Aside from the obvious annoyances that stray animals cause, fighting with wanted animals, for example, they are a health hazard and an economic drain. Stray animals do not receive shots or any other form of veterinary care. As a result, strays may carry fleas, ticks, rabies, parvo, heartworm, and/or distemper. They spread these diseases by biting humans and other animals, by defecating in public places as well as on private lawns, and by rummaging in dumps and trash cans (Humane Society of the United States, 1989). The health of strays has an adverse effect on the health of both humans and wanted animals.

6   The economic drain these animals cause is, more often than not, absorbed by taxpayers. Humane Societies, where most strays and abandoned animals end up, use tax money to defray the expense of caring for and eventually euthanizing these pets. In 1997, 13,157 dogs and cats were left in the care of the Doña Ana County Humane Society. Of these, 78 percent, 10,208 animals, were euthanized. Twelve percent, 1,554 animals, were adopted, and ten percent, 1,395 animals, were returned to their owners. The total cost for the care of these animals was $321,762, half of which was paid by taxpayers. The other half was made up by donations and service charges. Over the past ten years, there has been a 23 percent increase in the number of animals impounded by the Doña Ana County Humane Society (P. Angell, personal communication, May 7, 1998). It can be assumed that this increase reflects a trend in the overall population of pets in Doña Ana County as well as throughout the nation. Despite the number of animals euthanized, the number of strays just keeps growing.

7   Nationwide, the numbers are staggering:

- In six years, one female dog and her female offspring can produce 13,120 puppies, and this is a conservative estimate (P. Angell, personal communication, May 7, 1998).
- Some 70,000 puppies and kittens are born every day in the United States. At this rate an estimated 25.5 million puppies and kittens are born in the United States in a year (Humane Society of the United States, 1989).
- Only 7.5 million animals are destroyed, nationwide, by Humane Societies every year (Humane Society of the United States, 1989).

8   Assuming that in one year Humane Societies euthanized only those animals born in that same year, there would still be a *whopping 18 million puppies and kittens* needing loving homes in our nation. Even if half of these animals die from disease or neglect during the first few months of their lives, taxpayers will still be responsible for the care of *nine million animals.* Let's make a few more assumptions here. Let's assume that half (4.5 million) of these animals were kept from breeding, leaving the other half to breed at that rate of 13,120 animals every six years. Only half of the breeding animals would be female, so we need only concern ourselves with 2.25 million animals, less than one-tenth of the original 25.5 million dogs and cats born in one year. If this small fraction of all the animals born in a single year and their offspring are allowed to breed unchecked for six years, our nation will be faced with the responsibility of caring for *over 29.5 billion (mostly unwanted) pets!* How much clearer can it be that euthanization can't solve this problem?

9   These numbers show how important it is to find some way of preventing these animals from breeding as soon as *possible!*

10   The most obvious and effective of these methods of accomplishing this goal is the sterilization of pets. Two operations are involved in the sterilization of animals. The first

of these is spaying, in which the ovaries are removed from a female dog or cat. The second is castration, or neutering, in which a male animal's testes are removed.

11   The chief objection most people have to this form of population control is the expense, which can run from $35 for a small male cat to $120 for a very large female dog. The cost goes even higher if the female animal is in heat at the time of the operation. However, this cost is nothing when compared to the amount the owner may pay if complications arise during a beloved female pet's pregnancy. An emergency cesarean section for a small dog costs about $350. This price increases for larger animals. Treatment for prostate cancer, a condition that may affect unsterilized male dogs or cats, also costs several hundreds of dollars (A. Lewis, personal communication, May 14, 1998).

12   In addition to these high veterinary costs, numerous incentive programs exist to encourage people to sterilize their pets. Many animal welfare programs offer spay/neuter operations at a reduced price. The Doña Ana County Humane Society has a financial aid program set up to assist low income families who want to have their pets sterilized (P. Angell, personal communication, May 7, 1998). Further, many states offer reduced spaying and neutering costs to make the procedure more affordable (American Society for the Prevention of Cruelty to Animals [ASPCA], Government Affairs, 1998). For these reasons, cost is not a legitimate excuse for anyone to avoid sterilizing their animals.

13   Another reason people often refuse to have their female pets spayed is the myth that a female dog or cat must have at least one litter in order to lead a healthy life. Nothing could be further from the truth. The earlier a female pet is spayed, the healthier she will be as she ages. According to the American Society for the Prevention of Cruelty to Animals (ASPCA), a female pet spayed before the age of sexual maturity, at about six to nine months, faces only one-seventh the risk that a full female faces of developing mammary cancer. Spaying a pet also reduces the animal's risk of developing other expensive to treat and potentially fatal conditions such as breast cancer and pyometra (a pus-filled uterus) (ASPCA, 1998).

14   Other popular myths that prevent people from sterilizing their pets are that the operation will be dangerous and painful for the pet, that after the surgery the animal will become fat and lazy, and that the operation will cause the animal's personality to change. The first of these should be taken with a grain of salt. There is only a very slight risk to any animal undergoing this common procedure, and it takes only two to three days for a dog or cat to recover if given proper care. Second, sterilization cannot make an animal fat or lazy. Only lack of exercise and an unhealthy diet can cause that. Responsible owners can prevent a pet from becoming obese by monitoring food intake and exercising the pet regularly. Finally, any changes that take place in an animal's personality after sterilization will be to the owner's benefit. Spaying or neutering a pet destroys its desire to mate, causing it to wander from home less frequently. The animal will be less territorial, making it less eager to fight or to mark its territory (the owner's home and yard) with urine. Also, a sterilized cat or dog is less likely to attack a person without provocation and is just as loyal as an animal that has not been spayed or neutered (ASPCA, 1998).

15   Despite the euthanization of large numbers of dogs and cats every year by Humane Societies across the nation, the pet population continues to grow at an alarming rate. This increase creates health and economic problems for every person in this country and can best be controlled by one method: the sterilization of pets by responsible owners. Despite the many objections pet owners may find to this operation, there is no reason not to spay or neuter a pet. The benefits of sterilization, for dogs and cats as well as for owners, far outweigh any risk or inconvenience the pet or owner may experience.

REFERENCES

American Society for the Prevention of Cruelty to Animals. (1998). Why spay or neuter?: This low cost surgery offers you and your pet many, many advantages. Retrieved May 8, 1998 from the World Wide Web: http://www.aspca.org/spay.htm

American Society for the Prevention of Cruelty to Animals, Government Affairs. (1998). New York State Animal Population Control Program. Retrieved May 8, 1998 from the World Wide Web: http://www.aspca.org/apcp.htm

Berthiaume, B., Cornielle, C., Forrest, K., Funai, D., Nachmann, M., Shrugrue, T., & Tisdale, C. (1996). Have you ever tortured an animal?: Are you sure? There are many ways in which we indirectly abuse animals. Retrieved May 8, 1998 from the World Wide Web: http://www.geocities.com/College Park/6280

Humane Society of the United States. (1989). *Be a PAL: Pet Overpopulation Fact Sheet* [Brochure]. Washington, DC: Author.

Checklist: Critiquing a Problem/Solution Essay

1. In a sentence, state the problem the essay addresses. In another, state the solution. How clearly are both the problem and the solution stated?
2. How is the problem developed or explained? What examples or details does the writer give to show that the problem truly is a problem?
3. How has the solution been justified or supported? What alternative solutions are considered and discussed? How has the writer shown that the proposed solution is better than any alternatives discussed?
4. How likely is the introduction to catch the reader's attention?
5. How effectively does the conclusion finish the paper?
6. At what points is the reader likely to disagree with or be resistant to the argument presented? How has the writer addressed these concerns?
7. What ethos has the writer presented in this paper; that is, how does the writer appear to be engaged, knowledgeable, and fair?
8. How effectively is any material quoted from an outside source incorporated into the flow of the paper? Is the documentation (both in-text and bibliography) correct?
9. Does the paper adhere to conventions of usage, mechanics, and format? Correct any errors you find.

P A R T *Three*

Research

I n *Searching Writing,* Ken Macrorie comments on the researcher's natural curiosity in examining a topic:

> Look at a two-year-old grabbing books off a shelf, seeing how they open, ripping pages, finding out how they taste. Not much different from a kitten first time out of his box. Apparently, we're all born curious. Inside or outside school, research should be like that, but usually isn't.

Macrorie touches on several important points concerning research. First, humans really are curious; we're more than willing to look into things and do so frequently, because we want to know more about them. Although it's true that we make snap decisions about some things, more often than not we consider our options; we examine an idea or a topic or a product to make up our minds about it, especially when what we're considering is of major consequence. Futhermore, research permeates our lives. If you're a comparison shopper, you're a researcher. When you are contemplating a major purchase (e.g., a car or a guitar) and read brochures or check on the reliability or reputation of what you want to buy, then you're a researcher. Whatever its purpose, research should be as explorative and even as messy a process as that which Macrorie attributes to his two-year-old "reader."

Admittedly, looking into things and comparison shopping aren't the kinds of activities that drive most academic research. Students usually engage in research projects because they've been assigned. A biology student, for example, may be required to study the behavior of burrowing owls. He may sit under a tree at various times over a period of weeks, watching a burrow and taking notes on such matters as when the owls emerge from it, what they feed on, and how they interact with each other as well as with other animals, including the researcher himself. Those notes then inform the research report, in which the writer interprets the notes and uses them to support any generalizations he may make about the behavior of burrowing owls. A chemical engineering student may be required to conduct a lab experiment to determine the viscosity of various fluids; she conducts the experiment under controlled conditions and then writes a report presenting her findings and her interpretation of them. A student in a literature class may be asked to write an essay about the importance of a particular theme in a given poet's work. He will read several of her poems, but he will also need to read what other critics have said about her and her poetry. The research paper this student writes will include not only his interpretation of the poems but also his consideration of the critics' comments.

Note that interpretation figures prominently in the three examples of research writing just described. Ideally, research writing embodies the writer's interpretation of the topic. It should entail in-depth inquiry into a subject of the writer's choosing. It should be a springboard to discovery as the writer attempts to find new information to help her make up her own mind about a topic or support or modify a tentative position on the topic. The best research writing, then, should begin in curiosity and convey the excitement the writer feels in interpreting and making discoveries about the topic and, perhaps, about herself.

At times, student research papers seem to resemble a collection of facts and quotes, strung together in some semblance of order but not really making any particular point. Such papers have no definite shape; they have no discernible beginning, middle, and end. Because they have been written for no particular purpose or audience, they lack direction. At least part of the the problem students have with research writing stems from misconceptions about what a research paper should be and about what it means to conduct research. Research writing, even when assigned, should begin as a question the writer has about a particular topic. Thus, the writer's initial job is to probe the topic in search of an answer. The paper becomes an account of the writer's exploration of the topic; it presents her understanding of its importance and her stance on it.

Research writing, even when driven by a teacher's assignment, need not be drudgery, need not be boring for either the student writer or the teacher. Our goal in Chapter 12 is to present strategies that will help you engage with and manage a research project, which is one of the most comprehensive yet natural uses of writing that you may make.

What's your view of writing a research paper? Beginning an assigned research project, many students groan as they envision themselves seated in a library until late at night, slaving away at huge piles of books, picking a pithy quotation from one source, taking a telling statistic from another. But research should not entail this kind of drudgery. Although it is true that research requires you to use outside sources, your research should begin in curiosity. You should begin by asking a question about a particular topic, so that your initial job is to probe the topic in search of an answer. Once you have found an answer, or at least a tentative answer, to your question and so have adopted a stance on the topic, you may structure your writing to achieve one of the aims we talked about in Part Two.

Inform. Is there a topic you want to know more about? Use a research assignment to investigate the topic and then to inform others of what you learn.

Evaluate. Do you have to choose the better of two options? How will you make that choice? Use a research assignment to examine both options thoroughly, compare them, and then make an informed choice.

Argue. Do you have a topic you feel strongly about or a position you want to convince others about? Use a research assignment to develop support for your position.

Researching and Writing

CHAPTER *12*

Solve a problem. Do you know of something that needs to be fixed or needs to be changed? Use a research assignment to consider the problem, weigh various potential solutions, and then present what you think is the best solution.

A research paper written to fulfill one of these purposes will not be a mere re-hashing of other writers' ideas. By presenting *your* investigation, *your* serious, comprehensive look into a topic, you'll move away from the research paper as a simple collection of facts and quotations.

At the same time, you'll need to follow certain conventions. Research writing necessarily involves using sources beyond your own imagination. Using someone else's work can be fruitful, as it lets you

expand your own knowledge and so present a more comprehensive essay to a reader,

engage another writer in a "discussion" to develop your own perspective,

marshal support for your perspective, so that your reader may see you as a more informed, more convincing authority than he might otherwise, and

sharpen your research and interpreting skills, which will be required in much of the work you'll be asked to do as a college student.

When you use sources, you must avoid plagiarism. You must also report the results of your inquiry in such a way that other researchers can use your findings if they so desire. As you follow the guidelines in this chapter, you should achieve a necessary balance between content and convention in research writing.

Exercise 12.1

What is the best experience you've had with writing a research paper to date? The worst? Write a paragraph about each of these experiences. Next, develop a list of traits for a good research paper or research process. Then, compare your list with those of your classmates to help you clarify and expand your list. Finally, use the expanded list as a checklist to help guide your research writing.

Writing Strategy

RESEARCH NOTEBOOK

A research project requires that you to keep an accurate record of all you do to complete it, from start to finish. One of the best ways to create and maintain this record is with a research notebook—a notebook that is separate from any learning or reading log your instructor may have you keep. In your research notebook, you may

- make a timeline of important dates, including the project's final due date and your own schedule for major elements, such as the date for completing a first rough draft and the date your review group will meet to discuss one another's drafts,
- keep dialogue notes for everything you read,
- make complete bibliographical entries for all the materials you research,
- keep all of your notes from other activities you undertake, such as conducting interviews, and
- keep all your prewriting and drafts.

A research notebook will help organize your entire project by holding all related materials together in one place. Get a large, three-ring binder, notebook paper, a set of dividers, and several full-page, clear plastic sleeves to hold index cards and scraps of non–standard-size paper on which you may take notes.

TOPIC SELECTION

What makes a research topic workable? For our purposes, we'll assume that the essay you submit will be 1,500 to 2,500 words, about 6–10 double-spaced pages, so you'll have to pick a topic you can develop in those limits. Your topic may be something close to you and thus personal, or it may be as broad as a local or even a national problem. Whether personal or global, your topic needs to be one on which you can find information, whether you find it in a library, through field work, or on the Internet.

Sometimes you will have a free choice of topics for your writing. Then, your task becomes one of finding the right topic, one you want to spend a good bit of time with. But how do you find this topic? Identifying your interests is the most logical starting point. When you begin a research assignment, you may know, or at least have some idea of, a topic. If you're blank, however, look through your Interest Inventory (see p. 9) to see if any topic appeals to you immediately. Your inventory should reveal your expertise on several subjects. It should also tell you that you feel strongly about a number of issues. From such topics as these, ones in which you have expertise and about which you feel strongly, can come strong research papers.

Although you will at times be free to choose any subject you wish, at other times you will not. Either your instructor will ask you to find a subject in a specific context (e.g., the American colonial period) or will limit you to an even narrower subject (e.g., George Washington's battle strategies in several important battles during the American Revolution). In such instances, your job is to make the subject your own, that is, to find a topic of significance in it so that your paper reveals your thinking about the topic.

One of the best ways to begin searching for a topic is to freewrite, so that you uncover what you do and do not know. You may already know a good deal about such subjects as the colonial period or Washington's battle plans if such subjects have been assigned in the context of the course you are taking on early American history. If you are not assigned a subject specifically but may choose your own, then we suspect you will pick one you are familiar with or want to know more about. Whichever the case, begin by freewriting. Ask such questions as "What interests me about this topic?" and "What do I know about this topic?" Then, work toward answering those questions as you freewrite.

Exercise 12.2

1. If you have even a tentative topic for a research project, then use it as you complete this exercise. If you don't have a topic, pick one of the following subjects and freewrite on it for 15 minutes, asking questions you think are appropriate. Then read back over your freewriting and look for a focal point, something that might serve as the basis of a research project. If you find such a point, why do you think it might work for a research paper?

   nuclear energy
   alternatives to nuclear energy
   good (bad) study habits
   history of a favorite sport or hobby
   buying something (e.g., the best camera or microcomputer)
   benefits of some kind of exercise (e.g., running, swimming, biking)
   job opportunities for college students
   a social issue (e.g., drunk driving)
   a national, regional, or local environmental issue
   a campus issue

2. Later in this chapter, you will be assigned to write a research paper. If you are free to choose your own topic, begin thinking now about potential topics, or ask your instructor for suggested or assigned topics. Pick one, and freewrite on it for 15 minutes, asking appropriate questions. Then read back over your freewriting and look for a focal point, something that might serve as the basis of a research project. If you do not find one, freewrite for another 15 minutes; then look again. Continue working with this process until you find at least a tentative topic. Why do you think it might work into a research paper?

SEARCHING A TOPIC

We assume at this point that you have found at least a tentative topic, one you are curious enough about to spend some time exploring. How can you search the topic? How can you find, record, and make sense of information about the topic?

SOURCES OF INFORMATION

Once you've found a tentative topic, your next step is to survey sources to see what information is available. Depending on your topic, you may rely wholly on your library to support your research. Or you may find it necessary or desirable to do some kind of field search. Or you may use the Internet to investigate your topic. Then again, you may use a combination of two or even all three of these. No matter where you find sources of information, your job is not merely to string together facts and quotations; your job is to create some meaning out of the information you survey so that you report what you find of significance about your topic. In this light, you should see sources of information as springboards to discovery.

TAKING NOTES

As you read through your sources, look for ways to respond to them. Your job is not merely to quote from them but to develop your own ideas about them. With what in those sources do you agree or disagree? At what points are the thoughts of others consistent or inconsistent with your experience? What do you find of consequence in the information? Is there some action you think should be taken, or was some action taken that should not have been? Answering such questions as these as you explore sources can help you focus your thinking. What you find in researching a topic you should use first to help you settle your mind about the topic, to find a position on the topic, and then to support your position.

To work with your sources, you'll need to find some way to use the information you gather, some way to organize it so that you can access it easily at any point during the research process. One convenient way to to organize is with the traditional note-card system. When you take notes, use 3-by-5-inch index or note cards, recording one bit of information (e.g., a summary of a certain passage or a direct quotation) per card. Listing one bit per card makes it easy for you later on as you shuffle notes and move various citations around to find the most effective way to use the information. Note-card formats vary, but each card should carry at least this information:

1. The last name of the person you are citing (e.g., author or interviewee) or some other identification of the source (e.g., keyword of the title)
2. The source's call number, if it has one, or the web address or the database in which you located the source if the source comes from the Internet
3. The note itself
4. The page number you took the note from

Figure 12.1 shows a sample note card containing a direct quotation and a brief introduction to it. This note card refers to David Guterson's article, "No Longer a Fringe Movement," which appeared in the October 5, 1998 issue of *Newsweek*. We identified the passage for future reference by citing Guterson as its author. Were we working with an unsigned or anonymous article, we would have identified the passage using a key word from the article's title.

Guterson

In chronicling the rise of home schooling, Guterson cites the problem in public schools as a main reason: "A new wave of parents has chosen home schooling not primarily on its merits but because schools seemed mired in insolvable problems."

Newsweek 10/5/98
p. 71

FIGURE 12.1   Note Card with Direct Quotation and Introduction

If you find organizing note cards burdensome, then keep a notebook dedicated solely to your research project. As you read various sources, use dialogue notes to help you determine a given source's importance to your project. If you're using a laptop computer, you can keep your notes in files organized by author or topic. Whatever method you use—note cards, research notebook, or laptop—be sure to include complete bibliographical information about each piece you read. If you need to return to a particular source, you'll be able to locate it readily; if you decide to use it in your paper, you'll have the basis for the documentation you'll need to provide.

SUMMARIZING AND PARAPHRASING

At times, a source will not contain specific facts, statistics, or language you want to quote directly, or it will be too long for you to quote directly. Still, it may contain ideas you wish to use. If this is the case, you'll need to summarize those ideas, putting in your own words what you interpret as the passage's main point or points. If you incorporate a paraphrase or a summary in your research essay, you must document it, or you'll leave yourself open to a charge of plagiarism. (For a discussion of writing summaries and paraphrases, see Chapter 4.)

PLAGIARISM

Incorporating another person's words or ideas into your writing as your own is plagiarism. Even using short phrases and parts of sentences written by someone else constitutes plagiarism, unless you document those pieces properly. Documentation includes clearly identifying paraphrased and summarized materials in your text, with a reference to the appropriate source. It also includes identifying quoted materials in the text by placing a direct quote in quotation marks and providing a reference to its source. And it includes in-text citations, notes (such as explanatory footnotes, footnotes identifying sources, and endnotes), and a reference list (a bibliography or "Works Cited" list). Further, if someone helps you (perhaps as an editor), you must acknowledge that person's contribution to your writing on an acknowledgments page either immediately following your essay's title page or as the last page of your essay.

Failure to document sources properly is cheating, whether that failure is intentional or inadvertent. Because plagiarism is a matter of academic dishonesty, the penalty for plagiarism can be severe. Ask your instructor to define your university's policy concerning plagiarism.

LIBRARY SEARCH

Obviously, a library—your school's or a nearby public one—is a logical place to start. From past experience, you probably are familiar with some of the services and research opportunities a library offers. The following are typical:

1. *Catalog*—a listing of the library's holdings of books and journals that are bound or on microfilm or microfiche. These entries are usually alphabetized by author's last name, by book title, and by subject matter. Your library may have a card catalog, or it may have a computerized or on-line catalog accessed through a computer terminal.

2. *Periodicals*—current newspapers and popular, scientific, and professional journals to which the library subscribes. Most libraries have a reference section that houses periodicals.

3. *Interlibrary loan*—a system enabling a library to borrow books and periodicals it does not have from other libraries. If you cannot find a source you need, look into the feasibility of using interlibrary loan.

4. *Micromaterials*—collections of various materials (e.g., back issues of the *New York Times*) on microfilm or microfiche. Most libraries have microreaders available for patrons' use.

5. *Government documents*—collections of studies commissioned by agencies of the U.S. government. Certain libraries across the United States are designated document repositories and make these documents available to the public.

6. *Guides to periodicals and reference works*—indexes, bibliographies, or summaries of various reference works. The most widely used of these guides is the *Readers' Guide to Periodical Literature*, which lists articles in magazines and journals arranged alphabetically by subject matter and by author's last name.

7. *On-line catalogs and CD-ROM databases*—by typing in a few keywords, you may locate pertinent articles, books, and other sources in an on-line catalog. CD-ROM databases tend to be more subject-specific than are on-line catalogs; that is, a particular database is typically dedicated to a particular topic.

8. *Recent articles index*—a computerized index to articles published within the last three or four years on a range of topics. You may search such an index by subject area, by author, and by title.

Computer Tip

SAMPLE LISTING OF CD-ROM DATABASES

Although the following list is not exhaustive, it should give you an idea of the range of materials available to you through various electronic media in your library.

ABI/Inform (business)
Agricola (agriculture)
America, History & Life
Compendex (engineering)
Computer Select (computers)
Congressional Masterfile
Criminal Justice Abstracts
Econlit (economics)
ERIC (education)
Ethnic NewsWatch
GPO (U.S. government
 documents)

Medline (medicine)
MLA (literature and languages)
National Trade Bank Data
NTIS (technical reports)
PAIS (public affairs)
PsycLit (psychology)
Science Citation Index
Social Work Abstracts
U.S. Government Periodicals Index
Water Resources Abstracts

Another valuable source of information and assistance is the reference librarian, who can help you find what you're having trouble finding, become an independent user of the library, and learn to use such resources as a CD-ROM database. If you're having a particular problem in using your library, ask the reference librarian for help.

IDENTIFYING POTENTIALLY HELPFUL SOURCES

One of the more difficult tasks students face in conducting research is determining the relevance to their research project of the printed information they find. To discover what you think is important in a printed source, use the following strategies:

1. Preview a book by scanning the title, subtitle, table of contents, foreword, introduction, and conclusion. What was the author's purpose in writing the book? How pertinent is that purpose to your topic? Similarly, preview an essay or news item, scanning the title, introduction, conclusion, headings, and any graphics (tables, charts, or pictures).
2. Use the index of a book to locate particular information about your topic.
3. Use the bibliography of a book or article to locate additional sources relevant to your topic.

RELIABILITY OF PRINTED SOURCES

Not all printed sources of information are equally reliable, and part of your job as a researcher is to determine just how reliable your sources are. But how? Traditionally, the reliability of printed texts has been evaluated based on these five criteria:

Accuracy. What are the text's major premises? How well researched, supported, and documented do they seem to be? Does the text have an editor? Is the publisher likely to have employees whose job it is to check the facts of publications?

Authority. Who is the author? What are her credentials? What is her standing in the field? Who published the text? Both national and university presses generally require their publications to be well researched and well written, so that books from such houses are usually thought of as constituting reliable sources. Where does the essay or news item appear—in a national, regional, state, or local publication? We do not mean to imply that national sources are necessarily better than local sources. A statewide publication such as *Texas Monthly* (a well-written magazine concerning issues and topics in Texas) may well be a more reliable source of information on a particular topic than a nationally circulated gossip tabloid.

Objectivity. What biases are evident in the text? How fair does the writer's use of language seem? What is the nature of the text? Is it a political, social, or religious tract? A scholarly investigation of a particular topic? A piece of propaganda? What is its purpose, to sway a reader or to invite him to make up his own mind?

Currency. What is the publication date? Are the text's information and sources up-to-date?

Coverage. What is included or covered in the text? In how much depth? Are some topics given more thorough or more preferential treatment than others? Is such treatment warranted?

Whatever the kind of publication, your job is to determine the quality of the writer's treatment of the subject. The better that quality, the more reliable the source is likely to be.

Exercise 12.3

Using the topic you wrote about in an exercise earlier in this chapter or the tentative topic you have chosen for your research paper, locate in your library the following sources relating to your topic, listing the title, author, and call number for each:

> two books
> two essays in popular journals (e.g., *Time, Newsweek, Better Homes and Gardens, Popular Mechanics, National Geographic),* if applicable
> two essays in scholarly or professional journals, if applicable
> two items from a newspaper, including one from the *New York Times*
> two items from a CD-ROM database
> two government documents, if applicable

How reliable is each potential source? On what do you base your opinion?

FIELD SEARCH

Oftentimes, students overlook the value and appropriateness of using sources beyond those they find in a library. Field sources can be especially important for current community or campus issues, even for topics of national scope. If you have such a topic, you should not limit yourself to searching a library for information. Similarly, if one of your teachers is a noted authority on your topic, you should try to interview him, even though his writings may be available in your library.

Survey your campus or local community to locate potential sources. Use a local telephone book to find businesses or chapters of local and national civic organizations and special interest groups (e.g., environmental protection groups) that may be able to provide information about your topic. Many groups can furnish trade publications, pamphlets, brochures, and newsletters relevant to your search. To discover who is most concerned with your topic, read local and campus newspapers. Many individuals will be willing to talk with you about their points of view. Whereas using printed materials from groups is a relatively easy task, preparing to talk with someone is more difficult.

INTERVIEWS

An interview is a face-to-face meeting in which some topic is discussed. Interviews vary in formality, from discussion limited to questions submitted by the interviewer prior to the interview, to discussion that is not so limited, sometimes becoming an informal talk between two people who are interested in the same subject. Whatever the circumstances, these are some general guidelines you should follow to prepare for and conduct an interview:

1. Contact the person you want to interview as far in advance as possible to set up the interview. Identify yourself and your purpose clearly so that the interviewee will have some time to think about the general subject of the interview.
2. Prepare questions ahead of time to help you think your way through the interview. Decide what information you would like to receive, and frame questions to elicit it. Although you may use only some of these questions in the actual interview, preparing them will help you focus the interview. Ask pertinent, relevant questions; stick to the subject.
3. Include questions designed to establish the interviewee's credentials, such as who she is and how she came to be an expert on your subject.
4. Ask open-ended questions, those designed to elicit the interviewee's ideas and whatever facts she may know that you need. Ask for definition of terms or for clarification of points that are not clear to you. Open-ended questions let the interviewee talk at length about the subject and should elicit the information you seek.
5. In drafting and asking questions, remember that you are not an investigative reporter out to champion a cause or expose criminal activity. Questions should ask for information; they should not be of the "Do you still beat your wife?" ilk.
6. Take notes or use a tape recorder, but do not record secretly. Get the interviewee's permission to record ahead of time. If the interviewee is nervous, just talk with her and jot notes immediately after the interview.

7. At appropriate intervals and at the end, summarize the interview. Tell the interviewee what you have understood her to say so that she can clarify her position if need be.

8. As a courtesy, offer to provide the interviewee with a transcript of the interview and a copy of your paper—before the paper is due—so that she can see how you plan to use the interview. At that time, the interviewee can check facts and quotations for accuracy, which can strengthen your paper.

RELIABILITY   What is the person's status as an authority on your topic? Is she a nationally known figure? What is her background or education in the field? If your topic is more local than national in scope, what standing does your source have with respect to your topic? What qualifies her as an expert or authority? The more expertise your source has, the more reliable she may be.

Exercise 12.4

1. Find a topic of current interest in your local or campus community. What is at issue? Identify the thoughts of people on both sides. What is the position of each side? Find at least two published sources for each side, and summarize each. Identify at least one person on each side of the issue, and prepare a list of questions you would ask in an interview. If possible, interview these people, and summarize the results of your interviews. How reliable do you think the sources you have uncovered are? Why?

2. In a news magazine such as *Newsweek, Time,* or *U.S. News and World Report,* find an interview of a national business, political, or religious leader. Summarize the interview's content and its key points. How would you characterize the questions asked? The answers? Are there any questions you would have asked that were not asked? If so, what are they? Why would you ask them?

3. Arrange to interview one of your classmates. Prior to the interview, prepare a list of questions that ask things you would like to know about this classmate. After the interview, write a brief character sketch or biography of your classmate, and have him check your writing for accuracy.

QUESTIONNAIRES

Sometimes your topic will call for a survey of a sizable group of people. In such a case, interviewing will not be feasible. Instead, to reach this group, you may want to devise a questionnaire, a set of questions with spaces set aside for the recipients' responses. We see questionnaires often. For example, political pollsters use questionnaires to ascertain voter attitudes and then to predict a candidate's chances of winning, and advertising executives use them to ascertain consumer preferences before marketing a product.

Questionnaires survey primarily for two kinds of responses:

1. Factual information, such as frequency of product or facility use or kind of products or services used

2. Opinion, such as statements of agreement or disagreement with particular people (perhaps politicians or celebrities), respondents' perspectives on

particular issues, short statements about topics of particular interest or concern

Figure 12.2 shows an example of a questionnaire that could be part of a research project on how well a school library functions. Questions 1–3 ask for factual information, and questions 4–8 seek an opinion.

As you frame questions for a survey, try not to bias the responses; that is, try not to direct the respondents' responses to fit any preconceived notions you may have. As an example, look at question 7 in the library questionnaire. If the question read, "What should the library change its hours to?" what bias would it reveal?

In addition to posing topical questions to respondents, pollsters may also seek demographic information in an attempt to identify particular characteristics of the group being surveyed. In a political race, pollsters might ask respondents their age, gender, race, income level, education level, religious preference, status as homeowner or renter, marital status, and political affiliation. For our hypothetical library survey, appropriate demographic information would include the respondent's age, class (e.g., freshman), and major. Such information allows pollsters to describe a "typical" respondent so as to see trends or patterns in the responses and thereby enhance their analysis of the information. A researcher might find, for example, that 85 percent of the freshmen and 80 percent of the sophomores surveyed feel the library is something of a maze in which they have trouble finding what they need, but only 5 percent of the graduate students surveyed feel this way. The researcher could conclude from such responses that a comprehensive library orientation program is needed to help undergraduates learn how to use the library.

A final note about administering a survey: Your university may require that a researcher wishing to involve human subjects in any way get authority to do so from an appropriate university administrator. Before you distribute a survey, ask your instructor about your university's policy concerning such matters.

Exercise 12.5

Identify a current issue about which you are concerned. Devise a questionnaire of at least five questions to ascertain opinions of others on this issue. Administer the questionnaire to at least twenty people, drawing on as broad a range of respondents as possible. Summarize and analyze the results. How did your questions help shape the results?

OBSERVATION

The last form of field search we will discuss is firsthand observation. If your topic is about something of a physical nature (e.g., an environmental issue, campus parking facilities, campus bike traffic), one of the best ways of conducting research is to watch. If possible, observe the scene of your topic several times at different times of the day. Take notes; jot down your impressions of what you see; describe what you see; try to discern patterns in what you see. What is important about what you're observing? What does it mean?

FIGURE 12.2
Sample Research
Questionnaire

SURVEY OF SMITHSON LIBRARY

To respond to the following questions, circle or mark the most appropriate response.

1. How often do you use the library?
   Daily   Seldom
     1   2   3   4   5   6

2. What time of day do you most often use the library?
   Morning   Afternoon   Evening

3. For what purposes do you most often use the library? (Circle all that apply.)
   Reading   Studying   Typing   Researching   Other

4. How helpful are the following library personnel?

	Very helpful				Not helpful		
Reference librarians	1	2	3	4	5	6	No opinion
Reading room librarians	1	2	3	4	5	6	No opinion
Circulation librarians	1	2	3	4	5	6	No opinion
Interlibrary-loan staff	1	2	3	4	5	6	No opinion

5. To what extent are you able to find the resources you need in the library?
   Always   Seldom
     1   2   3   4   5   6

6. How adequate are the library hours for your needs?
   Adequate   Inadequate   Undecided

7. Should the library change its hours of operation?
   Yes ____   No ____
   If yes, should the library *increase* or *decrease* its hours? (Circle one.)

8. In the space below (and continuing on the back of this sheet, if necessary), please discuss your overall opinion of the library. Consider, for example, what its two primary strengths and weaknesses are. How would you address the weaknesses?

Spend an hour at a busy spot on campus. Describe the scene before you. Who is there? For what purpose? Are there any dominant patterns that emerge, things that are striking about what you see? If so, identify them. What makes them dominant or striking? What conclusions do you draw from your observation?

INTERNET SEARCH

One of the most promising and, at the same time, potentially frustrating aids to research is the information superhighway—the Internet. It is promising because of the vast amount of information it holds, ready for you as researcher to read, print out, and incorporate into an essay. Further, the Net opens lines of research that stretch beyond your local library. And you may use the Net for your research whenever a computer terminal is available to you, so you're not necessarily limited by the hours your library is open. But the Internet is potentially frustrating as well. First, it holds a vast amount of information, so much that you cannot possibly hope to review it all. Sometimes, the Net crashes and may be down for several minutes, several hours, or even several days as computer technicians work to restore service. But the biggest liability of the Internet as a ground for research involves the reliability of the sources available on it. Anyone can post anything on the Net, as evidenced by the web sites of hate groups and pornographers.

RELIABILITY OF INTERNET SOURCES

Because of the ease with which items can be posted on the Internet, you must consider the reliability of any Internet sources you want to use. The following questions for judging the reliability of Internet sources are based on the five criteria we listed for evaluating printed sources:

Accuracy. Does the information seem error-free? Is there any evidence of documentation of ideas? Is an editor or fact checker listed in the article? (Given the availability of the Internet and the ease of publishing on it, authors seldom rely on editors and/or fact checkers.)

Comment: There are no universally accepted standards for ensuring accuracy on the Internet.

Authority. Is the article signed—that is, is the author identified? If so, who is the author? What are his credentials? What is his standing in the field? Is the author someone you've heard of? Who sponsors the page on which the article appears? How reputable is this sponsor? Does the article offer links to information about the author and/or the sponsor?

Comment: It's often difficult to determine who has written an article on a web page; even when an article is signed, it's difficult to determine the writer's credentials. Further, the sponsor, if there is one, generally isn't listed, and it's often difficult to determine sponsorship from the web page's address.

Objectivity. What biases are evident in the text? How fair does the writer's use of language seem? What is the nature of the text? Is it a political, social, or religious tract? A scholarly treatment of a topic? A piece of propaganda? What is its purpose? To allow the writer to rant and rave about a particular topic? To sway the reader? To invite the reader to make up his own mind about the topic?

Comment: The Internet carries a lot of potentially useful information for a researcher. At the same time, it carries a lot of propaganda, some of which ventures into such realms as racism and hate. You must attempt to determine the writer's objectivity.

Currency. Is the web page dated? If so, what does the date mean; that is, is it the date the piece was originally posted on the Internet or when it was updated? How current are any links the text includes? Are the links still active, or have they moved or expired?

Coverage. What is included or covered in the text? In how much depth? Are some topics given more thorough or more preferential treatment than others? Is such treatment warranted? What does the web page carry that you can't find in potentially more reliable sources?

Our goal here is not to discourage you from using the Internet as a potential source for your research. But what you must keep in mind as you consider using information from web sites is this: *Anyone can post anything on the web.* You have to approach using such information just as you would buying a used car—with *caveat emptor,* "let the buyer beware," as your motto.

USING THE INTERNET

Your way into the Internet is your computer terminal and a web browser such as Netscape. Either use a specific command to open your browser or click on its icon. Once you have accessed your browser, you may use any of several search engines, which can help organize your search. Popular engines include Yahoo!, Lycos, Excite, Infoseek, AltaVista, and LookSmart. Each engine will give you different results because of its organization, so it may be helpful for you to use more than one engine, especially if you're not satisfied with the results that a given engine generates. Once you select a particular engine, you may use its subject index to begin, or you may use a keyword search.

A *subject index* is a listing of various topics or subjects that enables you to move quickly to a specific part of the Net. When you click on a subject heading, subtopics are displayed, and as you move deeper into the subject, you find increasingly narrow subtopics. For example, a search into the subject heading Education led to instructions for a specific line dance via this route:

Clicking on Education led to a departments heading that included K–12 and Universities and Colleges. Under the K–12 heading were three subtopics: Homework Help, Teacher Resources, and Special Education. Under the Universities and Colleges heading were three subtopics: Financial Aid, Fields of Study, and Graduate Schools. Clicking on Fields of Study led to a listing of a large number of fields of study offered by colleges and universities. Clicking on Dance led to a listing of types of dance, including Ballet, Jazz, and Country & Western. Clicking on Country & Western led to a listing of various home pages devoted to various kinds of country and western dances, and clicking on Kickit Line Dancing led to an alphabetized organizing grid for different line dances. Clicking on the Sh–Sj grid led to a list of dances in that range of the alphabet, and, finally, clicking on Shaggin' (Evelyn Young) led to step-by-step instructions on doing this particular dance.

What does all of this show? That there's a wide range of information available and that one very good search strategy is to browse, that is, to go into a particular topic area in which you may be interested, select promising or interesting sites, and see what's there.

A *keyword search* requires you to locate a box labeled something like Search the Web. Click on this box to place the cursor in it; type in one or two keywords, and either press Enter or click on the button labeled something like Search or Go Get It! In most cases, you'll be given the total number of hits generated by your search (a *hit* is a reference that includes at least one of your keywords) and then a listing of the sources. Usually, you can click on the title of an individual source to connect to it or call it up on your screen for review.

As noted, different engines are organized differently and so produce different results. A recent search for articles using the keyword "graffiti" generated these results: Excite, 32,798 hits; Infoseek, 29,860 hits; AltaVista, 273,710 hits. Not only does the number of hits vary, but the first several articles listed are not the same, so you'll probably want to use at least two engines for your search. Why so many hits? The Net is a web, so making connections is very easy. Every article with even the most remote tie to your keywords will be accessible. Hits will be displayed in groups of ten, with each entry carrying the article's title, its size (in kilobytes, Kb), a percentage indicating the relevancy of the article to your keywords (the higher the percentage, the more relevance), and either the first 20–30 words of the text or a brief description of the article's contents. You can't possibly read or even scan a large number of articles, so plan on looking closely at only the first 20 or 30, as these are likely to be the ones most germane to your search.

If the articles your search generated don't seem to be what you're looking for, try different keywords. If you've gotten an incredibly large listing of articles, then try narrowing the scope of your keywords (e.g., "lifesaving techniques" instead of "water safety"). If the number of articles seems too small, then try broadening the scope of your keywords. (Most search engines are designed to let you conduct a Boolean search, which lets you narrow the scope of your keywords by using "and" or "+" between terms. See the Help function of your search engine for more information on the correct format for a Boolean search.)

SAMPLE SEARCH   To give you an idea of what form an Internet search might take, let's follow Gardiner Rhoderick as he looks for information about the topic of his research paper, graffiti. You'll find a copy of Gardiner's paper in the Sample Student Process section at the end of this chapter (pp. 486–496).

Part of Gardiner's assignment was to incorporate at least two sources from the Internet, so he decided to conduct a keyword search. He logged on to the

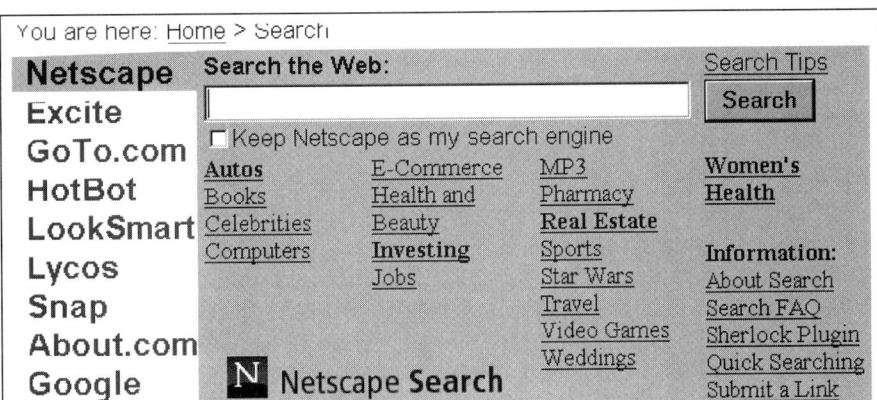

FIGURE 12.3
Netscape Search
Engine Screen

Internet and selected Netscape's search engine for his search (see Figure 12.3). In the box labeled Search the Web, Gardiner typed in the keyword "graffiti" and clicked on the Search bar. Netscape went to work, locating 138 potential web sites for Gardiner to consider and then listing them in order of likely relevance (see Figure 12.4).

FIGURE 12.4
Internet Search
Results

You are here: Home > Netscape Search > Search Results

Search Results for 'graffiti'

Reviewed Web Sites
11-20 of 138
Web sites reviewed and categorized by a team of editors.

- Metropol
  Metropol: Pictorial Document on the Lost Art of a Metropolis. presents a reverent and rare glimpse at the old school graffiti art masterpieces of Chicago
  http://members.xoom.com/metropolisms/
  found in: Arts > Visual Arts > Galleries > Online > Graffiti

- Art Crimes: Crayone
  Art Crime's feature on the work of Crayone
  http://www.graffiti.org/crayone/crayone_1.html
  found in: Society > Subcultures > Hip-Hop > Graffiti > Bay Area

- Underground Productions
  Underground Productions (UP) is a Swedish hip hop magazine. It covers the whole hip hop culture, graffiti, break dance, rap and foremost graffiti. The magazine was first published in the autumn of 91. The first issue was published in English in a print run of 320 copies.

One of the sites listed on the second Search Results page, Art Crimes, looked promising, so Gardiner clicked on it and worked his way back to the Art Crimes home page (see Figure 12.5). Sponsored by Susan Farrell and Brett Webb, this site offers a good bit of information about graffiti. You'll note that Farrell and Webb have organized their site into six categories. Because Gardiner needed sources for an academic paper, he decided to browse the Interviews & Articles section listed under Information & Resources. There, he found a listing of twenty-eight interviews of graffiti artists, twenty-six articles, and twenty-five researched discussions of graffiti. Scrolling through the researched discussions, Gardiner browsed several entries, deciding to use two as sources for his essay: Sherri Cavan's "The Great Graffiti Wars of the Late 20th Century" and Killian Tobin's "A Modern Perspective on Graffiti."

Gardiner's search was profitable. If he hadn't found the Art Crimes site as quickly as he did, he could have used Netscape's keyword feature to send the search engine on a different but related track. We noted that Gardiner's first keyword, "graffiti," yielded 138 potential sources. Of the first 10 of those hits, about half were positive about graffiti, and the other half were negative.

FIGURE 12.5   Art Crimes Home Page (www.graffiti.org)

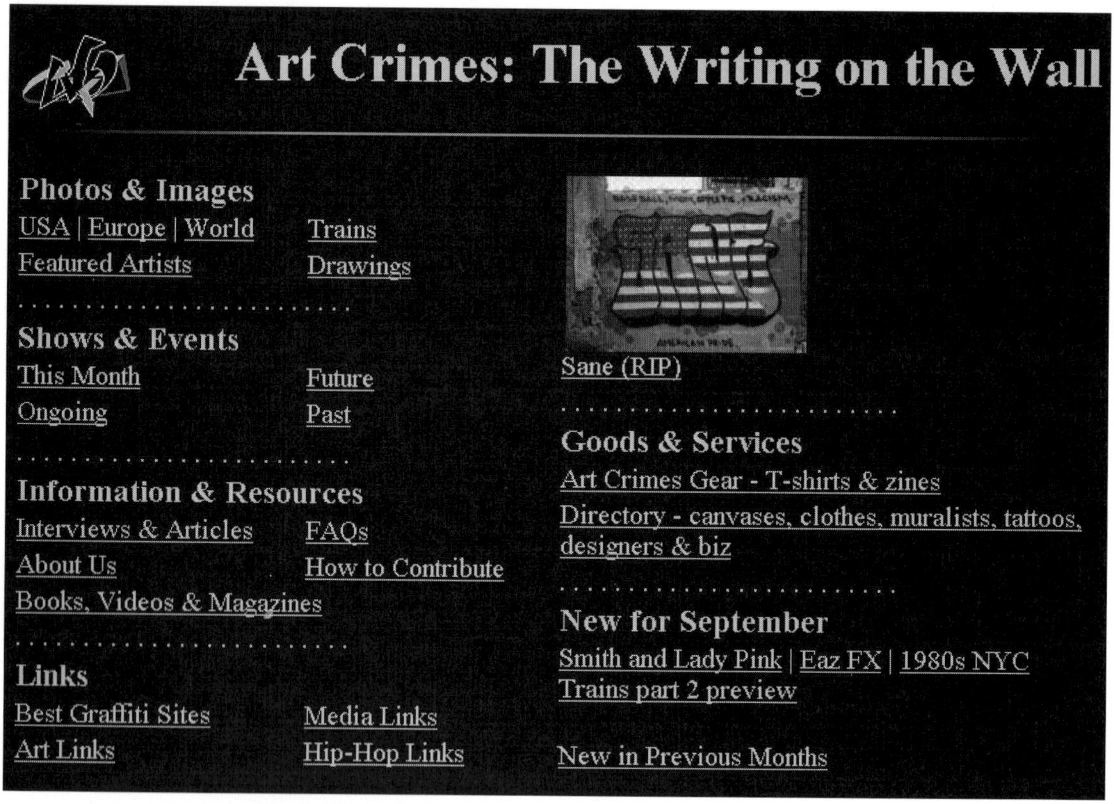

Art Crimes: The Writing on the Wall

Photos & Images
USA | Europe | World   Trains
Featured Artists   Drawings

Shows & Events
This Month   Future
Ongoing   Past

Information & Resources
Interviews & Articles   FAQs
About Us   How to Contribute
Books, Videos & Magazines

Links
Best Graffiti Sites   Media Links
Art Links   Hip-Hop Links

Sane (RIP)

Goods & Services
Art Crimes Gear - T-shirts & zines
Directory - canvases, clothes, muralists, tattoos, designers & biz

New for September
Smith and Lady Pink | Eaz FX | 1980s NYC
Trains part 2 preview

New in Previous Months

A different search yielded very different results. We decided to add "vandals" to "graffiti," so that "graffiti vandals" appeared in the Search box. That search identified about 150 potential sources; of the first 10 sites listed, all were negative about graffiti. The Internet offers you a wealth of sources to support your research; your job is to log on and go exploring.

Exercise 12.7

1. Using the search engine of your choice, base an Internet search on any of the following keywords: skateboards, grammar, the name of your favorite celebrity (e.g., singer or actor), president, skiing (snow or water), your home state, your hometown. Click on two of the first ten hits listed and read them. How reliable do these sites seem? On what do you base this assessment? Next, record the number of total hits your search generated and bibliographical information about the two sites you visited, including the relevancy rating.
2. Select either of the two sites you visited. Click on the More Like This link. Scan the first ten sites that come up and decide how similar to or different from your selected site they are.

Computer Tip

RESEARCH TOOL

Computers can be incredibly helpful research tools because of the access they offer to the Internet and because of their editing and storage capabilities. To use your computer more efficiently, try these strategies:

Bookmarking a site. Your search engine will allow you to identify a site for future reference and then store that site's Internet address in a file labeled Bookmarks. To enter a site as a bookmark, go to the site. Click on Bookmarks and then on Add Bookmark. Then, when you want to return to that site, all you need do is click on Bookmarks and then on the site you wish to retrieve.

Downloading a file. You may download or transfer a web page from the Internet to your computer. To download a page, click on File, then on Save As. At the prompt, type in the drive you wish the page to go to and then enter a file name. Hit the Enter key, and the file will be transferred to the drive you've designated.

Copying and pasting. You may copy part of a Net file to another file. Let's assume that you're working in Windows on your research paper. Keeping that file open, you may go to the Internet at the same time to find a source there that you need. When you locate that source, highlight the part you wish to copy and then click on the Edit heading. Under Edit, click on Copy. Then diminish the Internet screen by clicking on the minus (–) icon in the upper right-hand corner of the screen. Place the cursor in the still open research paper where you want the passage to appear; then click on Edit and then on Paste. The passage should appear. *Note: Be sure to document any material you import from any source to avoid plagiarism.*

HELPFUL INTERNET SITES

The Internet offers an incredible range of materials and sites to support your research. At times, it will be more practical for you to begin your search for information by accessing a site that is directly related to your topic. The sites listed below offer a range of materials, are easy to access, and provide links to other relevant sites.

ERIC (Educational Resources Information Center) <http://ericfac. occcard.csc.com/>   Maintained by Syracuse University, ERIC provides a bibliographical database for documents and journal articles related to education published since 1966.

Government Documents   The Government Printing Office (GPO) is responsible for printing reports from the various agencies funded by Congress and so by U.S. tax dollars. As you can well imagine, the GPO prints a tremendous number of reports and other materials that you may need to access during your research. The best way for you to do this is by going to your library's web site and searching for the GPO database. In all likelihood, your library will have links to these materials.

Indexes, Abstracts, Bibliographies, and Table of Contents Services <http://info.lib.uh.edu/indexes/indexes.htm>   Maintained by the University of Houston libraries, this site lists a wide range of links to indexes, abstracts, bibliographies, and table of contents services to help the researcher find such materials as journal, magazine, and newspaper articles, book chapters, and conference proceedings.

Library of Congress <http://lcweb.loc.gov>   This site affords access to the holdings and exhibits of the Library of Congress as well as links to other libraries, special topics databases, and other Library of Congress Internet resources.

Library Resources: Digital Libraries <http://www.indiana.edu/~vlib. digital.html>   This site provides links to a range of sites, including

The Modern English Collection   A collection of fiction, nonfiction, poetry, drama, letters, newspapers, manuscripts, and illustrations published from 1500 to the present. The site is sponsored by the Electronic Text Center at the University of Virginia.

D-Lib Program—Research in Digital Libraries   A monthly compilation of commentary, stories, and briefings, includes D-Lib Magazine, an on-line magazine of interest to web users.

The *New York Times* <http://www.nytimes.com>   The *New York Times* on-line, including archival materials. You'll have to register to use this site, but there's no cost, and registration is very easy.

Allyn and Bacon <www.abacon.com/compsite/>   This site contains very useful information about using the Internet to support your research. When you reach the Compsite home page, click on the Research icon (a flashlight with the word "research" written above it). You'll then be able to access information under these headings:

Search strategies and information
Evaluating Internet sources
Search engines and resources—a comprehensive list of search engines, including links to them
Citation and documentation
General resources for writing—links to on-line writing centers, which can help you with questions about your writing, including grammar and mechanics

Purdue University Online Writing Lab <http://owl.english.purdue.edu> This site is a comprehensive resource for writers. For example, it has over 130 handouts available on topics ranging from general writing concerns to spelling. It also includes sections on grammatical concerns and English as a second language.

In addition, a number of publications have their own web sites. The best way to locate these sites is by using a search engine and conducting a keyword search using the name of the publication. For example, you may access *Newsweek* by entering the magazine's name in an engine's Search for box. Your search will take you to <www.Newsweek.com>.

Computer Tip

MORE USEFUL INTERNET SITES

The Electric Library	http://www.elibrary.com
The Internet Public Library	http://ipl.org
The Internet Services List	http://spectracom.com/islist
The WWW Virtual Library	http://www3.org/pub/DataSource/bySubject/Overview.html
Inter-Links Journal List	http://www.nova.edu/Inter-Links/start.html

HyperNews   http://union.ncsa.uiuc.edu
HYTELNET   http://library.usask.ca/hytelnet

Exercise 12.8

1. Using the topic you wrote about in an exercise earlier in this chapter or the tentative topic you have chosen for your research paper, use a search engine to locate the following sources relating to your topic, listing the title, author, and web address for each.

   two books
   two essays in popular journals (e.g., *Time, Newsweek, Better Homes and Gardens, Popular Mechanics, National Geographic*), if applicable
   two essays in scholarly or professional journals, if applicable
   two items from a newspaper, including one from the *New York Times*
   an item you locate through the Library of Congress
   a government document, if applicable

   How reliable is each potential source? On what do you base your opinion?

2. Visit the Allyn and Bacon Compsite, and locate information on the following:

   documenting information
   evaluating information from the Internet
   problems with grammar and mechanics
   links to two search engines

INCORPORATING MATERIAL FROM SOURCES

To use your sources as effectively as possible, you need to be sure that each piece of information you use is clearly set in a context. Your reader needs to see just how you are using that information, for example, how particular information supports your ideas or how your interpretation of information fits with other material in your paper.

You can help the reader see how things fit by introducing passages smoothly. Passages that are not introduced are often abrupt. Either they intrude on the reader, interrupting the paper's flow, or they simply don't make sense because they aren't clearly connected to the rest of the paper. You can introduce a passage in a number of ways, as these hypothetical examples illustrate:

1. Preview the passage by identifying its main idea.

   A. B. Smith does not agree with the current criticism of President Gumbody's economic policies and vehemently attacks critics, saying, "Senator Jones can criticize our policies all he wishes—where are his alternatives? It's time for him to put up or shut up."

2. Connect the quoted material to information that precedes it.

Of this perspective, A. B. Smith states, "Now is not the time for divisiveness but for unity."

A. B. Smith comments on this criticism: "Let those who criticize our policies submit workable alternatives. So far, no one has, though we've continually challenged our detractors to do so."

A. B. Smith says that "to date, no suitable alternatives have been submitted," thus denying his opponent's claims to the contrary.

3. Make the passage an integral part of your own ideas.

Despite intense criticism, President Gumbody's supporters remain loyal because "the opposition has offered no workable alternatives."

The examples above involve shorter passages that fit within the boundaries of a sentence. If you quote longer passages, you'll need to inset them, and the format you'll employ will depend on the style guide you're using as the authority for your format. Two of the more widely used style guides recommend the following approaches.

1. Joseph Gibaldi, author of the *MLA Handbook for Writers of Research Papers* (1999, 5th ed.), states:

If a quotation runs to more than four lines in your paper, set it off from your text by beginning a new line, indenting one inch (or ten spaces if you are using a typewriter) from the left margin, and typing it double-spaced, without adding quotation marks. A colon generally introduces a quotation displayed in this way, though sometimes the context may require a different mark of punctuation or none at all. [. . .] A parenthetical reference to a prose quotation set off from the text follows the last line of the quotation. (81–82)

2. The *Publication Manual of the American Psychological Association* (1994, 4th ed.) says:

Display a quotation of 40 or more words in a free-standing block of typewritten lines, and omit the quotation marks. Start such a *block quotation* on a new line, and indent it five spaces from the left margin (in the same position as a new paragraph). Type subsequent lines flush with the indent. If there are additional paragraphs within the quotation, indent the first line of each five spaces from the margin of the quotation. Type the entire quotation double-spaced. (p. 95)

Note the differences between these two. First, the MLA recommends a bigger indentation than does the APA. Second, although both formats carry a page reference, the MLA format does not use "p." for page, whereas the APA format does. Which of these formats should you use? If your instructor doesn't specify a particular format, ask which she prefers you to use.

DOCUMENTING INFORMATION

Documentation, an essential part of any research project, involves both honesty and courtesy. You will use sources other than yourself in preparing a research paper, and you should credit those outside sources for the information you borrowed. Documentation, from start to finish, does at least these things:

1. Gives credit where it is due (a courtesy to the author you borrow from)
2. Provides readers with points for departure should they wish to use your research and your sources as the beginnings of their own work (a second courtesy)
3. Takes away any problem of plagiarism—that is, of your using someone else's words or thoughts without giving credit (a matter of honesty)

Documentation begins with an initial, or working, bibliography and includes citations in the text as well as a formal bibliography in the paper's final draft.

INITIAL BIBLIOGRAPHY

An initial bibliography is a list of potential sources, which you may keep on note cards, one source to a card, as a matter of convenience. A bibliographical note card should carry such information as the author's name (last name first, to make alphabetizing the final bibliography easy), the source's title, publication data, library call number (if applicable), and a very brief summary of the work's contents. A typical bibliography card is shown in Figure 12.6.

You probably will not use every source you survey initially, and your initial bibliography makes it convenient for you to retrieve more useful sources later. Just as you may not use all your initial sources, you may augment your bibliography as you find pertinent sources later in your project.

FINAL BIBLIOGRAPHY

The final bibliography, which you submit on a separate page as part of the final paper, may be either a list of only the works you cite in your paper itself or a list of all the works you surveyed in preparing your paper. If the former, you should title the page Works Cited, Bibliography, Literature Cited, or References. If the latter, you should title the page Works Consulted, which indicates that your list includes all works you surveyed during your research, whether your paper actually uses information from them or not. In any case, alphabetize each section of your bibliography by author's last name, and use the same entry format as that of your initial bibliography,

FIGURE 12.6 Typical Bibliography Card

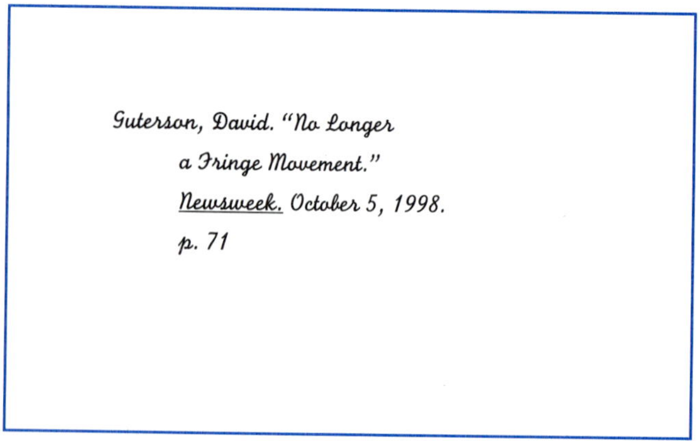

Guterson, David. "No Longer
   a Fringe Movement."
Newsweek. October 5, 1998.
   p. 71

whether that format is the one we suggested, a different one preferred by your instructor, or one established by a style manual in your field.

The following are sample entries for the kinds of sources you will be most likely to use. You'll note that two different formats are listed. The first is used by the Modern Language Association, and the second by the American Psychological Association.

Gibaldi, Joseph. MLA Handbook for Writers of Research Papers. 5th ed. New York: Modern Language Association, 1999.

American Psychological Association. (1994). Publication manual of the American Psychological Association (4th ed.). Washington, DC: Author.

These two manuals, two of the most widely used in the United States, carry information about various aspects of research writing, including documentation, manuscript preparation (e.g., spacing, margins, pagination, and binding), and mechanics of writing (e.g., spelling and punctuation). For writing papers in a particular discipline (e.g., agriculture, biology, or anthropology), consult the style manual adopted by experts in the field. If you do not know which manual is recommended for your discipline (the field of your major), consult one of your teachers for advice. Once you have chosen a style manual, become familiar with its conventions, and then be consistent in your use of it.

Some features of the MLA and APA styles are the same. Both specify double-spacing within and between entries. Both require that the author's name be placed at the left-hand margin, with subsequent lines indented half an inch (or five spaces). [Note, however, that the APA has a different style for papers that are being submitted for publication. In such cases, the author should indent the first line half an inch (or five spaces), and leave the remaining lines not indented; the typesetter then converts to a hanging indent.]

Moving beyond the basic layout, you'll notice several differences between the MLA and APA styles in the following entries. For example, although both formats require an alphabetical listing of authors by last name, the MLA format specifies that the author's name be given as it appears on the work's title page, whereas the APA format requires that only the initials of the author's first and middle names be used. Also, the MLA format specifies that the publication date be placed at the end, whereas the APA format specifies that it be placed in parentheses following the author's name. Here's how a book written by three writers would be documented in both these formats:

MLA   Young, Richard E., Alton L. Becker, and Kenneth L. Pike. Rhetoric: Discovery and Change. New York: Harcourt, 1970.

APA   Young, R. E., Becker, A. L., & Pike, K. L. (1970). Rhetoric: Discovery and change. New York: Harcourt.

Why the differences? Each style manual follows the traditional format established for its discipline.

The basic information that either format delivers includes the author's name, the title of the piece, and publication information (i.e., the date and place the piece was published). A correctly documented source should enable another researcher to locate that source with ease. If you have any questions concerning the elements of an entry, consult the style manual you are using.

BOOKS

1. Single author

Author's name as it appears on title page, last name first

MLA   Burke, Kenneth. The Philosophy of Literary Form. 2nd ed. Baton
          Rouge: Louisiana State UP, 1967.

Title of work (underscored)   *Edition*

Date of publication   *Where published and press*

Author's name, last name first, then initial

APA   Burke, K. (1967). The philosophy of literary form. (2nd ed.). Baton
          Rouge: Louisiana State University Press.

Title of work (underscored)

2. Two or more books by the same author

MLA   Burke, Kenneth. A Grammar of Motives. Berkeley: U of California
          P, 1969.

          ---. Language as Symbolic Action. Berkeley: U of California P, 1966.

APA   Burke, K. (1966). Language as symbolic action. Berkeley:
          University of California Press.

          Burke, K. (1969). A grammar of motives. Berkeley: University of
          California Press.

3. Two or three authors

MLA   Young, Richard E., Alton L. Becker, and Kenneth L. Pike. Rhetoric:
          Discovery and Change. New York: Harcourt, 1970.

APA   Young, R. E., Becker, A. L., & Pike, K. L. (1970). Rhetoric:
          Discovery and change. New York: Harcourt.

4. More than three authors

MLA   Britton, James, et al. The Development of Writing Abilities
          (11-18). London: Macmillan, 1975.

APA   Britton, J., Burgess, T., Martin, N., McLeod, A., & Rosen, H. (1975).
          The development of writing abilities (11-18). London: Macmillan.

5. Translation

MLA   Aristotle. Poetics. Trans. Hippocrates G. Apostle, Elizabeth A.
          Dobbs, and Morris A. Parslow. Grinnell, IA: Peripatetic, 1990.

APA   Aristotle. (1990). Poetics. (H. G. Apostle, E. A. Dobbs, & M. A.
          Parslow, Trans.). Grinnell, IA: Peripatetic.

6. Author and editor

MLA   Burke, Kenneth. <u>On Symbols and Society</u>. Ed. Joseph R. Gusfield.
Chicago: U of Chicago P, 1989.

APA   Burke, K. (1989). <u>On symbols and society</u> (J. R. Gusfield, Ed.).
Chicago: University of Chicago Press.

7. Edited collection

MLA   Skaggs, Calvin, ed. <u>The American Short Story</u>. 2 vols. New York:
Dell, 1985.

APA   Skaggs, C. (Ed.). (1985). <u>The American short story</u> (Vols. 1-2).
New York: Dell.

8. Government document

MLA   Chan, Amy. <u>The Use of Wetlands for Water Pollution Control</u>.
EPA Rept. 600/S2-82-086. Washington: GPO, 1982.

APA   Chan, A. (1982). <u>The use of wetlands for water pollution
control</u> (EPA Report No. 600/S2-82-086). Washington, DC:
U.S. Government Printing Office.

9. Author unknown

MLA   <u>Exploring Your World: The Adventure of Geography</u>. Washington:
National Geographic, 1995.

APA   <u>Exploring your world: The adventure of geography</u>. (1995).
Washington, DC: National Geographic Society.

ARTICLES

1. Article in a scholarly journal with continuous pagination

Authors' names as they appear on article, first author's last name first

Title

MLA   Schutz, Aaron, and Anne Ruggles Gere. "Service Learning and
English Studies: Rethinking 'Public Service.'" <u>College English</u>

Vol. no. and year published

60 (1998): 129-49.

Inclusive page numbers *Title* *Journal title (underscored)*

Authors' names

APA   Schutz, A., & Gere, A. R. (1998). Service learning and English

Year published

studies: Rethinking "public service." <u>College English, 60,</u> 129-149.

Journal and volume (underscored) *Inclusive page numbers*

2. Article in a scholarly journal without continuous pagination

MLA   Davis, Sherri Heckler. "The Zen Art of Prewriting." <u>New Mexico English Journal</u> 12.1 (1998): 21-23.

APA   Davis, S. H. (1998). The Zen art of prewriting. <u>New Mexico English Journal, 12</u>(1), 21-23.

3. Article in an anthology or collection

MLA   Britton, James N. "Language and Experience." <u>Explorations in Children's Writing</u>. Ed. Eldonna L. Evertts. Urbana: NCTE, 1970. 49-64.

APA   Britton, J. N. (1970). Language and experience. In E. L. Evertts (Ed.), <u>Explorations in children's writing</u> (pp. 49-64). Urbana, IL: National Council of Teachers of English.

4. Article in a newspaper

MLA   Dooley, Martha. "New Mexico's Welfare Plan Is 'All about Jobs.'" <u>Las Cruces Sun-News</u> 7 Aug. 1998: A1+.

APA   Dooley, M. (1998, August 7). New Mexico's welfare plan is "all about jobs." <u>Las Cruces Sun-News</u>, pp. A1, A3.

5. Editorial

MLA   "Highway Roadblocks Need Early Warning." Editorial. <u>Las Cruces Sun-News</u> 7 Aug. 1998: B7.

APA   Highway roadblocks need early warning [Editorial]. (1998, August 7). <u>Las Cruces Sun-News</u>, p. B7.

6. Letter to the editor

MLA   Fry, Thomas E. Letter. <u>Las Cruces Sun-News</u> 11 Dec. 1998: B7.

APA   Fry, T. E. (1998, December 11). Water wrongs [Letter to the editor]. <u>Las Cruces Sun-News</u>, p. B7.

7. Article in a magazine published weekly or biweekly

MLA   Chambers, Veronica, and Devin Gordon. "The Mommy Track." <u>Newsweek</u> 10 Aug. 1998: 62-63.

APA   Chambers, V., & Gordon, D. (1998, August 10). The mommy track. <u>Newsweek</u>, 62-63.

8. Article in a magazine published monthly or bimonthly

MLA   Howe, Steve. "Doing the Wild Thing." <u>Backpacker</u> Sept. 1998: 58+.

APA   Howe, S. (1998, September). Doing the wild thing. <u>Backpacker,</u> 58–62, 147.

9. Review

MLA   Petersen, Carol. "Composition and Campus Diversity: Testing Academic and Social Values." Rev. of <u>Academic Advancement in Composition Studies: Scholarship, Publication, Promotion, Tenure</u>, ed. Richard C. Gebhardt and Barbara Genelle Smith Gebhardt, and <u>Gender Roles and Faculty Lives in Rhetoric and Composition</u>, ed. Theresa Enos. <u>CCC</u> 50 (1998): 277-91.

APA   Petersen, C. (1998). Composition and campus diversity: Testing academic and social values [Review of the books <u>Academic advancement in composition studies: Scholarship, publication, promotion, tenure</u> and <u>Gender roles and faculty lives in rhetoric and composition</u>]. <u>College Composition and Communication,</u> 50, 277-291.

10. Article in a reference work (e.g., an encyclopedia)

MLA   Burns, Edward McNall. "Marshall Plan." <u>The World Book Encyclopedia</u>. 1965 ed.

APA   Burns, E. M. (1965). Marshall plan. In <u>The world book encyclopedia</u> (Vol. 13, pp. 186-187). Chicago: Field Enterprises Educational.

11. Anonymous article in a magazine

MLA   "Recruiters at the Gates." <u>Sports Illustrated</u> 10 Aug. 1998: 29.

APA   Recruiters at the gates. (1998, August 10). <u>Sports Illustrated,</u> 29.

ELECTRONIC SOURCES

1. CD-ROM database

Authors' names   *Article title*

MLA   Stewart, Ian B., and George G. Sleivert. "The Effect of Warm-up Intensity on Range of Motion and Anaerobic Performance."

Volume and issue number

Journal title (underscored) ——————— Journal of Orthopaedic and Sports Physical Therapy 27.2

Server accessed and date posted to server

Date and inclusive page numbers ———— (1998): 154-61. Abstract. CD-ROM. SilverPlatter. Mar. 1998.

Material accessed and type of medium

APA   Stewart, I. B., & Sleivert, G. G. (1998). The effect of warm-up —— *Article title*

Authors' names

Publication date ———— intensity on range of motion and anaerobic performance

[CD-ROM]. The Journal of Orthopaedic and Sports Physical —— *Journal title*

Therapy, 27(2), 154-161. Abstract from: SilverPlatter File:

Inclusive page numbers ———— Sport Discus Item: 454824   *Material accessed*   *Server accessed*

Server's ID info. for article

2. Web page

MLA   Cavan, Sherri. "The Great Graffiti Wars of the Late 20th Century."

Information about type of material accessed ———— Home page. 14 Apr. 1998 <http://userwww.sfsu.edu/~kazbeki/

grafwars.html>. *Date retrieved*   *URL*

APA   Cavan, S. The great graffiti wars of the late 20th century.

Date retrieved and from where ———— Retrieved April 14, 1998 from the World Wide Web: http://

userwww.sfsu.edu/~kazbeki/grafwars.html —— *URL*

3. On-line book

MLA   Crane, Stephen. The Red Badge of Courage. New York, 1895. 7 Nov.

1998 <http://etext.lib.virginia.edu/etcbin/browse-mixed-new?

id=CraCour&tag=public&images=images/mode>.

APA   Crane, S. (1895). The red badge of courage [On-line]. Available:

http://etext.lib.virginia.edu/etcbin/browse-mixed-new?

id=CraCour&tag=public&images=images/mode

4. On-line journal article

MLA   Heavey, Bill. "Spinning at Large." Field and Stream May 1998. 22

Oct. 1998 <http://www.fieldandstream.com/features/0598.

atlarge.html>.

APA   Heavey, B. (1998, May). Spinning at large. Field and Stream.

Retrieved October 22, 1998 from the World Wide Web: http://

www.fieldandstream.com/features/0598.atlarge.html

5. On-line review

MLA   Soergel, Dagobert. Rev. of WordNet: An Electronic Lexical

Database, ed. Christine Fellbaum. D-Lib Magazine Oct. 1998.

17 Oct. 1998 <http://www.dlib.org/dlib/october98/

10bookreview.html>.

APA   Soergel, D. (1998, October). [Review of the book WordNet: An electronic lexical database]. D-Lib Magazine [On-line]. Retrieved October 17, 1998 from the World Wide Web: http://www.dlib.org/dlib/october98/10bookreview.html

6. On-line newspaper article

MLA   Erlanger, Steven. "Clinton Reopens Mideast Talks; Hopes to Wrap Up Agreement." New York Times on the Web 22 Oct. 1998. 22 Oct. 1998 <http://www.nytimes.com/library/world/mideast/102298mideast-talks.html>.

APA   Erlanger, S. (1998, October 22). Clinton reopens Mideast talks; Hopes to wrap up agreement. The New York Times on the Web. Retrieved October 22, 1998 from the World Wide Web: http://www.nytimes.com/library/world/mideast/102298mideast-talks.html

7. E-mail

MLA   Dent, Nancy Burns. E-mail to the author. 8 Aug. 1998.

Note: The *Publication Manual of the American Psychological Association* (4th ed., 1994, pp. 173–174) stipulates that personal communications, whether letters, e-mail, or memoranda, not be included in a reference list because these "do not provide recoverable data." However, such communications should be cited in the body of your essay in a parenthetical expression like this one, for example: (N. B. Dent, personal communication, August 8, 1998).

8. MOO or MUD

MLA   "Finding Time for Your Own Professional Development." Online posting. The Netoric Project's Tuesday Cafe. 25 Aug. 1998. ConnectionsMOO. 11 Dec. 1998 <http://bsuvc.bsu.edu/~00gjsiering/netoric/logs/TC082598.TXT>.

Note: This citation is for the archived log of a discussion that took place on August 25, 1998.

According to APA guidelines, electronic communications such as on-line postings by discussion groups are not included in the reference list. They should be cited in the body of your essay, like e-mail messages.

9. On-line bulletin board

MLA   "Families, 4-H, Nutrition News--Feb. 1996." 1 Feb. 1996. 2 Jan.

1999 <http://www.bbpages.psu.edu/penpages_reference/

28603/286031000.html>.

Note: Again, APA style calls for citing on-line bulletin board postings in a parenthetical format in the body of your essay, with no entry in the reference list.

OTHER SOURCES

1. Music recording

Title   *Recording company*   *Date issued*

Artist — **MLA**   Griffith, Nanci. Other Voices/Other Rooms. Elektra, 1993.

APA   Griffith, N. (1993). Other voices/other rooms [CD]. Nashville:

Recording company — Elektra Entertainment. *Date issued*   *Title*   *Medium*   *Company location*

2. Film or video recording

MLA   Camelot. Dir. Joshua L. Logan. Perf. Richard Harris, Vanessa

Redgrave, Franco Nero, David Hemmings, Lionel Jeffries, and

Laurence Naismith. Warner Bros., 1967.

APA   Warner, J. L. (Producer), & Logan, J. L. (Director). (1967).

Camelot [Videotape]. Burbank, CA: Warner Bros.

3. Interview that you conducted

MLA   Williams, Jennifer A. Personal interview. 26 June 1998.

Note: The *Publication Manual of the American Psychological Association* (4th ed., 1994) does not list a format for a personal interview, presumably because an interview would not yield "recoverable data" (see pp. 173–174). However, you should cite a personal interview in the body of your essay in a parenthetical expression. The format for such a citation is this: (interviewee's name, personal communication, date). For an example of such a citation, see Kristina Geray's essay "The Pet Overpopulation Problem" in Chapter 11.

4. Advertisement

MLA   ComforTemp DCC. Advertisement. Backpacker Sept. 1998: 12-13.

Note: The *Publication Manual of the American Psychological Association* (4th ed., 1994) does not list a format for citing an advertisement.

5. Television program

MLA   "The Triumph of Evil." Frontline. PBS. WGBH, Boston. 26 Jan. 1999.

APA   Robinson, M. (Producer). (1999, January 26). The triumph of evil. Frontline. Boston: WGBH.

6. Performance

MLA   Chavez, Denise, perf. Women in the State of Grace. National Museum of Women in the Arts, Washington. 20 Apr. 1996.

APA   Chavez, D. (Performer). (1996, April 20). Women in the state of grace. [One-woman show]. Washington, DC: National Museum of Women in the Arts.

Note: This list of sample references is not exhaustive. If you need to cite a source we have not listed here, consult the style manual you're using for the proper format.

CITATIONS

Citation formats vary as widely as bibliographical formats, and yours will depend on the style manual you choose as your guide. In all but a few disciplines, *in-text citations* are accepted as the standard citation format because they provide a quick and easy form of notation. An in-text citation consists of a parenthetical reference to the complete bibliographical reference, which will appear in the Works Cited or References listing at the paper's end. In the following examples, we present first the MLA citation form, then the APA form.

MLA   In Language, Leonard Bloomfield advocates a commonsensical or utilitarian approach to questions of grammar, stating, "Grammatical doctrine should be accepted only where it passes a test of usefulness, and even then it should be re-shaped to suit the actual needs" (506).

APA   In Language, Leonard Bloomfield (1933) advocates a commonsensical or utilitarian approach to questions of grammar, stating, "Grammatical doctrine should be accepted only where it passes a test of usefulness, and even then it should be re-shaped to suit the actual needs" (p. 506).

Here the source is identified in the sentence by title and author, and the page from which the quote was taken appears in parentheses at the end of the passage.

MLA   In Language, we find the idea that "grammatical doctrine should
       be accepted only where it passes a test of usefulness, and
       even then it should be re-shaped to suit the actual needs"
       (Bloomfield 506).

APA   In Language, we find the idea that "grammatical doctrine should
       be accepted only where it passes a test of usefulness, and
       even then it should be re-shaped to suit the actual needs"
       (Bloomfield, 1933, p. 506).

In the above examples, the source is identified in the sentence, and the author and page reference are listed in parentheses following the passage.

If you need to use two or more works published by the same author, MLA style calls for identifying each work with an abbreviation of its title.

MLA   Bloomfield states that "grammatical doctrine should be accepted
       only where it passes a test of usefulness, and even then it should
       be re-shaped to suit the actual needs" (Language 506).

APA   Bloomfield (1933a) states that "grammatical doctrine should be
       accepted only where it passes a test of usefulness, and even
       then it should be re-shaped to suit the actual needs" (p. 506).

In the APA example, the parenthetical 1933a refers the reader to the reference list for the work's complete bibliographical information. APA style specifies that two or more works published by an author in the same year be listed alphabetically by title in the reference list. The suffixes "a," "b," and so on are then added to the year of publication for identification in in-text citations. Since APA style includes the publication date in the text, it readily differentiates between works by the same author published in different years.

In-text references are easier for the writer to use than footnotes because the latter require the writer to gauge how much space to leave at the bottom of the page. However, in-text references do not provide as much immediate information as *footnotes* or *endnotes,* which are complete references placed either at the bottom of the page on which the referenced materials appear (footnotes) or on a separate note page at the end of the paper (endnotes). If you are studying in a discipline that specifies either footnotes or endnotes in research papers, refer to that discipline's standard or recommended style manual for format information.

WRITING ASSIGNMENT

Engage in a research project. Find a subject you are or can become curious about; then, to begin, ask several questions that you think your research might answer or that you want it to answer. As you explore your topic, keep in mind our discussion of the reliability of sources. To help organize your project, keep a research notebook in which you place all notes, drafts, and photocopies you may make. Your instructor may want you to submit all such materials with your final draft. And keep in mind the four potential purposes for a research paper listed at the start of this chapter: to inform, to evaluate, to argue, or to solve a problem.

SAMPLE STUDENT ESSAY

The following research essay is by Clarita Brown, a writing student at New Mexico State University (NMSU). Consider these questions as you read and then respond to Clarita's essay:

1. What is the essay's purpose? Is its intention to inform, evaluate, argue, or solve a problem?
2. Identify the essay's thesis. What assertion does it make? How effectively does the essay develop this thesis?
3. Who would be an appropriate reader for this essay? How well does Clarita address this reader?
4. How effective are the introduction and conclusion?
5. How well does Clarita use outside sources? How does she incorporate them in her essay? How reliable do they seem to be?
6. Which style manual has Clarita used in documenting the paper? Are her citations and references correctly formatted?
7. Write a paragraph in which you talk about both the strengths and the weaknesses of the paper. What's your overall assessment of this essay?

THE AMERICAN INDIAN MOVEMENT AS A COUNTERCULTURE

CLARITA BROWN

1   There are many definitions of what people consider a "counterculture" to be. If a counterculture is a group of people that goes against the normal system of society in order to voice their ideas and thoughts on changing problems in that society, then the American Indian Movement (AIM) is a strong, proud counterculture. Like the Civil Rights Movement, AIM fights against federal oppression and societal mistreatment and helps Native Americans find a sense of unity, empowerment and support. As AIM co-founder Dennis Banks put it, "AIM's position has always been to create the seed, plant the seed, develop it a little, and then move on" (Record and Hocker 21). This seed consists of unity, power, and support.

2   The American Indian Movement was founded in 1968 in Minneapolis by Dennis Banks and George Mitchell. It was a small organization that did not get any national recognition until it took several actions to let everyone know Native American struggles are not over.

3 The first event was in November, 1969, when a group of students, including some AIM members, protested on Alcatraz Island. They demanded the land be used for Indian schools, basing their demand on the "provision of an act passed on July 31,1882 (*22 Stal.*181)" (Churchill and Wall 119).

4 The second event happened in 1972 in Washington, DC, when AIM organized a protest called "The Trail of Broken Treaties" to protest unjust treatment by the government. More than 1,000 Native Americans traveled to Washington, where they took over the Bureau of Indian Affairs (BIA) headquarters for a few days. Before leaving Washington following negotiations, "the occupiers packed away twelve tons of BIA files to take back to their respective reservations" (Weyler 54). These files exposed shady connections between the BIA and some corporations and corrupt deals to take over Indian land by unscrupulous resource developers. Among the artifacts was a letter to the BIA regarding two elderly women who had been beaten to death on a Wisconsin reservation. The BIA had only filed the letter and refused to set out an investigation (Weyler 55). AIM members wanted documentation of BIA abuse, and they found it.

5 The third and most important event was a 71-day standoff at Wounded Knee, South Dakota, on the Pine Ridge Reservation. "In 1973, the federally installed regime of tribal president Richard 'Dickie' Wilson was attempting to transfer the barren but uranium-laden northwestern eighth of the reservation—an area known as the Gunnery Range—to the Interior Department" (Churchill 40). Spurred by this and by the Pine Ridge people's struggle to survive in nearly third-world conditions, AIM stepped in to give the people a voice. Confronting AIM were the FBI, the US Army, US marshals, and local law enforcement. In the end, two AIM members were killed by gunfire, AIM leaders surrendered, and the federal government proclaimed victory. But it was an empty victory, because AIM did what it set out to do, which was to give Native Americans a national voice. They became a counterculture to be dealt with.

6 AIM, like some countercultures, uses actions of protest to let people know what is wrong with the way society treats them, or in the case of Pine Ridge Reservation, how society lacks concern for Native American well-being. Pine Ridge is a third-world in the United States' backyard. People there live in shack-like homes, drink contaminated water, and try hard just to live day to day. These are only a few of the reservation's problems; in addition, "close to half of all Pine Ridge residents—including a growing number of teenagers—battle alcoholism, which contributes to high rates of suicide and Sudden Infant Death Syndrome, and an increasing incidence of abuse of the elderly" (Record and Hocker 22). People on reservations do not have the resources or money to take care of these problems, and society remains blind and does not help. AIM, like the Civil Rights Movement, tries to spread awareness of these problems to the public through protests and other actions.

7 Like all countercultures, AIM finds itself out of the mainstream society when its members decide to take up a cause and protest. What they want to do is cause change, and sometimes yelling, misconduct, and going against the societal norm form the only way to do it. As J. Milton Yinger says in *Countercultures,* "[Such actions] represent efforts to create a cultural world in which new identities can be formed or tenuous ones validated and strengthened around congenial values and norms" (38). AIM is trying to get society's attention focused on the problems Native Americans face on their reservations, and if they need to shout or even break the law, then so be it.

8 Besides the problem of getting society's attention, the United States government has unfairly treated AIM and its members, because of their strong voice. The standoff at Wounded Knee would have never escalated to a 71-day standoff or to gunfire if the government had not flexed its muscles in an attempt to show who was boss. A coun-

terculture becomes a target when it becomes a threat to the status quo, and the US government made AIM its target. Witnesses at Wounded Knee reported that the "federal army" brought automatic weapons, snipers, armored personnel carriers, and about 130,000 rounds of ammunition (Record and Hocker 17). AIM responded by fighting back with a ragtag group of individuals armed with old 30–30's. Whether coming up with their own arsenal and using it was illegal or a form of self-defense, AIM resisted and two members died.

9   From Wounded Knee came a national understanding of Native American struggles and mistreatment. Famous supporters, like Robert Redford, joined their cause. An AIM leader in the stand-off, Russell Means became an actor and has starred in major motion pictures, but still strongly and actively supports AIM. "What Wounded Knee told the world was that John Wayne hadn't killed us all [. . .]. Suddenly billions of people knew we were still alive, still resisting" (White 39).

10   Another outcome of the Wounded Knee siege was the making of the movie *Thunderheart*. This movie, set in the poor Pine Ridge Reservation, tells of AIM's cause and shows how intertribal war continued after the siege. Mysteriously, "more than sixty other American Indian Movement supporters were killed on Pine Ridge during the next thirty months" after Wounded Knee (Churchill 41). *Thunderheart*, a movie about a Native American FBI agent trying to solve these killings, captured on film the poverty of Pine Ridge and the terrible living conditions there, and it served to spread the word about AIM and the problems of Native Americans.

11   Unlike some countercultures that come and go, AIM thrives. Today there are chapters of AIM in several states, which include New Mexico, Arizona, and California. AIM is very well organized and has created specifications for its members to follow. Members are expected to follow six principles, which include requiring them to be drug and alcohol free, to fight for their cause, and to fight for as long as they can. The most important principle is the sixth, which reads, in part, "AIM is for everyone [. . .]. AIM philosophy [. . .] is that you work with the people not above the people [. . .] AIM is willing to risk their reputation even when it is unpopular at the time [. . .]. And AIM is ready to battle and risk their lives for the people" (Means par. 7). Members are not asked to pay a fee or fill out a membership card; they show their membership by becoming and remaining active in AIM.

12   AIM's sixth principle is one which mainstream society has the most difficulty understanding. It is hard to imagine that a group of people would be willing to give their lives for a cause that society looks upon blindly. But members must risk losing their jobs and even their families when they are asked to leave for a cause in any part of the United States, at any time (Means par. 7). In mainstream society the family is a key part, and someone in this society could never visualize leaving their family for a group of activists.

13   Mainstream society looks down on AIM and most countercultures because they don't see the importance of fighting for change and what one truly believes in, so AIM keeps shouting. Some people, even Native Americans, believe AIM has put their own people in danger and caused mayhem within the Native American community. But others say with AIM's help there is a sense of togetherness and power within Native American communities. Elmer Bear Eagle, a veteran of Wounded Knee, said, "What I took away from Wounded Knee 1973 was a feeling of freedom, a feeling of real pride, being here with the people, with everybody" (Record and Hocker 17). Even as a Native American not directly involved with AIM, I always feel a sense of pride come over me when I see videos of AIM members sitting in front of the BIA building with their red berets and red AIM clothing. I used to think I would not do anything like that, but now I don't know what I would do in a situation like that. I am thankful for the American

Indian Movement because they give me a voice, make me proud, and fight for a better way of life for all Native Americans in the United States.

WORKS CITED

Churchill, Ward. "A Force, Briefly, to Reckon With." *The Progressive* 61.6 (1997): 39–41. Online. *Proquest Direct.*17 July 1998 <http://lib.NMSU.EDU/resources/dbpqd.html>.

Churchill, Ward, and Jim Vander Wall. *Agents of Repression: The FBI's Secret Wars against the Black Panther Party and the American Indian Movement.* Boston: South End, 1988.

Means, Sherry. "Introduction to the American Indian Movement:101." *American Indian Movement Website.* 17 July 1998 <http://www.dickshovel.com/aim101.html>.

Record, Ian, and Anne Pearse Hocker. "A Fire That Burns: The Legacy of Wounded Knee." *Native Americas: Akwe:kon's Journal of Indigenous Issues* Spring 1998: 14–25.

Weyler, Rex. *Blood of the Land: The Government and Corporate War against the American Indian Movement.* New York: Everest, 1982.

White, Richard. "The Return of the Natives." *The New Republic* 215.2 (1996): 37–44. Online. *Proquest Direct.* 20 July 1998 <http://lib.NMSU.EDU/resources/dbpqd.html>.

Yinger, J. Milton. *Countercultures: The Promise and Peril of a World Turned Upside Down.* New York: Free, 1982.

SAMPLE STUDENT PROCESS

The essay we'll follow in our discussion of a sample student research project was written by Gardiner Rhoderick, a first-year student at NMSU. Gardiner chose a problem/solution framework for his paper, a decision that guided not only the format for the paper but his research as well.

PREWRITING

Gardiner began by jotting this very quick Bug List (see p. 431):

> no skate park in Las Cruces
> too much control—police, school
> graffiti paintovers
> no respect for artists
> too much emphasis on winning
> writing classes at 8:30 in the morning
> specified writing process—too many drafts
> too many restrictions on doing my thing

From here, he decided to write about graffiti. His interest in this topic was timely, for during the semester in which he wrote the essay, a number of articles about the Las Cruces program to paint over graffiti were published in the local paper. Gardiner framed a fairly broad statement of the problem and then responded to questions designed to help him explore the problem statement with an initial audience firmly in mind.

Problem statement: Graffiti artists are misunderstood because graffiti is associated with gang problems.

1. Who can solve the problem you're dealing with? Who has the authority or power to change things?

The general public is capable of solving the problem, but the true authority to change the problem lies in the hands of law enforcement officials.

2. What is this person's role in the problem? Did he create the problem? Or is his role one of oversight, of being responsible for, say, enforcing a policy or practice that you may argue against? Or is he a concerned individual who has no particular official involvement with the problem but might be able to influence the eventual outcome—for example, a taxpayer and a voter living in a city that is in the process of deciding how to solve the problem of traffic congestion.

The public really doesn't have a role, but is more of a victim concerning the problem.
They are more like concerned citizens who could immediately influence the outcomes of the problem.

3. What does he already know about the problem? Is he likely to see it as a problem?

They understand the basic underlying fault of the problem, but not the reasons or the motivation for it.

4. What does he need to know to take the action you think he should take?

The public needs to go through a thorough educating process to understand all the background concerning the problem.

5. How opposed is he likely to be to your solution? Why?

The acceptance of the solution is likely to be ignored, seeing as how there is a tremendous bias towards the people who partake in the problem.

RESEARCH STRATEGIES

The assignment specified that Gardiner use at least four sources to support his writing and that two of those had to be Internet sources. His final bibliography has five entries: three books and two articles he found on the Internet. Because the books were published by reputable publishers and accepted by the NMSU library, Gardiner felt there was little question of their reliability. And he decided that the Internet sources were reliable as well. Unlike many Internet articles, both of these were signed by their authors, so it would be possible to check further into their credentials as authorities on the topic of graffiti. Further, Sherri Cavan, author of "The Great Graffiti Wars of the Late 20th Century," has a home page through San Francisco State University and signs her article in this way:

Sherri Cavan, Ph.D.
Department of Sociology
San Francisco State University

These credentials show that Dr. Sherri Cavan is a university faculty member.

Initially, Gardiner might have questioned the reliability of the essay by Killian Tobin, "A Modern Perspective on Graffiti." Gardiner found it on a web site promoting graffiti, so there's a question of potential bias. The web site has as the first part of its address http://graffiti.org. The "org" portion of the address indicates that the site is sponsored by a private organization (rather than a government agency or an educational institution)—in this case, one with commercial interests, listing graffiti-related items such as videotapes for sale. Further, in promoting graffiti, the site is promoting an activity that's illegal in most, if not all, communities. As noted earlier in this chapter, Gardiner found Tobin's article by browsing the site. He settled on the article because it offered support for his position that what society needs is a new way of looking at graffiti. Further, the tone of the article is not shrill. The bulk reports on problems surrounding graffiti and how graffiti has come to be seen as less than desirable by the public. Only the last paragraph offers Tobin's opinion, but even that paragraph is written with a very controlled, scholarly tone. And the article is not only signed but also lists a 1995 copyright date. Although the article does not carry any research references, Gardiner judged it to be reliable enough to support his writing.

ROUGH DRAFT

With his research notes in hand, Gardiner wrote and then revised the following draft for an in-class peer review session:

1   For the past 20 years graffiti has been evolving into a problem of insurmountable circumstance. Scrawls and messages adorn a spot in every city in the country (maybe the world) and is costing the United States billions of dollars every year to eliminate. Whether made by the stroke of a marker or the spew of a spraycan, the marks left on dumpsters, back alleys, business walls, bathrooms, rooftops and road signs are considered by the majority of the US population to be a sign of decay and hostility.

2   Graffiti is seen as a threat to the general public. The appearance of graffiti shows signs of supposed gang activity, therefore promoting gangs, and ultimately promoting violence. Graffiti is to blame for the decrease in general property value, neighborhood deterioration, and poor business development. These consequences of graffiti are more than disturbing, but are made worse by the misconception of what graffiti actually is. The context in which the word has fallen into (and the media created) has evoked a mood of disgrace, disgust and anger among the public community.

3   Modern graffiti as we know it began in 1973 by a man who wrote "Taki 183" (his moniker and the street on which he lived) on every flat surface in New York City. His graffiti, or "tag," became somewhat of a novelty, and local New Yorkers were amused when they caught a glimpse of the moniker. He was given media coverage, an article in the New York Post, and quickly became somewhat of a celebrity. Soon, as others saw what Taki was doing, more and more graffiti began to emerge. Other doers of graffiti, or "writers" as they have come to be called, began mimicking Taki's actions. As the graffiti population increased, the diversity among the forms of graffiti did also. Simple tags gave way to calligraphic signatures. When this was out done, stylized letters began to emerge,

soon murals began to pop out all over the city of New York, and finally graffiti took its form: as a stylistic interpretation of the alphabet. Graffiti ignited across the country and the world, and a sub-culture of thousands were soon taking to the streets, armed with a spraycan.

4   The actual date of the prohibiting of graffiti is unclear. Although at first enjoyed by many, by the early eighties, graffiti suddenly became an eyesore. Abatement programs were started across the country to eliminate the problem. The media stepped in, and this is where the war on graffiti began.

5   On one hand, we have the anti-graffitist, which accounts for the majority of the population (including the media). They condemn graffiti, stereotype its members, believe in harsh punishment for offenders, and are quick to neglect the qualities inherent in graffiti.

6   On the other hand, we have a sub-culture consisting of tens of thousands of members. They embrace graffiti. They believe in the artistic merit of graffiti, but also realize the illegal aspect of it. They offer no explanation as to why they do it, and at the same time, have a hard time understanding why themselves.

7   Graffiti has been mistaken for nothing but a scrawl on a wall. Its members have been stereotyped to oblivion and their "art" has been misconstrued among the public. Writers continue to produce graffiti, no matter what the consequence, knowing that what they do is wrong. So the problem arises: How do we stop graffiti? The answer is: you don't.

8   It is a known fact that graffiti will never be eliminated completely. There will always be someone engraving a tree, writing their name in concrete, or taking to the streets. The solution to the problem of graffiti is lessening its occurrence. In order to do this, the public must be educated. Misconceptions of graffiti and its creators need to be addressed and properly cleared up. Ideas of gangs, violence, and hostility need to be dealt with as well as informing who and what writers are all about. Acceptance of the art must also be pushed. Local businesses have endorsed graffiti projects on their walls, and although completely legal, the appearance of it still scares and shocks the public. More effort must be placed on opening up the people's eye to the artistic aspect of graffiti.

9   The concept of graffiti as an accepted art form is highly radical. But so is spending billions of dollars a year to cover it up. When a balance is reached between the toleration and prohibiting of graffiti, the problem itself will decline, and so will the cost of controlling it. If graffiti goes unnoticed and no action is taken, the walls of the country will be full of graffiti, while the pocketbooks of its citizens will be empty.

One of Gardiner's classmates responded to the draft by answering the questions on a peer review sheet.

1. What problem has the writer taken on? How clearly worded is the problem statement?

Legalizing graffiti. It is not very clear. You can easily make an assumption, but it is not said in the essay. It is not: "legalize graffiti."

2. How effectively has the writer explored the problem? Consider such questions as these: Why is the problem a problem? How widespread is it? Who is affected by it? What is its impact?

The writer explores the problem well, however, you need a few more details, figures, and etc., how much does it cost to cover graffiti, how much does it cost to have police take care of taggers, how many cops are on task forces? What about laws that say residents must clean-up graffiti w/in two weeks of it being there? How much property is affected? How many homes, businesses, and other buildings?

3. What solution or solutions does the writer offer? How clearly stated is the essay's thesis, that is, the solution? Has the writer cast it as an argumentative thesis? If not, make suggestions for revision.

How will you educate people about graffiti? How can you prove graffiti does not promote violence and gang activity? You need to state your thesis a lot more clearly.

4. What support has the writer offered for the solution? How effective is this support? Are you convinced that the solution is feasible or workable?

You need to show how an educated community could deal with and understand graffiti. Is education the only solution or just a start?

5. Who is the reader for this essay; what audience has the writer chosen? How effectively has the writer addressed that reader's potential concerns? What other audience concerns can you identify that the writer has either chosen to ignore or simply didn't know should be addressed? Make specific suggestions for revision.

I feel the reader is already involved with graffiti. You need to work on addressing those who know very little of graffiti. Show how you can save money and raise property values with the art work being displayed in the neighborhood. Maybe discuss designated tagging areas or even tagging licenses. You may also want to explore the tagger's view of his art a little more.

6. Pay particular attention to each paragraph's development. Identify the topic sentence for each paragraph. How does that topic sentence support or develop either the problem or solution section of the paper? How effectively does each paragraph support or develop its topic sentence? Make specific suggestions for revision.

The topic sentences are very good. However, there needs to be more support. In ¶4, how was it enjoyed? What made it an eyesore? It is just like that throughout the essay.

7. How many sources has the writer used? Are these documented correctly? To what extent has the writer incorporated and introduced quoted material smoothly and effectively? Make specific suggestions for revision.

Sources are not clearly documented. There are not many quotes. You may want to look at local graffiti—the mural across from Baskin Robbins.

Gardiner also had a conference on the draft with Bill, his instructor, who raised the following points:

1. Where are your sources? Remember that you have to include them, introduce any quoted material, and then document them correctly. I'm really concerned about this, because your draft doesn't show any notations or references at all.
2. Can you smooth out the introduction a bit? You make it seem that graffiti is a very recent phenomenon, but it's been around just about forever.

3. 2nd ¶—this seems out of place. You may want either to move it somewhere else in the paper or just delete it altogether. What does it add?
4. Taki ¶—opening sentence seems too broad and sweeping to me. This paragraph is one, by the way, that must be documented, because it contains specific materials that you took from somewhere—where?
5. You make a lot of unsupported assertions in this paper. The best way to strengthen these is to provide material from sources. Here's an example: you say at one point (¶7) that graffiti art has been "misconstrued" among the public. Why not quote somebody on this? Look at the source you're using about Denver's attempts to stamp out graffiti.

   Overall, if you're going to convince a reader like me that there's a value in certain styles of graffiti and that it's not all gang-related, you need to define terms more clearly so that I can understand what you mean by the kind of graffiti we as a society ought to value as legitimate art. A final note—what title will you give this piece?

After reviewing both his classmate's and Bill's comments, Gardiner wrote this summary assessment of the draft, focusing on what he thought worked well and what needed more work:

> The purpose of this essay is to help educate those that see graffiti as a harmful crime done out of violence. My paper goes into the explanation of why graffiti exists, why some do it, and what it should be seen as. The essay has a basic, overall strong-point. That is its ability to bring in the average Joe of sorts, those that want to see graffiti abolished, and suddenly realize the essay is pro-graffiti, although still addressing the issues that are pertinent to them. The work serves as more of an educational tool. It informs those who are unclear about the aspects of graffiti of the false bias they are more than familiar with. The language is intended for a mature audience, mostly because this is the audience that needs to make the difference, or rather, the change. The conclusion seems the most weak to me. Next time, I plan on developing a smoother, more "resolving" type of ending. I feel the conclusion ends too abruptly. And obviously I have to do the sources thing.

Gardiner also wrote a second, more focused audience analysis.

AUDIENCE ANALYSIS 2

1. What do you want your readers to understand or gain from reading your paper?

I would like my readers to take what I've said into consideration and thoroughly comprehend the aspects of graffiti which are commendable and should be given at least some form of acceptance.

2. What attitudes are your readers likely to have toward your topic? What aspects of that attitude have you addressed in your paper?

Most readers will have an attitude of negativity towards the topic. Maybe not so much with the ideas the essay addresses, but with the problem we're dealing with in general. I have tried to include the main reason for the bias in the essay, as well as sharing new information that they might not have known.

3. What do your readers already know about your topic? What do they need to know?

The reader already understands the basic principle behind the problem. What they need to know is the separation between the two forms of graffiti, understanding the artistic value of true graffiti, and learning about the bias that they themselves practice.

4. What questions are your readers likely to have about your topic? How effectively have you answered them?

I feel that the questions they would ask are far and few in number. This problem deals with more of informing what the people have never heard of.

5. What particular action do you want your readers to take, if any? Is your writing compelling enough to make them want to take this action? Why or why not?

I would like my readers to open their minds a little more and be willing to accept graffiti for its artistic merit. I feel that no matter what kind of motivation my paper has, people care so little about the problem, or listening to solutions, that any attempt would be in vain.

6. Is there any part of your paper that may make your readers reject your thinking? If so, how effectively have you prepared them for this material?

I should hope not.

7. Is there any aspect of your paper that is likely to surprise your readers? If so, does this surprise serve your purpose? If not, how may you more effectively prepare your readers for this material?

I would hope the fact that I am not looking for legalization of graffiti would cause somewhat of a surprise. In a reflective way it serves a purpose, but not in dealing with the situation.

With all this advice and planning at work, Gardiner produced the draft that follows. As you read it, consider the same questions you used in responding to Clarita's essay, paying special attention to the questions about a thesis statement, its support, and the use of outside sources.

FINAL DRAFT

YES, IT'S GRAFFITI, BUT IS IT ART?

GARDINER RHODERICK

1   The history of graffiti is a long one. Petroglyphs carved in rock and figures painted on the walls of caves stand as reminders that ever since humans learned that they could inscribe something on a wall, somebody has had the desire to leave his mark. Today these marks—graffiti—have evolved into a problem of insurmountable circumstance. Scrawls and messages adorn every city in the country and cost the United States billions of dollars every year to eliminate, four billion in 1995 alone (Walsh, 1996). Whether made by the stroke of a marker or the spew of a spray can, the marks left on dumpsters, back alleys, business walls, bathrooms, rooftops and road signs are considered by the majority of the United States population to be a sign of decay and hostility.

2   Modern graffiti emerged in the late 1960s or early 1970s by people like "Taki 183" (his moniker and the street on which he lived). "Taki 183" appeared on nearly every flat surface in New York City. Taki's graffiti, or "tag," became somewhat of a novelty, and local New Yorkers were amused when they caught a glimpse of the moniker. He was given media coverage, was the focus of an article in the *New York Times,* and quickly became somewhat of a celebrity. Soon, as others saw what Taki was doing, more and more graffiti began to emerge. Other perpetrators of graffiti, or "writers" as they have come to be called, began mimicking Taki's actions.

3   As the number of graffiti writers increased, the forms of graffiti became diverse. Simple tags gave way to calligraphic signatures. When writers became bored with simple tags, stylized letters began to emerge. These consisted of two-dimensional letters, usually filled with two to three different colors. Eventually, they grew into complex multi-colored masterpieces, and soon murals began to pop out all over the city of New York. Graffiti became a form of rebellious self-expression, a way for anyone to say "I'm here and I count." The graffiti artist as rebel held great appeal, and a sub-culture of thousands soon took to the streets, armed with spray cans, creating street art.

4   Art and popular culture scholars began to analyze and discuss graffiti in the context of street art. In 1975, Robert Sommer classified street art as:

> Professional art. Art legally introduced into a public place.
> Folk art. Created by nonprofessionals according to a traditional pattern to be displayed in their own spaces, e.g., harvest figures or a creche.
> Naive art. Created by nonprofessionals according to individual inclination to be displayed in their own places.
> People's art. Anonymous art in a public space.
> Chance art. The unintended creation of an attractive display, e.g., paint peeling on a building wall which reveals interesting hues and textures, or the accidental formation of rocks at Delaware Water Gap that resembles an Indian head.
> Graffiti. Inscriptions on rocks, walls, etc. Most graffiti are not art. (p. 13)

People's art and graffiti are both "extralegal" (Sommer, 1975, p. 15) and are often confused. Tobin defines "artistic graffiti" as a new art form that "is a modern day offspring of traditional graffiti that has elevated itself from just scrawling words or phrases on a wall, to a complex artistic form of personal expression" (par. 1). Most people, however, do not make this distinction, and the confusion concerning graffiti begins here.

5   Graffiti has been mistaken for nothing but a scrawl on a wall. Its writers have been stereotyped to oblivion as society's outcasts (gangsters and dopers), and their art has been misconstrued among the public. Supposedly, graffiti shows signs of gang activity, therefore promoting gangs, and ultimately promoting violence. The context which the word has fallen into (and the media created) has evoked a mood of disgrace, disgust and anger among the public.

6   The actual date of the prohibiting of graffiti is unclear. Although at first enjoyed by many, by the early eighties, graffiti had become an eyesore. Abatement programs were started across the country to eliminate the problem. The media stepped in, correlating modern graffiti with gang members and violent overtones. News stories focused on costs and property damage, never once revealing the essence of artistic graffiti, and this is where the war on graffiti began.

7   Typical of anti-graffiti programs was one begun in Denver, Colorado, during the 1980s. It involved an extensive article and ad campaign to alert Denver's citizens of the graffiti blighting their city. Farrell (1993) characterizes this campaign as biased and aggressive:

To maximize the sense of threat and violation, verbs such as "attack," "destroy," and "rob" are frequently paired with "graffiti vandal" and "graffiti vandalism." In a public service announcement aired on local television, Mayor Frederico Peña claims that "each day the citizens of Denver are being robbed, robbed by graffiti vandalism on their public and private property" (*In the Public Eye*, 1989). . . . Significantly, such phrasing implies not only violent assault, but an aggressive intentionality on the part of the "graffiti vandal," who doesn't "write" or "paint," but "attacks" and "robs." (p. 138)

Because most people associate it with gang activity, graffiti has been greatly misunderstood. And the war only continues.

8   On the one hand, we have the anti-graffitist, which accounts for the majority of the population (including the media). They condemn graffiti, stereotype its members, believe in harsh punishment for offenders, and are quick to ignore the qualities inherent in graffiti. Anti-graffitists have been known to respond violently. Dr. Sherri Cavan, a sociologist at San Francisco State University, reports that "a youthful tagger [was] shot and killed by an armed citizen intent on protecting public property from enemy attack. The Los Angeles County district attorney's office declined to file charges against the gunman . . . " (par. 14).

9   On the other hand, we have a sub-culture that Cavan calls the "aerosol nation" (par. 3) consisting of tens of thousands of members. They embrace graffiti. They believe in the artistic merits of graffiti, but also realize the illegal aspect of it. They offer no explanation as to why they do it, and at the same time, have a hard time understanding why themselves. Writers continue to produce graffiti, no matter what the consequence, knowing that what they do is wrong. So the problem arises: How do we stop graffiti? The answer: we don't.

10   Graffiti will never be eliminated. Someone will always engrave a tree, write his name in concrete, or use a spray can to mark the streets. The solution to the problem is not legalization. Nor is it a complete lockdown on graffiti and its perpetrators. The solution is tied to how artistic graffiti is defined. Misconceptions of artistic graffiti and its creators need to be addressed and properly cleared up, so the public must be educated about it. Ideas of gangs, violence, and hostility need to be dealt with, as well as informing who and what writers are all about. Acceptance of this art form must also be pushed. Local businesses have endorsed graffiti projects on their walls, but, although completely legal, the appearance of graffiti on business-sponsored walls still scares and shocks the public. More effort must be placed on opening up the people's eye to the artistic aspect of graffiti.

11   The first step in keeping the streets clean is making a delineation between what artistic graffiti actually is and isn't. A simple marking, made with a pen, marker, or spray paint, has been the traditional definition of graffiti for years. What hasn't been given attention is the new strand of artistic graffiti we have today. This complex and intricate style of painting has never been addressed, and most have no idea it exists. This is why, when we speak in terms of graffiti, many have their mind made up, quickly taking a solid stance on the issue. This is where the problem of an uninformed society comes into play.

12   The second step is a tolerance of sorts. Those who continue to scar the streets, making an ugly mess for the public to see, are more than worthy of being the target of mainstream America. Their useless marks do nothing but create an eyesore, and the activities of these individuals should be stopped. What should be tolerated (perhaps not legalized, but at least tolerated) is the unprecedented artistic version of graffiti. Although technically violating the law, the motives and skill behind the current movement is in no way lethal, in no way a direct sign of hostility, in no way a gang-instigated crime.

13   Contrary to popular belief, the average graffiti artist comes from a white middle-to upper-middle-class family. Their ages range between twelve and thirty years old, and they are never involved in gangs or gang violence (Walsh, 1996, p. 10). They do what they do, not to instill fear, but to inform the public, maybe as indirectly as possible, of the problems they have experienced in their upbringing and culture. Even though some may be politically motivated, while others are in it for themselves, their common goal is to share what they create with the rest of the world. They retreat to dilapidated urban areas, the forgotten areas of society, and add life with bold color, design, and complexity. Unfortunately, their efforts are usually unnoticed or, when noticed, misunderstood, leaving viewers with nothing but a negative response. The murals that can take hours on end to produce are all too quickly blotted out in a matter of minutes.

14   Even when graffiti makes a positive contribution to society, authorities work to stamp it out. A large mural (a piece of "people's art" or "artistic graffiti") painted on a drugstore wall by a group of art students under the direction of their teachers was almost immediately "painted over by the building owner as a 'routine maintenance procedure' " (Sommer, 1975, p. 94). Farrell (1993) tells of a more troublesome incident in Denver. In 1989, an AIDS outreach group had commissioned a group of Denver's more famous graffiti artists to paint a series of murals about AIDS prevention measures, including a hotline number. The positive impact was immediate as officials saw a marked increase in the number of calls to the hotline. These murals were promptly attacked by anti-graffitists, and officials declared them signs, not art, that were illegal because the artists did not have permits to paint them. The ploy worked, and the murals were painted over (pp. 182–183). People who see artistic graffiti as non-art need to take another look.

15   The third step is to push the acceptance of artistic graffiti. More businesses using it as a type of advertising or decoration will help the public come to accept and enjoy it. Cities have found that if they endorse a city-sponsored wall, "tagger" graffiti declines dramatically. Sommer (1975) cites several examples of the respect artistic graffiti has enjoyed:

> Artist Arnold Belkin painted a large mural for a playground in the Hell's Kitchen of New York City. Belkin was able to develop a large amount of community support for the mural; a year afterward, there was not a single extraneous spot, line or number defacing the mural. . . . Jerry and Salla Romotsky, an artist-writer team in Los Angeles who have followed the activities of Chicano street gangs in decorating neighborhood walls, found that gangs rarely disturb actual works of art. While many barrio walls have literally been covered with script, genuine murals have been spared. There have been a few instances where murals have been hit, but these are the exceptions rather than the rule. (pp. 21–22)

Walls decorated with artistic graffiti are respected and devoid of useless scribbles. The more artistic graffiti is seen in a dignified manner, well-done and completed, the more the public will begin to understand what it really is: art.

16   The concept of graffiti as an accepted art form is highly radical. But so is spending billions of dollars a year to cover it up. When a balance is reached between tolerating artistic graffiti and prohibiting tagging, the problem itself will decline, and so will the cost of controlling it. Art needs to be valued, not painted over because of unwarranted fear of gangs and drug dealers.

REFERENCES

Cavan, S. The great graffiti wars of the late 20th century. Retrieved April 14, 1998 from the World Wide Web: http://userwww.sfsu.edu/~kazbeki/grafwars.html

Farrell, J. (1993). *Crimes of style: Urban graffiti and the politics of criminality.* New York: Garland.

Sommer, R. (1975). *Street art.* New York: Links Books.

Tobin, K. (1995). "A modern perspective on graffiti." 1995. *Art crimes: The writing on the wall.* S. Farrell and B. Webb (Eds.). Retrieved April 14, 1998 from the World Wide Web: http://graffiti.org/faq/tobin.html

Walsh, M. (1996). *Graffito.* Berkeley, CA: North Atlantic Books.

Checklist: Critiquing a Research Essay

1. What is the purpose of this research essay—to inform, evaluate, argue, or solve a problem?

2. What is the thesis? How effectively does it fulfill the purpose you identified above?

3. Who is the intended audience? At what points in the essay is the reader likely to disagree with the writer? How effectively has the writer anticipated and addressed those disagreements? Are there any places in the essay that are likely to surprise the reader? If so, how well has the writer prepared the reader for them?

4. How does the paper begin? What did the writer intend the introduction to do, specifically? How effective is the introduction in identifying the topic, establishing the writer's stance or position on it, and bringing the reader into the paper?

5. What support is offered for the thesis? In what order? How convincing are the examples, statistics, illustrations, and other kinds of support? How appropriate is the support for the audience?

6. How appropriate for the reader is the language used in the paper? Is it too formal? Too colloquial? How appropriate is it for the subject?

7. How does the essay end? What did the writer intend the conclusion to do, specifically? How effectively does it close or round out the essay?

8. What is the essay's title? How effectively does it represent the paper to the reader? How appropriate is it for the topic?

9. Which style manual has the writer used? Are outside sources used and documented correctly? How effectively are materials from sources introduced? How effectively is information (e.g., quotations and summaries) from those sources integrated into the text?

10. Does the paper adhere to conventions of usage, mechanics, and format? Correct any errors you find.

PART Four

Special Writing Tasks

At first glance, the two chapters in this unit may seem to be very different. Chapter 13 offers instruction in in-class writing, whereas Chapter 14 suggests ways to refine writing and showcase it in a portfolio. The hurried, information-packed writing you do when you are attemping to show a teacher what you have learned about a subject might seem diametrically opposed to the leisurely and reflective writing you do when revising, polishing, and reflecting on your works in the process of assembling a writing portfolio. From another perspective, however, these types of writing share a very important similarity: They involve assessment.

WRITING AND ASSESSING

Writing and assessing are almost inseparable. Every time we put words on paper, we are inviting evaluation or criticism. But the more we come to think of writing as a process, the more we can push that kind of assessment into the background. As we do so, we move from a one-sided view in which writing is seen as a product to be assessed, or judged, to a broader perspective that includes the role writing can play in helping us become assessors or evaluators.

ASSESSMENT VIA ESSAY EXAMS   The first chapter in this part deals with a type of writing that many students dread—the essay examination. We have often heard arguments (from both students and teachers) against this type of writing. They suggest that if a teacher uses students' writing *only* to find out whether they have learned the course material, no *real* writing has been done. Such arguments often characterize the essay exam as an exercise in which students are asked to regurgitate information given by a teacher rather than to do any real thinking (or composing). Those who hold this view often advocate that essay exams be replaced by "objective" tests that measure what students know but inflict far less pain on teachers and students.

We will answer these arguments in some detail in Chapter 13. For now, we focus on one of the chief benefits of the essay exam: It allows students to use writing to express themselves. Students literally answer questions in their own words. In doing so, they connect things in ways that show their understanding of the subject matter at hand. It makes an important difference whether a writer says

> Japan bombed Pearl Harbor, and the United States declared war on Japan immediately.

or

> Because Japan bombed Pearl Harbor, the United States declared war on Japan.

The second sentence makes a stronger causal link. As another example, consider the following two sentences having to do with slavery and the U.S. Civil War:

> The Civil War was about slavery.

or

> The Civil War cannot be discussed without reference to the question of slavery.

The second sentence suggests that the writer understands the complexity of the connection between slavery and that war, an understanding that is not evident in the first sentence.

Our claim here, then, is that the writing done on essay exams allows a type of assessment that can be achieved in no other way. An objective test can assess whether a student has learned facts and rote definitions. However, if teachers want to assess students' grasp of ideas and concepts, they must have them write essays, since ideas and concepts are not reducible to the types of words and phrases used in objective tests.

ASSESSMENT VIA PORTFOLIOS   In Chapter 7, we examined ways to use writing as a means of forming and expressing value judgments. In Chapter 14, we will explore another use for writing, as a tool for assessing writing. At first glance, this may seem strange—using writing to assess writing—but when you think about it, it isn't. In the reflective essay you will write for the portfolio assignment, you will find it very useful to engage in written conversation with yourself in which you identify (and exemplify) your strengths, weaknesses, and progress as a writer. Of course, your teacher will probably use your reflective essay and the other writing in your portfolio as a means of assessing or evaluating your work in this course. Although you may dread this kind of assessment and wish it weren't necessary, it is. The good news is that the portfolio allows your teacher to see your growth as a writer in a much fuller sense than she could if she assessed your work only on the basis of the several finished products you produced during the course of the semester. A portfolio also allows your teacher to take into consideration your assessment of your own work.

WRITING BEYOND THIS COURSE

The title of this part is "Special Writing Tasks." What makes them "special" is that they prepare you in ways the other writing assignments in this text do not for specific types of writing you will do beyond this course. Writing for essay exams is required in many university courses. However, you will no doubt find that this type of on-demand writing does not disappear when you complete your college education. It is hard to imagine a profession that does not require the ability to put thoughts together in writing under time constraints. Whether you are an attorney, an architect, a biologist, or a nurse, you will have to report in writing what you know about many crucial situations. Likewise, a writing portfolio will prove useful to many of you in getting your first job and/or in moving from one job to another. Thus, the special writing tasks in the following chapters should prove useful to you now and throughout your professional life.

You will likely take many essay examinations in your college career. Given the amount of time and effort these essays require, you may wonder why so many teachers continue to make them an integral part of their examinations. They do so because they believe preparing for and writing essays fosters a different kind of learning than does objective testing. Consider your own reaction to essay examinations. How does it change your behavior in a classroom when a teacher informs you that a test, or at least a part of a test, will be an essay? As teachers who give essay examinations in our language and literature classes, we hope these exams encourage students to take notes in class, read and take notes on the assigned readings, and, in general, prepare themselves to explain and reflect on the course materials. It is one thing to know that you will be responsible for determining which item in a list of potential causes of World War I should be excluded (in a multiple-choice test); it is quite another to know that you could be asked to write an essay in which you discuss the historical period in question.

What difference, you may ask, does it make how I am tested if the result is to ensure that I know the causes of World War I? That is a good question. In a sense, the rest of this chapter will serve as our complete answer to it. But let's begin with a brief answer first.

As we've stressed throughout this text, writing is a powerful learning tool. In preparing for an exam, you should write summaries and paraphrases, which

Essay Examinations

C H A P T E R 13

means that you'll translate information you have been given into your own words. In doing so, you'll come to know that information in a way that you would not if you were preparing for a multiple-choice test, because essay exams require you to interact with and think about the information you have been given and thereby add depth to your learning.

To explore this point more fully, let's think about what happens when we listen to a set of directions for finding a place in a rather large city. We know we should write them down, but sometimes we aren't able to do so. What happens? What happens is that after two or three turns, we find that we can't play back (that is, "say back") the directions we have been given. In effect, we didn't learn the material. However, if someone were to give us a test in which they listed the various roads we would need to take to get to the location, we might well be able to recognize the roads that were mentioned and to label as wrong any roads that were not mentioned. That knowledge, however, will not get us to our location.

But what if we had drawn a map at the time we were given the directions? Even if we mislaid that map, the chances of our getting to the right place would increase if we had taken the time to draw it. In a sense, we would have imprinted the map (with various relationships among the roads we would be traveling) in our minds as we were drawing it. When we write things down (or draw pictures that represent relationships), we come to own that information in ways that we do not otherwise.

We believe there is a similar process at work when writing is used in academic settings. Think of the hypothetical history course we referred to. If you have memorized the list of causes of World War I, you will be able to list them on an objective test or exclude a wrong answer on a multiple-choice test. However, an essay examination on this material might ask you to discuss why most historians agree that one event was a cause of the war, but many disagree about the cause/effect relationship between another event and the war. You wouldn't be well prepared for such an examination if all you had done was memorize a list of causes. Now, suppose a year or two later you are studying the history of art during the pre–World War I period. If you studied for an essay examination in your previous history class and thus had to construct your own "map" of that historical period, you may well have a backdrop of historical information on which to build your new knowledge about the art movements of this period. A listing of the causes of World War I, even if you remembered the list, would likely be of little value to you in this new course of study.

If this were the only benefit of writing essay examinations, it would be a significant one, but there is more. Writing actually encourages you to think for yourself. We have been talking about the causes of World War I as if there were some official list of these causes in history books. Of course, that is not the case. Every historian of the period has his own list of causes. Historians will certainly agree on many of the causes, but they will disagree on various other causes, and even when they do agree on items in the list, they will differ as to the relative importance they assign these causes. As you become an active learner in your history class, you will read what the writers of your texts have to say on the matter, you will listen to the comments of your teacher, and, if you are truly interested in the subject, you may do other reading on your own. After engaging in this type of learning, you may actually be excited by the prospect of answering an essay question that asks you to evaluate potential causes of this war. Your study of this subject and the actual writing of this essay will allow you to develop your own insights about this subject. In such a situation, your writing will allow you to enter into the process by which knowledge is made rather than stand outside as a consumer of others' writing.

PACKAGING THE PROCESS

At the outset of this chapter, we need to say a bit about the type of writing required in essay examinations, as compared with the writing we have been encouraging you to do to this point. From the beginning of this text, we have emphasized writing as process. Although there is no correct number of drafts that a piece of writing should go through and no prescribed amount of time that should elapse between the beginning and completion of that writing, we have encouraged you to engage in activities that require you to take more, rather than less, time in your writing process. In Chapter 1, we suggested various ways of exploring your topics and finding different angles from which to approach topics. In Chapter 3, we offered advice on ways to improve your writing by reseeing it after getting it on the page. As its name makes clear, however, the essay examination does not allow you the luxury of reflecting on what you have said and reconceptualizing your essay. But that does not mean that you cannot bring a process approach to essay-exam writing. In fact, if anything, your writing process in this situation is even more important than in other, less stressful writing situations.

The process of writing an essay examination begins long before you sit down to write it. Your approach to a course requiring essay examinations is a part of this process. As you read materials for this course and as you attend class sessions, you should begin reflecting on the issues being introduced in the course. As you do, you should ask yourself what kinds of information your teacher stresses. Your teacher will have her own ways of signaling what are particularly significant ideas. The headings in your textbook should also give you insight into the writer's judgments as to what is important and how important concepts are linked to each other. You will remember that Chapter 4 introduced dialogue notes as a way of reading materials actively. You may find this reading strategy particularly helpful as you reflect on the materials in your texts and on the class notes you take. At first, it may seem strange to think about using your classroom notes as a springboard to writing; when you think about it, however, you may see how your classroom notes can become a kind of text you can explore as you seek to understand the major concepts being presented in class.

Assuming that you have developed a basic understanding of the course material, you are ready to write the essay exam. As we noted, you will benefit greatly by developing a process approach to this type of writing. The in-class process begins with careful reading of the questions to determine *what* the teacher wants in your answer and *how* you may best structure your response. Once you have decided what is being asked and how you want to structure your answer, you can construct a thesis sentence and an outline for your essay. Then, *and only then*, should you begin writing your essay.

We cannot emphasize this last point too strongly. There are important differences between in-class writing and out-of-class writing. Some writers may find it helpful to begin writing out-of-class assignments before they have a clear idea of what information will be included. Writers who are willing and able to discard major portions of a rough draft may use this kind of freewriting to help them find what they want to say. There is no time, however, for such extensive prewriting in an essay examination. Although you may usually feel free to cross out and write over a line here and there, to polish your writing by striking over a word and inserting a more precise one, and to make any editorial changes you have time for, you probably will not have time to reconceptualize your essay once you have begun. You are committed to following the course that you charted before beginning to write the essay.

It is crucial, as you write your essay, that you have confidence in your plan; there is no time for wondering whether you have read the question correctly and whether the material you are offering later in the answer is connected to material earlier in the answer. To put it positively, if you have a clear sense of where you are heading in an essay and how the various parts of the answer fit together to fulfill the requirements of the assignment, you will find that you can produce a reasonably well-developed answer in a short time. Therefore, you can afford to take the time you need at the beginning to plan your essay. It isn't possible to say just how much time you should take for planning, but a rule of thumb we have found useful is to allow around one-fourth of your time for planning. If you have 15 minutes for an essay, you can afford 3 or 4 minutes for planning; a 30 minute period may allow for 7 or 8 minutes of planning; and with an hour, you may plan for up to 15 minutes. Your planning times may vary, but if you are taking considerably more or less than one-fourth of your time for planning, you may benefit by attempting to move closer to this guideline.

Writing Strategy

SUMMARY OF THE ESSAY-EXAM PROCESS

Before the Exam

1. Take careful notes on readings, class lectures, and class discussions. Review them daily.

2. Use your notes from class and readings as springboards for entries in your dialogue notebook. In this notebook, you might also attempt to devise and answer questions your teacher could ask on an exam.

   During the Exam

3. Read the exam question carefully, determining *what* type of information the teacher is asking for and *how* you can structure your essay.
4. Construct a thesis for your essay.
5. Outline your essay.
6. Write the essay.
7. Reread the essay, if there is time, making local corrections.

PLANNING YOUR ESSAY'S CONTENT

Most teachers do not set out to write a specific type of essay question. However, nearly all of the questions we have seen in college classroom situations make use of one or more of the following four processes: summary, synthesis, evaluation, and interpretation. Both summary and synthesis are ways of informing a reader about a given topic. Evaluation keeps the focus on the subject but also introduces the writer's value judgments concerning that subject. And interpretation focuses on the meaning a writer finds in a subject. It is no accident that these four processes are closely related to Chapters 6 through 8 in Part Two, which spotlight the subject. On rare occasions, teachers may offer you the opportunity to make a personal response to course material (with a focus on you as writer) or ask you to write a persuasive essay (which spotlights a reader's reaction to what you have to say about the subject). In most essay-examination situations, however, teachers will want you to focus on the subject in question.

For purposes of discussion, we will treat each of the four processes separately. But, as we shall see later, many, if not most, of the essays you'll encounter in actual exam situations will combine two or more of them.

SUMMARY

On the surface, summary would seem to be no more than saying back to the teacher what the teacher or a source such as a textbook has said. It is not that simple, however. In summarizing, you are responsible for putting other people's thoughts into your own words. But summary is made more difficult by the need for brevity. Unlike a paraphrase, which allows you the luxury of a word-for-word translation, summary requires you to put others' ideas into your own words and to condense their thoughts into a form that will suit your purposes without misrepresenting what they have said. Deciding what to include and what to leave out requires mastery of your source. (For more on summary, see pp. 106–108 in Chapter 4.)

Here are examples of essay-exam questions that ask students for summaries:

1. According to the writers of our textbook, what is the evidence that the language used by animals (even when humans work with animals extensively) is different in kind (not just in degree) from human language?

2. What is a linguistic universal? What are some examples of linguistic universals? Why is the concept of linguistic universal important to modern grammarians like Noam Chomsky?

3. What is whole language instruction? Why do the authors of our textbook oppose it?

4. In class we talked about several "first generation" modern dancers. Write a brief discussion of two of these. Be sure to talk about what these dancers see as the purpose of dance and how they view the relationship between dance and musical accompaniment.

SAMPLE SUMMARY ESSAY

The following essay was written by a professor of dance and theatre at the University of North Carolina at Charlotte (UNC–Charlotte) as a sample for the students in her introductory dance classes. It answers question 4 above.

Two of the most important early modern dancers were Isadora Duncan, an American dancer, and Mary Wigman, a German dancer. Duncan helped establish a new kind of dance by means of her artistic daring. She was the first to express the inner feelings of human beings without the artifices, the contrived invention, the traditional methods and the vocabularies used in the ballet. Duncan's movement allowed the natural gestures of the body, freed from acrobatic exaggeration, to express themselves from an inner compulsion. She did not use the traditional costume of the ballet, but instead danced barefooted in a simple Greek-style tunic. She did not interpret or visualize the music in movement, but used music as the impetus to express the feelings that came from her soul, where (she believed) movement had its origins.

In Germany, Mary Wigman developed a form of modern dance influenced by Dolcroze and Rudolph von Laban. Her dances were introspective. She was determined to free dance from its bondage with music and often danced with no musical accompaniment at all. She felt that the dance should determine its own structural form; thus she often had music composed to fit her dances. She was very concerned with the concept of "space." She did not believe that dancers should ever see themselves as working in a vacuum; rather, they should see the space around them as symbolic of the human environment. Wigman rejected no movements, however odd or superficially ugly, if she felt they expressed what she wanted to communicate.

Duncan and Wigman, then, contributed much to the development of modern dance. Both dancers helped to free dance from its attachment to outward form—preferring to see it as arising from meaning that came from within the dancer—and both saw music as serving the needs of dance.

COMMENTARY   This sample provides the information the question asks for, and it does so in the terms used in the question—what the dancers saw as *the purpose of dance* and the dancers' views of *the relationship between dance and musical accompaniment*. Note also that the essay begins with a very brief, one-sentence preview of the content and ends with a brief summary that captures the similarities between the contributions of these dancers. The simple structure reflects the question, which asks for a discussion of two dancers. The writer provides a paragraph of information on each dancer and then closes the essay with a paragraph describing the two dancers' impact on modern dance.

SYNTHESIS

Often a teacher will ask you to draw together and put into your own words other people's thoughts, and to do so in a condensed form. The teacher who asks you to synthesize two different sources assumes that although the sources may have differing things to say about a subject, an astute reader can see useful ways of bringing them together.

Synthesis does not have to be restricted to discussion of information that comes from sources, however. Any question that asks you to look at two or more things from a perspective that brings them together is calling for synthesis. For example, question 7 below asks the essay writer to consider Chomsky's theory of language development and Piaget's theory of language development from the perspective of language theory itself. In doing so, it requires synthesis as the writer sorts through the various issues involved in language development and compares and contrasts the approaches of these two philosophers. Likewise, question 5 asks the writer to build a frame that will help bring together—perhaps by means of comparison and contrast—the various problems European countries face today. The question could have called for a simple listing of countries' individual problems; however, in asking for a discussion of the various "types" of problems the countries face, the question calls for a synthesis.

These essay-exam questions ask for synthesis:

5. According to the various articles we have read on the United Kingdom, France, Spain, and Germany, what are the major types of problems that modern-day Europe must contend with? Illustrate these types by discussing specific problems in individual European countries.
6. Edelman talks about politics being a series of pictures from which a pattern emerges or on which a pattern is imposed. Would Hedrick Smith ("The Image Game") agree or disagree with Edelman? Be specific in justifying your answer.
7. In what ways do Noam Chomsky and Jean Piaget seem to agree about language development in humans? What would seem to be important areas of disagreement between the two?

SAMPLE SYNTHESIS ESSAY

The following essay was constructed by Ron Lunsford from several written in response to question 7 above. He uses it as a model for students in his Introduction to Language course.

Noam Chomsky and Jean Piaget do agree about several aspects of how humans develop their language abilities; however, there is a crucial difference in their theories about language development. Let's look at similarities first. Both Chomsky and Piaget recognize the importance of nature in the development of speech. Both men believe that humans are born with innate structures in the brain that allow for language development. Just as a bird has an instinct for how to build a nest, a human is born with innate abilities when it comes to language. Here Chomsky and Piaget could be contrasted with the most extreme behavioristic position (as explained by Skinner in *Verbal Behavior*), in which the human being is seen as a *tabula rasa,* or blank slate, when it comes to language. While they discount this behavioristic position, Chomsky and Piaget would agree with Skinner (and with each other) that nurture plays a role in language development. Both would point to feral children as examples of the importance of one's environment and would agree that young children must have some interaction with speakers of language if they are to develop their own abilities to speak. However, when we get to the exact role that this interaction plays and to what is going on in the brain of the child as it develops its language ability, we see important differences between the theories of Chomsky and Piaget. Piaget agreed with some aspects of the behaviorists' stimulus-response approach to learning. Chomsky does not believe in language learning per se. Rather, he believes that a child "grows" his language abilities much like a tree grows from a seed. Except in those matters that are language specific, the child does not try various language moves and see what the responses to those moves are. A bird does not "learn" how to collect twigs for a nest; it knows that instinctively. Similarly, the human child knows which moves are possible in language and which are not. This leads to two other very important differences between Chomsky and Piaget. Chomsky believes that there is likely a specific language learning component in the brain—what he has sometimes referred to as a language organ. Piaget subscribed to a much more general learning mechanism in which various abilities are developed. Chomsky also believes in a universal grammar, which captures the ways in which all human languages are alike. The shape of the language organ would be determined by this universal grammar. Piaget's theories did not include such a grammar. Thus, we can see that while there are some important similarities between the theories of Chomsky and Piaget, when it comes to language development, their differences are striking—since Chomsky does not really believe that language is learned.

COMMENTARY   Since Ron put together the best parts of several good essays he received, this sample is likely a more complete answer than most teachers would require in an essay examination. However, it does illustrate some characteristics that all teachers will be looking for in questions that ask for a synthesis. Since a synthesis is a blending together, it will include both likenesses and differences. Note that this sample essay devotes approximately equal time to the ways in which Chomsky and Piaget are alike and the ways in which they differ. These comparisons and contrasts provide the basic structure of the essay, as the introduction (the first sentence) announces. Note the ways in which this comparison/contrast structure is alluded to by the transitions within the essay. The end of the essay is signaled by the word "thus" at the beginning of the last sentence. In this sentence, we are told again that there are important similarities in these two philosophers' theories and we are reminded of the one crucial difference in their theories—the question of whether humans actually *learn* language.

There are a few other important points to make about this sample essay. Since this is a technical subject, Ron must deal with such specialized terms as "feral child," "behaviorism," "innate," "universal grammar," and "learning" (in the sense in which "learning" is used in this essay). Although it is crucial that the context of the essay make it clear that the writer understands these terms (as it does), it is not necessary for each term to be defined as it is used. Doing so would slow down the process of writing (and reading) the essay too much. As a second point, note that Ron is presented with a ticklish problem in that Chomsky and Piaget technically disagree about whether humans actually learn language. It would be easy to talk about the ways in which Chomsky and Piaget differ (and are similar) in their views of language learning. But since the viability of this term is one of the issues on which they differ, Ron is careful to talk about the differences (and similarities) in their views of the development of language abilities. Note also that since Piaget died in 1980 but Chomsky is still alive, Ron decided to use the past tense in discussing Piaget's views and the present tense in discussing Chomsky's.

EVALUATION

In Chapter 7, we noted that evaluation requires a writer to judge a subject in terms of such qualities as its worth (good or bad), effectiveness (effective or ineffective), usefulness (beneficial or not beneficial), or significance (important or unimportant). We stressed the importance of developing criteria for evaluation in an evaluation process. For example, if you want to say that a given work of art is excellent, it is crucial that you first establish the criteria to use in judging a work of art and then measure that work by means of those criteria.

Evaluative criteria are no less important in an essay examination. However, in this writing situation, the criteria are often supplied for you, and your success will depend on how well you use them. For example, if a teacher asks whether Jimmy Carter was an effective president and you respond by listing only the many admirable personal qualities of President Carter, you are not likely to receive a high mark on the exam. In some very open assignments, you may well develop your own criteria for evaluation, but in a history class that has focused on the effectiveness of various U.S. presidents, you would not have this freedom. Your judgments must be offered in the context of the criteria developed in that class.

Here are examples of essay-exam questions that ask for evaluations:

8. In this course, we have read several novels written in the last half of the twentieth century. If you had to choose one of these as the best novel written in this historical period, which would it be? What criteria would your choice be based on?

9. It could be argued that no two religious leaders have had more impact on twentieth-century U.S. politics than Dr. Martin Luther King, Jr., and Dr. Billy Graham. As our readings have helped us see, Dr. King affected public policy by means of public campaigns in which he openly called for connection between faith and public policy, whereas Dr. Graham avoided direct public statements about matters of state, instead implicitly supporting the candidacy of certain politicians by means of his

private associations and talks with these candidates. In your opinion, which of these clergymen will prove to have had the most significant impact on public policy in twentieth-century United States? Why?

10. During the health-care reform campaign (in President Clinton's first term), were the Harry and Louise ads effective? Why or why not? Be specific in your explanation.

SAMPLE EVALUATIVE ESSAY

Jason Wise, a student enrolled in a course titled Communication and Public Advocacy, wrote the following essay in response to question 10.

> I believe the "Harry and Louise" advertisements were effective. They met several of the characteristics that successful television advertisements must meet.
>
> They were personal. Each viewer took something a little different away from their viewing. Even people as close as husband and wife would see the advertisements differently. The husband would identify more closely with Harry, the wife with Louise.
>
> The ads were self-disclosive and relied on autobiographical evidence. What we knew about Harry and Louise was what they told us in the ads. Each ad became a vignette, shedding a little more light on just who these people were, making them seem more real. We ended up feeling as if we really knew them.
>
> The ads were visual and made good use of associational grammar. We saw shots of these two people sitting at their kitchen table paying bills, something most of us could identify with. The ads didn't dwell on linear arguments to make their point; rather they made quick references to topics that pointed to problems in the Clinton plan, such as uninsured or underinsured illnesses and not being able to take a new job for fear of losing insurance coverage.
>
> An additional proof of the ads' effectiveness is the interest they created about this topic. The ads spawned spoofs; they were mentioned in monologues by Letterman and Leno, and they generated ad bites that were broadcast on national news. All in all, then, these were very effective advertisements, and helped defeat the Clinton health plan.

COMMENTARY   There is nothing flashy about this essay, but it is successful because it shows that Jason knows some of the major criteria that should be used in evaluating the effectiveness of advertisements. Note also that Jason begins and ends his essay in very straightforward ways, making his evaluation of the ads very clear. The structure of the essay is provided by the basic criteria that Jason uses to evaluate these ads—their personal nature, their ability to make viewers identify with these people, their visual qualities, and their ability to generate interest. It is worth noting that Jason disagreed with the author of the textbook used in the course, who had evaluated the ads as ineffective. Jason chose to write in support of his own opinion that the ads were effective; because he supported his opinion, his essay was seen as satisfactory. Had he chosen to agree with the textbook's author, Jason could have structured his response as a summary, much like Kim Coan's essay (pp. 522–523). Note that Kim mentions two crucial criteria for effective ads that Jason does not mention: the degree to which an ad reaches the people it is attempting to influence and the degree to which those people understand the point(s) being made by the ad. Nevertheless, Jason received credit for being able to think about this issue for himself and for using some of the criteria mentioned in the text and in class.

INTERPRETATION

When we interpret, we say what a text, an event, an artifact, or an object means; we derive this meaning in indirect rather than direct ways. For example, when we attempt to say what a certain character's actions in a novel mean, we have to look at those actions in the context of other factors such as the character's other actions, the actions of other characters in the novel, and the themes the author is working with in the novel.

It may not be so obvious that interpretation of a text involves more than simply decoding the words of that text. For example, if a character in a novel says, "These bags are heavy," you can arrive at a literal meaning for those words by reading them and understanding that they mean the bags weigh a lot. However, in order to know what these words mean in the context of the novel, you must know much more. If the character who says them is carrying three bags and walking with another person who is not carrying anything and who is healthy and strong and kindly disposed toward the speaker, you'll likely interpret the words as a request for assistance in carrying the bags. If, on the other hand, both characters are equally burdened and if there has been something of an uneasy silence between the two speakers, you may well interpret the words as an attempt to establish some sort of rapport and to indicate general good will.

Context will play a crucial role in the kinds of interpretation you will be asked to do in essay examinations. Consider, for example, question 12 below, which calls for a discussion of how U.S. actions in Iran in the 1970s might be seen as a cause for the taking of U.S. hostages in 1979. To answer this question, the writer probably would begin by listing actions taken by the United States. But that list would not be a sufficient answer. An interpretation requires an examination of the actions in light of what was taking place in Iran and, perhaps, in various other parts of the world in which the United States was involved. An interpretation of U.S. actions in Iran during this historical period could involve an insightful look into the many events and actions that provide the context in which these actions occurred.

This discussion should make it clear that evaluation involves interpretation, since evaluation requires making judgments about a given topic in light of certain criteria for making those judgments. In a sense, the criteria provide the context we have been talking about. We have separated evaluation from interpretation, however, because of the frequency with which students are called on to make evaluations and because of the formal nature in which the context (that is, the evaluative criteria) is set out in evaluation.

Here are examples of essay-exam questions that ask for interpretation:

11. One of the most striking scenes in *The Great Gatsby* occurs when Nick first meets Daisy as she and Jordan Baker sit on (or seem to float above) the couch in Tom Buchanan's living room. Briefly explain the significance of this scene in relation to the novel as a whole.

12. What was the role of the United States in Iran during the rule of the shah? How might that role be seen as a cause for the taking of U.S. hostages in Iran in 1979?

13. As we have seen, one of the most frequent themes in literature is the quest motif. Analyze the ways in which this motif is used in at least two of the following novels: *The Adventures of Huck Finn; Moby Dick; The Great Gatsby; Ulysses; The Invisible Man; Henderson, the Rain King.*

14. In "Revolution in Grammar," Nelson Francis offers three definitions of "grammar," distinguishing between what he labels as Grammar 1, Grammar 2, and Grammar 3. If you had to classify our two textbooks by means of these categories, where would you put them? Is this easy or hard? That is, does one (or both) of them seem to belong in more than one category? Is one of the books harder to classify than the other? Why?

15. Geography, government, social structure, and economics are all factors that mold historical development. Which one of these areas was the major factor molding North Carolina's development during the period from 1670 to 1770? Why? How did the factor you chose mold developments in the other areas mentioned? Be sure to use specific events in your essay to support your opinion.

SAMPLE INTERPRETATION ESSAY

The following essay by Matthew Reep, a UNC–Charlotte student, was written for his class in North Carolina history. It is a response to question 15.

The geography of North Carolina was the most important factor in molding its history. North Carolina's geography played an important role in shaping its government, its social structure, and its economic development.

North Carolina history began with exploration of the North Carolina coast, by early explorers such as Ralph Lane and John White. The North Carolina coast was a frequent landing point for English ships; thus, the first settlers to North Carolina arrived, and settled, there.

Later on, Black Beard played an important role in the development of North Carolina. From his base on the North Carolina coast, Black Beard intercepted trade ships traveling between Norfolk and Charleston. Although not officially sanctioned by the North Carolina government, Black Beard had a relationship with Governor Eaton that allowed him to store his loot in the governor's barns and store houses.

For many years to follow, the majority of North Carolina's trade and commerce were centered at the North Carolina coast. As one might imagine, this trade affected North Carolina's social structure. The rich and powerful men of North Carolina lived and held offices in the eastern part of the state. While the East continued to prosper, the western part of the state was undeveloped frontier country. Citizens of western North Carolina were seen as backward and awkward, while the eastern citizens were educated and polished.

Of course this geographical dominance by the East led to economic dominance as well. Many eastern citizens were made wealthy by the trade and commerce that were taking place there, while the western citizens were poor in comparison. The North Carolina government was also affected by eastern geographical dominance. Nearly all early North Carolina governors came from the eastern part of the state. Likewise, most of the members of the Legislature of the Royal Colony lived in the eastern part of the state. The number of counties in the East, as compared to the west, reflected, and perpetuated, the power base in the East. The geographical, social, and economic dominance of the East led to its central political role. When England began to put pressure on its colonies, through trade embargos and so forth, the eastern part of the state felt this pressure much more keenly than the west. It is no wonder, then, that the resistance to England, in the Revolutionary War, was centered in the East.

In conclusion, the geography of North Carolina was the most important factor in its development. North Carolina's geography greatly influenced its economic development, its social structure, and its government.

COMMENTARY   Matthew understands that the essay question calls for an interpretation. He knows that he can choose whatever factor he wishes (geographical, economic, social, or political) and make a case in support of it. He also knows that he must connect whichever factor he chooses to the other factors. In fact, the other three factors—economics, social issues, and politics—provide the context that allows him to interpret (that is, to show the meaning of) geography.

Matthew begins his essay with a one-sentence thesis that is set up for him by the essay question. He adds another sentence in which he lets the reader know that he will look at geography in terms of the other factors, thereby creating a very brief introduction for the essay. Note also that since this essay is several paragraphs long, Matthew uses a separate concluding paragraph of two sentences to sum up his argument.

PLANNING YOUR ESSAY'S STRUCTURE

After you decide what your teacher is asking for—summary, synthesis, evaluation, interpretation, or some combination of these—you should decide how to structure your essay. As we saw in Part Two, essays that spotlight the subject will employ one or more of the expository modes: process, comparison, definition, causality, analysis, and classification. You will probably find in the wording of the question itself some indication of what structuring devices are available to you.

Below we categorize some of the essay-exam questions presented earlier, along with some additional questions, according to the expository modes that provide their organization. The type of question in terms of the four processes discussed above is indicated in the second column.

Process

What are the main stages in language learning?	Summary
What are the various stages of the life cycle of a honeybee?	Summary
Describe the process by which a federal law is enacted in the United States.	Summary

Comparison

According to the writers of our textbook, what is the evidence that the language used by animals (even when humans work with animals extensively) is different in kind (not just in degree) from human language?

Summary

In what ways do Noam Chomsky and Jean Piaget seem to agree about language development in humans? What would seem to be important areas of disagreement between the two?

Synthesis

Explain the difference between phonemic and phonetic transcription.

Summary

It could be argued that no two religious leaders have had more impact on twentieth-century U.S. politics than Dr. Martin Luther King, Jr., and Dr. Billy Graham. As our readings have helped us see, Dr. King affected public policy by means of public campaigns in which he openly called for connection between faith and public policy, whereas Dr. Graham avoided direct public statements about matters of state, instead implicitly supporting the candidacy of certain politicians by means of his private associations and talks with these candidates. In your opinion, which of these clergymen will prove to have had the most significant impact on public policy in twentieth-century United States?

Evaluation

Definition

What is a linguistic universal? What are some examples of linguistic universals? Why is the concept of linguistic universal important to modern grammarians like Noam Chomsky?

Summary

What is whole language instruction? Why do the authors of our textbook oppose it?

Summary

Causality

According to the authorities we have read in this class, what were the main causes of World War I?

Summary

What was the role of the United States in Iran during the rule of the shah? How might that role be seen as a cause for the taking of U.S. hostages in Iran in 1979?

Interpretation

Analysis

As we have seen, one of the most frequent themes in literature is the quest motif. Analyze the ways in which this motif is used in at least two of the following novels: *The Adventures of Huck Finn; Moby Dick; The Great Gatsby; Ulysses; The Invisible Man; Henderson, the Rain King.*

Interpretation

One of the most striking scenes in *The Great Gatsby* occurs when Nick first meets Daisy as she and Jordan Baker sit on (or seem to float above) the couch in Tom Buchanan's living room. Briefly explain the significance of this scene in relation to the novel as a whole.

Interpretation

Classification

According to the various articles we have read on the United Kingdom, France, Spain, and Germany, what are the major types of problems that modern-day Europe must contend with? Illustrate these types by discussing specific problems in individual European countries.

Synthesis

In "Revolution in Grammar," Nelson Francis offers definitions of "grammar," distinguishing between what he labels as Grammar 1, Grammar 2, and Grammar 3. If you had to classify our two textbooks by means of these categories, where would you put them? Is this easy or hard? That is, does one (or do both) of them seem to belong in more than one category? Is one of the books harder to classify than the other? Why? — Interpretation

OVERLAPPING TERMINOLOGIES

The above list might seem to indicate that the four processes are separable, but they actually overlap, as the following essay-exam question illustrates:

> Our readings and class discussions have made it clear that television has had an impact on nearly every area of our lives, from values of children raised on television to the choice of detergents one has in a supermarket. One area in which television has had tremendous impact is sports. Discuss the significance of television's role in making modern-day professional sports what they are.

From one perspective, this essay could be structured as a causal analysis. You could discuss the various effects that television (the cause) has had on modern-day professional sports. Viewed from another perspective, the topic could be structured using comparison. That is, you could choose to compare modern-day sports with sports in an earlier time and show the tremendous differences caused by television. Clearly, in answering this question, you would include both causal analysis and comparison. The choice of which to use as an overriding structuring device would be up to you.

Similarly, deciding in which category to place a given essay topic is complicated. The following essay-exam question was categorized as "Summary":

> What is a linguistic universal? What are some examples of linguistic universals? Why is the concept of linguistic universal important to modern grammarians like Noam Chomsky?

The first two sentences in this question ask the writer to summarize information that has been given in sources; they ask how the sources define "linguistic universal" and what examples they offer. But in answering why this concept is important, the writer moves into the realm of evaluation. So why have we identified this question as a summary? We have done so because we see it as asking the writer to summarize an evaluation made by a linguistic authority. If the writer were being asked to come up with this judgment on his own, we would call this an evaluation.

As another example, consider the following question, which was also categorized as calling for summary:

> According to the writers of our textbook, what is the evidence that the language used by animals (even when humans work with animals extensively) is different in kind (not just in degree) from human language?

In this case, it is clear that an interpretation was made by an authority on language. This authority studied evidence (i.e., characteristics of animal language and characteristics of human language) and interpreted this evidence to mean that animal language and human language are different in kind. The question, however, does not call for the student writer to interpret the material but rather to summarize the main points made in a source.

The key difference between summaries and syntheses, on the one hand, and evaluations and interpretations, on the other, is the degree to which they ask you to take an active role in interpretation and evaluation. Clearly, any information the teacher asks you to summarize or synthesize is likely to contain evaluations and interpretations; if it did not, the teacher would not deem it worth including on an examination. However, in more advanced classes, you will often be asked to be an active participant in the making of knowledge by doing your own evaluating and interpreting. That is why it is crucial for you to know the difference between these processes. If a question asks for evaluation or interpretation, but you offer only summary, you will not satisfy the requirements of the assignment.

ESSAYS THAT ASK FOR PRACTICAL APPLICATIONS

One specific type of interpretation that students often encounter in essay examinations is the practical application essay. Many teachers like these essays because they allow students to show that they see connections between what they have studied in class and everyday activities and events. We have already seen an essay that could have easily been turned into a practical application essay. Jason Wise wrote an essay in which he evaluated the effectiveness of certain advertisements in a health-care campaign. In doing so, he used the principles for creating effective ads as a framework for his evaluation. A practical application assignment might have asked him to create an advertisement and then to show why it would be effective in achieving the ends it was designed to achieve. Here are additional questions asking for practical application essays:

16. If the media shifted from using a strategy schema to a problem-policy-performance schema, do you think their metaphors would change? Why or why not? If they did, in what ways? Give specific examples in explaining your answer.
17. You're the president of the United States, and you've decided to stop all funding to the National Endowment of the Arts because of obscenity in publicly funded art. What arguments of legitimacy would you use to support your decision? Why? Which arguments would you avoid using? Why?
18. As you know, the normal pronunciation of the "s" in the plural "boys" is "z." Explain why this is the case. If a native speaker of English did not use this form, would he be more likely to leave the "s" off entirely or to pronounce the "s" as "s"? Explain your answer.

19. A successful architectural design must combine form, space, and site in such a way that the building on the site seems to be a logical outcome of that site. Choose a site and describe it in terms of the site characteristics we have been discussing in class. Then discuss some basic outlines of a building that would be appropriate for that site.

20. You're the challenger running against the incumbent in an eastern North Carolina district that includes several large hog-farming operations. The incumbent, an ardent environmentalist, has attacked you in a television ad for accepting contributions from the hog industry. The wording of the television ad suggests that the industry has bought your vote. The visuals are of filthy hog-farming operations and a dirty stream. It is true that you have accepted some sizable contributions from the groups the ad mentions. The ad is hurting you in the polls, so you have decided that you are going to respond. How will you respond to that ad? Use Kathleen H. Jamieson's discussion of counterattack in *Dirty Politics, Deception, Distraction and Democracy* (New York: Oxford UP, 1992) to explain your response.

SAMPLE PRACTICAL APPLICATION ESSAY

Robbie Grier, a UNC–Charlotte student enrolled in the course Communication and Public Advocacy, wrote the following essay in answer to question 20.

There are three key ways of responding to attack ads:

1. Attack with a similar type ad;
2. Use a propositional ad—one that uses many words to counter the claim of an attack ad;
3. Reframe the attack by
   —redefining the context or examples given;
   —forewarning of manipulation;
   —distancing yourself from the attacker with humor;
   —citing credible sources to counter the attack;
   —dissociating oneself from the attack;
   —admitting one's mistake.

In this example, I might try to redefine the context in which the contribution has been made. I would show that my support for the issues surrounding hog farming existed prior to this contribution. Thus, rather than buying my vote, the contribution was an exercise of their right to support a candidate whose views tend to match theirs.

I would also use humor to diffuse the situation. If my opponent referred to unnamed sources, for example, I could use an ad depicting one of my opponent's "campaign workers" interviewing hogs for their opinions.

I might cite credible sources to show that the hog industry does not have the negative environmental impact attributed to it. In doing so, I could change the issue from my acceptance of a contribution to the hog farming industry itself, an issue on which most voters would side with me.

By means of such strategies as these, I might be able to turn an attack on me into a negative for my opponent and a positive for me.

COMMENTARY   Robbie charts a straightforward plan for his essay at the beginning by summarizing the principles he has learned about countering attack ads. From there, he has only to show how he will implement his plan.

PLANNING SAMPLE ESSAYS

Below are several possible essay questions. For each, determine what process or processes the question calls for—summary, synthesis, evaluation, interpretation, and/or application. Then determine what expository modes you would likely use in writing this essay and which of those modes you would use to provide the essay's overall structure.

21. Pick two of the following decades and discuss what course of action you would have taken to deal with the problems faced by the colonists of North Carolina during that time. Be sure to identify the problems and use facts: (a) 1675–1684; (b) 1720–1729; (c) 1760–1769.

22. Contrast the theatrical conventions, themes, and audiences of the Restoration theater of late-seventeenth-century England with those of the bourgeois tragedy of eighteenth-century England.

23. Leadership has always been a problem for North Carolina. During the period from 1660 to 1775, what individuals provided the best leadership for the colony? Be sure to discuss their accomplishments and the obstacles they had to overcome.

24. Explain the relationship between the terms "enthymeme," "responsive chord," "nonverbal communication," and "electronic media." In what way(s) are these concepts important for political communication?

25. What are ad bites? Why have they become popular? Why is Jamieson concerned about them?

26. You've decided to run for mayor of Las Cruces, New Mexico, and you've decided to make an appeal based on myth. Which American myth would you use for your appeal? Using the general characteristics of myths, explain your choice.

27. In many works we have studied, characters experience an initiation or illumination—a recognition about themselves, a situation, or another person. Choose three pieces of literature we have studied and show how they depict this experience. What is the nature of the illumination? Does the recognition promise change for the better or is it presented as coming too late, or as ironic?

28. How has the media's notion of newsworthiness given rise to the pseudo-event? Be very specific in your explanation. Use an example to illustrate your answer.

29. Using as your examples a play by Shaw, a story by Lawrence or Mansfield, and a story from Joyce's *Dubliners,* discuss how these writers represent various social classes. What conflicts and problems do their characters experience? Who has power? Who is powerless and why?

30. North Carolina's early history has been dictated by series of conflicts and their resolutions. Culpeper's Rebellion, the North Carolina Regulator

movement, and the American Revolution were major conflicts influencing North Carolina's development. Compare the causes of these events, show their similarities and differences, and indicate how the results aided or hindered North Carolina's unity.

31. Hugh Lefler writes, "Geographical factors contributed to economic differences in agriculture, industry, and trade in the various regions. Economic differences created social distinctions. Racial and social factors were involved in religious rivalries. And all of these factors contributed to political controversies." From your knowledge of North Carolina history, comment on the validity of the above quotation. Be sure to describe the political controversies and relate the statement to them. Which factor had the greatest impact on political controversies? Why? Be sure to use facts.

Writing Strategy

PLANNING ESSAY-EXAM ANSWERS

Ask yourself these questions as you plan an essay to answer an examination item:

1. Is this primarily a summary, synthesis, evaluation, interpretation, or application essay?
2. If it is a summary or synthesis essay, are evaluative or interpretive issues being summarized or synthesized? If so, what are they?
3. If it is an evaluation essay, are you free to choose your own criteria for evaluation? If so what criteria will you use? If criteria are assumed, what are they?
4. What expository mode provides the overriding structure for your essay?

ADDITIONAL SAMPLE ESSAYS

Below are four additional sample essays. Analyze each of these by answering the following questions:

1. What type of essay is it? Summary, synthesis, evaluation, interpretation, or application? Does this essay call for more than one of these processes?
2. What expository mode provides the essay's primary structure? Does it use other modes? What are they?
3. Using criteria outlined in this chapter, how effective do you find the essay?

David Wilson, a student enrolled in a course on theater history at UNC–Charlotte, wrote the first essay in response to question 22 (p. 518).

The comedy of manners of the Restoration period in England focused on the fashions and foibles of the upperclass while bourgeois tragedy throughout 18th century Europe focused on middle class heroes and heroines. These two types of theater performed very different functions for very different audiences. The theatrical style—the types of characters portrayed and the ways in which these characters were portrayed—also changed very much from Restoration theater to the domestic tragedies of 18th century Europe.

The comedy of manners thrilled and delighted the audiences of the Restoration with its broad gestures and declamatory delivery. Its language contained double entendres and its actors included women on the stage, some of whom appeared in tight fitting pants—or "breeches roles." The Restoration theater was in rebellion against the strict morals of the Puritans, who had closed the theater from 1642 until 1660. The audiences for these plays consisted of noble families, literary and artistic types, and people in the service industry—including "orange wenches," coachmen, and prostitutes, there to meet clients. The plays of this period contained themes that would appeal to such audiences, with social pretension and sex high on the list. Characters in the plays included gossipers and stock characters whose names usually described their personalities.

The audiences who came to Restoration plays came more for the social scene than to watch the play. They would discuss the play loudly, flirt with the orange wenches and wait for the play to end so they could rush back to meet the man who played the part of a woman. Since the audience was so loud, actors had to speak in loud voices and to speak toward the audience instead of to the other actors. They also used broad sweeping gestures to keep the audience's attention. These performances required very limited and sketchy rehearsals, since most of the show involved actors standing front and center delivering lines and then stepping back to let the next actor speak.

While this bombastic style was still around in the early 18th century, many actors began moving toward a more natural speech style. The theater of this period began to move away from the bawdy stock characters of Restoration theatre and toward more individual characters. With this change came more rehearsal time, since these characterizations required practiced actors. One publication that helped mark the end of Restoration bawdiness and the beginning of morality in 18th-century, middle-class theatre was Jeremy Collier's *A Short View of the Immorality and Profaneness of the English Stage,* an attack on the sexual overtones of Restoration theater.

The bourgeois tragedies that followed appealed to the rising new middle class. The heroes and heroines of these plays were drawn from the middle class and their themes reflected the problems and the values of the middle class. Since more and more people were introduced to learning and philosophy during this time, the vulgarity of the previous century was rejected. Since wars were being fought for economic rather than religious reasons, religion was becoming more personal; people were turning to religion to help them understand the world they lived in and their place in that world. The plays of this period openly appealed to the emotions, and good was pitted against evil, with the virtuous rewarded and the wicked punished.

The changes from Restoration to 18th-century England and Europe were profound. Those changes were very much reflected in the major changes that took place in the theater as it evolved from the bawdy and bombastic plays of the Restoration to the middle class morals of the 18th-century theatre.

ESSAY 2

The second sample essay was written by Ann Long while studying British literature at UNC–Charlotte, in response to question 29 (p. 518).

The divisions of social class are depicted in strikingly different ways by the writers we have been introduced to this term. While some, such as Wilde and Shaw, chose humor to highlight the contrasts between the classes, others, such as Mansfield and Joyce, chose a more serious method to examine the conflict. Whether humorous or serious, the writers make it clear that the upper and lower classes are in conflict.

In Shaw's play, "Mrs. Warren's Profession," social power belongs to Sir George. He is the traditional English "gentleman," complete with title and money. He is able to do as he pleases, investing in business as he sees fit without the interference of the surrounding society. As his partner, Mrs. Warren would appear to have power, but as she tells her daughter, the only way women like her have to get money is to use their appearance to please men. So, Mrs. Warren's power comes not from social position, but rather from an ability to peddle her feminine wares. Of this, Sir George has taken advantage simply because he can.

However, Mrs. Warren's daughter, Vivie, does not understand her mother's predicament. She tells her mother that even the very poor have choices. They may not be able to choose to be royalty, but they can choose whether to make money by rag-picking or selling flowers. Vivie, a modern woman who believes she is the captain of her own ship, cannot see how Mrs. Warren was powerless as a young woman; nor can she understand why her mother cannot now give up this wicked life.

But Vivie realizes that she has not been fully in control herself, since she has been dependent upon her mother's money. She feels that she must take control and leave her mother. Ironically, when Vivie leaves, Mrs. Warren takes some control of her life by refusing to shake hands as she bids her ungrateful daughter "adieu."

Shaw's satire is powerful, and the humor is not without its pain; in contrast, we confront the pain caused by the indifference of the higher classes directly in Mansfield's "The Garden Party." The death of a lower-class gentleman who lives at the foot of the hill is of great concern to little Laura. But the rest of her well-to-do family is unable to arrive at the same sensibility, which has so upset Laura. They are aware of "the little cottages" at the bottom of the hill and the people in those cottages, but they see these cottages as "the greatest possible eyesore," and they do not think the people in them have a right to live so close to them.

In short, the people at the bottom of the hill are offensive to those at the top of the hill. And of course, the power lies with those at the top. Certainly they do not have the power to defy death, but they are able to ignore the hardship of others as they pursue a "pretty" life. They are insensitive about this power, as Laura's mother reveals when she offers to "send that poor creature some of this perfectly good food." She believes the food will be a great treat for the children.

She fails to see that this basket of food is of no comfort, and will be seen as a symbol of their "above-it-all" attitude. Had there been real concern for the grieving family, they would not have sent a child, Laura, to do an adult's work.

Mansfield is hard on the upper class, but she cannot approach Joyce's harshness. In "The Dead," Joyce draws a firm line between the social position of Lily, the gatekeeper's daughter, and Gabriel, the hostess's nephew. When Lily rebuffs Gabriel's innocent interest in her, Gabriel is very distressed. Is he this sensitive, or is it the fact that the rebuff comes from a gatekeeper's daughter? Gabriel is a worldly-wise man of the upper class, but in reality he has less power than Lily. He is completely powerless in his relationship with his wife, Gretta.

As these works illustrate, all three of these writers—Joyce, Mansfield, and Shaw—are concerned with the struggle between the classes and the issues of what kind of power (and control) members of the upper class and the working class have.

ESSAY 3

The third essay was written in response to question 28 (p. 518) by Cherish Smith, a student in Communication and Public Advocacy at UNC–Charlotte.

An issue does not necessarily have to be important to be newsworthy. If it will likely raise the ratings of the news, the press will consider it newsworthy. Thus, the press considers an event newsworthy if it is *personal, dramatic, novel, consistent with a theme,* and *observable.* This conception of what makes for news has given rise to the *pseudo-event.* This is an event that is created so that it can be "covered" by the news. Reporters are supposed to "cover" the news, not "create" it. But the line between "covering" and "creating" gets blurred in the pseudo-event because these events are manufactured to be covered. With an eye to what the press considers to be newsworthy, those who create pseudo-events make sure that they are *dramatic, intelligible, repeatable,* and *easy to disseminate.* These events are easily covered by the press, with such matters as lighting and outlets for camera hookups taken into consideration when they are planned. Since pseudo-events are *dramatic* and often produce conflict, they attract the media. Conflict is an ongoing news theme. Pseudo-events are most often novel. If the issue is ongoing, the pseudo event must be staged in a novel way. A good example was Dukakis and his tank rides. The message was meant to be intelligible: "I'm for use of traditional weapons." The event was easily disseminated and dramatic. Reporters found it easy to cover.

ESSAY 4

Kim Coan, a student enrolled in the course Communication and Public Advocacy, wrote the last sample essay in response to question 10 (p. 510).

According to the writer of our text, Jamieson, the Harry and Louise ads were not effective advertising; but they were effective public relation tools. They didn't work as advertisements because they just scraped the surface of health care reform. However, when the Clintons attacked the ads, a conflict was created and the media picked up on this conflict. The media went on to show ad bites of these advertisements. Since these ad bites were picked up in excess of

700 times, people came to know the names, Harry and Louise; this was great public relations. But the real issues of health care reform were not made clear by these ads. When polls were taken, people were found to remember the names, Harry and Louise, but they could not connect facts of the issue being debated with these names.

Exercise 13.1

Here are some questions you may want to use to practice your essay-examination skills.

1. Examine the two essays in Chapter 6 that deal with the term "nigger" (pp. 174–179). In what ways do the two writers, Gloria Naylor and Michel Marriott, agree about the use of this word? In what ways do they disagree?

2. In her essay entitled "One Road Taken" (pp. 278–280), Kacey Atwood argues that Robert Frost's poem, "The Road Not Taken," concerns itself with those times in life when a person chooses the right course of action in the face of what might be easy, but wrong, choices. One could read the poem very differently. Explain how the poem could be read as a poetic statement that life often presents us with choices that are not at all clear-cut.

3. Antonya Nelson's "In the Land of Men" (pp. 255–262) ends with the narrator pondering a choice. Is this story as open-ended as it seems? Has Nelson prepared the reader in any way for the narrator's decision? What evidence can you offer from the story to support your viewpoint?

4. Julie Titone and Sherman Alexie comment on the decline of salmon populations using different genres to do so. Titone wrote an essay (pp. 415–418); Alexie wrote a poem (p. 271). How do these two pieces of writing help you understand the importance to the Northwest of a healthy salmon population?

You have no doubt heard the word "portfolio" used in various contexts. An artist may assemble a portfolio of works to submit when applying for admission to an art institute. A dabbler in the stock market builds a stock portfolio. A graphic artist may take a portfolio with examples of previous projects to a meeting with a potential client. These various uses of the term "portfolio" refer to a collection of materials. In this chapter, we'll talk about your writing portfolio as a place for you not only to collect samples of your writing but also to reflect on them.

By the end of your writing course, you'll have had a great deal of feedback from your teacher on your writing. And you may have had the opportunity to get your classmates' opinions on your writing. In the long run, however, the person whose opinion matters most when it comes to your development as a writer is you. Your teacher and your classmates will not always be there to suggest ways in which your writing can be improved. Your progress in the future will be directly related to your ability to read your own writing critically; assembling a portfolio gives you the opportunity to hone this important writing skill.

Portfolios

CHAPTER 14

TYPES AND PURPOSES
OF WRITING PORTFOLIOS

There are many different ways of assembling a writing portfolio. You may include all of the writing you do in a given writing course, as Bill's portfolio assignment requires (see pp. 528–529). If you do not include all of your writing, however, you will need some means of selecting certain works. The selections you make should depend on the purpose you wish the portfolio to serve.

If the purpose of your portfolio is to help you gain entry into a prestigious writing program or to secure a job as a writer, you will likely choose your most polished pieces of writing. In such a situation, you might be interested only in finished pieces of writing, leaving out all the earlier drafts that helped you get to the finished writing.

On the other hand, if you intend to submit your portfolio to the director of writing at a university in hopes of attaining credit for a course more advanced than the one you are currently in—as students can do at UNC–Charlotte, where Ron teaches—you will want to take into consideration the types of writing required in that course and be sure to submit samples that demonstrate your ability to do such writing. You will also probably want to include samples of your prewriting and drafting processes, since the ability to work through the writing process is highly valued at schools such as UNC–Charlotte.

The kind of portfolio we envision in this chapter is somewhat like the one you might submit for credit in a course, but it goes a bit further in helping you reflect on your strengths and weaknesses as a writer and chart a course for your continued development. Additionally, it allows you the opportunity to demonstrate your developing writing skills to your teacher. Such a portfolio will likely include two or three pieces of finished writing, demonstrating a range of rhetorical aims. For at least one of those pieces, the portfolio will include all the writing you did for the various stages. Finally, the portfolio will contain a reflective essay in which you discuss your progress as a writer, using the writing samples in the portfolio to illustrate that progress.

PUTTING THE REFLECTION IN YOUR
REFLECTIVE ESSAY

We have used the reflective essay in our own teaching for a good many years now, and we are convinced of its worth as a tool for personal assessment and growth. However, we are also aware of its dangers and pitfalls. In asking you to write a reflective essay, your teacher will be asking you to walk a tightrope between reflection and evaluation. To succeed, you must keep in mind the clear distinction between these assignments. You are being asked to reflect on your growth and development as a writer. It is your teacher's task to evaluate your work in the course.

If it is not your task to evaluate your work or your effort in this course, what exactly do you do in reflective writing? Rather than asserting that you have learned a great deal about writing in this course, you should concentrate on what you have learned about your writing. You may begin with a thesis such as the following: "Here are the major things I have learned about my writing in this course." Note that this assertion does not argue that your writing has reached the A level, or even that it has gotten better; your argument, should you choose to frame your essay with an argumentative thesis, is that you have learned something about your writing.

It is worth mentioning a few other things about this process. First, note that we are suggesting that you discuss what you have learned about your writing, rather than what you have learned about writing in general. We do so because we want to help you resist the temptation to turn your reflective essay into a description of the course you have just taken. Second, note that you need not argue that your writing has gotten better during the short time you have been in this writing course. We hope it has. However, starting from a thesis that your writing has improved may well lead to a focus on such empirical evidence as grades: "I was writing C minus papers at the beginning of the course and by the end I was writing B plus papers, so I should receive an A for the progress I have made." This is not what we would want from our students, and we suspect it is not what your teacher will be looking for. Improvement in the quality of one's writing is slow and incremental. If you have learned some things about your writing that will allow you to work knowledgeably on improving it in the future, you have achieved a worthy goal.

Just as the reflective essay does not call for evaluation of you or your writing, it does not call for an evaluation of your writing course or your teacher. It is tempting to turn this assignment into what Ron calls a panegyric. (See his reflective essay assignment on p. 528.) You may well feel that this has been the best course you have ever taken and that your teacher has made very real contributions to your growth as a writer. If so, that is wonderful. You will probably have the opportunity to write an evaluation or respond to a questionnaire evaluating the course and its teacher. Save that material for that opportunity. Here, your focus should be on what you have learned about your writing.

You may be wondering what is left. "If I can't evaluate myself, if I can't talk about what the course covered, and if I can't talk about how wonderful the course was and what a great teacher I've had in this course, what, then, is a reflective essay?" We may begin an answer to this question by examining what "reflection" means literally. If you look at the surface of water in the proper sunlight, you may well see a reflection of yourself in the water. The first step in reflective learning is the seeing. In the reflective essay we are envisioning, your writing for this course will take the place of the water; that is, you will look for your reflection, as a writer, in that work. This is not to suggest, however, that you should limit your analysis to finished pieces of writing. You can learn much about yourself as a writer by looking carefully at the ways in which your writing developed from draft to draft. And as the essays that follow illustrate, you may well want to reflect on what you have learned about your writing in conversations (and peer-group workshops) with members of your class. Once you begin to look carefully at the work you have done in this class, you will find much on which to reflect.

SAMPLE PORTFOLIO ASSIGNMENTS

Here we present examples of our most recent portfolio assignments.

Ron's Portfolio Assignment

Your portfolio should include the following:

- two revisions of papers written during this semester
- a piece of writing done this semester in another class (optional)
- a reflective essay

The two revised papers need not be the two you received the highest marks on. Choose essays that help illustrate your progress as a writer in this course. Since the papers will have already undergone extensive revision, you may well not need to do major revisions on the papers at this point. However, I suspect that you will find that despite the revising you have done, there are local matters that can be attended to in one last polishing. Strive to make the papers as "finished" as you can.

The piece of writing from another course is optional. If you choose to include an outside piece of writing, submit a cover note that gives the writing assignment and other pertinent information. Also, explain what you think you learned in writing this essay and why you like the writing you produced in responding to this assignment.

The reflective essay is the crucial element in this project. In it, you will attempt to chart your course as a writer during the last semester—or longer if you choose. We will discuss this essay in class, but I will answer here a few questions that I anticipate your asking. The essay should be from 1,000 to 1,500 words long. It may be organized as an autobiography in which you detail your progress as a writer in something of a narrative form. In this case, your style of writing is likely to be somewhat informal. On the other hand, you may choose to approach your writing analytically, talking about particular areas that you have worked on during this semester. Such a paper may be a bit more formal than the narrative, but it need not be formal. In either case, you should feel free to address us as a class, to assume the background knowledge that we all have (and to use that knowledge in framing your discussion), and to refer to our class discussions and to interactions you have had with your classmates. Whatever its form, your discussion should include specific references to the writing that you have included in your portfolio. In a sense, these pieces provide the evidence for the claims you are making. Finally, let me urge you not to turn this into a panegyric in which you are the perfect student, I am the perfect teacher, and this is the perfect class. Please strive to take a clear-eyed, honest look at yourself as a writer through the lens of the papers in this portfolio.

Bill's Portfolio Assignment

For your final assignment, you will submit a portfolio that consists of all the writing you have done in this class, together with a reflective essay about your work. [This assignment is based on one in *Paideia,* edited by Kristina Fury and Kimberly Whitehead (New York: Forbes, 1998).]

Reflective Essay   For your final essay for this semester, you'll submit an argument about what you've learned as a writer, drawing for examples on your experience in the class. This essay is a reflective self-assessment that will involve you in reviewing all of the work you've done this semester so that you can discuss what you've learned about writing, reading, thinking critically, and researching.

As you begin thinking about this essay, which should be from three to five pages long, you may respond to these questions:

1. What have I learned? What have I learned that's important? How will it help me academically, personally, and/or professionally?
2. What contributed to my learning? What particular assignments, techniques, and/or activities really helped? How can I demonstrate this? What evidence from my course materials can I use to support my assertions here?
3. Why are these things important to me? What will I be able to do as a result of this course, either as a student or as a professional, once I graduate?
4. How have I developed as a writer, as a student? What specific skills, techniques, and strategies have I learned that will help? What are my strengths as a writer? What do I do well? What are my weaknesses? What do I still need to work on; what skills do I still need to develop as a writer?

Because this essay is an argument, you'll need to support your assertions with detail, with evidence, for example, from your writings and your responses to readings this semester. One way to begin is to look back at the course's purpose statement at the very beginning of your syllabus:

Through a sequence of reading, writing, and workshop exercises, you will

*   become familiar with the composing process and learn to adjust it to accomplish various writing tasks,
*   develop analytical reading and critical thinking skills,
*   develop expository and argumentative writing skills,
*   develop research skills, and
*   use collaborative learning in various contexts.

Have you done these things? How effectively? To what extent?

SAMPLE REFLECTIVE ESSAYS

Here we offer reflective essays written by students in our classes. You will note that essays by two of these students (Ali Duffy and Steve Duran) have been used as models in this text (Ali's personal essay is on pp. 142–143; Steve's informative essay is on pp. 207–210).

REFLECTIVE ESSAY

ALI DUFFY
ENGLISH 1103—FALL, 1997
UNC–CHARLOTTE

1   As I complete my first semester as a college freshman, I have come to dwell in my writing rather than to languish in it. I am inspired to write rather than being drilled and programmed to write. My biggest improvements have been internal ones. Through the

process of composing five different papers, I have learned to focus on a specific audience, manage my time, critique globally, and edit extraneous information out of my papers.

2   There is a reason my friends used to call me the "Procrastination Queen." Throughout high school, I could put off writing papers until the night before they were due, and still receive an A. However, I now realize how critical drafts are to a final work. Of course, drafts require time. Before coming to college, the only managing of time I had ever had to do was fitting in my five minutes of homework into my busy dance schedule. Although I have had to make a few sacrifices here, I appreciate my time more now that I have to schedule things. I now have to find time for drafts and revisions, but it is worth doing so, in part because my concept of drafting has changed. In high school I didn't bother to take the time to make global revisions, but this semester, the revisions and drafts of my position paper alone took over a month

3   Of the five papers we wrote this term, the position paper and the persuasion paper were the hardest for me because I couldn't focus on an audience. For example, in my persuasion paper about abortion, I didn't know whether to soak it with emotion or state my case with a calmer, more balanced approach. I made the mistake of aiming the paper at people who are unsure of their views on abortion, rather than to a more appropriate audience of pro-choice advocates. In revising this paper for my portfolio, I feel that I focused more on my specific audience by adding emotional stories about abused and neglected children, and explaining more graphically the repercussions of "back-alley" abortions. I feel that my voice is more powerful and my audience is more apparent.

4   The words "local" and "global," in reference to critiquing, were not parts of my vocabulary until well into this semester. Through the peer critiques we did in class, I have learned to make more global suggestions to others. For example, when critiquing the in-class piece about sex education written by Emily Weast, I noted that Emily had no mention of the media in her introduction even though she included a whole paragraph on media in the body of the paper. Also, I suggested that Emily spread out her statistical information throughout the paper, instead of concentrating it all into one paragraph. These exercises in critiquing other papers has paid off in my own revisions. In my most recent revision on my evaluation essay, I completely restructured my quotes from *Miss Saigon* to put more overall emphasis on the characters and the music. These are not the kinds of revisions I am used to making. Learning to critique globally has forced me to read my own papers differently—to see them in a more neutral and objective way.

5   Ever since I was in middle school, teachers have made comments on my papers, such as "too much information," "not focused enough," and "cut the fat." My pattern was to get so anxious about writing, and finishing a paper, that I would include all the information I could find on the subject and end up having extraneous and unrelated sections in my paper. I am beginning to learn to weed out superfluous material and develop the material that is pertinent to my topic. My least favorite paper this term, the argumentative (position) paper about smoking in public, was full of unnecessary information, which made the piece confusing for the audience. I was vague in my comments about smoking in public places; I failed to mention what the current smoking laws are and was thus not able to focus on specific laws and regulations that I wanted to see changed. The paper had too many statistics that did not really serve any purpose. For example, what does the fact that 2.3 percent of the United State's crops are tobacco have to do with current smoking regulations?

6   I have noticed a change in my writing this term in all of my courses. My papers are more focused and my sense of audiences and topics is clearer. I also find that my papers are developed more fully because I take the time to make real revisions from draft to draft. I believe these changes will serve me well in the writing I do for the rest of my college career and, indeed, in my entire life.

COMMENTARY Ali came to UNC–Charlotte with a good deal of ability and confidence in her writing, as the example of her writing in Chapter 5 illustrates. Thus, it would be false of her to present what Ron often refers to as an "I once was blind, but now I see" reflective essay. Ali needs to talk about the ways in which she can learn to improve on her already excellent writing skills. And she does.

Ali's reflective essay is well organized—in fact, it is a bit too organized in some ways. That is, Ali begins with a formulaic thesis sentence in which she outlines what she has learned in this class. She has learned to manage her time, to make global (as opposed to local) revisions, to pay attention to audience, and to work on extraneous material that often appears in her writing. Two of these matters—audience awareness and global versus local revision—are major components of the class instruction; however, Ali applies them to *her* writing, showing where she has begun to put these principles into practice.

Two other matters are worth mentioning. First, note that Ali talks about some of the activities of her writing group. Discussion of such matters usually adds important information to any reflective essay, since no two writing groups function alike and no two students learn the same things in writing-group discussions. Second, note that although Ali talks about how her writing has developed over time, the organization of her paper is essentially analytical. That is, she has chosen the second of the two methods outlined in Ron's assignment.

AGGIE MAGIC TRICKS

KARA EDEWAARD
ENGLISH 111H, FALL 1998
NEW MEXICO STATE UNIVERSITY

1   As I start to contemplate writing this paper, I begin by making a list of all the possible things that I have learned during the semester, then I select a few that changed my writing technique, and now I ponder why these skills helped me with such a transition. It all started on that first day in English 111, when I was given our course syllabus. I could not believe that we were going to learn how to deal with the composing process, analytical reading and critical thinking skills, expository and argumentative writing skills, research skills, and collaborative learning. It all seemed like too much. At any rate, I thought that I already had good writing technique. I did not believe I had room for further improvement. I soon changed my mind, as I developed the skills that aided in this writing.

2   The first step in this improvement was to read works written by other authors. By reading assorted essays, I was able to view different techniques for writing on defined topics. The essay "Dark Side of Tomatoes" by Raymond Sokolov illustrated how to present information with some humor and a catchy introduction. Sokolov opens by telling his audience about an experience as a boy biting into a nice juicy tomato: "I bit into one; juice spurted on my cheeks. . . ." This personal narrative reels the audience in and makes them look at the tomato in another light. Sokolov also adds a bit of humor, because after all how serious can anyone take tomatoes. I enjoyed this essay and have

learned to incorporate some of these techniques into my writing. Another essay that I learned from was Dr. Martin Luther King's "I Have a Dream." Dr. King uses analogies that a wide audience can relate to. His analogy of the "bad check" that America has issued Black Americans increases the impact of his essay. Another device that King uses is repetition. He is able to press the urgency of the fight for freedom by repeating the word *now*. By being exposed to all sorts of writing styles, I was able to incorporate them into my essays.

3   I was able to learn a great deal about how to produce a paper in English 111. I've learned how to write down all of the major ideas I have, and then to develop those ideas by means of various prewriting techniques. After I have found all of the ideas that I want to include in my paper, I then think about what kind of audience I will be writing to. Once my audience is chosen I can then assemble my ideas in a rough draft. During this semester I wrote on NMSU Online Registration. I decided that my audience would be the students on campus. By choosing this audience, I was able to go into more detail, because many of the students would know exactly what I was talking about. Since my audience had prior knowledge, I could manipulate my topic to a greater extent by incorporating details that a different audience would not know about.

4   Researching and developing the ideas through writing occur at the next stage. I have found that many topics will become strong essays once they are thoroughly researched. When writing about NMSU Online Registration, I found alternative sources by conducting interviews with the writer of the system and with a student who uses an online registration system at another school. I used these two interviews to find out more background on the system and to see what other systems were like compared to ours. Once a paper has been fully researched and outlined, the writing must begin. This process includes writing and then revising. All papers need to be revised at least once after the paper has been written. This revision includes correcting all mistakes (grammar, spelling), making sure that the ideas connect, and that the audience will relate to the topic. Once these tasks have been finalized, the paper is ready.

5   I believe that the biggest lesson I have encountered over the semester has been to explain each idea extensively. I was so determined to make my writing brief that I did not see that my audience was missing out on the details that I did not convey. The details are the most essential part of writing; I know that I still need to work on expanding details in many of my papers, but I have realized that without specifics the audience will not get the meaning that I intend. I am working on making my writing better in this way.

COMMENTARY   Like Ali's essay, Kara's is a bit more formulaic than we might like. She is committed to demonstrating that she has learned a great deal in this course, and she does so. It isn't until near the end of the paper, however, that she gets to an issue (development) that turns the lens directly onto her writing—as opposed to writing in general. She (and we) would probably have learned more about her writing had she spent more time talking about how she is learning to provide the details and specificity needed in her writing. Although we could wish for more of this type of information, Kara does personalize her discussion by using an example of her writing, the essay on on-line registration, to illustrate what she has learned about the writing process.

STEVE WANTS AN A

STEVE DURAN
ENGLISH 111H, FALL, 1998
NEW MEXICO STATE UNIVERSITY

1   Chances are, writing will be a necessary part of life up until the time when the Sun finishes the nuclear reactions of hydrogen in its core and expands its outer layers so far as to encompass the earth, raising all of our body temperatures to well above 5,000 degrees. Since this won't happen for another four or five billion years, I suppose it might be worthwhile to learn some skills in writing.

2   I've always enjoyed writing, ever since the day I learned to write my name with a thick blue crayon. I practiced my new skill extensively, drafting my monosyllabic work on every surface in the house. My earliest work, circa 1984, I believe, was titled "Steve Wants a Cookie," and was first drafted on the wall of the kitchen. Unfortunately, later that day, a vicious case of writer's block struck with such brutality that I was forced to delay future drafts until the next day. Even more unfortunate, upon returning to my work, it had been white-washed, and my proposal had not been appreciated or taken to heart as I received no cookie. It seems my work did not receive favorable reviews from the household critics. I have learned that all writers must accept criticism, and I do believe that my work has substantially progressed. My writing goals have also evolved from "Steve Wants a Cookie" to "Steve Wants an A."

3   With that in mind, let me review what I have learned about my writing. This past semester, I have learned the value of a discovery draft, rough draft, and peer reviews. In the past, I found no use for these nuisances, and I must admit I still look upon them with something less than favor. But whether I like them or not, I now appreciate their value. Before this class, when I had a paper to write I would just wait until the day before the deadline, then spend all day and night writing. I did fine this way, although I spent a good eight or nine hours straight on a paper, which can drive any normal person to the outer perimeters of their sanity. I would sit in my hard wooden chair, staring at a blank computer screen until an idea popped into my head. Then I'd take the idea, put it into words, think about it, revise it, and finally type it out. This is a lot of work for my little pea-brain, so as you can imagine, this was a time-consuming process. Was there a better way to write? Of course not. There couldn't be.

4   As painful as this is to admit, I was wrong. As I have learned this semester, there is a better way. With a discovery draft, I could get all my ideas on paper, just to have them out of my head, free from all that other garbage floating around in there. Once down on paper, I could read and evaluate it and see if it made sense. Then, I could organize those ideas into more coherent sentences and paragraphs that might make sense to someone else besides me. Next, I would give it to some other poor slob to find my mistakes for me. Once read by normal people, it becomes clear what I need to do better and what few things I have done right. Then all I have to do is completely overhaul my paper, and I am done. It is amazing how such a simple process has for so long evaded such a simple mind.

5   In learning to write for different purposes, I also learned how to use language for each purpose. In "Intricacies of an Idiot," I evaluated just what makes Homer Simpson so entertaining. It all boiled down to the fact that Homer is a foolish, lazy, incompetent moron and I, on the other hand, am . . . well, less of a foolish, lazy, incompetent moron and therefore have the right to laugh at his shortcomings. In that essay, I found that use

of language that is appropriate to my audience was critical to adequately evaluating Homer. I tried to use as many different descriptive adjectives as I could to keep it colorful, but after a certain point, there simply are no more synonyms for "lazy" and "moron."

6 Writing with my audience in mind is another important lesson I learned this semester. I never used to think about what my readers would think; I just wrote until I liked what I wrote. But I overlooked an important factor, which I call the B/S factor. Yes, the Boredom/Suicide factor is an important way to measure how well I had written for my audience. If my readers are continually drifting off into Slumberland or threaten to kill themselves (or me), chances are I have not written particularly well for my audience.

7 In "The Space between Your Ears," an essay about the mental side of golf, I tried to use technical terms for golfers, but still keep it understandable and interesting. In essays where the author presents information or explains a process, most often boredom is almost inescapable. So I tried to use language and humor that even non-golfers could understand. I used references to other sports to let non-golfers relate to my ideas. I tried to write for my main audience (golfers) while keeping a secondary audience (non-golfers) in mind. This creates a balance that is critical in maintaining a low B/S level.

I also learned that I must take my audience into account in controversial papers. In " . . . And Justice for Some," I took a stand that the death penalty is a necessary part of the justice system. Even though I was writing for an audience that strongly disagreed with my ideas, I acknowledged the good points in their arguments, and then respectfully informed them that they were wrong and I was right. Even though I am sure they despise me and my ideas, and desire to see me given a life sentence in prison for that essay, I am sure I convinced them that I actually deserve the death penalty.

8 In my paper entitled "The Deceptive Logic of Math," I approached my readers in a different way. I took the position that math is illogical and useless in real life. By itself, I am sure anyone may be willing to give me five seconds to prove my point, but I also included my belief that anyone who disagreed with my theory should be shipped off to a deserted island where they would be exploited for my own personal gain. I don't think I made any new friends in this essay, but I proved my point.

9 I learned many important things this semester. First, focusing on reading strategies helped me get through boring or difficult essays by making me pay the right kinds of attention. I also learned that discovery drafts, rough drafts, and peer reviews are not unnecessary wastes of time; they are very necessary wastes of time. I learned that I must keep my audience in mind when writing papers. I don't want my readers to become violent with boredom while reading my paper—unless that is the purpose of my paper; then I hope they become as violent as possible. I've learned to be respectful to my critics. And for my final argument to he who has the power, I believe my work has dramatically improved—as a direct result of this course—from "Steve Wants a Cookie, "to "Steve Wants an A." Although my well crafted title states my argument as clear as can be, allow me to sum it all up by saying: Steve wants an A . . . although, he would settle for a cookie.

COMMENTARY We present Steve's essay as an example of a rather creative approach to the reflective essay. Steve decided to write a humorous essay in which he spoofs the kind of grade consciousness a reflective-essay assignment might seem to encourage. Rather than presenting a thesis such as "I have learned a good deal about my writing in this course," Steve tells his reader outright that his thesis is "Steve wants an A in this course." Within the framework of this spoof, however, Steve lists many important principles of good writing. And, more important, he shows how he has applied these principles in his own writing.

PART Five

Style

Exactly what is writing style? Few words are more pervasive in our language than "style." We talk about a style of dress, a hair style, a style of playing tennis, a business style, and, of course, a writing style. In each of these cases, a large part of the meaning is carried by the modifier—from "of dress" in the first case to "writing" in the last. A style of dress is very different from a style of playing tennis, but the two phrases are similar in that both draw attention to individuality. All people wear clothes and many add accessories such as purses and jewelry. But no one person puts these elements together in exactly the same way as any other person. So, we can talk about one person's style of dress as a way of focusing on that person's individuality. This, then, is one meaning for the word "style." There is another meaning, however, which is evident in the sentence: "She has style." What exactly does it mean to have style? To begin with, we know that it is a good thing. One would rather have style than lack it. Beyond that, what do we know about having style? In this sense, the word "style" is associated with a certain quality of right- ness. Although we cannot quite put our finger on why it is so, we have the feel- ing that a person with style will know what to wear at the appropriate time, will say the right things, and, in general, will make those around him comfortable. When you are with a person who has style, everything is as it should be.

We have moved a good way from our initial question of what writing style is, but we can return to that question by looking at the three essays featured at the beginning of this part: Henry Louis Gates, Jr.'s "Change of Life," Amy Tan's "Mother Tongue," and Joan Beck's "The Government Cannot Protect You." There is something right about these essays. In the next two chapters, we will look at excerpts from these and other essays to gain insight into what it is that makes essays feel right, what makes us comfortable with them. Here we want to preview some of what we will be saying in those chapters by offering our definition of writing style in light of our understanding of how language and thought are connected. This may seem a grand undertaking, but to undertake less would be to offer a superficial definition of the term.

According to one theory, there is no separating language and thought. You may be familiar with this view from readings in which thinking in various languages is analyzed. In one famous example, it was argued that the Hopi Indians had only two words for color, "hot" and "cold," and that they could not perceive any difference between green and blue since both are "cold" colors. Those who are most knowledgeable about the way human minds work do not give very much credence to this view of the connection between language and thought. It seems clear that people are capable of many thoughts that their language does not allow them to express. If we were to accept the view that language and thought are inseparable, there would be no need to talk about writing style. All writers would simply say what they mean and be done with it.

Does that mean, then, that we can talk about finding what we want to say and then going back to refine or polish what we want to say? Is style really reducible to polish? We don't believe that it is. But if we can't say style and thought are inseparable and yet are unwilling to see style as mere polish or ornamentation, where does that leave us? We can answer this question best by referring to a couple of passages from the essays presented on pages 538–546. First, let's examine the fifth paragraph from Beck's "The Government Cannot Protect You":

> Most AIDS activist groups are much more concerned about people who already have AIDS than about preventing others from becoming infected. Most laws dealing with AIDS are intended to help and shield the HIV-positive, not to safeguard others. Protecting yourself from getting AIDS is something you have to do for yourself.

There is much to say about the style of this paragraph, as we will explain in some detail in Chapter 16, but for now we want to focus on the choice of the word "shield." This is one of the choices that makes us feel that this piece has the kind of rightness we associate with good style. How did Beck choose the word "shield"? Did she think of it at the moment she thought of the idea she wanted to represent? Or did she begin with a vague sense of the meaning she wanted to convey and then choose "shield" from the various words she might have chosen—much as one might think about a young male human and choose from such words as "boy," "lad," "urchin," and "wight"? We really can't say. We can say that Beck could have left the word "shield" out entirely and not lost the point she is making; that is, she could have asserted that most of the laws are designed to help people who are HIV-positive, not to safeguard others. But there is more, so much more, that Beck wants us to get from the word "shield." With this word come associations with wars and battles and ideas of partial protection and of something standing between a person and some type of danger. There is also a slight suggestion, at least to us, of obfuscation, of something getting in one's way and keeping one from seeing something else. So when Beck chooses "shield," there is a resonance with so many other things in the essay that the choice feels right.

Now, let's consider a second passage taken from the fifth paragraph of Gates's "Change of Life":

> [. . .] She began to buy cloth too, bolts of material for some future occasion. Before long, there were galvanized garbage cans filled with bolts of cloth. A sense of need, born of a childhood of scarcity, now came upon her, spurring a pack rat's notion of providence—a contained panic about running short. [. . .]

Here we focus on Gates's use of the word "contained." This word works wonderfully to describe the overall behavior of Gates's mother—everything about her actions speaks of a woman who is so desperate that she must do something. Yet, her methodical actions arise from the assurance she has that there is no need to rush; nothing will change anything. The word "contained" also works marvelously here because of the previous sentences in which the reader is told of the mother's filling galvanized garbage cans—which could also be called containers—with bolts of cloth, in an effort to protect against the nameless harm that is to come to them. Gates knows, at some level, that he could have said "container" instead of "can," but since he didn't, he can trigger this word for the reader and thereby draw attention to the fact that garbage cans contain—both in the literal sense of being containers and in the metaphoric sense of being a part of the process by which his mother busies herself with action that keeps her panic in some kind of check.

So, what is the point of these analyses? As we indicated earlier, we do not know at what stage in her writing process Beck decided on the word "shield." Likewise, we don't know when Gates decided on the phrase "contained panic." However, we would argue that these are the kinds of choices that often come about after a writer is well into an essay. We can imagine that in working on a second or third version of his essay, Gates suddenly changed a phrase like "reserved panic" to "contained panic." He knew that he was working toward the idea that this panic was in no way wild or flailing. In rereading his work, he may have realized—either consciously or unconsciously, and it wouldn't matter which—that "contained panic" would pick up the resonance of the garbage cans and allow him to use those cans as a kind of concrete symbol for the terror of his mother. Now, is this kind of revision mere ornamentation? We think not. Rather, we see it as the way writers give us that wonderful comfort that comes when all the right words are in the right places.

This last point brings us to the thoughts of Kenneth Burke, who provides us with the inspiration for this part on style. Burke defines style as "ingratiation." What exactly might he mean by this? Throughout his writings, Burke illustrates the ways in which writers use language to draw readers into a place where they are receptive to what the writers have to say. A writer's style, then, is the language she uses to make readers comfortable with what she is saying. Style is not what is being said; however, the reader will not hear what is being said, at least not fully, if the style is not right. The two chapters in this part are dedicated to helping you work on this crucial aspect of your writing.

HENRY LOUIS GATES, JR.

CHANGE OF LIFE

1 Though I didn't realize it at the time, probably the biggest reason I joined the church was Mama. Mama, who knew so well how life could kill the thing that made you laugh, who remembered at every funeral what a person had hoped to be, not what he had become, seemed to be dying herself, before my eyes.

2 It came with menopause, and that's how we talked about it. Because we never had the vocabulary to talk about what it turned out to be, a depressive disorder that never quite left her. In fact, she was never the same again, but of course permanence is something you recognize afterward. I can say that a veil passed over her life, dimming her radiance, and then never quite lifted away.

3 I was twelve and she was forty-six when it started, and it was beyond my comprehension. I only knew that something had eclipsed the woman who gave birth to me and raised me, and that nothing I could do seemed to restore things. I was powerless, and so was she. Mama's "change" was the great crisis in my life, the crossroads of my childhood. I was devastated.

4 It was when Mama got sick that I began to withdraw from other kids. She'd talk about dying for hours. She told me to prepare for her death. She'd tell me she was in a lot of pain. And then she would cry. No amount of love could help. I'm very sick, she would say, and I believe I'm going to die. You'll live with your father, and things will be OK. But it is important that you prepare yourself, she repeated.

5 I noticed smaller changes. Mama, the fearless one, suddenly became afraid of dogs. She started to alter physically, as well. Mama used to do exercises devoutly and weighed a trim ninety-eight pounds. At about this time, though, she gained fifty or sixty pounds. Then the clutter in our home started, because she would buy canned goods obsessively, as if to stock a bomb shelter we didn't have. She began to buy cloth too, bolts of material for some future occasion. Before long, there were galvanized garbage cans filled with bolts of cloth. A sense of need, born of a childhood of scarcity, now came upon her, spurring a pack rat's notion of providence—a contained panic about running short. Running out. Going without. Needing and not having. Even as the house became cluttered with her acquisitions, she became obsessed with cleanliness, spending a good part of each day vacuuming. Vacuuming and dusting. I liked trying to help her, and would cook, and clean, and even iron sometimes. I would read the pamphlets that started appearing all over our house, with titles such as "The Phases of Eve" and "The Change of Life," so that I might get a handle on this crazy, evil thing that had entered our lives.

6 I could not break the spell, no matter how ardently I labored. The depression only deepened that year, and I watched her grow sadder every day.

7 The night they took her away to the hospital, she hugged me as if that was the end. I cried until I fell asleep, afraid that she would die, afraid that I was responsible. And if I was, as I suspected, responsible, I had a good idea how.

8   You see, I had developed all sorts of rituals. I would, for instance, always walk around the kitchen table only from right to left, never the other way around. I would approach a chair from its left side, not the right. Mama had hung a beautiful oak crucifix in the hall that connected our bedrooms and the toilet, and I would nod my head as I passed it, just as I had seen my father do at the Episcopal funeral of his father. I got into and out of the same side of bed, slept on the same side, and I held the telephone with the same hand to the same ear. But most of all, as if my life depended on it, I crossed my legs right calf over left, and never, ever, the other way around.

9   Until one Sunday. For a reason that seemed compelling at the time, probably out of anger or spite, I decided that day to cross my legs in reverse. It was a dare, an act of defiance, a deliberate tempting of fate. And it took place just after Sunday supper, at about 1:00 p.m. Mama had not felt like getting dressed that day. She was having "hot flashes," as she'd started to call them, and felt "disconnected," disembodied from herself. She was going to die, she said to me, over and over and over that day. She'd had one "spell" in the middle of a funeral, just a couple of Sundays before. I wasn't there, but I heard that my aunts Helen and Hazel had taken her out of the church to Hazel's house, where the post-funeral meal was being served. Talking crazy talk, was the way Daddy still describes it. Out of her head.

10   And on this afternoon, the sense of illness lay so heavy you could have gathered it in your hands like snow and rounded it into balls to throw. We all waited for something terrible to happen. And then it was Mama who told me, through her tears, that she had to go to the hospital, that she didn't know when she would be coming back, and that if she shouldn't come back, I must never forget that she loved me.

11   She didn't die. After her hospitalization of four or five days she started taking a lot of pills prescribed by the doctors, which accumulated like everything else. She had weathered acute depression, but despite real improvement, she did not emerge healthy and whole, as I had dared to hope. Her phobias would evolve in unpredictable ways. In later years, she developed a fear that objects resting on a table or a countertop would fall off the edge. She would go around the house pushing objects farther back from perilous edges. It puzzled and vexed me: I'd point out, in a reasoning tone, that it would take an earthquake to produce the results she feared. But Mama felt her life had been shaken by just such an earthquake; she knew how easy it was to fall off the edge.

12   As did I in my own way. My metaphor was an untethered craft, battered by frigid waters, too far out for me to bring back to shore.

13   But Mama wasn't the only one to change. I could never shake the idea that if only I hadn't dared fate to punish me, by crossing my legs the wrong way around, Mama wouldn't have become sick and gone to the hospital. It was a sense of guilt so enormous that I couldn't talk about it. Except to Jesus. That Sunday when Mama went away, I started to atone. I prayed all day, all evening, and the next day: if God would just let Mama not die, as she was convinced she was going to do, I would give my life to Christ and join the church.

14   After enough time had passed to show that the Lord had kept His side of the covenant, it fell to me to fulfill mine. When I announced my intention to join the church, Daddy thought I'd taken leave of my senses. Mama, quietly wrestling with her own devils, was more tolerant, of course, but even I saw that she hoped I would outgrow it. If you go into this thing, Daddy said quietly, scarcely able to believe his ears, don't do it halfway. And don't be a quitter. Nobody likes a quitter.

15   Nobody my age had joined the church in years, at least not the Methodist church. I had been thinking about doing it for several months, since I had turned twelve. It was 1962. Each time in the service when Reverend Mon-roe would invite all who wished to make Jesus their personal Savior to come forward and enter the circle, I had been

tempted to go. But I waited until a Sunday afternoon service in Keyser. Reverend Monroe had two churches, you see; he preached at Walden in Piedmont, but his primary pulpit was in Keyser, and he'd shuttle from one to the other, preaching in one and then the other, each Sunday.

16 I sat there throughout the service, nervous and tense. My stomach was doing flip-flops. I thought he'd never read the invitation; I thought he'd never stop that boring sermon.

17 When finally he did, I found myself rising mechanically, stumbling out of the pew, wandering to the front of the church, standing right in front of Ralph Edell Mon-roe, and wondering what would happen next. Nobody quite knew what to do. It had been so long since anyone joined the church that no one could remember what came next. Monroe stumbled through the book of rites until he found the right page, and then he asked me the prescribed questions.

> Do you here, in the presence of God and of this congregation, renew the solemn promise contained in the Baptismal Covenant, ratifying and confirming the same, and acknowledging yourselves bound faithfully to observe and keep the covenant, and all things contained therein?
>
> Have you saving faith in the Lord Jesus Christ?
>
> Do you entertain friendly feelings towards all the members of the Church?
>
> Do you believe in the doctrines of the Holy Scriptures as set forth in the articles of religion of the Methodist Church?
>
> Will you cheerfully be governed by the Discipline of the Methodist Church, hold sacred the ordinances of God, and endeavor, as much as in you lies, to promote the welfare of your brethren, and the advancement of the Redeemer's kingdom?
>
> Will you contribute of your earthly substance according to your ability, to the support of the Gospel, Church, and poor, and the various benevolent enterprises of the Church?

18 Yes, yes, and yes! I answered as forcefully as I could, and the reverend proclaimed the reception address:

> We welcome you to the communion of the Church of God; and in testimony of your Christian affection and the cordiality with which we receive you, I hereby extend to you the right hand of our fellowship; and may God grant that you may be a faithful and useful member of the Church militant till you are called to the fellowship of the Church triumphant, which is without fault before the presence of God.

19 Then, departing from the text, he invited everyone in the church—all of them older women—to march single file to the front and welcome me into the fold. God bless you, Skippy, each one said, shaking my hand warmly, or hugging me, or running her hand over my forehead or across my head. That part was so beautiful that I couldn't help but cry. I stood there crying and shaking hands, until everyone had passed by. Then I sat down again.

20 The first thing I did after joining the church was to go down to the Five and Ten Cent Store, to the school-supply section, where they stocked the boxes of twelve, twenty-four, and sixty-four Crayola crayons. There I discreetly placed $1.18, in change, down between the neatly stacked cartons. I had stolen a box of crayons when I was six, and wanted to atone for my sin by repaying the store, with interest, for my crime.

21 I began to cook most of the evening meals for the family. When Mama felt like doing the cooking, I would bake: cakes and corn pudding. I still remember the two Betty Crocker

cookbooks she had. They were the same shade of green as the *Webster's Dictionary* that Daddy used for doing the crossword puzzles every day. I loved to cook *with* Mama, just to be near her, to be talking with her. But I was constantly frustrated that we never had all the ingredients a recipe would call for, so I couldn't ever get it exactly right. What is oregano? I'd ask my mother, unsure how to pronounce it. And what in the world was cumin? I'd spend hours searching for a recipe that called only for ingredients that Mama stocked. They were few and far between. Furthermore, Betty didn't season with bacon drippings or ham hocks, and she didn't cook the vegetables long enough to suit us.

22   For the next two years, I didn't play cards, I didn't go to dances, I didn't listen to rock and roll; I didn't gamble or swear, as my classmates did. I didn't ever lust in my heart—except once or twice for Brenda. I went to church, and read the Bible, and spent a lot of time thinking about questions that it turned out Miss Sarah and even Reverend Mon-roe weren't prepared to answer for me.

23   I enjoyed my time alone: I had to, since I hardly went anywhere during these two years, except for school and church. It gave me distance from Daddy and Rocky, neither of whom seemed to be crazy about the person I was becoming. It gave me space to think about Mama's change and a way to use my prayers to help her. It gave me a way to stop thinking so much about nuclear war. For the world now seemed a dangerous place, and the Cuban missile crisis of 1962 provided bleak confirmation. We all went to bed one night thinking that we were going to die in some terrible, horrible, nasty way. I prayed and prayed until I fell asleep. Ain't no use worrying about bomb shelters, Daddy had said. It won't help much. I just wanted to be at home when it happened with Mama and Daddy and Rocky. I was worried that Daddy might not get to Heaven, as much as he cussed and played cards. The church would help with my worries about Vietnam, where my cousin Jay had been sent. His mother, Aunt Marguerite, was so up-set she stopped reading the papers.

24   Larger things began to worry me, now. After I became a Christian and was saved, I was terrified that an angel would show up in my room, bearing some ominous message from God, or that such a message would appear in the form of Writing on the Wall. Miss Sarah would talk of that all the time. I agonized constantly that a bad-news message from God would delineate my role in life, my obligations to God and to our people. That was one of the reasons I was afraid of the dark. I was terrified of the Visitation that would make me an agent of salvation. More concretely, I feared that one day I'd open my mouth and somebody else's voice would come out, as the Spirit possessed me to do its bidding.

25   I didn't want to be like that. I didn't want to be an automaton controlled by heav-enly remote. What I did feel was that God spoke His will to my heart if I asked what I should do in a given situation. I still ask, and, generally, I still hear. Sooner or later.

26   In those days, I spent long hours wondering about, and worrying about, God, Je-sus, being born again, eternal life, Hell, the Devil, why bad things happen to good peo-ple, why good things happen to bad people, and what is right and what wrong.

27   In the end, as I say, joining the church gave me a space of my own, and I found so-lace in that solitude, long after I realized that the time had come to part ways with our small white wooden church.

AMY TAN

MOTHER TONGUE

1   I am not a scholar of English or literature. I cannot give you much more than per-sonal opinions on the English language and its variations in this country or others.

2   I am a writer. And by that definition, I am someone who has always loved language. I am fascinated by language in daily life. I spend a great deal of my time thinking about the power of language—the way it can evoke an emotion, a visual image, a complex idea, or a simple truth. Language is the tool of my trade. And I use them all—all the Englishes I grew up with.

3   Recently, I was made keenly aware of the different Englishes I do use. I was giving a talk to a large group of people, the same talk I had already given to half a dozen other groups. The nature of the talk was about my writing, my life, and my book, *The Joy Luck Club.* The talk was going along well enough, until I remembered one major difference that made the whole talk sound wrong. My mother was in the room. And it was perhaps the first time she had heard me give a lengthy speech, using the kind of English I have never used with her. I was saying things like, "The intersection of memory upon imagination" and "There is an aspect of my fiction that relates to thus-and-thus"—a speech filled with carefully wrought grammatical phrases, burdened, it suddenly seemed to me, with nominalized forms, past perfect tenses, conditional phrases, all the forms of standard English that I had learned in school and through books, the forms of English I did not use at home with my mother.

4   Just last week, I was walking down the street with my mother, and I again found myself conscious of the English I was using, and the English I do use with her. We were talking about the price of new and used furniture and I heard myself saying this: "Not waste money that way." My husband was with us as well, and he didn't notice any switch in my English. And then I realized why. It's because over the twenty years we've been together I've often used that same kind of English with him, and sometimes he even uses it with me. It has become our language of intimacy, a different sort of English that relates to family talk, the language I grew up with.

5   So you'll have some idea of what this family talk I heard sounds like, I'll quote what my mother said during a recent conversation which I videotaped and then transcribed. During this conversation my mother was talking about a political gangster in Shanghai who had the same last name as her family's, Du, and how the gangster in his early years wanted to be adopted by her family, which was rich by comparison. Later, the gangster became more powerful, far richer than my mother's family, and one day showed up at my mother's wedding to pay his respects. Here's what she said in part:

6   "Du Yusong having business like fruit stand. Like off the street kind. He is Du like Du Zong—but not Tsung-ming Island people. The local people call putong, the river east side, he belong to that side local people. The man want to ask Du Zong father take him in like become own family. Du Zong father wasn't looking down on him, but didn't take seriously, until that man big like become a mafia. Now important person very hard to inviting him. Chinese way, come only to show respect, don't stay for dinner. Respect for making big celebration, he shows up. Mean gives lots of respect. Chinese custom. Chinese social life that way. If too important won't have to stay too long. He come to my wedding. I didn't see. I heard it. I gone to boy's side, they have YMCA dinner. Chinese age I was nineteen."

7   You should know that my mother's expressive command of English belies how much she actually understands. She reads the *Forbes* report, listens to *Wall Street Week,* converses daily with her stockbroker, reads all of Shirley MacLaine's books with ease—all kinds of things I can't begin to understand. Yet some of my friends tell me they understand 50 percent of what my mother says. Some say they understand 80 to 90 percent. Some say they understand none of it, as if she were speaking pure Chinese. But to me, my mother's English is perfectly clear, perfectly natural. It's my mother's tongue. Her language, as I hear it, is vivid, direct, full of observation and imagery. This was the language that helped shape the way I saw things, expressed things, made sense of the world.

8   Lately, I've been giving more thought to the kind of English my mother speaks. Like others, I have described it to people as "broken" or "fractured" English. But I wince when I say that. It has always bothered me that I can think of no way to describe it other than "broken," as if it were damaged and needed to be fixed, as if it lacked a certain wholeness and soundness. I've heard other terms used, "limited English," for example. But they seem just as bad, as if everything is limited, including people's perceptions of the limited English speaker.

9   I know this for a fact, because when I was growing up, my mother's "limited" English limited *my* perception of her. I was ashamed of her English. I believed that her English reflected the quality of what she had to say. That is, because she expressed them imperfectly her thoughts were imperfect. And I had plenty of empirical evidence to support me: the fact that people in department stores, at banks, and at restaurants did not take her seriously, did not give her good service, pretended not to understand her, or even acted as if they did not hear her.

10   My mother has long realized the limitations of her English as well. When I was fifteen, she used to have me call people on the phone to pretend I was she. In this guise, I was forced to ask for information or even complain and yell at people who had been rude to her. One time it was a call to her stockbroker in New York. She had cashed out her small portfolio and it just so happened we were going to go to New York the next week, our very first trip outside California. I had to get on the phone and say in an adolescent voice that was not very convincing, "This is Mrs. Tan."

11   And my mother was standing in the back whispering loudly, "Why he don't send me check, already two weeks late. So mad he lie to me, losing me money."

12   And then I said in perfect English, "Yes, I'm getting rather concerned. You had agreed to send the check two weeks ago, but it hasn't arrived."

13   Then she began to talk more loudly "What he want, I come to New York tell him front of his boss, you cheating me?" And I was trying to calm her down, make her be quiet, while telling the stockbroker, "I can't tolerate any more excuses. If I don't receive the check immediately I am going to have to speak to your manager when I'm in New York next week." And sure enough, the following week there we were in front of this astonished stockbroker, and I was sitting there red-faced and quiet, and my mother, the real Mrs. Tan, was shouting at his boss in her impeccable broken English.

14   We used a similar routine just five days ago, for a situation that was far less humorous. My mother had gone to the hospital for an appointment, to find out about a benign brain tumor a CAT scan had revealed a month ago. She said she had spoken very good English, her best English, no mistakes. Still, she said, the hospital did not apologize when they said they had lost the CAT scan and she had come for nothing. She said they did not seem to have any sympathy when she told them she was anxious to know the exact diagnosis, since her husband and son had both died of brain tumors. She said they would not give her any more information until the next time and she would have to make another appointment for that. So she said she would not leave until the doctor called her daughter. She wouldn't budge. And when the doctor finally called her daughter, me, who spoke in perfect English—lo and behold—we had assurances the CAT scan would be found, promises that a conference call on Monday would be held, and apologies for any suffering my mother had gone through for a most regrettable mistake.

15   I think my mother's English almost had an effect on limiting my possibilities in life as well. Sociologists and linguists probably will tell you that a person's developing language skills are more influenced by peers. But I do think that the language spoken in the family, especially in immigrant families which are more insular, plays a large role in shaping the language of the child. And I believe that it affected my results on achievement tests, IQ tests, and the SAT. While my English skills were never judged as poor, compared

to math, English could not be considered my strong suit. In grade school I did moderately well, getting perhaps B's, sometimes B-pluses, in English and scoring perhaps in the sixtieth or seventieth percentile on achievement tests. But those scores were not good enough to override the opinion that my true abilities lay in math and science, because in those areas I achieved A's and scored in the ninetieth percentile or higher.

16 This was understandable. Math is precise; there is only one correct answer. Whereas, for me at least, the answers on English tests were always a judgment call, a matter of opinion and personal experience. Those tests were constructed around items like fill-in-the-blank sentence completion, such as "Even though Tom was _____ Mary thought he was _____." And the correct answer always seemed to be the most bland combinations of thoughts, for example, "Even though Tom was shy, Mary thought he was charming," with the grammatical structure "even though" limiting the correct answer to some sort of semantic opposites, so you wouldn't get answers like, "Even though Tom was foolish, Mary thought he was ridiculous." Well, according to my mother, there were very few limitations as to what Tom could have been and what Mary might have thought of him. So I never did well on tests like that.

The same was true with word analogies, pairs of words in which you were supposed to find some sort of logical, semantic relationship—for example, "*Sunset* is to *nightfall* as _____ is to _____." And here you would be presented with a list of four possible pairs, one of which showed the same kind of relationship: *red* is to *stoplight, bus* is to *arrival, chills* is to *fever, yawn* is to *boring.* Well, I could never think that way. I knew what the tests were asking, but I could not block out of my mind the images already created by the first pair, "*sunset* is to *nightfall*"—and I would see a burst of colors against a darkening sky, the moon rising, the lowering of a curtain of stars. And all the other pairs of words—red, bus, stoplight, boring—just threw up a mass of confusing images, making it impossible for me to sort out something as logical as saying: "A sunset precedes nightfall" is the same as "a chill precedes a fever." The only way I would have gotten that answer right would have been to imagine an associative situation, for example, my being disobedient and staying out past sunset, catching a chill at night, which turns into feverish pneumonia as punishment, which indeed did happen to me.

17 I have been thinking about all this lately, about my mother's English, about achievement tests. Because lately I've been asked, as a writer, why there are not more Asian Americans represented in American literature. Why are there few Asian Americans enrolled in creative writing programs? Why do so many Chinese students go into engineering? Well, these are broad sociological questions I can't begin to answer. But I have noticed in surveys—in fact, just last week—that Asian students, as a whole, always do significantly better on math achievement tests than in English. And this makes me think that there are other Asian-American students whose English spoken in the home might also be described as "broken" or "limited." And perhaps they also have teachers who are steering them away from writing and into math and science, which is what happened to me.

18 Fortunately, I happen to be rebellious in nature and enjoy the challenge of disproving assumptions made about me. I became an English major my first year in college, after being enrolled as pre-med. I started writing nonfiction as a freelancer the week after I was told by my former boss that writing was my worst skill and I should hone my talents toward account management.

19 But it wasn't until 1985 that I finally began to write fiction. And at first I wrote using what I thought to be wittily crafted sentences, sentences that would finally prove I had mastery over the English language. Here's an example from the first draft of a story that later made its way into *The Joy Luck Club,* but without this line: "That was my mental quandary in its nascent state." A terrible line, which I can barely pronounce.

20   Fortunately, for reasons I won't get into today, I later decided I should envision a reader for the stories I would write. And the reader I decided upon was my mother because these were stories about mothers. So with this reader in mind—and in fact she did read my early drafts—I began to write stories using all the Englishes I grew up with: the English I spoke to my mother, which for lack of a better term might be described as "simple"; the English she used with me, which for lack of a better term might be described as "broken"; my translation of her Chinese, which could certainly be described as "watered down"; and what I imagined to be her translation of her Chinese if she could speak in perfect English, her internal language, and for that I sought to preserve the essence, but neither an English nor a Chinese structure. I wanted to capture what language ability tests can never reveal: her intent, her passion, her imagery, the rhythms of her speech and the nature of her thoughts.

21   Apart from what any critic had to say about my writing, I knew I had succeeded where it counted when my mother finished reading my book and gave me her verdict: "So easy to read."

JOAN BECK

THE GOVERNMENT CANNOT PROTECT YOU

1   There's a *life-death message* in the final report of the National Commission on AIDS. But the report concentrates so hard on blaming political leaders for not doing more about the epidemic the message is lost between the lines of anger and frustration.

2   No cure for AIDS is in sight, the commission's report notes. A vaccine is years away. HIV continues to be a slow, inexorable killer, mostly of adults in the prime of *life*.

3   But, as the report should have stressed in language strong enough to burn into the brains of us all, you can generally protect yourself from getting AIDS.

4   The government isn't going to guard you from getting AIDS. It can't. President Bush couldn't. President Clinton can't. The White House's new AIDS coordinator, Kristine Gebbie, can't either, no matter how urgently AIDS groups pushed for that post to be created. Neither can the governors, mayors, members of Congress, corporate executives or community and religious leaders the commission's report blames for not doing more.

5   Most AIDS activist groups are much more concerned about people who already have AIDS than about preventing others from becoming infected. Most laws dealing with AIDS are intended to help and shield the HIV-positive, not to safeguard others. Protecting yourself from getting AIDS is something you have to do for yourself.

6   Doctors can't cure you if you get AIDS. They can only postpone your death, treat some associated illnesses and keep you feeling a little better as you slowly die. All the politically correct attitudes, all the anti-discrimination laws, all the political activism, all the red AIDS ribbons, all the support groups, all the finger-pointing can't change the basic facts about this epidemic.

7   The same sober assessment about the lack of substantial progress against the AIDS epidemic was sounded repeatedly in Berlin in June, when thousands of scientists met at the annual international conference on AIDS. The lack of encouraging scientific news included studies pointing up the limited benefits of AZT, the primary drug used to treat HIV infections and AIDS.

8   Prevention is now the only way to stop the epidemic from continuing to spread widely and rapidly throughout the world, scientists repeatedly emphasized at the Berlin conference.

9   HIV does not infect humans easily, like the common cold. It is not genetic, the result of an unlucky mistake in DNA coding. Its cause is known, unlike most forms of cancer. AIDS, like it or not, is an infection acquired by having sex with an infected partner (anal-receptive sex is particularly risky) or sharing a needle with an infected intravenous drug user.

10   Exceptions include babies of HIV-positive mothers, people inadvertently transfused with HIV-positive blood, accidentally infected health care workers and a few cases for which the cause has not been established.

11   The hard fact is that those who want to protect themselves against HIV infection and AIDS can almost certainly do so by not sharing intravenous drug needles with an infected person and by having sex only within an established monogamous relationship with a partner who is free of HIV.

12   Why is it so hard to push this message clearly and explicitly? For one reason, it's widely assumed that changes in sexual behavior in the last three decades have made the message of premarital abstinence and marital fidelity naive and obsolete. Never mind that two generations ago, it was considered the social norm (whatever the exceptions in practice).

13   So those who are trying to prevent the spread of AIDS are relying on messages about "safe sex," which generally means condoms. Condoms can substantially reduce the risk of acquiring HIV from an infected partner as well as the chances of getting other sexually transmitted diseases, which in turn increase susceptibility to HIV. But condoms have a high failure rate as a contraceptive, and the AIDS virus can much more easily slip through microscopic holes in a condom than can a much larger sperm. A woman can usually become pregnant only about two days a month. The sexual partner of a person with HIV is always at risk.

14   Even so, an increasing number of schools are making condoms available to students, sometimes over the strenuous objections of parents who feel the implicit message is that sex is okay and expected of teenagers and that more immature young people—not fewer—will be at risk.

15   It is also difficult to shape messages about sexual behavior so they will be acceptable to minorities and to gays who are at higher risk of AIDS than the population as a whole. But excessive sensitivity, exaggerated political correctness and concern about seeming to blame the victims can sometimes dilute the cautions too much.

16   We do need much more scientific research about AIDS—and more money to pay for it, even though AIDS research is now better funded than work on other diseases which claim many more lives. We do need support and good care for persons with AIDS and HIV. We do need an end to residual prejudice, discrimination and unjustified fears of infected people.

17   We do need more treatment facilities for drug abusers, although the high rate of recidivism is discouraging. Needle exchange programs have ardent backers, although critics are concerned about supporting what is self-destructive behavior regardless of the risk of AIDS.

18   We do need more empowerment for women, in the United States and especially in many Third World cultures, so they can protect themselves from the sexual demands of high-risk men and from dangerous sexual practices.

19   But while we are working on all these difficult things, it would help to broadcast clearly and loudly the message of individual responsibility for avoiding HIV and individual power to do so, instead of blaming the government for not doing more.

Mark Twain probably put it best when he said, "The difference between the almost-right word and the right word is [. . .] the difference between the lightning bug and the lightning." But how exactly will you know when you have selected the right word in a given situation? As you have more and more experience as a reader and a writer, you will become more and more skilled at this important task. There is no substitute for this experience. There are, however, some basic concepts about word formation and about how words work that will help you hone your skills in finding the right word for a given writing situation.

WHAT IS A WORD?

In written language, we have little difficulty in determining what is, or is not, a word. Letters that are separated by a space from other letters represent a word. Thus, "black" and "bird" are both words since they are separated by spaces from the other words around them. However, "blackbird" is one word, since there is no space between the two parts of this word. It seems right to say that "black" and "bird" are separate words, and "blackbird" is one word, since a blackbird is different from a black bird: A black bird is a bird that is black; a blackbird, on the other hand, is a particular type of bird.

Working with Words

C H A P T E R 15

However, the breaks between words are not always so logical. Consider the following examples:

high school	high school
can not	cannot

In the first case, two words, "high" and "school" can be used to mean something quite different from "a school that is high." A high school is a type of school, just as a blackbird is a type of bird. Yet, the graphic system for English represents "high" and "school" as separate words. On the other hand, there seems little difference between "can" and "not" presented as two separate words and "cannot" presented as one word.

It is strange, isn't it, that something that seems so simple and straightforward as the concept of *word* can be so complicated when we take time to examine it carefully? We all know what a word is. Yet, when it comes to explaining to someone else exactly what we know, we find ourselves faced with a problem that is far from simple. And that is but one of the complexities of human language that we meet head on when we talk about words. The way in which words and thought connect is another.

THE SYMBOLIC NATURE OF WORDS

Intellectually, we all know that the connection between a word's sound and its meaning is arbitrary. That doesn't stop us from *feeling* that there is an inherent connection between the words we use to refer to something and the thing itself. When we learn a foreign language, we tend to think of the word our native language uses for a thing or a concept as the right word for what we are talking about; we see the foreign word as a substitute for this correct word. In learning French, for example, we would see the word "chien" as a translation for "dog." But "chien" and "dog" are really just *symbols* that represent an idea, or concept, in our minds. And that is what symbols do—they represent, or stand for, something else. When we think of symbols, we tend to think of certain rituals or artifacts that are rich in associative meaning. For example, the cross has a rich history of symbolic meaning for anyone familiar with the Christian religion. However, words can also be symbols; in fact, all words are symbols, since they stand for some thing or idea. This is just another way of saying the word and the thing or idea it represents are not one and the same.

We know that it is a convention of the English language to use the word "dog" to refer to certain furry, four-legged animals. If we were speaking another language, we would choose another set of sounds to represent these creatures. Indeed, even when using English, we are not obligated to equate the sound "dog" with such an animal. We could also use some of the following symbols: "miniature collie," "Tucker," "my companion," "small animal," "cur," "fleabag," "furry friend," "barking machine," and so forth.

Take a minute to list the various words you use to refer to a person or object that is important to you. Choose something with which you can associate at least three different terms. Examine the situations in which you use these various terms. How do they differ? Are there any differences in the meanings you associate with them?

You may object that we are stretching a bit in referring to a dog in the preceding paragraph as a "barking machine"; certainly it would take a very specific context to make this the right choice for the writer's meaning. But, as Exercise 15.1 should help you see, selecting the right word is not simply a matter of matching labels with preordained meanings. The situation and the shade of meaning the writer wants to convey in that situation help determine what word he chooses.

A RHETORICAL PERSPECTIVE

The point of this discussion is that choosing the right word in any given situation is a rhetorical act. By this, we mean that in selecting words you must take into consideration your audience and your purpose in writing for that audience. If you are spotlighting the subject, your goal is likely to be clarity: You want your reader to understand exactly what you are saying about your subject. If you are spotlighting the writer, your goal is likely to be self-expression: You want your reader to experience what you have experienced. Finally, if you are spotlighting the reader, your goal is to move the reader toward some action.

We do not mean to suggest that any of these goals is absent in a given writing situation. You will not disregard clarity simply because you are spotlighting the writer or the reader. However, clarity will probably not be the most important factor in selecting words in these cases, as it might well be when the spotlight is on the subject. By the same token, expression of your personal feelings will not be the focus in writing intended to persuade the reader, even though you may well tell a personal story, as Dr. Martin Luther King, Jr. does in "Letter from Birmingham Jail"(pp. 371–381), in order to move your reader toward the action you want her to take.

STRATEGIES FOR WRITING THAT SPOTLIGHTS THE SUBJECT

The focus in informative writing is on conveying information clearly. The successful writer will give readers the impression that they are looking through words to the writer's meaning. Any words that draw attention to themselves will probably be less effective than they might otherwise be. In informative writing, the premium is on precision.

The most important tool you can have for achieving precision is a command of words. Finding the right word for a given situation will often involve choosing one word from three or four that are very close in meaning. For example, you could characterize a conversation between two people as "conversing," "talking," or "chatting," since these three words have relatively similar meanings. And these are not the only possible choices, of course. Depending on the situation and your purposes in writing about the conversation, you could also use such words or phrases as "confab," "powwow," "meeting of the minds," "tête-à-tête," and "dialogue" to represent what is taking place between the two people. So how do you choose? If you have a firm grasp of the various subtle differences in meaning that readers will take from these words, you can make the proper choice to convey your intended meaning. The differences in meaning may be subtle, but they do exist. For example, as one moves from "conversing," to "talking," and then to "chatting," there is a movement from somewhat formal to informal to very informal. One *converses* with important people in important situations. One does not usually *converse* with friends in a bar.

We see other subtle differences in meaning when we look at the second group of words. In "confab," " powwow," and "tête-à-tête," there is some hint that the matter being talked about is a problem or issue of some sort. But "confab" implies that the two parties communicating are working together toward the resolution of the problem or the issue. Thus, if you and a friend are trying to decide how best to get your roommate to clean up the bathroom, you might *confab* about the matter. Both "tête-à-tête," and "powwow," however, allow for some possible conflict, as might happen when the two people on either side of an issue meet with each other. Thus, if you talk with your roommate directly about the issue, the two of you might have a *tête-à-tête* or a *powwow*. Note that even though the element of confrontation is here, there is also a very strong sense that the conversants are talking to each other and hearing each other. To have a tête-à-tête, or a powwow about an issue is very different from having an *argument* about the issue.

Exercise 15.2

Reread paragraph 7 of Amy Tan's "Mother Tongue" (p. 542). On the whole, Tan's language in that paragraph is very direct and clear. However, in a few places she uses rather formal words. For example, she says that her mother's expressive language "belies" how much her mother understands. Also, she tells us that her mother "converses" with her stockbroker daily. What less formal words or phrases might Tan have used in place of these two words? What would she gain or lose in making such changes?

LEARNED AND POPULAR WORDS

In the paragraph you examined for Exercise 15.2, Tan uses a learned word, "converses," rather than its popular counterpart, "talks." Learned words are words that have come into English from another language, such as Greek, Latin, or French. We call these *learned words* because the languages they have come from are languages known by the most well-educated speakers of English. *Pop-*

ular words, on the other hand, come from the people. For speakers of English, popular words are words that have been in the language at least since the Middle English period (roughly 1100 to 1500 C.E.) or, in most cases, since the Old English period (roughly 700 to 1100 C.E.). The word "converse" came into the English language from French, which in turn took the word from Latin. "Talk," on the other hand, can be traced all the way back to Old English.

Here are examples of pairs of learned and popular words:

Popular Words	Learned Words
help	assist
start	commence
tell	convey
talk	converse
small	petite
right	correct
leave	depart
come	arrive
choose	select
hard	difficult
bad/evil	sinister

Why do we have such matching sets of words? Are the learned words simply available to us when we want to impress someone with our vocabulary? As you have no doubt already surmised (figured out?), it's more complicated than that. The learned words do add an element of formality and respect. When Tan says that her mother "converses" daily with a stockbroker, the word "converses" does carry with it a suggestion of her mother's intelligence and business sense. But there is more to the difference than formality. The history of the word "converse" carries with it a sense of long familiarity with, and much knowledge about, a subject. One may *talk* about the weather, knowing nothing, or very little, about meteorology. However, when one *converses* about a subject, it is assumed that one knows quite a bit about it.

Such a list as the one offered here makes it clear that no two words are absolutely interchangeable. Even if we could start with two words that were completely synonymous, they would not remain that way. Either one of the words would disappear, or one of them would tend to be used in a certain set of circumstances and the other in another set of circumstances and, as a result, the two would develop slightly different meanings. We can see this process at work with the first pair of words in the list of examples. "Assist" has come to be used in more formal situations, to the point that one who assists is sometimes given the title of "assistant." One might *assist* a doctor who is operating on a patient. However, one would likely *help* a child with her homework.

Exercise
15.3

Despite the very real purpose that learned words can serve, there is no shortage of humor aimed at those who tend to use overly pretentious language. You may have heard of the alleged cheer used at a university where the students were reputed to be enamored of their intelligence:

Repel the blackguards,
Repel the blackguards,
Force them to relinquish the spheroid.

Another easy target is the malapropisms of a character such as Archie Bunker (from the television situation comedy *All in the Family*). Archie often talked about being "exacerbated" with the younger generation, when he actually meant "exasperated."

Then there is the story of a political candidate who won an election by spreading the word that his opponent had a daughter who was a thespian in New York City and a son who had been seen openly matriculating at a local university.

There is another story about a plumber who once wrote to a research bureau saying that he had used hydrochloric acid to clean out sewer pipes and inquiring if there was any possible harm in doing so. According to the story, he received the following reply: "The efficacy of hydrochloric acid is indisputable, but the corrosive residue is incompatible with metallic permanence." The plumber took this reply as a compliment and sent a thank-you to the person who wrote it. After two or three interchanges with higher and higher officials, a top scientist wrote the plumber saying; "Don't use hydrochloric acid. It eats hell out of the pipes." The plumber finally understood.

Find a couple of examples of your own (from your readings or from your own or other people's experience) of humor that arises from pretentious language. In each case, what causes the humor? Who, or what, is being made fun of? What, if any, point about language does the story (or situation) make? (By the way, if you don't know the word "malapropism," you will want to look it up. Have you or your friends used any malapropisms recently?)

Exercise 15.4

Choose three pairs of words from the list of examples of popular and learned words, and explain the difference in meanings you assign to the words in each pair. Look up the words in an unabridged dictionary, preferably the *Oxford English Dictionary*, to see whether the historical meanings of the words correspond with the differences you see in the words' meanings. Then, use each of the words in a context that helps illustrate the differences you intuit. Are there any pairs in the list that seem completely interchangeable to you? Why or why not?

Exercise 15.5

We would expect popular words to predominate in your writing. This is as it should be, because good writing cannot be equated with "big" words. In fact, any time you use a learned word when you could have chosen a popular word, you should have a definite reason for doing so. To gain some insight into your word choices, review an essay you have written in this course, preferably one that spotlights the subject. Look carefully at a paragraph or two in that essay, focusing on any learned words you find in that passage. How many do you find? Are these words well chosen? Why or why not?

TECHNICAL LANGUAGE AND JARGON

We are all familiar with caricatures of professional jargon as pretentious and incomprehensible. However, writing that spotlights the subject often makes use of some type of specialized language. After all, specialized language is really just an extension of the symbolic power inherent in all language. As we saw earlier, the symbol "dog" may be used to represent a particular kind of furry animal. Without such symbols, how would we convey thoughts about this animal? We could adopt the methods of the philosophers at the Academy of Lagado in Jonathan Swift's *Gulliver's Travels:* Rather than using words, they carried around all those things they might want to refer to in sacks on their backs. That might have strengthened their backs, but it surely weakened their communication. Alternatively, we could agree to use language but decide to keep it simple, clear, and direct—that is, to avoid all specialized language. In that case, we could refer to a dog as a "furry animal." No one would have to learn the technical term "dog." Of course, we would have to take pains to make sure to communicate important differences between this particular furry animal and another with a large bushy tail and a white stripe down its back. It would not take too many unfortunate encounters with the latter animal to make us willing to learn a technical term.

We hope this example makes the point that we all use specialized language. Of course, one person's technical language is another person's jargon; jargon is any language that is incomprehensible to us. Thus, we want to be careful not to frustrate readers with terms they do not know. On the other hand, the more we know (and can assume that our readers know) about a given topic, the more shortcuts the language affords us. Individuals trained in language studies would find it very hard to converse with one another without such terms as "clause," "*t*-unit," "free modifier," "modality," "transformation," "independent clause," and "gerund." Those in health care could not do their work without such terms as "cardiovascular system," "CAT scan," "EKG," and "PET." Individuals trained in computer science find useful such terms as "modem," "bit," "byte," "ROM," and "RAM."

The three specialized fields mentioned above—language study, health care, and computer science—are very much a part of our lives; to one degree or another, we have had to learn terminologies from these fields to edit our writing, talk with our doctors, and master our personal computers. However, new areas of specialization are continually evolving. As they do, they introduce specialized terms that at first seem foreign and perhaps, unnecessary to us. For example, an article by Gary T. Marx that appeared in *Whole Earth Review* and dealt with technological intrusions into daily life contained the following terms: "personal communication device," "information leakage," "biometric monitoring," "UHF channels," and "infinity transmitter." Our natural tendency, when we see such terms, is to question their necessity. We look at a phrase such as "personal communication device," and ask why it's used. Why does a cell phone have to be made to sound fancier by being called a "personal communication device"? This is a reasonable question, and if the writer meant what we mean by "cell phone," that term would have been more appropriate. However, the article in which the term appears makes it clear that the writer is referring to many different devices, including cell phones, cordless phones, beepers, and room monitors for infants. Therefore, the term "cell phone" would have been inappropriate because in this essay's context it would be too narrow. The writer had to resort to a more general term—not to confuse his readers or to impress them but to communicate more correctly what he intended.

Communication is the key. Technical language for one audience may well be jargon for another. The more technical you can afford to be, the more precise and economical you can be in language use. The economy of technical language comes, in part, from its frequent use of acronyms and abbreviations. Even though these shortcuts can be distracting to those unfamiliar with the terms, it would be rather time-consuming if we had to say, for example, "North Atlantic Treaty Organization" every time we wanted to refer to what we commonly call "NATO."

Exercise 15.6

Reread Amy Tan's essay, "Mother Tongue," in the introduction to this part. In this piece, Tan deals with the complicated issues of how language and thought are connected. In particular, she discusses ways in which Asian Americans may be affected by the lack of English, or of "proper" English, in their homes. She also talks about the ways in which those who speak a nonstandard language are treated in U.S. society. Does Tan use technical terms? If so, are you familiar with them, or do they seem like jargon to you? Note any that you feel unsure of.

Exercise 15.7

What areas do you have expertise in? If you need to do so, look back at your responses to the Interest Inventory (on p. 9), particularly items 4 and 5. Pick one of these areas and list some of the technical language you have to know in order to understand conversations about this subject. Are there particular technical or professional journals or magazines that deal with topics in this subject? If so, what kinds of specific knowledge can we assume the readers of these publications have?

Exercise 15.8

The following passage is from a seminal article on style by Monroe C. Beardsley, entitled "Style and Good Style":

The clearest way to say what style is, I think, is to say what a *difference* in style is. Take two sentences or parts of sentences, S1 and S2. We say that they differ in style when two things are true about them. First, they differ to some extent in *meaning*. And second, the difference is not on the plane of overt or explicit meaning, but on the plane of covert or implicit meaning. The distinction between explicit and implicit meaning is one that requires a certain amount of analysis to elucidate, but let me say in a general way what sorts of things I have in mind, and leave it to the examples to clarify the distinction. Implicit meaning includes what we would ascribe to the connotations rather than to the plain dictionary sense of a word, and it includes what we would consider to be merely suggested, or hinted, or intimated by a sentence rather than what the sentence plainly states.

It is relatively easy to see what we are talking about when we compare two similar English expressions with respect to their style. If they don't differ at all in meaning, there is no difference in style (but this, as Pascal says, is almost impossible, for if there are different words, or the same words in a different order, there is almost certain to be some difference in meaning, however small and subtle). If the meanings differ in some explicit way, there is no difference in style. It follows from this analysis that the concept of style is inherently comparative, and therefore variable with the context of concern. To isolate a particular stylistic feature in any discourse is always to think of a particular element of implicit meaning in terms of which that discourse might differ from some other one. This is the first of my two theses, then: that style is detail of implicit meaning.

Write a brief answer to each of the following questions:

1. How does Beardsley's passage compare to our comments on style in the introduction to this part? What connections can you make between Beardsley's passage and what we said?
2. Do you find many learned words in this passage? Choose one or two words and examine them carefully. Write a brief essay in which you explain how they help Beardsley achieve his purpose in this passage.
3. Does Beardsley use technical or professional language? Are there terms you do not know? Examine one or two terms carefully, explaining whether they seem to be useful technical terms or problematic jargon.
4. What type of audience do you imagine this essay was written for? Be as specific as you can in terms of the audience's education and interest in and knowledge about this topic. How do you know these things?

Exercise 15.9

After you have read this passage from a book by Ernest Pascarella entitled *How College Affects Students,* answer the questions that follow:

With the development of more sophisticated, user-oriented statistical packages such as SPSS (Nie, 1983) and SAS (SAS Institute, 1985), the power of multivariate analysis has become available to novitiate and experienced researchers alike. Arguably, the consequences of this have not been uniformly positive. The uninformed use of sophisticated analytical routines is often more likely to obfuscate and mislead than to clarify. Nevertheless, the impressive advances in computing power during the last twenty years have permitted scholars to analyze large and complex national data sets with relative (though perhaps not absolute) ease and efficiency. Such analyses have made major contributions to our understanding of such issues as the impact of college on status attainment and the influence of institutional characteristics on learning. Moreover, they represent a new emphasis or direction in the research literature, which is not nearly so apparent in the studies reviewed by Feldman and Newcomb.

1. What audience do you think this book was written for? Why? How heavily does the writer depend on learned words? On technical language? How appropriate is the language in this passage for that audience? (Here is another way of asking this question: Do you think the technical language and the learned words used in this paragraph are necessary?)
2. Assuming that you agree with us that this piece is not very appropriate for college students, identify words or phrases that need to be explained. Look up any words you do not know. Then rewrite the passage in a fashion that would make it appropriate for an audience of college students.

STRATEGIES FOR WRITING THAT SPOTLIGHTS THE WRITER

The focus in personal writing is the writer's experience. The spotlight is on how she sees the world, as opposed to how others may see it. We often talk about good writing of this type as being descriptive and original, as opposed to information-oriented writing, which we often think of as impersonal and objective. Of course, these contrasts do not hold up in fact. Good writers will find ways to bring originality and vivid description to all types of writing, but they will find that personal writing offers them the best opportunity to hone their descriptive writing skills.

DESCRIPTIVE WRITING

Writer-focused writing spotlights the way the writer sees the world. We do not mean that all descriptive writing describes what the writer literally *sees;* the writer could very well describe a feeling or a complicated situation. It is worth noting, however, that in talking about these nonsensory experiences we have already employed (without even thinking about it) a metaphor that compares them to sensory experiences. What do we mean when we talk about "feelings"? Aren't we, in some sense, comparing an internal state of being to the external sensory act of touching something? We also talk of "seeing" someone's point of view or of "hearing" what someone is saying (in the sense of understanding). It is clear that the senses—both literally and metaphorically—play a crucial role in helping a writer understand her perspective (or point of view) in a given situation or on a given subject. If the writer can help us *see* a scene or a situation the way she *sees* it, she can help us understand her perspective, as the passages below illustrate very well. The first is from Lee Abbott's "The True Story of Why I Do What I Do," which we discussed in some detail in Chapter 4 (pp. 92–95).

> The hours passed that Sunday afternoon as they always do when I cast myself back into the dangerous tides that are my past: the clock above the antique writing desk chiming on the quarter-hour, the father wandering between the refrigerator and liquor cabinet, Pee Wee Reese or Dizzy Dean saying in the TV room what the Dodgers were doing; the son in another room cobbling together in his fertile but screwy imagination a tale of swashbuckling and hair-raising, a narrative of guns and grateful bimbos and nick-of-time derring-do. We were in our elements, him and me: one, the older, tuned to the stupid clatter of the exterior world; the other, the younger flesh of him, tuned to the twilight interior world of fetch-and-keep, of fantasy. [. . .]

The next passage is from one of the essays featured at the beginning of this part on style, Henry Louis Gates, Jr.'s "Change of Life" (p. 540).

> I sat there throughout the service, nervous and tense. My stomach was doing flip-flops. I thought he'd never read the invitation; I thought he'd never stop that boring sermon.
>
> When finally he did, I found myself rising mechanically, stumbling out of the pew, wandering to the front of the church, standing right in front of Ralph Edell Mon-roe, and wondering what would happen next. Nobody quite knew what to do. It had been so long since anyone joined the church that no one

Derek: Did you and Alicia _____ the town last night?

Lorenzo: No, by the _____ I got to her house, it was raining _____ and _____. So we decided to kick _____ and take _____ a movie on TV.

Derek: What was the movie about?

Lorenzo: It was about a country preacher whose wife was cheating on him with a young man in the town. The preacher hit the young man in the head with a _____ bat and killed him. The preacher ran away to an even more isolated place and started a small church for that community. While he was helping people in this community his heart was _____ ing because he could not be with his children and with his mother, who was very sick. Soon he got the news that his mother had _____ away. It was almost more than he could take. But he kept working in this new community and the people really _____ up to him. However, one man in the congregation found out about the preacher's past and _____ him _____ to the authorities. The movie ended as the authorities came to the church where he was preaching to arrest him. In the last scene, the preacher is handcuffed and put into a squad car to be taken to jail.

Now compare your insertions with the words that were originally in this passage, which are shown below.

Derek: How's it going, Lorenzo?

Lorenzo: Fine and dandy, couldn't be better.

Derek: Did you and <u>Alicia</u> do the town last night?

Lorenzo: No, by the time I got to her house, it was raining cats and dogs. So we decided to kick <u>back</u> and take in a movie on TV.

Derek: What was the movie about?

Lorenzo: It was about a country preacher whose wife was cheating on him with a young man in the town. The preacher hit the young man in the head with a ball bat and killed him. The preacher ran away to an even more <u>isolated</u> place and started a small church for that community. While he was helping people in this community his heart was breaking because he could not be with his children and his mother, who was very sick. Soon he got the news that his mother had <u>passed</u> away. It was almost more than he could take. But he kept <u>working</u> in this new community and the people really looked up to him. However, one man in the congregation found out about the preacher's past and turned him in to the authorities. The movie ended as the authorities came to the <u>church</u> where he was preaching to arrest him. In the last scene, the preacher is handcuffed and put into a squad car to be taken to jail.

You may not have filled the blanks with the exact words that were taken out, but we would guess that for the most part you were able to predict what was left out. You could do so because much of our language consists of idioms and dead metaphors. An *idiom* is a collection of words that means something different from what those words mean in isolation. For example, Derek asks Lorenzo if he and Alicia "did the town last night." This is an idiom that is very hard to translate. But it is clear that these words together mean something quite different from their usual meanings.

Idioms are a mainstay of our ordinary language. For example, in his second line, Lorenzo uses the idiom "by the time." This means something roughly equivalent to "when." Many other idioms indicate that we are giving little attention to the language we are using in a given situation. When Derek asks Lorenzo how it's going, Lorenzo responds "Fine and dandy." He is not giving serious thought to saying how he is doing—or at least his choice of words would seem to indicate that he is not. In fact, Lorenzo may not be feeling well at all. He may be assuming, perhaps rightly, that in this situation the greeting is formula and no original language is required. We see another example of this lack of attention in his statement that it was "raining cats and dogs." This seemingly picturesque way of speaking has become so common that it means no more than would the phrase "raining hard." If Lorenzo simply wants to convey that the rain was heavy, either "raining hard" or "raining cats and dogs" will suffice; neither is very original.

The second type of language we find in this passage is what has come to be called *dead metaphors*. As you know, a metaphor is a comparison without "like" or "as." Thus, the sentence "Jaime is a lion" is a metaphor in which Jaime is being compared to a lion. This is a simple, straightforward kind of metaphor, a type we seldom see in sophisticated writing. Much more frequent are metaphors in which a comparison is made subtly, through the use of unusual word choices. As an example, we might say, "Jaime roared his answer." Since humans cannot literally roar, we are comparing Jaime to a lion, or at least to some animal that can be said to roar. A more usual word choice would be "gave" or "offered," as in "Jaime gave a reply," or "Jaime offered a response."

With this understanding of metaphor, we are in a position to bring to life—to speak metaphorically—the dead metaphors in the passage we have been examining. The first one is in the first question that Derek asks Lorenzo: "How's it going?" There is an underlying metaphor here that compares one's day-to-day existence to a journey of some sort. So, Derek is asking Lorenzo for a report of how he is doing on his journey. This has become so commonplace, however, that we seldom see the greeting "How's it going?" as metaphorical. Rather, we tend to react to it much as we would react to an idiom.

A second dead metaphor occurs in the narrative of the movie, where the preacher's heart is said to be "breaking" because he is away from his children. There are two metaphors here. In the first, the preacher's emotions are identified with his heart. There is no literal connection between a person's heart and how he feels emotionally about things; and in fact, various cultures ascribe emotions to different parts of the human anatomy. In the second part of this metaphor, the human heart is compared to some physical object that is capable of breaking into parts. Again, when we hear about hearts breaking, we seldom think of this as metaphorical language. This metaphor has become a routine part of our discourse; thus, it can be said to be a dead metaphor.

Select a passage you wrote in an earlier essay—preferably one that spotlights the subject. Read the passage to determine what underlying metaphors you used, and then attempt to rewrite the passage without these metaphors. For example, in the passage describing the plot of the movie (p. 558), rather than saying that the preacher's heart was breaking, Lorenzo could have said that the preacher was very sad to be away from his children. Rather than saying that the preacher's mother passed away (a part of the metaphor that compares life to a journey, in which being born is arriving and dying is leaving), Lorenzo could have said that the mother died. After you have rewritten your passage, trade papers with a classmate and check to see that each of you has removed all metaphors from his or her passage. Do you find any that escaped attention? Do you disagree as to whether a certain example is actually an underlying metaphor? Write a paragraph detailing what you found in this process.

As you no doubt discovered in working through Exercise 15.11, it is impossible to remove metaphorical language from your writing—even writing that is designed to communicate information in a very clear and straightforward way. Metaphor is integrally connected to the thinking that we do in writing. Of course, you do not want to rid your writing of metaphors, but rather to cultivate your ability to use metaphors of all types effectively.

We have looked at unoriginal metaphors. Now, let's compare that kind of metaphor with the original metaphors you will want to learn to use in writing that focuses on your experiences. First, consider a passage from Dennis Gilbert and Joseph Kahl's "How Many Classes Are There?" a subject-oriented analysis of social classes.

The line between middle class and working class has been blurred by trends which have reduced the traditional differences between blue-collar and white-collar employment. A declining income differential, the increasing routinization of clerical tasks, and the corresponding drop in the prestige value of a white collar per se, have all served to close the gap between shop and office. Viewed in terms of major occupational groupings, the problem centers on the sales, clerical, and craft categories. Our way of dividing these between middle and working class is based on a distinction between workers whose jobs are highly routinized, closely supervised, low in prerequisite training or education, and low in pay, and those who are in the opposite situation. On this basis, we had no trouble placing semiprofessional jobs and the lowest-paid managerial jobs in the middle class or operatives in the working class. The assembly-line character of modern office work and the low salaries associated with most clerical jobs led us to place clerical workers in the working class. We split sales workers into two groups: those engaged in retail work and "others." The latter group includes insurance salesmen, real-estate agents, manufacturers' representatives, and other people who work quite independently and have much higher incomes than the retail workers. Our decision to place most craft workers and foremen in the middle-class is based on similar considerations. They are well paid, skilled, and relatively independent in their work. Moreover, the prestige attached to such occupations places them well above other blue-collar workers. [. . .]

Gilbert and Kahl make use of several metaphors. None of these metaphors is fresh or original; yet they are effective. The structure of the passage, classification, is provided by a key metaphor: Various workers in our society are represented on a huge graph. Gilbert and Kahl talk about a "line" between classes and a "gap" between various classes. They also talk of "dividing" workers into various groups, of "splitting" various groups, and of "placing" people into various groups. This metaphor transforms people into elements that can be manipulated in a graph in various ways.

Embedded within this large metaphor is a second metaphor (or comparison). Gilbert and Kahl talk about "low" salaries and "high" salaries and about jobs with "low" and "high" prestige. This is such a common metaphor that it is very hard to separate the words "low" and "high" from their literal meanings. We tend to think that talk of a high salary is straightforward, literal language. But in fact, it is not. What exactly is a high salary? Is $10,000 high? Is $150,000 high? Many of us would say that the first is not and the second is. But if we were workers in an undeveloped country, we might well see $10,000 as quite high. And if we were professional basketball players, we might think of $150,000 as remarkably low.

Whenever we begin to make relative judgments, such as "high" and "low," we begin to think of salaries in terms of a graph, and then the words "high" and "low" become automatic. When we represent salaries on a graph, the higher the salary, the higher the line representing that number. In certain horizontal graphs, higher salaries would be represented by longer lines, but it is telling that we seldom see salaries represented this way. We would guess that this is because people are so attracted to the metaphor of "high" and "low." This may be in part because it is such a seemingly natural step to another metaphor in which "high" is good and "low" is bad. This latter metaphor may come from a much more general human equation, perhaps tapping into humans' basic instincts. Throughout the history of humankind, high places have been associated with good things, and low places have been considered not good. Another way to come at this metaphor is to say that "up" is good and "down" is bad, and another possible explanation for this metaphor is the natural association between "more" and "up" and between "less" and "down." For example, if a person has a vat containing grain and puts more grain into the vat, the level of the grain in the vat goes up. If grain is taken out, the level goes down. Gilbert and Kahl are tapping into this general metaphor, then, when they talk about high and low-salaries and high- and low-prestige jobs.

Gilbert and Kahl use another very specific kind of metaphor, known as *metonymy*, when they talk of "blue collar" and "white collar" workers. Metonymy involves using a term that is closely associated with a topic to represent that topic. For example, on Ron's campus, the chancellor and the provost of the university have their offices on the fifth floor of a building called the Reese Building. When certain faculty members talk about the actions of the chancellor or the provost, they often refer to them as actions taken by Reese or by the fifth floor, since these two terms are so closely associated with these officials. We see the same process at work when a king or a queen is referred to as the Crown— since crowns are so closely associated with kings and queens. In the United States, we see this process at work when actions taken by the president are referred to as being taken by the White House. Thus, in talking about blue-collar and white-collar workers, Gilbert and Kahl are using a metonymy with a very long history; traditionally, those who work at laboring jobs have worn blue (or at least not white) shirts, and those in management have worn white shirts.

Our analysis should make it clear that the metaphorical language used in reading and writing is closely aligned with our thinking processes. Metaphors are so naturally a part of our thinking that we seldom recognize them as metaphors or comparisons. How else could we think about these things without making these comparisons?

Now, consider another passage, from Datus Proper's "Dark Hollow," a writer-oriented essay (see pp. 132–135 for the full essay).

> Watching a good fly is like watching a bird dog that knows what it's doing. You have faith. Almost every pool has at least a small fish—in the middle, where a trout can hold in slow water and foray into the current for a passing snack, or in the calm patch above a boulder, or in little eddies at the head of the pool. When the fly dallies over just the right spot, the fish responds. A little one is a sparkle, making up its mind and pouncing in the same instant. A big trout is a shadow, a lovely lazy rise without fuss.

When we look at the original metaphorical language in a passage such as this one, we see the same thinking processes at work as in Gilbert and Kahl's passage. However, in this second passage, the writer's metaphors jump out at us because they are fresh and original. We have not thought of these comparisons before.

Consider the *simile* (comparison using "like" or "as") in the first sentence of this passage: "Watching a good fly is like watching a bird dog [. . .]." Compare the metaphor here with the metaphors in the passage about social classes. Although you have certainly heard people talk about blue- and white-collar workers and about high and low salaries, we suspect that you have not heard of comparing watching a fly (an artificial fishing lure) to watching a bird dog. Your first response is probably to wonder just how these two very different activities are alike. If so, then Proper has been successful in presenting an original metaphor to you. It is his job to draw out the similarities for you, as he attempts to do in the rest of the paragraph.

The metaphorical language does not end here, of course. A bit later, Proper tells us that the fly "dallies" over the right spot. Here is another very specific type of metaphor, called *personification*. When we personify something, we bring it to life. In speaking of a fishing fly as being capable of dallying—that is, seeming to trifle, or to waste time—Proper gives it the characteristics of living beings capable of purposeful actions. Again, the language here offers readers a fresh view of this scene. How many readers will have thought of fishing flies as being capable of "dallying"? Not many, we suspect. It is important to note, however, that once a reader thinks about this description, she can see a reason for the comparison. As the fly hovers in the water, it seems to move slowly and without direction, in a way that might be thought of as dallying. If the writer had spoken of the fly as "croaking its joy at being in the water," this would be fresh language. But flies don't croak, and unless the writer can help the reader see some way in which a fly can be like something that croaks, the original language serves no purpose.

We'll mention two other rather striking metaphors in the passage by Proper. In the first, a small fish is seen as a "sparkle" and a larger fish is seen as a "shadow." Both of these are examples of metonymy. As we said above, metonymy is a kind of metaphor in which something closely associated with a subject is made to stand for, or represent, that subject. Proper wants readers to see the smaller fish as moving swiftly through the water and catching sunlight in such a way as to reflect that light in sparkles. He thus uses the metonymy of seeing that small fish as a "sparkle." Similarly, the larger fish moves more slowly and, rather than reflecting light in sparkles, blocks the sun so as to cast a shadow. This shadow associated with the large fish also comes to represent it, in a second metonymy.

In what sense can we say that these two metonymies, "sparkle" and "shadow," are original? Once we see what the writer wants us to see, the logic of the metonymy is clear—small fish do catch light and reflect it in ways that a sparkling diamond might, and large fish do produce shadows in the water. However, the language here is much more creative than language that refers to statements made by the president as statements made by the White House, because this latter metonymy has become a part of everyday speech. The "sparkle" and "shadow" metonymies were there waiting to be discovered, and since Proper discovers them for us, we see his language as fresh and original.

Exercise 15.12

Although we encourage you to strive for original and fresh metaphors in your writing—particularly in writing that focuses on the writer—you will find that even in this type of writing, you will often use standard, or dead, metaphors. Below are passages that contain several metaphors that Gates uses in his essay "Change of Life" (pp. 538–541). What is being compared to what in each example? Note that some passages may contain more than one metaphor. Which of these metaphors are original and which are dead metaphors? Do you have difficulty in deciding in some cases? Write a brief discussion of your findings.

1. I can say that a veil passed over her life, dimming her radiance, and then never quite lifted away. (paragraph 2)
2. I only knew that something had eclipsed the woman who gave birth to me [. . .]. (paragraph 3)
3. Mama's "change" was the great crisis in my life, the crossroads of my childhood. (paragraph 3)
4. [. . .] she would buy canned goods obsessively, as if to stock a bomb shelter [. . .]. (paragraph 5)
5. [. . .] spurring a pack rat's notion of providence—a contained panic about running short. (paragraph 5)
6. I could not break the spell, no matter how ardently I labored. (paragraph 6)
7. And on this afternoon, the sense of illness lay so heavy you could have gathered it in your hands like snow and rounded it into balls to throw. (paragraph 10)

8. She had weathered acute depression [. . .]. (paragraph 11)
9. But Mama felt her life had been shaken by just such an earthquake; she knew how easy it was to fall off the edge. (paragraph 11)
10. My metaphor was an untethered craft, battered by frigid waters, too far out for me to bring back to shore. (paragraph 12)
11. Mama, quietly wrestling with her own devils, was more tolerant [. . .]. (paragraph 14)
12. My stomach was doing flip-flops. (paragraph 16)
13. In the end, as I say, joining the church gave me a space of my own [. . .]. (paragraph 27)

Exercise 15.13

Examine an essay you have written in this course—preferably one that spotlights the writer. List several metaphors used in that essay, and label them as "dead" or "original." Then create at least three original metaphors and work them into your text.

STRATEGIES FOR WRITING THAT SPOTLIGHTS THE READER

Writing spotlights the reader when its goal is to affect the reader in some way. In this type of writing, the words the writer chooses must do more than allow the reader to understand the writer's thoughts; they must move the reader to be receptive to those thoughts. For this task, the writer depends on the power that language has to affect readers emotionally.

DENOTATION AND CONNOTATION

You are probably familiar with the terms *denotation* and *connotation*. If so, you know that the denotative meaning of a word is the meaning found in a dictionary, whereas the connotative meaning is the meaning we associate with a word because of the various situations, or contexts, in which we have encountered that word. For example, the word "flower" has a denotative meaning of "a plant cultivated for its blossoms." Its associational meaning, however, may be very different. If you think of lovely flowers given to you by a boy- or girlfriend, you may have very pleasant associations for this word. But what if someone associates "flower" with the deaths of several loved ones? This person's associational meaning for this word will likely be quite different.

Actually, words have more than denotative and connotative meanings. Once again, Kenneth Burke helps us see this with an analysis in one of his essays, "Mind, Body, and the Unconscious." Using the word "dog" as his example, Burke assigns it five types of meaning:

1. The personal associative meaning that each individual brings to the word. A person who was frightened early in life by a dog may always bring this meaning to the word "dog."
2. The meanings that arise from the sounds of the letters in the word. We know that "dog" rhymes with "hog." This would not be a part of the

meaning of "dog" in French, since the words for "dog" and "hog," *chien* and *cochon,* do not rhyme.

3. The dictionary definition of the word.

4. The idea that the definition in 3 attempts to represent. This one is a bit more difficult. Although the dictionary definition of the word "dog" has to cover everything from a chihuahua to a husky, we have a sense that some dogs are more in the center of what the word "dog" means than are others. Have you ever heard someone say, "Now *that's* a dog"? If so, that person was referring to this idea.

5. The total of associational meanings that go with the word because of the various contexts in which it appears. Here we are talking about everything that goes with "dog"—from kennel, to dog food, to hunting, to fleas.

As you can see, Burke's system is complicated. Actually, it is even more complicated than it appears here, since we have simplified quite a bit with our paraphrase. We are most interested in Burke's distinction between personal associations (1) and public contextual meanings (5). If you associate a pleasant summer at the beach with the word "dog," because the only time you were close to a dog was that summer you spent at the beach with your cousins and their dog, that is a personal association. Other people may have very different personal associations with this word. However, you, and most other people, probably associate doghouses, fleas, and faithfulness with dogs. These are the types of connotations the writer builds on in effective writing.

Exercise 15.14

Think for a minute about the associations you bring to the words "lawyer" and "attorney." Both regularly refer to someone with a law degree who makes a living by working in the legal profession. The connotations of the two words are quite different. A person with an office in a house just off Main Street may be called a lawyer. A person who has just been named as a partner in a prestigious big-city law firm will more likely be referred to as an attorney. If we look more closely, however, we find that these two words do not have exactly the same denotative meanings. An attorney is someone who is given the legal right to act in place of someone else. Of course, lawyers are often given such power, but someone could be an attorney without being a lawyer. That is, "attorney" is a broader term than "lawyer."

The following pairs of words are similar to the pair we've just considered: professor/teacher; evening/night; preacher/pastor; singer/musician. In each case, explain the difference in denotative meaning. Then, attempt to capture your sense of the connotative differences in the two words' meanings. Finally, speculate on how the two words' differing contexts have helped create this connotative difference in meaning.

The connotative meanings of words also often reveal the writer's attitude toward a person or situation. If you receive a gift that didn't cost very much and that you don't like, it is "cheap," but if you like it, it is "inexpensive." A person who is careful with her money is "frugal" if you like her, "cheap" or "tight" if you don't. If a person is on your side, he is "firm" or "resolute"; if not, he is "obdurate" or even "pigheaded."

If you look some of these words up in a dictionary, you will find that what we are calling a connotative meaning has made its way into the dictionary, or denotative, definition as a third or fourth possible meaning for the word. This makes us face two important facts: First, language is always changing, though that change tends to be slow. Second, the line between a word's denotation and connotation is very difficult to draw.

Exercise 15.15

1. For each of the sets of words below, state what you see as the shared denotative meaning. Then, determine which words you would label positive, which neutral, and which negative. On what do you base your labeling? Write sentences that cause readers to see the words as you do. In addition to these positive/negative differences, what other differences do you see between these words? Are these additional differences denotative, connotative, or both?

   thin, scrawny, lean, gaunt, slender, lanky, scraggy
   rash, heady, impetuous, hasty

2. For each of the words below, develop a set of synonyms. Then, rank your words from most positive to most negative. If you were to use each word to describe someone or something, how would your attitude toward that person or thing change as your language changed?

   lazy   small   satirical   sweet   large   motive   feisty

It is tempting to think of connotations as something added to the denotative meaning. But the connotative element of language is an integral part of the meaning we convey to others. To get more insight into the role connotation plays in the overall impact of writing, let's look at a passage from Jonathan Kozol's essay "Distancing the Homeless" (the underlining is ours).

But there may be another reason to assign labels to the destitute. Terming economic victims "psychotic" or "disordered" helps to place them at a distance. It says that they aren't quite like us—and more important, that we could not be like them. The plight of homeless families is a nightmare. It may not seem natural to try to banish human beings from our midst, but it is natural to try to banish nightmares from our minds.

So the rituals of clinical contamination proceed uninterrupted by the economic facts described above. Research that addresses homelessness as an *injustice* rather than as a medical *misfortune* does not win the funding of foundations. And the research which is funded, defining the narrowed borders of permissible debate, diverts our attention from the antecedent to the secondary cause of homelessness. Thus it is that perfectly ordinary women whom I know in New York City—people whose depression or anxiety is a realistic consequence of months and even years in crowded shelters or the streets—are interrogated by invasive research scholars in an effort to decode their poverty, to find clinical categories for their despair and terror, to identify the secret failing that lies hidden in their psyche.

We could examine many of the words in this passage, but we will limit ourselves to the underlined words in the second paragraph: "contamination," "interrogated," "invasive," "decode," and "clinical." Much of the weight of Kozol's argument is carried by these words. What exactly does Kozol want his readers to think, and feel, as a result of this passage? He wants us to think that something is very wrong with the way people who are homeless are being treated and that this treatment is being caused in part by the failure of certain key people to understand who homeless people are. He wants us to feel anger and distrust of the motives of those responsible for this problem. The words we have underlined help him achieve this goal.

What do we know about something that is "contaminated"? We know that it is tainted, spoiled, perhaps rotten. Of course, clinical data are not literally spoiled or rotten, but Kozol wants us to feel some of the same things for this data-gathering process that we might feel about something that is rotten. The second underlined word, "interrogated," means questioned. Anyone who is asking questions can be said to be interrogating. However, our associations with this word are likely to conjure up images of dimly lit precinct houses where hardened criminals are being questioned and perhaps abused by detectives who have themselves been hardened and contaminated by the very process in which they are participating. To say that homeless people are being interrogated by researchers is to make it clear that the homeless people are not the only ones in this situation who have lost their way.

This view of researchers is made more clear when we are told that they are "invasive." This can be a technical term for any medical procedure that compromises the integrity of the patient's body. In our everyday use of the word, however, things that are invasive are harsh and threatening. To speak of research scientists as invasive is to present them in a decidedly unfavorable light.

The final two words we have underlined, "decode" and "clinical," continue this very unfavorable view of these research scientists. To "decode" means literally to translate something so that it may be understood. However, decoding is associated with a mechanical, rote—even statistical—process. It is also associated with spying and espionage. Similarly, the denotative meaning of "clinical" is objective, analytical, controlled, and methodical. The secondary meanings of this word, however, suggest that the research scientists are dispassionate and impersonal. So, these researchers, whose goal should be to find ways to help their fellow human beings, are approaching homeless people as if they were a package of statistics and numbers, without regard for their essential humanity.

Exercise 15.16

Reread the following passages from essays presented in Chapter 10 (we added the underlining).

The news organizations' reticence about mentioning the actual nature of abortion may arise in part from a chink in the gleaming semantic armor that otherwise encases the subject. *The abortion advocates forgot to re-name the body parts encountered in abortion.*

Presumably the "conscientious practitioners" of abortion (as the AMA now calls them—in slight departure from its own earlier description of them as "modern day Herods"), would be <u>loath</u> to <u>admit</u> to killing unborn children. They would rather say that they *terminate pregnancies,* an odd assistance for a process that invariably terminates itself.

As long as the discussion is couched in such <u>genteel</u> terms, there isn't much room for primitive, natural words like "arm" and "leg." They are <u>goucheries</u>. On the other hand, if we could simply introduce a few Choice words into the vocabulary, then our mass media would no longer need to <u>shy</u> away from the topic of abortion techniques. The unborn child won't be called a child but just a "fetus" (Latin for "offspring"), and the arm is only a "potential arm" or, say, a "brachium."

Michael Heaphy, "Dismemberment and Choice"

The Italian philosophy of life espouses high-energy confrontation. A male student makes a vulgar remark about your breasts? Don't <u>slink</u> off to <u>whimper</u> and simper with the campus <u>shrinking violets</u>. Deal with it. On the spot. Say, "Shut up, you jerk! And crawl back to the barnyard where you belong!" In general, women who project this take-charge attitude toward life get harassed less often. I see too many <u>dopey</u>, immature, self-pitying women walking around like melting sticks of butter. It's the Yvette Mimieux syndrome: Make me happy. And listen to me weep when I'm not.

Camille Paglia, "Rape and Modern Sex War"

Write a brief explanation of how the connotations of the underlined words in each passage help the writer achieve the overall purposes of the essay. Also note any other words that you find particularly effective. Explain their effectiveness. ▪▪

Exercise 15.17

Examine a passage (a paragraph or two) from an essay you have written in this course—preferably one that spotlights the reader. Revise this passage, attempting to use the connotations of words to help you achieve your purpose. Then, write a brief discussion of the changes you have made in this process. ▪▪

TONE

We all know what the word "tone" means when a parent says to a child, "Don't use that tone with me." The parent is reacting to something in the sound of the child's voice. What the child has said may be perfectly acceptable, but the way he has said it—the actual intonation in his voice—is taken as an intent to give offense.

We may be less sure of what "tone" means for written texts. If tone were limited to literal sound, we would not be talking about tone in writing. But a writer can reveal her tone toward another person through the words she uses. We could not hear Heaphy's voice when he wrote:

As long as the discussion is couched in such genteel terms, there isn't much room for primitive, natural words like "arm" and "leg." They are goucheries.

But we did know something about his attitude toward the people who use this "genteel" language.

One way of talking about tone is to say that a writer's tone can reveal his attitude toward any one of the three elements in the rhetorical triangle—the writer, the subject, or the reader. When the writer is spotlighted, he often adopts a tone that reveals an attitude toward himself. One of the most common tones in this type of writing is a humorous one, as is the case in the following brief passage from *Leaving Home* by Garrison Keillor:

> When I burst upon the radio business in 1963 as the friendly announcer of "Highlights in Homemaking," I badly wanted my voice to sound like that of Orson Welles, as rich and smooth as my mother's gravy on Sunday pot roast, and I succeeded so far as to sound at least brown and thick and lumpy, and then the pretense was too hard to keep up, and by the time "Prairie Home" rolled along, my voice had drifted back toward center and sounded more like my dad's.

Clearly, Keillor is taking a humorous tone toward himself in this passage. The clash between "burst upon the radio business," which suggests a grand and important beginning of his career, and the role he played (as announcer for a nondescript homemaking show) makes it clear that Keillor sees his early aspirations in a comical light. This tone is continued with the humorous metaphor in which he wants his voice to sound like his mother's "rich and smooth" gravy, but finds that it actually sounds "brown and thick and lumpy."

The writer can also reveal an attitude toward her subject. In writing that spotlights the subject, it is often helpful to begin by asking whether the writer is treating the subject seriously or not. An informative essay by a nuclear scientist having to do with the dangers of nuclear energy is likely to be quite serious. An essay in which a columnist for a local newspaper talks about the trials and tribulations of choosing a pair of shoes to wear to a wedding is likely to be light and humorous. Most examples of informative writing will assume tones somewhere between these two extremes, and a careful analysis of the writer's attitude toward her subject will allow the reader to place the tone somewhere on a continuum, with these two examples as the poles of that continuum.

Such a continuum is not very helpful in evaluating the tone of persuasive writing, however, because a serious attitude toward the subject is a given in this situation. Writers of persuasion essays do sometimes say things they do not mean, though. For example, when Heaphy describes the AMA's description of doctors performing abortions ("conscientious practitioners") as a "slight departure" from their earlier description ("modern day Herods"), he really means that there has been not a slight but a tremendous change in the position of this organization. His intent is to ridicule the organization's lack of consistency as well as its current position. We describe such a tone as *ironic,* since Heaphy is saying the opposite of what he means. Heaphy assumes that his readers will understand what he really means to say and be persuaded, in part, by his wit.

Heaphy's essay is a prime example of what authors can do with tone once they decide not to address those who hold the opposing point of view. This decision frees them to take what is often referred to as a *satirical tone*—one in which those opposed to the author are held up for ridicule, often by means of humorous language. We see another example of this strategy in the passage quoted from Paglia's essay, in which she counsels young women not to "slink off to whimper and simper with the campus shrinking violets." Here she presents a somewhat comical and very negative view of those who take a different view from hers. Her attitude toward these women is clear; she has little respect for them.

Such tones are in sharp contrast to the tone a skilled writer will use when he is talking to an audience that holds a position different from his. As an example, consider the following passage from Jerry Z. Muller's essay "The Conservative Case for Abortion" (Chapter 9, pp. 315–318):

> The right-to-life movement regards human "life" as a good—a claim most of us are broadly inclined to accept. But the right-to-life movement goes further. It regards *all* human life as a good, regardless of the mental, emotional or intellectual capacities of the individual. To right-to-lifers, keeping alive anencephalic infants (children missing all or most of their brains) is a moral imperative. The right-to-life movement regards every degree of human life as equal to the most complete development of human life: that is why the moral status of a fetus two weeks into its development is the same as that of children and adults.

Even though Muller's argument may well be rejected by those favoring the right-to-life position, they will not find his language nearly as inflammatory or as insulting as will those who oppose the positions taken by Heaphy and Paglia. Muller keeps his tone appropriate for addressing an audience that takes a position opposite to his.

Exercise 15.18

Imagine a situation in which you are writing to an audience that agrees with Muller on the issue of abortion. Rewrite Muller's passage above, using language that takes a satirical tone toward those who oppose that point of view. Would your rewritten passage be more persuasive for those already leaning toward Muller's argument? Why or why not?

Exercise 15.19

Contrast two passages from essays you have written—one passage from an essay written to those who disagree with your argument (a position essay) and one passage from an essay written to persuade those who already accept or lean toward your argument (a persuasion essay). In a brief essay, explain the differences in tone you find in these two passages.

Twain said "The difference between the almost-right word and the right word is [. . .] the difference between the lightning bug and the lightning." He could have said that choosing the right word is where the rubber meets the road. We're glad he didn't. Aren't you?

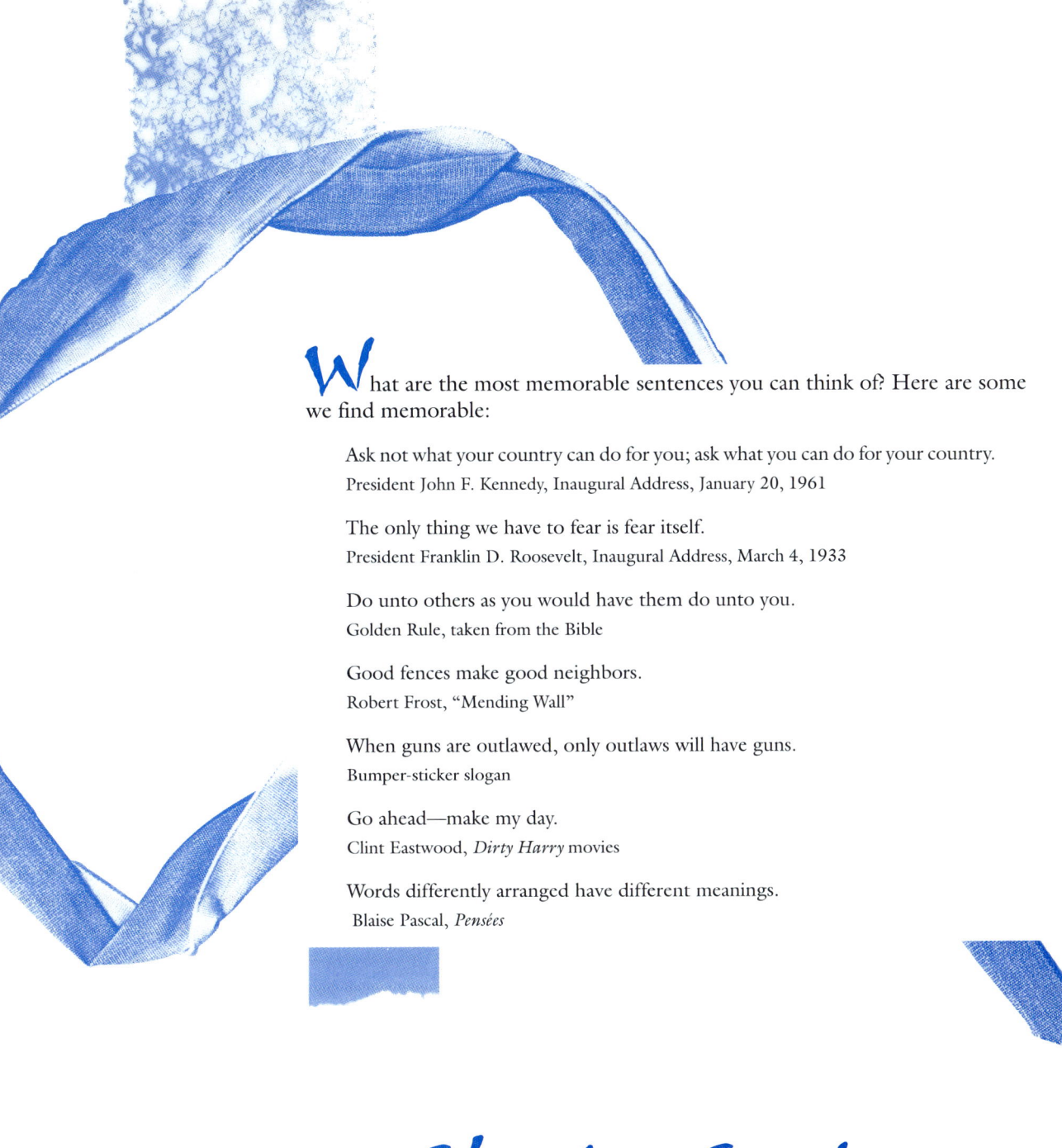

What are the most memorable sentences you can think of? Here are some we find memorable:

Ask not what your country can do for you; ask what you can do for your country.
President John F. Kennedy, Inaugural Address, January 20, 1961

The only thing we have to fear is fear itself.
President Franklin D. Roosevelt, Inaugural Address, March 4, 1933

Do unto others as you would have them do unto you.
Golden Rule, taken from the Bible

Good fences make good neighbors.
Robert Frost, "Mending Wall"

When guns are outlawed, only outlaws will have guns.
Bumper-sticker slogan

Go ahead—make my day.
Clint Eastwood, *Dirty Harry* movies

Words differently arranged have different meanings.
Blaise Pascal, *Pensées*

Shaping Sentences

C H A P T E R 16

These sentences are memorable for more than one reason. In the first two cases, the sentences were uttered by famous people on momentous occasions. In all of the cases, there is a certain playing with language that calls attention to itself—something that suggests we should pay special attention to what is being uttered.

It is significant that when people want to say something that will be remembered for posterity, the unit they use is the sentence. Do you remember anything that came before or after any of the sentences quoted above? Probably not. We asked you to think of memorable sentences, but if we had asked for memorable "sayings," would you have thought of phrases or clauses instead of sentences? We suspect not. When the shapers of these sentences formed them, they knew that the unit we would remember would be the sentence, the basic building block of discourse.

SENTENCE STRUCTURE

If we agree that the sentence is the basic unit of discourse, it seems like a good idea to begin with a simple definition of "sentence." Unfortunately, there isn't one. The only certain thing we can say about the (written) sentence is that it is the unit that occurs between a capital letter at the beginning of a string of words and a period (or question mark or exclamation point) at the other end of that string. This is not very helpful, of course, since *sentence fragments* also often begin with a capital letter and end with a period.

There are, to be sure, other definitions of "sentence." We are all familiar with the traditional definition of a sentence as a complete thought. But what exactly is that? Which of the following are complete thoughts?

Wow, what a day!
You want what?
Yes, she is.

All of these can be punctuated as separate units, but what does it mean to say they are, or are not, complete thoughts? Their meaning is clearly dependent on the other units around them—as is true of all sentences.

Yet another definition is that a sentence is a complete thought with a subject and a predicate that contains a finite verb. Once we begin to define the sentence from this grammatical perspective, it is possible to develop various categories of English sentences, according to the types of finite verbs they contain and the types of complements these verbs take. This kind of grammatical analysis is not very helpful, however, in talking about what makes effective and ineffective sentences. And that is what we want to turn our attention to in this chapter. In the pages that follow, we offer various strategies available to you as you write and revise sentences in essays that are designed to achieve the rhetorical goals presented in Part Two. We have avoided grammatical terms as much as possible, attempting to illustrate the strategies clearly so that you can learn to use them by imitation. However, in some cases, it proved to be too awkward not to use basic grammatical terms.

Although we don't think you need to understand all of the intricacies of grammar in order to write successful sentences, the terms make it easier for us to explain what you will see happening in the examples we provide. When we use grammatical terms in the text, we will provide a brief explanation in an accompanying Time Out, like the one that follows.

Time Out

A *finite verb* is a verb with tense. Thus, in "John lived in Chicago," *lived* is a finite verb, since it is in the past tense. If the verb were *lives*, it would still be a finite verb, since it would be in the present tense. However, in the sentence, "Living in Chicago taught me a lot," *living* is not a finite verb, since it does not have tense.

A RHETORICAL PERSPECTIVE

As we said above, our focus in this chapter is on the way sentence structure can help you achieve your rhetorical purpose in writing. From this perspective, we are concerned not with correct and incorrect sentences, but with more and less effective ways of shaping sentences. Below we will explain and give examples of many different ways of building sentences. Our goal is to increase your awareness of the many choices you can make in constructing sentences as you write or, perhaps more usefully, as you revise your writing.

As we discuss these choices, it will be helpful to return to the rhetorical triangle, a concept we introduced in Part Two, Writing Occasions. Even though a writer can use any type of sentence in any rhetorical situation, we can make certain connections between rhetorical purposes and sentence strategies. Thus, we will organize our treatment of strategies for building sentences into those strategies that seem most useful when the spotlight is on the subject, those that seem most useful when the spotlight is on the writer, and those that seem most useful when the spotlight is on the reader.

STRATEGIES FOR WRITING THAT SPOTLIGHTS THE SUBJECT

When writing spotlights the subject, the other elements in the rhetorical triangle—writer and reader—should take supporting roles. We consider such writing good if it gives us the feeling that we can see through the language of the writer to the message that she wants to give us. Thus, sentences that call attention to themselves, in the ways the sentences at the beginning of this chapter do, will not be the norm in such writing. Rather, you will want to work toward clear, readable sentences that convey the meanings you intend in a straightforward manner.

But just how do sentences convey meanings? We said in Chapter 15 that words are the primary unit of meaning in the language. However, words do not carry all of the meaning. Think back to Pascal's statement that words differently arranged have different meanings. Then, examine these two sentences:

> The exhausted woman remembered she had to attend a school play that night.
> Exhausted, the woman remembered she had to attend a school play that night.

The words are the same, but the meaning is different. The woman in the second sentence seems more "exhausted," because the writer elected to bring this descriptive word to the front of the sentence and use it as the lens through which readers view the rest of the sentence. It is clear from this example that a part of the meaning of any sentence comes from the way the writer puts the words together to form that sentence.

The decisions we make when we arrange the words in a sentence reveal how we want the parts of the sentence to be related to each other. How are relationships between various units in our writing fashioned? And how do we signal a reader that relationships are important? Before we say more about these matters, we need to look briefly at relationships between sentences. Consider the following sentences:

> Jaime left the party. Bill, however, stayed at the party. Therefore, I had a good time at the party.
> Jaime left, but Bill stayed at the party. Therefore, I had a good time at the party.
> Since it was Jaime, rather than Bill, who left, I had a good time at the party.

In all three versions, the writer lets us know what the relationships between various parts of her story are. However, as we move from the short, choppy sentences in the first version to the single sentence in the last version, the writer is making more sophisticated connections. She is using her command of sentence structure to let us know what connection she wants us to focus our attention on and to move the other connections into the background, as supporting information that should not share the spotlight with the one important connection. We can illustrate what the writer is doing in each case by labeling connections between sentences in bold capital letters, connections between clauses within sentences in bold lowercase letters, and connections within clauses in lowercase italic letters.

> Jaime left the party. [CONTRAST] Bill, however, stayed at the party. [CAUSE] Therefore, I had a good time at the party.
> Jaime left, [contrast] but Bill stayed at the party. [CAUSE] Therefore, I had a good time at the party.
> Since it was Jaime, [contrast] rather than Bill, who left, [cause] I had a good time at the party.

Time Out

A *clause* is a group of words with a subject and a verb. An *independent clause* can stand by itself as a complete sentence: "John left the party." A *dependent clause* cannot stand by itself; it must be attached to another clause to be meaningful. Leaving a dependent clause to stand on its own—for example, "When Jaime left the party"—creates a sentence fragment.

Let's look at another example. Here is a passage from an essay entitled "Distancing the Homeless," by Jonathan Kozol:

> A misconception, [**time/cause**] once it is implanted in the popular imagination, is not easy to uproot, [**time/cause**] particularly when it serves a useful social role. [**CAUSE**] The notion that the homeless are largely psychotics who belong in institutions, *[contrast]* rather than victims of displacement at the hands of enterprising realtors, spares us from the need to offer realistic solutions.

We have used the system explained above to identify the connections in this passage. In order to demonstrate how the connections work in Kozol's passage, we have rewritten it, attempting to keep the basic information he presents but changing the connections between the various parts of the passage.

> *Our Rewriting of Kozol's Passage*
>
> Once a misconception is put into the popular imagination, [**time/cause**] it is not easy to uproot. [**?**] A misconception is particularly hard to uproot [**cause**] if it serves a social role. [**ASSOCIATION**] For example, there is a misconception about who homeless people are. [**ASSOCIATION**] Some people believe the homeless are largely psychotics, *[contrast]* rather than people who have been displaced by enterprising realtors. [**CAUSE**] Since these people believe psychotics belong in institutions, [**cause**] they do not have to come up with realistic solutions for a problem.

Note that Kozol is able to highlight the principal assertion he is making by focusing on a key causal relationship—that between the two sentences in the passage. He wants to tell his readers that the misconception that people who are homeless are basically psychotics is hard to uproot because it allows us to avoid the hard work of coming up with solutions to this problem. Compare Kozol's passage to our version. We have attempted to present all of the information he presents, but since the sentences are shorter, we lose focus. We do get to his key assertion in the connection between the last two sentences in our passage, but by that time the reader has had to deal with several other relationships between sentences, without any clear directions from us as to how things connect. Note that it is hard to see exactly what relationship exists between the first and second sentence in our rewritten version. Note also that we are forced to label two other relationships as associations. This is the most general and easiest connection available to us. We can always say that one item "goes with" another in some sense, as is evident in the writing of very young writers, who tend to put everything together with "and."

Exercise 16.1

Using the system introduced earlier, label the connections in a paragraph from one of the essays presented at the beginning of Chapter 6 or an essay selected by your instructor. How clear are the connections within and between sentences? Can you see ways in which connections could have been made more effectively?

BASIC TOOLS FOR BUILDING SENTENCES

The large number of tools available for sentence building can be intimidating. In presenting these tools, we do not mean to suggest a paint-by-the-numbers mentality in which you go through the list of options available to you as you construct each sentence in a paper. Rather, we hope that these tools may be useful to you in analyzing the patterns of connections you typically make in your writing and in thinking about ways to make your sentences more purposeful in the revising stage of your writing.

For the most part, the strategies we offer can be grouped together under what is commonly called *sentence combining*. The ability to write longer sentences will make you a better writer. When short sentences are used purposefully, however, they can be very effective tools for good writers, as we shall see in some of the examples later in this chapter. Good writers know how (and when) to use both short and long sentences.

One way to make sentences longer is to combine shorter sentences to create longer ones. When you want to connect two ideas, you have two basic choices: You can connect the ideas in such a way as to signal their equality, using *coordination,* or in such a way as to spotlight one idea and place the other in a supporting role, using *subordination.*

COORDINATING TOOLS   Given two sentences, you may use coordination in the following ways:

Two Sentences Combined into One Compound Sentence

Jaime left the party. Marta stayed on for a while.

becomes Jaime left the party, and Marta stayed on for a while.

or Jaime left the party, but Marta stayed on for a while.

or Jaime left the party; however, Marta stayed on for a while.

or Jaime left the party; nevertheless, Marta stayed on for a while.

or Jaime left the party; therefore, Marta stayed on for a while.

Two Sentences Combined into One Simple Sentence

Jaime left the party. Marta also left the party.

becomes Jaime and Marta left the party.

576   Part Five   Style

	Jaime left the party. Marta stayed on for a while.
becomes	Jaime, not Marta, left the party.
or	Jaime, but not Marta, left the party.
	They elected Jesse. They elected Moira.
becomes	They elected Jesse and Moira.

Time Out

A *simple sentence* is one that contains only one clause. A *complex sentence* contains an independent clause and at least one dependent clause. A *compound sentence* contains at least two independent clauses. And a *compound-complex sentence* contains at least two independent clauses and at least one dependent clause.

Note that coordinating conjunctions, such as "and," allow us to join clauses with a simple comma; however, conjunctive adverbs, such as "therefore," require semicolons between clauses. Despite their differing requirements as to punctuation, however, all items that allow for coordination may be grouped rather simply in terms of the four primary relationships they establish between ideas. We can use terms provided by Kenneth Burke to represent these four relationships: association, opposition, sequence, and consequence. Here are various connectors that suggest these relationships:

Association	Opposition	Sequence	Consequence
and	but	next	therefore
in addition to	yet	first, etc.	so
furthermore	notwithstanding	finally	as a consequence of
further	however		thus
moreover	rather		
	on the other hand		
	whereas		

Time Out

The coordinating conjunctions are

and	but	for	yet	so
or	nor	both/and	either/or	neither/nor

Conjunctive adverbs are too numerous to list here.

One of the keys to clear writing is the care that you take in making connections. It makes a great deal of difference whether you say

> Jaime left the party, and Marta stayed with me.

or

> Jaime left the party, but Marta stayed with me.

The second sentence suggests that Marta might have been expected to leave with Jaime; whereas the first makes no such assumption. Return to a paragraph you have written in an earlier paper, and examine the connections between the sentences in that paragraph. Rewrite the paragraph, attempting to make connections as clear as possible. Then, write a brief analysis of how your changes affected the meaning of that paragraph.

SUBORDINATING TOOLS   There are several ways to create more sophisticated sentences using subordination. One type of subordination occurs when two sentences are combined into one complex sentence in which one clause modifies the other. In such a sentence, one clause takes center stage, and the other plays a supporting role. Below are examples of this type of sentence combining. In these examples, the words "something" and "sometime" in italics indicate places where one sentence will be built into the other. The italicized word in the combined sentence serves to connect the two sentences.

Two Sentences Combined into One Complex Sentence

He will come *sometime*. We will leave.
becomes   *When* he comes, we will leave.

We will wait until *sometime*. He will arrive.
becomes   We will wait *until* he arrives.

Josie will not pass the test unless *something*. Josie works hard.
becomes   *Unless* Josie works hard, she will not pass the test.

Josie will pass the test if *something*. Josie works hard.
becomes   *If* she works hard, Josie will pass the test.

Josie was warned about the test. Josie did not spend her time wisely.
becomes   *Although* she was warned about the test, Josie did not spend her time wisely.

The person will likely make a high grade. The person will study hard.
becomes   The person *who* studies hard will likely make a high grade.

Josie did not do well on the test. Josie did not study enough.
becomes   Josie, *who* did not study enough, did not do well on the test.

We chose a place. This is the place.
becomes   This is the place *that* we chose.

The car chose that moment to fail me again. The car has always been a problem.
becomes   The car, *which* has always been a problem, chose that moment to fail me again.

Below are several model sentences that were formed by using the strategies just presented. Under each of these models are two sentences that can be combined to form one sentence with that structure. Produce that sentence. Then, create a sentence of your own with a structure like that of the model sentence.

Example   The boy whom they called refused their request.
              The tree was in a protected forest.
              They cut down the tree.
Solution   The tree that they cut down was in a protected forest.
              The man who likes hot dogs is my father.

1. That is the man who ran for Congress.
   That is the person.
   The person works hard.
2. The dog that bit the letter carrier was held for observation.
   The trees were cut back.
   The trees were blocking the drivers' vision.
3. If the results prove positive, the team is likely to publish its findings.
   The game will likely be canceled.
   The weather does not improve.
4. Until the report is finished, we will not know what our profits are.
   The coach will not allow the player to return to the team until *sometime*.
   The player apologizes for her mistakes.
5. Although the crash destroyed both cars, no one was hurt in the accident.
   The house is in a good location.
   The house did not sell for its full value.

A second type of subordinating relationship is formed when one clause is built into, or embedded in, another clause. Below are examples of various embedded structures. The place where the embedded structure will appear is indicated by "something." The connecting agent in the combined sentence is in italics.

Two Sentences Combined into One Complex Sentence with an Embedded Structure

              Jesse said *something*. Jesse would not come to the party.
becomes   Jesse said *that* he would not come to the party.

Note: The connector "that" is often optional. It could have been omitted in the combined sentence above.

              Something is sad. Melinda will not come to the party.
becomes   It is sad *that* Melinda will not come to the party.

              Something will determine your fate. You will do *something* about this problem.
becomes   What you do about this problem will determine your fate.

Note: The connector "what" actually takes the place of the placeholder "something" in both the main sentence and the embedded sentence. This pattern is repeated in the next several sentences.

	I like *something*. You said *something* in the meeting.
becomes	I like *what* you said in the meeting.
	I believe *something*. He says *something*.
becomes	I believe *whatever* he says.
	I am not sure of *something*. He will choose *something*.
becomes	I am not sure *which* he will choose.
	I will choose *something*. *Something* will come first.
becomes	I will choose *whichever* comes first.
	I don't know *something*. Alphonse received his promotion.
becomes	I don't know *whether* Alphonse received his promotion.
	Something was hotly debated. He will come.
becomes	*Whether* he will come was hotly debated.

Note: Usually when "whether" is used as a connector, "or not" is optional—although purists may insist on its inclusion. Note also that "or not" may be separated from "whether": "*Whether* he will come *or not* was hotly debated."

We have illustrated how two clauses can be joined together and how one clause can be embedded in another. There is yet another way to combine clauses: One clause can be collapsed into another by making its main verb into an *ing* verbal or an infinitive. Let's take a look at how these two processes work.

	Jon likes *something*. Jon reads the paper on Sundays.
becomes	Jon likes *reading* the paper on Sundays.
	By *something*, Ruth was able to pass the test easily. Ruth studied a great deal.
becomes	By *studying* a great deal, Ruth was able to pass the test easily.
	Something is harder than it looks. Someone plays the guitar well.
becomes	*Playing* the guitar well is harder than it looks.
	The team likes *something*. The team wins on the road.
becomes	The team likes *to win* on the road.
	Something was an obsession with him. He finished the job.
becomes	*To finish* the job was an obsession with him.
	Their goal was *something*. They win the championship.
becomes	Their goal was *to win* the championship.

Time Out

We have already seen two verbals: the gerund and the infinitive. A *verbal* is a nonfinite form of a verb. Another way of saying this is that a verbal does not have tense. The three verbals we shall deal with are the *infinitive* (the form with "to," such as "to win"), the *gerund* (the form with an *ing* ending, such as "reading"), and the *participle*. The participle has two forms, present and past. A *pre-*

sent participle is an *ing* form of a verb, just like a gerund. The difference between participles and gerunds is that gerunds act like nouns—that is, they fit into the noun slot of a sentence—whereas participles act like adjectives. Thus, in the following sentence, "winning" is a participle: The winning team celebrated loudly. We can turn the participle into a participial phrase as follows: After winning the game, the team celebrated loudly. The *past participle* is one of the principal parts of a verb. It also acts as an adjective. In the following sentence, "defeated" is a past participle: The defeated players were very quiet in their locker room. We can turn this participle into a participial phrase as follows: Defeated by an error in the last inning, the players sat quietly in their locker room.

Exercise 16.4

Below are several model sentences that are formed by using the strategies just presented. Under each model are two sentences that can be combined to form one sentence with the same structure as that of the model. Produce that sentence. Then, create a sentence of your own with that structure.

1. I did not know whether he was the best person for the job.
   The man did not know *something*.
   The house was priced too high.
2. Their chief goal was to make it through the semester.
   Joan's wish was *something*.
   Joan wanted to go to Disney World.
3. I will abide by whatever the board members want to do.
   My friend wants to say *something*.
   I will support *something*.
4. It is unlucky that the team's best player was hurt before the tournament.
   Something is likely.
   The parts will arrive by this time tomorrow.
5. They were sure they could succeed by following the advice of their parents carefully.
   The organizers improved attendance at the reunion by *something*.
   The organizers chose a more central location for the event.
6. The experts know the team has little chance of winning.
   The teacher realizes *something*.
   Jon is trying hard to do his homework correctly.
7. We will listen to what we want to.
   They respect *something*.
   The experts have *something* to say.

As we said earlier, we are not suggesting that you write sentences in some mechanical fashion. However, there is certainly a connection between your ability to exploit the tools of language and your ability to express what you mean to others. It is instructive to note that even though Amy Tan, in "Mother Tongue" (featured at the beginning of this part), wishes for the ability to express herself in some form more basic than language, she cannot do so. In fact, she is able to make her points about language only because she has mastered the tools we have been discussing here, as the next exercise illustrates.

Exercise 16.5

Examine paragraph 15 of Tan's essay, "Mother Tongue" (pp. 543–544). Label the connections between sentences and clauses in this paragraph as we labeled the connections in the passage from Kozol's essay (see p. 575). How many of the tools presented above does Tan use in her paragraph?

STRATEGIES FOR WRITING THAT SPOTLIGHTS THE WRITER

When we say that a particular piece of writing spotlights the writer, we mean that the writer's main goal is to give her reader insight into her feelings and experiences. As we pointed out in Chapter 5, writers often use narrative and descriptive modes in personal writing. These modes allow the writer to evoke for the reader a sense of being in on an action while it is taking place, of experiencing some thing or event through the senses of the writer.

This passage is from Henry Louis Gates, Jr.'s "Change of Life," one of the essays featured in the introduction to this part:

> I noticed smaller changes. Mama, the fearless one, suddenly became afraid of dogs. She started to alter physically, as well. Mama used to do exercises devoutly and weighed a trim ninety-eight pounds. At about this time, though, she gained fifty or sixty pounds. Then the clutter in our home started, because she would buy canned goods obsessively, as if to stock a bomb shelter we didn't have. She began to buy cloth too, bolts of material for some future occasion. Before long, there were galvanized garbage cans filled with bolts of cloth. A sense of need, born of a childhood of scarcity, now came upon her, spurring a pack rat's notion of providence—a contained panic about running short. Running out. Going without. Needing and not having. Even as the house became cluttered with her acquisitions, she became obsessed with cleanliness, spending a good part of each day vacuuming. Vacuuming and dusting. I liked trying to help her, and would cook, and clean, and even iron sometimes. I would read the pamphlets that started appearing all over our house, with titles such as "The Phases of Eve" and "The Change of Life," so that I might get a handle on this crazy, evil thing that had entered our lives.

Here is another very descriptive passage, from "Under the Influence" by Charles Russell Sanders:

> My father drank. He drank as a gut-punched boxer gasps for breath, as a starving dog gobbles food—compulsively, secretly, in pain and trembling. I use the past tense not because he ever quit drinking but because he quit living. That is how the story ends for my father; age sixty-four; heart bursting, body cooling and forsaken on the linoleum of my brother's trailer. The story continues for my brother, my sister, my mother, and me, and will continue so long as memory holds.
>
> In the perennial present of memory, I slip into the garage or barn to see my father tipping back the flat green bottles of wine, the brown cylinders of

could remember what came next. Mon-roe stumbled through the book of rites until he found the right page, and then he asked me the prescribed questions.

These passages are certainly descriptive. The reader has a sense of being placed in the middle of a scene, of seeing things just as the author saw them. Of course, this is an illusion; we cannot literally see what the author saw. To do that would require the scene to be filmed. But words can do what no camera can, as Abbott makes clear when he tells us, at an earlier point in his essay, that the stories writers tell come from their desire "to fix on the page a moment, suffered or made up, when something—one puny thing or idea or person—revealed itself and so turned off the Boom-Boom-Boom which usually deafens us to ourselves." This passage helps us understand that the important element in personal writing is not *what* the writer sees, but rather *how* he sees things. In the stories they have given us, Abbott and Gates are presenting a personal vision of a scene, and by means of that scene, a personal vision of an important relationship in their lives. No camera could capture this vision. If any of us had been present at the moments being described, we would not have seen or understood what Abbott or Gates saw and understood.

Exercise 15.10

Let's examine some of the verb phrases in Gates's passage. Gates describes himself as "rising mechanically, stumbling out of the pew, wandering to the front of the church, standing right in front of Ralph Edell Mon-roe, and wondering what would happen next." Then the pastor, Mon-roe, "stumbled through the book." These verb phrases describe, but they do much more. They give the reader the sense that the narrator doesn't know exactly what he is doing, that he is acting very much like the "untethered craft" described in paragraph 12 of Gates's essay. The other characters in the passage, especially the pastor, are also unsure of themselves. Of course, the uncertainty in this scene is tied to the overall theme of the uncertainty a young boy experiences when the very anchor of his existence—to continue the metaphor of the small craft—is taken away from him.

With Gates's passage as an example, return to a passage in a paper you have written in this course—preferably one in which the spotlight is on the writer. Examine your word choice in that passage, and, where possible, make it more descriptive and more attuned to the overall purpose of your essay. When you have done so, write a brief discussion of how the language in your revised passage helps readers experience the scene as you, the writer, experienced it.

ORIGINAL WRITING

What do we mean when we say that writing is original? Since writing is made up of words, we can probably best explain what we mean by talking about originality in language. Not all of the language we use is original. A very large part of it is routine and automatic. To see what we mean, put the first word that comes to mind in each of the blanks in the following passage:

Derek: How's it _____, Lorenzo?
Lorenzo: Fine and _____, couldn't be _____.

whiskey, the cans of beer disguised in paper bags. His Adam's apple bobs, the liquid gurgles, he wipes the sandy-haired back of a hand over his lips, and then, his bloodshot gaze bumping into me, he stashes the bottle or can inside his jacket, under the workbench, between two bales of hay, and we both pretend the moment has not occurred.

What sentence strategies do Gates and Sanders use to bring their narratives to life? It is clear that they use many of the strategies of coordination and subordination that we have discussed. But they employ other strategies as well. The first of these is what is often referred to as the *cumulative sentence.* Below is a cumulative sentence and another version of the sentence cast as a *periodic sentence,* the opposite of a cumulative sentence.

Cumulative

The man and woman sat at the red light, in complete resignation, his hands still dirty from a long day's work, her back still bent from hours of stooping to pick row after row of beans.

Periodic

The man with his hands still dirty from a long day's work and the woman whose back was still bent from hours of stooping to pick row after row of beans sat in complete resignation at the red light.

As these sentences illustrate, the periodic sentence withholds its basic structure until its end. Another way of putting this is to say that we don't know what the subject of the sentence (in this case, "the man and woman") is doing until the end; in this example, the main verb, "sat," occurs only seven words from the end of the sentence. In the cumulative sentence, the reader gets the basic picture clearly in his mind at the beginning—the man and woman sat in complete resignation—and then he is ready for additional information.

Cumulative sentences thus allow the writer to use longer sentences with more detail, to add color and texture to his writing, without confusing or disorienting the reader. Three key elements characterize the cumulative sentence: *ing (or ed) phrases, appositives,* and *absolutes.* Skilled writers use these tools in various sophisticated ways, but the strategies themselves are not all that complicated. With the *ing* (or *ed*) structures, we simply take a sentence with an *ing* or *ed* verb and build it into another sentence—for example:

	The man stayed up all night.
	The man was listening to the jazz musicians.
becomes	The man stayed up all night listening to the jazz musicians.

	The boy could not sleep at all that night.
	The boy was excited about the appointment he had at the Driver's License Bureau.
becomes	The boy, excited about the appointment he had at the Driver's License Bureau, could not sleep at all that night.

The appositive structure is one of the most useful tools you can employ in descriptive writing. It provides you the opportunity to rename some word or phrase in your original sentence and add more detail about this word or phrase.

In each of the sentences below, the appositive is in bold. The word that the appositive renames is in italics. (Note that we are also using some of the strategies discussed earlier in this chapter.)

> Franco gave the keys to the boy.
>> The boy was a small figure.
>>> The small figure was seen against the overwhelming massiveness of the truck.
>> The boy was about to drive the truck.

becomes   Franco gave the keys to the *boy,* a small **figure** seen against the overwhelming massiveness of the truck he was about to drive.

> She proceeded with a confidence.
>> She did not know she had *something*.
> She was a woman.
>> She had now made a choice.
>>> The choice would surely be revisited at many different crucial points in her life.

becomes   A **woman** who had now made a choice that would surely be revisited at many different crucial points in her life, *she* proceeded with a confidence she did not know she had.

Time Out

As we'll see later in this chapter, the appositive is one of the basic schemes in sentences. It allows us to rename any noun in a sentence. Here are examples of appositives:

John, the captain of the team, hit the winning home run.
They gave the prize to Jerry, the last person to be so honored in that old high school.

In the first case, "John," a noun functioning as the subject of the sentence, is renamed by another noun, "captain." In the second case, "Jerry," a noun functioning as an indirect object, is renamed by the noun "person."

The last strategy we will examine in this section is called the *absolute phrase*. An absolute structure is a combination of one independent sentence and a second assertion that is made by a subject and a verbal—a present or past participle. This sounds more complicated than it is. Consider the following sentences:

Hands were waving frantically.
Frederico approached the car hurriedly.

We can form the following absolute structure from these two sentences:

Hands waving frantically, Frederico approached the car hurriedly.

The subject of the participle is often modified by a noun or pronoun in the possessive case. Thus, an even more likely absolute structure is

His hands waving frantically, Frederico approached the car hurriedly.

Time Out

An absolute phrase is a difficult concept to define. It is easier to illustrate, so let's start with several illustrations:

Their **hopes** *dashed,* the members of the team left the arena.
With **hands** *raised* and **hearts** *lifted,* the worshipers proclaimed the good
    news of their salvation.
They seemed ashamed, **heads** *down* and **eyes** *fastened* on the ground.

In an absolute phrase, some comment is made on some aspect of the information in the main clause. An absolute phrase must have a subject and a participle. In the examples above, the subjects are in bold and the past participles are italicized. As the second and third examples illustrate, these phrases often contain more than one subject and verb.

Perhaps it will help to look at a few more examples of absolutes.

	The team's chances of winning were shattered.
	The team dedicated itself to making the score respectable.
becomes	Its chances of winning shattered, the team dedicated itself to making the score respectable.

	The jury was dismissed.
	The attorneys spoke freely.
becomes	The attorneys spoke freely, the jury having been dismissed.

	The teacher had called the roll.
	The students began to talk softly.
becomes	The teacher having called the roll, the students began to talk softly.

Note: If one of the sentences has a verb in a perfect tense, the tense of that verb in the combined sentence will be present perfect.

So is that all there is to forming absolutes? Not quite. As you can see by examining these examples, there is always a relationship between the two elements that are combined into an absolute structure. In the first of our example sentences, Frederico's hands were waving frantically *as* he approached the car. In another example, we see an additional relationship of time: *After* the team's chances of winning have been shattered, it can dedicate itself to a second goal—a respectable score. In the third example, there is an inherent connection between attorneys in a court of law and the jury in that court. In addition, there seems to be a causal relationship here; that is, *since* the jury has left the room, the attorneys may speak freely. When you create absolutes, be sure that you (and your readers) know what the relationships are between the elements being combined. You would not write the sentence "Hands waving frantically, Frederico approached the car hurriedly" if the hands waving frantically belong to people in the car or to bystanders. The hands must belong to Frederico, since he is the only person in the sentence that the absolute phrase is attached to.

Exercise 16.6

Examine the passages by Gates and Sanders at the beginning of this section (pp. 582–583) to determine how many examples of *ing* or *ed* phrases, appositives, and absolutes you can find there. Does one writer seem to use certain strategies more than the other writer does? If so, can you speculate as to why?

Exercise 16.7

Below are several model sentences formed by using the strategies just presented. Under each of these models is a series of sentences that can be combined to form a sentence with the structure of the model sentence. Produce that sentence. Then, create a sentence of your own with the same structure.

1. One of my favorite teachers, a choral director, died recently.
   The man ran to help the boy.
   The man was large.
   The man was a fire fighter.
2. She moved quickly, darting through the field like a rabbit startled by a hunter.
   The speaker answered slowly.
   The speaker stared at the audience.
   The speaker was like an animal.
      The animal was frozen by fear.
3. Eyes darting, nostrils sniffing the air, the deer stood frozen in the clearing.
   His legs were pumping.
   His lungs were gasping for air.
   The cyclist seemed fixed in his determination.
4. My grandmother told her story, her hands gesturing gently in the air.
   The fire truck's siren was piercing the silence.
   The fire truck rounded the corner.
5. The little boy sat down beside all the dental hygiene magazines, eased himself into what he hoped was a blind spot for the nurse as he awaited the inevitable.
   The little deer moved across the glen.
      The little deer glided softly across the glen as *something*.
         The boy watched in awe.

6. They last saw him on Friday, swimming fearlessly in the high waves and waving to them in utter glee.

    The mayor arrived at noon.

    The mayor was shaking hands with everyone in sight.

    The mayor was kissing every baby she could find.

7. Felicitá left the office quickly, dejected and hurt by the careless way corporate America treated those who had given so often at the office.

    The insurance adjustor arrived late.

    The insurance adjustor was frustrated.

    Something angered the insurance adjustor.

    Many delays hindered *someone.*

    Some people try *something.*

    Some people perform their jobs well.

8. Bill watched as Felicitá left, his hands folded protectively against his chest, his face guarded lest he give any offense to her or the company.

    The woman glared as *something.*

    Tom approached.

    Tom's clothes were torn and tattered.

    Tom's eyes were imploring *something.*

    She gives him some slight assistance.

To this point, we have discussed some of the grammatical structures that make up cumulative sentences. You may have noticed, however, that some of examples we have presented are not, strictly speaking, cumulative. To take a very simple example, consider the appositives in the following sentences:

> Battling the disease continued to motivate Harold, a fighter who would not be slowed down by pain that would have left normal humans utterly defeated.
>
> Harold, a fighter who would not be slowed down by pain that would have left normal humans utterly defeated, continued to battle the disease.
>
> The man who ordered the investigation and subsequently was implicated as a co-conspirator in the robbery eventually proved his innocence.

In the first example, the appositive comes after the main clause, making the sentence clearly cumulative. In the second, the appositive breaks the flow of the sentence, separating subject and verb. However, note how easy it is to understand this sentence, as compared to the third sentence, which is hard to understand even though it is perfectly grammatical. What makes the difference? The first two sentences contain *free modifiers,* and the third contains a *bound modifier.* To process the simple assertion "the man proved his innocence," the reader has to deal with all the information in the clause attached (bound) to "man"—"who ordered the investigation and subsequently was implicated as a co-conspirator in the robbery." It is not just any "man" who was implicated; rather, it is "the man who ordered the investigation and subsequently was implicated as a co-conspirator in the robbery."

Like cumulative sentences, free modifiers allow us to process the main elements of a sentence separately from the extra information we are given about those main elements. Thus, they make for ease in reading. Let's look at two more examples:

Bound Modification

Her assumptions that everything would work out if they just waited patiently and that if they didn't there wouldn't have been anything worth doing about the matter anyway weighed heavily on him.

Free Modification

Her assumptions troubled him—the assumption that everything would work out if they just waited patiently and the assumption that if they didn't, there wouldn't have been anything worth doing about the matter anyway.

In the first sentence, the reader must process a very long subject—from "Her" to "anyway"—without knowing what the verb of the sentence is. Until he gets to that verb, the reader must hold all of the information in the subject in his memory to come up with a meaning for the sentence. Competent readers can do this, but it requires considerable effort. In the second sentence, the writer gives the reader a clear sense of what is being asserted—*something* "troubled him." When the reader gets to the long appositive at the end of the sentence, he knows that he is getting detail that will make clear the meaning of the *something* slot of the sentence—in this case, the slot filled by the phrase "Her assumptions."

As these examples show, free modification works well at the end of a sentence. However, modifiers can be free in any part of a sentence, as the underlined portions of the sentences in this passage from Gates's "Change of Life" indicate:

> I noticed smaller changes. Mama, the fearless one, suddenly became afraid of dogs. She started to alter physically, as well. Mama used to do exercises devoutly and weighed a trim ninety-eight pounds. At about this time, though, she gained fifty or sixty pounds. Then the clutter in our home started, because she would buy canned goods obsessively, as if to stock a bomb shelter we didn't have. She began to buy cloth too, bolts of material for some future occasion. Before long, there were galvanized garbage cans filled with bolts of cloth. A sense of need, born of a childhood of scarcity, now came upon her, spurring a pack rat's notion of providence—a contained panic about running short. Running out. Going without. Needing and not having. Even as the house became cluttered with her acquisitions, she became obsessed with cleanliness, spending a good part of each day vacuuming. Vacuuming and dusting. I liked trying to help her, and would cook, and clean, and even iron sometimes. I would read the pamphlets that started appearing all over our house, with titles such as "The Phases of Eve" and "The Change of Life," so that I might get a handle on this crazy, evil thing that had entered our lives.

The key to using free modifiers successfully is to signal your readers when they are dealing with elements in the main clause and when those elements are being given supporting detail. There are reliable ways to do this. When you begin a sentence with a subordinating conjunction, such as "before" or "until," experienced readers will know that they are reading a subordinate clause and that the subject of the sentence will likely come immediately after the comma at the end of the clause. Likewise, experienced readers will recognize participles (present, *ing,* and past, *ed*) as likely introducers of free modifiers.

> Feeling vaguely sad and unsettled, the woman turned to the immediate business at hand.
> Ashamed and totally saddened by the unexpected developments, the man stumbled toward some words of condolence.

Free modifiers that come within a clause must be signaled by punctuation. In many cases, commas will be enough to let readers know that they are being offered additional detail; in other cases, dashes or parentheses will signal a break in the flow of the sentence structure. These are examples of internal free modifiers:

> Jaime gave the window a rap, a very timid tap, and proceeded to climb down the ladder.
> The horse pulled to a sudden stop—neighing and rearing on its hind legs—and just as quickly the snake lunged halfway up the horse's flank.

Keep in mind that the most likely place for free modifiers is the end of the sentence. As we have seen, writers signal readers that these elements are free by separating them from the rest of the sentence. To do so, they use such marks of punctuation as commas, dashes, and colons.

Exercise 16.8

Examine a passage (two or three paragraphs long) from one of your essays spotlighting the writer. Determine whether the sentences in the passage are primarily periodic or cumulative. Rewrite several of the periodic sentences as cumulative sentences. Then, determine the percentage of words occurring in free modifiers in each of the passages—the original and the revised. Does the percentage of words in free modifiers increase? Do you see any improvement in the descriptive and/or narrative quality of the essay? Explain.

Exercise 16.9

Choose one essay from the sample essays at the beginning of Chapter 5 and one from either Chapter 6 or Chapter 7. Analyze a passage of two or three paragraphs from each essay, determining the ratio of cumulative to periodic sentences and the percentage of words occurring in free modifiers. Then, write a paragraph explaining whether your findings seem consistent with the information in this chapter.

Exercise 16.10

We have seen how appositives can be helpful in the production of cumulative sentences. We can also create free modifiers that rename other elements in a sentence. For example, examine the following sentence:

> She was walking, ambling rather aimlessly, down the road.

In this sentence, the verb "walking" is renamed, or elaborated on, by the free-modifying phrase "ambling aimlessly." Sentences can often be combined to form more complex sentences with free modifiers that rename a verb, an infinitive, or a gerund. Here is an example in which the combination uses free modifiers that re-name the verb:

Example   They swung futilely, trying to hit that nemesis knuckleball.
           They flailed at it with rib-racking fury.
           They hacked at it in hurried, aborted swings.
           They missed it with all of their might.

Solution   They *swung* futilely, trying to hit that nemesis knuckleball,
           flailed at it with rib-racking fury, **hacked** at it in hurried,
           aborted swings, and **missed** it with all of their might.

Combine the following sets of sentences in a similar way, renaming the infinitive in the first case and the gerund in the second.

1. They wanted to win the game.
   They wanted to prove that they really belonged in the tournament.
   They wanted to regain the respect had been lost in last year's tournament.
   They wanted to feel some pride again in themselves.
2. The judges managed to keep straight faces by making an effort.
   The judges were stifling incipient bursts of mirth.
   The judges were actually thinking of the most boring parts of their own lives.
   The judges were conjuring up intimations of their own mortality.

STRATEGIES FOR WRITING THAT SPOTLIGHTS THE READER

Writing spotlights the reader when its goal is to affect the reader in some way. In this type of writing, sentences must do more than say what the writer means; they must conform to the meaning of the words in such a way as to make the reader receptive to that meaning. In the abstract, these may seem rather strange concepts. Let's turn to specific explanations of how the shape of sentences can affect a reader.

SENTENCE RHYTHM

We begin our discussion of strategies for spotlighting the reader with attention to sentence length. We all know that we can write very short sentences, such as

   It can't.

and longer ones, such as

   The White House's new AIDS coordinator, Kristine Gebbie, can't either, no
   matter how urgently AIDS groups pushed for that post to be created.

But is a longer sentence always better? Sentences do get longer as writers develop their skill—to a point. However, in and of themselves, longer sentences do not make for more effective writing. As you experiment with longer sentences, you will be able to use them to accentuate your shorter sentences and add rhythm to your writing. The more you focus on your reader, the more attention you will want to give to sentence rhythm.

Readers do not like to read a long succession of sentences that are nearly the same length. As a case in point, examine the two passages below. Paragraph A comes from one of the essays featured at the beginning of this part, Joan Beck's "The Government Cannot Protect You." (The numbers in brackets indicate the number of words in the preceding sentence.) Paragraph B is a rewritten version that attempts to make the sentences more nearly equal in length. Note how much more effective Beck's original paragraph is in establishing a rhythm.

A. The government isn't going to guard you from getting AIDS. [10] It can't. [2] President Bush couldn't. [3] President Clinton can't. [3] The White House's new AIDS coordinator, Kristine Gebbie, can't either, no matter how urgently AIDS groups pushed for that post to be created. [23] Neither can the governors, mayors, members of Congress, corporate executives or community and religious leaders the commission's report blames for not doing more. [23]

B. The government isn't going to guard you from getting AIDS, because it isn't able to do so. [17] Neither President Bush nor President Clinton has the power to protect you from this disease. [15] AIDS groups pushed very hard for a White House AIDS coordinator, but this person can't protect you from AIDS. [19] The AIDS Commission blames many different leaders for not doing more to stop AIDS. [14] However, neither the governors, mayors, members of Congress, corporate executives or community or religious leaders can protect you against AIDS. [20]

When reading the sentences of good writers, such as Beck, we have the feeling that the sentence length is determined by content. For example, consider the second, third, and fourth sentences in Beck's passage, which contain a total of 8 words. Beck could easily have combined these sentences into one; however, she achieves a rhythm that helps her say more effectively what she wants to say with short sentences. She wants to emphasize a negative assertion here—that no one can protect a person from AIDS. In these short sentences, she follows one negative with another, thus increasing their impact. Then, after the three short sentences, she gives us two relatively long sentences, both 23 words long. What is the effect of these longer sentences? There is a sense in which the length of the sentences contributes to the overall meaning Beck is conveying. It is as if the three very short sentences represent the futile attempt to stop AIDS. It's as if the structure says, "Can't stop it here . . . can't stop it here . . . and can't stop it here." And then the flood gates open, and the two long sentences flow over the reader with the information that no one and nothing can protect a person from this disease. In this passage, the rhythm of the sentences works to emphasize the message given in the words of the text.

Exercise 16.11

Examine the finished paper and a draft of an essay you wrote earlier in this course—preferably one that spotlights the reader. Determine the average sentence length for both versions of this essay. Then, decide which paragraph in the finished essay has the best sentence rhythm. This may be a bit difficult at first, but you need to begin working on feeling this rhythm. Now, write a brief analysis of what happened to the sentences in the paragraph you selected during your revising process and what contributes to the paragraph's rhythm.

SENTENCE SCHEMES

We are now ready to return to the memorable sentences we examined at the beginning of this chapter (see p. 571). These sentences seem designed to capture our attention not just by what they say, but by their very structure. They do so by employing what have traditionally been called *sentence schemes.*

What exactly is a sentence scheme? In its usual meaning, a "scheme" is some type of plan or design. When we talk of sentence schemes, we are talking about design or structure. There are as many different schemes for sentences as you can think of labels for different ways of putting words together. The classical rhetoricians developed a number of these labels. The following definitions and examples, from Edward Corbett's *Classical Rhetoric for the Modern Student,* constitute a small part of their list:

antithesis—juxtaposition of contrasting ideas, often in parallel structure

> Many things difficult to design prove easy to perform.

anastrophe—inversion of natural word order

> People he had known all his life he didn't really know.

apposition—placing side by side two coordinate elements, the second of which serves as an explanation of the first

> Men of this kind—soldiers of fortune, pool-hall habitués, gigolos, beach-combers—expend their talents on trivialities.

anaphora—repetition of the same word or group of words at the beginnings of successive clauses

> We shall fight on the beaches, we shall fight on the landing grounds, we shall fight in the fields and in the streets, we shall fight in the hills.
> Winston Churchill

antimetabole—repetition of words, in successive clauses, in reverse grammatical order

> Ask not what your country can do for you; ask what you can do for your country.
> John F. Kennedy

In some cases, writers use schemes such as these to draw attention to a specific sentence in the hope that that sentence and the speech it comes from will be etched in the minds of those who hear or read it. That is surely what happened with such sentences as "The only thing we have to fear is fear itself," and "Ask not what your country can do for you; ask what you can do for your country." Although you may not be writing prose that will establish your place in history—at least not during this writing class—you may enjoy experimenting with these and other schemes to see what kinds of interesting sentences you can create. Schemes allow you the chance to do much more than add ornamentation to your writing; they offer the means to combine meaning and style in a way that makes your writing more likely to move readers toward the actions you want them to take.

This is exactly what Beck is able to do with the sentence structures in her essay. Earlier, we talked about the rhythm she creates by the use of short and longer sentences. There is much more to Beck's sentence style, as we can see by examining her use of sentence schemes. Specifically, she relies heavily on two sentence schemes: anaphora and antithesis. Here are some key examples of her use of anaphora:

> *All the politically correct attitudes, all the anti-discrimination laws, all the political activism, all the red AIDS ribbons, all the support groups, all the finger-pointing* can't change the basic facts about this epidemic.

> *We do need* much more scientific research about AIDS—and more money to pay for it [. . .]. *We do need* support and good care for persons with AIDS and HIV. *We do need* an end to residual prejudice [. . .]. *We do need* more treatment facilities for drug abusers [. . .]. *We do need* more empowerment for women [. . .].

Exercise 16.12

Try your hand at rewriting the passages in Beck's essay from which the examples above were taken, removing the anaphora. Rewrite all of the material replaced by ellipses. (See pp. 545–546) for the full text of Beck's essay.) Be careful to keep the meaning of the passage as close to the original as possible. Then, write a brief discussion of what is lost in your revision. In what sense have you changed the meaning of the passage?

What is lost in your rewrite in Exercise 16.12? We would guess that you miss the rhythm and the voice in Beck's essay. Beck's essay reads very well; you can almost hear it as you read silently. But her sentence structures do more than add ornamentation. They add to the message that the AIDS problem is getting larger and larger. In the first example sentence above, the reader feels burdened with the weight of futile efforts to stop this disease. In the second example—the passage beginning with "We do need much more"—the reader feels somewhat daunted by all of the ways in which we are not doing enough to stop AIDS. Thus, the sentence schemes carry an important part of the meaning. And there is more.

To appreciate the role that antithesis plays in this essay, look first at its very beginning. In her first two sentences, Beck sounds her theme:

> There's a *life-death message* in the final report of the National Commission on AIDS.

> But the report concentrates so hard on blaming political leaders for not doing more about the epidemic the message is lost between the lines of anger and frustration.

Beck's theme is one of contrast; she wants to contrast what is being said about AIDS with what should be said. Or, to put it another way, she wants to contrast what is being heard with what should be heard. She keeps readers attuned to this theme throughout her essay by the antithetical nature of her sentence structures, as these examples illustrate:

> Most AIDS activist groups are much more concerned about people who already have AIDS *than* about preventing others from becoming infected.
> Most laws dealing with AIDS are intended to help and shield the HIV-positive, *not* to safeguard others.
> We do need much more scientific research about AIDS—and more money to pay for it, *even though* AIDS research is now better funded than work on other diseases which claim many more lives.
> We do need more treatment facilities for drug abusers, *although* the high rate of recidivism is discouraging.
> Needle exchange programs have ardent backers, *although* critics are concerned about supporting what is self-destructive behavior regardless of the risk of AIDS.
> But while we are working on all these difficult things, it would help to broadcast clearly and loudly the message of individual responsibility for avoiding HIV and individual power to do so, *instead* of blaming the government for not doing more.

Exercise 16.13

Analyze one of the essays presented at the beginning of Chapter 10. Then write a paragraph or so in which you discuss the ways the writer's use of sentence structuring supports his or her theme.

We began this chapter by quoting some famous and memorable sentences. That is also how we began the previous chapter on words—by quoting a well-known sentence by Mark Twain. Why do you suppose we didn't begin that chapter by quoting some very useful words? In Ron's case, he might quote such favorite words as "obfuscate," "disingenuous," "disambiguate," "deracinate," "disinterested," and so forth. Of course, it makes no sense to speak of quoting words. Words don't belong to any person. When we use the word "disambiguate," we don't need to give a reference to the person (or dictionary) that introduced us to this word. But if we use such sentences as the following, we rightly feel it necessary to give credit to the person who first uttered or wrote the sentence:

> Words differently arranged have different meanings.
> Blaise Pascal

> The difference between the almost right word and the right word is [. . .] the difference between the lightning bug and the lightning.
> Mark Twain

Why? Because the sentence is the basic unit of expression. You and I may want to convey similar meanings—and we may well use many of the same words, since words are the basic units of meaning and they belong to all of us. However, we will not put the words together in the same way; we will not express ourselves in exactly the same way. Thus, writing begins with the sentence. Careful writing begins with the care we take in shaping our sentences.

Acknowledgments

Chapter 2

page 39: Gilbert Highet. *Explorations*. New York: Oxford University Press, 1971, 306–307.

page 48: Datus Proper, "Dark Hollow," *Field & Stream,* July 1993.

pages 48–49: Camille Paglia. "Rape and Modern Sex War." From *Sex, Art and American Culture* by Camille Paglia. Copyright © 1992 by Camille Paglia. Reprinted by permission of Vintage Books, a division of Random House, Inc.

page 49: Gloria Naylor. "Mommy, What Does 'Nigger' Mean?" *New York Times,* February 20, 1986. Copyright © 1986 by The New York Times. Reprinted by permission.

page 49: Stacy Birch. "What a Child Deserves" (student writing).

page 51: Camille Paglia. "Rape and Modern Sex War." From *Sex, Art and American Culture* by Camille Paglia. Copyright © 1992 by Camille Paglia. Reprinted by permission of Vintage Books, a division of Random House, Inc.

page 51: "Common Decency" by Susan Jacoby. Copyright © 1991 by Susan Jacoby. Originally appeared in *New York Times Magazine*. Reprinted by permission of Georges Borchardt, Inc., for the author.

page 52: Louis Barbash. "Clean Up or Pay Up." Reprinted with permission from *The Washington Monthly*. Copyright by the Washington Monthly Company, 1611 Connecticut Ave., NW, Washington, DC, 20009, 202-462-0218.

page 53: Julie Titone. "Balance of Power: Can Endangered Salmon and Hydroelectric Plants Share the Same Rivers?" *Earthwatch*, September/October, 1992. Julie Titone is a staff writer for the *Spokesman-Review* newspaper of Spokane, Washington, and Coeur d'Alene, Idaho.

pages 53–54: George Orwell. "Politics and the English Language," in *Shooting an Elephant and Other Essays*. New York: Harcourt, Brace and World, 1950, 90–91.

pages 54–55: Loren Eiseley. "The Brown Wasps," in *The Night Country*. New York: Charles Scribner's Sons, 1971, 232.

page 55: Louis Barbash. "Clean Up or Pay Up." Reprinted with permission from *The Washington Monthly*. Copyright by the Washington Monthly Company, 1611 Connecticut Ave., NW, Washington, DC, 20009, 202-462-0218.

page 56: Susan Douglas. *Growing Up Female with the Mass Media*. New York: Times Books, 1995, 302.

pages 58–59: Datus Proper, "Dark Hollow," *Field & Stream,* July 1993.

page 59: Camille Paglia. "Rape and Modern Sex War." From *Sex, Art and American Culture* by Camille Paglia. Copyright © 1992 by Camille Paglia. Reprinted by permission of Vintage Books, a division of Random House, Inc.

page 60: Gloria Naylor. "Mommy, What Does 'Nigger' Mean?" *New York Times,* February 20, 1986. Copyright © 1986 by The New York Times. Reprinted by permission.

page 60: Stacy Birch, "What a Child Deserves" (student writing).

pages 61–63: Rebecca Thomas Kirkendall, "Who's a Hillbilly?" *Newsweek,* November 27, 1995, 22. All rights reserved. Reprinted by permission.

Chapter 3

page 65: Donald M. Murray. *The Craft of Revision.* Ft. Worth, TX: Harcourt Brace Jovanovich College Publishers, 1991, 1.

pages 86–87: Marisol Vargas, "Mirror Image" (student writing).

Chapter 4

page 89: Mortimer J. Adler. "How to Mark a Book." *Saturday Review of Literature,* July 6, 1940, 11.

pages 90–92: Denise D. Knight. "No Hunting Here, Please." *Newsweek,* October 5, 1998, 16. All rights reserved. Reprinted by permission.

pages 92–95: Lee K. Abbott. "The True Story of Why I Do What I Do," in *Puerto del Sol.* Las Cruces: New Mexico State University Press, 1988. Lee K. Abbott is the author of six collections of short stories, most recently *Wet Places at Noon,* and the director of the MFA program in creative writing at The Ohio State University.

page 96: Lorna Dee Cervantes. "Freeway 280," in *Emplumada.* Pittsburgh: University of Pittsburgh Press, 1981. Published by permission of the *Latin American Literary Review.*

pages 100–102: Denise D. Knight. "No Hunting Here, Please." *Newsweek,* October 5, 1998, 16. All rights reserved. Reprinted by permission.

page 107: Otto Friedrich. "The Computer Moves In." *Time,* January 3, 1983, 14–24.

pages 111–113: Geoffrey Cowley. "Vaccine Revolution." *Newsweek,* July 27, 1998, 48–49. © 1998, Newsweek, Inc. All rights reserved. Reprinted by permission.

pages 120–124: Shelby Steele. "A Negative Vote on Affirmative Action." Copyright © 1990 by Shelby Steele. From *The Content of Our Character* by Shelby Steele. Reprinted by permission of St. Martin's Press, Incorporated.

Chapter 5

pages 132–135: Datus Proper, "Dark Hollow," *Field & Stream,* July 1993.

pages 135–137: Steven Barboza. "My Conversion." *New York Times,* April 24, 1993. Copyright © 1993 by The New York Times. Reprinted by permission.

pages 138–139: Arlene Yusnukis. "Purple Mountains' Majesty" (student writing).

pages 140–141: Daniel Kinken. "At the MAC" (student writing).

pages 142–143: Ali Duffy. "The Dance" (student writing).

page 148: Lee K. Abbott. "The True Story of Why I Do What I Do," in *Puerto del Sol.* Las Cruces: New Mexico State University Press, 1988. Lee K. Abbott is the author of six collections of short stories, most recently *Wet Places at Noon,* and the director of the MFA program in creative writing at The Ohio State University.

pages 161–163: Chris Miller. "Gringos on Safari" (student writing).

Chapter 6

pages 166–169: Elisabeth Kübler-Ross. "On the Fear of Dying." Reprinted with the permission of Simon & Schuster from *On Death and Dying* by Elisabeth Kübler-Ross. Copyright © 1969 by Elisabeth Kübler-Ross.

pages 169–171: "Gender Gap in Cyberspace" by Deborah Tannen. *Newsweek,* May 16, 1994. Copyright Deborah Tannen. Reprinted by permission. This article is based in part on material from the author's book *You Just Don't Understand* (Ballantine, 1997).

pages 172–173: Michael Kinsley. "Orwell Got It Wrong." Reprinted with permission from the June 1997 *Reader's Digest.* Copyright © 1997 by The Reader's Digest Assn., Inc.

pages 174–176: Gloria Naylor. "Mommy, What Does 'Nigger' Mean?" *New York Times,* February 20, 1986. Copyright © 1986 by The New York Times. Reprinted by permission.

pages 176–179: Michel Marriott. "Rap's Embrace of 'Nigger' Fires Bitter Debate." *New York Times,* January 24, 1993. Copyright © 1993 by The New York Times. Reprinted by permission.

pages 180–182: Kelly McGinley. "Investing in Your Future" (student writing).

pages 183–184: Joshua Morris. "The Middleton Inn: An Architectural Triumph" (student writing).

page 187: "Gender Gap in Cyberspace" by Deborah Tannen. *Newsweek,* May 16, 1994. Copyright Deborah Tannen. Reprinted by permission. This article is based in part on material from the author's book *You Just Don't Understand* (Ballantine, 1997).

page 187: Elisabeth Kübler-Ross. "On the Fear of Dying." Reprinted with the permission of Simon & Schuster from *On Death and Dying* by Elisabeth Kübler-Ross. Copyright © 1969 by Elisabeth Kübler-Ross.

page 189: Deborah Schiffrin. *Approaches to Discourse.* Cambridge, MA: Blackwell, 1994, 56.

pages 194–195: John Holt. *How Children Learn,* rev. ed. New York: Delacorte/Seymour Lawrence, 1983, 84–86.

pages 196–197: Jonathan Kozol. *Savage Inequalities: Children in America's Schools.* New York: Crown, 1991, 84–85, 92–93.

pages 198–199: Meir Shalev. "If Bosnians Were Whales." *New York Times,* January 1, 1992. Copyright © 1992 by The New York Times. Reprinted by permission.

page 200: Jonathan Kozol. "The Human Cost of an Illiterate Society." In *Illiterate America.* Garden City, NY: Anchor Press/Doubleday, 1985, 22–29.

pages 207–210: Steve Duran. "The Space Between Your Ears" (student writing).

Chapter 7

pages 213–221: Mark Twain. "Fenimore Cooper's Literary Offenses." *North American Review,* no. CCCCLXIV, July, 1895.

pages 221–222: Ellen Goodman. "Beauty Industry on Rampage." *Las Cruces Sun-News,* October 21, 1997, A-10. © 1997, The Boston Globe Newspaper Co./Washington Post Writers Group. Reprinted with permission.

pages 223–224: Stacy Birch. "What a Child Deserves" (student writing).

pages 225–227: Michelle Lebsock. "Gillian Welch: Music's 'Next Big Thing' " (student writing). Lyrics from Gillian Welch's CD *Revival* used by permission from Warner Brothers.

pages 242–243: Bridget McCollam. "Adult Audiences Only" (student writing).

Chapter 8

pages 247–255: Joyce Carol Oates. "Shopping." *Ms.,* March 1986, 50+. Copyright © 1986 by Ontario Review Inc. Reprinted by permission of John Hawkins & Associates, Inc.

pages 255–262: Antonya Nelson. "In the Land of Men," from *In the Land of Men* by Antonya Nelson. © 1992 by Antonya Nelson. Reprinted by permission of Frederick Hill Associates Literary Agency.

pages 263–267: José Armas. "El Tonto del Barrio," in *Cuentos Chicanos.* Rudolfo Anaya and Antonio Marquez, eds. Albuquerque: University of New Mexico Press, 1984. Copyright José Armas.

pages 268–269: Kate Chopin. "The Dream of an Hour." *Vogue,* December 6, 1894, 360.

page 270: Robert Frost. "For Once, Then, Something," from *The Poetry of Robert Frost,* edited by Edward Connery Lathem. Copyright 1916, 1923, © 1969 by Henry Holt and Company. Copyright 1944, 1951 by Robert Frost. Reprinted by permission of Henry Holt and Company, LLC.

page 271: Sherman Alexie. "That Place Where Ghosts of Salmon Jump." Reprinted from *The Summer of Black Widows.* © 1996 by Sherman Alexie, by permission of Hanging Loose Press.

pages 272–273: Sherman Alexie. "The Powwow at the End of the World." Reprinted from *The Summer of Black Widows.* © 1996 by Sherman Alexie, by permission of Hanging Loose Press.

pages 273–275: Kelly McGinley. "The Shopping Ritual" (student writing).

pages 276–278: Jessica Lynn Edwards. "The Price of Freedom" (student writing).

pages 278–280: Kacey Atwood. "One Road Taken" (student writing). Poem by Robert Frost, "The Road Not Taken," from *The Poetry of Robert Frost,* edited by Edward Connery Lathem. Copyright 1916, 1923, © 1969 by Henry Holt and Company. Copyright 1944, 1951 by Robert Frost. Reprinted by permission of Henry Holt and Company, LLC.

pages 305–307: Kristina Geray. " 'How Exhausting It Is' to Keep Up Appearances" (student writing).

Chapter 9

pages 310–312: Phil Gramm. "Don't Let Judges Set Crooks Free." *New York Times,* July 8, 1993. Copyright © 1993 by The New York Times. Reprinted by permission.

pages 312–314: Jack B. Weinstein. "The War on Drugs Is Self-Defeating." *New York Times,* July 8, 1993. Copyright © 1993 by The New York Times. Reprinted by permission.

pages 315–318: Jerry Z. Muller. "The Conservative Case for Abortion." Reprinted by permission of *The New Republic.* © 1995, The New Republic, Inc.

pages 319–321: "Common Decency" by Susan Jacoby. Copyright © 1991 by Susan Jacoby. Originally appeared in *New York Times Magazine.* Reprinted by permission of Georges Borchardt, Inc., for the author.
pages 321–323: Heather Cully. "The Age Requirement for Teen Drivers" (student writing).
page 334: Martin Luther King, Jr. "Letter from Birmingham Jail." Reprinted by arrangement with The Heirs to the Estate of Martin Luther King, Jr., c/o Writers House, Inc. as agent for the proprietor. Copyright 1963 by Martin Luther King, Jr., copyright renewed 1991 by Coretta Scott King.
page 348: John Shelton Reed. "For Pollsters, 'More' Doesn't Always Mean 'Better'," in *Society by Agreement: An Introduction to Sociology.* Earl R. Babbic, ed. Belmont, CA: Wadsworth, 1977, 59.
pages 360–362: Emily Weast. "Learning about Sex" (student writing).

Chapter 10

pages 364–366: Michael R. Heaphy, "Dismemberment and Choice." © 1992 by National Review, Inc., 215 Lexington Avenue, New York, NY, 10016. Reprinted by permission.
pages 367–370: Camille Paglia. "Rape and Modern Sex War." From *Sex, Art and American Culture* by Camille Paglia. Copyright © 1992 by Camille Paglia. Reprinted by permission of Vintage Books, a division of Random House, Inc.
pages 370–381: Martin Luther King, Jr. "Letter from Birmingham Jail." Reprinted by arrangement with The Heirs to the Estate of Martin Luther King, Jr., c/o Writers House, Inc. as agent for the proprietor. Copyright 1963 by Martin Luther King, Jr., copyright renewed 1991 by Coretta Scott King.
pages 382–384: Jaime Sherrill. "Zero Tolerance for Abuse" (student writing).
pages 384–386: Jaclyn Talbert. "Justice for Those Who Have Shown Us No Mercy" (student writing).
pages 391–392: J. Edgar Hoover, *Law Enforcement Bulletin* 30, June 1961.
pages 392–393: Pete Hamill. "Crack and the Box." *Esquire,* May 1990, 63.
page 393: Jaime Sherrill. "Zero Tolerance for Abuse" (student writing).
page 394: Martin Luther King, Jr. "Letter from Birmingham Jail." Reprinted by arrangement with The Heirs to the Estate of Martin Luther King, Jr., c/o Writers House, Inc. as agent for the proprietor. Copyright 1963 by Martin Luther King, Jr., copyright renewed 1991 by Coretta Scott King.
pages 404–407: Alysia Tucker. "No More" (student writing).

Chapter 11

pages 410–415: Louis Barbash. "Clean Up or Pay Up." Reprinted with permission from *The Washington Monthly.* Copyright by the Washington Monthly Company, 1611 Connecticut Ave., NW, Washington, DC, 20009, 202-462-0218.
pages 415–418: Julie Titone. "Balance of Power: Can Endangered Salmon and Hydroelectric Plants Share the Same Rivers?" *Earthwatch,* September/October, 1992. Julie Titone is a staff writer for the *Spokesman-Review* newspaper of Spokane, Washington, and Coeur d'Alene, Idaho.

pages 418–421: Randy Fitzgerald. "The War Against Witnesses." Reprinted with permission from the December 1998 *Reader's Digest*. Copyright © 1998 by The Reader's Digest Assn., Inc.

pages 422–425: Andrew Overton. "Change" (student writing).

page 435: Louis Barbash. "Clean Up or Pay Up." Reprinted with permission from *The Washington Monthly*. Copyright by the Washington Monthly Company, 1611 Connecticut Ave., NW, Washington, DC, 20009, 202-462-0218.

pages 443–446: Kristina Geray. "The Pet Overpopulation Problem" (student writing).

Part Three

page 447: Ken Macrorie. *Searching Writing*. Rochelle Park, NJ: Hayden Book Company, 1980, 54.

Chapter 12

page 465: Netscape search engine screens. Portions copyright Netscape Communications Corporation, 1998. All rights reserved. Netscape, Netscape Navigator, and the Netscape N logo are registered trademarks of Netscape in the United States and other countries.

page 466: Art Crimes home page. Art Crimes copyright © 1994–1998 by Susan Farrell and Brett Webb. All rights reserved.

page 471: Joseph Gibaldi. *MLA Handbook for Writers of Research Papers*. 5th ed. New York: Modern Language Association, 1999, 81–82.

page 471: *Publication Manual of the American Psychological Association*. 4th ed. Washington, DC: American Psychological Association, 1994, 95.

pages 483–486: Clarita Brown. "The American Indian Movement as a Counterculture" (student writing).

pages 492–496: Gardiner Rhoderick. "Yes, It's Graffiti, But Is It Art?" (student writing).

Chapter 13

page 506: Thanks to Professor Sybil Huskey, chair of the Dance and Theatre Department at the University of North Carolina at Charlotte, for the essay that appears on this page. Thanks also to the following other members of the UNC–Charlotte faculty who provided examples of their students' writing for this chapter: Professor Mark Pizzato, Dance and Theatre; Professor Anita Moss, English; Professor Richard Leeman, Communication Studies; Professor Albert Maisto, Director of University Honors; and Dean Edward Perzel, Professor of History. And thanks to the students whose essays we included: Kim Coan, Robbie Grier, Ann Long, Matthew Reep, Cherish Smith, David Wilson, and Jason Wise.

Chapter 14

pages 529–530: Ali Duffy. "Reflective Essay" (student writing).

pages 531–532: Kara Edewaard. "Aggie Magic Tricks" (student writing).

pages 533–534: Steve Duran. "Steve Wants an A" (student writing).

Part Five

pages 537, 538–541: Henry Louis Gates, Jr. "Change of Life." From *Colored People* by Henry Louis Gates, Jr. Copyright © 1994 by Henry Louis Gates, Jr. Reprinted by permission of Alfred A. Knopf, Inc.

pages 541–545: Amy Tan. "Mother Tongue." Copyright © 1990 by Amy Tan. First published in *The Threepenny Review*. Reprinted by permission of the author.

pages 536, 545–546: Joan Beck. "The Government Cannot Protect You." *Chicago Tribune*. Reprinted with permission of Knight-Ridder/Tribune Information Services.

Chapter 15

pages 554–555: Monroe C. Beardsley. "Style and Good Style," in *Reflections on High School English: IDEA Institute Lectures 1965,* Gary Tate, ed. Tulsa: University of Oklahoma Press, 1966, 91–105.

page 555: Ernest Pascarella. *How College Affects Students: Findings and Insights from Twenty Years of Research.* San Francisco: Jossey-Bass, 1991, 3.

page 556: Lee K. Abbott. "The True Story of Why I Do What I Do," in *Puerto del Sol.* Las Cruces: New Mexico State University Press, 1988. Lee K. Abbott is the author of six collections of short stories, most recently *Wet Places at Noon*. He is the director of the MFA program in creative writing at The Ohio State University.

pages 556–557: Henry Louis Gates, Jr. "Change of Life." From *Colored People* by Henry Louis Gates, Jr. Copyright © 1994 by Henry Louis Gates, Jr. Reprinted by permission of Alfred A. Knopf, Inc.

page 560: Dennis Gilbert and Joseph A. Kahl. "How Many Classes Are There?" in *The American Class System,* 4th ed. Belmont, CA: Wadsworth, 1993, 309–310.

page 562: Datus Proper, "Dark Hollow," *Field & Stream,* July 1993.

pages 566–567: Jonathan Kozol. "Distancing the Homeless." *The Yale Review,* Winter, 1988, 153–167.

pages 567–568: Michael R. Heaphy, "Dismemberment and Choice." © 1992 by National Review, Inc., 215 Lexington Avenue, New York, NY, 10016. Reprinted by permission.

page 568: Camille Paglia. "Rape and Modern Sex War." From *Sex, Art and American Culture* by Camille Paglia. Copyright © 1992 by Camille Paglia. Reprinted by permission of Vintage Books, a division of Random House, Inc.

page 569: Garrison Keillor. *Leaving Home.* New York: Penguin, 1987, xviii.

page 570: Jerry Z. Muller. "The Conservative Case for Abortion." Reprinted by permission of *The New Republic.* © 1995, The New Republic, Inc.

Chapter 16

page 575: Jonathan Kozol. "Distancing the Homeless." *The Yale Review,* Winter, 1988, 153–167.

page 582: Henry Louis Gates, Jr. "Change of Life." From *Colored People* by Henry Louis Gates, Jr. Copyright © 1994 by Henry Louis Gates, Jr. Reprinted by permission of Alfred A. Knopf, Inc.

pages 582–583: Charles Russell Sanders. "Under the Influence." *Harper's,* November 1989, 68.

page 588: Henry Louis Gates, Jr. "Change of Life." From *Colored People* by Henry Louis Gates, Jr. Copyright © 1994 by Henry Louis Gates, Jr. Reprinted by permission of Alfred A. Knopf, Inc.

pages 591, 593, 594: Joan Beck. "The Government Cannot Protect You." *Chicago Tribune.* Reprinted with permission of Knight-Ridder/Tribune Information Services.

page 592: Edward Corbett. Classical Rhetoric for the Modern Student. New York: Oxford University Press, 1965, 464–478.

Index

Burnett, Frances Hodgson *(The Secret Garden)*, 16

Camera eye, as writer's vantage point, 287
Carter, Jimmy, 509
Castoreno, Adam, 34, 35–36, 46
Catalogs, 148–149
Causal fallacy, 351, 353
Causal reasoning, 336–337
Causality
  claims of, 341–342
  mode of, 129, 199–200, 514
Cavan, Sherri ("The Great Graffiti Wars of the Late
    20th Century"), 466, 487–488
CD-ROM databases, 455–456
Cervantes, Lorna Dee ("Freeway 280"), 95–97,
    103, 104
"Change," 421–425
"Change of Life," 536, 537, 538–541, 556–557,
    582, 583, 588
Character, literary, 286–287
Chomsky, Noam, 506, 507–509
Chopin, Kate ("The Story of an Hour"), 268–269,
    276–278
Chronology, use of, in personal essay, 151–152
Citations, in-text, 481–482
Clarity, need for, in informative essay, 190–192
Classical Rhetoric for the Modern Student, 592
Classification mode, 129, 235–236, 514
Clauses, 575, 576–582
"Clean Up or Pay Up," 52, 55, 410–415
Climax, in literary texts, 286
Clustering, 16–18. *See also* Association
Coan, Kim, 510, 522–523
Cohesion, paragraph, 54–56
Comma splices, 79
"Common Decency," 51–52, 129, 319–321
Comparison mode, 129, 195–199, 514
Complex sentence, 577
Compound-complex sentence, 577
Compound sentence, 577
Computer facilities, 6
Computers, 5–6, 79
  and brainstorming, 11
  and dialogue notes, 115–116
  and exploratory questions, 28–29
  and fonts, 81
  and footers, 81
  and formatting text, 80–81
  and freewriting, 15–16
  and global revisions, 72

and headers, 81
and interest inventory, 9–10
as research tool, 455–456, 467–470
and revising text, 66
Conclusion, as element of essay, 58–61
Conflict, in literary texts, 286
Conjunctions, coordinating, 577
Conjunctive adverbs, 577
Connotation, 564–568
Consequence
  and coordination, 577
  questions of, 23, 24–25, 27–28, 116–117
"Conservative Case for Abortion, The," 129,
    315–319, 327, 570
Contributing cause, 350
Cooper, James Fenimore, 213–221, 236
Coordinating conjunctions, 577
Coordination, of ideas, 576–578
Corbett, Edward (*Classical Rhetoric for the Modern
    Student*), 592
Corder, Danielle, 14–15
Cowley, Geoffrey ("Vaccine Revolution"),
    111–115
"Crack and the Box," 392–393
Criterion-based evaluation, 212, 229–230,
    232–233, 236, 237
Cully, Heather ("The Age Requirement for Teen
    Drivers"), 321–325, 326, 333
Cumulative sentence, 583–587

"Dance, The," 141–144, 145, 146, 151–152
Dangling modifiers, using Search function to find,
    79–80
"Dark Hollow," 48, 49, 58–59, 104, 132–135,
    145–147, 152, 562–563
Databases, CD-ROM, 455–456
Dead metaphors, 558–560
Definition, fallacy of, 351–354
Definition mode, 129, 236, 514
Denotation, 564–567
Dependent clause, 575
Description
  mode of, 129
  use of, in persuasion essay, 391–392
Description mode, 129
Detail, use of, in personal essay, 148–149, 152–153
Dialogue
  as feature of personal essay, 147–148, 153
  imaginary, 337–339
Dialogue notes, 111–116, 117–118, 297–299